Late Medieval Castles

Late Medieval Castles

Edited by
Robert Liddiard

THE BOYDELL PRESS

First published 2016
The Boydell Press, Woodbridge
ISBN 978 1 78327 033 0

The Boydell Press is an imprint of Boydell & Brewer Ltd
PO Box 9, Woodbridge, Suff olk IP12 3DF, UK
and of Boydell & Brewer Inc.
668 Mt Hope Avenue, Rochester, NY 14620–2731, USA
website: www.boydellandbrewer.com

A catalogue record for this book is available
from the British Library

Contents

Illustrations

5 **Meaningful Constructions: Spatial and Functional Analysis of Medieval Buildings**

6 *Mota, Aula et Turris*: **the Manor-Houses of the Anglo-Scottish Border**

7 **Lulworth Castle, Dorset**

The editor, contributors and publishers are grateful to all the institutions and persons listed for permission to reproduce the materials in which they hold copyright. Every effort has been made to trace the copyright holders; apologies are offered for any omission, and the publishers will be pleased to add any necessary acknowledgement in subsequent editions.

Acknowledgements

The original source details for the articles in this volume are listed below, alphabetically by author. The editor and the publishers are grateful to all authors, institutions and journals for permission to reprint the materials for which they hold copyright. Every effort has been made to trace the copyright holders; we apologise for any omission in this regard, and will be pleased to add any necessary acknowledgement in subsequent editions.

N. Coldstream, 'Architects, Advisors and Design at Edward I's Castles in Wales', *Architectural History* 46 (2003), 19–35.

C. Coulson, 'Fourteenth-Century Castles in Context: Apotheosis or Decline?', *Fourteenth-Century England* 1 (2000), 133–151.

C. Coulson, 'Some Analysis of the Castle of Bodiam, East Sussex', *Medieval Knighthood* 4 (1992), 51–107.

C. Coulson, 'Specimens of Freedom to Crenellate by Licence', *Fortress* 18 (1993), 3–15.

C. Coulson, 'Structural Symbolism in Medieval Castle Architecture', *Journal of the British Archaeological Association* 132 (1979), 73–90.

P. Dixon, 'The Donjon of Knaresborough: the Castle as Theatre', *Château-Gaillard* 14 (1990), 121–139.

P. Dixon, '*Mota, Aula et Turris*: the Manor-Houses of the Anglo-Scottish Border', in *Manorial Domestic Buildings in England and Northern France*, ed. G. Meirion-Jones and M. Jones, Society of Antiquaries Occasional Papers, Vol. 15 (London, 1993), 22–48.

P. Dixon and B. Lott, 'The Courtyard and the Tower: Contexts and Symbols in the Development of Late Medieval Great Houses', *Journal of the British Archaeological Association* 146 (1993), 93–101.

G. Fairclough, 'Meaningful Constructions: Spatial and Functional Analysis of Medieval Buildings', *Antiquity* 66 (1992), 348–366.

P. A. Faulkner, 'Castle Planning in the Fourteenth Century', *Archaeological Journal* 120 (1963), 215–235.

J. Goodall, 'Lulworth Castle, Dorset', *Country Life* (13 January 2000), 43.9, 34–39.

C. McKean, 'A Scottish Problem with Castles', *Historical Research* 79 (2006), 166–198.

T. McNeill, 'Castles of Ward and the Changing Pattern of Border Warfare in Ireland', *Château-Gaillard* 17 (1996), 127–133.

R. K. Morris, 'The Architecture of Arthurian Enthusiasm: Castle Symbolism in the Reigns of Edward I and his Successors', in *Armies, Chivalry and Warfare in Medieval England and France*, ed. M. J. Strickland (Stamford, 1998), 63–81.

M. C. Prestwich, 'English Castles in the Reign of Edward II', *Journal of Medieval History* 8 (1982), 159–178.

C. Taylor, 'Medieval Ornamental Landscapes', *Landscapes* 1 (2000), 38–55.

M. A. Whitaker, 'Otherworld Castles in Middle English Arthurian Romance', in *The Medieval Castle: Romance and Reality*, ed. K. Reyerson and Faye Powe (Dubuque, 1984), 27–45.

Editor's Preface

Late Medieval Castles is a companion to *Anglo-Norman Castles* (2003), a volume that brought together a series of historiographically significant articles on castles and castle-building in the period from the Norman Conquest to the early thirteenth century. The format and themes of the present collection are broadly comparable with the earlier book, but with the focus on those castles dating to the period *c.*1250–1500.

In the course of bringing *Anglo-Norman Castles* to publication the somewhat arbitrary cut-off date of *c.*1225 seemed unsatisfactory for a number of reasons. On a practical level, there were highly relevant articles that could not be included because the subject matter fell outside the chronological range of the volume. A more scholarly concern was the fact that a number of issues pertinent to castle-building in the eleventh and twelfth centuries could not be satisfactorily addressed without reference to subsequent developments in the thirteenth and fourteenth. Allied to this, a focus on Anglo-Norman building (no matter how justifiable in historical terms) does perhaps contribute, albeit unwittingly, to the erroneous idea that the eleventh and twelfth centuries are the most important centuries for castle-building, a time when the 'true' castle is to be found, and that the period that follows, particularly after 1300, is something of an anti-climax. The present volume should therefore be seen as a continuation of the broad themes discussed in the introduction to *Anglo-Norman Castles*, with the aim of pursuing them in a late medieval context.

In the years since 2003 there have been a number of important publications in the field of castle studies, and castles continue to be a source of controversy and to provoke debate. Despite the fact that the availability of some secondary material has been made easier through electronic access, I have been consistently reminded by academic colleagues that a compilation such as this is worthwhile, both for the student reader and those seeking a path into the specialist secondary literature. This author at least also believes that there is value in bringing together in one place a series of important contributions that have defined the subject and which also illustrate a diversity of approaches. The papers here do not represent, and are deliberately not intended to represent, a collection of the most recent pieces of published work; rather, they have been included for their historiographical value: their contribution to a specific problem or issue, their wider impact upon castle studies and as a demonstration of the range of research undertaken on the medieval castle by scholars from a variety of backgrounds. I am acutely aware that there are chronological and geographical gaps (the focus here is on the British Isles), but the contents undoubtedly reflect the general historiographical trends in English castle studies, and the Guide to Further Reading at the end of the volume includes additional material.

I should like to thank Charles Coulson for commenting on an early draft of this introduction and also Oliver Creighton, Gillian Eadie, Christian Frey and Tom McNeill for bibliographical assistance and their thoughts on possible articles for inclusion. My thanks also go to Rohais Haughton, Caroline Palmer and Rob Kinsey at Boydell & Brewer for all their efforts on seeing this volume through to publication. Parts of this introduction are based upon R. Liddiard, 'English Castle-Building', in *Princely Rank in Late Medieval Europe*, ed. T. Huthwelker, J. Peltzer and M. Wemhöner (Ostfildern, 2011), 48–63.

Abbreviations

ANC	R. Liddiard (ed.), *Anglo-Norman Castles* (Woodbridge, 2003)
CBA	Council for British Archaeology
CCR	*Calendar of Close Rolls*, 67 vols (PRO Texts and Calendars, 1892 onwards)
CChR	*Calendar of Charter Rolls*, 6 vols (PRO Texts and Calendars, 1903–27)
CFR	*Calendar of Fine Rolls*, 22 vols (PRO Texts and Calendars, 1911–62)
CIPM	*Calendar of Inquisitions Post Mortem*, 20 vols (PRO Texts and Calendars, 1904–95)
CNRS	Centre National de la Recherche Scientifique
CPR	*Calendar of Patent Rolls*, 60 vols (PRO Texts and Calendars, 1891 onwards)
Foedera	*Foedera, Conventiones, Litterae, et Acta Publica*, ed. T. Rymer, amended edn by A. Clarke and F. Holbrooke, 4 vols in 7 (Record Commission, 1816–69)
HKW	R. A. Brown, H. M. Colvin and A. J. Taylor, *The History of the King's Works* (2 vols, London, 1963)
HMSO	Her Majesty's Stationery Office
NAS	National Archives of Scotland
NMR	National Monuments Record
NRAS	National Register of Archives for Scotland
RAI	Royal Archaeological Institute
RCAHM (Scotland)	Royal Commission on the Ancient and Historic Monuments of Scotland
RCAHM (Wales)	Royal Commission on the Ancient and Historic Monuments of Wales
RCHME	Royal Commission on the Historical Monuments of England
VCH	Victoria County History

A Note on the Text

In order to bring a degree of consistency to the volume, footnote references for the majority of articles reproduced have been re-cast in a house style. In places this has meant some heavy editing of material, although this has chiefly involved issues of presentation. For those four pieces that contained Harvard-style referencing and separate bibliographies these have been retained, albeit with some standardisation of the order of information; a decision was taken not to convert such references to footnotes as it was felt that to do so would interfere with the original integrity of the piece in question. In the course of pulling the volume together a small number of obvious typographical errors were encountered; these have been corrected and where possible references to forthcoming work have been updated or revised.

It is hoped that this volume successfully treads the line between bringing a degree of editorial cohesion to a collection of articles that display wide variation in scholarly conventions, while at the same time retaining the intellectual coherence of the individual contributions. Any errors or inconsistencies are entirely the responsibility of the editor.

Introduction

Robert Liddiard

The importance of the period 1250–1500 to the history of castellated buildings is most readily seen in the construction of some of the finest examples of medieval secular architecture in the British Isles.[1] A number of the most significant and instantly recognisable medieval castles such as Caernarfon, Warkworth and Raglan were built after 1250 and, in a tangible link to the past, significant Anglo-Norman fortresses such as Windsor and Kenilworth were often transformed by extensive and radical modification in the centuries after their initial construction. The 'castles' of this period encompassed a diverse range of buildings that included the palatial fortresses of the Crown and nobility, the country seats of the wider baronage and the crenellated manor houses of minor gentlemen. Common to all, however, were the trappings of fortification – symbolic or otherwise – that were required to mark them out as the homes of an aristocratic class that claimed leadership in warfare as a prerogative well beyond the Middle Ages.[2] The word 'castle' was also applied to the purpose-built artillery forts of the Henrician period, which marked a significant turning point in the history of English fortification; for all their novelty in planning and execution, their moats, portcullises and rounded towers betray a distinctly medieval influence.[3]

The later Middle Ages witnessed important changes in the design of domestic ranges and lodgings, the development of the castle at this time being intimately bound up with the broader process described by Anthony Emery as 'the first great era of country house building' in England and Wales.[4] From c.1300, there was a general trend for noble buildings to become larger, architecturally more elaborate, and more intricate in their spatial organisation. Evidence for such changes is found in both the 'trophy houses' of the aristocracy and also in the

---

[1] For general architectural overviews, see R. Branner, *Gothic Architecture* (New York, 1961); P. Frankl and P. Crossley, *Gothic Architecture* (New Haven, 2001), N. Coldstream, *Gothic Architecture* (Oxford, 2002); for the English contribution to castle architecture, see J. Goodall, *The English Castle* (New Haven, 2011).

[2] J. R. Hale, *War and Society in Renaissance Europe, 1450–1620* (Leicester, 1985), 130; C. M. Storrs and H. M. Scott, 'The Military Revolution and the European Nobility, 1600–1800', *War in History* 3 (1996), 1–41.

[3] J. R. Hale, 'The Defence of the Realm, 1485–1558', *The History of the King's Works, 1485–1660*, vol. 4, Part ii, ed. H. Colvin (London, 1982); A. Saunders, *Fortress Britain* (Liphook, 1989).

[4] A. Emery, *Medieval Houses* (Princes Risborough, 2007), 7.

greatest castles of the realm.[5] The achievement should not be underestimated: the
mid-fourteenth century re-building at Windsor, for example, resulted in a castle
that could boast a level of domestic sophistication not rivalled elsewhere until
well into the post-medieval period.[6] What separated the house from the castle
was, of course, the presence of fortifications. The English aristocracy raised great
residences in some number and of considerable complexity during this period,
but only in some cases did they decide to provide their buildings with apparatus of defence. The precise motivation for the fortified element has represented
something of a bugbear for scholars: specifically, whether the defensive apparatus
– battlements, gatehouses, arrowloops and so forth – chiefly represented a serious
response to military insecurity or was the manifestation of a militant aristocratic
architectural style that social rank demanded. While the two were not of course
necessarily mutually exclusive, considerations surrounding this key issue have
formed the basis of much of the writing on English castles and lie at the heart of
many of the contributions to this volume.

Castles and Late Medieval Society

The most influential explanatory framework in English castleography for the
changing form of castles in the two centuries following 1300 is one that portrays
the period as one of prolonged and piecemeal decline.[7] Prior to this date, a corresponding 'rise' had taken place during the two centuries following the Norman
Conquest of 1066, a process often couched in terms of a teleological evolution
between attacker and defender as castles evolved in response to the growing complexity of siege warfare. The high point of this process was the castle-building programme undertaken by Edward I in North Wales, which represented the pinnacle
of English medieval military engineering, something made more significant by
the international dimension provided by the influence of the continental builder,
Master James of St George.[8] Thereafter, the military role of the castle diminished
and was replaced with a more obvious concern for domestic provision; its fortifications were now an architectural 'sham' that merely hinted at serious purposes.
Once deprived of its 'serious' military apparatus, a noble building ceased to be a

---

[5] See the comprehensive treatment in A. Emery, *Greater Medieval Houses of England and Wales,
1300–1500* (3 vols, Cambridge, 1996–2006).
[6] C. Wilson, 'The Royal Lodgings of Edward III at Windsor Castle: Form, Function, Representation', in *Windsor. Medieval Archaeology, Art and Architecture of the Thames Valley*, ed. L. Keen
and E. Scarff, British Archaeological Association Conference Transactions 25 (Leeds, 2002),
15–93.
[7] A. Hamilton Thompson, *Military Architecture in England During the Middle Ages* (London, 1912);
H. Braun, *The English Castle* (London, 1936); R. Allen Brown, *English Castles*, 3rd edn (London,
1976); M. W. Thompson, *The Decline of the Castle* (Cambridge, 1987); D. J. Cathcart King, *The
Castle in England and Wales* (Beckenham, 1988); M. W. Thompson, *The Rise of the Castle* (Cambridge, 1991). For historiographical commentary, see C. Coulson, 'Cultural Realities and Reappraisals in English Castle Study', *Journal of Medieval History* 22 (1996), 171–208.
[8] A. J. Taylor, 'Master James of St George', *English Historical Review* 65 (1950), 433–57.

castle and so its history blended with, and then became subsumed within, that of the mansion.[9] An increased emphasis on domesticity in residential building, coupled with the emergence of purpose-built artillery fortifications by the developing nation-state, led to a divorcing of the twin elements integral to the castle – fortification and residence – during the sixteenth century. From c.1500 the story of defences leads to bastions, Vauban and stop lines, while that of domesticity to the rise of Palladianism and the country house.[10]

This idea that the period after 1300 represented a retreat from the more warlike characteristics of a previous age is ultimately based on the unarguable evidence that there were at this time important structural changes in castle design and that by the sixteenth century some contemporaries were expressing the view that castle-building had ceased.[11] Following the Edwardian conquest, the construction of new castles by the Crown almost came to an end, and those projects that were undertaken, such as Queenborough, appear to represent something of a disappointment when compared to a surviving architectural masterpiece such as a Conwy, Warwick or a Bolton.[12] The importance of the castle to warfare also diminished. At a national level, siege activity after 1300 was minor in comparison to the twelfth and thirteenth centuries, in part because much of England's military efforts were directed overseas.[13] The prohibitive costs involved in making a castle defensible caused many fortresses to be undermanned and under-equipped and consequently ineffectual during periods of organised conflict. By the end of the fifteenth century the castle had become almost irrelevant to the outcome of campaigns; during the Wars of the Roses battles, rather than sieges, were the decisive military events.[14]

The idea of decline also took inspiration from, and contributed to, more general characterisations of late medieval English society. One of the perceived problems facing the English aristocracy at this time centred on the practice of retaining men in return for money – 'bastard feudalism' – which, it has been argued, had the unpleasant side effect of large numbers of armed brigands contributing to lawlessness.[15] The possible architectural ramifications of bastard feudalism were discussed in 1946 by Douglas Simpson in an influential paper in which he inter-

[9] Brown, *English Castles*, chapter 4.
[10] For the classic account of the 'rise and fall' of the castle, see Brown, *English Castles*, for thoughts on the sixteenth century, see M. Johnson, *Behind the Castle Gate: From Medieval to Renaissance* (London, 2002).
[11] Thompson, *Decline*, 110.
[12] Something perhaps highlighted by the lack of surviving fabric at Queenborough: see H. M. Colvin (ed.), *The History of the King's Works, Vol. 2: The Middle Ages* (London, 1963), 793–804.
[13] R. Liddiard, *Castles in Context* (Macclesfield, 2005), 70–8.
[14] J. Gillingham, *The Wars of the Roses: Peace and Conflict in Fifteenth-Century England* (London, 1981); A. Goodman, *The Wars of the Roses: Military Activity and English Society, 1452–97* (London, 1981).
[15] The secondary literature on this subject is extensive. For the issues at stake and historiographical review, see M. Hicks, *Bastard Feudalism* (London, 1995) and the key works by K. B. McFarlane, *The Nobility of Later Medieval England* (Oxford, 1973) and *England in the Fifteenth Century* (London, 1981); P. R. Coss, 'Bastard Feudalism Revised', *Past and Present* 125 (1989), 27–64; D. Crouch,

preted the physical separation of ranges of lodgings and self-contained accommodation blocks seen at some fourteenth-century castles as a response by lords who were fearful of the retainers billeted within the castle walls.[16] In comparison with the systematic and clearly defined obligations for manning during the period of 'true' feudalism, such as castle-guard, the castles' fall from grace as an institution seemed compelling.

Perhaps most importantly, the form of the castle also changed: architecture became increasingly decorative and less overtly 'military', and residential considerations more integral to new designs. The emergence in the fourteenth century of the true 'courtyard castle', in which the defensive and domestic arrangements were combined in a single unitary plan, represented an important development in the history of high-status architecture, stressing again the increasingly peripheral status of the castle to the history of warfare. Even successful veterans of the Hundred Years War often chose to build from their acquired riches residences for which the term 'Old Soldier's Dream House' seemed most appropriate.[17] The elegant façades of castles like Herstmonceux or Thornbury seemed to command the attention of art historians, rather than scholars of military science.

An Age of Decline?

It is as well to point out at the start that a significant number of the articles in this volume take issue with the 'decline' thesis, and by extension, the idea of a preceding 'rise'. Many prefer instead to see the later medieval period as one of continuing development, at times almost a celebration of long-held ideals about what a castle represented. It is important to note that much of the research on castles has been undertaken concurrently with broader re-assessments by social and political historians of late medieval society and feudal relations.[18] The rehabilitation of the late medieval aristocracy into the cultural mainstream, rather than caricatures of 'robber barons', provides an essential backdrop to any evaluation of the buildings into which they poured money and resources and whose outward appearance and internal furnishings reflected directly on their lordship and estate.[19]

The particular significance of the late medieval period to English castle-building

D. A. Carpenter and P. R. Coss, 'Debate: Bastard Feudalism Revised', *Past and Present* 131 (1991), 165–203.
[16] W. Douglas Simpson, '"Bastard Feudalism" and the Later Castles', *Antiquaries Journal* 26 (1946), 145–71.
[17] C. Hohler, 'Kings and Castles: Court Life in Peace and War', in *The Flowering of the Middle Ages*, ed. J. Evans (London, 1966), 140.
[18] For general works, see D. Crouch, *The Image of Aristocracy in Britain 1000–1300* (London, 1992); P. R. Coss, *The Knight in Medieval England 1000–1400* (Stroud, 1993); C. Given-Wilson, *The English Nobility in the Late Middle Ages* (London, 1987); D. Crouch, *The Birth of Nobility* (London, 2005).
[19] Perhaps best seen in art historical analysis: J. Alexander and P. Binski (eds.), *Age of Chivalry: Art in Plantagenet England 1200–1400* (London, 1987); P. Binski, *Westminster Abbey and the Plantagenets* (London 1995); and architectural history: J. Bony, *The English Decorated Style: Gothic Architecture Transformed 1250–1350* (New York, 1979); N. Coldstream, *The Decorated Style* (London,

as a whole concerns Charles Coulson's 'Apotheosis or Decline?', which, although concentrating on the fourteenth century, offers a critique of the 'rise and fall' thesis. This has at its core the nineteenth-century study of castle buildings as 'military architecture' and has as its terms of reference the classification of the fortified elements, which both mark out a building as a castle and their survival lending itself to typological analysis. The 'functional, almost brutal' assessment of castle architecture by Viollet le Duc in particular proved highly influential to a group of scholars responsible for putting English castelology on to its modern footing.[20] The 'military' character of the buildings of the earlier period was also underlined by the work of the historians Ella Armitage and J. H. Round, who placed the castle firmly as a Norman import brought to England after 1066 and at the heart of the warlike feudal society established after the Norman settlement.[21] The impression given by the massive stone hulks of Anglo-Norman fortresses dovetailed neatly with then current ideas of the nature of the feudal baron who used his castle as a base for private war. The Edwardian castles built in the aftermath of the English conquest of North Wales spoke equally eloquently about the military power of the castle in the hands of a successful warrior king. The further away castles moved from 1300, however, the greater their domestic character and so all the more contrast with those of previous centuries.

As Coulson explains, the fundamental point here is that the very concept of the castle going into decline after 1300 is ultimately predicated on this idea of a military 'rise' beforehand. The purpose of the Anglo-Norman donjon, or 'great tower', assumes some significance at this point, as its status as a 'building of last resort' represents a crucial part of the teleological progression to the Edwardian castles of the late thirteenth century. A number of case studies have, however, drawn attention to the military weakness of donjons both individually and as a group: the typology of donjon design does not sit easily within the orthodox evolutionary framework, and the list of military deficiencies highlighted at sites as diverse as the White Tower, Orford and Hedingham makes it increasingly difficult to accept the idea of something akin to an arms race taking place during the eleventh and twelfth centuries.[22] Moreover, a considerable body of evidence suggests that many donjons had important ceremonial purposes where the access to the

1994); but also socio-economic treatments, for example, C. Dyer, *Standards of Living in the Later Middle Ages* (Cambridge, 1989).

[20] E. E. Viollet le Duc, *An Essay on the Military Architecture of the Middle Ages*, trans. M. MacDermott (Oxford, 1860); M. W. Thompson, 'The Military Interpretation of Castles', *Archaeological Journal* 151 (1994), 439–45.

[21] J. H. Round, 'The Castles of the Conquest', *Archaeologia* 58 (1902), 313–40; E. S. Armitage, *The Early Norman Castles of the British Isles* (London, 1912).

[22] T. A. Heslop, 'Orford Castle and Sophisticated Living', *Architectural History* 34 (1991), 36–58, reprinted in R. Liddiard (ed.), *Anglo-Norman Castles* (Woodbridge, 2003), 273–96; P. Dixon and P. Marshall, 'The Great Tower at Hedingham Castle: a Reassessment', *Fortress* 18 (1993), 16–23, reprinted in Liddiard, *Anglo-Norman Castles*, 297–306; P. Dixon, 'The Myth of the Keep', in *The Seigneurial Residence in Western Europe AD 800–1600*, ed. G. Meiron-Jones, E. Impey and M. Jones, British Archaeological Reports, International Series 1088 (Oxford, 2002), 9–13; E. Impey (ed.), *The White Tower* (New Haven, 2008).

building and the internal arrangement of rooms were contrived to underline the authority of the builder.[23] Such observations are important, suggesting as they do that developments after 1300 have significant antecedents in the Anglo-Norman period. In short, if applying military credentials to fourteenth- and fifteenth-century castles finds the buildings wanting, then this is unlikely to represent decline in traditional form as the same is true of those of the twelfth and thirteenth.[24]

If doubts exist over a military 'rise' prior to 1300, then the status of an Edwardian 'apogee' during the 1280s and 1290s can also be downplayed. The excellent state of preservation of the principal Edwardian castles, together with their long tradition of study, has possibly enhanced their significance to the story of English castle-building.[25] As Nichola Coldstream explains in her 'Architects, Advisers and Design' the concentration of surviving castellation in North Wales is unique in the British Isles, but she questions the role of the royal builder Master James of St George as a genius designer and the presence of a distinctive Savoyard connection in elements of the buildings. In preference, Master James emerges as a director of works of exceptional ability, and the castles themselves as being more English in inspiration, at least in their key structural elements. Such an argument emphasises the place of the Edwardian castles in the mainstream of general architectural developments rather than as a watershed between 'rise and fall'. As monuments to a successful conquest of his Welsh neighbours, Edward I's castles remain spectacular, but as the yardstick by which to judge their fourteenth- and fifteenth-century successors their status is perhaps doubtful.

As Dixon and Lott argue in 'Tower and Court', a number of important continuities of architectural form can be traced across the supposed high point of military architecture at the end of the thirteenth century. In common with unfortified residences, the basic building block of the domestic accommodation of the late medieval castle comprised the hall, with private apartments and service buildings off either end. From as early as the twelfth century it was convenient to arrange these structures around a courtyard, and at new castles, particularly after c.1350, the trend was clearly towards a regular arrangement. If the courtyard provided one thread of continuity from the earlier to the later Middle Ages then the tower was another. The donjon was still seen after 1300 as an appropriate vehicle for lordly display, especially as a symbol of royal authority. Below the level of the Crown and greater magnates, towers attached to halls also retained their importance as markers of lordly status. Although technically based around courtyards, the vertical form of castles such as Old Wardour and the donjon of Warkworth

---

[23] P. Dixon, 'Design in Castle-Building: The Control of Access to the Lord', *Château Gaillard* 18 (1998), 47–57; P. Marshall, 'The Ceremonial Function of the Donjon in the Twelfth Century', *Château Gaillard* 20 (2002), 141–51; *idem*, 'The Great Tower as Residence in the Territories of the Norman and Angevin Kings of England', in *Seigneurial Residence*, ed. Meiron-Jones *et al.*, 27–44; R. Turner, 'The Great Tower, Chepstow Castle, Wales', *Antiquaries Journal* 84 (2004), 233–316.

[24] C. Coulson, 'Peaceable Power in Norman Castles', *Anglo-Norman Studies* 23 (2001), 69–95.

[25] J. Goodall, 'The Baronial Castles of the Welsh Conquest', in *The Impact of the Edwardian Castles in Wales*, ed. D. M. Williams and J. F. Kenyon (Cardiff, 2010), 155–65.

reflected the continued importance of height as a visual focus for castle architecture. The fifteenth century in particular witnessed something of a resurgence, as the examples at Tattershall, Buckden, Ashby-de-La-Zouch and Raglan still demonstrate. Crucially, none of this need be seen as evidence of decline or 'sham' fortification; rather, they stand for a continuation of long-held ideals of what castle-building represented, adapting to new circumstances.

Perhaps the most significant of these new circumstances, and almost certainly one of the principal drivers of change, is to be found in aristocratic lifestyles. In a trend beginning in the late thirteenth, which became pronounced in the fourteenth, the number of residences maintained by the Crown and aristocratic families were reduced, with resources concentrated on a smaller number of properties that were often expensively re-built or re-fitted.[26] As both a cause and effect, magnatial itineraries became more restricted and many castles became almost continuously occupied, albeit not garrisoned. At the same time, albeit with some fluctuation, the size of households increased.[27] In addition, detailed work by Woolgar has emphasised the increasingly strict and graded stratification within households that necessitated more complex spatial arrangements. Located within the castle walls at any one time might be a diverse group of people and attendants including the temporarily resident lord and lady, close and extended family, permanent skeleton staff, additional household servants and visiting guests with their own households. The competing demands of privacy, order, efficient management and the observance of etiquette all necessitated a building that could accommodate the increasing demands placed upon it.

A greater complexity to residential buildings post *c.*1300 can in part be explained by this increasing sense of hierarchy within the household; indeed, some of the best evidence for these changes comes from castles themselves, with the proliferation of halls, chambers, household accommodation and services. Although most medieval mansions had only a single court, there was a trend from the fifteenth century for a second, again driven by a need for more space and also for increased privacy for the lord and his immediate family.[28] Given that 'the plan and appearance of a medieval house reflected the social structure of the family and household it was built to accommodate' and was 'essentially an envelope to contain a household'[29], the knock-on effects on built structures are those discussed by Patrick Faulkner in his seminal 'Castle Planning in the Fourteenth Century'. Faulkner charted the increasing sophistication of residential planning over the course of the later Middle Ages and, in all but name, raised

---

[26] C. M. Woolgar, *The Great Household in Medieval England* (New Haven, 1999); Emery, *Greater Medieval Houses*, vol. 3, 'Household Expansion, Chambers and Lodgings', 27–39.

[27] See in particular Wooglar, *Great Household*, and C. Given-Wilson, *English Nobility*; K. Mertes, *The English Noble Household, 1250–1600* (Oxford, 1988); J. M. W. Bean, *From Lord to Patron* (Philadelphia, 1989).

[28] C. K. Currie and N. S. Rushton, 'Dartington Hall and the Development of Double-Courtyard Design in English Late Medieval High-Status Houses', *Archaeological Journal* 161 (2004), 189–210.

[29] Quotations from Emery, *Medieval Houses*, p. 123 and p. 119 respectively.

an early question mark over the whole 'decline' thesis.[30] Although subsequent decades have seen changes in the interpretation of some building types – such as a move away from the idea of the first-floor hall house – Faulkner's analysis of the domestic arrangements of castles remains highly influential.[31] In a series of case studies he demonstrated the increase in scale of late medieval domestic apartments and, in pioneering use of spatial analysis, also their increasing complexity over time. The thirteenth century, despite rapid changes in castle enclosures, was relatively static in terms of residential development. The accommodation and domestic facilities were essentially separate entities, linked around a curtain wall. The requirements for more permanent lodgings at the turn of the thirteenth century led to a multiplicity of separate 'units' of accommodation and services. By the late fourteenth century, however, the 'courtyard' castle of quadrangular forms as at Bolton and Bodiam, allowed the full integration of defences and domestic facilities.

Faulkner's analysis influenced a good deal of later work (albeit not always fully acknowledged), and successfully bridged the gap in the study of secular and ecclesiastical buildings; in a particularly telling remark, it judged that when approached from the point of view of domestic planning, the great house or castle were 'the same'. His work has since been taken further by scholars who, using similar techniques, have demonstrated the complexity of access arrangements in later medieval buildings and how they reflected changing attitudes to privacy, authority and gender.[32] Fairclough's discussion of Edlingham in Northumberland is a case in point. Here the chronological development of the building comprised a somewhat nostalgic moated hall-house built by Sir William Felton c.1300, later extended with a solar tower, chambers, gatehouse and surrounding walls c.1360, with a third phase in the sixteenth century that saw the site taking on a more regional role and the creation of a 'pseudo-courtyard house'. The changing use of space within the building reveals a sequence potentially at odds with a straightforward reading of the architectural history of the fabric. The outward elaboration of the castle curtilage during the 1360s and later was somewhat 'illusory'; despite the external appearance of force, the works undertaken actually increased the level of 'openness' in the castle as a whole and consequently its vulnerability to attack. The significance of the gatehouse lay in its facing on to the public area of the outer court, as a liminal structure between the castle and the outside world and the more 'public' and 'private' areas within the enclosure itself.

---

[30] See also Faulkner's 'Domestic Planning from the Twelfth to the Fourteenth Centuries', *Archaeological Journal* 114 (1958), 150–83.

[31] For changing interpretations of the hall house, see J. Blair, 'Hall and Chamber: English Domestic Planning 1000–1250', in *Manorial Domestic Buildings in England and Northern France*, ed. G. Meirion-Jones and M. Jones (London, 1993), 1–21, reprinted in Liddiard, *Anglo-Norman Castles*, 307–28; on medieval building archaeology more generally, see J. Grenville, *Medieval Housing* (Leicester, 1999).

[32] J. R. Mathieu, 'New Methods on Old Castles: Generating New Ways of Seeing', *Medieval Archaeology* 43 (1999), 115–42; A. Richardson, 'Gender and Space in Medieval Royal Palaces c.1160–c.1547: A Study in Access, Analysis and Imagery', *Medieval Archaeology* 47 (2003), 131–65.

Recognition of the complex development of just a single castle such as Edling-ham brings into sharp relief the problem that any broad-brush characterisation of castle-building in the late Middle Ages will inevitably mask distinctive regional patterns, which often display considerable variation. The north of England, for example, witnessed an upsurge in fortification across a broad social spectrum in the period 1360–1430.[33] Philip Dixon's analysis of the Anglo-Scottish Border in his '*Mota, Aula et Turris*' provides a valuable discussion of buildings below the level of the great magnate. Dixon rejects the stereotype of the Border region as a violent backwater clinging to conservative building styles. Instead, he identifies a series of phases of building that took place as a response to changing social and economic circumstances, both national and regional. The Anglo-Norman inheritance of the region was one of relatively few castles and manor houses that reflected both Norman and indigenous traditions, but with stone ground-floor halls without aisles and services as a particular style. By the end of the thirteenth century there was a move to develop the storied chamber or solar block that was either detached or at the high end of the hall, which by the end of the fourteenth had culminated in the development of the almost free-standing tower house. Such houses came to be found in considerable numbers in northern England, Scotland and Ireland, and attest to the vigour of sub-regional fortification in the late medieval period. In terms of sheer numbers, the tower house stands as a tangible reminder that the lordly tower had lost none of its potency at the end of the Middle Ages.[34]

That domesticity may have become more evident at later castles did not detract from the status of the castellated building. Yet it remains the case that castle-building did, at some point, cease. The time-frame and reasons for the end of the castle is a subject for a monograph in its own right, but scholars are now more comfortable than they once were of pushing the chronology of castle-building beyond the traditional period boundaries of the Renaissance and Reformation. In terms of design, the single-pile courtyard house remained the dominant plan for the noble residence in England down to the Civil War, and, as John Goodall explains, even those castles that took on a more classical form, such as Thomas, Lord Bindon's Lulworth built in 1608, had an internal spatial organisation that was distinctly medieval in character. The existence of what might be termed the 'post' or 'sub' medieval castle has particular resonance in Scotland where, as Charles McKean argues, the continued energy of crenellated residences was not the result of ignorance of Renaissance thinking, but rather a confident national

---

[33] Emery, *Greater Medieval Houses*, vol. 1, 21–9; A. King, 'Fortresses and Fashion Statements: Gentry Castles in Fourteenth-Century Northumberland', *Journal of Medieval History* 33 (2007), 372–97.

[34] See also P. Dixon, 'Tower Houses, Pelehouses and Border Society', *Archaeological Journal* 136 (1979), 240–52; C. Tabraham, 'The Scottish Medieval Tower-house as Lordly Residence in the Light on Recent Excavation', *Proceedings of the Society of Antiquaries of Scotland* 118 (1988), 267–76; T. Barry, 'Harold Leask's "Single Towers": Irish Tower Houses as part of Larger Settlement Complexes', *Château Gaillard* 22 (2006), 27–33.

architecture in which the demonstration of lineage through building was a cherished virtue. Particular styles of building can be closely related to changes in political circumstances: the mid-sixteenth-century penchant for rounded towers, for example, reflected the then currently close connections with France. Crucially though, Scottish nobles at this time favoured a nostalgic rather than contemporary French style because of the benefits of identity and pedigree that such a form provided. Particularly telling are the comments to the Earl of Ancrum 1632 requesting that the battlements on the main tower at Ancrum House be retained 'for that is the grace of the house, and makes it looke lyk a castle, and henc so nobleste'. Such remarks might suggest that it was only when aristocrats decided that crenellated residences – and their associated internal spatial ordering – ceased to have the connotations of lineage, authority and military leadership that they had in earlier periods that the castle went into terminal decline.

Symbolism and the Battle for Bodiam

Underpinning many of these interpretative trends is an implicit assumption that there was something more fundamental at work in the motivation for crenellated buildings than the 'rise and fall' thesis might allow. The exact purposes behind the construction of 'military' architecture have probably proved the most contentious issue in castle studies since the early 1990s. The seminal piece on this subject is Charles Coulson's 1979 article 'Structural Symbolism in Medieval Castle Architecture', which in many respects set the tone for much future research, particularly in the period after 1990; much of the 'revisionist' approach to the medieval castle, either directly or indirectly, owes an element of its ideological scope to this particular article.

Over thirty-five years since its publication, it is instructive to see the case that it makes, since the qualifications and nuances are easily overlooked, and the whole thesis has perhaps subsequently become too easy to over-simplify. In essence, the thrust of the argument is that in interpreting castles 'military purpose should not *uncritically* (my emphasis) be ascribed on the ground alone of some architectural semblance of fortification'. It is important to note that the military role of the castle, its potential to defend lives and chattels, or its possible deterrent effect is nowhere denied; rather, a basic defensibility is accepted and fully acknowledged, whereas what Coulson terms 'social purposes' were more important than any military function *per se* and frequently overrode the concern for out-and-out defensibility. As is to be expected from the *pugnatores* who raised them, the architecture took on a militant military style in which nostalgic sentiment was a prominent, and sometimes principal, element.[35]

Such military 'symbolism' was sometimes derived from the building of particularly efficient fortifications or by lavish accommodation, but for most

---

[35] Ideas pursued in recent work on the sociology of medieval battle, R. Jones, *Bloodied Banners: Martial Display on the Medieval Battlefield* (Woodbridge, 2010).

castles the 'military' features were deliberately chosen to evoke specific responses: the ideas of chivalry, splendid living and a sense of a noble past and aristocratic lineage. The elements that spoke most readily of warfare, such as gatehouses, towers, battlements and moats, were singled out for attention and became a marker of social status because their association with 'front rank' fortifications represented the position – actual or perceived – of the builder. Such 'artistry with function' fits effortlessly into explanations of medieval ecclesiastical architecture, but sits uneasily within the traditional 'form follows function' rationale of castle studies.

The importance of this noble style to late medieval aristocrats is also found in the issue of 'licences to crenellate', ostensibly permission from the Crown to subjects wishing to construct their own fortifications. The licences that appear from *c.*1200 onwards in the records of government have often been interpreted as the vestiges of, at its most extreme, a restrictive policy by the Crown towards baronial building that was potentially detrimental to royal authority. Medieval monarchs' claims to rights over the fortifications of their subjects ultimately derived from Carolingian Europe, but the extent to which restraints could be placed on fortress building in the eleventh and twelfth centuries, apart from rare cases when kings decided to make it their business, has been doubted.[36] The Anglo-Norman background is of crucial importance for the understanding of licences to crenellate in the later medieval period, as such documents do not necessarily represent straightforward evidence for a practice of restricting fortification that pre-dated the systematic keeping of royal records.

As Coulson demonstrates in 'Specimens of Freedom to Crenellate by Licence', rather than evidence of restriction, the extra *cachet* of a licence from the king for a building that advertised aristocratic rank was sought out as a sign of royal favour by a range of established nobles, prelates and successful courtiers alike.[37] Analysis of those licences that were issued also presents a series of problems if they were intended to restrict building. A number of major 'front rank' fortresses with the potential to resist the king, such as Beeston in Cheshire, were never licensed, yet the humblest castles, such as Braybrooke in Northamptonshire, were, something that raises the central problem of the restrictive thesis: if a fortress such as Caerphilly was required to withstand a medieval siege, why was the Crown so concerned to license buildings that many archaeologists would not hesitate to classify as manor houses?[38] Furthermore, the sheer number of

---

[36] See R. Eales, 'Royal Power and Castles in Norman England', in *Medieval Knighthood* 3, ed. C. Harper-Bill and R. Harvey (Woodbridge, 1990), 49–78, reprinted *ANC*, 41–67; C. Coulson, 'The Castles of the Anarchy', in *The Anarchy of King Stephen's Reign*, ed. E. King (Oxford, 1994), 67–92, reprinted *ANC*, 179–202.

[37] Note that the piece reproduced here is a shorter version of a more detailed discussion: C. Coulson, 'Freedom to Crenellate by Licence: An Historiographical Revision', *Nottingham Medieval Studies* 38 (1994), 86–137, at 113; see also *idem*, 'Hierarchism in Conventual Crenellation: An Essay in the Sociology and Metaphysics of Medieval Fortification', *Medieval Archaeology*, 26 (1982) 69–100.

[38] Coulson, 'Freedom to Crenellate by Licence', 113.

unlicensed sites (many of which are extant, or their locations known today) that
would have received licences had the Crown been enforcing a policy of restriction
suggests that successive monarchs were hardly doing anything of the sort.[39] What
might be true indices of defence, such as width of walls, are conspicuous by their
absence in the wording of licences themselves, and this, together with the sheer
range of structures licensed (urban dwellings, religious houses and, at least in one
case, a garden wall) and the similar arrangements in place for the privileges of
imparking and warrens, makes the argument that licences were elective, rather
than restrictive, a strong one.[40] Furthermore, the idea that the architecture of
castles can be interpreted within the context of a codified military style goes a
considerable way to reconciling apparently contradictory elements in the analysis
of specific buildings.

A case in point is Bodiam castle in Sussex, which, at least historiographically,
is probably the most significant English castle of the late medieval period. During
the 1990s the castle famously became the 'touchstone' of the general debate over
the military role of castles.[41] Charles Coulson's article on Bodiam is included here
as it remains the most detailed and authoritative account of the architecture of
the building and of the circumstances surrounding its construction. The arguments over the defensibility of the castle are well-worn and will not be repeated in
detail here, but Coulson's argument concerning Bodiam raises wider issues that
can usefully be applied elsewhere, particularly for the fourteenth century, when
an almost obsessive preoccupation with the subtleties of social rank permeated
gentry culture.[42]

The challenge in interpreting Bodiam lies in the fact that it defies simple or
easy explanation. The quadrangular plan and the sophistication of the domestic
arrangements fit the broader thesis of the increasing importance of residential
elements in castles, but the technologically advanced gunports and wide moat add
an overtly military sense, suggesting that Bodiam represents the final swansong
of the 'real' castle. The case for the latter is supported by the wording of the licence
to crenellate, which states that the castle was intended to resist the king's enemies,
and the exceptionally well-preserved fabric, which allows some (albeit necessarily imprecise) attempt to be gained of the overall impression that the builder, Sir
Edward Dallingridge, intended. The impression is undeniably militant. Detailed
analysis of the building, however, finds that the gunports are ill-positioned for a

---

[39] See the number of range of structures that did, and did not, receive licences listed in D. J. Cathcart King, *Castellarium Anglicanum* (New York, 1983).

[40] For a discussion of licences to impark, which show some remarkably similar characteristics, see
S. Mileson, *Parks in Medieval England* (Oxford, 2009), chapter 5.

[41] D. Stocker, 'The Shadow of the General's Armchair', *Archaeological Journal* 149 (1992), 415–20; D.
J. Turner, 'Bodiam, Sussex: True Castle or Old Soldier's Dream House?', in *England in the Fourteenth Century: Proceedings of the 1985 Harlaxton Symposium*, ed. W. M. Ormrod (Woodbridge,
1996), 267–77; J. Goodall, 'The Battle for Bodiam Castle', *Country Life* 16 (1998), 58–63; M. Johnson, *Behind the Castle Gate: From Medieval to Renaissance* (London, 2002).

[42] P. Coss, *The Origins of the English Gentry* (Cambridge, 2003), 216–38; G. Harriss, *Shaping the Nation, England, 1360–1461* (Oxford, 2005), 136–54.

military purpose, some of the internal arrangements would frustrate any defence and the moat would have been easily drained.

In general terms, the castle's construction cannot of course be divorced from wider local and national issues such as French raiding of the south coast, an unpopular royal administration and social tension following the Peasants' Revolt of 1381. Ironically, Bodiam's state of preservation and visual appeal, the latter owing much to the activities of Lord Curzon, encourage an uncritical emphasis on these 'headline' issues at the expense of some of the less obvious motivational factors behind Dallingridge's decision to build. Particularly relevant is the structure of power in late fourteenth-century Sussex, where the absence of an intermediate group of magnates between gentry and nobility fostered assertiveness on the part of the former, resulting in conflict with, in Dallingridge's case, the leading magnate of the realm, John of Gaunt. An alternative view, accordingly, sees Bodiam not as a response to the demands of national defence, but as part of an aristocratic re-assertion of authority in the specific circumstances of foreign war, aftermath of civil revolt and, perhaps decisively, are by a man from the upper gentry recently on the receiving end of greater lord's wrath, but who had not escaped from the experience altogether badly. The general architecture of the building is archaic and nostalgic, which carries connotations of lineage, yet is juxtaposed with self-deprecating defensive elements that speak of power in the present.

Perhaps the strongest testament to the continued esteem for crenellation in the late medieval period is the fact that it remained a suitable aristocratic building style despite, as Michael Prestwich explains, the well-documented failure of castles to play a decisive part in national conflict and political dispute. As was the case in the Anglo-Norman period, the cost of maintaining a garrison of any kind for any length of time was prohibitively high and consequently was rare.[43] Partly as a result, there was a lack of any kind of clearly defined defence network of castles intended to resist major strategic threats, such as the English border with Scotland. In practice, Scottish incursions into England by-passed major fortresses, which in themselves could do little to inhibit either the activities of raiding parties or larger invading armies. Major castles could, however, feature prominently in local disputes, specifically in complaints connected to national events when castellans associated with the royal household could find themselves and their buildings the source of resentment. This latter point does serve to emphasise the value of a fortress in wider politics, physically on the rare occasion it needed to be defended, and psychologically as a tangible sign of lordship and political authority during periods of factional strife.

In recognition of the difficulties of adequate manning, borders that required active defence necessitated particular arrangements. In 'Castles of Ward', Tom

---

[43] See J. Moore, 'Anglo-Norman Garrisons', *Anglo-Norman Studies* 22 (2000), 205–60; M. Prestwich, 'The Garrisoning of English Medieval Castles', in *The Normans and their Adversaries at War: Essays in Memory of C. Warren Hollister*, ed. R. P. Abels and B. S. Bachrach (Woodbridge, 2001), 185–200.

McNeill examines the provisions for castle-based military operations in thir-teenth- and fourteenth-century Ireland. A distinction can profitably be made between those major fortresses that marked the expansion of lordship, and those 'castles of ward' whose purpose was to house small garrisons on a temporary basis. The latter were a 'mixed bag' of crudely defensible enclosures intended for the defence of minor places in a given zone. In periods of raiding the incum-bent troops could be bolstered by local levies and then directed against raiders attempting to despoil the lordship. Such arrangements barely warrant the term 'system', but offer a valuable case study into how the problem of defending terri-tory was conducted during this period. The rather ephemeral nature of the chosen examples is indicated by the fact that they became redundant after c.1350 when their supporting lordships fragmented, a reminder that in order to be successful and enduring, border castles required both the mechanisms and the political will to make them effective.[44]

If strong lordship was a prerequisite for effective defence, then the often intri-cate arrangements that were made to ensure that visitors had a suitably intimi-dating approach to a lord in residence bring the role of the castle as the physical embodiment of authority into sharp focus. As Philip Dixon makes clear in his analysis of Knaresborough in Yorkshire, the elaboration of entrances to buildings could often extend to something akin to stage management. The unusual form of Knaresborough's donjon can, in part, be explained by its political purpose. Its construction was part of a policy of showcasing royal authority in the north of England during a period of baronial disquiet at the role of Piers Gaveston. The desired effect was partly achieved by the design of the building itself, but also in carefully choreographed access arrangements. Particularly striking is the juxta-position of an elaborately decorated approach with anteroom and a contrastingly sparse audience chamber in which nothing detracted from the visual impact of the lord's throne lit via its own window. The tower was intended for Gaveston himself, and its message would have been principally directed at Thomas of Lancaster, who had a well-documented hatred of the royal favourite. As a display of kingly power in the north, the donjon was as much an example of royal propaganda through building as the better-known Caernarfon a generation earlier, opening up the possibility of similar political overtones to other significant works.[45] It also offers an important reminder of the revisionist case, that stately architecture is not neutral or passive and certainly not a sign of fear or weakness: it is almost always militant, but not always military.

---

[44] See the lack of arrangements for the Edwardian castles, M. Prestwich, 'Edward I and Wales', *Edwardian Castles*, 1–7.

[45] One of the most obvious is the near contemporary of Knaresborough, Dunstanburgh in North-umberland, where the possible Arthurian connotations of the site and its political motivation are discussed in A. Oswald, J. Ashbee, K. Porteous and J. Huntley, *Dunstanburgh Castle, Northum-berland*, Archaeological, Architectural and Historical Investigations (London, 2006).

The Cultural Castle

The themes of propaganda and late medieval chivalric culture meet in Richard Morris' 'Arthurian Enthusiasm', which discusses the extent to which Edwardian castles can be read as an architectural embodiment of Arthurian romance. It was Arnold Taylor who originally raised the possible symbolic connotations of the Roman Empire and Arthurian legend in Edward I's Caernarfon, but while the specific connotations with Constantinople may now be replaced by a general idea of *Romanitas*, the 'overkill' of Edward's building programme and its political dimensions are not in any doubt.[46] Morris explores the idea that the architecture of Caenarfon might reflect a more unambiguous association with a cult of King Arthur. Edward's Arthurian interests are well-documented, and the 1284 'round table' tournament at Nefyn on the Lleyn peninsula is a suggestive context for the cultural image of the castle in Edward's court.[47] The elaboration of the turrets that project above the Eagle Tower battlements, the geometry of the mural towers, the elaborate castellated ensemble and the view across the water of the Menai Strait are all suggestive of the 'fairy tale' castle, but moreover, as Whitaker demonstrates in 'Otherworld Castles', they are all images that find resonance in romance literature of the day. The depiction of castles in medieval romances remains an understudied topic, but there is a wide range of literary material that is available for study and has considerable potential to reveal the significance of the castle to the medieval mind.[48]

The castle in literature represents hierarchy and order, and serves as a specific literary device that allows heroes to show off their supreme virtues in a fantasy world where constraints of normal existence do not apply. The imagined castle reflects this ideal: walls are of marble and studded with precious stones, they are well proportioned and designed, have tortuous approach, are well-lit, and usually sumptuously decorated and warm. Their supernatural characteristics belong to a tradition of writing concerning the Otherworld, a place of temporal pleasure, but also inhabited by the dead. Thus the literary hero experiences all the ambiguities of the castle: magnificent in its form, but also containing horror and pain. In Romance literature it is normally a paranormal being that predetermines the hero's journey to and through the castle buildings; how the knight reacts to the challenges he faces reveals the true nature of his virtue: skill at arms, abstinence, humility, self-discipline and courtesy.

Literary descriptions of entries and exists also serve as a reminder of the fact that the castle, real or imaginary, did not exist in isolation from its landscape. While the element of fantasy in literary depictions has always been treated with

---

[46] A. Wheatley, 'Caernarfon Castle and its Mythology', *Edwardian* Castles, 12–39.

[47] The Arthurian connections with castle-building are unsurprisingly close in Cornwall and pre-date the Edwardian interest; see O. J. Padel, 'Tintagel in the Twelfth and Thirteenth Centuries', *Cornish Studies* 16 (1988), 61–6.

[48] See also, M. Thompson, 'Castles', in *A Companion to the Gawain-Poet*, ed. D. Brewer and J. Gibson (Cambridge, 1997), 119–30; A. Wheatley, *The Idea of the Castle in Medieval England* (York, 2004).

caution by historians, the work of landscape archaeologists has shown that, while the ideals may be subject to hyperbole, the idea of making a castle magnificent in its setting was very much a medieval reality. Christopher Taylor discusses the contribution of landscape studies to late medieval castles in his discussion of 'ornamental landscapes'. The landscape context of castles has been the subject of much research in the past decade, and has almost become a sub-discipline in its own right.[49] Some conclusions have been directed at arguments of defensibility – the interpretation of a gunport, for example, might be altered depending on whether it overlooks a pre-prepared field of fire or a formal garden – whereas others have a greater relevance to aristocratic mentality and perception of the natural environment. As Taylor explains, remnants of what have come to be termed 'ornamental' or 'designed' landscapes comprise the archaeological remains of former ponds, lakes, parks and moats that were once integral to residential buildings. The origins of such settings undoubtedly lie in the Anglo-Norman period, but the fourteenth century in particular may have seen important developments, particularly in the conjunction of parkland and water. The latter point is significant, confirming as it does the similar conclusions about the period reached by scholars working on architecture and spatial organisation of buildings. As partly aesthetic schemes capable of sustaining symbolism and imagery that blur the distinction between economics, allegory and parody, the landscape contexts of castles are vitally important in determining what these buildings meant to their contemporaries.[50]

The general historiographical thrust of the pieces reprinted here should be clear to the reader, and it should be self-evident that castles have been the subject of a good deal of analysis and debate. Much ink has been spilt in an effort to re-interpret military decline as development; and interdisciplinary study has aided an awareness of the cultural, political and landscape context of the late medieval castle.[51] It is important to note that such arguments have not always gone uncontested.[52] Such discussion and debate is welcome so long as it means that castle studies does not drive itself up an intellectual cul-de sac.[53] Many of the arguments over 'decline' are based upon a relatively small number of elite buildings that do not always do justice to the full range of fortified structures in

---

[49] See O. H. Creighton, *Castles and Landscapes* (London, 2002); *idem, Designs Upon the Land* (Woodbridge, 2009).

[50] Which may reflect distinctly medieval sensibilities: R. Liddiard and T. Williamson, 'There by Design? Some Reflections of Medieval Elite Landscapes', *Archaeological Journal* 165 (2008), 520–35. I am grateful to Charles Coulson for originally pointing out some of the problems of the Bodiam landscape to me as far back as the year 2000.

[51] Compare the approach taken in R. Allen Brown, *Castles* (Aylesbury, 1984) and O. Creighton and R. Higham, *Medieval Castles* (Princes Risborough, 2003).

[52] C. Platt, 'Revisionism in Castle Studies: A Caution', *Medieval Archaeology* 51 (2007), 83–102.

[53] O. Creighton and R. Liddiard, 'Fighting Yesterday's Battle: Beyond War or Status in Castle Studies', *Medieval Archaeology* 52 (2008), 161–9; see also thoughts on a research agenda in O. H. Creighton, 'Castle Studies and Archaeology in England: Towards a Research Framework for the Future', *Château Gaillard* 23 (2008), 79–90 and also a wide-ranging review of Emery's *Greater Medieval Houses*: M. Cherry, 'Review Article: *Greater Houses of England 1300–1500 Vol.3: Southern England'*, *Antiquaries Journal* 87 (2007), 411–15.

the late medieval landscape.[54] Historiographically, the long view is undeniably helpful; as modern scholars strive for the 'holistic' approach to the castle it is instructive to see the conclusions of those writing before the military orthodoxy of the twentieth century became fully established.[55] It is, however, abundantly clear that some of the old certainties about castles have been replaced by doubts. While it may be true in some respects to say that scholars might be more uncertain about castles than they may have been hitherto,[56] the contents of this volume (and its companion *Anglo-Norman Castles*) will hopefully stand as an example of how much we already *do* know about castles. There are many fruitful avenues for future research in castle studies, but all are required to take account of the formidable scholarship that has gone before.

[54] The most obvious example being town walls, which for reasons of space could not have its own contribution be accommodated here, but see C. Coulson, 'Battlements and the Bourgeoisie: Municipal Status and the Apparatus of Urban Defence in Later-Medieval England', in *Medieval Knighthood* V, ed. S. Church and R. Harvey (Woodbridge, 1995), 119–95, and O. Creighton and R. Higham, *Medieval Town Walls, An Archaeology and Social History of Urban Defence* (Stroud, 2005).
[55] For the idea of a 'wrong turn' in castle studies, see the extended discussion in C. Coulson, *Castles in Medieval Society* (Oxford, 2003).
[56] Johnson, *Behind the Castle Gate*, 176–83.

1

Fourteenth-Century Castles in Context: Apotheosis or Decline?[1]

Charles Coulson

Convention has dealt harshly with English castle-architecture after the 'great days' of Edward I. The fourteenth century can boast such remarkable structures as Thomas of Lancaster's additions to Pontefract[2] (Yorks.), Edward III's sumptuous rebuilding at Windsor[3] (Berks.), Edmund of Langley's Fotheringhay (Northants.), with its once-allusive 'fetterlock' plan,[4] and the surviving spectacular north-east front of the Beauchamps' Warwick.[5] Yet paradoxically, these and lesser displays of power (such as Bodiam, Bolton, Cooling, Donnington, Lumley, Maxstoke, Nunney, Raby, Sheriff Hutton, Shirburn, Wardour, Wingfield and Wressel) tend to disappoint popular expectations. These and many others, less familiar, can seem too 'domestic'. 'Castles' must be 'seriously fortified' and above suspicion of being castellated palaces. Appreciating them correctly calls for a different approach. It is not enough to accept residence as a proper purpose, but reduced to a subordinate by-product of 'strategic necessity'.[6] Although the concept of 'castles of chivalry' has modified the utilitarian and 'functional' approach, the stigma of 'decline' persists.[7] Architectural historians, with a different interpretative agenda, rely more on individual structure and detail – but as Paul Frankl noted, 'there is, as yet, no terminology for the styles of military architecture, and this is a subject to which more thought might profitably be devoted'.[8] This remains the position.

The unity of medieval noble architecture, when contemplated entire, overwhelms the specialisms 'religious', 'military', 'civil', 'domestic', or merely

---

[1] The help of Nigel Saul in getting this article into final form is most gratefully acknowledged. These notes minimise references and eschew subsidiary controversies. See C. Coulson, 'Cultural Realities and Reappraisals in English Castle-Study', *Journal of Medieval History* 22 (1996), 171–207 (with bibliography); also Castle Studies Group, *Newsletter* 12 (1998–9), 43–50.

[2] *HKW*, plate 51 (as before destruction in the Civil War).

[3] M. W. Thompson, *The Decline of the Castle* (Cambridge, 1987), 50–1 (upper ward, plan).

[4] J. D. Mackenzie, *The Castles of England: Their Story and Structure* (2 vols, London, 1897), i, 320–2, 326–7.

[5] Important redating and analysis: R. K. Morris, 'The Architecture of the Earls of Warwick in the Fourteenth Century', in *England in the Fourteenth Century*, ed. M. W Ormrod (Woodbridge, 1986), 161–79.

[6] Notably D. J. Cathcart King, *Castellarium Anglicanum: An Index and Bibliography of the Castles in England, Wales and the Islands* (2 vols, New York, 1983) i, xivff.

[7] E.g. C. Platt, *The Castle in Medieval England and Wales* (London, 1982), chaps 7 and 8; H. Braun, *The English Castle* (London, 1936), chaps 4 and 5.

[8] P. Frankl, *Gothic Architecture* (trans. D. Pevsner; Harmondsworth, 1963), 246.

ecclesiastical and secular, initiated by Arcisse de Caumont (1802–73). But art-historical method still genuflects to architectural Darwinism.[9] Only recently has 'the
survival of the fittest' fallen from favour as prime mover of castle-development.
Doubts have most crucially focused on the twelfth century. Matthew Strickland
has emphasised the powerlessness, quite often, of unsupported English castles
in face of even ill-equipped Scots. In 1173, the major fortress of Warkworth was
abandoned as 'indefensible against a major Scottish invasion', although it was
always 'a fortified seigneurial residence' discharging 'the administrative functions
of lordship'.[10] Because the military hypothesis began with 'the Normans', any revision has deep historical implications, especially for the castles of the fourteenth
century. Detailed discussion must begin with a reappraisal of the early castles.

The point that needs stressing above all is continuity of design. Domestically,
after all, no plan lasted longer than that of the ground-floor hall-chamber-kitchen
etc. house.[11] From the 1420s the new aesthetic of brickwork imported a change
more conspicuous than real. Stone remained a noble material, as is evidenced
by Ashby-de-la-Zouche, Haddon, Raglan, Sudeley and elsewhere. The Lancastrian and Yorkist castle merges into the Tudor with almost insensible gradation
and was anticipated by the fourteenth-century version. The Renaissance was
very largely atavistic. Next to the hall-plan, no elements lasted longer than the
gatehouse, courtyard and tower.[12] Neither the Wars of the Roses nor domestic
peace after 1487 had much effect on planning or construction. Moats only slowly
disappeared. Castellation continued. Fenestration expanded steadily but without
significant changes in tempo.

The traditional schema devised to accommodate perceptions of the peculiar
British experience of 'castles' has been an obstruction. It proposes a simple progression from 'truly military', via ambivalent but still 'genuine', to semi-convinc-
ing with a long tail of 'sham' castles and (disgraceful) follies. Perceptions of the
Conquest colour everything. When we regard the thousand or so replacement
lordly seats of the Norman settlement[13] not as campaign castles (though some
were, either ephemeral or surviving as administrative centres) but as grandiose
variants of the supplanted Anglo-Saxon thegn's *burh* (castles in most features but
name), the whole picture changes.[14] Earthworks are often hard to evaluate and

---

[9] E.g. G. Webb, *Architecture in Britain: The Middle Ages* (Harmondsworth, 1956), 70–1.
[10] M. Strickland, 'Securing the North: Invasion and the Strategy of Defence in Twelfth-Century Anglo-Scottish Warfare', in *Anglo-Norman Warfare*, ed. M Strickland (Woodbridge, 1992), 209–19.
[11] M.E. Wood, *The English Medieval House* (London, 1965), drawing on (T. H. Turner); J. H. Parker,
Some Account of Domestic Architecture in England (4 vols in 3, Oxford, 1851–9).
[12] P. Dixon and B. Lott, 'The Courtyard and the Tower: Contexts and Symbols in the Development of Late Medieval Great Houses', *Journal of the British Archaeological Association* 146 (1993),
93–101, 146.
[13] E.g. B. English, 'Towns, Mottes and Ring-Works of the Conquest', in *The Medieval Military Revolution*, ed. A. Ayton and J. Price (London, 1995), 45–61.
[14] A. Williams, 'A Bell-House and a Burh-Geat: Lordly Residences in England before the Norman
Conquest', in *Medieval Knighthood* 4, ed. C. Harper-Bill and R. Harvey (Woodbridge, 1992), 221–
40, reprinted *ANC*, 23–40. Overview: C. L. H. Coulson, *Castles in Medieval Society: Fortresses in
England, France and Ireland in the Central Middle Ages* (Oxford, 2003). R. Eales, 'Royal Power

few have been excavated. With the few but highly significant early stone 'keeps' the focus sharpens: so many survive and in such good order that nearly all the difficulties encountered in interpreting the majority earth and timber castle simply disappear.[15] Other castle towers, those with upper-floor lordly display 'doorways', opening into mid-air, suggest a direct borrowing, perhaps surprising, of a late-Saxon feature,[16] strengthening the inherent probability that early castles were not utilitarian. Symbolism, in all its aspects, was there from the first. With the stone 'great-towers' of c.1077–c.1135 affinities with the fourteenth century, when most of them were still in use, become strikingly close. They are often minutely domesticated, sometimes with extravagant ostentation, especially outwardly (Norwich, Rising), expressive of palatial sub-Carolingian princely grandeur[17] (Colchester, London) and household amenity (e.g. Rochester). There can be little doubt that considerations of power and prestige played a key role in their construction.

The ideas now being established cast grave doubt upon the whole military rationale hitherto applied variously to all but a handful of medieval castles. Instead of rational and soberly purposeful expenditure, we find, just as with the Norman great churches, pure and showy ostentation, especially by sheer size and conspicuous display. Hedingham tower (Essex),[18] Norham (Northumb.) and Portchester (Hants.) must be mentioned. Bramber (Sussex), Ludlow (Salop.) and Richmond (Yorks.) had gates transformed into lofty towers. Visual impact was crucial. The small group of thin-walled early 'proto-keeps' were only slightly less assertive and equally 'unmilitary'. Seignorial display was served also by the grand 'country house' centrepiece of Castle Acre (Norfolk), later converted to a tower to conform with fashion.[19] Military determinism was as out of place in the twelfth century as it was in the fourteenth.

It is becoming clear that what we tend to regard as untypical and degenerate in fourteenth-century castles in reality were authentic original characteristics. Whether the standard fourteenth-century 'palace-castle' be written back into the twelfth century (cf. Newark, Old Sarum), or, more logically, the latter be recognised as enduringly establishing the *genre*, makes little difference. Lack of linkage

and Castles in Norman England', in *Medieval Knighthood* 3, ed. C. Harper-Bill and R. Harvey (Woodbridge, 1990), 48–78, reprinted *ANC*, 41–67.

[15] R. Higham and P. Barker, *Timber Castles* (London, 1992). For review of excavations of castles, see J. Kenyon, *Medieval Fortifications* (Leicester, 1990). C. Coulson, 'Peaceable Power in English Castles', *Anglo-Norman Studies* 23 (2001), 69–96.

[16] D. Renn, 'Burhgeat and Gonfanon: Two Sidelights from the Bayeux Tapestry', *Anglo-Norman Studies* 16 (1994), 177–98.

[17] The seminal paper is P. Heliot, 'Sur les residences princieres baties en France du 10e siècle au 12e siècle', *Le Moyen Age* iv, 10 (1955), 27–61, 291–319.

[18] P. Dixon and P. Marshall, 'The Great Tower at Hedingham Castle: A Reassessment', *Fortress* 18 (August 1993), 16–23, reprinted *ANC*, 297–306. Issues generally explored at the White Tower symposium, April 1999. Turrets present problems at Hedingham and elsewhere.

[19] C. Coulson, 'The Castles of the Anarchy', in *The Anarchy of King Stephen's Reign*, ed. E. King (Oxford, 1994), 81–4. T. A. Heslop's work is crucial: 'Orford Castle: Nostalgia and Sophisticated Living', *Architectural History* 34 (1991), 36–58; and *Norwich Castle Keep: Romanesque Architecture and Social Context* (Norwich, 1994).

between architectural fact and political rationale is clear, almost equally, from both. If one represented 'decline', so did both. Even Richard I's *donjon* at Château Gaillard by Les Andelys, in Normandy, backed onto the chalk precipice and seemingly a place of last resort if there ever was one (though not in the 1204 siege), is now shown to have been essentially another hall of private audience, neither residence nor refuge despite its impressive missile-resistant prow and (sometime) machicolation. The 'martial face', to use Michael Thompson's apt phrase,[20] appears always to have been part of the architectural performance – not a pretence at all, since expressive features were always variously ambivalent and dual- (or multi-) purpose, but at least as sophisticated as the great churches. Accordingly, there was no contradiction in combining windows closely with crenellated (even machicolated) parapets, as at Nunney *c.*1373 (Somerset) or at Raglan *c.*1430–70 (Gwent) and at La Ferté Milon,[21] a feature which is a commonplace of the palace-castles like Sheriff Hutton and Wressel. Conspicuously, at Wardour (Wilts.) the fenestration is part of the design (1393). The soldierly *panache* of Bodiam is restrained by comparison – which makes exactly the impact it was unquestionably designed to do. But their intentions and our impressions can be far apart. It is troubling to find few if any measures of even internal security reflecting the effects of bastard feudalism, whereas hierarchified apartments for household and guests are ubiquitous. The 'true castle' is so elusive essentially because, as now conceived, it scarcely ever existed. That Edward Dallingridge's castle of Bodiam (1385–*c.*1391) was true to its cultured age is only to be expected. That it also conformed, as many castles variously did, to a long-running image making them more not less, 'castles' – in the proper, contemporary sense – may be less obvious.[22]

A raft of new explanations – or, rather, of old ones hitherto confined to churches and to post-medieval mansions – needs to be applied to castles. Personality was all-important. Richard II's sumptuous rebuilding in 1396–9 of the lodgings in the inner bailey of the Roman *castellum* and Norman castle of Portchester presents no problems or surprises.[23] Architecturally it made Richard's cultured mark just as one would expect – but, perhaps, expectations go too far. So very different a monarch as Henry II, in apparently dissimilar circumstances, built at Dover (1179–89) the last and most lavish of the English 'square keeps', as astonishing in its self-indulgence as anything built in the fourteenth century.[24] Perhaps only Warwick or the 144-feet tall tour *d'orgueil* of Largoët en Elven (Morbihan) achieve the

---

[20] Thompson, *Decline of the Castle*, chap. 5.

[21] J. Mesqui and C. Ribéra-Pervillé, 'Les châteaux de Louis d'Orléans et leurs architectes (1391–1407)', *Bulletin Monumental* 138, 3 (1980), esp. 320–3.

[22] C. Coulson, 'Some Analysis of the Castle of Bodiam, East Sussex', in *Medieval Knighthood* 4, ed. C. Harper-Bill and R. Harvey (Woodbridge, 1992), 51–107, *passim*. N. E. Saul, 'Bodiam Castle', *History Today* 40 (Jan. 1995), 16–21.

[23] *HKW*, 790–1; plate 49. The works at Portchester were probably initiated for the benefit of Roger Walden, the treasurer and later archbishop of Canterbury, who, with his brother, was keeper of the castle from 1395: *CPR (1391–6)*, 568, 572.

[24] J. Goodall, 'The Key to England', and 'In the Powerhouse of Kent', *Country Life* (18 and 25 March 1999), 45–7, 110–13.

same sublime fantasy.[25] Dover shows that if so seemingly 'serious' a castle could have so 'frivolous' a centrepiece then hardly any castle can be thought anywhere to lack a 'non-military' aspect. Certainly, the element of pure propaganda, even of ego-trip, was so widespread that no castle was a 'fortification' in the nineteenth-century sense.[26] Victorian romanticism is more relevant than Victorian militarism. Much wider sympathies are required to understand, for example, Louis IX's stupendous castle of Angers (1230s), enclosing, dwarfing and eclipsing the ancient Angevin comital palace. When Edward II in 1307–11 wished to impose his favourite Gaveston upon the lordship and tenantry of Knaresborough (Yorks.), he built for him a *donjon*, in twelfth-century style containing a lord's hall of audience reached by way of a spuriously defended stairway. Attendants' rooms were accessible directly from outside, linked by a private stair with the audience chamber on the first floor. Philip Dixon does not hesitate to describe these arrangements as theatrical.[27] Edward I's North Welsh castles, Caernarfon especially, condition our minds towards accepting 'the castle as theatre'. If so, Dover's manner, austere and elegant in sparing quality detail rather than flamboyant, is classical drama. As is habitual the 'keep' flaunts the imagery of war in truly 'chivalric' style. The details of the extended processional stairway, here carried up to the second storey and elaborated with successive spectacles and obstacles, repay detailed examination and support very radical conclusions.[28]

Just as Bodiam refutes military determinism[29] as applied to castles of the period of the Hundred Years War, so does Dover 'keep' deny its supposedly warlike generation. Intellectuals enjoy metaphysics, as a rule, but this tends in military matters to go into reverse. Some process of psychological compensation may be the cause.[30] This factor perhaps explains why castles have received only a fraction of the art-historical, biographical and structural attention devoted especially to the great churches. Castles have been thought to be self-explanatory expressions of the notion that 'form follows function', to the architect,[31] and to the historian and archaeologist, a no-go area under martial law. Arguing the obvious thus becomes surprisingly difficult. Because the architectural details are often equivocal, surely deliberately so, castles' conspicuous-ness, impressive bulk, sophisticated design (as Sandy Heslop has demonstrated for Orford), exorbitant elaboration and pure power-statement, are frequently all we are left with. In the ordinary village, of

[25] E.g. J. Mesqui, *Châteaux Forts et Fortifications de la France* (Paris, 1997), 209–10.

[26] General discussion: D. Stocker, 'The Shadow of the General's Armchair', *Archaeological Journal* 149 (1992), 415–20.

[27] P. Dixon, 'The Donjon of Knaresborough: The Castle as Theatre', *Château Gaillard* 14 (1990), 121–39; and 18 (1998). Compare *HKW*, 689–90.

[28] R. Allen Brown, *Dover Castle* (London, 1966), 17–26.

[29] C. Coulson, 'Structural Symbolism in Medieval Castle Architecture', *Journal of the British Archaeological Association* 132 (1979), 75.

[30] C. Coulson, 'Hierarchism in Conventual Crenellation…', *Medieval Archaeology* 26 (1982), 69–100. R. Allen Brown, 'The Status of the Norman Knight', reprinted in *Anglo-Norman Warfare*, 140.

[31] Giles Worsley, *Daily Telegraph*, 1 August 1998, A6.

course, a modest stone castellated manor house stood out as clearly as the church, and was often close to it. Because there was no civilian authority of Roman type, and military display marked out the upper classes, their building proclaimed the power of arms. Crenellation was ubiquitous. A great lord was strong enough to project his power psychologically. Henry II's resources exempted him from the guns or butter dilemma. The greater the lord the more was left over from the cake for the icing, to use a perhaps more apt metaphor. But it is still very striking how normal it was for residence to prevail over security. Much can be learned from the details of the buildings. Faced, for instance, with such ragged remnants as the Nevilles' Penrith[32] (Cumb.) or Richard Abberbury's Donnington (Berks., licensed 1386) a message less complete but still consistent is conveyed by refinements denoting high-status apartments (door-heads and jamb-enrichment, the provision of vaulting and its type, built-in fittings, window size and type, fireplaces, latrines, access routes, ante-rooms etc.). Status-discernment has been brought to a fine art, notably in the 1960s by Patrick Faulkner[33] and in the *Summer Meeting Proceedings* of the Royal Archaeological Institute. The socio-architectural method is most systematically applied across an enormous and varied field by Anthony Emery's *Greater Medieval Houses of England and Wales, 1300–1500*. Emery's three-volume handling of the vast mass of sporadically known material will, when complete, be highly important, both for his data and his analysis. Castellated building is not separated into artificial 'defensible' and 'non-defensible' categories but each 'house' is allowed to speak for itself. The licences to crenellate, cited from my own (unpublished) work, are equally catholic, encompassing buildings (towns also) of every type. This freedom from conventional trammels, combined with exemplary architectural scholarship, recalls the cultural sensitivity of the pioneering *Some Account of Domestic Architecture* of J. H. Parker (1851–9). Much progress in the field has been made since Parker's day, and Emery's book will firmly locate castles within a large tradition. To this body of architecture the fourteenth century makes a massive contribution.

The current reorientation of analysis towards the architectural provision for spectacular public occasions and solemn, more private meetings, combined usually with accommodation of graduated rank exactly agrees with the fourteenth century. Precedents now show, in addition, that exorbitantly ambitious building was wholly within, indeed of the essence of, castle-building. The chivalric context, of pageantry and war-cult, is helpful but still too narrow for an aesthetic phenomenon so wide-ranging as castellation. One genre, royal and great lord triumphalism, should be brought in. Buildings from Roman Imperial triumphal arches onwards (and even before) have celebrated *gloire* of the Louis XIV type. Henry II's *bâtiments de gloire* continued throughout his reign. Philip II's conquest

---

[32] A. Emery, *Greater Medieval Houses of England and Wales, 1300–1500* (Cambridge, 1996), i, 132–6, discusses Neville building as a whole.
[33] E.g. P. Faulkner, 'Castle-Planning in the Fourteenth Century', *Archaeological Journal* 130 (1963), 215–35.

of Normandy was celebrated with new round *donjons* in the duchy and else-where. Mention of Louis IX's Angers has already been made. Edward I's castles, especially in North Wales, are familiar. Arnold Taylor originated the suggested imperial allusion (to Constantinople) of Caernarfon's banded masonry and Eagle Tower, in 1963,[34] long before the vogue for castle psychology, when he was Chief Inspector of Ancient Monuments. That his interpretation has now, by the usual processes of creeping certitude, become established 'fact' does not invalidate it but does sound a note of caution against the bandwagon effect. Motives were always too complex to be reduced to 'prestige versus functionalism'. Conwy's four (and unnecessary) lofty stair turrets to the royal apartments in the eastern courtyard offer general, but rather intangible, corroboration. Superfluity of any kind is as diagnostic as unexpected omission. The extravagant 'overkill' of the whole Welsh programme is architecturally very clear. Richard Morris's survey of Arthurian allusion is more specific, so far as that is possible.[35] These motivational approaches inevitably promise more than they can always deliver; but they rein-vigorate castle study, restoring it to the cultural mainstream and opening up new lines of awareness to break down the sterile rigidities of 'military architecture'.

The fourteenth century in particular stands to benefit. Many more of the aris-tocratic seats of this period must be brought within the acceptable canon as 'cas-tles'. The intermediate term 'fortified manor house' lacks social as well as archi-tectural reality and is perhaps best discarded. Similarly, 'fortification', as usually understood, is an obstruction. As Michael Prestwich showed in 1982, even major castles played a very subordinate role in the troubles of Edward II's reign.[36] They were irrelevant unless it was decided to man and munition them beforehand. That some divorce, not absolute but a very clear separation, must be accepted of warfare from the architecture is perhaps less obvious. Castles, of whatever size or degree of military appearance, were all vulnerable to attack (to burglary, no less) if not fully manned and stocked – which was very costly and exceptional. They did not exert the almost mesmeric local 'control' sometimes propounded. All, however, were with trivial exceptions essentially 'seignorial domestic' in charac-ter. The fact is most conspicuous, and best recognised, in France. The construc-tion of a more or less castle-like mansion (e.g. Moor End, Northants.) therefore blended status imperatives, resources and local politics.[37] Edward Dallingridge celebrated his establishment in east Sussex by building his spectacular castle at

---

[34] *HKW*, 370–1, plate 15; cf. A. J. Taylor, *Caernarvon Castle* (London, 1953), 15–18. Very generally A. Tinniswood, *Visions of Power: Ambition and Architecture from Ancient Rome to Modern Paris* (London, 1998).

[35] R. Morris, 'The Architecture of Arthurian Enthusiasm', in *Armies, Chivalry and Warfare in Medi-eval Britain and France*, ed. M. Strickland (Stamford, 1998), 63–81. Cf. J. G. Edwards, 'Edward I's Castle-Building in Wales', *Proceedings of the British Academy* 32 (1944), 15–81.

[36] M. Prestwich, 'English Castles in the Reign of Edward II', *Journal of Medieval History* 8 (1982), 159–78: also R. Eales, 'Castles and Politics in England, 1215–24', *Thirteenth Century England* 2 (Woodbridge, 1988), 23–43, reprinted *ANC*, 367–88.

[37] E.g. G. Meirion-Jones, ed., *The Seigneurial Domestic Buildings of Brittany*, First Interim Report 1983–5, European Vernacular Architecture Research Unit (London, 1986). For Moor End, see e.g.

Bodiam, whereas King Richard's own half-brother, John Holland, later (1397) briefly duke of Exeter despite the presence of the Courtenay earls at Powderham and Tiverton, contented himself with a double-courtyard palace at Dartington by Totnes in an almost unfortified style. That there was an alternative to ostentatious 'fortification' is most important. At Penshurst (Kent) the ex-mayor of London, John de Pulteney, opted for it. Most interestingly the licence to crenellate obtained in 1393 by his successor John Devereux was for a more castellated version. John de la Mare's Nunney (Somerset) represents the opposite choice – he built a tall, machicolated but widely windowed and slightly flimsy tower-house (licensed 1373) in complete contrast with, for example, Haddon Hall (Derbys.).[38] Wherever we look, the ascendancy of image over utilitarianism is evident. In the countryside, within towns, and in nobles' suburban seats, battlements, gatehouses, turrets and castle-panoply proclaimed their owners' pretensions (in the sense of social insecurity) not their fears. By often combining crenellation with cognate privileges of imparking, road-diversion and petty jurisdiction, the licences complement the built record. In the south and east of England, the various 'invasion scares' repeat in the chancery rolls the same message of privilege dominating defence. Just how these opportunities for social control were exploited is most fully shown by the opportunistic aggrandisement of the urban patriciates.[39]

Corroboration is condensed in the 'licences to crenellate', documents which by bulk and character are so typical of the fourteenth century and in particular of the administration of Edward III. The licences are a comprehensive social phenomenon, of *arrivisme* chiefly, affecting all the propertied classes. To run one's eye down the list of licensees is to receive a selective architectural companion to political biography. An appropriate proportion of lay and ecclesiastical magnates figures among the mass of the sub-baronial gentry, many of them obscure with purely local positions to assert, others dignifying their home base for careers at Court.[40] Few generalisations are admissible. Sir Thomas Wake of Liddel had licence in 1327 'to strengthen his dwelling-house of Cottingham, co. York, with a wall and to crenellate the same'. He had ready access, directly or by proxy, to the Chancery, a factor noticeable under Mortimer and Isabella, Edward II and Richard II, but notably less so under Edward III. Cottingham (now swallowed up by Hull) had come to the Wakes with the heiress of the Stutevilles (themselves

CCR (1345–8), 270; T. F. Tout, *Chapters in Administrative History* (6 vols, Manchester, 1920–33), iv, 180.

[38] A. Emery, *Dartington Hall* (Oxford, 1970); Thompson, *Decline of the Castle*, chap. 4, 52–4. CPR (1340–3), 331; (1391–6), 164; (1370–4), 367.

[39] C. Coulson, 'The 'Salvation of the Realm' and 'the Saving of Privilege': Castles and their Lords, c. 1337–1413' (in preparation); also 'Battlements and the Bourgeoisie: Municipal Status and the Apparatus of Urban Defence in Later-Medieval England', in *Medieval Knighthood* 5, ed. S. Church and R. Harvey (Woodbridge, 1995), 119–95.

[40] C. Coulson, 'Freedom to Crenellate by Licence: An Historiographical Revision', *Nottingham Medieval Studies* 38 (1994), 86–137; also C. Coulson, *Castles, Kings and Courtiers: Fortifying, Privilege and Defence in England, Ireland and Wales* (in preparation); also Coulson, 'Hierarchism in Conventual Crenellation'.

licensed for the established castle there, in 1201). On Baldwin Wake's death (1282) it was described as 'A capital messuage, well built with a double ditch and enclosed by a wall'. Thomas's own inquisition of 1349, taken at Cottingham, suggests that he had done no building – a not uncommon phenomenon. His licence was largely a coming-of-age gesture of possession. The place, with its park, capital seat of the barony, was 'ruinous' although costing only five marks a year to keep up. Administrative routines, as usual, continued regardless. During Thomas' minority the expansive burgesses of Hull, themselves exploiting licences' éclat, had encroached on the lordship with new roads, as he had alleged. His brief disgrace after Henry of Lancaster's armed demarche at Bedford apparently emboldened the prior of Spalding to try, with the monks of Crowland, to put pressure on Wake's rights in the marshes of Deeping and Bourne (Lincs.). In both confrontations licences tested local and regional strengths. This series of events accords entirely with the archaeology, stubbornly uninformative and prosaic though it tends to be.[41] As usual, physical danger of any kind passed the buildings by.

'Fortification', throughout the period, predicated not defence essentially but noble style. *Fortalicium* was not 'fortlet' but indifferently the whole, or the component elements, of a *forteresse*, a term encompassing our 'castle', walled towns and virtually the whole range and panoply of castellated building. The metaphysics were of the essence. The usage, and the medieval perception of the built landscape, survive strongly in John Leland's *Itinerary* (c.1535–43). He reflected also traditional site-nomenclature. By popular and official accolade the castle-style was accorded primarily to the place's dynastic renown; it was not an assessment of defensibility. These titles long preceded the 'seriously defended residence' definition. The numerous survivors on the ground were systematically recorded and perpetuated by the Ordnance Survey. Following up these 'castles' in all their diversity from the map gives a very instructive new perspective. The nomenclature is a linguistic palimpsest conveying an authentic tradition which orthodoxy, for nearly a century now, has suppressed.[42]

Fortification, in this comprehensive sense, advertised nobility. In the same way, and almost more extensively, large halls, kitchens and reception suites proclaimed lavish hospitality and numerous household dependants.[43] Abbatial kitchens are famous (Glastonbury, Durham, Fontevrault), but Raby castle (Co. Durham), Bolton and Stanton Harcourt (Oxon.) show comparable 'secular' examples. This propaganda of conspicuous consumption is less of a confidence trick

---

[41] *Rotuli Chartarum* (Record Commission, 1837), i, 89b; *CPR (1321–4)*, 7; *(1327–30)*, 31, 33; *(1330–34)*, 87, 411; *CCR (1333–7)*, 116; *CIPM*, ii, p. 260; ix, pp. 201, 233; x, pp. 552–4; Mackenzie, *Castles of England*, ii, 217–18. Coulson, 'Battlements and the Bourgeoisie', 161–5.

[42] F. Wilkinson's, *The Castles of England* (London, 1973) defies orthodoxy by map work; cf. King, *Castellarium Anglicanum*. See also the Moated Sites/Medieval Settlement Research Group *Reports*, 1–13, ed. R. Daniels, (Hartlepool, 1985–98).

[43] E.g. D. Crouch, *The Image of Aristocracy in Britain, 1000–1300* (London, 1992), esp. 252–80; C. Given-Wilson, *The English Nobility in the Late Middle Ages* (London, 1987), esp. chaps 4 and 5. C. M. Woolgar, *The Great Household in Late Medieval England* (New Haven and London, 1999).

than the ambiguities of 'fortification'. The fourteenth-century integration of the
castle-plan and more organised layout of apartments, offices and curtilage clari-
fies their relationship to the whole, reducing the previous, rather bogus, sense of
(timber) apartments camping out within a defensive girdle (e.g. Peter of Savoy's
Pevensey, c.1250). By comparison the earlier plan looks more 'military', and the
later castle less 'genuine'. The superbly ingenious Percy tower-house and castle
at Warkworth (c.1400) was saluted in the 1538 survey as a 'very propere howsse'.
Very obviously, Pevensey looks much less 'domestic' than Lumley (Co. Durham),
licensed in 1392.[44] Such quadrangular ranges of intricately linked rooms around
small courtyards, which are the 'normal' fourteenth-century type, may be closer
in appearance to Tudor mansions – but they are no less 'castles' for all that.

Cost-effectiveness hardly ever agrees with aristocratic display. The over-exact
correcting of the ideas propagated by Sir Walter Scott of medieval bravado and
individualism[45] has meant that the praise lavished on the post-medieval 'prodigy
house' has not been applied to its medieval counterparts. Piers Gaveston's *donjon*
at Knaresborough, provided by Edward II to glorify his upstart favourite is, like
Warwick, Bodiam, Herstmonceux, Pierrefonds and Saumur, perfectly authentic
fantasy. But William Burges' 'restoration' in 1875–9 of Castell Coch (Glamorgan)
for Lord Bute is still unjustly taken to represent the unacceptable face of medievalism. Such exuberance, it is thought, could not possibly be right. Viollet le
Duc's great *Dictionnaire Raisonné de l'Architecture Française*, hostile though it is
to neo-classicism as 'contrary to the national spirit', is still imbued with strenuous sanity and sensitive knowledge of medieval literature and lifestyle, which his
Dictionnaire du Mobilier confirms. The loss of much of his romantic vision is to
be regretted. It is possible to be excessively dour, unemotional and historicist.
Wordsworth may go too far in anathematising 'the nicely calculated less and
more' actually to be found at King's College Chapel, but the timber Octagon of
Ely cathedral (c.1322) is a handy epitome of inspirational construction. Warwick's
Caesar's Tower, in particular, with its lobed plan and double summit is no less
poetic,[46] representing the apogee of late-decorated Geometric and Perpendicular
castle-building in England. It would be a pity if only art historians were uninhibited enough to appreciate the castles of this vital and inventive period.

Admittedly, scant remnants survive. Loss or neglect of the middling, knightly,
castles has skewed the physical record; but Edward III's adroit focusing of noble
prestige upon his court (even before the French wars) means that architectural
emulation is quite fairly reflected in the licences to crenellate. Ruan Lanihorne
(Cornwall, 1335), which belonged to the Larchdeacons, was once 'a very substantial complex, probably of quadrangular form, perhaps with an outer court, and
with seven towers'.[47]

[44] (Turner and) Parker, *Domestic Architecture*, iii, 202–6; Emery, *Greater Medieval Houses*, i, 117–21,
    144–8; *CPR (1391–6)*, 188.
[45] E.g. R. A. Brown, 'The Status of the Norman Knight', 141.
[46] Plans and sections in S. Toy, *The Castles of Great Britain* (London, 1953), 204–5.
[47] P. Rose and A. Preston-Jones, 'Medieval Cornwall', *Cornish Archaeology* 25 (1986), 173.

In 1341, Sir Reginald Cobham nominated Austin Lodge (*Orkesdene*, Kent) and Sterborough, (*Pringham*, Surrey) for licence, but seems only to have built at the latter. Quadrangular Sterborough, like Ruan Lanihorne, once had seven towers, with a moat and gatehouse. It was described in 1369 as 'a chief messuage, wherein is a *forcelettum ad modum castri* with a very strong wall, and a park with deer measuring a league in circuit'.[48] Sterborough clearly upheld the Cobhams' prestige, but self-aggrandisement could sometimes be dissembled. Applying in 1340 for licence for Triermain (Cumb.) once 'a substantial rectangular castle, said to have had turrets on two of the corners', Roland de Vaux added that it lay 'in the march of Scotland'.[49] In *c*.1380, John, Lord Cobham, at Cooling on the potentially vulnerable Hoo Peninsula of Kent, actually apologised. The still extant enamelled copper plate which he had displayed to passers-by on his machicolated outer gatehouse declared that his patriotism was so enthusiastic that he was 'mad in help of the cuntre'.[50] Perhaps it is the castle saying it was 'made to help the country'. Denying self-interest was then politically correct. In an earlier phase, understatement was more appropriate, despite Warwick. Maxstoke nearby is another 'fortress in the castle manner'. Exteriorly intact and still splendid, it illustrates many of the themes discussed here and merits detailed attention.[51]

Whether classified as 'a fortified manor-house', or described more correctly as 'a castellated country house', Maxstoke was a castle meant by William de Clinton, whose earldom died with him in 1354, like Dallingridge's Bodiam, to perpetuate his personal renown in the Clinton family. Outfacing mortality was always a prime mover of architecture. Clinton had it licensed initially to John, his nephew and heir, then more correctly (but still retrospectively) in his own name (12 February 1345),[52] having already abandoned the old manor-house to the priory he formally refounded in 1336. His motives could hardly be clearer, or more typical; which makes the handful of 'defensive' quirks all the more revealing. There can be no question that his castle was a very fine house, originally with apartments on all four sides of the quadrangle. It satisfied the Staffords, earls and dukes (1438–83), almost unaltered, and then (with some domestic remodelling), Lady Margaret Beaufort. In 1521, it was considered a possible temporary residence for Henry VIII himself. With a good moat, separated from the walls (slightly over 5 feet thick) by a wide bank ('berm'), large (28-feet diameter) octagonal towers at the four corners, and a lofty gatehouse opposite the apartments remaining, but altered, along the west and north-west sides, Maxstoke is demonstrably castellar

---

[48] *CIPM*, xii, pp. 326–9; *CPR (1340–3)*, 304.

[49] *CPR (1338–40)*, 417.

[50] W. Scott-Robertson, 'Coulyng Castle', *Archaeologia Cantiana* 11 (1877), 128–44: facsimile of plate, plan, accounts, *CPR (1377–81)*, 596.

[51] N. Alcock, P. Faulkner and S. Jones, 'Maxstoke Castle, Warwickshire', *Archaeological Journal* 135 (1978), 195–235: plates viii–x: plans, sections, documents, etc.; M. Binney, *Country Life* (11 and 18 April 1974), 842–5, 930–3: plates 1, 3, 9, 10 reproduced here (as Figures 1–4) by permission of Country Life Picture Library.

[52] *CPR (1343–5)*, 431, 444.

Figure 1. Maxstoke Castle. The gatehouse. Original 'sheds' to berm, large central windows, loop lights, nominal drawbridge recess, miniaturised battlements.
(*Country Life* Picture Library)

(see Figure 2). Its style, however, is markedly lower-key than nearby Warwick, perhaps out of *parvenu* tact. In similar fashion, Bishop Rede of Chichester may have aimed to defer with a castle less assertive still to Arundel, further down the Arun, when building Amberley castle (licensed 1377) with showy crosslet-oillet quasi-gunloops, but without towers. Genuflecting to the dominant *caput* was normal in France. Leland's hint that Fulbrook castle, built by John, duke of Bedford, 'was an eyesore to the Erlis that lay in Warwicke Castle, and was cause of displeasure between each lord', is a possible clue to earlier Beauchamp–Clinton undercurrents.[53]

[53] *CPR (1377–81)*, 76. L. Toulmin Smith, ed., *The Itinerary of John Leland, 1535–43* (repr. London, 1964), ii, 47–8.

Figure 2. Maxstoke Castle from the south-east. Moat (undefended), wide berm,
gatehouse flank, windows, loop lights, chimneys, low walls.
(*Country Life* Picture Library)

Maxstoke's combination of palatial accommodation[54] with potentially defensive features – drawbridge-recess (non-functional) and shoot, 'murder-holes'
in the gate-passage, battlement (merlon not crenel) cresting, crenel shutters
etc. – affords valuable paradigms for the castle-style of the whole century. If the
language of strategy or defence were to be employed, note would be taken of
such 'civilian' elements as the frontally slender turreted and windowed gatehouse
(Figure 1) which 'controlled' the wall-walks all around the castle – in the sense
that they were very awkwardly accessible only, or mainly from it. From within
the resemblance to, and anticipation of, the gatehouses of a host of great houses,
palaces, conventual precincts and colleges down to the early Stuart period is
especially striking. One would note also the undoubtedly original single-storey
sheds or outshuts, 'encumbering' both exterior flanks (fitted out for comfortable
low-status occupation) with doorways to the open 'berm' or grassy verge within
the moat, from which mere ladders could easily reach the wall-top. The 'curtain walls' at Bodiam (licensed 1385) and Shirburn (Oxon., 1377) rise higher and
impressively direct from the water, although Rotherfield Greys (Oxon., licensed

---

[54] Alcock *et al.*, 'Maxstoke Castle', esp. 222–4, exemplify Patrick Faulkner's important accommoda-
tion-suite analysis using purely 'domestic' criteria of planning.

1346, 1348) and Nunney are like Maxstoke in having a bank within the moat.[55] Loops for crossbows (always the garrison weapon) occur only at the top of the gatehouse, where they are most conspicuous. Such a place, very typically, cannot be crudely classified.

When the literary evidence is fully evaluated it is likely to confirm that such architectural hints as these at Maxstoke alluded to an idealised castle-image, certainly closer to the story of the *Sangreal* than to Scott's *Torquilstone* or Conan Doyle's *La Brohinière*; but also remote from the barbarities of popular legend. The great barbican of Warwick was not so much 'a killing ground'[56] as a hypothetical declaration of power over men's lives (an attacker would have gone around the back, by the old curtain and motte). The 'we could kill you if we wished' message reveals not so much the destructive side of medieval civilisation as the continual desire to sublimate, legitimise, and even escape from, its brutality. While rising above and transcending violence, fortification reflected a society in which fighting was commonplace. It acknowledged the realities of power but made a gesture of defiance as well. It was always an element of castellated display to flaunt threats. Archbishop William of Corbeil's tower-palace at Rochester, apart from a drawbridge and numinous portcullis (both always elemental symbols) but otherwise almost devoid of defensive devices, has nevertheless in its original surviving parapets joist holes for projecting hoards or bratticing.[57] A show of defence was the more eloquent when labour services might be involved. Dover tower's processional ramp has a drawbridge pit. Had the original interior plan of the King's Gate, Caernarfon, been executed the redundancy of superfluous devices would have seemed all the greater. The obstacle-course of Dallingridge's main (but not lesser) entry at Bodiam boasts its full ingenuity. Such 'vain and ridiculous excess' smacks of literary hyperbole. It was unquestionably enjoyed, indeed revelled in. Such devious stratagems were far from automatic. Many obvious 'defensive' tricks were deliberately missed, not incompetently forgotten. Machicolated overhanging parapets, as on Cooling's outer gate where almost oversize for emphasis, are quite rare compared with fourteenth-century France (unless over entries). Angled entrances, in the flank of a tower, were practically inconvenient (compare Lacy's gate at Denbigh) and rare, in England. Good sites for 'flanking' loops often sport windows instead. Protected wall-walks and mural galleries are distinctly uncommon. Such instances of deliberate neglect of defensive opportunity are omnipresent and very telling.

At Maxstoke, indifference not ignorance is the sole explanation. Lack of care is ruled out by the evidence of planning forethought afforded by every original feature. Given the enduring domestic convenience of Maxstoke for a large residential household, its explicit 'military' details imbued with the chivalric cult can

---

[55] *CPR (1374–7)*, 434; *(1345–8)*, 514; *(1348–50)*, 36.
[56] D. King, *The Castle in England and Wales: An Interpretative History* (Beckenham, 1988), 156.
[57] Celebrated in the later city seal: R. Allen Brown, *English Medieval Castles* (London, 1954), 172 (end-piece; caption transposed with p. 9).

Figure 3. Maxstoke Castle. Entrance passage, detail of vault. Outer vault, 'murder holes', portcullis chase, inner ribbed vault. (*Country Life* Picture Library)

be no less deliberate. The manner of fortification here is relaxed, almost casual, but not perfunctory. Other periods (e.g. the late-twelfth and late-fourteenth centuries) and particular regions (Wales and the Borders) adopted a more militant and 'French' style. So Maxstoke's few 'genuine' defences draw the eye, as they were obviously meant to do. Before the double-leaved door (still covered with iron sheeting embossed with Stafford motifs) and the rather thin portcullis, three holes in the gate-passage vault 'cover' the entry (Figure 3). They are quite large, square, the lateral pair slightly canted out of the vertical towards the axis. Traditionally called 'murder holes', they could have been used to put out a fire; or be spy-holes enabling the gates to be kept closed to the last moment, then courteously opened on demand (as today to Black Rod or in the enthronement ceremony at a cathedral). These apertures are elaborated into an aesthetic element, very typically, in the Ricardian vault of the Bloody Tower (ex-Garden Tower) entry, London, and at Bodiam, by piercing the bosses at the intersections of the ribs. Faces peering from above might intimidate the visitor, making him feel properly small and vulnerable before meeting the castle's lord. Identifying him, after he had removed any helmet, would be possible, In a Decorated or Perpendicular cloister walk it would be the arms and cognisances of benefactors to which the visitor would look up. Seignorial territoriality was much the same whether expressed by saints' statues over the archway to a religious precinct, or by heraldic emblems over a castle gateway. The establishment was appropriated by the lord's badge, as were his servants and dependants. Ambiance has to be conjured up from such signs.

Maxstoke needs no 'reconstruction' – which is almost to be regretted, since properly based drawings can greatly contribute to conveying atmosphere, making ruins live.[58] The more populist methods should not be scorned. The plain, minimalist, even atavistic quality of Clinton's battlements, however, is far from dumb. Whereas the trend-setting summit of the Eagle Tower at Caernarfon with its trio of turrets, twenty years earlier, had raised mouldings down the vertical edges of the merlons, so that each crenel (embrasure), with its projecting drip-mould along the sill, is visibly framed, Clinton opted for a quite stark simplicity. Against the trend to ornamentation, his crenel sills are almost flat, the embrasures rather wide relative to the merlons, and the whole parapet (like the wall) somewhat thin. The differentiation between castle-style and church-crenellation is neglected but subtle and illuminating. In both secular and religious use, battlements usually screen leaded (or flagged) gutters – as the creasings show was the case as Maxstoke. But the careful severity here is remarkable. Instead of Caernarfon's coping statuary (most elaborate on the barbican at Alnwick) and elaboration of roll-mouldings, Maxstoke has an angular coping to the merlon with an exaggeratedly deep doubled exterior drip (Figure 4). There is the same suggestion of the *primitif* in the sloping, wide grooves for the pivots of hanging crenel-shutters at either end of the merlon. If they were ever fitted, the shutters would have reduced the exposure of the wall-walk. But both features are incongruous,[59] both suspiciously crude and over-scale as though purposely conspicuous from outside.

Deterrence, by displaying potential resistance to attack, was effected by ostentation of wealth and power in all prominent ways, including the whole architectural gamut. Castles were simply the most visible of the many appurtenances of rank and influence. C. Northcote Parkinson neatly expressed the reaching of this point of immunity, reinforced by exaggeration as 'the flunkey puzzle' and 'the hound barrier'.[60] Unfortunately bluff can be called. In 1357, Clinton's proud Maxstoke was breached. Unusually, if the wording of *oyer and terminer* commissions is to be believed, regarding such aggravated burglaries, it was the walls and

---

[58] E.g. E. E. Viollet le Duc, *Histoire d'une Forteresse* (Paris, 1874), and *idem, Essai sur L'Architecture Militaire au Moyen Age* (Paris, 1854); B. Morley, 'Hylton Castle', *Archaeological Journal* 133 (1976), 12 1 b; and 'Wardour Castle, Aspects of Fourteenth-Century Castle Design', in *Collectanea Historica: Essays in Memory of Stuart Rigold*, ed. A. Detsicas (Maidstone, 1981), 112: also T. Ball, 'Castles on Paper', *Fortress* 2 (1989), 2–15.

[59] Military interpretation in Viollet le Duc, *Dictionnaire de L'Architecture Francaise du XIe au XVIe Siècle* (Paris, 1854–68 etc.), in the article 'Croneau', e.g. figs 8, 11, 12, 13. At Cardiff castle, SW curtain, the shutters have been 'restored', by William Burges. Examples of 'submissive' fortifying in C. Coulson, 'The Sanctioning of Fortresses in France: "Feudal Anarchy" or "Seignorial Amity"', *Nottingham Medieval Studies* 42 (1998), 38–104.

[60] *Parkinson's Law* (London, 1957), 74–80.

Figure 4. Maxstoke Castle. Battlement detail. Groove in coping of merlon as for the pivot of a hanging crenel-shutter. (*Country Life* Picture Library)

not the doors that had been 'broken'. As usual, physical 'breaking', theft and finally assault of persons were the almost ritualistic stages described. The pillaging of Westenhanger, Kent, in 1382, and of Lewes in 1383 were more serious but similar.[61] Without manning and stocking well beyond habitual levels, all castles were open to opportunistic attack, and still more to organised assault. For the most part, the buildings show that the risk was acknowledged but, wherever inconvenient, largely ignored.

Root and branch reappraisal of the reasons for fortification has reached the point where the question has become: how far did military events involve English castles at all? That they did so only in special circumstances is already clear. Even the turmoil of the Scottish border did not make much difference. Of course, 'strategic' aims (where genuine) were more natural to royal castles. Their building and use have been quite fully studied, but they were not the normal experience of castles, in the fourteenth century or more widely. For the silent majority one must look elsewhere. The general motives and impact of urban fortification, in relation to the Scots, to the Maritime Lands administration, and to municipal ambition were much more representative of the norm. It is worth repeating that towns as varied in situation as Canterbury, Carlisle, Coventry, Harwich, Hull, Ipswich,

[61] *CPR (1354–8)*, 651; *(1381–5)*, 133, 259, 319, 548.

King's Lynn, London, Newcastle, Norwich, Rye and Yarmouth pursued their own aims. Oligarchies shrewdly exploited every opportunity, manipulating often factitious crises to keep mustering and control of their own manpower, as well as of their walls, gates, ditches and taxes (e.g. murage), in their own hands. Carlisle was notably skilful at this vital self-defence. Upstart Hull worked the privilege system to out-manoeuvre archiepiscopal Beverley (*c*.1320–30), and Harwich successfully pleaded 'fortification' (*c*.1350–5) to jostle aside ancient Ipswich.[62] It is a commonplace that defence did not operate in a socio-political vacuum: but perhaps less obvious how enmeshed in local self-interest was the construction of town walls. This scenario, not one of continual warlike ferment, accords with the architecture of town and castle alike. Notions of central direction become highly questionable.

The focus of effort applied to fortresses is on manpower, and on the social control exercised by military pretext, leaving 'fortification' in, at most, an ancillary position. Compulsory defence-residence, for example, was applied to coastal and marcher estates, and thus to any suitable habitation – but initiatives were often not central but selfish and local.[63] Fortresses, rather than ordinary manor-centres, tend to be specified in Irish mandates, as the insecure pattern of 'English' settlement dictated,[64] but in England from the start of the 'French' war (1337) castles were incidental to the operation. One of very many examples must suffice here. The courtier Thomas de Aledon (*Daldon*) discharged his duties for his Hampshire lands by getting an exemption, to last 'while he is in co. Kent with his household, men-at-arms and archers ... on the custody of the maritime land and preservation of the peace there'. Actually, at Boughton Aluph, east of Ashford, about 12 miles from the sea at Hythe, he was apparently then building a finely engineered manorial church next to his manor-house. Heraldic glass flaunted his connections and the large crossing-tower on slender piers advertised the high-class masons at his command. Next spring (May 1339) he sought a licence to crenellate, to dignify the house directly.[65]

Aledon naturally had his own agenda, but 'private' fortification might relate more directly to 'public' priorities. In July 1341 the need to supplement local leadership in the North evoked a commission headed, as traditionally, by the bishop of Durham, the earl of Lancaster, and Lords Percy and Neville, who were empowered to ensure that the nobility 'stayed powerfully' there 'for the defence of the realm'. Ambition, boosted by magnate and royal notice, is the likely stimulus for a series of near-contemporary licences to crenellate: Thomas de Muschamp received licence for Barmoor, Robert de Manners for Etal, and Robert de Ogle ('king's yeoman') for Ogle with licence also to impark there (all Northumberland).

---

[62] Coulson, 'Battlements and the Bourgeoisie', 149–56, 161–5, 184–6.

[63] E.g. *CCR (1354–60)*, 114 (Scottish march); *(1337–9)*, 179 (Maritime Lands' principles); *CPR (1338–40)*, 149–50, 271 (early detailed example). In general, H. Hewitt, *The Organization of War under Edward III* (Manchester, 1966), chap. 1.

[64] E.g. *CFR (1356–68)*, 224, 303, 308; *CCR (1337–9)*, 328, 423–4; T. Rymer, ed., *Foedera* (Record Commission, 1825), III, i, 434.

[65] *CCR (1337–9)*, 626; *CPR (1338–40)*, 253.

These licences were issued in May 1341, two months before the issue of the formal commission.[66] Licences followed for Widdrington (Northumb.), Newton-in-Makerfield (Lancs.), and in 1342 for. High-Head (Cumb.), Kexby and Monkton (Yorks.); in 1343, Bothal and Crawley (Northumb.) were also licensed.[67] Architecturally the associated building in 'the northern style' (to employ David King's term) responded primarily to their owners' new prominence, under magnate leadership, when Edward III was often absent in France. The visual impact of battlemented hall-chamber blocks, towers and of 'barmkin' enclosures in great variety, reproducing *en petit* magnatial Alnwick, Brancepeth, Raby and Warkworth, still substantially conveys the 'baronial' feeling that their builders desired. There could be no better display of confident power than, for instance, a Robert de Manners of Etal refusing to skulk in some comfortless, unheated and inconvenient 'border hold'.[68]

Castellation was not, of course, alone in its distance even from the brutal aspects of war. Where it survived, castle-guard enhanced its original symbolism (it had never on its own been militarily viable) continuing to express the knightly fellowship of the tenantry of the great castellanies. The alarms of war were formulaic feudal occasions, systematically manipulated to keep dependency active. One example of this recognitory and pro forma type of summons, in Prince Edward's duchy of Cornwall castellanies in 1351–61, may be mentioned. Because the justifying circumstances had always to be 'necessity' of war, something more than remote possibility had to be made out. Only the rendability of fortresses, on the Continent, was due at the over-lord's arbitrary will.[69] Fortunately, with the French war, or the Scots, Crown and magnates had no lack of pretext.

Of the four capital castles of the duchy,[70] the diminutive 'shell-keep' on its early ringwork with attached bailey at Restormel was antiquated but kept up; Trematon, by Saltash, on the Tamar estuary, was old but more capacious; inland Launceston, with its township, baileys and thirteenth-century cylindrical *donjon* with 'chemise', on the motte, had the greatest dignity: but remote Tintagel on its Atlantic coastal headland was ruinous, almost deserted[71] and seemingly nugatory. The 'safety of his duchy of Cornwall and of the people of the county in this time of war' could scarcely be effected by having 'the defects of the said castles made good', at Tintagel least of all. It was very largely a chivalric ritual to summon the fief-holders to 'repair' (*recte?* 'prepare') their respective sections of the battlements of Restormel in 1361. Putting up the hoards or *bretasche*, then, in due

---

[66] *Foedera* II, ii, 1171; cf. *CPR (1340–3)*, 253; *ibid.*, 179, 221. See A. Goodman, 'The Defence of Northumberland: A Preliminary Survey', in *Armies, Chivalry and Warfare* (1998), 161–72.

[67] *CPR (1340–3)*, 289, 304; *(1343–5)*, 30, 143.

[68] Etal: Emery, *Greater Medieval Houses*, i, 91–2.

[69] E.g. C. Coulson, 'Valois Powers over Fortresses on the Eve of the Hundred Years War', in *Armies, Chivalry and Warfare* (1998), 147–60, and references.

[70] Cf. N. Pounds, 'The Duchy Palace at Lostwithiel, Cornwall', *Archaeological Journal* 136 (1979), 203–17.

[71] E.g. *Register of Edward the Black Prince* (4 vols, London, 1931), ii, 185 (1361).

course, carefully marking each component for reassembly before taking them down and storing them for the winter, ready for the next summons, was punctiliously stipulated (one is reminded of play-equipment).

Many comparable military duties were of so limited an occasion as to have recognitory significance only. And here it was not much more.[72] Armed men (one per fief) were, it is true, put on three-days' notice to go to 'garrison' each of the four castles, but regardless of their different defensive potential. If guard duty had to be done, the regular forty-day watch, with paid service beyond that if called for, were terms put in as though to refresh memories – but no general paid impressment was envisaged at all.

Just as an emulatory cluster of licences to crenellate in the north (1341–3) saluted the July 1341 cooperation, so it is chiefly social motives that are to be inferred for licences obtained by knights of the castellanies of Launceston and Trematon and others around 1335. Sir John Larchdeacon of Ruan Lanihorne, already noted, was one of them. Much caution is needed over such protestations of danger as those made in 1347 by 'the men of Cornwall' (and of Devon) to obtain a tax-remission. At least so far as an architectural linkage and possible permanent and purposive building may go, royal works not excluded, other lines of investigation are likely to be more productive.[73]

The medieval idealisation of 'the castle' is one such avenue, already referred to. Professor Van Emden, in 1984, gave some hint of the powerful literary image of the fortress.[74] It is reinforced by pictorial art.[75] Olga Grlic and Sandy Heslop have in hand an important study, *Twelfth-Century Castles and the Architecture of Romance*, which will explore the interaction of literary and physical realisations. Such trans-disciplinary work is vital. Much of the correlation between the literary figure and surviving buildings (including cases of patrons associated with both) that they propose will shed methodological light on the English fourteenth-century castle as well, just as does the other twelfth-century work now in progress. There is considerable potential in applying to castle-design analogies drawn from the whole range of late medieval literature, as Michael Thompson has shown regarding the *Green Knight's Castle* and Tom McNeill in relation to the *Roman de la Rose*.[76] It is a dimension to which J. H. Parker and Viollet le Duc were always

---

[72] *Ibid.*, 9, 185; *CIPM*, v, 48 *(1309)*; e.g. xiv, 4–5, 92, 209–10 *(1374–75)*; xv, 191–2, 211–12 *(1381–82)* etc.

[73] E.g. *CPR (1334–8)*, 75, 77, 79, 238, 473; *CFR (1347–56)*, 15; C. Coulson, 'Battlements and the Bourgeoisie', *passim*.

[74] W. Van Emden, 'The Castle in some Works of Medieval French Literature', in *The Medieval Castle: Romance and Reality*, ed. K. Reyerson and F. Powe (Dubuque, IA, 1984), 1–6. See also contributions by M. Whitaker (27–46), M. Dean (147–74) and E. English (175–98).

[75] E.g. A. Mackenzie, 'French Medieval Castles in Gothic Manuscript Painting', *The Medieval Castle*, 199–214. Also M. Meiss, *French Painting in the Time of Jean de Berri* (London, 1967); and generally, C. Hohler, 'Kings and Castles: Court Life in Peace and War', in *The Flowering of the Middle Ages*, ed. J. Evans (London, 1966), 133–78.

[76] My thanks are made to Professor Heslop for sending advance details of his project. M. Thompson, 'The Green Knight's Castle', in *Studies in Medieval History Presented to R. Allen Brown*, ed. C. Harper-Bill, C. Holdsworth and J. L. Nelson (Woodbridge, 1989), 317–25; T. McNeill, *English Heritage Book of Castles* (London, 1992), 109–11.

sensitive, but which subsequently, in English scholarship especially, fell victim to academic specialisation and to the overflow into architecture of military, techno-logical and utilitarian systems of explanation.

Another area of active growth is the landscape aspect, due especially to the work of Paul Everson of the Royal Commission on Historical Monuments.[77] It is salutary to think of Bodiam as a water-girt *château de plaisance* and to remem-ber that contemporary Bolton was built with a laid-out 'model village' extend-ing from Richard Scrope's castle gates, almost in the Capability Brown manner. Eighteenth-century likenesses to medieval parks and landscape 'design' will yield increasing insights. 'Bowers' and 'pleasances', such as Henry V's at Kenilworth (complementing John of Gaunt's great hall-suite), and Richard II's summer house at Sheen Palace, will show castles in their setting opening out into the country-side, together with park lodges, in a manner hitherto strange for 'the castle'.[78]

So many different contextual and other facets have to be kept in focus at the same time to comprehend the castle in the fourteenth century, and not just the conspicuous new buildings of the period, that a swift overview risks degenerating into a list or a mere jumble. To expect to avoid these pitfalls would not be realistic. Pre-eminently, the noble life-style must be the dominant and unifying idea, both individually and collectively.[79] Finding that Henry II's Dover was, in its different way, quite as fantastical as Jean de Berry's Méhun sur Yèvre,[80] and that showman-ship was an original as well as a later feature of castellation, merging almost seam-lessly into the Tudor and Renaissance era, is surely the central insight.

To avoid ending on an unrepresentatively elevated note let us consider finally the typically humdrum situation of Lady Elizabeth de Burgh, at her ancestral castle of Clare (Suffolk) in 1360.[81] Only the very tall motte, of East Anglian pres-tige type, is now visible. It was one of the several residences belonging to Lady Elizabeth, who was Edward III's aunt and one of the coheiresses of Gilbert, last of the de Clare earls of Gloucester. So as to prevent her dependants from being arrayed in Essex for coastal preparedness, Lady Elizabeth asked that she might keep them in Suffolk, over 25 miles inland but nominally nonetheless 'on the sea shore during the present perils in parts adjoining her castle of Clare'. It is not the dilapidation of the castle (inland Shoreham, Kent, in 1371 was no different[82]) nor

---

[77] E.g. contribution to Coulson, 'Bodiam Castle', *Fortress* 10 (1991), 7, 15; and P. Everson, '"Delight-fully Surrounded with Woods and Ponds": Field Evidence for Medieval Gardens in England', in *There by Design: Field Archaeology in Parks and Gardens*, RCHME Conference (November 1996), 31–8.

[78] McNeill, *Castles*, 83; *HKW*, 245–6, 684 (Kenilworth); Index.

[79] Conveniently, M. Girouard, *Life in the English Country House* (New Haven and London, 1978), chap. 1, 'The Power Houses'; chap. 2, 'The Medieval Household'. See also n. 43 above.

[80] J.-F. Finó, *Fortresses de la France Médiévale* (Paris, 1970), 404–7.

[81] *CCR (1360–4)*, 19–20. J. C. Ward, 'Elizabeth de Burgh, Lady of Clare (d. 1360)', in *Medieval Lon-don Widows, 1300–1500*, ed. C. M. Barron and A. F. Sutton (London, 1994), 29–46.

[82] *CCR (1369–74)*, 286 (alias 'Lullingstone').

the economy with truth,[83] which matters here, but the fact that such a primitive and largely neglected early earth and timber castle not only still did duty administratively (which was normal) but that it provided a worthy residence for a wealthy and highly connected dowager in the last months of her life.[84]

---

[83] For the evasions of the abbot of Bury St Edmunds in 1377–86, see *CCR (1374–7)*, 504; *(1377–81)*, 13, 37; *(1381–5)*, 555–6; *(1385–9)*, 174.

[84] Jennifer Ward's *English Noblewomen in the Later Middle Ages* (London, 1992) provides general context. C. Coulson, *Castles in Medieval Society*, part 4, deals with specific problems of widows, minors, dowagers and heiresses. For more information on Elizabeth de Burgh, see Jennifer Ward (ed.), *Elizabeth de Burgh, Lady of Clare (1295–1360): Household and Other Records* (Woodbridge, 2014).

2

Architects, Advisors and Design at Edward I's Castles in Wales

Nicola Coldstream

The concentration of military architecture in North Wales from Flint in the east to Anglesey in the west is unsurpassed anywhere in Great Britain. Some of the castles are attributable to the wars fought between the princes of Wales and Edward I of England in 1277, 1282 and 1294/5. Others were built several decades earlier, by both the Welsh and the English.[1] Of these, some were slighted and left in disrepair after Edward's conquest, but the English took over and modified some others, notably Castell-y-Bere, Criccieth and Dolwyddelan. This article is primarily concerned not with them, but with the castles built *de novo* around Snowdonia by Edward after his various campaigns: Flint and Rhuddlan founded from 1277, Conway, Caernarfon and Harlech from 1283, and Beaumaris from 1295.[2] Their location reflects the outcome of the wars, with Flint and Rhuddlan founded in the east after Llywelyn ap Gruffudd had retreated into Snowdonia; Conwy, Caernarfon and Harlech closer to Snowdon after Llywelyn's defeat and death; and Beaumaris on Anglesey after the Welsh uprising of 1294/5. These castles are judged to be the apogee of military architecture in the late thirteenth century. Imposing and stylish, they represent all that was required in a fortified castle at that time: a visible, formidable presence that dominated its surroundings; defensive strength in walls, mural towers, and gatehouses equipped with multiple portcullises and murder holes; and domestic apartments suited to the administrative and judicial duties that the constable would dispense in peacetime. The buildings seem to follow a common pattern in planning and detail, which suggests not only that their construction was centrally controlled, but that they were designed by the same architect. A. J. Taylor collected the documentary evidence of central control in *The History of the King's Works* in 1963;[3] but in 1950 he had already affirmed that the architect of the castles was James of St George, Master of the King's Works in Wales.[4] Master James's presence in Wales was already known, but there was doubt whether he was a mason or an administrator. Taylor established

---

[1] The castles of the princes of Wales include Castell-y-Bere, Criccieth, Dolwyddelan, Dolbadarn and Ewloe. Degannwy, originally a Welsh castle, was rebuilt by Henry III.

[2] Edward also built castles at Builth and Aberystwyth in mid-Wales. They will not be considered here.

[3] *HKW*, 293–408.

[4] A. J. Taylor, 'Master James of St. George', *English Historical Review* 65 (1950), 433–57. See also n. 5, below.

unequivocally that he was a mason, and, further, he discovered that Master James actually came from Savoy, where he had been building castles for the counts. In a series of articles written over more than twenty years Taylor built up his case for the significance of James of St George as a master architect and military engineer, and for the equal significance of the connexion with Savoy, which supplied many constructional and stylistic elements for the castles in Wales.[5] Taylor's discoveries were based on the detailed analysis of both buildings and building records for Wales and Savoy. Stimulated by an inspired guess, his feat of research is justly famous. Taylor evoked a military architect of genius, who brought his experience in Savoy to create the finest castles in Britain, the equal in style and grandeur to any in medieval Christendom. He wrote of 'a master of military design' who produced at Beaumaris 'a consummate example of his art'.[6] Although Taylor did not ignore the contribution of Edward I, in his reading the figure of James of St George becomes a creative military engineer in the manner of Vauban or van Coehoorn. He bestrides the castles, not only as organiser and builder, but also as a source of symbol, meaning, and design itself. Yet Taylor did not make his own meaning entirely clear. His conclusions imply that the architect was taking over from the patron in initiating new forms of defence. Since this development is normally associated with the late fifteenth, rather than the late thirteenth, century it warrants further investigation. Did James of St George contribute new thinking to castle design or was he an unusually well-documented master mason who carried out his patron's commands?

Taylor's picture of Master James is very much the product of its time. Only a few years before his first article on the subject, John Harvey had published his own study of Henry Yevele, subtitled 'The Life of an English Architect', in which he had apparently demonstrated that, despite the comparative scarcity of information, it was possible to write the biography of a medieval mason.[7] Yevele, like Master James, was presented as an architect of exceptional talent. Following the distinction between architects and masons established only from the sixteenth century, someone who could be described as an architect could be seen as a more

[5] These articles, published in many different journals between 1950 and 1977, have been collected in A. Taylor, *Studies in Castles and Castle-Building* (London, 1985). Unless otherwise stated, all references to Taylor's work will be to that volume, which is continuously paginated. Individual articles cited are: 'Castle-Building in Thirteenth-Century Wales and Savoy', The Albert Reckitt Memorial Lecture, 1977, *Proceedings of the British Academy* 63 (1977), 265–92 (*Studies*, 1–28); 'The Castle of St. Georges-d'Espéranche', *Antiquaries Journal* 33 (1953), 33–47 (*Studies*, 29–44); 'Master James of St. George', *English Historical Review* 65 (1950), 433–57 (*Studies*, 64–98); 'Castle-Building in Wales in the Later Thirteenth Century: the Prelude to Construction', in *Studies in Building History: Essays in Recognition of the Work of B. H. St. J. O'Neil*, ed. E. M. Jope (London, 1961), 104–33 (*Studies*, 99–128); 'The Date of Caernarvon Castle', *Antiquity* 26 (1952), 25–34 (*Studies*, 129–38); 'Who was "John Pennardd, Leader of the Men of Gwynedd"?', *English Historical Review* 90 (1976), 79–97 (*Studies*, 209–30); 'Stephen de Pencestre's Account as Constable of Dover Castle for the Years Michaelmas 1272–Michaelmas 1274', in *Collectanea Historica: Essays in Memory of Stuart Rigold*, ed. A. Detsicas (Gloucester, 1981), 114–22 (*Studies*, 249–56).
[6] Taylor, *Studies*, 79.
[7] J. H. Harvey, *Henry Yevele c. 1320 to 1400. The Life of an English Architect* (London, 1944).

individualistic and creative being than a mere stonemason. Medieval architects whose lives and careers could be mapped would enjoy the status accorded to Wren, Hawksmoor or Scott. Yet neither Master James nor Yevele enjoyed any kind of artistic independence. Many studies made since the 1950s, including Taylor's own further researches into the authorship of the castles in Wales, have revealed, either purposely or as a by-product, that the masons' work had a necessary hinterland in the number and variety of people involved in constructing a major building.[8] The question turns on the matter of design. This is still very puzzling. In general, although we now have a better idea of how buildings were set out and who drew up the designs, we still know little of the relative contributions to their appearance of patrons, advisers and master masons. Taylor himself provided many clues to this process in Wales but he did not pursue their implications; nor did he alter his original conclusions. While his identification of James of St George's origins and the Savoyard elements in the castles in Wales are not in doubt and will certainly not be challenged here, his interpretation of the documents and the building fabric ignore details that offer a modified narrative of what happened in North Wales and why Master James was summoned there. This alternative view questions whether it is appropriate to see him as an architect essentially ahead of his time.

Beaumaris was the only castle never to be completed and, except for Caernarfon, which was unfinished in 1294/5 and was occupied for six months during the Welsh rebellion, the castles were unchallenged during the Middle Ages. By the early fourteenth century Wales had ceased to be a political or military issue and, exemplary though the castles may have been, as castles they went out of fashion very soon after they were built. They were slighted in the Civil War, but although they have lost some walls, towers and domestic buildings their military frameworks have survived remarkably well. We can follow their course of construction in detail in the extant building accounts, writs and letters, which deal with supplies, manpower and progress reports. All the castles were situated by the sea to enable them to be supplied easily,[9] and the differences between them reflect both their functions and their sites. As intended centres of government, three – Rhuddlan, Conwy and Caernarfon – were attached to new, walled towns. Conwy and Caernarfon seem to have a more ceremonial demeanour, which suggests that it was at either of these that the king and queen were expected to reside when they visited Wales. The plan of Caernarfon, elongated and with a central waist, was dictated by the presence of a Norman motte, round which the eastern part of the castle was laid out. The rhomboid plan of Rhuddlan and the pentagonal outer curtain of Beaumaris were made possible by the flat coastal terrain, whereas Harlech and Conwy had to conform to the rocky outcrops on which they were founded. The castles have quadrangular inner wards, and mural towers, which are mostly

---

[8] E.g. S. Murray, *Building Troyes Cathedral. The Late Gothic Campaigns* (Bloomington and Indianapolis, 1987); R. Goy, *The House of Gold. Building a Palace in Medieval Venice* (Cambridge, 1992).

[9] *HKW*, 293, 309; M. Prestwich, *Edward I* (London, 1988) (hereafter *Prestwich*), 208.

Figure 1. Harlech Castle, the gatehouse from the east, showing spiral putlog holes and semicircular arches. (*Photo: Author*)

Figure 2. Harlech Castle, south curtain showing the flat latrine (*above*) and the corbelled type (*below*). (*Photo: Author*)

cylindrical or part-cylindrical, although there is much variation, and Caernarfon has octagonal or part-octagonal towers (the latter also built at Conwy). At Flint the south-east tower is detached and strengthened. The two ends of Conwy are defended only by barbicans, but Rhuddlan, Harlech, Beaumaris and Caernarfon concentrate their defensive strength in powerfully towered gatehouses, with, at Harlech and Beaumaris, an outer curtain with mural towers, fully concentric at Harlech, adapted at Beaumaris.[10]

The features that Taylor isolated as Savoyard rather than English or Welsh occur at one or more of this group. They include the use of spiralling or inclined putlog holes for scaffolding, a technique hitherto unknown in English building; fully semicircular arches in doorways (Figure 1); distinctive, wide windows with segmental arches and tracery; crenellations adorned with pinnacles; and two types of latrine shaft, a shallow projection built into the angle of a tower and the curtain wall, and a projecting, semicircular corbelled structure (Figure 2).[11] He noted other parallels between the two areas in the use of quadrangular plans with corner towers, which had wooden floors at every level, and a strengthened

[10] A. Taylor, *Rhuddlan Castle*, 3rd edn (Cardiff, 1982); A. Taylor, *Harlech Castle*, 3rd edn (Cardiff, 1997); A. Taylor, *Caernarfon Castle and Town Walls*, 5th edn (Cardiff, 2001); A. Taylor, *Conwy Castle and Town Walls*, 4th edn (Cardiff, 1998); D. Renn and R. Avent, *Flint Castle Ewloe Castle*, rev. edn (Cardiff, 2001); A. Phillips, *Beaumaris Castle* (Cardiff, 1961).
[11] Taylor, *Studies*, 3–4.

corner tower at Yverdon on Lake Neuchatel, which was built in association with a new town. Yverdon was only one of several castles that the counts of Savoy were building in the 1260s and 1270s; others include Chillon on Lake Geneva, the castle-palace at St Georges d'Espéranche, east of Vienne, and smaller works in the Viennois at Voiron, La Cote-St-Andre and St Laurent du Pont.[12] Castles built by local lords included Grandson on Lake Neuchatel and Champvent. The counts were also extending their influence over the Alps – commanding the Mont Cenis and Great St Bernard passes – and into the territory of the bishops of Sion in the upper Rhone valley. In the 1250s the future Count Peter had built towers at Conthey, Brignon and Saillon; after the Savoyards seized the castle at Martigny in 1260 they built there the tower of La Batiaz, and further reinforced Saillon. In 1279–80, Count Philip built the tower of Saxon, between Saillon and Martigny. Finally, the Bishop of Sion took La Batiaz in 1280–1, and made repairs there.[13] It was in these buildings, and further south at San Giorio in the Val di Susa, that Taylor found parallels for the unusual elements in the castles in Wales, parallels so close that the segmental windows of Harlech are almost exactly the same size, as well as the same design, as windows at Yverdon and Chillon.[14] James of St George worked as a mason at Yverdon, at first with his father, and at Chillon; between 1273 and 1275 he travelled extensively between Count Philip's building works all over Savoy, from Aosta to the Viennois and Vaud.[15] The names of the resident masons at the various sites are not all recorded, but at Saillon Taylor found Francis the mason, whom he equated with John Francis, who worked at Conthey and Brignon; at Saxon and Falavier, Tassin of St George; and also at Saxon, Tassin's brother Gilet and one Beynardus.

Edward I's discovery of James of St George can be explained through the family and political connexions between England and Savoy. As a granddaughter of Count Thomas of Savoy, Edward's mother, Eleanor, had provided fruitful opportunities for Savoyards to make their fortunes in England: her uncle Boniface became archbishop of Canterbury. Other Savoyards who were close to Edward, and came to England to settle or to visit, included his friend and crusading companion, Otto de Grandisson (or Grandson), and, later, the future Count Amadeus of Savoy. Owing to complex feudal arrangements going back over time, the kings of England were the counts' overlords for a number of strongholds that commanded routes to the Alpine passes. In 1273, on his leisurely journey home from the Holy Land after his accession, Edward passed through Savoy so that his great uncle, Count Philip, could do homage for them. The ceremony took place at Philip's new castle-palace of St Georges d'Espéranche, whence Master James is thought to have taken his surname.[16] Edward would have seen the new house and, presumably, heard about the mason on whose expertise Philip was coming to rely.

[12] Taylor, *Studies*, 41.
[13] Taylor, *Studies*, 12–14.
[14] Taylor, *Studies*, 9.
[15] Taylor, *Studies*, 11, 93–6.
[16] Prestwich, *Edward*, 83–4.

There is no doubt that Edward I came to regard James of St George very highly. The earliest reference to him in Wales is in the summer of 1278, when 'Magistro Jacobo Ingeniatori [military engineer]' was sent to Wales 'ad ordinandum' the work on the castles.[17] This term can cover matters of design. By the following year Master James was one of the keepers of the works in Wales, one of those in charge of the operation. In the campaign of the 1280s, when Caernarfon, Conwy, Harlech and the alterations to Criccieth were in building simultaneously, James of St George was appointed Master of the King's Works in Wales, which gave him control of construction in all its aspects. This post he retained in the building campaigns of 1295–6.[18] But there are further, unusual signs of the king's approval: James's wages were consistently higher than those of all the other named masons, and from 1284, with the status of king's sergeant, he received a grant for life from the Wardrobe of 3s. per day, 8 marks annually for clothes, and a pension for his widow. This grant was made specifically 'pro bono et laudabili servicio'.[19] James was made Constable of Harlech in 1290, an administrative appointment; he was also sent to Gascony in the late 1280s on a mission that apparently had nothing to do with building.[20] By this time, Master James had become one of Edward's trusted royal servants as well as his Master of the Works in Wales, and, later, in Scotland.

The evidence of James of St George's high status, his role as Master of the Works, and the elements in the castles that can have come only from Savoy, indicate that he was chiefly responsible for their design. Yet there are difficulties that Taylor never addressed, both in the fabric of the castles and in alternative readings of the documentary record. Interpretation of the fabric is not as straightforward as it seems, particularly concerning the nature of the stylistic parallels that Taylor sought to explain. The majority of the details that are peculiar to north Wales and Savoy are not serious contributions to offensive and defensive planning, but a method of construction – inclined or spiral putlogs – and architectural embellishments – window designs, crenellations and latrine shafts. Some embellishments are not even related to Savoy: while the pinnacles of Conwy may have been inspired from the Val di Susa, its faceted chimney-stacks were thoroughly English, with an earlier parallel at Tonbridge Castle in Kent.[21] More general aspects of planning, such as the quadrangular trace and strengthened towers, were not, as Taylor was aware, exclusively Welsh and Savoyard.[22] Both were devised from the early thirteenth century in the war-torn regions of France and Britain: in north and west France at Dourdan and Le Coudray-Salbart during the conflicts between Philip II Augustus and the Plantagenets; along the Marches

[17] Taylor, *Studies*, 64.
[18] Taylor, *Studies*, 67, 71.
[19] Taylor, *Studies*, 68.
[20] Taylor, *Studies*, 72–3.
[21] D. Renn, 'Tonbridge and other Gatehouses', in *Collectanea Historica: Essays in Memory of Stuart Rigold*, ed. A. Detsicas (Gloucester, 1981), 98 and fig. 17.
[22] Taylor, *Studies*, 40.

of Wales – Usk – where the powerful Marshall Earls of Pembroke and Hubert de Burgh, Earl of Kent, were responsible for innovatory castle designs; and in the castle built in Dublin by the justiciar, Meiler Fitz Henry.[23] Although Taylor cited the strengthened corner tower of Yverdon as a precedent for Flint,[24] the Yverdon example is not an isolated tower but part of the curtain wall. Those of Dourdan and Le Coudray-Salbart are more persuasive precedents, since they are both isolated by a ditch; but the closest parallel to Flint is perhaps at the newly built port of Aigues-Mortes on the Mediterranean coast, whence Edward had set out for the Holy Land in 1270. The isolated Tour Constance, built in the 1240s, is larger, but closely resembles the arrangement at Flint.[25]

The essential, defining element in the design of Rhuddlan, Caernarfon, Harlech and Beaumaris is, however, the strengthened, twin-towered gatehouse (Figure 1). This is the feature upon which the defensive and ceremonial strength of the castle is focused. The twin-towered gatehouse originated in roughly the same area – on both sides of the English Channel – and at the same time as the quadrangular trace with mural towers. The outer defences of Chepstow had a twin-towered gatehouse by the late twelfth century, and Dover by 1216;[26] Philip Augustus built one at Dourdan before 1220.[27] By the 1230s towered gatehouses were rising in several places, apparently again those associated with Hubert de Burgh, including Beeston in Cheshire and Montgomery in mid-Wales, the latter a royal castle, as was Degannwy, a Welsh castle taken and refurbished with a towered gatehouse by Henry III in the 1240s.[28] Llewelyn the Great had built one at Criccieth. In the next generation Richard de Clare, Earl of Gloucester (d. 1262), or his son Gilbert built the gatehouse at Tonbridge, Kent, probably by 1265; and between 1268 and 1271 Gilbert de Clare constructed the inner ward, with two gatehouses, at Caerffili in South Wales.[29] Finally, from 1275, Edward I's alterations to the entrance of the Tower of London included the Middle and Byward Towers, both twin-towered gatehouses.[30] The gatehouses of Rhuddlan, begun in 1277, were the next in sequence. This steady succession of gatehouses had produced a generation

[23] P. Curnow, 'Some developments in military architecture c. 1200: Le Coudray-Salbart', *Proceedings of the Battle Abbey Conference on Anglo-Norman Studies* 2 (1979), 42–62; J. Knight, 'The Road to Harlech: Aspects of some Early Thirteenth-Century Welsh castles', in *Castles in Wales and the Marches. Essays in honour of D. J. Cathcart King*, ed. J. Kenyon and R. Avent (Cardiff, 1987), 75–88; J. Mesqui, *Châteaux Forts et Fortifications en France* (Paris, 1997), 138–41, 153–4.

[24] Taylor, *Studies*, 8.

[25] Mesqui, *Châteaux Forts*, 15–16; Prestwich, *Edward*, 211.

[26] R. Avent, 'The Late 12th-Century Gatehouse at Chepstow Castle', *Château Gaillard* 20 (2002), 27–40; J. Goodall, 'Dover Castle and the great siege of 1216', *Château Gaillard* 19 (1998), 97–9.

[27] See above, n. 23.

[28] Knight, 'The Road to Harlech', above, n. 23. Knight's suggestion (p. 83) that the quadrangular plan with a strengthened tower travelled from France to Savoy and came to Wales with Master James direct from Savoy rather than from parts of France that were well known to the English is an ingenious attempt to conform to Taylor's influential views. L. Alcock, 'Excavations at Degannwy Castle, Caernarvonshire, 1961–6', *Archaeological Journal* 124 (1967), 192–6 and fig. 2.

[29] Renn, *Tonbridge*; see also D. Renn, *Caerphilly Castle* (Cardiff, 1989).

[30] *HKW*, 720–2.

of experienced builders in England and Wales. In Savoy, however, twin-towered gatehouses did not exist. Thirteenth-century Savoyard fortifications consisted of towers, some isolated, some in association with walls. The idea of concentrating the main defence on a heavily fortified gatehouse was unknown, or at any rate untried. When James of St George arrived in England he may never have seen such a structure, and can certainly never have designed or built one.

In essence, then, the context of the castles in Wales is not Savoyard but Anglo-French, a milieu that was familiar to Edward I but not to James of St George. In addition we should take into account to distinct differences in quality between the works in Wales and those in Savoy. For Taylor, Master James had a true designer's eye, not only for symmetry but for the graceful lines of towers. Taylor saw a striking resemblance between the towers of Saillon and Conwy,[31] and his belief in Master James's abilities as a designer perhaps led him to discount the lower standard of construction in Savoy. The castles in Wales are architecturally in a different class, showing evidence that deep, serious thought went into their appearance and intended impression. To adapt Pevsner's famous comparison, if in Wales we have architecture, in Savoy we merely have building.[32] Against this it could be argued that the conditions in Savoy did not allow Master James to display the talents that emerged when he came to Wales; but in that case, it is difficult to see how Edward I could possibly have predicted that the ugly duckling at work in Savoy would turn into a swan in Wales.

Yet the documents affirm that, from the 1280s at any rate, Master James was Master of the King's Works in Wales, the man in charge of building the castles. For Taylor, the mutual confirmation of documents and building style, a concurrence that is rare in medieval studies, was enough to make James of St George the originating genius of these buildings. Taylor did, however, hedge his bet by including royal advisers in the original concept and in deciding where the castles should be sited.[33] Yet we have seen that the stylistic argument is equivocal in that this type of castle was outside Master James's experience; and the written records are neutral on the subject of design. In Savoy he is found directing the works, and this is broadly true of his traceable activities in Wales. Only once is there even a hint of the design process, when in summer 1278 he was sent 'ad ordinandum' the work on the castles. This term is interpreted to mean design, but it can also mean setting out.[34] Setting out the plan and the elevation should be a continuous activity; but by the summer of 1278 Flint, Rhuddlan, Builth and Aberystwyth had already been started, and there is no evidence that Master James designed them all over again, although the gatehouses of Rhuddlan do pose a problem since they seem to be of a less 'advanced' type than either the Clare and London gatehouses or those of the 1280s (Figure 3). Each tower has a stack of

---

[31] Taylor, *Studies*, 6.
[32] N. Pevsner, *An Outline of European Architecture*, 7th edn (London, 1973), 15.
[33] *HKW*, 293.
[34] N. Pevsner, 'Terms of Architectural Planning in the Middle Ages', *Journal of the Warburg and Courtauld Institutes* 5 (1942), 232–7.

Figure 3. Rhuddlan Castle, south-west gatehouse, showing interior of towers.
(*Photo: Author*)

single rooms with no linkage between the towers above the entrance passage. This inconvenient arrangement may show that the gatehouses were never intended for residential use; but it could alternatively be seen as an amateurish first effort by Master James. If so, the records do not reveal it. The writs, letters and building accounts for Wales concern progress reports, wages and supply of materials. They note the day-to-day activities only of those who were paid at task, as, for instance, John Flauner, who did specific works at Conwy in 1286.[35] The very senior masons were paid quarterly or annual salaries, and how they actually earned them was rarely recorded, except when they did work at task or were paid expenses for visits to building sites or to Edward's court. The records for Wales are not peculiar in this: building accounts in general very rarely mention the process of design. We should not expect them to reveal James as the designer, and the fact that they do not in no way denies the possibility. Yet this is at best negative evidence. The only castle at which he was named master mason was Beaumaris, the last to be built. If we accept Shelby's view that the master mason was always the designer – and cathedral works, which continued for years with changes of master mason, warn us to be careful about this – we might accept that by the 1280s, when he was placed in overall charge of the works in Wales, Master James had learned enough to design a gatehouse.[36]

---

[35] Taylor, *Studies*, 115; *HKW*, 344–5.
[36] L. R. Shelby, 'The Role of the Master Mason in Medieval English Building', *Speculum* 39 (1966), 387–403.

It seems reasonable, however, to suppose that he received help. Taylor speculated that the king and his advisers were present at the initial planning stages,
but Master James's fellow masons must also be taken into consideration. By this
time there were many masons in England who could have instructed him. Master
Bertram has a good claim to have inaugurated the gatehouses of Rhuddlan. He
had been the unfortunate subject of a letter sent to the king in April 1277 from the
surrendered Welsh castle of Dolforwyn, in which the writer, probably Amadeus
of Savoy, said that he did not trust the mason Master Bertram with making the
repairs to the building.[37] Described, like Master James and others, as *ingeniator*,
Bertram was by now at the end of a career that is documented from 1248 until his
death in 1283/4. Although he seems to have specialised in siege engines, he was
also a stonemason. He was in charge of making the king's engines at the Tower of
London in 1276, and had therefore seen the Tower's new gatehouses for himself.
Despite the complaints from Dolforwyn, he was placed in charge at Rhuddlan
several months before James of St George arrived there to set out the works, and
had by that time made considerable progress.[38] (The unusual plan of the gatehouses could, indeed, be seen as his work, except that it is most unlikely that the
choice of elements for any feature of the castles was left to the master mason.)

A more likely tutor to James of St George, however, although undocumented
in this context, is Robert of Beverley, master mason and keeper of the works
at Westminster Abbey and the Tower of London.[39] He was one of the leading
masons of the day. Throughout the 1260s, Robert was employed in royal works at
Westminster and Windsor, and also worked in the City of London on churches
and bridges. Between 1269 and 1272 he sporadically 'viewed the accounts' for the
works at Westminster Abbey, which suggests that his own work there was much
reduced. In 1271 Robert became Surveyor of the royal works at several places in
the south, including Windsor and the Tower of London. From 1275 he designed
the new outer ward and barbican at the Tower, including the twin-towered gatehouses; for once, there is no doubt about the designer, since he was supplied
with materials for making templates for mouldings. He remained keeper of the
works at the Tower and Westminster until his death in 1285. Chronologically, the
London gatehouses come between the two Clare castles at Tonbridge and Caerffili
and Rhuddlan. The plans of the two Clare gatehouses are so similar that they are
almost certainly by the same designer.[40] Tonbridge is a particularly fine building
(Figure 4): made throughout of ashlar, it was constructed with great attention to
detail in mouldings and ornament, with hood moulds to windows and fireplaces
ending in stiff-leaf foliage or finely carved headstops. Gilbert de Clare entertained

---

[37] Taylor, *Studies*, 5.
[38] Taylor, *Studies*, 5 n.2; 68 n.4; 115; 127 n.90; 253 n.23; *King's Works*, 1035–7; J. Harvey, *English Medieval Architects. A Biographical Dictionary down to 1550*, rev. edn (Gloucester, 1984), 21.
[39] Harvey, *English Medieval Architects*, 23–5; *King's Works*, *passim*; H. Colvin (ed.), *The Building Accounts of King Henry III* (Oxford, 1971), 416–22.
[40] Renn, *Tonbridge*, 98 and fig. 18.

Figure 4. Tonbridge Castle, gatehouse from the north. (*Photo: Author*)

Edward I there in 1274 on his way to his coronation,[41] and Edward may well have borne the Tonbridge gatehouse in mind when he later commissioned those for the Tower.

Tonbridge has details indicating connexions both to Westminster Abbey and north Wales: a beautiful corbel head, with grimacing expression, which is close to work at Westminster, and the fragment of a faceted chimney shaft like those at Conwy.[42] The architect of Tonbridge and Caerffili is not recorded, but it is well within the accepted limits of methodology to suggest that he could have been Robert of Beverley. Tonbridge is dated before 1265s only on circumstantial evidence, but Caerffili was built between 1268 and 1271, at a time when Robert's duties at Westminster were very light. While nothing in the record associates him with either castle, nothing prevents the possibility.

The significance of this lies in the relation of Caerffili to the castles in North Wales (Figure 5). Concentric, and built to a high specification, with two sets of twin-towered gatehouses on its east and west sides and cylindrical towers, Caerffili resembles the later castles so closely that it must have served as some kind of model.[43] Yet, because it needed such comprehensive restoration in the nineteenth and twentieth centuries, there is always a faint suspicion that although the restorers, the Marquesses of Bute, were scrupulous in their methods, they could not help having in mind an image of the better-preserved northern castles.

[41] Renn, *Tonbridge*, 100–1.
[42] Renn, *Tonbridge*, n. 21, pl. XVII.
[43] Renn, *Caerphilly Castle*, 16–19; 34–5.

Figure 5. Caerffili Castle, inner ward from the north. (*Photo: Author*)

Caerffili, as it is now, may look more like, say, Harlech, than it did in the late thirteenth century. Be that as it may, six years before the North Welsh wars began, there already existed in South Wales a castle built to the specification and in the style that Edward was to order for the north.

If Robert of Beverley did design Caerffili, he would have had an important part to play in training Master James; but even if he did not, he could still be significant: there is no evidence that James ever visited Caerffili, but he could certainly have inspected Robert's new gatehouses at the Tower when he attended the king's court at Westminster in May 1278,[44] by which time he had also seen the beginnings of the new gatehouses at Rhuddlan. Rhuddlan cannot be attributed to Master Robert: at this time he was busy in the south, and while he could theoretically have sent templates to Wales, he would have had to make visits of inspection, and no such visits are recorded.

In Wales itself a number of masons worked closely with Master James, and some, at least, contributed to the castle designs. A master mason normally recruited his journeymen as part of his contract, and it was only the extent of the building programme in Wales that forced the impressment of masons that is such a striking feature of the works organisation.[45] Several men who appeared in the records of Savoy, all known to James of St George, were brought to Wales, evidently recruited by him. There must have been problems of language between the visitors and the English masons, and how the Savoyards integrated with the English workforce is not clear, nor is the part played as intermediaries by the clerks, who could presumably speak French, if not the dialect spoken by the men of Savoy. Taylor discovered that the Savoyard John Francis worked at Conwy and

[44] Taylor, *Studies*, 65.
[45] *HKW*, fig. 25.

Beaumaris, Gilet of St George and Beynardus were at Aberystwyth, and Beynardus again at Harlech.[46] He drew attention to the similarities between John Francis's works at Saillon and Conway, and those of Gilet of St George and Beynardus at Saxon and Harlech.[47] Master James had not been closely concerned with either Saillon or Saxon. The towers of Conwy that for Taylor so closely resemble those of Saillon should perhaps be attributed not to James but to John Francis, who may also have imported the design of the corbelled latrine found at Harlech, which was built at La Batiaz only after 1280–1, when Master James was in Wales and could not have seen it.

Master James's two leading English colleagues in Wales were Walter of Hereford and Richard of Chester. Walter of Hereford was in charge of the works at Caernarfon from 1295, completing the south curtain after the Welsh rebellion. He was already a distinguished mason, having been master at Edward I's newly founded abbey of Vale Royal from 1278 to 1290, and at the same time master mason of Winchcombe Abbey.[48] Although Walter did not set out the south curtain at Caernarfon, John Maddison has isolated certain styles of moulding that he attributed to him, so that Walter was able to influence details of the design if not the whole scheme.[49] John Harvey believed that the design of the castles was the joint responsibility of Walter of Hereford and James of St George together with Richard of Chester.[50] Richard, also known as the Engineer, was from 1281 the highest-paid mason after James of St George, receiving the same wage as Robert of Beverley. Like Master James, he attained the status of king's sergeant and received a life pension.[51] He was already named the King's Engineer in 1272–3, and was with the advancing army in 1277; but the next few years are obscure and he may have been busy on his interests in Chester, where he became a substantial citizen. In 1283 Edward ordered his clerk, William de Perton, 'to cause to be brought divers tools and other necessaries, as our beloved Richard the Engineer will tell you, for making ditches at Aberconwy. You are also to cause to come to Conwy masons and quarry-breakers, as the same Richard will tell you.'[52] Richard helped to make the timberwork for the royal apartments built by James of St George at Conwy. Taylor saw him as James's 'right-hand man'.[53] That Edward should personally discuss matters of building with him suggests that he was as highly trusted as James of St George, and his presence at a number of building sites in the early stages suggests that he was part of the design team.

Taylor was not too willing to see the master and undermasters as a design

[46] Taylor, *Studies*, 12–13, 16–17, 19–20.
[47] Taylor, *Studies*, 12–13, 19–20; *HKW*, 1038–9.
[48] Harvey, *English Medieval Architects*, 136–7.
[49] J. M. Maddison, 'Decorated Architecture in the North-West Midlands – An Investigation of the Work of Provincial Masons and their Sources' (Unpublished Ph.D. Thesis, University of Manchester, 1978).
[50] Harvey, *English Medieval Architects*, 137.
[51] Taylor, *Studies*, 68 and n.4; Harvey, *English Medieval Architects*, 178–80, under Lenginour.
[52] Taylor, *Studies*, 74, 116–17.
[53] *HKW*, 393.

team, but he did allow that the king's advisers and the king himself might have influenced the castle designs. The advisers formed the king's intimate circle of household knights and clerical officials of the Wardrobe, the department that financed the operation.[54] Master James worked with household knights in both Wales and Savoy. The records of the building works in Savoy are patchier than for the king's works in Wales, but they give a consistent, if sketchy, impression of the organisation. As in most building programmes of any size, administrators and masons worked together. In the 1260s the keeper of the count's works was Peter Mainier, who is recorded at Yverdon, Romont and Chinon.[55] Another administrator was Sir John Masot, a household knight who was closely involved not only with paying wages but with design: he is recorded first at Saillon in 1261, where he was to settle the form of a tower, and its site.[56] In the 1270s, together with another household knight, Petrus de Langis, Masot frequently worked in association with James of St George. Among several Savoyards given administrative duties in North Wales was Sir John de Bevillard, who in 1285/6 supervised the works at Conwy and Caernarfon and, with James of St George, allocated the masons' tasks. He was Constable of Harlech from 1285 until his death in 1287.[57] Taylor, however, discounted his influence.[58] Another Savoyard knight, thought to be 'probably influential',[59] was William de Cicon, first the Constable of Rhuddlan, then, as the seat of administration moved westwards, the Constable of Conwy. The names of other household knights appear occasionally, but their activities are unspecified. The wardrobe clerks – William de Perton and Robert de Belvero at Rhuddlan, Hugh of Leominster at Caernarfon, and Walter of Winchester at Beaumaris – organised wages and supplies; evidence for their advice on design is neutral. A similar neutrality surrounds most of the senior Wardrobe officials, regarded as Edward's inner council, part of his familia or close household. Nothing associates the Treasurers, Keepers and Stewards for the 1270s and 1280s with the castle-building programme; nothing rules them out.[60] For two other officials, however, there is evidence of a kind. John Benstead, Controller of the Wardrobe in 1295, made surveys and other military preparations, and even fought in Scotland as a banneret, giving up his clerical orders. Edward described him as 'our clerk who stays continually by our side'.[61] The other cleric who was almost constantly with Edward until his death in 1292 was the Chancellor, Robert Burnell. Again, there

---

[54] Taylor, *Studies*, 116; T. F. Tout, *Chapters in the Administrative History of Medieval England*, ii (Manchester, 1920), 156; Prestwich, *Edward*, 138. The knights were mostly bannerets, men of higher status.
[55] Taylor, *Studies*, 11, 24.
[56] Taylor, *Studies*, 12.
[57] Otherwise known as Bonvillars. Taylor, *Studies*, 213, 216, 221–2; Prestwich, *Edward*, 151.
[58] Taylor, *Studies*, 224.
[59] Prestwich, *Edward*, 209.
[60] The Treasurers were Joseph de Chauncy, Richard Ware and John Kirby; the Keepers, Thomas Bek and William Louth; the Stewards, Hugh FitzOtho, Robert Fitzjohn and John de Montalt: Prestwich, *Edward*, 138–9, 145, 234–5.
[61] Prestwich, *Edward*, 142; Tout, *Chapters*, ii, 19–20, 141.

is no evidence that Burnell gave any advice on the design of castles; but his own house, Acton Burnell in Shropshire, has domical vaults that betray the influence of vaults at Caernarfon.[62]

Edward I had other intimates, among the fighting men. The greatest seem to have been his two Savoyard friends, his cousin Amadeus of Savoy and Otto de Grandisson. Amadeus was at Montgomery in 1277, and was possibly the writer of the letter that condemned Master Bertram. He led the army at Chester in 1282. Otto de Grandisson, who, Prestwich speculated, 'doubtless had a part to play'[63] was a lifelong companion to Edward; he became Justiciar in North Wales and Constable of Caernarfon, although he was seldom in Wales after 1284.[64] Together with John de Vescy and Roger de Clifford, Otto was present at the ceremonies of homage at St Georges d'Espéranche in 1273. Taylor surmised that Robert Tibetot and Payn de Chaworth were also in the party.[65] Vescy and Grandisson were sent to occupy Anglesey in August 1277, and, with Tibetot, were among those who negotiated peace with Llywelyn in November. Payn de Chaworth, who was Edward's commander in South Wales, built the quadrangular inner ward of Kidwelly castle.[66] The presence of these men at Philip of Savoy's new palace is important to Taylor's case, since it helps to explain how certain features were transmitted from Savoy to Wales: the quadrangular plan, the flat garderobe projection, the polygonal towers, and the arrangement of the domestic quarters. Thus, by inference and some special pleading, Edward has the expert advice of a group of men who were with him in Savoy, experienced in military architecture and able to gain the king's attention.

They may have contributed advice but it would be as well not to exaggerate it. They may, equally, have stayed in favour by acquiescing in decisions that the king had already made. In 1273, the Welsh war was by no means inevitable. The idea of Edward's friends making notes of their surroundings for use in castles that were intended to be built after such a war does not ring true;[67] and we have seen that Payn de Chaworth could have built a quadrangular ward at Kidwelly without having visited Savoy. Without going so far as to say that the influence and contribution to design of Edward's *familia* of cronies and officials are factoids, we should note how far arguments in their favour are based on speculation and wishful thinking.

A more persuasive contributor is the king himself. Both Taylor and Edward's biographer, Michael Prestwich, agree that Edward decided the essential elements of the castles, from their sites to their component parts. Given their political, let alone their military, importance, it could scarcely be otherwise. Although no written evidence of his detailed instructions survives from the Welsh campaign,

[62] Maddison, 'Decorated Architecture', 72, 104.
[63] Prestwich, *Edward*, 209.
[64] *Ibid.*
[65] Otherwise known as Tiptoft. Taylor, *Studies*, 29.
[66] Taylor, *Studies*, 180; J. Kenyon, *Kidwelly Castle*, rev. edn (Cardiff, 1990), 28–34.
[67] Prestwich, *Edward*, 170–5.

a memorandum sent by Edward to James of St George in 1302 concerning the castle of Linlithgow is revealing.[68] This document, which is effectively a contract, instructs James to build a twin-towered gatehouse and two towers on the water at either end of the palisade, with a change of material from stone to timber, all of which Edward has already explained to him. That all building contracts were the culmination of detailed discussion is self-evident, but this is further evidence that Edward did not necessarily act through advisers but talked directly to his master masons without intermediaries. Elements of plans and details in the castles in Wales reflect the king's personal wishes. The twin-towered gatehouse is one of his contributions. He also preferred cylindrical, half-round or polygonal – as distinct from D-shaped – towers, and was probably responsible for the extensive provision of latrines. Edward was evidently careful about hygiene, perhaps again influenced by the efficient arrangements at Tonbridge. Not only were many latrines built into the new castles, but he added them to the towers, Dolwyddelan for example, that he took over from the Welsh. Edward, at least, may genuinely have noted the design of the flat latrine shaft on his visit to St Georges d'Espéranche.

It is Caernarfon, however, that demonstrates the true role of Master James of St George. Caernarfon differs from the other royal castles in having bands of masonry in contrasted colours in its curtain wall and polygonal towers (Figure 6). (The latter occur otherwise only at Denbigh, which was built under licence by Henry de Lacy, Earl of Lincoln.) In 1950 Taylor thought that this difference in style showed that Caernarfon must have been designed by someone other than James of St George, possibly Walter of Hereford, master mason in 1295.[69] Later he changed his mind, arguing that the entire castle had been set out in the 1280s, when James was Master of the King's Works in Wales and Walter was busy elsewhere;[70] he explained the differences in detail by suggesting an elaborate ceremonial and symbolic function for Caernarfon. The castle, near the site of Roman Segontium and the birthplace of Magnus Maximus, the legendary father of Constantine, had taken on the imagery of Christian imperialism, manifest in the reproduction of the banded walls and polygonal towers of the Theodosian walls of Constantinople. Caernarfon was also chosen as the place for Queen Eleanor to give birth in 1284 to the 'first royal child to be born in Wales since the two last princes of Gwynedd'.[71] Richard Morris has developed the symbolism of Caernarfon by adding an Arthurian element.[72] In these readings, the appearance of Caernarfon is symbolic and political, the imposition of Edward's claim to Wales, his identification with the Christian heroes Constantine and Arthur, and the continuity of his line. That the baby turned out to be the future Edward II

[68] Taylor, *Studies*, 79–81.
[69] Taylor, *Studies*, 71.
[70] Taylor, *Studies*, 137; *HKW*, 391.
[71] *HKW*, 371 and n. 2.
[72] R. Morris, 'The Architecture of Arthurian Enthusiasm: Castle Symbolism in the Reigns of Edward I and His Successors', in *Armies, Chivalry and Warfare in Medieval Britain and France*, ed. M. Strickland, Proceedings of the 1995 Harlaxton Symposium (Stamford, 1998), 63–81.

Figure 6. Caernarfon Castle,
banded masonry on the
Queen's Tower. (*Photo: Author*)

is, however, fortuitous, since its parents could not possibly have known that the
child would be a boy, and in any case his elder brother, Alfonso, was still alive and
thus heir to the throne;[73] yet Caernarfon, whether Constantinian or Arthurian or
both, represented something special to Edward. Master James is most unlikely to
have put political and symbolic ideas into Edward's head; nor does Taylor suggest that he did, preferring the possibility that a member of Edward's entourage
supplied a description of the Theodosian walls, which Master James, having built
polygonal towers at St Georges d'Espéranche, could construct at Caernarfon.[74]
The polygonal towers and striped masonry must have been requested by the king,
along with the other main decorative feature of Caernarfon, the carved figures

[73] As late as 1987, however, Taylor argued that Caernarfon was deliberately chosen as Edward's
birthplace, citing evidence that the lower floors of the Eagle tower were built unusually fast to be
ready in time. See A. Taylor, 'The Beaumaris Castle Building Account of 1295–1298', in Kenyon
and Avent, *Castles in Wales and the Marches*, 126.
[74] *HKW*, 369–71; Taylor, *Studies*, 41.

Figure 7. Caernarfon Castle, remains of parapet figures on Chamberlain Tower.
(*Photo: Author*)

and heads, remains of which adorn the coping stones of the battlements of the towers, including those built in the campaign of the 1280s (Figure 7).[75]

Caernarfon, then, owes its appearance to Edward I, and demonstrates clearly that Master James, far from initiating design, merely obeyed his master's orders, whether they were for particular features, as at Linlithgow, or for what those features were to look like. Taylor's own successive interpretations of Caernarfon bring out the inherent conflicts in his argument. He stresses Edward I's contribution to design, but still he privileges the architect. It is indeed true that Edward was not trained in the mason's craft and could not have taught James of St George how to design the castles he wanted, including the gatehouses. Nevertheless, it was Edward who ordered the elements of the castles, and many of their details that Taylor identified closely with James himself were built by his undermasters. In one sole respect does Master James seem to have a particular claim to unique expertise: planning the domestic apartments. Taylor emphasised the identical plan of hall, chamber and chapel, even at the same side of the inner ward, at St Georges d'Espéranche and Conway, which is perhaps not fortuitous.[76] Otherwise his personal contribution to the castle design is not discernible.

Yet it is scarcely likely that Master James was summoned all the way from Savoy merely to arrange the bedrooms. Luckily, the documents, which for all their abundance conceal so much, do unequivocally reveal the reason why Edward asked for him. The subtext makes clear that James of St George was a consummate organiser. There may have been nobody in England – not even Robert of Beverley – thought capable of supervising the new works in Wales, but in Savoy Master James had supervised over a vast area and difficult terrain a large number

[75] A. Taylor, *Caernarfon Castle and Town Walls*, 5th edn (Cardiff, 2001), pp. 31–2. I thank Jeremy Ashbee for drawing my attention to the heads on the earlier towers.
[76] Taylor, *Studies*, 15–16.

of building programmes that were in progress simultaneously, from fortifications to new towns, from Vaud to the Viennois, the Alps and the Val di Susa. Fortifications and new towns were the two kinds of building work that really appealed to Edward, the founder of *bastides* in Gascony, and Hull and Winchelsea in England, to say nothing of the new towns at Flint, Rhuddlan and Conway. He also had a habit of calling in particular experts for specific tasks, such as the specialist diggers of canals whom he brought from East Anglia for water defences.[77] It was for his organisational skills, rather than his perceived abilities as a military engineer, that James of St George was appointed to Wales.

Taylor's discoveries in Savoy were an outstanding piece of research, and their romantic circumstances are seductive. His argument, built up over so many publications, is persuasive; but it makes too great a claim for the genius of one man at the expense of the many. Neither the documents nor the buildings support the notion that James of St George anticipated his innovatory successors in later centuries. They show, in more detail than we are normally vouchsafed, that Master James was a typical master mason of his day. There is nothing unusual in the summons to Wales from Savoy. Medieval masters were frequently called over long distances: obvious examples are Etienne de Bonneuil who went from Paris to Uppsala and Mathias of Arras, who was called to Prague from the south of France. Nor were the builders of the castles in North Wales any more talented than those of Tonbridge and Caerffili; and equal talent was displayed in church building by the builders of castles. In the context of his day Master James was notable only for his exceptional ability to execute orders to the king's satisfaction, from which flowed the honours and privileges that single him out. As such he was typical of those whom Edward trusted and with whom he worked most closely. Edward possessed consistency of purpose and extreme competence, both of which characterise his Master of the Works in Wales. Construction of the castles depended on James's organising skills, but their design did not. Master James probably contributed less to the design of the castles than someone entitled 'master mason' would normally expect. Not only did he build according to specific instructions, but many of the elements attributed to him were supplied by his undermasters. We should see these buildings as essentially collaborative works at every stage, from setting out to the final touches. Taylor, whether intentionally or not, placed too much emphasis on a master mason because he was well documented. Medieval records, owing to the patchiness of their survival, can mislead in this respect. That Master James's collaborators were less fully recorded is no reason to write them out of history. To do so distorts our understanding of how this extraordinary building campaign was carried out.

---

[77] *HKW*, 319; Taylor, *Studies*, 27.

Acknowledgements

Versions of this paper were given at seminars at the University of Virginia, Charlottesville, the Courtauld Institute, and Warwick University. I am grateful for comments and suggestions made on those occasions. For help with specific problems I would particularly like to thank Jeremy Ashbee, Richard Eales, John Goodall and Derek Renn. Judi Loach suggested useful changes to the text.

3

The Courtyard and the Tower: Contexts and Symbols in the Development of Late Medieval Great Houses

Philip Dixon and Beryl Lott

The final two centuries of the Middle Ages are conventionally considered a period in which castles and castle-building were in decline. The 'Decline of the Castle' and 'Decline' are the titles of chapters dealing with this period in books written by Allen Brown.[1] In each case the contrast with what went before is strongly emphasised: the previous chapters are named 'The Perfected Castle' and 'Apogee'.[2] In the same vein, these final centuries after *c*.1300 have been described as 'the period of decline in use but survival in fantasy' in an authoritative account, significantly entitled *The Decline of the Castle*.[3] Our view of this period is different. We consider that the castles of the later Middle Ages show a steady development, not a decline, and the main elements of that development can already be traced in buildings of the 'Golden Age'.[4]

Our themes, the symbols of the courtyard and the tower, are visible in the arrangements of 1283 at Caernarvon.[5] The King's Gate of this castle was a novel

[1] R. A. Brown, *English Medieval Castles* (London, 1953), 89; *idem*, *English Castles* (London, 1976), 128.

[2] Brown, *English Medieval Castles*, 60; *English Castles*, 95.

[3] M. W. Thompson, *The Decline of the Castle* (Cambridge, 1987).

[4] Though this is our present starting point, all the elements are as clear in the twelfth century. At this period can be found (a) rectangular (bishop's and king's) courtyard houses (for example, Old Sarum, Sherborne, Newark, Wolvesey Palace, Windsor Castle [Henry II's palace in the upper ward] or Corfe Castle [the Gloriette], the first two with attached solar towers), (b) great halls with adjacent solar towers (for example Norham, Northumberland: P. Dixon and P. Marshall, 'The Great Tower in the 12th Century: the case of Norham Castle', *Archaeological Journal* 150 (1993), 410–32, and (c) free-standing donjons with ceremonial rather than domestic function (for example, Castle Hedingham, Essex: see P. Dixon and P. Marshall, 'The Great Tower at Hedingham Castle: A Reassessment', *Fortress* 18 (1993), 16–23, reprinted *ANC*, 297–306.

[5] For a discussion and floor plans of Caernarvon, see Royal Commission on Ancient and Historical Monuments in Wales and Monmouthshire, *Caernarvonshire* II (1960), 124–50. A reasonable reconstruction of the King's Gate is given in S. Toy, *The Castles of Great Britain* (London, 1953), 245; the angled gate has analogies with the complex triple-towered gateway at Denbigh, Clwyd, which was being built from 1282. Though the masons at Denbigh are not known, it is likely that royal workmen were involved (*HKW*, 333–4). A construction of the next generation, the new gate and adjacent donjon at Knaresborough, was probably similar to Denbigh, and was built at the expense of Edward II. It too was probably constructed by royal craftsmen, though their names

and complex affair placed to divide the interior of the castle into two halves. The entrance passageway beyond the central polygonal chamber directed traffic at right angles westwards into a lower courtyard.[6] This contained the principal hall and its services, and a series of accommodation lodges in mural towers. All this is a conventional arrangement: what is much odder is that this lower courtyard contained also the visual focus of the castle, the Eagle Tower, emphasised particularly from the outside by its greater size and by its termination in a triple crown of turrets, originally given additional importance by the placing of sculptures of eagles on its battlements. The purpose of this striking design is a strong statement of the fulfilment of the *Dream of Macsen Wledig* in the person of Edward I and his son, a statement whose propaganda must have been obvious to the defeated Welsh aristocrats. The symbolism of all this has been examined by Dr Arnold Taylor,[7] who further identified the Eagle Tower as the intended residence of the king's Justiciar of Wales and first constable of the castle, Edward's loyal supporter Otto de Grandson, and his conclusions seem now to be accepted. However, what has not been explained is why this significant element of the symbolism of the castle was placed in the lower ward, and not (where one might expect) in the inner bailey. While the Justiciar was provided for in the Eagle Tower, accommodation for the constable or his military deputy was arranged around the hall on the top floor of the King's Gate.[8] The two royal officials – keeper of Caernarvon and viceroy of the principality – were thus catered for at the main entrance and in the lower courtyard. The third household, to be accommodated in the unfinished ranges in the upper ward, must thus be that of the king himself. The arrangement closely resembles the bipartite design of Conway.[9] Here the hall and lodgings occupy the lower courtyard entered from the town, while the more remote eastern bailey formed a tiny courtyard house for the king and queen, with an external gate to the

are not known: P. W. Dixon, 'The Donjon at Knaresborough: The Castle as Theatre', *Château Gaillard* 14 (1988), 122.

[6] Access to the courtyards from the unfinished King's Gate is problematic. Toy shows only one passage, leading westwards to the lower bailey; it appears that he considered that the eastern bailey was reached only by the Queen's Gate: *Castles of Great Britain*, 245, 171. The Royal Commission conjectured, probably correctly, that passages opened both eastwards and westwards from the polygonal chamber at the back of the gate: *Caernarvonshire* II, 14.1.

[7] *HKW*, 370–1. Magnus Maximus the Roman Emperor (or usurper), killed in 388, was in Welsh folklore the hero and ancestor to the descendants of Cunedda, the princes of Gwynedd. His supposed body was discovered in 1283 and reburied in the church at Caernarvon in the presence of Edward I, a political ruse identical to that carried out later by Edward in the case of the reburial of King Arthur at Glastonbury, and coupled here with the birth of the new Prince of Wales on the building site at Caernarvon in April 1284. For Edward's own conventional but strong religious beliefs, see M. Prestwich, 'The Piety of Edward I', in *England in the Thirteenth Century*, ed. W. M. Ormrod (Woodbridge, 1986), 120–8.

[8] For the arrangement of the Constable's Hall and apartments, see Toy, *The Castles of Great Britain*, 245.

[9] For the plans of Conway, see RCAHM (Wales), *Caernarvonshire* 11 (1956), 46–55, and for discussion *HKW*, 337–54. Here too there was deliberate capturing of the *mise en scène* of the displaced Welsh prince's regime. An old hall, known as *Aula Lewelini*, was incorporated with some difficulty into the town defences, to serve for the king's son Edward, the Welsh prince's successor, until its dismantling and removal to Caernarvon in 1316: *HKW*, 353–4.

waterside similar to the placing of the Queen's Gate at Caernarvon. The additional element in this comparison is the placing of the Eagle Tower in the lower bailey at Caernarvon. The reason for the difference, and for the choice of polygonal towers and decorative banding imitated from the Theodosian walls of Constantinople, was that this was to be the chief place in the new principality, and so required a seat for both the king and his lieutenant. In this context the preservation of the eleventh-century motte of Robert of Rhuddlan, awkwardly cramping the layout in the centre of the new upper courtyard, is an explicit emphasis of the importance of the *Dream*: the motte had been (incorrectly) identified as the ancient seat of Prince Macsen himself, and was now explicitly being taken over and made part of the household arrangements of the principality's new overlord.[10] The bipartite nature of Caernarvon as the English king's main seat in Wales conveyed the double theme of dominion and residence to his new subjects, and was not likely to be misunderstood. This sort of symbolism must have been much in the minds of the designers after the killing of the last prince of Gwynedd, Llewellyn ap Griffith, since it was echoed at the same time at Harlech Castle, like Caernarvon begun in August 1283. As part of the building of the new castle at Harlech, the wooden hall of Prince Llewellyn's manor at Ystumgwern was dismantled, and was brought to be re-erected on specially built footings within the courtyard, to signify the supplanting of the old dynasty by the new.[11]

Caernarvon, then, combined a tower-house for the royal official with a courtyard house for the king himself, and it is notable that the king's house itself was given little architectural emphasis other than the understated skirt of masonry around the base of 'Macsen's' motte. We may suppose, then, that at this period at any rate the king required no architectural emphasis, while the symbolism of *dominium*, the donjon or great tower, might appropriately be given to a royal official. Are there any other structures that confirm this view? The design of the donjon at Flint Castle (1277) is significant here, since from the outside it appeared to be a massive cylinder dominating the castle in the same fashion and in the same position as that of the mighty donjon of Coucy near Soissons, the clearest

---

[10] For a discussion of the evidence behind these points, see Arnold Taylor's analysis in *HKW*, 369–71; Dr Taylor, however, considers that the motte of the 1080s was in fact identified by Edward or his advisers as that of Earl Hugh, to emphasise 'not new gain but due reconquest'. The point cannot be established beyond doubt, but in view of the short duration of the Norman conquest of Gwynedd, and the successful Welsh overthrow of Robert of Rhuddlan, this was surely not a good message to convey; and so it seems more plausible that the antiquity of the waste mound had been lost sight of, and that its careful treatment was a part of the Macsen theatricals. For Edward's concern with the political advantages of the use of legends one should consider his participation in the 'discovery' and subsequent ceremonial reinterment of the bones of King Arthur at Glastonbury: M. Prestwich, *Edward I* (London, edn of 1990), 120. As Bradley rightly observes 'the past was being used in a much more active manner, in order to promote or protect the interests of a social elite': see R. Bradley, 'Time Regained: the Creation of Continuity', *Journal of the British Archaeological Association* 140 (1987), 1–17, esp. 14–15.

[11] For this, see A. Phillips, *Harlech Castle* (London, 1961), 20.

Figure 1. Interior of the great tower at Flint Castle, viewed from the entrance, showing
the narrow chambers surrounding the central area, probably a small courtyard.
Photo: © Philip Dixon

statement of seigneurial power in the thirteenth century.[12] In its interior, however,
there was no provision in the great tower at Flint for any lordly accommodation,
no hall, no audience chamber, but instead very cramped apartments arranged
around a central courtyard (Figure 1). The intended occupant, as Taylor has
pointed out,[13] was to be another royal official, probably the justiciar of Chester
when hearing the pleas of the Crown at Flint. As a king's officer he required only
an external display of power. Accordingly, his domestic arrangements within the
donjon were suitably bleak. In the same fashion, Edward II's new great tower
at Knaresborough Castle (1309), probably part of a complex gate similar to the
King's Gate at Caernarvon, or the baronial castle of Denbigh (1282 and later),
contained only a throne room, necessary services and attendants' rooms, and
an upper private chamber, all intended to emphasise the authority of the king's
favourite, Piers Gaveston.[14]

[12] E. Lefèvre-Pontalis, *Le Château de Coucy* (Paris [n.d., *c*.1910]); F. Enaud, *Coucy* (Paris, 1978),
39–41.
[13] *HKW*, 317n.
[14] P. W. Dixon, 'The Donjon at Knaresborough: the Castle as Theatre', *Château Gaillard* 14 (1988),
121–39.

While the donjon might thus be the symbol of royal authority invested in the hands of others, during the fourteenth century the king's own houses continued the theme of the courtyard, a palace within the curtilage of the castle, and this approach was increasingly taken up by the king's barons both in the rebuilding of older castles and in the design of new works.[15] Edward III's most expensive work, the rebuilding of the upper ward at Windsor Castle, converted a conventional later twelfth-century courtyard with hall, services and chambers into a huge courtyard house with integrated suites of apartments,[16] a pattern paralleled, for example, by the attempt by the Marshalls to squeeze a new courtyard house into the outer ward of the old castle of Chepstow.[17]

The dominance of these courtyard houses in new castle planning of the later fourteenth century is now well accepted.[18] Chillingham, Northumberland (rebuilt as a courtyard after 1344), Bolton, Yorkshire (1378 and after), and Bodiam, Sussex (1383) provide examples of courtyards lacking any significant architectural focus. But the symbolism of the tower, even in England, was never lost to view. Edward III's new coastal defence castle at Queenborough, Isle of Sheppey, for example, was constructed about 1360 with a symmetrical central courtyard, but the drawing by Wenceslas Hollar before its destruction in the seventeenth century shows a structure dominated by its great central block.[19] Such a dominating courtyard, if the usage at Henry III's new castle at Degannwy is any guide, might be referred to as a donjon, the name for the old symbol of dominance transferred to the new structural form.[20] At the level of the barons, the castle of Old Wardour, Wiltshire, was built about 1380 as a courtyard castle whose open court was tightly squeezed into a yard surrounded by apartments, so that its external appearance was of a wide-spreading tower,[21] while the Percy rebuilding of Warkworth, Northumberland, perhaps of c.1390, included a great tower on the old motte so designed that a full suite of baronial apartments was contrived around a courtyard reduced to the extent that it became no more than a narrow light well.[22]

---

[15] The development and planning of the fourteenth-century courtyard castles has been outlined by P. A. Faulkner, 'Castle Planning in the Fourteenth Century', *Archaeological Journal* 120 (1963), 215–35. Courtyard houses were part of the residential requirements of both bishops and kings in the twelfth century, and were built by John at Corfe (the Gloriette) and by Henry III in the lower bailey at Windsor: see above, n. 4, and for a general statement of Edward I's own preference, see M. Prestwich, *Edward I* (London, edn of 1990), 164 ['Castles were not in fact much favoured. He seems to have preferred to stay at the manor in Windsor park, rather than in the castle there …'].

[16] W. St John Hope, *Windsor Castle* (London 1913) ii, 568; *HKW*, 872–82.

[17] Faulkner, 'Castle Planning in the Fourteenth Century', 216–18; J. Knight, *Chepstow Castle* (London, 1992).

[18] See, for example, the treatment of the subject by Anthony Emery, *Darlington Hall* (Oxford, 1970).

[19] *HKW*, 795 for a plan, and pl. 47B for Hollar's drawing.

[20] L. Alcock, 'Excavations at Degannwy Castle, Caernarvonshire', *Archaeological Journal* 124 (1967), 190–201, esp. 194–5.

[21] R. B. Pugh and A. D. Saunders, *Old Wardour Castle, Wiltshire* (London, 1968).

[22] W. D. Simpson, 'Warkworth, a Castle of Livery and Maintenance', *Archaeologia Aeliana* 4th ser. 15 (1938), 115–36; M. J. B. Hislop, 'The Date of the Warkworth Donjon', *Archaeologia Aeliana* 5th ser. 19 (1992), 79–92, argues convincingly for a date in the 1380s or 1390s, and discusses the plan. For a much later, and much less convincing, date of c.1520, see L. Milner, 'Warkworth Keep,

Figure 2. South Kyme, Lincolnshire: solar tower of moated manor house, showing traces of link to demolished hall.
Photo: © Philip Dixon

Free-standing residential tower-houses, or solar towers attached to halls, con-tinued to be built throughout the thirteenth and fourteenth centuries, chiefly in the northern parts of England and at a lower social level than these principal baronial and royal castles.[23] Notable examples of these towers include Haughton, Northumberland (*c.*1270),[24] Stokesay, Shropshire (*c.*1280 and 1305),[25] Longthorpe,

---

Northumberland: A Reassessment of its Plan and Date', in *Medieval Architecture and its Intel-lectual Context*, ed. E. Fernie and P. Crossley (London, 1990), 219–37.

[23] For the transition between hall-and-solar tower and tower-house, see P. W. Dixon, 'From Hall to Tower: the Change in Seigneurial Houses on the Anglo-Scottish Border after *c.*1250', in *Thir-teenth-Century England* 4, ed. P. Coss (Woodbridge, 1992), 85–107, and for a wider study of the region, see P. Dixon, '*Mota, Aula et Turris*: the Manor Houses of the Anglo-Scottish Border', in *Manorial Domestic Buildings in England and Northern France*, ed. G. Meirion-Jones and M. Jones (London, 1993), 22–48.

[24] See Dixon, 'From Hall to Tower', 94, 102.

[25] R. A. Cordingly, 'Stokesay Castle, Shropshire: the Chronology of its Buildings', *Art Bulletin* 45 (1963), 91–107; J. Munby, *Stokesay Castle* (English Heritage Guidebook, 1993).

Figure 3. Buckden, Huntingdon: brick tower of bishop of Lincoln, added close to the (now demolished) great chamber c.1480.
Photo: © Philip Dixon

Peterborough (c.1300),[26] and Crawley (1343) and Edlingham, Northumberland (c.1380).[27] All of these were solar towers, private apartments beside more public halls. They were clearly defensible, but the emphasis seems to be more on the signalling out of the lord's apartments above the roofs of an adjacent range of buildings. A clear example of this is the very tall tower-block built with large decorated windows dating to about 1360 (Figure 2), next to the now vanished hall at the moated manor at South Kyme, Lincolnshire, by the Umfravilles, a once significant family somewhat impoverished during the fourteenth century by the loss of their Scottish estates.[28] A little later than this was the building of a detached

[26] E. C. Rouse, 'The Wall Paintings at Longthorpe Tower', *Archaeologia* 96 (1955), 1–57; Rouse, *Longthorpe Tower* (Official Guide, 1955).
[27] Dixon, 'From Hall to Tower', 106, 89–90; G. Fairclough, 'Edlingham Castle: The Military and Domestic Development of a Northumbrian Manor. Excavations 1978–80: interim report', *Château Gaillard* 9–10 (1982), 373–87, and 'Edlingham Castle', *Transactions of the Ancient Monuments Society*, new ser. 24 (1984), 40–60.
[28] For a plan of Kyme, see A. Emery, 'Ralph, Lord Cromwell's Manor at Wingfield (1439–c.50): its Construction, Design and Influence', *Archaeological Journal* 142 (1985), 317; for the inheritance

small solar tower near the unfortified hall at Halton, Northumberland, somewhat stronger than Kyme, but in a more troubled area, and owned by a much less
important family.[29]

During this period in France, however, a change is visible in the design of
new castles. At first the arrangement of a courtyard house within a curtain can
be seen to influence royal castles (as, for example, Angers). Subsequently the
design spread to the comital and less important structures, such as those at Najac
(Aveyron) or Échiré (Deux-Sevres), matching the patterns in England.[30] From
the middle of the fourteenth century onwards, however, we can see a small but
significant group of important castles in which the donjon forms a protected residence for the royal or ducal owner. Among the first is Pierrefonds, where Jacques
Harmand has identified a first phase, perhaps about 1360, with a massive tower-
house with projecting angle towers.[31] This fortified manor was converted into a
courtyard castle, dominated by a complex of towers, at the end of the century.
At this time the new castle of Vincennes to the south of Paris was constructed
around the royal hunting lodge. Here the king's house took the form of a huge
free-standing tower in its own bailey, surrounded by the tower-houses of the
courtiers arranged around a great and largely empty courtyard.[32] The social and
political overtones of this transition have yet to be worked out in detail. Until
they are, it seems plausible to suppose that the collapse of royal authority during
the first stages of the Hundred Years War had led to a perception that the king
needed to reassert his status using the same architectural motifs as were current
among his subjects. At Vincennes this symbolism included the association with
royal authority of the unity of king and court, a message made quite explicit in the
fifteenth-century painting of Vincennes rising above its forest included in the *Très
riches heures* of the Duc de Berry.[33] To be sure, troubled times might suggest to a
castle designer the advantages of a strong house for his patron, but the linking of
tower building with the supposed anarchy of late medieval feudal relationships,
propounded by Douglas Simpson,[34] and restated less baldly by Anthony Emery[35]
is a misunderstanding of the personal security of individual lords: even Charles
V at the lowest point of his fortunes is to be found living in an unfortified palace

of Kyme and the subsequent decline of the Umfravilles, see W. Percy Hedley, *Northumberland
Families* I (Newcastle, 1970), 212, 214–15.

[29] P. Dixon and P. Borne, 'Halton Castle Reconsidered', *Archaeologia Aeliana* 5th series 6 (1978),
131–9.

[30] J. Mesqui, *Châteaux et Enceintes de la France Médiévale: de la défence à la résidence* I (1991), 83
sees these as stages in which seigneurs passed from dominance of the land to economic dominance (thirteenth century), and thence to *domination culturelle* in the fourteenth century.

[31] J. Harmand, *Pierrefonds, la Forteress D'Orléans: les Réalités* (Le Puy-en-Velay, 1982); *idem*, 'Le
manoir d'Orléans à Pierrefonds', *Bulletin de la Société Nationale des Antiquaires de France* (1960),
159–74. For a brief discussion, see *Medieval Archaeology* 30 (1986), 216–17.

[32] Mesqui, *Châteaux et Enceintes de la France Médiévale* 1, 182: see also 145–8, 218.

[33] *Les Très Riches Heures du Duc de Berry*, ed. Jean Lognon (London, 1969), illus. 13 (12v).

[34] W. D. Simpson, '"Bastard Feudalism" and the Later Castles', *Antiquaries Journal* 26 (1946), 146–71.

[35] A. Emery, 'The Development of Raglan Castle and Keeps in late Medieval England', *Archaeological Journal* 132 (1975), esp. 151, 169–72, 186.

Figure 4. Vez (Oise): late fourteenth-century residential great tower, characteristic of the late medieval French donjons. *Photo: © Philip Dixon*

at Loches (where he was visited by Jeanne d'Arc), and not in the great tower of the castle.[36]

The re-emergence of the donjon as a symbol of royal power by *c.*1400 was followed by its increasing use in baronial castles as we can see at Vez (Oise) (Figure 4): the trends here are more difficult to follow, since in most areas the lesser lords were still marking their lordship by the use of towers, and the novelty accordingly is only perceptible at the highest social rank. One of the most striking examples of the new style is the enormous free-standing tower-house at Largoët near Lorien, built about 1430 by the steward of the Dukes of Brittany,[37] a donjon whose polygonal design with its prominent and decorative tiers of battlements provides us with a probable source for the English towers of the middle of the fifteenth century. In England the most prominent of the new towers is probably Ralph Lord Cromwell's great solar block built against a comparatively small hall within the small thirteenth-century castle at Tattershall, Lincolnshire, between 1434 and 1440.[38] This, however, is perhaps less a member of the new wave, and more a continuation of the older tradition of hall-and-solar-tower, for Tattershall

---

[36] Anon., *Le Palais Royal de Loches* (Loches, 1987), 4.

[37] For drawings of Largoet, see Mesqui, *Châteaux et Enceintes de la France Médiévale* 1, 150–1 and fig. 172.

[38] W. D. Simpson, 'The Affinities of Lord Cromwell's Tower-house at Tattershall', *Journal of the British Archaeological Association*, 2nd ser. 40 (1935), 177–92; for details of the background and the cultural context of Cromwell's new building, see Emery, 'Ralph, Lord Cromwell's Manor at Wingfield'.

Figure 5. South Wingfield, Derbyshire: accommodation tower added to ranges c.1440.
Photo: © Philip Dixon

looks across the marshes to Kyme, whose owners the Umfravilles (sometimes allies and sometimes rivals) had previously dominated the lowlands from the solar tower attached to their hall.[39] The new tower at Tattershall greatly surpasses that at Kyme: Cromwell's success in national politics, as Treasurer, was here being underlined.[40] During the same period Cromwell was also building a new courtyard house to replace a small ringwork castle at South Wingfield in Derbyshire.[41] The initial arrangements here owed little to the new fashion for a great tower, and consisted simply of a hall, chambers and services at the centre of the ringwork. Changes of design during the building added accommodation ranges across the southern side of the ringwork, to form a courtyard, part of which was still timber-framed in its outer walls.[42] At a late stage in the development of the house,

[39] For Kyme and the Umfravilles, see above, n. 28. Others, more concerned with the 'mainstream' developments of curtain walls and courtyard castles than with the survival of towers throughout the Middle Ages, have considered Tattershall an anachronism: see A. Hamilton Thompson, *Medieval Military Architecture* (London, 1913), 318.

[40] M. W. Thompson, *Tattershall Castle* (National Trust Guide, 1975): see also Emery, 'Ralph, Lord Cromwell's Manor at Wingfield', 276f. In this connexion it is interesting to note the *rebus* of the Treasurer's purse on the fireplaces at Tattershall, and the placing of the audience chamber right at the top of the tower, where it would be most impressive to the lords who visited Cromwell.

[41] The most detailed and authoritative account is Emery, 'Ralph, Lord Cromwell's Manor at Wingfield', 276–339. For the campaigns of building, see M. W. Thompson, 'The Construction of the Manor of South Wingfield', in *Problems in Economic and Social Archaeology*, ed. G. de G. Sieveking, I. H. Longworth and K. E. Wilson (Cambridge 1976), 457–38. For a brief summary of the alternative sequence, see P. W. Dixon, 'South Wingfield Manor', *The Nottingham Area* (Archaeological Journal, supplement to volume 146 (1989)), 57–9.

[42] S. Lucy, 'The Kitchen Area at South Wingfield' (Unpublished BA dissertation, University of Nottingham 1987).

Figure 6. Nottingham Castle: reconstruction of royal apartments and solar tower of *c*.1480 (model by P. Dixon and D. Taylor, based on antiquarian drawings and excavations). *Photo: © Philip Dixon*

Figure 7. Warwick Castle; remains of the unfinished Bear Tower, begun by Richard III as a rectangular great tower. *Photo: © Philip Dixon*

however, the wooden external walls were rebuilt in stone (leaving the inner walls in timber), and parts of the new ranges were demolished and replaced by a massive and dominating tower separating the new inner courtyard from the buildings of the outer court (Figure 5). The external appearance of the high tower as a donjon, however, is illusory: it was for display alone and was not intended to be a lord's residence, for the family lived in unprotected chambers on the other side of the courtyard. The tower was much more mundane inside, and its ground floor contained a large communal latrine, entered from the courtyard, while its upper levels provided chambers, which (though large and well appointed) may have been no more than superior guest rooms similar to the apartments in the lodging ranges.[43] It is difficult to avoid the conclusion that, at a relatively late stage in the construction of Wingfield, Cromwell or his architect decided that his new double-courtyard great house lacked the focus of a tower as a symbolic motif of his lordship, even though the layout of the manor's accommodation left little function for the new building.

The free-standing lord's house continued to be built through the fifteenth century. Closest to Largoët in its design is the Yellow Tower of Gwent at Raglan Castle, an isolated tower-house placed in a dominant position beside the entrance in a manner similar to that of the thirteenth-century castles of Coucy or Flint. The date of the building of this addition to the early castle remains uncertain. Emery argued for the period around 1460, and linked the construction at Raglan, and that of other English towers, with the growing unrest at the beginning of the Wars of the Roses.[44] Others have considered an earlier date, perhaps in the 1430s, as more likely:[45] this would place it in date very close to that of the great tower of Largoët, and make the similarity in appearance the more telling. To the period from 1450 to 1480 belong the tall tower blocks at Buckden, Huntingdonshire (Figure 3), and Ashby de la Zouch in Leicestershire.[46] Both were self-contained residences dominating their courtyards, that at Ashby more clearly fortified, though even here the underground passage to the kitchen provided convenience at the expense of strength. Two further buildings of this period, residential towers added to the earlier castles of Tutbury, Staffordshire (1457–60)[47] and Warwick, confirm the continuance of the tower-house design into the second half of the century. The Bear Tower at Warwick, in particular, though left incomplete and

---

[43] This sequence described here differs considerably from the analysis of the building by Emery, 'Ralph, Lord Cromwell's Manor at Wingfield'. The archaeological evidence for the changes is clear-cut, however, and has been presented by Beryl Lott in an unpublished BA dissertation, 'A Study of the West Range and High Tower at South Wingfield Manor' (Nottingham 1991).

[44] Emery, 'The Development of Raglan Castle', 186.

[45] A. J. Taylor, *Raglan Castle* (Ministry of Works Official Guide, 1950); J. R. Kenyon, *Raglan Castle* (Cadw Official Guide, 1992), 5.

[46] T. L. Jones, *Ashby de la Zouch Castle* (Official Guide, 1953 and later editions); M. W. Thompson, 'Buckden Palace', *Archaeological Journal* 124 (1967), 250–5; RCHME, *Huntingdonshire* (London, 1926), 34–8; W. D. Simpson, 'Buckden Palace', *Journal of the British Archaeological Association* 3rd ser. (1937), 121–32.

[47] R. Somerville, 'Tutbury Castle', *Archaeological Journal* 120 (1963), 276–8.

finished as a low postern gate (Figure 7), seems from its remains to have been intended as a detached tower-house on the scale of Tattershall or Ashby, with octagonal angle towers, a massive structure, which would presumably have dominated the adjacent tall slender fourteenth-century towers on the entrance façade.[48]

In the meantime, solar towers continued to be constructed in new building. Two royal works are significant here. In the last years of his reign Edward IV began to rebuild the state apartments within the middle ward of the important royal castle at Nottingham. Though these were demolished after the Civil War, drawings and descriptions, confirmed by the evidence of excavation,[49] show that these took the form of a crescent of buildings with large canted bays, built in stone on the first storey, and in timber above, where the state apartments themselves lay (Figure 6). The work was completed after his brother's death by Richard III, who spent much of his reign in Nottingham. The great polygonal tower, presumably built by Edward, though now known as Richard's Tower, which was attached to the new buildings, seems from its position and from Smythson's plan to have formed a privy chamber opening from the more public galleries.[50] At the very end of the century Henry VII demolished much of Humphrey of Gloucester's palace at Greenwich, and rebuilt it as a new courtyard house, in which the great hall projected from the eastern side of the courtyard, and the royal apartments formed the northern side.[51] This arrangement echoes that proposed for Notting-

[48] No detailed study of this work has been published. For its incomplete state, see J. Leland, *Itineraries* (ed. L. Toulmin-Smith), II (London 1910), 40. The date is 1483–5: see Peter Curnow, unpublished MS at Society of Antiquaries of London (1971). For a view of this façade of the castle in the eighteenth century, see Thompson, *The Decline of the Castle*, 77. The tower's builder, Richard III, while Duke of Gloucester and lieutenant in the north, had been responsible for the addition of the apartment block in the gate known as the Red Tower to the castle of Penrith, about 1475, and added a polygonal tower (similar to that at Nottingham) to the buildings on the motte at Sandal Castle, W. Yorks, in 1484: *HKW*, 828.

[49] For the excavations, see C. Drage, *Nottingham Castle: A Place Full Royal* (Nottingham, 1990); the layout of the buildings was recorded by the architect Robert Smythson in 1617, and the dominant bulk of Richard's Tower is given us by an illumination of 1551 and Speed's map of 1614: *ibid.*, pls 5 and 6. The model from which Figure 6 is derived was constructed by P. Dixon and D. Taylor, and is held in the Nottingham Castle Museum.

[50] The great hall of the original castle is missing from Smythson's plan (for reproductions of which see *HKW*, pl. 48 and Drage, *Nottingham Castle*, 29) and had presumably been removed by 1617: a single wall, however, is visible on the drawing between the chapel and the kitchen beside the gate of the middle bailey, and may represent the original screens passage of a hall, which projected into the bailey, producing a small inner royal courtyard defined on the south by the hall, and on the north by the state apartments, and entered, like Whitehall, London, or Haddon Hall, Derbyshire, through the cross passage of the great hall.

[51] For the planning, see P. W. Dixon, *Excavations at Greenwich Palace 1970–1* (London, 1972); for further discussion of the Tudor layout based on the excavations and on the documentary evidence, see Colvin *et al.*, *History of the King's Works* 4 (London, 1982), 96–123, and S. Thurley, 'Greenwich Palace', in *Henry VIII: A European Court in England*, ed. D. Starkey (London, 1991), 20–5. Thurley, perhaps through unfamiliarity with the English sites, traces the design of the tower-like royal lodging as far afield as urban palaces in Burgundy, but this is quite unnecessary, as English parallels are immediately to hand. Duke Humphrey's earlier palace seems to have consisted of a principal apartment to the north along the riverside, ending at its western end

Figures 8–9. Misericords
in chancel of Manchester
Cathedral, perhaps
showing Lathom House,
Lancashire.
Photo: © Philip Dixon

ham Castle, and the principal royal apartments of the new palace closely resem-
bled those of Nottingham. They lay along the riverside, and consisted of a suite of
state rooms ending in a privy chamber contrived within a tower, which formed
the dominant architectural motif in all views of the palace before its demolition
in the seventeenth century (Figure 10).[52] Greenwich was probably the last of the
royal palaces designed with such emphasis on a solar tower, and the symmetry of
the Renaissance buildings of France and Italy made it increasingly unfashionable.

 in a kitchen, with a courtyard or garden on its southern side. No other buildings (for example,
 a return range on the west or south) were located in the excavations: Duke Humphrey's house
 therefore seems either to have been either a single riverfront range, or to have had any further
 buildings to the east, beyond the excavated area.
[52] For views by Antonius van der Wyngaerde *c.*1558, see Colvin, *HKW* 4, pls 4, 5, and for the palace
 in the seventeenth century, see *Walpole Society* 35 (2), pl. 6.

Figure 10. Greenwich Palace, London: view from the south, showing great tower rising above the river front, anon, *c*.1620.

Figure 11. Entrance front of Holme Pierrepoint Hall, Nottinghamshire, of *c*.1500.
Photo: © Philip Dixon

It is no surprise, however, to find the style continuing for a while among the lesser lords. At Gainsborough, Lincolnshire, probably during the 1490s, a tall solar tower was built at the end of the family rooms.[53] The unfinished palace at Thornbury,

---

[53] P. Linley (ed.), *Gainsborough Old Hall* (Lincoln, 1991).

Figure 12. Holme Pierrepoint Hall in the seventeenth century from Thoroton's
Antiquaries of Nottinghamshire.

Gloucestershire (1511–22) was similarly dominated by its solar,[54] as was the contemporary moated manor house of Compton Wynyates, Warwickshire.[55]

While Henry VII was building at Greenwich his craftsmen were constructing
a palace on a quite different plan at Richmond on Thames.[56] Drawings before the
destruction of this palace in the seventeenth century show that it consisted of
two principal courtyards, symmetrically arranged, with the principal apartments
arranged around a small inner courtyard, and appearing from the outside as a
massive block of buildings rising tower-like above the outer court. A parallel to
this can be seen in the mid fifteenth-century courtyards at Knole, Kent,[57] and a
very similar arrangement on a smaller scale was formerly to be seen at Holme
Pierrepoint, Nottinghamshire (Figures 11, 12), whose entrance front with little

[54] For the incomplete plan, see M. Howard, *The Early Tudor Country House: Architecture and Politics 1490–1550* (London, 1987), 79; the Duke of Buckingham's private tower is well shown in an
eighteenth-century view reproduced by Thompson, *The Decline of the Castle*, 63.

[55] For this, see S. R. Rigold, 'Compton Wynyates', *Archaeological Journal* 127 (1975), 218–20. Similar
towers were created even later, during the rebuilding of monasteries after the Dissolution, for
example, the chamber block created as a tower at the end of the first-floor apartment in the west
wing at Lanercost Priory, Cumbria.

[56] For plans, early illustrations and discussion, see Colvin, *King's Works* 4, 222–34 and pls 18, 19; for
excavations, see P. Dixon, 'Excavations at Richmond Palace', *Post-Medieval Archaeology* 9 (1975),
103–16.

[57] For a plan, see P. Faulkner, 'Some Medieval Archepiscopal Palaces', *Archaeological Journal* 127
(1970), 140–4; the eighteenth-century bird's-eye view by Kip is reproduced in Thompson, *Decline
of the Castle*, 59.

emphasis on the gateway is reminiscent of Knole.[58] An important link, now lost, in the design of these late fifteenth-century palaces is the Stanleys' great house at Lathom, near Ormskirk, Lancashire, referred to as 'the Northern court', and said by the eulogist of the Stanley earls of Derby to be the model that influenced Henry VII in his palace building. In view of the family connexion, it is likely that the Stanley misericords in the chancel of Manchester Cathedral, several of which show what seems to be parts of the same great house (Figures 8, 9), are the sole known representations of Lathom, showing a heavy gatehouse in a courtyard range with polygonal roofed towers, nine in the inner ward (which may be the towering structure in one of the carvings) and nine in the outer, according to the poet.[59]

After the beginning of the sixteenth century the principal design in new building work took the form of courtyard houses, mostly lacking a single dominating focus,[60] except on occasion for emphasis on the gateway, an element that can be traced back to the 'Golden Age', for example at Harlech or Denbigh or Dunstan-burgh, and followed through the fourteenth and fifteenth centuries, particularly in the entrances to monasteries such as Thornton, Lincolnshire (1380), and in Cambridge University colleges, notably Trinity and St John's.[61] Prominent examples of this style can be seen in Bishop Waynflete's gatehouse at Esher Place of the 1480s and his construction of a giant porch tower across the screens passage at Farnham, Surrey, between 1470 and 1475.[62]

The buildings we have discussed in this short survey are very varied, and include both castles and unfortified great houses. The distinction between the two is often hard to make, though there is a clear trend for the great houses of any particular stratum of upper society to become larger during the fifteenth and the sixteenth centuries, and for the developments within both new and old castles to include increasingly spacious and integrated domestic lodgings. But the

---

[58] Holme Pierrepoint Hall, a small brick palace, is said to have been constructed soon after 1500: the surviving roof of the south range seems a little archaic for this date. The dominating inner courtyard was demolished during the eighteenth century, but is visible in a perspective view published in John Thorsby's, *Thoroton's Antiquities of Nottinghamshire* (Nottingham, 1790), 181: see Figure 12.

[59] For literary references, see I. F. Baird, *Scottish Feilde and Flodden Feilde: Two Flodden Poems* (New York, 1982), verse 5i, and J, N, Hales and F J Furnival (ed.), *Bishop Percy's Folio Manuscript: Ballads and Romancesi* (1867), 313–40. The Earl of Derby is called 'King of [the Isle of] Man', and so the date should be before 1521. We are most grateful to Dr Jennifer Lewis, who is preparing a thorough study of this important site [now published as J. Lewis, 'Lathom House: The Northern Court', *Journal of the British Archaeological Association* 152 (1999), 150–71], for discussion on these points and for her advice, and for her introduction to the Stanley misericords at Manchester Cathedral.

[60] For a recent discussion of the sixteenth-century styles, see Howard, *The Early Tudor Country House*, which, however, omits both Lathom and Greenwich.

[61] Thornton: see A. W. Clapham and P. K. Baillie Reynolds, *Thornton Abbey Humberside* (revised edn, Department of Environment Guidebook, 1974); for the gatehouses of St John's College (1490s) and Trinity College (1510s), see RCHME, *The City of Cambridge* (London, 1960).

[62] For discussion, see M. W. Thompson, '"Fox's Tower", Farnham Castle, Surrey', *Surrey Archaeological Collections* 58 (1960), 81–94.

story of the later Middle Ages is a development, not a decline. Throughout the medieval period castles are always 'in decline', that is, inadequate or even surplus to the requirements of the next generation in a kaleidoscope of shifting politics, economy and social status.

Our two themes, the courtyard and the tower, are constants during this period, and provide a symbolic core in the design of great houses. The resulting architecture is influenced by the social and political contexts of the day: a shell for the overt symbolism of social power, which had force even in the seventeenth century, when the Earl of Ancrum, discussing the modernising and civilising of Ancrum House, advised leaving the battlements of the dominating tower, 'for that is the grace of the house, and makes it looke lyk a castle, and henc so nobleste …'[63]

[63] *Correspondence of Sir Robert Kerr, first Earl of Ancrum, and his son William, third Earl of Lothian,* I, 62, Bannatyne Club (Edinburgh 1875): quoted in RCAHM (Scotland), *The County of Roxburgh* II (1956), 485.

4

Castle Planning in the Fourteenth Century

P. A. Faulkner

The form and content of any building is the expression of its designer's brief, and that brief will, almost inevitably, contain conflicting elements. Overshadowing the development of the medieval castle as a building is the conflict between its military and its domestic functions. The form taken at any particular time is bound to be a compromise between these two issues, which will not only vary in relative importance but will each one vary as techniques in their respective fields develop. Although in this paper it is proposed to follow trends in domestic demands and observe their effect on the form of the castle, this aspect should not properly be treated in isolation, and if little mention is made of the military element it must be remembered that this is, nevertheless, always present. It is proposed to analyse three individual fourteenth-century buildings as a means of determining these trends, but before doing so the position reached in the previous century must be summarised, first as to what may be established as the basic requirements for a household in terms of plan form and secondly as to how this was used to provide the accommodation demanded in the greater castles, thereby demonstrating something of the approach of the designers of that time to this particular problem.

Through the thirteenth century two common house plan forms dominate, the upper or twin hall type and the end hall or hall and chamber-block type.[1] The upper hall house, which tended to die out towards the end of the century, consists essentially of two identical floor plans, superimposed on each other, each containing a hall with an inner chamber attached at one end.[2] It may appear in more elaborate form with additional chambers attached to both hall and inner chamber while still retaining its twin nature providing for two households.[3] Of the two forms the hall and chamber-block plan is the more persistent. It was the basic form before the Conquest and, though temporarily swamped by the upper hall house, returned to increasing favour as the thirteenth century progressed. Its elements are a group or groups of chambers associated with a common hall. In its simplest form it appears as a ground-floor hall with a two-storey block of chambers at one end,[4] providing for a single household. A number of groups of

---

[1] P. A. Faulkner, 'Domestic Planning from the Twelfth to the Fourteenth Centuries', *Archaeological Journal* 115 (1958), 150–83.

[2] Examples are Boothby Pagnell, Christchurch Castle hall and the guest-houses at Fountains Abbey.

[3] Kidwelly Castle hall and Harlech gatehouse.

[4] King John's House, Warnford, Infirmarer's Lodging, Peterborough Abbey.

such chambers, each self-sufficient, allows a number of households to be associated with a common hall.[5] The chamber groups may vary from an elaborate suite of many rooms to a single-chamber lodging.[6]

Throughout the following paper it is assumed that the occurrence of a plan form that may be identified with one or other of these two types establishes the provision of accommodation for an independent household.

In terms of the earlier Middle Ages a castle may be described as a collective defensive position in which the lord, his household and the households of his dependants might live in common safety. The form taken by the defences as such was dictated by military techniques and will not be discussed here. It is hoped to demonstrate that the form taken by the accommodation remained static through the thirteenth century in spite of considerable advances in the design of the defensive system by the examination of four castles in their thirteenth-century state – Corfe, Chepstow, Caerphilly and Beaumaris.

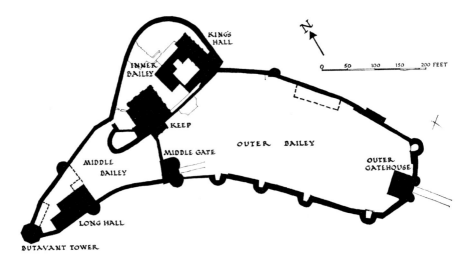

Figure 1. Corfe Castle: the thirteenth-century buildings.

Corfe presents a defensive system based on the keep and bailey principle. Within this, its domestic planning is based on a series of some six or seven loosely connected but unrelated residences (Figure 1) all of the highest order; two in the King's Tower or keep, still in use as royal residences at this time,[7] and another in the embryo courtyard house built early in the century. The outer bailey appears to have contained only one permanent residential building, the gatehouse. The

---

[5] Ludlow Castle had three chamber-blocks attached to the great hall.
[6] The Lodgings in the SE tower at Goodrich etc.
[7] D. Simpson, 'Development of Corfe Castle', *Proceedings of the Dorset Natural History and Archaeological Society* 73 (1951), 71–84.

Middle Gate, standing in isolation, provided one, if not two, more while the western portion of the middle bailey is treated as a group residence with buildings incorporating the old Long Hall.[8] All these are residences in their own right of one or other of the basic forms already noted such as can be paralleled anywhere from the late twelfth century onwards.

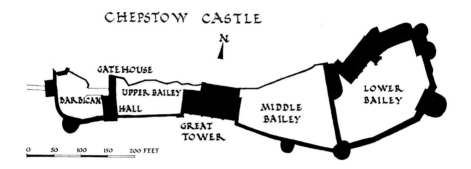

Figure 2. Chepstow Castle.

Chepstow (Figure 2), like Corfe, is an existing castle being enlarged as a result of the increasing domestic demands of the thirteenth century rather than to achieve any improvement in military fortification. At the beginning of the century the defences had already been improved when the middle bailey was equipped with mural towers and loops in the curtain; a barbican thrown out to, the west and a new hall and gatehouse added to the upper bailey. In the last quarter of the century, however, not only was the Great Tower itself improved but concurrently what amounted to a new palace was planned at the eastern end of the site (Figure 3). The extent to which this lower bailey existed before is immaterial. It was transformed by the works of 1270 onwards into a courtyard surrounded by domestic buildings. The more secure northern side is clearly the principal. In itself it consists of two halls, the more important, western, hall clearly Roger Bigod's own. This had a chamber block at each end, one over the pre-existing gate to the middle bailey, the other over service rooms planned in common with the eastern hall, which had its own chamber block next the gatehouse. This group undoubtedly looks forward in its planning to the following century but retains, however, its individuality as a block in the same way in which the slightly earlier adjoining gatehouse is planned as a separate entity incorporating a twin hall residence in the manner of Harlech.[9] Beyond lies Marten's Tower, a further independent residence arranged over a working military lower floor. It has a private chapel and precautions are taken to defend it from both the bailey and the wall

---

[8] RCHME, 'Excavations in the West Bailey at Corfe Castle', *Medieval Archaeology* 4 (1960), 29–55.
[9] Faulkner, 'Domestic Planning', 158.

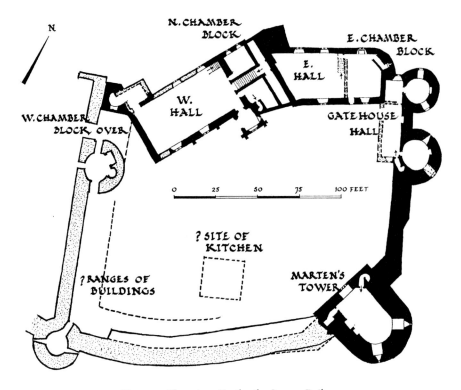

Figure 3. Chepstow Castle: the Lower Bailey.

walk. The thirteenth-century arrangements along the south and west sides of the
bailey cannot now be determined, though there is some suggestion that a kitchen
lay in this area, perhaps freestanding in the Ludlow manner. These buildings at
Chepstow, though largely planned as a single campaign, are still conceived as a
series of entities placed around the curtain. They may not be so widely spaced
as those at Corfe but there is, even so, no attempt at unification into a single
building.

The more regular layout at Caerphilly (Figure 4) appears at first sight to have
achieved some measure of unity yet, here again, the conception is that of a series
of independent residential points placed around a pattern of curtain walls, which
have now assumed a geometric form dictated by the latest military techniques.
The residences, a principal and some eight others, are unrelated to one another
except insofar as they form part of a common defensive system. Those in the
inner ward are of the chamber-block type grouped around a common great hall.
There are at least two suites. The western extends to the west side of the inner
ward while the eastern includes the chapel, the whole group displaying some
conflict between military and domestic design as it spreads across the inner curtain into the outer ward. The remaining residences are all of the twin hall type:
two in the great gatehouse on the eastern works; in the east gatehouse of the
inner ward where one is provided with a private chapel; others in the two western

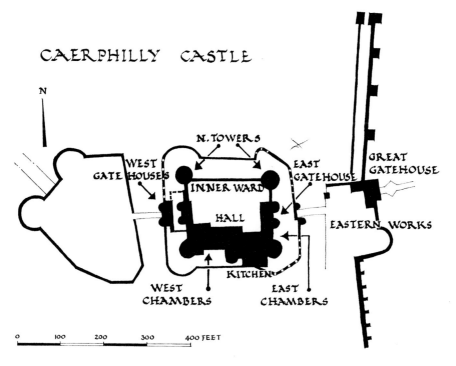

Figure 4. Caerphilly Castle.

gatehouses and probably in. the northern angle towers of the inner ward. Any advance that the regular and geometric layout of Caerphilly represents clearly lies in the military field only. The staccato domestic planning of Corfe is still the rule.

Beaumaris exemplifies the classic concentric castle (Figure 5). The circumstances under which the Edwardian castles were built – single overall royal control, nationwide resources and political pressure – were clearly such as to produce intensive technical development. What was achieved was the perfection of a type already in existence. As at Caerphilly, Beaumaris was planned to provide a series of residences, of which the principal was to have been of hall and chamber block type against the east side of the inner ward with chambers at either end incorporating the Rusticoker Tower to the north and others with access to the surviving private pews of the chapel to the south. In addition two great twin hall residences were planned in the northern and southern gatehouses, in size and elaboration the equals of that against the curtain. Further household units were accommodated in the upper floors of the north gate and, probably, of the Gate-next-the-Sea, while still more may have been intended against the west side of the inner ward. Even here the castle takes the form of a series of houses attached to a symmetrical defence system. It is the defences that are seen as a whole, not the accommodation within.

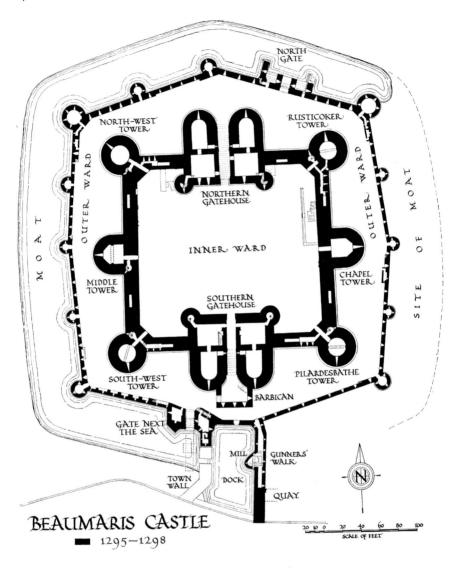

Figure 5. Beaumaris Castle.

To sum up the position at the end of the thirteenth century, the castle, assuming that what was provided was, in fact, the requirement, demanded provision for a number of households all of noble rank dominated by one of even superior station. It will be seen from the examples quoted that the satisfaction of the military and domestic demands were treated as separate problems, which were, nevertheless, beginning to interact. Two trends are discernible; first, there was an increasing demand for permanent accommodation of a high order within the castle and secondly the defences, in becoming more ordered and regular, tended to concentrate the room available for domestic building into a relatively smaller space, generally quadrangular in form. The reconciliation of these conflicting demands of expansion and contraction was a problem that thirteenth-century designers failed to solve, or perhaps even to recognise. In any consideration of the treatment of this problem in the following century it must be remembered that it was not one that remained static.

It is hoped in the following studies of Goodrich and Bolton castles to analyse the accommodation provided in comparable buildings at the beginning and at the end of the fourteenth century and thus to demonstrate the elaboration of domestic demands over the period and the manner in which these were integrated into a single concept. Following this an attempt is made to use the principles so established to elucidate the planning of the late fourteenth-century castle at Bodiam.

Goodrich Castle, Herefordshire
(Figure 6)

Goodrich Castle, in its present form, was built by the Valence Earls of Pembroke in the opening years of the fourteenth century. As it stands it is the work of one period, the only substantial vestige of earlier building on the site being the small non-residential twelfth-century keep and the only later work being confined to minor alterations.[10] To this extent, then, it can be said to be an unfettered design of its time, representing the up-to-date demands of its near-royal builder. Not only is the building of one date but it is sufficiently complete to enable us to appreciate the whole extent of the accommodation provided and to identify its component units. We appear to be faced with a single building more or less quadrangular. Closer examination, however, reveals the castle, not as a single dwelling but as a series closely planned into one whole, marking the first step beyond the stage reached at Beaumaris.

Of the buildings ranged round the central courtyard the keep, preserved at the rebuilding of the castle, does not appear to have been converted to any domestic use and is, therefore, with the prison beside it, omitted from this analysis. First must be noted the kitchen, between the keep and the south-west tower and connected to all other parts of the castle by pentices, and the chapel next to the gate; both of these stand on their own giving common service to the rest of the castle. In the latter the accommodation is grouped around three halls placed along sides of the court, the Great Hall, to the west, a north hall and an east hall. The four towers are occupied by chambers and service rooms, those in the north-east tower being arranged over the gate passage and chapel.

The three halls each form the basis of a hall and chamber-block group. The great hall is served by the chambers in the south-west tower. Two doors in the south wall imply the existence of two rooms at hall level in the tower, and the

---

[10] A gallery was inserted in the chapel with a door to new first-floor accommodation made between the N hall and the gatehouse. A door was cut between the ante-room and the great hall.

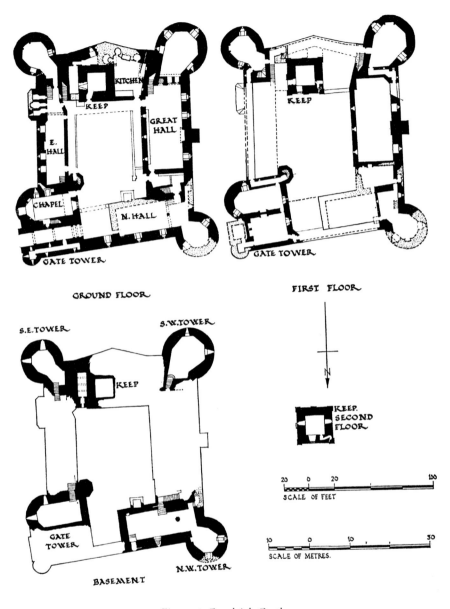

Figure 6. Goodrich Castle.

absence of garderobe or fireplace suggests that they were service rooms. A third door in this wall leads to a cellar below while the stair at the south-east angle rises to the door of the great chamber at first-floor level with a fireplace in the south wall and a garderobe in the passage through the north wall. The north hall and the north-west tower form a further group. The hall is entered at its south-west angle through an ante-room that adjoins the great hall. The connecting door is later. Along the south side of this ante-room is a bench. At hall level, partly in the north-west tower, is a chamber with a fireplace above which is the great chamber, also with a fireplace, which was reached by a stair descending into the western end of the hall. This chamber extends over the west end of the hall in a manner curiously reminiscent of the Great Tower at Chepstow; *en suite* with it is an inner chamber over the ante-room with a garderobe to the west.

A stair in the ante-room leads to the lower north hall similar in size to that above. This has no fireplace and, significantly, there is access, defended by port-cullis and drawbar, direct into the outer bailey.[11] The hall is provided with a cham-ber in the north-west tower and has a garderobe. On the east side of the court an octagonal turret contains the stair leading to the chambers over the gatehouse. This is essentially a two-chamber lodging with a larger outer chamber or hall and an inner chamber beyond, both with fireplaces, the latter with a garderobe. The two small chambers over the outer gate are ruined beyond recognition. In assessing the importance of this lodging it is worth remembering that the outer chamber is only slightly smaller than the hall of the Harlech gatehouse. South of the chapel, the east hall departs somewhat from the pattern so far noted in that it has an entrance at either end and is separated from its chambers in the south-east tower by a lobby out of which opens what can only be described as a battery of three garderobes. Leading from this lobby are two doors, one to the ground floor of the south-east tower, a chamber with walldrain and fireplace, the other to the chamber below. From the adjacent pentice a stair leads to the first-floor tower chamber also with walldrain and fireplace. At the northern end of the east hall a stair descends to a cellar below the chapel.

It remains to be seen to what extent this division into units can be used to interpret the accommodation provided by the early fourteenth-century planners of Goodrich. In an attempt to determine the most likely occupant of each an obvious criterion is the degree of luxury displayed and the measure of that must be the amenities provided. Of the furnishing and manner of decoration of the rooms, nothing, of course, survives. All that is left are the permanent architec-tural features; the doors, windows and fireplaces. In some buildings there is a clear gradation in the detail of these features, and it is reasonable to suppose that the richer the foliage, the more elaborate the moulding, the finer the ashlar, the higher the degree of the occupant.[12] There is no such gradation at Goodrich, the detail in all the lodgings and chambers is similar and it is of a high standard, elegant though restrained. It can only be assumed that such uniformity of stand-ard implies parity of rank among the occupants. This point must be made, for it implies that here is no accommodation for men-at-arms or common soldiers but only for those comparable in degree to the owner. A second criterion is the scale

---

[11] Extensive remains of the stables have recently been uncovered in the outer bailey W of the great hall.

[12] Particularly stressed at Ludlow in the E chamber-block.

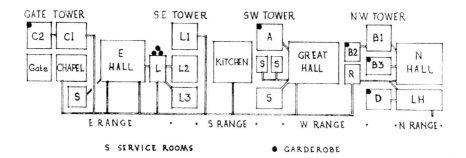

Figure 7. Goodrich Castle: planning diagram.

or amount of accommodation provided in each of the units and the individual interpretation of those units. This can, perhaps, best be done diagrammatically.

In the illustration (Figure 7) the 'boxes' each represent a room and the connecting lines the circulation between them. By virtue of their position and treatment the Great Hall and North Hall with their respective chamber blocks are clearly the most important. It is suggested that, of these, the North Hall is designed as a residence for the owner while the Great Hall, with its single great chamber (A), is reserved for the principal guest. If, as seems probable, the Great Hall is already at this time regarded as something of a status symbol,[13] it is understandable that its occupant would be one worthy of the highest compliment who could be served in state but who would not regard the castle as a permanent home. On the other hand, the private suite of great and inner chambers (B1 and B2) attached to the north hall allows for a household with additional accommodation in the lower chamber (B3) for a noble dependant; if, indeed, this hall was that of the owner it would serve as a court hall and would appropriately have a waiting room attached. In the ante-room (R) this is provided, equipped with a bench and interposed between the hall and the entrance from the court; a similar arrangement exists at Conway.[14] Also connected with the ante-room is the lower hall (LH). Of a lower standard of finish this would be suitable for the squires attached to the owner's household, with its inner chamber (D) reserved for the chief among them. There are noticeably no stables in the inner bailey, and quick access to those in the outer bailey may well have been part of the designer's brief and explain the postern at this point.

There are two points to note in relation to the lodging (C1 and C2) in the gate tower. First it has no hall, and second it occupies the traditional position over the gate for the constable or permanent custodian of the castle.[15] It would fit this purpose well, for such an official would not need a hall for ceremonial, and even

[13] At Conway there was no connection between the royal apartments and the great hall.
[14] At Windsor a stone bench was provided in the cloister outside the King's chamber. R. A. Brown, *English Medieval Castles* (London, 1953).
[15] Constable's Tower is the gatehouse tower at Dover.

in the lord's absence the courts would presumably continue to be held in the lord's hall. The compactness of this lodging and the command it gives over the gate make this allocation more than probable in which case it would have been the only permanently occupied portion of the castle.

It has already been remarked that the east hall does not conform to the normal hall and chamber-block pattern. The hall and the chambers in the south-east tower (L1, 2 and 3) each have individual access and the garderobes that serve them are grouped in the common lobby (L). Here would seem to be a plan for communal living on a scale comparable to that of the owner. Such a set of conditions would meet the requirements of those of noble rank who came to the castle, not so much in their own right but in the train of either principal guest or owner; living together in their own hall but each, or each set, provided with their own lodging. The kitchen and chapel, be it noted, would serve all halls *via* the pentice.

To sum up, we can say that the castle was called upon to provide permanent accommodation for the owner and his squires, for a state guest and those who travelled in his train and for a permanent constable or sheriff. We can, in addition get some idea of the accommodation that satisfied such persons and see that the castle was equipped to serve as the headquarters of a civil lordship. All this is superimposed upon its essential military form, skilfully combined into a single building clearly seen as a whole. Skilful as it is, however, it would seem that the designer saw it still as a series of units placed one against the other. Unified, perhaps, to a greater degree than had been the case hitherto but not to the extent that was to be achieved later in the century when the requirements of even more elaborate domestic ritual could be fully integrated with military necessities into a single conception. There can be few buildings where this achievement can be better studied than at Bolton Castle in Yorkshire.

Bolton Castle, Yorkshire
(Figure 8)

Bolton castle was built on a fresh site in the last quarter of the fourteenth century by Richard, Lord Scrope. The contractor for half the building, at least, is known to have been John Lewin.[16] Its advantages as a subject of study lie, not only in sits completeness, but in the fact that it must, being self-contained, of necessity include within one building all the permanent accommodation demanded, not only the halls and chambers but stables, mills, stores and kitchens. Stark and uncompromising in exterior appearance, the castle contains within every luxury known to the time. It is quadrangular, generally three-storied with five-storied angle towers, one of which, the kitchen tower, has collapsed.

To some extent the quadrangular courtyard form of Bolton may be seen as a direct development from the inner bailey at Goodrich, while the germ was already apparent at Chepstow.

---

[16] L. F. Salzman, *Building in England* (Oxford, 1952), 454.

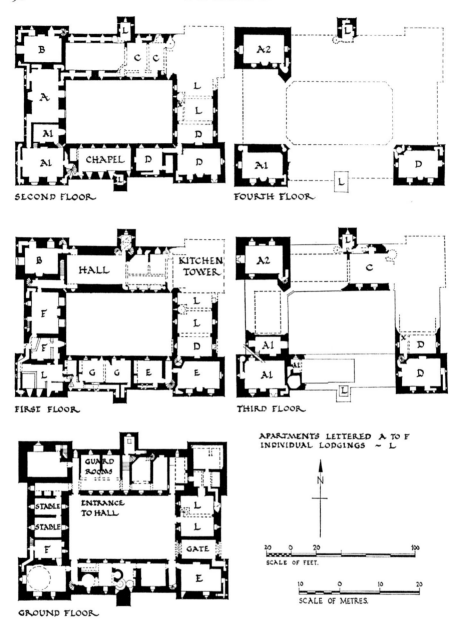

Figure 8. Bolton Castle.

Once again it is noticeable that the major rooms show little variation from a uniformly high standard from which it may be concluded that accommodation within the castle was reserved for those of comparatively high rank; those of lesser rank can, perhaps, be identified with the inhabitants of the villages around, only called upon to serve within the castle when it was occupied.

On analysis, the accommodation within the walls can be broken down into no less than eight major household units and some twelve lesser lodgings all integrated into one unified conception. The greater part of this accommodation is arranged above the ground floor, which is, in the main, reserved for service rooms. Of the suites of living rooms and lodgings, the principal are arranged in the western range, though focused on the great hall in the north range, which is, in turn, balanced in the south range by the chapel. The plan provides for a series of hall and chamber groups on the one hand and of individual lodgings on the other, a division that, more marked here than at Goodrich, was hardly to be found in the thirteenth-century castle, but one that was to develop in the following centuries.

The planning of the greater apartments at Bolton is related to the great hall, the entrance to which, and indeed to all the principal apartments, is in the north-west angle of the court through a not particularly imposing door. At this point the visitor and his horse part company, the visitor along a wide right-angled corridor, flanked by guardrooms, to the stair leading to the hall. This is entered at first-floor level through a vaulted lobby at the north-east angle. The route is marked with some architectural distinction.

Associated with the great hall and placed at its ends are groups of chambers, (B) to the west and (C) over the service rooms to the east. The hall in this case serves more than its usual two chamber blocks for beyond the door in the south-west angle is a lobby reminiscent of the Goodrich ante-room, leading to a further hall (A) on the second floor only slightly smaller than the great hall. The second-, third- and fourth-floor plans show this inner hall to have, yet again, two chamber blocks (A1 and A2) attached to it.

On examining the southern and larger of the groups (A1), it is seen that the large second floor chamber, occupying the south-west tower, has separate access to the chapel stair and to the private pew, and that, with its four attendant chambers, it forms yet another hall and double chamber-block group – the third in the series. A fourth (F) lies below on the first and ground floors below the inner hall (A).

These groups in the western and part of the northern range form the extent of the principal accommodation. The eastern and part of the southern range are given over to lodgings as opposed to suites, which, themselves, fall into three groups – first the single-chamber lodgings, marked (I) on plan, six in the east wing and three in each of the north and south turrets; second the multiple chamber lodgings, of which there are two: (G) of two chambers and (D) of six chambers. Thirdly, there is the suite marked (E), with a hall on the first floor of the south-east tower, a high room with clerestory lighting, a kitchen to the west of it and, below, a chamber on the ground floor. In its independence this hall appears to parallel the isolated eastern hall at Goodrich.

A detailed diagrammatic analysis of these apartments follows; the left-hand half of the diagram (Figure 9) shows the layout of the great suites.

It would seem axiomatic in medieval domestic planning of the scale under consideration that the most remote apartment shall be reserved for the most

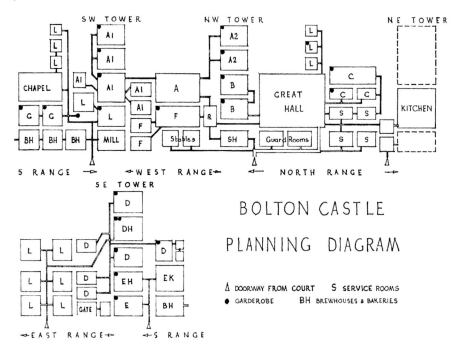

Figure 9. Bolton Castle: planning diagram.

select occupant and that difficulty of personal access shall be a mark of rank. It is, therefore, reasonable to suppose that the innermost set of chambers, those centred on the second-floor great chamber in the south-west tower, should house the most important person. The group (A1) is arranged with two pairs of inner chambers, one above and one to the right, both leading off the great chamber to which is also attached a private pew overlooking the chapel. It is suggested that this group is designed to accommodate the principal guest and his household or households with, so to speak, a king's and queen's side. The whole group forms a complex chamber-block to the main inner hall (A). This is balanced at the nominal lower end of the hall by a suite of two chambers (A2) in the north-west tower comparable to those in the south-west. It was traditional up to this time for the owner's suite to be placed over the lower block of hall and chamber-block houses, as, for example, in the Bishop's Palace at Wells. These rooms, some of the finest in the castle, could reasonably be allocated to Lord Scrope's own household, sharing the privacy of the inner hall, to which only the privileged would have access, with his principal guest.

Below this inner hall is another unit of hall and block of two chambers (F), to which access is only to be had through the lobby or ante-room (R), and, attached to the upper end of the great hall a suite (B) of great and inner chamber in the north-west tower. Either of these would provide accommodation for a person of high rank, one, indeed, so exalted as to merit a private hall. The suite (C) attached to the lower end of the great hall has characteristics that require more consideration. It occupies the traditional owner's position and has dual access to the great hall and service rooms. It is marked, in fact, as being the apartment of one who is intimately connected with the owner and who is interested in the economy of the castle. This would suggest the permanent residence of Lord Scrope's High Steward.

On the ground floor of the north-west tower is an isolated chamber or hall of some size (SH). With connections to the lobby or ante-room above and to the entrance passage and stables, it provides an exact parallel with the lower north hall at Goodrich and, perhaps, served the same purpose, providing accommodation for the squires of those who occupied the great suites in the western range.

It has already been noted that the accommodation falls into two main divisions, the households and the individual lodgings. Of the latter, twelve are single-chamber lodgings. The north and south turrets both contain a set of three small lodgings (L), each group with access to a common garderobe, the northern suggesting accommodation for pages or those whose duties required them to be in attendance in the great hall with which the lodgings are associated.

The southern group are similarly associated with the chapel. In 1399 Scrope founded a chantry of six priests at Bolton. Doubtless these chambers, with two men to each, were their lodgings.

Of the group of six single-chamber lodgings (L) in the east range little need be said beyond noting the systematic manner of their planning and that each chamber is provided with independent access from the court.

The chambers in the south-east tower appear to have been designed to meet a special case. Here are six chambers (D) radiating from a central great chamber or hall (DH), which is significantly provided with two garderobes. Three of these chambers are arranged over the gate, two larger ones in the south-east tower and one thrown out on its own in the south range. This last is commonly known as the Auditor's chamber. It has attached to it two small rooms, one of which appears to have been designed as a strong-room, which makes the allocation reasonable, more particularly if the whole group is considered as serving as the offices and accommodation for the administrative staff of the lordship (perhaps the bailiffs of the outlying manors), with the upper chamber in the south-east tower reserved for the bailiff of Bolton itself or principal officer of rank. This suggestion is strengthened if again, the increase of pomp and circumstance of an establishment such as Lord Scrope's be considered, for it will be seen that there has been promotion throughout; the bailiff occupies the normal position of the constable over the castle gate, the constable or high steward has been promoted to the owner's position at the low end of the hall while the lord himself occupies new quarters at the low end of the private inner hall.

The suggestion has already been made that the hall in the south-east tower (EH) served the same purpose as did the east hall at Goodrich in providing for those who used neither the lord's hall nor the inner hall. The provision of a separate kitchen (EK) implies that it is a hall that would be in use when the lord is absent and consequently the great hall and its kitchen out of use, its position near the permanent quarters of the administrative staff being thus logical.

The achievement of Bolton is its clear conception as a single building integrating into one whole the many and varied demands of a great and defendable mansion. Its value to us lies in its expression of these demands which in themselves reflect the manner in which its inhabitants lived and the use to which they put such a building. While the comparison between Goodrich and Bolton is not necessarily valid, it may, nevertheless, serve as a pointer to some of the changes taking place over the span of the century. The most obvious is the great increase in the numbers accommodated in buildings of nearly the same ground area – Goodrich, in fact, being slightly the larger; secondly, there is an increased elaboration of the plan representing a more elaborate mode of life; thirdly, doubtless arising out of the last, a more marked differential scale of accommodation that has resulted in the growth of the individual lodging, and lastly, the decrease in the size of the hall, now clearly a formal apartment.

At the end of the fourteenth century the integrated planning of Bolton was by no means an isolated phenomenon. It is, though, remarkable in the completeness that enables us to analyse its workings and come to a better understanding of some of its less complete contemporaries. One such is Bodiam Castle in Sussex.

Bodiam Castle, Sussex
(Figure 10)

Built by Sir Edward Dalyngrigge under a licence dated 1385, Bodiam had a very definite military role to play; it is, nevertheless, in the terms of the licence, 'a house fortified'. To whatever extent its external appearance may be due to the influence of the romantic poets or to the military engineers its plan form is similar to that at Bolton. It is quadrangular with intermediate turrets on the long sides and angle towers. It differs in that greater care is taken to achieve architectural symmetry. Generally the buildings are only two-storied rising to three in the turrets. The spaciousness of the court and the generous fenestration give its interior a far more open and domestic character than that of Bolton.

The south range contains the ground floor great hall with its great chamber on the first floor extending over the first bay of the hall and the ground floor buttery and pantry. There is no sign of access to this chamber, but lack of windows on the south side of the hall suggests a stair at this point.[17] Below, the central passage between the service rooms leads westward to the kitchen rising through two stories. From the kitchen access is gained to the south-west tower, which contains a basement cellar, a ground-floor lodging with fireplace and garderobe and, above, a dovecote.

---

[17] The face of this wall was rebuilt in the course of the 1920 restorations, and any evidence that might have existed for this stair destroyed.

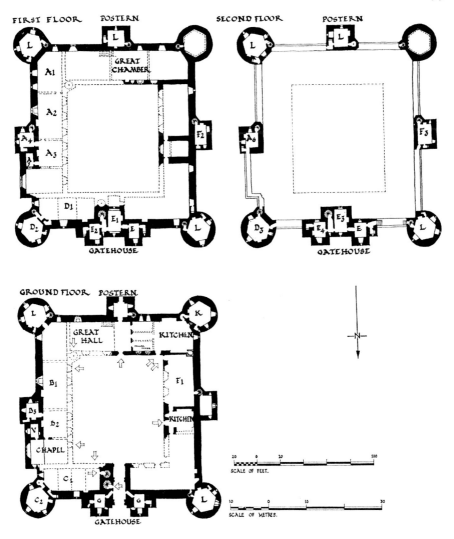

Figure 10. Bodiam Castle.

The entrance to the great hall is roughly on the axis of the court. Opposite, in the south wall of the hall, is the postern gate and above this, accessible from the gate passage, two single-chamber lodgings each with fireplace and garderobe. Forming an eastern chamber block to the great hall and reached only through the large ground floor room in the south-east angle of the court, the south-east tower contains three single-chamber lodgings, one on each floor.

The eastern range is planned as a third and more elaborate chamber-block attached to the great hall. In this it resembles the western range at Bolton, which occupies the same relative position to its great hall. On the ground floor of this range is a suite consisting of a hall (B1), beyond which is a great chamber (B2) with an inner chamber (B3). Above is the principal suite. The inner wall of the courtyard is missing here, only its foundations and those of a stair in the south-east angle of the court remain. Lack of any other renders it certain that a stair in this position gave access to the upper suite, while comparison with Bolton and other examples suggests that the stair would lead from the upper end of the hall to the outer chamber of the suite (A1). There being no evidence for a fireplace in this room, and the fact that the suite beyond is complete without it, would argue that the room was an ante-room or audience chamber in the manner already demonstrated at both Goodrich and Bolton. The remaining chambers continue the usual sequence of an inner hall (A2), marked by the only crenellated fireplace in the castle, a great chamber (A3), an inner chamber (A4) with garderobe in the east tower, with a third chamber (A6) above. Bolton again provides a parallel in the way in which a private pew (A5) is attached to the great chamber of this, the principal suite, overlooking the chapel, which occupies the northern end of the east range. The main body of the chapel is entered from the courtyard, serving the whole of the castle.

The northern range, from the north-east tower to the gatehouse, contains, on the ground floor, a hall of considerable size (C1) and a chamber in the tower (C2). A stair at the western end of this hall leads to the suite (D), a replica of that below with an additional chamber (D3) on the second floor of the north-east tower.

In the gate passage are the entrances to the guardrooms and the stair leading to the lodging (E) above. This is in two floors; the first floor with two chambers (E1) and (E2) on either side of the stair lobby, both with fireplaces, and a further chamber in the west gate turret without a fireplace. The principal rooms of this lodging are on the second floor where the passage between the chambers (E3) and (E4) is treated with a ribbed vault and foliage corbels, the only example of such enrichment in the castle.

The layout of the north-west angle is obscure on both floors though the tower itself has an individual lodging on the ground floor and a stair leading to two others above, each with fireplace and garderobe. The remainder of the west range is occupied by a small kitchen rising through two stories with a first-floor gallery across its east side; between this and the main kitchen is a hall (F1) on the ground floor with attached chambers (F2) and (F3) in the west tower, and above it a fur-ther similar hall, with tall two-light mullion and transome windows to the court, accessible only from the gallery across the kitchen. The loss of so much of the courtyard wall and of the internal partitions leaves a considerable amount of the planning to conjecture. The diagrammatic analysis that follows will, it is hoped, justify the assumptions made. From the diagram (Figure 11), which continues the conventions already used, the great hall is seen to fall naturally into its place as the focus of the plan and as the centre of a hall and multiple chamber-block layout. The great chamber appears as a formal apartment not, by late fourteenth-century standards, equipped as a living apartment. It can only, therefore, have served for the entertainment of guests rather than for their accommodation – a foretaste of the drawing room to come.

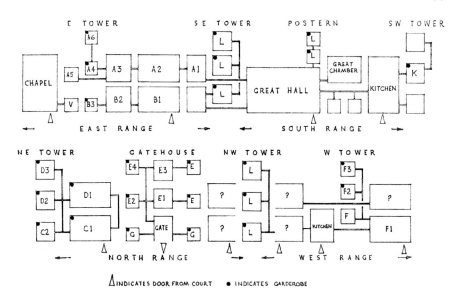

Figure 11. Bodiam Castle: planning diagram.

The great suite (A) does not split, as at Bolton, to provide lavish guest accommodation, so that it may be taken to have been reserved for Sir Edward Dalyngrigge himself, who, even so, required an ante-room before his inner hall and a private pew overlooking the chapel. If, on the parallel of Bolton, this area is taken as being earmarked for the use of the owner and his principal guests it will be noted that the guest accommodation varies in content, for here we have, in addition to the household suites (A) and (B), three individual lodgings (L). Though still suitable for guests of rank their presence, in the lower standard that it implies, may reflect the difference in status between the guests of Sir Edward and those of the Lord of Bolton.

Beyond the chapel, in the north range, are two halls or great chambers (C1) and (D1) placed one above the other, with the north-east tower acting as chamber block to both. The condition of the building leaves the behaviour of the stair between the suites and the gatehouse in some doubt. It would be more logical if this were to provide direct communication between the upper hall and the court. It may be possible that that was, indeed, the case. These two suites, together with all the apartments between the gatehouse and the hall, form the extent of the major guest accommodation and that of the owner, embracing the owner's own household, a great chamber for formal entertainment, three further household suites, one of primary importance, and three individual lodgings. The lodgings in this context are illustrative of the growing tendency, already noted, towards the abandonment of the household suite for guests of rank.

The six chambers in the upper floors of the gatehouse clearly form a single unit, which might be considered as forming a twin upper hall house were they not of so late a date. As it is they must be looked on as a multiple-chamber unit no doubt serving their traditional purpose in providing accommodation for the constable of the castle.

Reverting to the group associated with the great hall, there are three further single lodgings to be noted, two in the south or postern tower, which, on the analogy of Bolton, may be assigned to the pages and one in the south-west tower with cross-communication between the kitchen and service rooms, which would probably house the steward.

The condition of the castle renders detailed reconstruction of the west range difficult. A broad comparison with Bolton, however, may serve to lead to some general conclusions as to the purpose of these apartments. It was argued that the same relative area at Bolton was reserved for the administrative staff of the lordship. A feature there was the provision of a hall and kitchen, which, it was suggested, was for the use of those who would not sit at the lord's table and who, in any case, would need to be catered for when he was not in residence. Such a hall and kitchen exist here at Bodiam and could serve the same purpose. In this case it would be reasonable to make a tentative allocation of the suite of chambers in the west tower to the chief bailiff and of the individual lodgings in the north-west tower to those of the outlying manors. Beyond this it is difficult to be more explicit.

Conclusions

In their similarities, Bodiam and Bolton are expressions of the same approach to the planning of a great castle-residence and as such belong to the same class, both bearing the hallmark of the late fourteenth-century planner, the ability to produce an integrated plan that solves the domestic and military problem in a single architectural conception. That this was no sudden development but a gradual growth out of the problems of the thirteenth century has been demonstrated by the comparison between Goodrich and Bolton. The choice of these particular buildings is arbitrary. No claim is made that they are unique; on the contrary, each is claimed to be typical of the trends of its own period.

Of the conclusions that may be reached from their study, some must be stressed in particular. First, the device, which persists through the whole medieval period up to the mid-fifteenth century of division into households. The great house or castle, for from this point of view they are the same, is not a single house but a series of houses finally integrated into one building but still a series of houses. The surviving contract for Bolton refers to the apartments as houses, even making the distinction between these and the individual lodgings or chambers: 'tous les meson et chambres avanditz …', all the houses and lodgings aforesaid are to have doors, fireplaces, privies and other necessaries included in the work. Secondly, the multiplication of halls is a natural corollary of the first point. In Goodrich, in Bolton and in Bodiam the lord's hall is in each case separated from the great hall: in Goodrich in the north range, in Bolton in the west range on the second floor and in Bodiam in the east range on the first floor. Thirdly, the separation of the castle into two main divisions: one part for use when the lord was in residence, which must have been rare enough, another for the administration of the lordship, probably permanently occupied. No special provision, other than the guardrooms, was considered necessary for the small permanent complement of purely military personnel,[18] for it must be remembered that, in time of war or strife, just as the castle itself was dual purpose so were its inhabitants; both the lord and his bailiff were knights, and just as a bishop could be a chancellor or a prior a politician, so could a soldier be a steward and a castle a house.

---

[18] The permanent garrison at Pembroke was only two mounted sergeants-at-arms and ten footmen. The guardrooms would be adequate for these (*Liberate Rolls*, 37 Henry III, 26 May).

5
Meaningful Constructions: Spatial and Functional Analysis of Medieval Buildings

Graham Fairclough

Spatial analysis has enjoyed a considerable vogue in archaeological studies over the past two decades, though usually applied in prehistoric contexts. The paper applies well-tried techniques to the analysis of complex high-status medieval buildings and demonstrates their superiority in terms of data (especially when used in parallel) on social function and status over subjective analysis based on notions of symbolic or functional characterisation.

Spatial analysis is a widely used term in current archaeological practice, but it describes many disparate approaches tht do not always share the same objectives or methods (e.g. Boast & Yiannouli 1986, 136). It can be used, for example, to denote patterning of artefact distribution from site excavation (e.g. Mytum 1989a; Ellison 1987; Fisher 1985) or from field-walking (Hietala 1984; Hodder & Orton 1976). Very commonly, however, it is used to investigate architectural space (Hillier & Hanson 1984; Foster 1989a; Samson 1990; Dickens 1977). This is the usage in the present paper, which is concerned with spatial analysis as a means of exploring how architectural space has been consciously sub-divided and allocated in the past. There are several other methods of reading the architecture of past societies, notably those that rely on symbolic analysis and attempts to associate buildings with particular social functions (e.g. Richards 1990; Johnson 1986; Coulson 1979), and these will also find their way into the margins of the present paper. One useful framework for the present paper is that offered by Markus: the relationships, as articulated and taught by buildings, of self to self; of self to others (the inhabitant/visitor dichotomy that underlies Hillier & Hanson's theories); and of both self and others to the larger, cosmic Other (Markus 1982, 6).

A starting-point of all these approaches, and of this paper, is that the fundamental structures of a society condition the ways in which groups negotiate rights over space within a building. This insight is far from restricted to archaeological studies, being a commonplace for example in a large body of architectural theory and in the field of environmental behavioural science. That 'culture is the main influence on the use of space', taking culture as embracing social relationships, has been a main theme of such studies since the 1960s (Rapoport 1969; 1990, 223). The same concept is also the basis of Hillier and Hanson's work, which recognises that the relationship between space and society is reflexive and mutually deter-mining (Hillier & Hanson 1984, ix–x; Samson 1990, 14), and in this context the importance of buildings (which more than any other artefact or social construct concerns the use and control of space) is hard to over-state.

Buildings are perhaps our principal evidence for culture and society in much of the past (especially in historic periods), and they can offer a rich source of data for social patterning and relationships. In addition, buildings are also significant because they are rarely (at least for pre-industrial periods) standardised, and they can therefore often bring us closer to individual decision-makers such as archi-tects, designers and users. Indeed, because of their frequent longevity they can also illustrate social change over the long term more effectively than other types of artefact. Understanding change and adaptation can tell us more about the past than mere reconstruction of 'original' structures (see e.g. Banning & Bird 1987; Atkin et al. 1985). Finally, buildings have the advantage that the basic (data for studying this evidence is becoming increasingly available through the results of almost incessant archaeological building recording, usually as part of conserva-tion work, which provides the detailed stone-by-stone records and interpretive studies to allow us to 'read' historic buildings in order to draw wider social, as well as merely art-historical, conclusions.

Many of the more formal techniques of spatial analysis currently in use have been developed within architectural theory during the 1970s and 1980s, and rely principally on morphological analysis. This is not the place for an overview. Many summaries of the techniques already exist in archaeological literature (e.g. Dick-ens 1977; several contributors to Samson 1990; Foster 1989a; Mytum 1989b) as well as in accessible architectural works (e.g. Steadman 1983). Particularly nota-ble are those techniques that have found successful archaeological applications (Steadman 1983, 201–46; Brown 1990b). Most recently, Rapoport's summary of over twenty years' development of environmental behavioural study (EBS) has much of relevance to archaeology, not least because he himself sees archaeology as one of the disciplines that comes closest to EBS in terms of aims, methods and approach (Rapoport 1990). EBS is directly relevant to spatial studies of build-ings (or settlements) – 'material aspects are not primary (and) ... cognitive and symbolic approaches are essential ... meaning (is) more important than mere instrumental function' (Rapoport 1990, 187).

Among these many techniques, the one most commonly adopted by archae-ologists is the theory of space created by Hillier and Hanson (1984). They them-selves applied the theory, during its early development, to historic sites (e.g. the Ambo kraal in Hillier & Hanson 1984, 164–75). Several archaeological studies in recent years have taken up the techniques (principally access analysis of buildings but also axial analysis of settlements) offered by their pioneering work (Foster 1989a; Chapman 1990). But while recognising from the first the historic dimen-sion of their work, Hillier and Hanson had as their starting-out point a desire to form a social theory that would facilitate contemporary design; an agenda as clear as that indicated from the Postscript to *The social logic of space* (with its prescription for the only spatial pattern that would allow the development of a society 'democratically deployed in space' (1984, 262)), however desirable, is not necessarily suited to archaeology with its overriding concern with historical and cultural specificity. The extent to which the usefulness and validity of access analysis is strained when applied to the past will be partly explored later, but the observation has been made already by others (Brown 1990a). Nonetheless, it is difficult to analyse historic space in buildings without being indebted to Hillier and Hanson's main premises: that 'spatial organisation in society is a function of differentiation' (1984, 142–3), that basic dichotomies can be identified between concepts of aggregation and containment (1984, 11--13) and of ideological and transactional space (in some circumstances reversed) (1984, 20–1), and that there is a correlation between the nature and organisation of society and the degree of order imposed on building form and use of space (social relations become more formal as they become less frequent – 1984, 235).

One of the more fully worked-out archaeological applications of access analysis is worth brief consideration. This is the paper on Orkney brochs by Sally Foster in *Antiquity* (Foster 1989a), which, with a subsequent more detailed paper (Foster 1989b), elegantly demonstrates the value of this technique in interpreting past cultural uses of these buildings in terms of social or political organisation. At

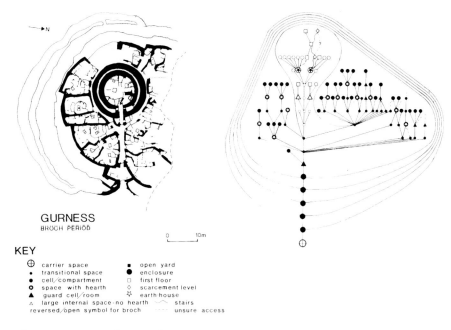

GURNESS
BROCH PERIOD

0   10m

KEY

⊕ carrier space   ■ open yard
• transitional space   ● enclosure
• cell/compartment   ☐ first floor
○ space with hearth   ◇ scarcement level
▲ guard cell/room   ⚚ earth house
△ large internal space-no hearth   stairs
reversed/open symbol for broch   unsure access

Figure 1. Access analysis used at Gurness, from Foster 1989a. Each symbol represents a discrete bounded space. Lines denote access between spaces. The vertical scale of the diagram measures depth from a common starting point, in this case the entrance to the broch complex.

Gurness, for example (Figure 1), the technique highlighted the degree to which strangers were excluded from parts of the building group, the higher status of the upper levels of the broch itself and the extent to which the surrounding 'out-buildings', in contrast to the broch itself, were essentially open to the outside world. This in turn informed further interpretation of social organisation, development and change through time. Others have used this (e.g. Yiannouli & Mithen 1986) and similar methods for the comparative analysis of types or groups of buildings (for instance, Gilchrist 1988a, or Cromwell quoted in Mytum 1989b, 351–3).

Access analysis emphasises control, however, and this can sometimes leave too little room to take account of function and use. Hillier and Hanson were most concerned with movement, encounter and direction of access between visitors and inhabitants. Relationships between inhabitants, which are generally central to a building's use, planning and meaning, are less visible in such analysis, which, as merely axial settlement analysis 'interpreted for permeability' (Hillier & Hanson 1984, 147), has greater emphasis on access and control than on either symbolic or practical function. The reasons for access, and the frequency and nature of movements and encounters, tend not to be considered in detail and other methods are required to contextualise and explain. It is the first theme of this paper to try to explore broader ways of seeing.

A second theme of the present paper is that it is just as valuable to study more recent buildings in this way, as it is to study prehistoric buildings, even if they survive more completely than prehistoric buildings such as Orkney brochs. There can be a tendency to, suggest that rigorous analysis of space is less suited to buildings of more recent date, because, paradoxically, their better survival and associated documents are taken to suggest that meaning and significance are self-evident. Architectural spatial theory, of course, originated to study and analyse modern spaces precisely in order to understand hidden social mechanisms, and indeed the better and more complete the survival of a building, the better chance we have of understanding its social meaning. The existence of documentary evidence should be no disincentive to try to look at deeper structures below and beyond contemporary understanding. Knowledge of medieval politics and society derives from documentary sources, which are the product of writers who did not set out to explain the inner workings of their social organization, and who, even had they attempted to do so, would perhaps not have been capable of sufficient detachment or understanding. Beyond this, documents are often heavily overlaid and coloured, if not actually distorted, by centuries of historical interpretation and reconstruction. Few of the questions we ask about life in, say, a fourteenth-century English house are readily answered by the contemporary documentation of mundane household accounts, 'lists of servants' rules (ideal rather than practical, one guesses), the barest bones of legal proceedings. Spatial analysis, in common with other archaeological methods, allows us in some measure to validate, calibrate or re-interpret contemporary documentation. At best it can inform an expansion or re-assessment of our own historically derived perceptions. There is certainly no reason to restrict the archaeological use of rigorous analysis and interpretation of space to prehistoric society and structures.

Planning Analysis

Both themes are illustrated by looking at an older archaeologically based technique, first devised in the 1950s by Patrick Faulkner (another architect), to analyse high-status medieval houses. This was as part of his work for the Ministry of Public Buildings and Works on the repair of historic buildings, and his research grew from the need to understand buildings before intervening in their historic development. His methods used 'planning diagrams' to illustrate the interrelationship and functions of rooms within complex buildings (Faulkner 1958; 1963). They have been subsequently used by later writers, either explicitly (e.g. Dixon 1978; Fairclough 1982; Gilyard-Beer 1977) or implicitly (e.g. Morley 1976; 1981; Emery 1970; 1985), and many students of buildings use the technique as an analytical tool without taking the results to formal publication. Faulkner's 'planning diagrams' and Hillier and Hanson's 'access analysis' have features in common, but they also offer different opportunities. Neither monopolises understanding of archaeological buildings and sites, and as indicated already many complementary alternative approaches exist (e.g. Gilchrist 1989; Johnson 1986).

Faulkner started with the now-familiar assumption that a building's plan indicates function and purpose, revealing the 'mode of living of those for whom the building was designed' (1958, 150). His emphasis on design is useful, but we need now a parallel acknowledgement of the equal importance of hidden and unspoken expressions of status or power. Like access analysis, planning diagrams involve schematic representation of a building's layout and plan. They emphasise functional relationships, generally from the viewpoint of someone using the building, rather than the actual spatial arrangement of rooms in a building. While access analysis focuses on an outsider's (a stranger's) experience of a building, and thus principally on questions of movement and control, privacy and independence (facets of function but not the whole picture), planning analysis is also about access, use and purpose, and is as much concerned with interaction between occupants of a house as it with their relations with strangers. In Markus's terms, access analysis tends to look at self/other relations; planning diagrams take in these, but they can also see self/self relationships (and to an extent self/other to Other, although this is better considered by cognitive and symbolic analysis) (Martin 1982, 6). Thus, in planning diagrams, a room's relationship to another is often determined, for example, not by physical location but by access to and from other related rooms. Bolton Castle illustrates the contrast between the siting of the rooms forming linked suites and their position on the functional diagram (Faulkner 1963, 228, reproduced as Figure 2 here).

Faulkner's planning diagrams did, however, stop short of fully schematic representation. His diagrams, like Bolton, generally shadow the general shape of a building, and indeed there is often no advantage in departing from actual, visible

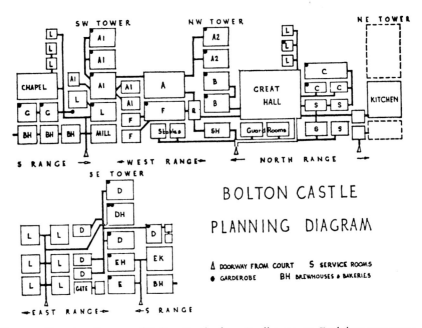

Figure 2. Planning diagram of Bolton Castle, from Faulkner 1963. Each box represents, approximately proportional to floor area, a single room in the building. While arrangement mainly follows the actual layout of the building, and vertical scale is provided by the building's successive floor levels, the relationship and grouping of rooms allows analysis of functional planning.

layout. But it may sometimes be instructive to disregard physical form more completely in order to draw similarities or contrasts within groups of buildings. It is the value of this analytical tool that it guides us towards an understanding of buildings and their cultural meaning by giving priority to meaning and function rather than to form and design. This recalls Rapoport (1990, 187) – cognitive and symbolic meaning is more important than instrumental function: 'Meaning is the main function.' Giving priority to internal relationships rather than to external form or design can filter from a building's planning the less significant 'background noise' such as aesthetics and design (the symmetry of a building like Warkworth (Northumberland) – did not prevent highly complex spatial planning), topographic variation – differences of design on constrained urban sites or within pre-existing enclosure as opposed to 'greenfield' sites – or cultural pressures – like late medieval northern British preferences, militarily dictated or not, for tower-shaped houses. Gilchrist's application of access analysis to monastic planning, identifying common attributes between buildings despite local differences, is a good example of this (Gilchrist 1989a).

Faulkner's work also confirms the value of spatial analysis in historical periods, especially if used in conjunction with other methods. His planning analysis altered our perception of the nature of medieval high-status households. These

were already ostensibly relatively well understood both from contemporary documents and recent historical studies, but the detailed reality (Mertes 1988; Given-
Wilson 1986) only became fully apparent after Faulkner's (and others') work. Spatial analysis of the medieval household's principal artefact, the physical remains
of the buildings that accommodated and supported it, has to be laid alongside the
evidence from contemporary documents. Girouard recognised the same parity of
built with written sources in his classic work on the country house (1976, 14–80),
which has claims to belong to archaeology as much as to architectural history.

Faulkner's method is simple and useful but it is capable of some extension
and elaboration to embrace wider notions of function, symbolism and meaning.
It may benefit from underpinning, with more rigorous analysis borrowed from
more recent work. But before attempting this in the context of a particular building, it is worthwhile to look in more detail at some of the factors involved and
their application to medieval buildings.

Factors

Spatial analysis to interpret historic buildings needs to take account of a multiplicity of factors that affect meaning. Markus has identified three ways of categorising
building space – form (including boundedness and area), function (including
symbolic as well as instrumental function) and aformal space (Markus 1982, 5–6).
This framework is useful, allowing attention to focus on individual, more specific,
concepts of use and access such as function and status, movement and control,
community and independence. By analysing these factors within a building, it is
possible to form interpretations of social organisation.

Principal factors include the social importance or the functional role needed
to justify individuals' access to a particular space, or their 'ownership' (sole,
shared or subservient) of a room. The nature and form of boundaries to rooms
is significant, especially the way that entrances are treated. Here Hillier's statement that social relations are formalised as they become less frequent (Hillier &
Hanson 1984, 235) is relevant, as doors that display highest rank (architectural
detail, protective arrangement, remoteness through privacy) may be those that
are as infrequently used as they are formal (as in the different values put on front
and back doors in the use of terraced houses earlier in the twentieth century).
Alternatively, apparently opposite explanations may hold, and in some circumstances (such as entrances to fortified and high-status enclosures, or the main
entrance to public buildings) the most public, least private and lowest-ranked
doors are those singled out for greatest architectural promotion.

Social standing related to other members of a household can also be indicated
by the comparative position, size, furnishings and fittings of rooms as well as by
the interrelationships between rooms. At the same time, a room's relationship
(or access) to essential facilities e.g. kitchens, garderobe, specialised or defended
entrances) is also significant in appreciating status, and it is relevant to consider

whether that access is shared or monopolised. Finally, the relationship to parts of the house of higher (or lower) status is also meaningful.

In most prehistoric, and even many medieval, buildings, such detailed physical evidence may not exist; analysis of this type may nevertheless allow the construction of a number of models for reconstruction based on alternative interpretations of what does survive. Indeed, reconstruction based on informed extrapolation from spatial analysis can be a main gain of this approach, whatever period of building is being studied. It can, for example, be possible after spatial analysis to begin making sensible guesses about lost upper-floor arrangements of ruined buildings.

Three sets of factors in particular merit consideration, being those that tend to be understated in morphologically based spatial analysis. They constitute 'types of interface, a significant conceptual component of building analysis' (Hillier & Hanson 1984, 176), and thus inform our view of status and use.

Direction of access

It is important to consider the direction of access (from, for example, the form of door jambs and thresholds), as this often indicates the function of a room and the status and purpose of access. Movement through a building to this day is rarely entirely open or uncontrolled, so the presence of guarded, interrupted or privileged access needs to be taken into account, particularly with direct access either from outside the building (i.e. unregulated and unmediated by other rooms) or between areas of especially widely differing status. The most difficult forms of social control to identify are those that rely on little or no physical or visible signs, but only on well-understood systems of social knowledge – taboos, fear, authority, custom etc. (cf. Owen 1990).

At its simplest, direction of access, with its consequent implications for function and use, is resolved by a simple question: whether or not a room is closed from outside or from within, whether or not its users or occupants lock themselves into a room, as say, in a bedroom; or whether they close the door on its contents, as, say, in a store-room or prison. Such questions are only partly a matter of an 'insider' perspective. They are also linked to the process noted by Hillier and Hanson whereby the normal relationship (as seen for instance at Gurness, above, whereby inhabitants occupy the 'deep' parts of a building and visitors the 'shallow') is reversed (Hillier & Hanson 1984, 184). In a prison or a hospital, the inhabitants (the 'owners') are the staff, but they occupy the shallow, front rooms. The more transient occupants, the 'visitors', are the inmates, who paradoxically occupy the deep, most secure, rooms not for reasons of status or privacy but for reasons of security. Space thus indicates loss, not possession, of power.

But it is worth considering whether in fact we should perhaps regard the people (i.e. the social concepts of visitor and resident) as being reversed rather than the building. Those whom the building is intended to house (that is, in normal terms the residents or owners) are in this case those who are held against their wishes or at least against their preferences. Guards are visitors, even though in charge.

A partly analogous reversal is visible when looking at visitor responses to the type of ranked patterning of rooms in seventeenth-century royal palaces (and the greater houses) with an 'axis of honour' approaching the main bedchamber. The normal intention is to deny access at each stage to an increasingly large proportion of visitors so that only those closest in rank to the king are allowed to reach the highest rooms. There are two reversals – servants, and visitors of higher rank than the owner. The former need to have access (usually invisible access) to all rooms, and this is in some ways irrespective of status. The latter may not wish to reach the innermost rooms – it is the host, not the guest, who gains the social benefits in such a case – and such visitors have to be pulled inwards rather than being excluded. In other words, in such reversed situations the direction of movement indicated by architecture and planning are at odds with social pressure.

Nor is direction always a matter of worldly function, as the treatment of doors can sometimes indicate symbolic or psychological attitudes. At Chastleton House (Oxon.), for instance, designed *c*.1603, doorways from the house's two staircases (state and service) have floor-to-ceiling stone jambs. They have decorative mouldings only on one side of the doorway, and this side is the nominal or cognitive 'out-side'. This is straightforward in the case of the outer door, and of doors from the screens to the hall, while decoration on doors between the hall, state stair and the private chambers on the principal floors (i.e. ground and first) form a progression of successively more private rooms creating increasing 'depth' as more private areas are reached. Equally, it is normal that the service stair and rooms beyond (i.e. kitchen, servants' rooms, etc.) are treated as 'external', because when considered from the dominant perspective of the owners they belong to the 'other' world. But the topmost, second, floor, which is devoted in part to low-status rooms and in part to an attic Long Gallery for exercise, games etc. (Coop. 1986, 54–61), is also treated as external, and this is both unusual and significant. Whether approaching from the servants' stair or the private stair, someone entering the upper floor (and beyond it the roofs) would have passed through doors against the grain – i.e. both doors have jambs whose external chamfers face towards the gallery, as if the gallery was regarded in symbolic terms as external to the house. The jambs could easily have been reversed for the opposite effect, as on lower floors, and the designers' choice must be seen as having significance. The gallery, in other words, appears to have been regarded as a 'substitute outdoors', its externalness marked in stone. Only the lower two floors (principally hall, parlour, chambers etc. and associated stair) are, in this sense, fully internal to the house.

Purpose of access

Direction is not all, however. Doorways and rooms can be used by groups or individuals for several quite different purposes, and the simple fact of access does not of course always carry the same meaning to different groups in society. The most stratified societies rarely display a single hierarchy but rather a complex of interlinked circles and layers. A single individual is likely to have had more than one role in such complex social structures, and we should expect each of these roles to manifest themselves, not necessarily visibly at this remove of time, in building plans. The reversal of host–guest relationships when the guest is of higher status, and the effect of this on the meaning of the building, has already been noted.

As a simple example, not involving reversal, access analysis of the bedchambers of later seventeenth-century palaces and large houses such as Hampton Court and Holyroodhouse, for example, might identify more than one approach to an obviously paramount central room, the monarch's bedchamber. Each route would have allowed access to the central room, but for different functional reasons which were socially very unequal. On the one hand is the servants' approach to the bedchamber via backstairs and closet stairs. This is low-status (unless, again a reversal, when used for subversive purposes – cf. backstairs politics in Anne's reign, calling to mind today's equivalent, the denigratory 'kitchen cabinet') and primarily day-to-day functional rather than symbolic. On the other hand, there is the progression of state apartments leading from the public area of the palace through successive and increasingly private areas to the royal bedchamber. Checks and controls in the latter set (once passed) would have enhanced rather than diminished the status of a visitor, which is far from the case in the former set except in terms of whatever social ranking existed within the servants' population. In visual terms the distinction was sharp. While being seen and noticed was a primary reason for seeking to gain privileged access to the bedchamber, service access was in contrast barely visible; indeed it was as hidden architecturally as the state rooms were decoratively and physically highlighted – 'so contrived … that the ordinary servants may never publicly appear in passing to and from for their occasions there' (the architect Roger Pratt, quoted in Girouard 1976, 188, also 135–45).

Use and access

When looking at the purpose of access we moved closer to the broader question of functional meaning that is often at the heart of spatial analysis. It is not possible to consider purpose without looking at use and function. Foster, for instance, refers to the need to recognise functional zones, for instance areas with hearths, and her justified access maps (Foster 1989a, 47, figure 5) incorporate analysis of function as well as of access. Function in a room can be identified from a variety of evidence, much of which has already been mentioned – size, furnishings, treatment of floors, provision of light and heat, standard of decoration, possession of subordinate private chambers and, if so, whether these are shared, the proximity to or isolation from central rooms, relationship to defended or special(ised) entrances. There will also be functions that are implicit in the nature and meaning of access itself.

Taken with evidence derived from access analysis (for example, on whether access to service areas such as garderobe and rubbish disposal areas is shared or private, or on relationship to service and cooking areas), a knowledge of function allows a more rounded view of a building's purpose and its place in social life. Faulkner placed function on an equal footing with access, and his planning diagrams used basic access patterns as the matrix within which to locate function.

Applications

Spatial analysis has, as one of its aims, the measurement of a building or settlement in units or patterns that allow interpretation and comparison with other
sites. In other words, spatial analysis generates ways of seeing and understanding.
Three main applications, to some extent interlinked, for Faulkner's type of planning diagrams can be usefully identified for the purposes of the present paper
– the better understanding of individual buildings, the identification and study of
generic types of building and the broader study of social organisation.

Individual building analysis

At the simplest level, planning diagrams can facilitate a better and clearer understanding of an individual building in its social context. Gilyard-Beer, for example, used a planning diagram as part of his study of the late fourteenth-century
outer gate of Carlisle Castle, de Ireby's Tower (Gilyard-Beer 1977). As with all
gatehouses, though perhaps exceptionally, de Ireby's tower exhibits a multiplicity
of functions within a single form and within a framework of status and display.
These functions range first from architectural symbolism of the entrance (with
the implicit announcement of the power to restrict entry – 'marking the passage
between domains ... (is) ... the important event or act' (Rapoport 1990, 466)) to
more direct considerations of military defensibility, and secondly from residential to administrative uses.

The published planning diagram reveals three separate sets of accommodation in the tower. One is of some comfort and status for occupation by a senior
castle official. The other two sets provide chambers and prisons for the operation
of two separate jurisdictions, royal and county. At a different level, the various
defensive and symbolic aspects of access to the tower are revealed by the interrelationship of these three groupings to the gate-tower's wall-walk, barbican
and external spaces. Access to the roof and wall-walks of the tower was open
to the main residential rooms, while the wall-walk of the castle's main curtain
wall cannot be reached from these rooms. This separation was partly for practical
military reasons of independent defensibility but also worked as a reminder of,
and safeguard for, the strictly defined roles of separate jurisdiction within this
major royal castle which, as with any major medieval building, needed to contain several quasi-independent organisational structures. Analysis of space thus
illustrates the interplay and overlap of some of the administrative and political
spheres of influence in medieval Britain.

A study of South Wingfield, Derbyshire (Emery 1985) illustrates the value of
stylised rather than realistic or 'topographical' representations of space and planning in historic buildings. At the south end of the great hall built in the 1440s is a
multi-period and intricately planned group of chambers on three floors around a
small courtyard. Emery provides a good sequence of structural development, and
he clearly used the concepts, and perhaps the methods, introduced by Faulkner.
But no diagrams are published, and readers' understanding is hampered by the

absence, at least from the published report, of explicit formal spatial analysis. Access analysis or planning diagrams would provide a stronger framework for understanding this complex wing of the castle. Even a cursory look, with formal methods in mind, raises new questions – for example, re-interpretation of the large first-floor room as an audience chamber in a progression leading to the lord's chamber, rather than Emery's interpretation of it as a semi-public chamber-cum-hall at the centre of a network of rooms. Emery's interpretation puts this room and its occupant at the centre of a household suite, whereas a revised interpretation would suggest an intermediate stage in the transition to the increasingly private way of life demanded by later medieval lords, and often the subject of complaint by their social dependants (see e.g. Girouard 1976, 30, 45–7).

Generic classification

Secondly, there is value in a generic use of planning diagrams to identify categories of buildings which share common symbolism and function or which demonstrate common solutions to similar social situations. They can also do this by escaping from the superficial variations imposed by the vagaries of topography, form and design.

To take a straightforward example, there is a wide range of variation in the layout and design of late medieval manor-houses in northern Britain (even within a single county – see RCHME *Westmorland*), and planning diagrams can often reveal patterns and similarities within this wide range, which can in turn provide social explanations. There is also a well-known concentration of small towers in the same region. Analysis of solar cross-wings in H-plan halls reveals features similar to the vast majority of the free-standing towers of northern England: the frequent lack of internal communication from ground to first floor, but the prevalence of first-floor entries. which are now, but were clearly not originally, external; a lack within the tower of service rooms and thus their general inability to be self-contained. It is then apparent that in planning and spatial terms the towers are closely identical with the solar cross-wings, merely relict features of otherwise vanished larger houses (e.g. Fairclough 1980, 1983) – in other words, originally solar wings built tower-wise. Conversely, towers that are genuinely tower-houses or some other form in their own right can be clearly distinguished by similar methods.

Belsay (Northumberland) and in Scotland Chipchase and Elphinstone fall into one group (Simpson 1940; Cruden 1960, 131–41), while the polygonal south tower at Stokesay (Faulkner 1963, 112–13) – which to first appearance, even in its physical relationship to the hall, appears to be a typical solar tower – proves to be neither solar tower nor self-contained tower house, but a third category, a stack of independent one-room lodgings. A similar use of Faulkner-type planning, in association with other forms of analysis, has produced useful comparison between the twelfth-century keeps of Newcastle and Dover and the tower at Trim (Co. Meath, Eire) (McNeill 1990, 324–5, 332–3, figure 8). In short, planning diagrams provide diagrammatic and comparative quantification of features and combinations of attributes not always otherwise readily apparent.

Wider social modelling

Finally, here treated separately but obviously linked to and forming part of other applications, planning analysis can lead us to form and test theories of social organisation or architectural design. This is the application for which Faulkner most often used planning diagrams. Without publishing formal diagrams, he approached the question of twelfth- to thirteenth-century houses in this way (Faulkner 1958), showing the underlying social pattern of an architecturally well-known group of houses hitherto unconsidered in sociological terms. In a later, more influential paper (Faulkner 1963), he applied formal planning diagrams to fourteenth-century castle design, demonstrating that informed and systematic analysis of function and space can reveal important elements of the society to which buildings like Bodiam, Ludlow and Bolton belonged. His diagrams showed the domestic requirements that design sought to fulfil, and thus identified a form of complex medieval domestic planning –the multiple chamber house – which is specific to a particular cultural and social context.

In this plan-form, several sets of rooms ('households', each comprising more or less standardised categories of accommodation) are served by shared common facilities (kitchens, service areas and great hall, the latter being the central and defining feature of the system), but they are clearly ranked by factors such as size, luxury or position into a hierarchy reflecting relative social importance. This plan-form is peculiarly associated with the historically documented high-status medieval household. The pooling of resources, for defence or cooking, was not confined to the castles and houses of the great lords, but was found at lower levels of society and in urban and monastic communities. Similar collective strategies involving pooled resources occur elsewhere in medieval England, and it may seem that such practices derive from egalitarian structures. But in practice (as for example in the countryside of sub-divided field systems held in common) this ostensibly collective or egalitarian approach was rooted in strong lordship and social control, and it is therefore not surprising that shared resourcing and use of space reveals itself to us most clearly in castles, those contexts where lordship had strongest and most detailed interest.

The strength of Faulkner's method is shown by the ability of others to use its techniques to offer alternative social interpretations. Morley, for example, identified a plan-form – 'hall with lodgings' – which forms an exception proving Faulkner's rule (Morley 1981). Without publishing formal planning diagrams, but using a similar conceptual approach, Morley re-examined some of Faulkner's concepts, commenting that 'there is little point in analysing the way a castle is planned if we do not believe that the planning reflects the social status of the household'. He is, though, reluctant to give weight to planning analysis except where supported by 'hard historical evidence'. This cautious view is not, in fact, wholly borne out by his own work, which identifies a category of castle planning distinct from Faulkner's multi-household castles. Okehampton Castle is a typical example of this category – still the castle of a significant lord, but consisting not of a number of separate ranked households such as identified at Bolton by Faulkner, but of a small central household surrounded by equal-sized subordinate lodgings. Morley explains this as allowing greater flexibility when the status and nature of the groups requiring accommodation was unpredictable. Whether this is, in turn, a function of seasonal as opposed to more permanent occupation, a result of lower status of the castle's owner, or a question of chronological or regional differences still needs to be fully explored, but the contrast between multi-household and subordinate lodgings castles is nonetheless instructive.

A Case Study – Edlingham Castle, Northumberland

Some of the ideas outlined above may be best demonstrated by summarising aspects of work in progress from excavation results at Edlingham Castle in mid-Northumberland. This site was excavated by the Department of the Environment between 1978 and 1982, to allow fuller public display of the medieval structures, and to study the effects of warfare on the Anglo-Scottish marches and the development of the northern tower house and related traditions. Two interim accounts have been published (Fairclough 1982; 1984), both attempting to produce a social archaeological reading of the site. The first included spatial analysis, using Faulkner's techniques (Fairclough 1982, 387, figure 5) but based on incomplete archaeological and documentary evidence. The castle had a long and complex continuous sequence of development, which for present purposes has been simplified to three main periods (periods A to C on Figure 3). Although in most of the castle only the ground floors survives, and only the solar tower stands to anything like its full height over substantial areas, the evidence of the surviving remains, combined with cautious extrapolation from analogous buildings and, most of all, insights derived from planning and spatial analysis, allows a good measure of reconstruction.

The first buildings (a hall-house with associated kitchens standing within a moated enclosure (period A, Figure 3)) were erected in c.1300 for Sir William Felton, a member of Edward I's household. He came from a hitherto unimportant family of the minor gentry in Shropshire, but he was newly prosperous through advancement in royal service and a significant landowner in Northumberland through a profitable marriage to a local heiress. To mark his success, he built a large and impressive semi-fortified house on land that he had recently purchased in his own name in his wife's county. The house reflected in design and appearance a varied career as soldier, royal administrator and supervisor of royal fortified building work in Gascony, North Wales and Scotland. It identified Felton's place in society for contemporaries and continues to do so for modern historians. Principally, however, it expressed his social importance and wealth. The means of doing this (as is often the way with validation of social or institutional power) was

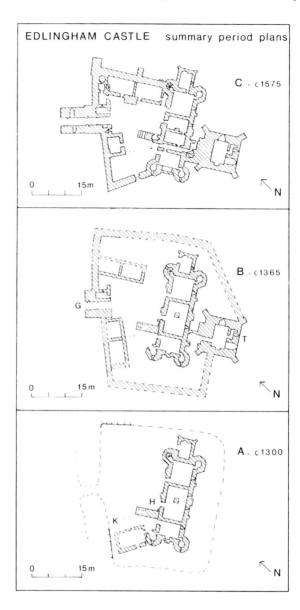

Figure 3. Summary period plans of Edlingham Castle, corresponding to the broad periods described in this paper, from the earliest moated enclosure with Hall House (A), through expansion and enclosure (B), to the latest integrated pseudo-courtyard house (C).

H = Hall House,
K = kitchens etc.,
G = gatehouse,
T = solar tower.

the use of an otherwise obsolete building type that looked backwards to earlier, anachronistic notions of lordship.

This house became inadequate for later requirements, and it was extended and improved by Felton's successors in their equally active, if less successful, pursuit of higher social status (period B, Figure 3). By this time (c.1360–70), however, the long wars with Scotland had brought a new architectural bleakness and an increasingly militarised society to Northumberland, which led Felton, still involved in military service, to choose a defensible form (a solar tower) for his new private chambers and to add a strongly fortified gate-tower and curtain walls to the hitherto hardly defensible house. The previous generation had used military forms that echoed the past and thus enhanced social standing, but the later military fashion by more solid practical pressures. This neither precluded the use of architecture to denote rank, nor reduced the relationship of the building's design to its social and architectural need for organised space, but it did make explicit the military power that the earlier generation had been able to leave as allusion.

By the mid to late sixteenth century, there had been further change (period C, Figure 3). The castle's then owners, the Swinburne family, formed part of a wide network of related Northumbrian families, but were content with a more local role at county rather than national level, and lacked the Feltons' grander military and political ambitions. Defence was still an important consideration in the areas, but the Swinburnes were not a military family, and their use of the house reflected this. Changes at this time were also part of a wider evolution in domestic planning. The differences between the Swinburne houses and either of the Felton houses were thus greater than the differences between the two Felton houses.

Before looking in detail at one period (for present purposes the second of these three periods), it is worthwhile to use a simple form of access analysis to explore change through time. The most immediately visible change between the first and second periods was architectural – the addition of towers, the increase in fortification, the proliferation of residential and service rooms. Access analysis shows further dimensions (Figure 4). The strengthening of defences in defences in periods B and C was illusory, especially by the later sixteenth century; enlargement of the gate-tower and the multiplication of checks and controls in the entry passage was negated by increased external openness elsewhere in the castle. As the point of 'transition between domains' (Rapoport 1990, 466), here the internal and external domains, the gatehouse was chosen for the major formal and public transition even though other transitions, equally important in functional but not in symbolic terms, occur elsewhere in the castle, both between the castle and the outside world and between parts of the castle. One reason for this may well be because in the fourteenth century the gate appears in fact to have been approached through an agricultural outer court (the 'home farm' of later terminology, rather like the courtyard of Roman villas such as Bignor-Scott 1990, 165–8), and this brought a perceived need to mark out in some special way the entrance into domestic, higher-status and more private areas of the castle.

But at the same time the shrinkage of the courtyard introduced direct access from the outside world, unmediated and uncontrolled, into the private chambers at the base of the solar tower, and thus almost in the heart of the castle. There was also direct entrance into the service and kitchen areas of the courtyard, lightly protected but not marked architecturally or spatially (e.g. in an axial sense) in any way, as befits a workaday entrance as opposed to one with wider meaning. The strong gatehouse therefore provided a façade but not a reality of defence, and it was principally successful in its non-military objectives of displaying power

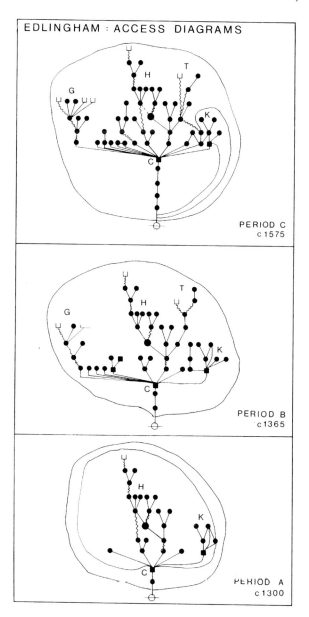

Figure 4. Diagrammatic representation of access patterns, for each of the three periods shown in Figure 3, showing expansion and change through time. The method used is a simplified version of that shown in Figure 1. The diagram is justified from the position of a visitor at the outer gate of the castle. Stairs are shown as wavy lines, to allow some correlation between depth and actual height; stairs also tend to have stronger attached controls over movement. Letters carry same meanings as in Figure 3, with C = main courtyard.

and status and in providing an extra level of independent, relatively high-status private accommodation. The diagram also reveals the independence of the gate-house from all other sections of the castle.

The access diagrams also show patterns of movement growing more complex through time. The hall continued to hold a central position, while subsidiary centres developed in a range of relationships to it. The hall in particular changed its role, becoming less important than the central courtyard as a focus of activity in its own right rather than as the main area for movement between other rooms. It came in some ways to have the function of a sort of secondary interior courtyard from which access was available to other rooms, i.e. a route for journeys through the castle, whereas in its earlier form it was more often a final destination.

These access diagrams therefore have uses, not least to allow a coherent reconstruction of missing upper floors. But, although successful in many ways, they also illustrate some shortcomings of the method. In part this may be because the two techniques put forward by Hillier and Hanson, access analysis of buildings and axis analysis of settlements, posit a sharper distinction than sometimes exists between individual buildings and settlements. Edlingham Castle is a complex of several buildings that shares some of the characteristics of settlements, particularly the integration into a whole of different types of space, including public open space (the courtyard), multi-purpose thoroughfares (gate passage, communication routes across the court and through buildings), and a range of buildings of different functional value and weight. While not a sufficiently large or aggregated complex to benefit from settlement axial analysis, it remains the case that building access analysis does not answer all questions. It can identify the main focus of movement, it can distinguish between 'inner' and 'outer' rooms and define 'depth', but more refined analysis is needed to take in other aspects of space and its use.

On the diagrams at Figure 4, several areas – courtyard, hall, kitchen and chambers – all stand out as being central to some degree, but each owes its position to different functions. Access is in itself no guide to this. In the same way, the deepest, innermost rooms have differing status and purpose: garderobes can appear in equivalent positions (whether used by chambers of widely varying rank or purpose, or providing a common facility for a lodgings block) and can appear as deep as the highest-status chamber or the inner recesses of the kitchen. Indeed, two of the four deepest rooms were garderobes. In Figure 4, the number of rooms with either multiple or multi-functional access (and on the period C diagram the existence of two other possible entry points) leads the diagram to be opaque. All these shortcomings are significant, and it is clear that access diagrams cope less successfully with more complex buildings.

Looking in detail at one period, period B, the later fourteenth century, has most potential – Figure 5 shows a first step towards applying to the mid-fourteenth-century house a method that both analyses space more fully and introduces a stylised representation of instrumental function as well. It uses the ideas of Faulkner's planning diagrams, without precisely reflecting the actual physical shape of the building, but still in more immediately legible form than access diagrams. Instead, the schematic symbolic planning of the castle is used – i.e. a visitor entering the courtyard would have found kitchen and service areas to the right, chambers to the left and the main house directly ahead and (with the main rooms at first-floor level) above, the solar tower rising higher again behind. This sequence of views is in itself indicative of contemporary perceptions of architecture and society. Figure 5 also emphasises the 'substructure' of social use and organisation, the vernacular so to speak, rather than any veneer of 'polite' design.

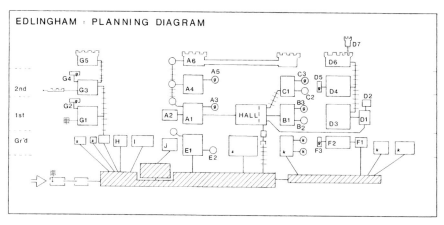

EDLINGHAM : PLANNING DIAGRAM

Figure 5. Planning diagram of period B (c.1365) at Edlingham, following the conventions shown in Figure 2. Access is indicated by lines between the boxes, whose size broadly represents floor area. Stairs are shown as ladders.
Al, G4, J etc. indicate main planning units of linked rooms sharing functions.
k = kitchen and related rooms, s = storage and offices, g = garderobes.
Shaded areas indicate courtyards. Vertical scale is based on floor levels. The distinction between primary high-status apartments (A to D) and secondary chambers and lodgings (E to J) is clear, the former normally complex aggregations 'behind' the hall, the latter (with the special exception of the gatehouse) being isolated, mainly single, rooms accessible direct from the courtyard.

In doing so, and in increasing the clarity of functional interrelationship, however, it risks loss of insights into aesthetic considerations of design and of planning related to the physical world. It also loses some of the clarity of access analysis in that it lacks the comparative vertical scale afforded by calibration against a common starting point ('justification'). To planning diagrams, therefore, needs to be added a much more rigorous matrix showing movement and access, while retaining the additional insights that planning analysis brings. Figure 6 attempts to provide this, by superimposing the planning on the access diagram. This gives many of the benefits of both techniques, in particular in relating function more closely to access. The method could be taken further, either by representing function, use and interior architecture more graphically, or by using room floor area (e.g. Austin 1989, 174–82) or volume as indices of status, wealth and function.

Finally, a useful further step is to add to these diagrams a model that categorises space by other attributes – such as function, gender, class or age (see e.g. Gilchrist 1988). These attributes could be superimposed on any of the matrices already discussed, but for the purposes of the present exercise, to demonstrate how spatial analysis should not completely lose sight of the outward form of a building, they are superimposed in Figure 7 on the actual layout, i.e. the non-schematic plan, of the castle. The use categories chosen concern class and functional divisions, because these are rather more evident in the fabric and plan of the building. Inevitably, the categories both overlap (the courtyard can be both

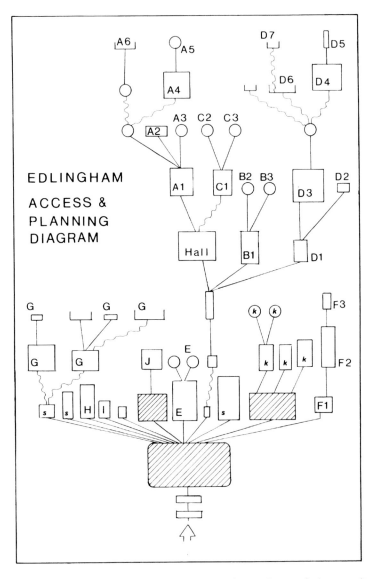

Figure 6. The planning diagram at Figure 5 transposed onto the justified access diagram at Figure 4. The more rigorous attention to the distance of rooms from a fixed point (the outer gate) demonstrates the relative contrast in depth between different sets of rooms. Significant contrasts include the relative shallowness, despite physical height, of the gatehouse upper chambers and roof (G), compared, e.g., to Hall House and solar tower upper floors (A–D). One chamber (E) has greater depth only because hidden behind a small courtyard, which secures privacy in accordance with status even though at ground-floor level. Kitchen rooms are similarly one level deep, though for reasons not of privacy and status but of concealment, and in later period (see C on Figure 4) a 'back door' opened through the enclosure wall allows concealment at a less deep level. Conventions as Figure 5.

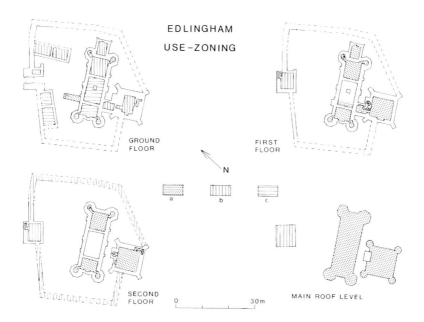

Figure 7. Use-zones, based on function-related status of rooms in period B. The three
categories are defined from the planning diagram at Figure 5.
a = primary private apartments (i.e. apartments A to D), b = secondary chambers or
lodgings (i.e. E to J), c = kitchens, offices, storage.
Further sub-division would be possible: the gatehouse could form a separate category.

private and public depending on circumstances, and are therefore not zoned on
the plan – zoning here would amount to identification of informal pathways) and
are oversimplified (the broad category 'private' does not allow detailed ranking by
status, while the gate-tower chambers should be zoned separately as a category in
their own right). A more refined approach, again beyond the scope of the present
paper, would seek to identify distinctions between age, gender, family relationship and job.

Even such a preliminary attempt begins to clarify more aspects of building use.
It shows the correlation of upper floors with high-status activity, and of control
of roof-tops with high-status use as well as for defence, although the Chastleton
example cited earlier shows that high and low status can co-exist on an upper
floor. There is also the question of whether we should not also take into account
the views obtained from roof tops as part of building (and wider landscape) planning, as control over access to views of the countryside may be taken to symbolise
control over use of the countryside itself. At lower levels, the diagram shows the
extent to which planning use-zones were related to physical layout, as explained
above.

Where fuller documentary evidence is available, as it is at Edlingham for the
later sixteenth century, it may be possible to use functional analysis to look more
closely at population, age-structure and inheritance. An inventory of 1572 (used

for a planning diagram in Fairclough 1982, figure 5) sets its listing of rooms into a formal tripartite division of the whole house deriving from partible inheritance, or co-parcenary (see Machin 1977; Dixon 1978). A similar division, less well-documented, appears to have occurred earlier, when in c.1400 the estate was divided to form a dower portion. There is thus the possibility, having used the 1572 document to elucidate the planning analysis and to identify spatial patterns deriving from partition, to recognise other instances of this practice. It is already clear that the three separate houses were not fully self-contained, but shared common cooking and defensive facilities. The use-zone analysis in Figure 6 can be applied to each of the three sixteenth-century subordinate homes as well as to the overall building. At the same time, spatial analysis should also distinguish long-term trends (like the tendency of household units to become smaller and less ranked as the medieval and early modern period advanced) from those arising from more locally specific changes – 'the structure of space within buildings (followed) new rules in accordance with changing social function within families and organisations ... and the interaction of these groups with society' (Markus 1982, 1).

From this preliminary statement on Edlingham, a number of major themes are emerging:

- It is useful to identify two distinct types of private chamber, 'primary' chambers linked directly to the hall in an aggregated pattern, and 'secondary' chambers which were isolated and free-standing. The distinction between chamber and lodging may cut across both types.
- The balance between these types changed over time. Isolated chambers became more common during the fourteenth century as the castle, and presumably Felton's influence and household, grew in size and complexity, and needed to accommodate a wider range of semi-independent retainers, kinsfolk and friends, all with their households. They declined in number during the sixteenth century as patterns of family life changed with the disappearance of satellite households requiring separate chambers, and an increased demand for groups of chambers.
- At the same time, and as part of this process, the proliferation of chambers aggregated to the hall encroaches on to public space. This was not a one-way process: it also resulted in an opening-up of more secluded private chambers and the 'un-privatisation' of the great chamber. The hall itself changed during the sixteenth century, losing roles as a central commonly shared room but gaining functions as an interchange or junction between other areas.
- There is an associated wider trend towards increased importance and scale of private space at the expense of public space; contemporary observers record precisely this, as early as the famous complaint of Piers Plowman that lords forsake their duties in the hall in favour of private lives (and unfulfilled public responsibilities) in the chamber.
- The courtyard remained throughout the period a principal element of the house, but its significance grew less, especially during the sixteenth century.

It was reduced in size, encroached on by new service areas and by-passed by new internal and external access.

- Service provision, perhaps surprisingly and with a few exceptions, remained more or less static during the period, despite expansion and changes in the type and numbers of chambers and therefore, presumably, in household composition. This also has implications for estimates of total population (including service staff and dependent groups) using the castle. It may be that household population remained fairly static, and that planning change was instead due to re-negotiation of individuals' relationships with each other and with the centre.

- Direct access from outside the castle, other than through the main gate, proliferates through time; even relatively central or 'deep' parts of the house came to have direct links with the outside world. This predictable process reflects increased emphasis on domestic function rather than military symbolism, but it is interesting that the process begins with service and lower-status areas, where convenient access was a matter of practicality; the high-status parts of the house remain guarded and controlled for the whole medieval period, although obviously for social not military reasons.

- It is also possible that we can recognise the declining status of servants (as medieval habits of educating children through service to social peers began to change) in their increasing invisibility, and changes in use of space may also indicate the need of owners to have more direct and visible links with the outside in order to emphasise status. In short, there may be situations in which the correlation of depth with high status is reversed as a means of hiding service areas.

Conclusion

Few very complex buildings even of the medieval period have yet been thoroughly examined to decipher their social signals. The present discussion on Edlingham is no more than preliminary, but it does confirm that more can be deduced than from subjective analysis built simply on notions of symbolic or functional characterisation. Further examples of its application to other medieval or later buildings would be valuable, although it may be that the techniques can only be usefully applied to high-status buildings of some complexity of planning. But some other building types have been looked at in this way – preliminary analysis of medieval urban buildings (Atkin et al. 1985, 251–9), houses and some settlements of the later Iron Age (e.g. Foster 1989a; Reid 1989; Heslop 1987; Fasham 1985). Furthermore, Austin's work at Thrislington (Austin 1984) and recent excavations such as West Cotton (Windell in preparation) and Burton Dassett (Palmer in preparation) may point the way for houses at lower social levels and encourage the study of peasant use of space in house and settlement. Roman villas also appear to be well-suited to this type of analytical approach (see Smith 1978; Scott 1990), especially now that some work, e.g. at Stanwick (Neal 1989; in preparation; Keevil 1990; in preparation), is offering the chance to understand more about the upper floors, and thus the overall planning, of these buildings. There must, finally, surely be other avenues of research: perhaps more challenging areas like non-physical aspects of spatial allocation and social division (the head-teacher's door syndrome!) or the concepts of inter-visibility and supervision in social planning. These are rather harder to see than divisions of space that are marked architecturally. And, finally, it may be possible to examine different layers of use or understanding of buildings – children living at Edlingham would not recognise (even if their parents did, which must be doubtful) the present paper's interpretation of their home.

Bibliography

Alock, N., P. A. Faulkner *et al.* (1978) 'Maxstoke Castle, Warwickshire', *Archaeological Journal* 135, 195–233.

Atkin, M. W., A. Carter & D. H. Evans (1985) 'Excavations in Norwich, 1971–78', Norwich Survey Part II, *East Anglian Archaeology* 26.

Austin, D. (1989) *The deserted medieval village of Thrislington, County Durham: Excavations 1973–74.* Lincoln: Society for Medieval Archaeology Monograph 12.

Banning, E. B. & B. F. Byrd (1987) 'Housing and the changing residential unit: domestic architecture at 'Ain Ghazal, Jordan', *Proceedings of the Prehistoric Society* 53, 309–26.

Boast, R. B. & E. Yiannouli (1986) 'Creating space', *Archaeological Review from Cambridge* 5 (2), 136–40.

Brown, P. E. (1990a) 'Comment on Chapman', in Samson 1990, 93–110.

—— (1990b) 'Analysing small building plans: a morphological approach', in Samson 1990, 259–76.

Chapman, J. (1990) 'Social inequality on Bulgarian tells', in Samson 1990, 49–92.

Coope, R. (1986) 'The Long Gallery: its origin, development, use and decoration', *Architectural History* 29, 43–84.

Coulson, C. (1979) 'Structural symbolism in medieval castle architecture', *Journal of the British Archaeological Association* 132, 73–90.

Cruden, S. (1960) *The Scottish castle.* Edinburgh.

Dickens, P. (1977) 'An analysis of historical house plans', in D. Clarke (ed.), *Spatial analysis.* London.

Dixon, P. W. (1978) 'Coparcenary and Aydon Castle', *Archaeological Journal* 135, 234–8.

Ellison, A. (1987) 'The Bronze Age settlement at Thorny Down – pots, postholes and patterning', *Proceedings of the Prehistoric Society* 53, 385–98.

Emery, A. (1975) *Dartington Hall.* Oxford.

—— (1985) 'Ralph, Lord Cromwell's Manor at Wingfield', *Archaeological Journal* 142, 276–339.

Fairclough, G. J. (1980) 'Clifton Hall, Cumbria: excavations 1977–79', *Transactions of the Cumberland & Westmorland Antiquarian & Archaeological Society* 80, 45–68.

—— (1982) 'Edlingham Castle: the military and domestic development of a Northumbrian manor', *Château Gaillard* 9–10, 373–87.

—— (1983) 'Fortified houses and castles', in P. Clack & J. Ivy (ed.), *The Borders*: 81–99. London: Council for British Archaeology, CBA Group 3.

—— (1984) 'Edlingham Castle, Northumberland: an interim account of excavations 1978–82', *Transactions of the Ancient Monuments Society* n.s. 28, 40–60.

Fasham, P. J. (1985) *The prehistoric settlement at Winnall Down, Winchester*. Winchester: Hampshire Field Monograp. 2.

Faulkner, P. A. (1958) 'Domestic planning in the 12th to the 14th centuries', *Archaeological Journal* 115, 150–83.

—— (1963) 'Castle planning in the 14th century', *Archaeological Journal* 120, 215–35.

Fisher, A. R. (1985) 'Winklebury hillfort – a study of artefact distribution from subsoil features', *Proceedings of the Prehistoric Society* 51, 167–80.

Foster, S. (1989a) 'Analysis of spatial patterns in buildings (access analysis) as an insight into social structure: examples from the Scottish Atlantic Iron Age', *Antiquity* 63, 40–50.

—— (1989b) 'Transformations in social space – the Iron Age in Orkney and Caithness', *Scottish Archaeological Review* 6, 34–55.

Gilchrist, R. (1988) 'The spatial archaeology of gender domains: a case study of medieval English nunneries', *Archaeology Review from Cambridge* 7 (1) (Women in Archaeology), 21–8.

—— (1989) 'Community and self: perceptions and use of space in medieval monasteries', *Scottish Archaeological Review* 6, 55–64.

Gilyard-Beer, R. (1977) 'De Ireby's Tower, Carlisle Castle', in M. Apted, R. Gilyard-Beer & A. D. Saunders (ed.), *Ancient monuments and their interpretation*: 191–210. Chichester.

Girouard, M. (1976) *Life in the English country house*. New Haven & London.

Given-Wilson, C. (1986) *The Royal household and the King's affinity*. New Haven.

Heslop, D. H. (1987) *The excavation of an Iron Age settlement at Thorpe Thewles, Cleveland 1980–82*. London: Council for British Archaeology, Research report 65.

Hietala, H. (1984). *Intrasite spatial analysis in archaeology*. Cambridge.

Hillier, W. & J. Hanson (1984) *The social logic of space*. Cambridge.

Hodder, I. & C. Orton (1976). *Spatial analysis in archaeology*. Cambridge.

Johnson, M. H. (1986) 'Assumptions and interpretation in the study of the Great Rebuilding', *Archaeological Review from Cambridge* 5 (2) (Space in Archaeology), 140–53.

—— (1990) 'The Englishman's home and its study', in Samson 1990, 245–58.

Keevil, G. D. (1990) 'Redlands Farm Villa', *Current Archaeology* 122, 52–5. In preparation. Excavations at Redlands Farm Roman Villa, South Stanwick, Northamptonshire. [see now Keevill, G. (1996) 'Reconstruction of the Romano-British at Villa Redlands Farm', in P. Johnson (ed.), *Architecture in Roman* Britain, York, CBA, 44–55.]

Machin, R. (1977) 'Barnston Manor and Aydon Castle', *Archaeological Journal* 134, 297–302.

Markus, T. A. (1982) *Order in space and society – architectural form and its context in the Scottish Enlightenment*. Edinburgh.

McNeill, T. E. (1990) 'Trim Castle, Co. Meath: the first three generations', *Archaeological Journal* 147, 308–36.

Mertes, K. (1988) *The English noble household*. Oxford.

Morley, B. (1976) 'Hylton Castle', *Archaeological Journal* 133, 118–34.

— (1981) 'Aspects of 14thcentury castle design', in A. Detsicas (ed.), *Collectanea Historica – Essays in Memory of Stuart Rigold*, 104–13. Maidstone: Kent Archaeological Society.

Mytum, H. (1989a) 'The recognition and interpretation of intra-site patterning … Walesland Rath', *Scottish Archaeological Review* 6, 65–74.

— (1989b) 'Functionalist and non-functionalist approaches in monastic archaeology', in R. Gilchrist & H. Mytum (ed.), *The archaeology of rural monasteries*, 339–61. Oxford: British Archaeological Reports, British series 203.

Neal, D. (1989) 'The Stanwick Villa, Northamptonshire – an interim report', *Britannia* 20, 149–68.

In preparation. Excavation at Stanwick Villa, Northamptonshire. [see now Crosby, V. & Muldowney, L. (2011) *Stanwick Quarry, Northamptonshire, Raunds Area Project, Phasing the Iron Age and Romano-British Settlement at Stanwick, Northamptonshire (excavations 1984-1992)*, English Heritage Research Department Report Series 54/2011.]

Owen, T. M. (1990) 'Cottage and stable loft: the relevance of non-material evidence in the study of material culture' (Presidential address), *Archaeologia Cambrensis* 139, 1–11.

Palmer, N. In preparation. Excavations at Burton Dassett, Warwickshire.

Rapoport, A. (1969) *House form and culture*. Princeton.

— (1990) *History and precedent in environmental design*. Princeton.

Reid, M. (1989) 'A room with a view: an examination of round houses', *Oxford Journal of Archaeology* 8/1, 1–40.

Richards, C. (1990) 'The late Neolithic house in Orkney', in Samson 1990, 111–24.

Samson, R. (ed.) (1990) *The social archaeology of houses*. Edinburgh.

Scott, E. (1990) 'Romano-British Villas and their social construction in space', in Samson 1990, 149–72.

Simpson, D. W. (1940) 'Belsay Castle and the Scottish Tower House', *Archaeologia Aeliana* (4th series) 17, 75–84.

Smith, J. T. (1978) 'Villas as a key to social structure', in M. Todd (ed.), *Studies in the Romano-British Villa*, 149–85. Leicester.

Steadman, J. P. (1983) *Architectural morphology*. London.

Windell, D. In preparation. Excavations at West Cotton, Raunds Area Project, Northamptonshire. [see now Chapman, A. (2010) *West Cotton, Raunds: a study of medieval settlement dynamics, AD 450-1450: excavation of a deserted medieval hamlet in Northamptonshire, 1985-89*, Oxford.]

Yiannouli, E. & S. J. Mithen (1986) 'The real and random architecture of Siphos: analysing house plans using simulation', *Archaeological Review from Cambridge* 5 (2) (Space in Archaeology), 167–80.

6

Mota, Aula et Turris: The Manor-Houses of the Anglo-Scottish Border

Philip Dixon

This paper surveys the seigneurial buildings of the Anglo-Scottish Border, and places the fortified buildings constructed between the eleventh century and the seventeenth century in their social and economic context. It shows that the development of these houses was a complex pattern in which the builders responded to changing needs of politics and lordship, which ended in a breakdown of the local feudal society in the late Middle Ages.

The Anglo-Scottish Border is an area famous for its castles, an area in which private fortifications abound, and in which, it has been said, 'nearly all men of any wealth at all occupied bastle-houses', that is to say, fortified farmhouses.[1] The common picture of the society and its architecture is one in which the rough and conservative North preserved Norman or even earlier habits to the end of the Middle Ages. The types of buildings, too, are seen as backward-looking: the towers of the fourteenth century and later which are so distinctive a feature of the area were based on Norman keeps: 'By this time [1386] the days of castle building in England were virtually over ... by this time the castle has yielded pride of place to the mansion house. But in the North of England, along the Scottish border where warlike conditions persisted, the old Norman tradition of a square keep or tower-house was never forgotten.'[2] Even Allen Brown followed this line: 'Northern fortification in the later Middle Ages shows a remarkable conservatism. Etal ... is essentially a lesser keep-and-bailey castle after the twelfth-century manner ... and Edlingham in Northumberland ... consists merely of a simple, walled enclosure with a square keep at one end and perhaps a gatehouse at the other.'[3] This echoes a view long held by students of the architecture of the Middle Ages, summed up by Hamilton Thompson: 'The pele-tower may be regarded as a direct survival of the rectangular keep in a simplified form.'[4] In this military society, therefore, there is for the student little prospect of tracing the progressive changes

---

[1] Ramm *et al.* 1970, 65.
[2] Simpson 1940, 76.
[3] Brown 1953, 91.
[4] Thompson 1912, 316.

to be found in southern England: '[Yanworth Hall, Westmorland] shows little development from the Norman keeps of a date two hundred years earlier. This fact alone indicates the still disturbed state of the Border country, which stifled progress towards that comfort in house design which the more settled South was already beginning to enjoy; peace and security have ever been necessary to house development.'[5]

These views are fundamentally misguided. It is true that there are many castles, towers and lesser fortified buildings on the Borders, and true, too, that these range in date from the eleventh to the seventeenth century. But a close examination shows that the building of them falls into distinct phases, and that, particularly in the thirteenth century, the seigneurial buildings of the Borders differed little from those outside the region: the history of manorial building in the region is a story of the recurrent ebb and flow of styles. It is the purpose of this paper to present a summary of the current results of a long-term survey of the medieval secular and military architecture of the Borders, and to draw out some conclusions about the social and economic context in which these structures were built.

Periods of construction

From about 1080 to about 1130 was a phase of earthwork castles, of both motte-and-bailey and ringwork type; in addition to earthwork castles whose buildings, now gone, were of timber, surviving structures in the region include castles with stone curtain towers on earthen banks, and stone halls and chambers within ringworks. After the first quarter of the twelfth century stone donjons were built on some of these sites, and the construction of great towers continued into the thirteenth century.

From about 1220 until the early fourteenth century almost all the new building on manorial sites took the form of stone halls inside courtyards, most of which can have been scarcely stronger than the moated sites of contemporary Midland and Eastern England.

During the second and third quarters of the fourteenth century we see the construction of new houses with solar towers of great strength, and curtain walls creating small but very defensible castles. These led, by the later fourteenth century, to the building of freestanding tower-houses.

The tempo of building slackened during the fifteenth century. From about 1500 until the early seventeenth century there was a second phase of the building of towers, which were distinguished from the earlier examples by their smaller size, and by the lower status of most of their builders.

These towers overlapped in date, from about 1550 to about 1620, with a remarkable group of very small, and often, roughly built, fortified houses whose owners were normally customary tenants. During this period unfortified manor-houses similar in their design to those built outside the Border region were introduced into the area.

[5] Lloyd 1931, 186.

The First Phase: the Early Castles

In strong contrast to the density of early castles in Midland England or the Welsh Borders, the Anglo-Scottish frontier was, it seems, poorly protected. Considering the size of the region, remarkably few castles can be identified. Bamburgh, the seat of the Anglian kings and earls, was fortified as early as the sixth century, and may have had continuously maintained defences thereafter.[6] The bishop's castle at Durham belongs to the first years of the Conquest, and contains masonry of the 1070s in its chapel. The king's castle of Newcastle upon Tyne was begun as a ringwork with at least one tower of stone after 1080.[7] During the reign of William Rufus another castle was begun at Carlisle on the western border, and at least by 1095 further castles stood at Tynemouth and perhaps at Morpeth, where the earthworks of the existing castle may be the *munitiuncula* referred to by Symeon of Durham.[8]

The archives of the North during these years are comparatively sparse, and some of the undated motte-and-bailey castles of the uplands may belong to this period. The creation of few indeed of the baronies and lordships of the area, how-ever, can with confidence be placed before the very end of the eleventh century, or even later,[9] and it seems likely that the castles that formed their *capita* belong to the period following the extinction of the earldom in 1095, perhaps after the settlement of 1106, when Henry I established his followers in forfeited estates.[10] The major castles at Prudhoe, Wark on Tyne, Wark on Tweed, Elsdon, Norham and Alnwick all probably belong to the first third of the twelfth century, and so too, perhaps, the less well-known mottes at Wooler (Northumberland), Liddel (Cumberland), and the colonising earthwork castles of Dumfries.[11] This pattern of early baronial castles seems to have become fixed by the 1150s or 1160s. This at any rate is the likely period for the building of the motte-and-bailey castle at Har-bottle in Coquetdale, or perhaps just its refortification, since Harbottle received the service of the territorial unit long known as The Ten Towns of Coquetdale, and so is likely to have been the centre of a pre-Conquest estate, and also there-fore the location of an early Norman *caput*.[12]

It is significant that even by this stage, nearly a century after the Conquest, there were proportionately fewer castles in the region of the Anglo-Scottish border than, for example along the Welsh border, or even in central England between Oxford and Leicester.[13] The distribution of these castles, too, is interesting. Figure 1 (upper) shows the pattern of known early castles, with an approximation of

[6] Hope-Taylor 1977, 292 and note 339.
[7] Knowles 1926; Harbottle 1982, esp. fig. 1.
[8] Symeon of Durham, *Opera Omnia*, 2 vols, ed. T. Arnold (Rolls Ser., Chronicles and Memorials, 75 London 1882–5), II, 225; Bates 1891, 3, n.11.
[9] Hedley 1968, 18–19.
[10] Kapelle 1979, 191–206.
[11] For a brief discussion, see Simpson and Webster 1985.
[12] Bates 1981, 5; *NCH* 15 (1940), 480; both of whom take a late date as likely; so, too, Blair 1944, 133–7.
[13] Renn 1968, map A; Cathcart-King and Alcock 1966.

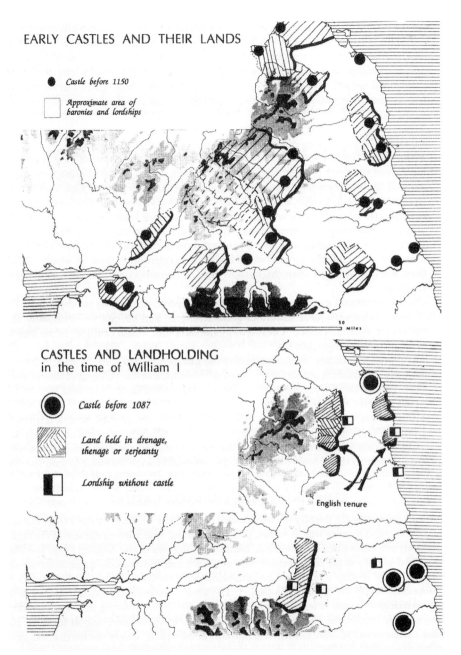

Figure 1. (upper). Map of castles before *c*.1150, showing the extent of their lordships (lower). Map of eleventh-century castles, English tenure, and lordships without castles.

their territories. Together they occupied a broad belt of uplands, agriculturally somewhat poor, which surrounded the much more fertile manors of the central Northumberland plain, and separated that area from the Scottish border. A similar pattern in the central uplands of Cumbria has been claimed to have been linked to the organisation of pre-feudal multiple estates, in which lordships shared in lowlands and highland transhumance areas.[14] The same may be true in these lordships on the Borders, for transhumance farming was the norm in the agricultural strategies of the Border uplands when documents survive, late in the Middle Ages.[15] A second distribution, however, suggests alternative reasons for the pattern. On Figure 1 (lower) are shown the very early castles, and two interestingly odd phenomena: in the first place the map shows a pattern of manors and baronies the *capita* of which, to the best of our knowledge, were never fortified, and secondly some lordships whose tenure, by thenage, drenage and serjeanty, sets them apart from the norms of feudal holding, together with the lands belonging to the ancient centre of Corbridge, some of which were subsequently detached and amalgamated with the feudal baronies of Bolam and Styford. We can see a discrete pattern in which the fortified *capita* surrounded areas containing lands with pre-Conquest tenures and manors that were never castellaries. Their occupiers were perhaps the survivors of the Anglian nobility discussed by Kapelle,[16] some of whom, at any rate, later claimed descent from Earl Gospatric,[17] and whose descendants gradually merged with the lesser Norman landlords, perhaps at a date too late to adopt the fashion of motte-and-bailey castles for their *capita*. It is likely enough that the manorial seats in these unfortified lordships were timber halls, such as the *aula* of the rich man of Tughall, burnt down by heavenly fire in 1069.[18] None is so far known to have survived, or has been excavated, in this area; the existence of stone chamber-blocks, today without any sign of a contemporary attached hall, suggests the former presence of such wooden buildings at a number of sites such as Aydon, Shield Hall, Heaton or Cresswell.[19]

Stone towers were built during the twelfth century at the most important of these early castles. The first were probably those at the two principal seigneurial *foci* of the early Borders, the castles of Carlisle and Bamburgh; both donjons share many features in common, and were perhaps built during the Scottish tenure of the North after the end of Henry I's reign.[20] Subsequent great towers at Newcastle, and then Brough and Brougham extend the date of the building of these structures

[14] Winchester 1987, 3.
[15] For discussion of this, see Dixon 1976, esp. 95–100.
[16] Kapelle 1979, 201–2.
[17] Hedley 1968, I, 12–14, 244–66.
[18] Reginald of Durham, ed. J. Raine (Surtees Soc., 1, 1835), chapter xvi, 30–1.
[19] For an excavated example elsewhere, see Dixon *et al.* 1989, esp. 410–12; and for further discussion, Dixon 1992.
[20] Colvin *et al.* 1963, 595–6, favour construction by David I; on the other hand McCarthy *et al.* 1990, 119–20, believe that Henry I was responsible: the argument turns in part on the use of the word *castellum*, and it should be noted that this is frequently used to refer to a town: see Coulson 1982.

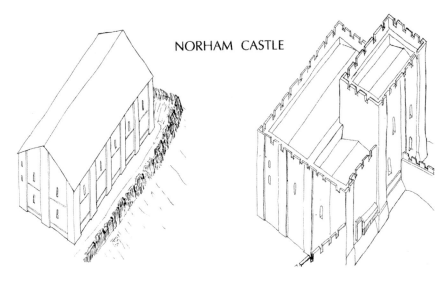

NORHAM CASTLE

Figure 2. The development of the great tower at Norham Castle, Northumberland,
from 1120 to c. 1170.

into the thirteenth century.[21] One of the most striking examples is the great tower
of the bishop of Durham's castle at Norham, a massive donjon considered to have
been constructed as a great tower in the 1150s or 1160s, and then repaired during
the fifteenth century.[22] Modern survey of this building, however, suggests a much
more complicated development (Figure 2), in which the first phase, probably
attributable to Bishop Ranulph Flambard c.1121, was a first-floor hall raised on a
vaulted basement, set within a ringwork, which had a stone gatehouse, but which
might have been simply fenced in timber. A second phase, perhaps the work of
Bishop de Puiset in the 1150s, involved the construction of a chamber-block parallel to the hall (making a double-pile building), one end of which rose above a
vault to create a small tower. A stone curtain of twelfth-century appearance may
belong to this phase. It seems that this remarkable and irregular complex survived in this form through much of the Middle Ages, reaching its present form of
a 'typical' rectangular great tower only as a result of massive rebuilding c.1400.[23]

By the middle of the thirteenth century there is some evidence to suggest that
these early castles were becoming obsolete. The decline of Wooler, a strategically
significant place on the flank of Cheviot, is a particularly striking sign of the general good order of the Borders. In an inquisition held in 1255 it was noted that
Isabella de Ford held one third of the capital messuage of Wooler, a derelict motte
(*mota vasta*) worth nothing.[24] Similarly the castle, which had been head of the

[21] Simpson 1949a; Charlton 1979.
[22] For a sensible general discussion, see Blair 1944, 137–41.
[23] Dixon and Marshall 1993, 410–32.
[24] *Cal. Inq. P. M.* 39 Hen. III, no. 40, printed in Bain, 1881–8, 1, 374–5, cf. also *Cal. Inq. P. M.*, I, no.
    341.

barony of Bolam, may have begun its decay as soon as the early thirteenth century, when Aline and John de Caux, coparceners of the barony, moved from Bolam to Harnham, setting up a new manor by subdivision, and built a hall at Shortflatt, abandoning the *caput*.[25] The alterations that were made to the motte at Mitford, Northumberland, may provide another example. The twelfth-century shell-keep was partially demolished, and a long rectangular building, with walls less than a metre thick, was built in place of the internal ranges within the shell. This hall-like structure was eventually replaced by the five-sided tower whose basement storey still stands on the motte. It seems likely that this sequence shows a partial demilitarising of the castle, presumably not earlier than the later twelfth century, succeeded by a refortification.[26] During this period the greater castles, of course, remained occupied as seigneurial seats; it is, however, notable how many of them (for example Alnwick, massively rebuilt after 1310, Mitford, repaired c.1300, or Warkworth, refurbished about 1330) were very substantially rebuilt during the fourteenth century, after the Anglo-Scottish wars began, suggesting that they too had not been kept in adequate repair.

The Second Phase: the Halls

The existence of stone halls in the region has long been known, at least since the first publication of Aydon in 1851.[27] What has emerged only in recent years is the wide range and the surprisingly large number of these buildings in an area generally thought to be dominated by towers. Surveys have now revealed at least twenty-six hall-houses in the Borders. The work continues, and more of these buildings may well await discovery.[28] The range of dates is wide, from the thirteenth to the fifteenth century, and there is more than one type of building represented, but the majority of these structures belong to the thirteenth century.[29]

The simplest of these buildings, and perhaps the earliest, is the hall that formed the first phase at Drumburgh, Cumbria. This was a long rectangular ground-floor hall, entered by a broad round-headed doorway of earlier thirteenth-century appearance. No internal divisions have been preserved, but the position of the door suggests that it gave access to the lower end of a hall at least eleven metres long, with a service room to its west and perhaps a small chamber at its upper end. A ground-floor hall of similar size survives as the core of Featherstone Castle, Northumberland. The entrance door here suggests a date of about 1260. Both ends of this hall have been rebuilt, but it may have contained services and

[25] Dixon 1988, 5; Dixon and Borne 1978, 234–9, esp. 235.
[26] The analysis is based on excavation, but these works (of the 1930s) were very unsatisfactory, and their publication includes no detailed plans or sections (Honeyman 1955).
[27] Parker and Turner 1851, 1, 148–9.
[28] For the distribution of these buildings, see Dixon 1988, 6. Surveys have been carried out by Philip Dixon, in association with Janet Sisson, Patricia Borne and Leslie Milner. Parallel work by Peter Ryder has revealed early halls at Corbridge (Low Hall) and Blenkinsopp.
[29] For a general account of the work on these buildings up to 1991, see Dixon 1992.

chamber like Drumburgh. Other ground-floor halls, heavily rebuilt, form the
earliest parts of the 'towers' at Rudchester (1285), Halton and Corbridge Low Hall
(both c.1300), and each may have contained at least services, and perhaps chambers, within a simple long rectangular plan.

Halls in which the principal accommodation lay on the first floor, raised above
a basement storey, form a distinct regional type. Dally Castle in North Tyndale,
the earliest known of these (apart, that is, from Bishop Flambard's hall at Norham
Castle), was under construction in 1237, when Sir David de Lindesey, later Justiciar of Lothian, was said to be building a house with wonderfully thick walls like
a tower.[30] Thirty years later, John Comyn the Competitor was granted licence to
crenellate the manor-house at Tarset, two miles distant from Lindesey's manor.
Both these structures were rectangular, with corner turrets, and the wording of
the documents suggests that the first-floor defended hall was hard to classify,
and perhaps was something of a novelty, since Dally was a *domum … ad modum
turris*, and Tarset was called not a hall but a *camera*.[31] A clearer example of a
first-floor hall has recently been excavated at Edlingham, where a ditched courtyard, looking like a typical moated site, and perhaps enclosed originally with a
palisade, contained a large rectangular building with polygonal corner turrets,
whose hall and chambers lay on its first floor, approached by an external stair.[32]

Few of these hall houses are sufficiently well preserved for the original arrangement of their accommodation to be certain. The clearest example is Aydon, of
c.1296 (Figure 3).[33] Here the appearance of an 'end-hall', that is to say a hall-and-
chamber on two floor levels, is illusory. The recent restoration has shown that
the lower hall had no communication with the lower chamber, but gave access
solely to service and store rooms at the lower end of the house. The ground-floor
chamber was almost certainly reached only from the first-floor solar, to which it
provided a secluded and secure inner room, with the most elaborately decorated
fireplace in the building. The chamber-block at Aydon was therefore conceived
of as a separate three-storeyed tower, probably built against the gable end of an
existing timber ground-floor hall, which was soon to be replaced by a new structure, containing an attendants' hall and stores on the ground floor, and a hall
and kitchen on the floor above. In its first phase the hall excavated at Edlingham
Castle appears to have had a similar arrangement of chambers in a three-storeyed

[30] Bates 1891, 55–6, locates the house at Dally. Honeyman in *NCH*, 15 (1940), 274, is more cautious
about this, since Lindesey was baron of Chirdon (about one mile to the north-east of the site),
but he correctly confirms the ruin at Dally as of the earlier thirteenth century on the evidence of
its architectural fragments, and is probably over-critical of the identification.
[31] *NCH*, 15 (1940), 243–7. The term suggests that the foundations at Tarset (excavated in the 1880s)
were the remains of a stone chamber block, and that the hall, and other buildings, lie undiscov-
ered elsewhere in the moated site. The site at Dally, however, is too confined to allow room for
other buildings.
[32] For an interim account of the excavations, see Fairclough 1982: the date of the hall itself is particularly uncertain, but it may be of the late thirteenth century.
[33] For discussion of the internal arrangements, see Dixon and Borne 1978, esp. 236.

Figure 3. Aydon Castle (Northumberland): the first floor-hall and the chamber block from the North.

block at the end of a two-storeyed hall;[34] in this case a separate chamber lay at the lower end of the hall, while the kitchen was below, next to the lower hall; kitchen and lower hall had access only from the courtyard, and food must have passed by the external stair to the hall. Unless the lower hall was used for service and storage, these functions must have been relegated to a separate building. During the fourteenth-century rebuilding, this arrangement with an integral, vertically set suite of chambers was abandoned, and a new strong chamber was added in a massive solar tower (Figure 4). Access to this was contrived through an anteroom at the lower end of the hall. The provision of this new accommodation led to a reworking of the chamber block at the upper end of the hall. Its ground-floor chamber seems now to have been separated from the upper storeys, and was connected by a new door with what had been an independent single room, to make a two-room set, with its own door to the courtyard. A similar set was also provided in the lowest storey of the new solar tower by the creation of an independent access through the end of the old lower hall. The result was to provide a series of separate apartments: the great hall now gave access to three family (or perhaps guest) rooms at its upper end and to a strong and grandly appointed set in the new tower (Figure 5), important rooms called in 1572 the 'Parlar' and 'the Brode chambre'. Separately entered suites of heated chambers lay on the ground floor of

[34] The discussion is based on the planning diagrams in Fairclough 1982, 387.

136 PHILIP DIXON

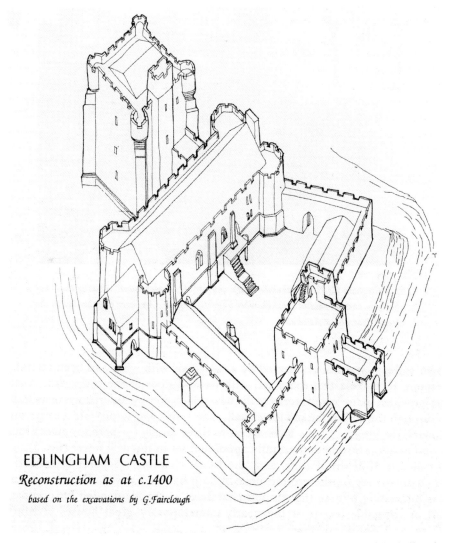

EDLINGHAM CASTLE
Reconstruction as at c.1400
based on the excavations by G.Fairclough

Figure 4. Edlingham Castle (Northumberland): reconstruction drawing of the hall and
courtyard with the solar tower of c.1370, based on the results of the excavations
by G. Fairclough.

both hall and tower. Their use is uncertain, but it is interesting to note that similar
chambers, perhaps intended for occupation by a steward or constable, occur at
the nearly contemporary great houses of Markenfield, Yorkshire, and Tulliallan,
Fife.[35]

---

[35] Miller 1985, esp. 104 ('Undercroft C'); RCAHM Scotland, 1933, 275–9: I owe this reference to
Mr John Dunbar. In its first phase Edlingham had a single independent chamber of this type at
ground-floor level.

Figure 5. Edlingham Castle (Northumberland): interior of the solar tower, showing the lower chamber, and the vaulted great chamber with its fireplace. An inner chamber lay on the second floor above the vault.

The complexity of the accommodation and the elaboration of the decoration in these halls indicates clearly enough the high status of their builders, a point that is demonstrated by the inventories and inquisitions of the thirteenth and fourteenth centuries. The lords who built and occupied the Border halls belonged at least to the minor nobility of Northumberland and Cumberland. Many, of course, were substantial lords who had lands elsewhere, such as David de Lindesey of Dally Castle, who was Justiciar of Lothian, or John Comyn of Tarset Castle,

Haughton Castle

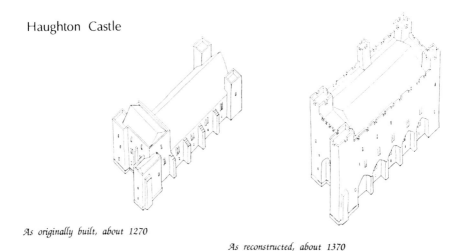

As originally built, about 1270

As reconstructed, about 1370

Figure 6, Haughton Castle (Northumberland): the first two stages in the development of
the castle from a first-floor hall and solar tower to a three-storeyed fortified hall block.

competitor for the Scottish throne, and brother-in-law to John Balliol. Others
held baronies (Langley, Aydon) or substantial manors (Haughton, Edlingham).[36]
The *Inquisitiones post mortem* of the early fourteenth century demonstrate the
devastation that followed the uprising against Edward I's nominee in Scotland.[37]
Tarset, once worth £246, was in 1314 only worth £5. 7s. 4d., while Aydon was
valued at no more than 14s. 7d. in 1322, and in 1326 Chirdon in North Tyndale
was worth 'nothing on account of the poverty of the country and want of beasts'
and the neighbouring manor of Snabdough 'worth nothing for want of tenants'.[38]
    During these years fortifications were added to the hall-houses: the hall at
Aydon was rebuilt with battlements and a small courtyard by 1305; by 1315 a larger
crenellated wall cut off the manor-house from the level ground to the north. A
round tower commanding the approach may have been added after 1346.[39] The
hall with solar tower at Haughton in North Tyndale was rebuilt twice during the
fourteenth century. In the first stage a barrel vault was inserted over the ground
floor, and a second floor, carried on broad arched machicolations, was built above
the hall; subsequently these arches were blocked in a thickening of the walls of the
first storey (see Figure 6). At Edlingham a new solar tower was built at the side

[36] For a fuller discussion of the society and of the collapse in the early fourteenth century, see Dixon
    1992.
[37] See in general Musgrove 1990, chapter 6; discussions of the collapse in Tuck 1971, and a modified
    view, emphasising the resilience of the area, in Tuck 1985, esp. 36–42.
[38] *NCH*, 15 (1940), 244–5; PRO, London, Chancery IPM, 25 Edward I (C133), file 81; 15 Edward II
    (C134), file 90, no. 2) (= *Cal. Inq. P.M.*, VI, no. 597); 19 Edward II (C134), file 96, no.14 (= *Cal. Inq.
    P. M.*, VI, no 693).
[39] See Dixon 1988, 32.

of the hall, perhaps about 1380, and perhaps in the same decade at Halton a small solar tower was built at a little distance from the hall of *c*.1300. Few indeed of the old halls remained without fortifications during these years. Unfortified examples may perhaps include the *camera* at Heaton beside Newcastle or the solar-block at Proctor's Stead near Embleton, both some distance from the border line itself. Even in these cases, however, protection of the site by curtain walls and ditches cannot be ruled out: we know that the old hall at Drumburgh was fortified in 1307, but the surviving remains show no traces of defences, which were thus presumably outworks. Far from the Border, at Old Hollinside in County Durham, the entrance to the hall was protected by a raised tower (Figure 7). In an exposed position close to the frontier the manor-house of Burgh, a first-floor hall, which about 1260 had replaced an earthwork castle, was abandoned and in ruins by 1362.[40]

Figure 7. Old Hollinside (County Durham): a thirteenth-century hall with chambers and services in attached wings, later fortified by the addition of a small tower over the ground-floor entrance.

The Third Phase: the Towers

The attached solar towers, or the chamber-blocks with their rooms arranged in a vertical series at the end of a ground-floor or first-floor hall, bridge the gap between the hall-house and the tower-house of the later Middle Ages. During the course of the fourteenth century nearly one hundred of the manor-houses of the Border area were rebuilt as towers. To understand how these buildings fit

[40] Hogg 1954, 129

into the rapidly changing politics of this period, it is clearly important to establish the precise date of these structures, but this has attracted a measure of controversy, with dates proposed in the early fourteenth or even the thirteenth century for such buildings as Corbridge, Chipchase and Belsay in Northumberland, or, among others, Drum and Hallforest in Aberdeenshire.[41] For none of these early dates is there good evidence. A *mansum* at Newlands by Belford was crenellated by licence in 1310; this was called a *turris* in the great list of Northumbrian fortifications of 1415,[42] and may therefore represent an early example of the type, but no trace now remains of the building. One cannot therefore judge either whether the house fortified in 1310 included a tower, or, if it did, whether it was no more than a solar tower such as are known at this date elsewhere in England.[43] The same is true of Eslington, whose fortification was licensed in 1335, which was called a *turris* in 1415, and a *toure with a barmekyn* [courtyard] in 1541.[44] During the period of the worst Scottish attacks between the death of Edward I in 1307 and the recovery after the battle of Halidon Hill (1333) old castles were put into order, but there is little sign of new fortifications in the Borders. An exception, the construction of a large new castle at Dunstanburgh after 1313, was probably due to the ambitions of Thomas, earl of Lancaster, and was not a response to local conditions. It is presumably no coincidence that Earl Thomas's conflict with his cousin Edward II, which saw the king and Gaveston making good use of the coastal castles at Tynemouth and Scarborough during their flight from the North in 1312, was followed within months by the earl's beginning the building of his own coastal castle at Dunstanburgh.[45] The earliest surviving new structures of this period in the region are the great towers at Etal (licensed in 1341) and Crawley (licensed in 1343).[46] Neither was certainly a tower-house: Crawley, which- lacks any evidence for an internal hall, was probably a massive solar-tower attached to less well protected buildings, whose foundations can still be traced as mounds inside the large ditched courtyard that surrounds the main building, and the tower at Etal (Figure 8), despite Knowles's description of the site as consisting of a keep and gatehouse,[47] seems to have been an elaborate accommodation block at one end of the principal range of a courtyard castle. It seems, then, that during the first part of this phase some of the new buildings were continuing the pattern of hall and solar-tower that had been established during the thirteenth century.

[41] Brown 1976, 131; Cruden 1963, 109–11; Wood 1965, 168, 175; Simpson 1938–9, I, xxix–xl; Simpson 1940, esp. 79–80.
[42] Bates, 1891, 8, 19.
[43] For example at Stokesay, Shropshire (1305), or Longthorpe near Peterborough of *c.* 1300.
[44] Bates 1891, 17, 43.
[45] Simpson 1949b, 1–25, esp. 7–13, argues that the castle was built for reasons of patriotism and public spirit; Blair 1949, 25–8, disagrees on the grounds of Earl Thomas' character, surely rightly; see in general Maddicott 1970, and, for the immediately preceding events, Dixon 1990, esp. 126–8.
[46] The great tower of Widdrington was licensed in 1341, and appears from the Buck engraving to have been an L-shaped tower house, but no trace of this building now remains.
[47] NCH, 11 (1922), 467–9, followed by Brown 1976, 91.

Figure 8. Etal Castle
(Northumberland): tower
built at the end of a range
of buildings in the 1340s.

During these years, however, we can see some transitional types. The castle
of Thirlwall near Gilsland, first referred to in 1369, has the rectangular plan with
angle towers to be seen in thirteenth-century halls, but its accommodation was
arranged vertically like a tower, in three low storeys, without the tall principal
room to be found in the earlier buildings. At Blenkinsopp the castle of 1340 seems
to have been a thick walled square-set building no more than 16 m long, set within
a tight rectangular chemise.[48] The structure appears to have been much more
like a tower than a hall, but the surveyors of 1415 chose to use the term *castrum*,
glossed by the less precise word *fortalicium* for the site, rather than *turris*.[49]

The last of the Northumbrian licences was that of 1378 for Fenwick Tower, but
Fenwick was in fact the first licensed fortification in Northumberland for over
thirty years. Bates, indeed, suggested that after the Scottish invasion of 1346 it
was crown policy to encourage the erection of fortified houses, which therefore
needed no special licence.[50] It is not clear whether this or some administrative
change was responsible for the hiatus; in Cumberland at any rate licences were
being granted as late as 1399, though mostly for buildings far to the south of the
Border; here too there is a very noticeable decline in numbers of licences after the
early 1350s.

---

[48] The best interpretation of this much rebuilt (and now demolished) building is given in an unpublished survey report by Ryder (1986).
[49] Bates 1891, 15. This is identical to their treatment of the moated site of Horton-iuxta-mare, but
such arguments from medieval terminology are extremely tentative: see Coulson 1982.
[50] Bates 1891, 11. For a more modern view of the significance of licences to crenellate, see Coulson
1993.

But can it be assumed that all or even most of the fourteenth-century towers that received no licence were therefore built after about 1350? Two considerations make this more plausible: the builders of the unlicensed towers were of similar social status to those whose fortifications received licence; there are therefore no grounds for suggesting that the former group of buildings were of small size or were built by men of lesser pretensions, or who hoped by their insignificance to escape notice. Secondly, though charters and similar sources occasionally refer to fortified buildings, none shows that any unlicensed structure predates 1350, and the earliest reference to the existence of a building for which no licence was issued is as late as 1365,[51] nearly twenty years after the end of the main North-umbrian series of licences. The implications of this negative evidence are shown graphically in Figure 9, which indicates a rapidly mounting tempo in building during the later fourteenth century. These implications are striking: after the pause during the earlier part of the century, between c.1350 and 1415 some seventy substantial towers were completed in Northumberland, and about half as many in Cumbria, a massive expenditure of resources in a period in which recovery from the crisis of the 1310s and the Black Death was still slow.[52]

Recognisable fragments of half of these fourteenth-century towers still sur-vive. Fifteen are small rectangular buildings, averaging about 10 m by 8 m in size, best exemplified by the vicar's towers at Corbridge (c.1390) and Ford, or the little chamber block at Halton, also of c.1390. Ten large rectangular towers (about 15 m by 10 m) were built with finer masonry details, corresponding to the greater resources of their builders. In other respects the layout of the large and small towers is similar: where evidence survives the entry was at ground-floor level beside a stair that led to the upper storeys. The ground floor, normally barrel vaulted, shows little sign of use as accommodation, and may have been used for storage. The first floor, normally a little loftier than the others, was presumably the hall: in two fifteenth-century examples (Newark on Yarrow and Comlongon) the entrance stair led to a screens passage and kitchen, partitioned off in timber from the hall itself. The upper storeys contained chambers, in the larger examples sometimes subdivided by partitions, with mural chambers including garderobes at the upper levels. The arrangements are so regular that a unique variant, at Chipchase (c.1400?) is particularly noteworthy: here the kitchen, and the screens passage from the newel stair, is on the top storey, and so the hall seems to have been built above the chambers.

Chipchase, and the similar great tower at Belsay,[53] are members of a small group of towers, including Cresswell in Roxburghshire, in which extra accommodation

[51] Bates 1891, 11, quoting *Cal. Inq. P. M.*, II, 270: this document refers, however, to the existence of a castle at Langley, which was a hall-house now refortified. The structure would require a licence less obviously than would a completely new building. For the date of the rebuilding of Langley (on architectural grounds c.1340 x 1360), see Dixon 1976, 32.

[52] For discussion of this, see Dixon 1992.

[53] Built c.1370: here the kitchen is in the basement, apparently as an afterthought. See Middleton 1910, 15; Simpson 1940, esp. 81.

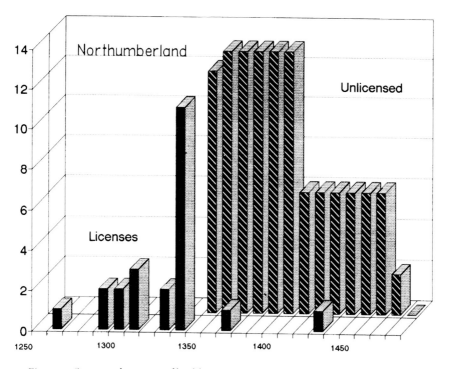

Figure 9. Suggested pattern of building activity in Northumberland before 1415, distinguishing between licensed and unlicensed fortifications.

was obtained by the construction of a wing or jamb, protecting from the main body of the building, and containing suites of private chambers. They belong, it seems, to the late fourteenth and fifteenth centuries, a date in keeping with their occurrence elsewhere, for example at Craigmillar near Edinburgh of c.1370. These are the first of the towers that can be considered true tower-houses, self-contained buildings enclosing kitchen, services, hall and sufficient chambers to accommodate a household. The extent to which in fact they were independent houses, however, remains very doubtful, and even Belsay seems to have been built to respect the end of earlier hall.

The Fifteenth Century

With the exception of the great gatehouse at Bywell, built about 1430, perhaps as a replacement for the old earthwork castle of Styford,[54] and the new great

---

[54] This is a motte-and-bailey castle in a wood at NGR NZ 027623, which seems to have escaped recognition. Styford was part of the barony of Bolbec, and Bywell a moiety of the barony of Balliol, but both baronies were held, from the late fourteenth century, by the Neville earls of Westmorland: *NCH*, 6 (1902), 75, 228.

Figure 10. Cocklaw Tower
(Northumberland): a
fifteenth-century tower-
house with first-floor hall
and mural towers.

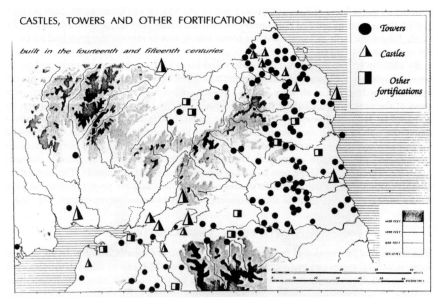

Figure 11. Distribution map of the fortified houses of the Border region belonging to the
fourteenth and fifteenth centuries.

gatehouse at Morpeth Castle, the new fortifications on the English side of the
border were all minor works. At Cocklaw (Figure 10), Branxton, Dilston, and at
the earlier halls of Low Hall, Corbridge and Cresswell, towers were built by small
landowners; where the builder can be identified, the other towers of this period
were built by more significant lords, Percies, Nevilles or Ogles, not as principal
houses, but as outliers on scattered portions of their estates, for example at Cockle

Park (after 1461), Hefferlaw (after 1470), or Hulne (1488). Because of the lack of good documentation during most of this period, what is known of the buildings comes mostly from surviving structures, and no estimate is possible of how many buildings have vanished without record, but it seems clear that many fewer tower-houses were now being built. The distribution pattern (Figure 11) closely resembles that of the preceding century, and the majority of the surviving buildings are of relatively small scale: thus they should be seen as the final stage of the major burst of building during the later fourteenth century.

The major fortifications on the Scottish side of the border date to the period before the outbreak of the wars of Independence. During the period of intensive building in England little may be found across the border, except the tower of Torthowald (?fourteenth century) and the English-built castle at Hermitage of c.1360. Numerous earth and timber 'towers' have been alleged,[55] but none survives, and the evidence is as flimsy as the supposed structures. There could hardly be a greater contrast between these and the sophisticated towers of England. The erection during the fifteenth century of a group of major towers in the Scottish side of the border indicates a change. The Douglases, with their seat at Threave, with its massive tower of c.1390, had before 1388 remodelled the courtyard castle at Hermitage to form a great tower,[56] and by 1423 they had begun a second great tower at Newark-on-Yarrow at the other end of the central uplands. Towers of similar size were founded by the influential Kers at Cessford and by the Murrays at Comlongon, both perhaps during the second quarter of the century. About the same time the powerful family of the lairds Johnstone built at Lochwood the tower that was to remain the principal house of the surname.

By 1485 by far the largest number of fortified houses lay on the coastal plain and in the adjacent uplands of Cumberland and Northumberland. Few indeed lay in the central border uplands. The builders of all were almost entirely landed men of considerable wealth, and most of the towers formed their principal houses, or the *capita* of substantial manors. In Scotland far fewer fortifications are known; in general their distribution was in the valleys below the uplands, and they formed the *capita* of the Norman baronies, or of the feudal magnates whose power increased at the expense of the crown during the later fourteenth century and the fifteenth century.[57] During the sixteenth century the picture changed radically. The majority of the new buildings lay within the central uplands. The interesting characteristic of the fourth and fifth phases of border fortification must therefore be seen as the massive development of stone buildings in this hitherto barren region (Figure 16).

---

[55] For example, by Simpson 1940.
[56] RCAHM Scotland 1956, 83.
[57] For discussion of this, see Smout 1969, 37–8.

The Fourth Phase: the Later Towers

The survival of late medieval fortified houses in the border zone is striking. In all, at least some structural traces can be found of about 250 houses that can be dated to the sixteenth century, and the names and descriptions of an even greater number, now demolished, may be found in documentary sources. During this period towers were constructed in every part of the region, from the outskirts of Newcastle to the furthest recesses of the upland dales. A few, such as Hoddam in Dumfriesshire, were massive structures, as large as the great seigneurial tower houses of the late fourteenth century. Most, however, were comparatively small; on average not much more than 15 m by 10 m in plan, and only three or four storeys high (Figure 12). The number of surviving examples is sufficient to allow us to see distinct regional types. Despite the widespread distribution of these towers, no single architectural style unites the whole of the Borders, but the variations in design and decoration do not conform to the internal political zones of the region, and on occasion can be seen to cut across the border line itself. To demonstrate the patterns, Figure 13 shows a selection of architectural features: the design of gunports and the treatment of the parapets of towers.

Few roofs survive from this period: the eighteen at present identified in the survey fall into three clear groups. To the west, in northern Cumbria, all have heavily jowled king-posts on cambered tie-beams, supporting side purlins. Examples range from the elaborate roof of Askerton Castle, with a dendrochronological date

Figure 12. Kirkandrews Tower (Cumberland): small tower-house of the later sixteenth century, built by one of the unruly members of the Graham surname.

of 1497, to the simple roof of the stonehouse at Cote House, perhaps of the later sixteenth century. In Northumberland, in contrast, king-posts of this date have not been observed, and the surviving roofs are simple principal-rafter trusses (sometimes with curved feet) with a cambered tie and a collar. A roof of this sort

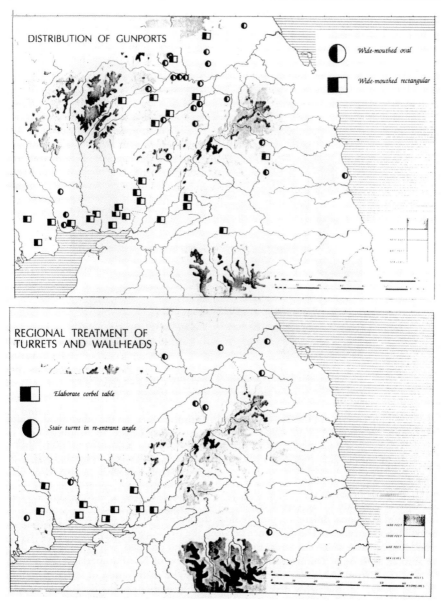

Figure 13. (upper). Distribution map of gunports, distinguishing between the rectangular and the oval versions of the wide-mouthed type (lower). Variations in the treatment of the wall-heads of towers, showing a division between styles of the West March and those of the Middle March.

at Aydon Castle has a dendrochronological date of 1543, and others belong to the end of the sixteenth and the early seventeenth century. Raised crucks have also been noted in late sixteenth-century stonehouses. In Scotland, however, where surviving roofs are still rarer, all the known roofs of towers belong to the early seventeenth century, and have braced common rafters with collars but without longitudinal stiffening.

The distribution of the types of gunports used in these towers, in contrast, show two separate centres of distribution. The more sophisticated of these, the wide-mouthed oval version, is concentrated in the Tweed valley. In Dumfriesshire, on the other hand, examples of this style are confined to the major work at Caerlaverock Castle, to building of the same period nearby at Bankend Tower, to the elaborate work at Amisfield of 1600, and to a lone example in the north, that of Lochhouse Tower, near Moffat. The shot-holes of the other West Marches towers are either the starker wide-mouthed rectangular type, or one of the more elaborate keyhole or dumb-bell patterns. This rectangular variety, however, is comparatively rare in the Tweed region. Both types allow a similar field of fire, and have no apparent functional difference, nor are there distinctions in date or in social status between the buildings concerned. The difference between the two schools emphasises local variations in building practice that cut across the Border line into England, where the western designs are similar to those of Dumfriesshire, while those few in Northumberland are similar to those of the Tweed. A similar pattern is shown by the distribution of styles of wall-head (Figure 13, lower), for the richly decorated blind machicolations of the Scottish West March spread into northern Cumberland, but not elsewhere in. the Borders, and the rounds at the wall-head (and the rare turrets in the re-entrant angle) of Northumberland are matched most frequently in the Tweed valley. This cross-border linking of schools of masons towards the end of the sixteenth century has been identified in the case of the Buckholm school of Roxburghshire, with its links in north Northumberland.[58]

The dating of the towers within the sixteenth century requires further discussion. In a synthesis of the Scottish tower-houses the period from about 1480 to 1560 has been described as 'the long pause' during which 'few tower houses of any consequence were built'.[59] An analysis of the architectural details of the border tower-houses suggests that the normal use of these features belongs to the second half of the sixteenth century:[60] wide-mouthed oval gunloops were apparently introduced by Italian engineers at Dunbar about 1520,[61] and are first found in the Borders between 1530 and 1540, and became common after 1560; four-centred doorhead and machicolated corbel-tables may be found in the fifteenth century, but occurred only rarely before c.1570; edge rolls and pilaster mouldings

[58] For discussion of this, see Dixon 1975.
[59] Cruden 1963, 144, 150–76.
[60] For more detailed discussion of these points, see Dixon 1976, 168–76.
[61] I owe this point to discussion with Mr John Dunbar.

are datable to the second half of the century, and trace their origin to the major works at Stirling (1538 x 1541). This tends to confirm the 'long pause' in the Scottish Borders. In England at least the pause is less obvious: in the area covered by the 1541 survey four towers had been built during the previous generation, and two more, and a number of 'bastells' were still under construction.[62] This seems to be a continuation, on a smaller scale, of the fifteenth-century pattern. Furthermore, the use of datestones, which underlies Cruden's chronology, is hazardous, since almost all bear dates of the second half of the sixteenth century or later; indeed, more than half belong to the period from 1590 to 1618. This is a common phenomenon: few of the hundreds of datestones collected by MacGibbon and Ross are earlier than 1560.[63]

The Fifth Phase: the Stone Houses, Bastles and Pelehouses

All the structures discussed so far have been at least of manorial status. During the sixteenth century, however, we find for the first time the survival of fortified buildings built by less important people. There is a greater variety of forms during this period, and a much wider range of contemporary records about the construction and their appearance: in consequence the written sources become of even greater significance in forming a picture of the fortified houses of the Border. This leads to problems, since the structures were described by contemporaries under a variety of names: tower, pele or peel, bastle-house, stronghouse, stonehouse and pelehouse.[64] These are terms that are not used consistently.[65] During the sixteenth century a stone tower could be called a pele: Helefyld Peel in Yorkshire, for example, had a gate and garrets,[66] and the phrase 'castle or pele' or 'tower or pele' is not uncommon.[67] This rather loose usage is found in the borders in the brief survey of 1561,[68] but at the beginning of the century in this region, a pele was still regarded as an earth and timber fortification, as it had been during the thirteenth-century conquests of Edward I. In this way, in the Debateable Land of the West March in 1528, a 'strong pele of Ill Will Armistraunges' was 'buylded after siche maner that it couth not be brynt ne distroyed unto it was cut

---

[62] Bates 1891, 49–50.

[63] MacGibbon and Ross 1887–92,

[64] The etymology of 'pele' and its forms are described by Nielson 993, and his conclusions are generally accepted; Wood 1965, 168n.

[65] In view of the variation in terminology, strict adherence to sixteenth-century usage is thus neither possible nor desirable: It is, however, thoroughly regretable that the term 'bastle' now in common usage has been limited to the class of small, usually roughly built, fortified houses: only one now-surviving building, Akeld Bastle, was certainly called a bastle in the sixteenth century, but the authors of Shielings and Bastles are obliged to describe this house as 'not typical', as being 'of more superior character' than the other stone houses discussed in their book (Ramm *et al.* 1970, 67). For the problems connected with consistent terminology, and the mistaken use of 'bastle', compare Dixon 1972 and 1979.

[66] *Letters and Papers of Henry VIII*, 12 pt i, no. 1321, ed. J. Gairdner (1890).

[67] *Ibid.*, 18 pt ii, no. 455; 19 pt i, no. 348; 19 pt ii, no. 664.

[68] Bates 1891, 52–3. The more detailed survey of 1541 has no such usage.

Figure 14.
Ferniehurst. Castle
(Roxburghshire):
chamber-block and side
of the hall of a very large
late sixteenth-century
L-shaped tower.

down with axes'.[69] The headsmen of North Tyndale in 1541 had similar buildings, described as

> very strong houses whereof for the most parte the utter sydes or walles be made of greatt sware [square] oke trees stongly bounde & Joyned together with great tenons of the same so thyck mortressed that yt wylbe very harde withoute greatt force & laboure to breake or caste down any of the said houses the tymber as well of the said walles as rooffes be so great & covered most parte with turves & earthe that they wyll, not easyly burne or be sett on fyere.[70]

None of these structures is now preserved, but they were familiar in Scotland even towards the end of the sixteenth century, when Bishop Leslie described the houses of the chieftains [*potentiores*] as pyramidal towers built of earth alone, which they call 'pailes'.[71] In England at this period slightly different terms were

[69] British Library, Cotton MSS, Caligula B vii, fo. 28.
[70] *Ibid.*, Caligula B viii, fo. 856d.
[71] 'Pyrarriidales turres quas pailes vocant ex sola terra': Leslie, 1578, 61; Dalrymple's translation of this passage in his edition of Leslie (ed. 1596, I, 98) calls these towers 'four nuiked', that is, square. An Act of 1535 'for bigging of strenthis on the Bordouris' distinguishes between barmkins of stone and lime to be built by landed men of 'ane hundreth pund land' and 'big pelis' of unspecified but certainly poorer material, to be built by 'landit men of smallar rent': *APS*, ed. Thompson, II, 1424–1567, 346.

Figure 15. Low Cleughs Field (Northumberland): pele-house built *c*.1600 by customary
tenants of the Crown lands.

used: we find 'stone house', 'a lytle stone house or pyle', 'bastell house', 'stone
houses or bastells', 'a stronge pele house of stone', or 'a lylte pele house or bastell'.[72]

The buildings themselves display wide a variation between elegant tall towers,
six or seven storeys in height (Figure 14), and squat, rough, gabled buildings little
different from the unfortified single-storeyed houses of the region. Though no
classification of these structures can be clear cut, three types stand out: the tower,
discussed in the previous section; the bastle, a large and normally well-built stone
house; and the pele-house, a similar but smaller structure (Figure 15). It is the last
that is now customarily designated 'bastle'.

These three types of fortified house show significant variations in the periods
during which they were built, and interestingly separate distribution patterns.
Towers are found throughout the period, perhaps more frequently after the
middle of the century. Their distribution (Figure 16) shows a marked concentration in the upland valleys, in particular of western and central Scotland, in
Dumfriesshire and Roxburghshire, and the density within the thin-soil uplands
of Liddesdale and Eskdale is very striking. In England they are rare in the East
March, and are found in only limited numbers in the Middle March, except
for those in the upland dales of Tyne, Rede and the headwaters of the Aln and
Coquet. The distribution of bastle-houses, on the other hand, avoids these upland
areas. Most common in the more fertile middle Tweed valley, they extend into the

[72] British Library, Cotton MSS, Caligula B viii, fos 636 ff: the descriptions of the buildings from
this manuscript were transcribed by Bates 1891, 29–49; the whole document, with many errors of
transcription, is published by Hodgson 1828, p. 3, vol. 2, 171–242.

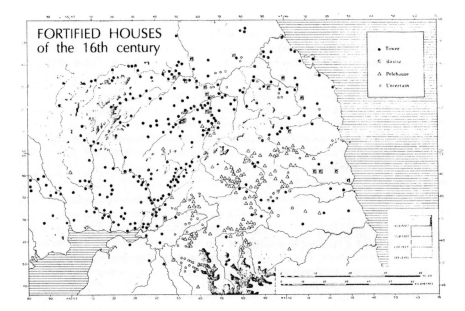

Figure 16. Map of towers, bastle-houses and pele-towers built during the sixteenth century, showing the variations in the patterns of distribution of each type.

lowlands of Northumberland, ringing the Border uplands. Documentary sources name over seventy buildings that no longer survive, which may have been what we would recognise as bastle-houses. Their distribution suggests an extension of the pattern across the somewhat higher land between the lowland plain and the Border dales, and in Gilsland, in northern Cumberland. The distribution of pele-houses is in stark contrast to that of the other types. These rougher buildings have a dense distribution pattern[73] in Gilsland, Bewcastledale and the Northumbrian uplands.

Lords and Reivers

In consequence of this sudden upsurge in building, fortified houses were built and owned by men of a social level far below that normally associated with private castellation. The occupants have been described as men 'not noticeably wealthier than their neighbours', and their society 'while far from being an egalitarian democracy, was extremely homogeneous', while 'all but the poorest families built for themselves a small fortified tower house'.[74] The situation, however, was somewhat different. The owners of tower-houses were likely to be cadets of the greater lords, or lairds and headsmen of their surnames, and to be worth at least

---

[73] In the Border area, at least: survey work in upper Clydesdale has revealed the ruins of several apparent pele-houses well away from the Border zone.
[74] Ramm *et al.* 1970, 65; Maxwell-Irvine 1970–1, esp. 217.

£150 sterling at their deaths. Even the small and poorly built pele-houses were occupied by relatively wealthy men – some of whom were as rich as the tower owners, though their formal status in society might seem lower, since most were customary tenants and not the freeholders or feu-holders of lordships. In short, the sixteenth-century tower-houses of England were built for members of the minor gentry, including the most substantial of the hereditary heads of surnames of the upland Borders. In Scotland the members of this social class were nationally even more significant, since a Border laird might be (like Scott of Branxholm) a Privy Counsellor. Within the Border dales on the English side, however, such chieftains as the Charlton of Hesleyside or the Heron of Chipchase (both families commonly including royal officials, and the occupants of towers) were uncharacteristic. In these dales the bulk of the society was organized in surnames under headsmen of considerably lesser standing, who lived in pele-houses.[75]

This remarkable Border society of thieves and riders has received considerable attention, chiefly by description of its final stages.[76] Its origins are less well known. There seem few grounds for claiming any great antiquity for the customs and social structure: indeed, during the thirteenth and the fourteenth centuries on both sides of the Border we can see a well-developed feudal society, with a hierarchy of local lords, the greatest the occupants of castles, and the lesser lords inhabitants of halls and towers. During the fifteenth century and the early sixteenth century, however, national politics led to the removal or muzzling of the feudal principals, the Percies, the Douglases and the Dacres, and the imposition by the Crown of direct, inadequate, rule. While the minor gentry of the lowlands remained aloof, the vacuum in the Border uplands was filled by clan and kinship leaders, the Crown tenants who were headsmen of the Border surnames.

Bibliography

Bain, J. ed. (1881–8) *Calendar of Documents Relating to Scotland*, 4 vols, Edinburgh.

Bates, C. J. (1891) *Border Holds*, published as *Archaeologia Aeliana* 2nd ser., 14.

Blair, C. H.vH. (1944) 'The early castles of Northumberland', *Archaeologia Aeliana* 4th ser., 22, 133–41.

——(1949) 'Editor's Note', *Archaeologia Aeliana* 4th ser., 27–9.

Brown, R. A. (1953) *English Medieval Castles*, 3rd edn (1976), London.

Cathcart-King, D. J. and Alcock, L. (1966) 'Ringworks of England and Wales', *Château Gaillard* 3, 126–7.

Charlton, J. (1979) *Brougham Castle*: Official Guide, London.

Colvin, H. M. *et al.* (1963) *A History of the King's Works*, I, London.

Coulson, C. (1982) 'Castellation in the County of Champagne', *Château Gaillard* 9–10, 351–6.

[75] For a full discussion of the range of wealth and the status of the builders and occupants of towers, bastles and pele-houses see Dixon 1979.

[76] For example, Fraser 1971; Tough 1927; Rae 1966; Watts and Watts 1975.

—(1993) 'Specimens of freedom to crenellate by licence', *Fortress* 18, 3–15.

Cruden, S. (1963) *The Scottish Castle*, revised edn, Edinburgh.

Dixon, P. W. (1972) 'Shielings and bastles: a reconsideration of some problems', *Archaeologia Aeliana* 4th ser., 50, 249–58.

— (1975) 'Hillslap Tower, masons, and regional traditions', *History of the Berwickshire Naturalists' Club* 40, 128–41.

— (1976) 'Fortified Houses on the Anglo-Scottish Border', unpublished D.Phil. thesis, University of Oxford.

— (1979) 'Towerhouses, pelehouses, and Border Society', *Archaeological Journal* 136, 240–52.

— (1988) *Aydon Castle*, London.

— (1990) 'The donjon of Knaresborough: the castle as theatre', *Château Gaillard*, 14, 121–40.

— (1992) 'From Hall to Tower: the change in seigneurial building on the Anglo-Scottish Border after *c.* 1250', *Thirteenth-Century England* 4 (Woodbridge), 85–107.

Dixon, P. W. and Borne, P. (1978) 'Coparcenary and Aydon Castle', *Archaeological Journal*. 135, 234–9.

Dixon, P. W. and Marshall, P. E. (1993) 'The Great Tower in the twelfth century: the case of Norham', *Archaeological Journal*, 150, 410–32.

Dixon, P. W., Hayfield, C. C. and Startin, W. (1989) 'Baguley Hall, Manchester: the structural development of a Cheshire manor house', *Archaeological Journal* 146, 384–423.

Fairclough, G. (1982) 'Edlingham Castle: the military and domestic development of a Northumbrian manor. Excavations 1978–80: interim report', *Château Gaillard* 9–10, 373–87.

Fraser, G. McD. (1971) *The Steel Bonnets*, London.

Harbottle, R. B. (1982) 'The castle of Newcastle upon Tyne: excavations 1973–79', *Château Gaillard*, 9–10, 407–18.

Hedley, W .P. (1968) *Northumberland Families*, 2 vols, I, 12–14; 244–66, Newcastle.

Hodgson, J., *et al.* (1820–58) *A History of Northumberland*, 7 vols, Newcastle upon Tyne.

Hogg, R. (1954) 'The manor-house at Burgh by Sands', *Transactions of the Cumberland and Westmorland Antiquarian and Archaeological Society* 2nd ser., 54, 129.

Honeyman, H. L. (1955) 'Mitford Castle' *Archaeologia Aeliana*, 4th ser., 33, 27–33.

Hope-Taylor, B. (1977) *Yeavering*, Department of Environment Archaeological Report 7, London.

Kapelle, W. (1979) *The Norman Conquest of the North of England*, London.

Knowles, W. H. (1926) 'The castle of Newcastle upon Tyne', *Archaeologia Aeliana* 4th ser., 2, 1–51.

Leslie, J. (1578) *De Origine Moribus et Rebus Gestis Scottorum*, Rome.

Lloyd, N. (1931) *A History of the English House from Primitive Times to the Victorian Period*, London.

McCarthy, M., Summerson, H. R. T. and Annis, R. G. (1990) *Carlisle Castle: A Survey and Documentary History*, HBMC(E) Archaeol. Rep. 18, London.

MacGibbon D. and Ross, T. (1887–92) *The Castellated and Domestic Architecture of Scotland*, Edinburgh.

Maddicott, J. R. (1970) *Thomas of Lancaster*, Oxford.

Maxwell-Irvine, A. M. T. (1970–1) 'Early firearms and their influence on the military and domestic architecture of the Borders', *Proceedings of the Scottish Antiquarian Society* 103, 192–223.

Middelton, A. (1910) *An Account of Belsay Castle*, Newcastle.

Miller, J. S. (1985) 'Restoration work at Markenfield Hall, 1981–4', *Yorkshire Archaeological Journal*. 57, 101–10.

Musgrove, F. (1990) *The North of England*, London.

NCH (1893–1940) *A History of Northumberland*, 15 vols, Newcastle upon Tyne.

Nielson, G. (1893) *Peel: Its Meaning and Derivation*, Glasgow.

Parker J. H. and Turner, H. (1851–9) *Some Account of Domestic Architecture in England*, 3 vols, Vol. 1 (1851), *From the Conquest to the End of the 13th Century*, Oxford.

Rae, T. I. (1966) *The Administration of the Scottish Frontier, 1513–1603*, Edinburgh.

Ramm, H. G., McDowall, R. W. and Mercer, E. (1970) *Shielings and Bastles*, London.

RCAHM Scotland (1933) *An Inventory of the Historical Monuments of the Counties of Fife, Kinross and Clackmannan*, Edinburgh.

RCAHM Scotland (1956) *The County of Roxburgh*, 2 vols, Edinburgh.

Renn, D. (1968) *Norman Castles in Britain*, London.

Ryder, P. (1986) *Blenkinsopp Castle* (Napper Collection Partnership, May 1986) [Unpublished].

Simpson G. G. and Webster, B. (1985) 'Charter evidence and the distribution of mottes in Scotland', in *Essays on the Nobility of Medieval Scotland* (ed. K. J. Stringer), 7–11, Edinburgh.

Simpson, W. D. (1938–9) *The Book of Dunvegan*, 2 vols (Third Spalding Club, 1938–9), Aberdeen.

—— (1940) 'Belsay Castle and the Scottish tower houses', *Archaeologia Aeliana* 4th ser., 17, 75–84.

—— (1949a) *Brough Castle: Official Guide*, London.

—— (1949b) 'Further notes on Dunstanburgh Castle', *Archaeologia Aeliana* 4th ser., 27, 1–25.

Smout, T. C. (1969) *A History of the Scottish People*, London.

Thompson, A. Hamilton (1912) *Military Architecture in England during the Middle Ages*, Oxford.

Thomson, T. and Innes, C. (ed.) (1814–75) *The Acts of Parliaments of Scotland* (Record Commission 1814–75).

Tough, D. N . L. (1927) *The Last Years of a Frontier*, Oxford.

Tuck, J. A. (1971) 'Northumbrian society in the fourteenth century', *Northern History* 6, 22–39.

—— (1985) 'War and society in the medieval North', *Northern History* 21, 33–52.

Watts, S. J. and Watts, S. (1975) *From Border to Middle Shire*, Leicester.

Winchester, A. (1987) *Landscape and Society in Medieval Cumbria*, Edinburgh.

Wood, M. (1965) *English Mediaeval House*, London.

7
Lulworth Castle, Dorset

John Goodall

Rescued from a ruin by a £5 million English Heritage conservation project, the historical richness of Lulworth Castle, Dorset, has been revealed in all its complexity as a stylish seventeenth-century hunting lodge on an essentially medieval plan.

'My castle, it is ruined,' Herbert Weld was heard to exclaim as he viewed the smouldering remains of Lulworth Castle, after a catastrophic fire in August 1929. The castle had been the home of his recusant family for nearly 300 years. An electrical fault in a linen cupboard is thought to have started the blaze, and it took firm hold before fire engines from the surrounding counties arrived. They brought the fire under control but ran out of water and were unable to supply their need from the nearby sea because, it was discovered, their hoses had different gauges and could not be linked together. Helpless, the family, staff, firemen, locals and a vast crowd of curious holiday-makers then watched the house being

Figure 1. Lulworth Castle from the east. (Robert Liddiard)

slowly consumed. Everything that could be salvaged was brought out, but most of the contents of the upper floors were lost.

For the next 50 years, the gutted masonry shell of Lulworth Castle stood open to the elements, overgrown with weeds and saplings. There were plans to restore it as the family house, but the cost was prohibitive and the proposal would have involved demolishing the upper storey of the building. The family built a new neo-Georgian house in the park (designed by Anthony Jaggard), and the castle was taken into the guardianship of Department of the Ancient Monuments (from 1983 known as English Heritage), with the intention that it would be preserved as an ornamental ruin. Between 1979 and 1983, it was cleared of rubble and consolidated. But it quickly became apparent that there were serious structural problems, which threatened the stability of the fabric. The use of soft chalk in the walls made them particularly vulnerable to water damage, and the whole building had to be temporarily secured with scaffolding.

English Heritage decided to roof and re-fenestrate the building. This approach had one important advantage, beyond the fact that it promised to preserve the castle in the long term. Since the fire had stripped down the interior, it was now possible to see the structural bones of the building, revealing how it had been altered over its 300-year history. It was only by roofing the structure that this architectural palimpsest could be protected and made accessible to the public. Visitors could then see at first-hand how archaeology could inform the study of the country house. To heighten the sense of this meeting between the two, it was further decided to restore the exterior to its appearance the day before the fire.

The task of recording, conserving and repairing Lulworth Castle was completed in 1998 after eight years' work, and has cost about £5 million, of which £1.5 m was provided by the Lulworth estate. The architects were Gilmore Hankey Kirke. The estate and the Weld family have been enthusiastic supporters of the work, and they now manage the property on behalf of English Heritage, an unprecedented arrangement. Glass plate negatives taken for an article published in *Country Life* in 1926 (9 January) have been of notable importance in the project, and are the single most important record of the building before the fire (Figures 7–8). Their quality allowed some of the details they capture to be scrutinised under high magnification.

Lulworth Castle was built by Thomas, 3rd Lord Bindon, and was probably largely completed between 1608 and 1610. It is situated just four miles from Thomas's house at Bindon Abbey, and was evidently intended as the focus and ornament of a new 1,000-acre park in the locality, which he had created in 1605. The great architectural patron and minister of state Robert Cecil, 1st Earl of Salisbury, was directly involved in encouraging the project, and in a letter of 1608 Bindon acknowledged that it was he who had 'laid the first foundation of the pile in my mind'.

The castle that Thomas built has changed little externally since its construction in the seventeenth century (Figure 1). It comprises a regular four-storey central block with a great drum tower at each corner. This striking design, sparingly

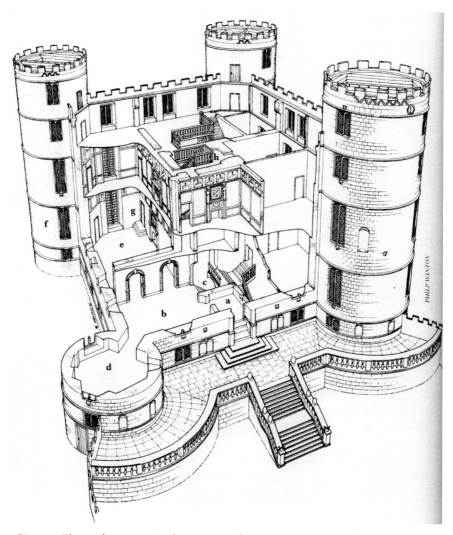

Figure 2. The castle as it was in the seventeenth century, cut away to show the interior at that time: a, entrance vestibule; b, screen passage; c, stair to kitchens and cellars; d, buttery; e, great hall; f, oriel chamber; g, door to main stairwell with access to chapel and upper floors; h, servants' stair.

detailed and crowned with castellations, makes unmistakable allusion to medieval castle architecture. But despite employing the architectural vocabulary of defence and adopting the title of castle, there is nothing military about Lulworth. The detailing of the exterior is rigorously symmetrical and clearly reflects the internal arrangements of the building: the floor levels of each storey are indicated by string courses, and the relative importance of each is expressed both by its height and by the size of its windows.

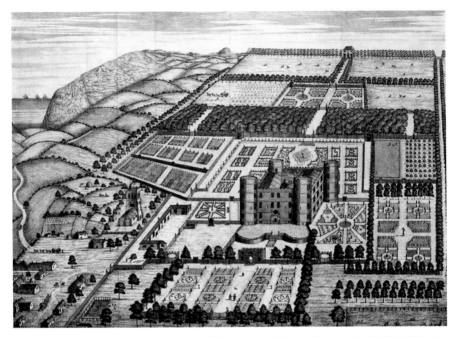

Figure 3. Lulworth in 1721. (Courtesy of The Dorset History Centre. Ref: D/WLC/P 53)

Considerable care was taken to make the approach to the building, already splendidly set to dominate the surrounding park, as impressive as possible. The principal façade is constructed in cut stone and decorated with mock arrow loops, niches and corbels cut as lions' heads, all details that are absent on the other, less visible, parts of the building. It was fronted by a low stone terrace, and the fine central doorway, flanked with statues, was approached up a wide flight of steps (Figure 4). A door formerly at basement level is thought to have been the original front door (Figure 9).

The terrace was heightened and extended in the eighteenth century to enclose three sides of the basement, but the original design is recorded in an engraving showing the castle and its grounds in 1721 (Figure 3). Also visible on the engraving is the seventeenth-century walled forecourt to the castle, with its two-storey gatehouse and a stable block set to one side of the building.

Before the fire, little was known about the original interior of the castle, which had been extensively altered in the eighteenth century. It is now apparent, however, that Lulworth followed an essentially medieval domestic plan, ingeniously compressed into a tower (Figure 2). The main entrance to the castle opened into a screens passage – an enclosed service area at the end of the great hall – by way of a vaulted vestibule. Immediately to the visitor's right, a stairway descended from this to the kitchens in the basement (Figure 5) and, to their left in the adjacent tower chamber, there was a buttery. The principal pair of doorways in the passage led into what one visitor described in 1635 as 'the stately hall'. At the upper end of this there was an oriel chamber in the tower, where the gentlemen of the

Figure 4. The main
entrance of the castle
today. (*Country Life*
Picture Library)

household dined, and, opposite it, a door to the main stairwell of the house. The
chapel opened off this, but the stair itself led to several suites of apartments. These
were arranged on two floors, with the most important, including the great chamber, on the lower. The upper floors and the roof – an essential area for recreation
– were also accessible up a central servants' stair.

Although contemporaries never referred to it as such, Lulworth Castle has
been described as a hunting lodge by architectural historians. Indeed, it has been
plausibly suggested that it was deliberately built with an eye to catering for James
I's love of the chase. Hunting lodges, and Lulworth in particular, are thought to
have played an important role in the development of domestic architecture in
England at the end of the sixteenth century. Not only did they appeal to their
owners as places of recreation, but the demise of the great household meant that
they were better adapted to the needs of seventeenth-century life than the medieval courtyard house. As a result, it was the hunting lodge with its integrated plan
that served as the model for the next generation of domestic architecture and

Figure 5. The vaulted basements of Lulworth Castle. (*Country Life* Picture Library)

Figure 6. Old Wardour Castle, Wiltshire: the remodelled symmetrical fourteenth-century façade. © Historic England Archive

Figure 7. Lulworth's saloon, formerly the great hall, as it was in 1926, when it was recorded by *Country Life*. (*Country Life* Picture Library)

Figure 8. The saloon as it is now. (*Country Life* Picture Library)

Figure 9. An original seventeenth-century door to the castle, possibly from the main entrance. (*Country Life* Picture Library)

from which the compact country house, familiar in later centuries, may trace its descent.

In consequence, it is no surprise that Lulworth is generally discussed for its forward-looking qualities and in terms of contemporary and later buildings. Nor is it surprising that its castle-like form is often presented as a curious, but essentially cosmetic, aspect of its design: fantastical evocation of archaic chivalric ideas, then in high fashion at court and reflected in other great contemporary commissions, such as Bolsover Castle, Derbyshire. But Lulworth Castle, like the buildings it is usually compared with, is arguably thoroughly medieval both in form and conception. As such, its feudal trappings should be seen not as an affectation of fashion, but as evidence of the survival of the medieval architectural tradition into the seventeenth century.

Compressing a house into a tower was an architectural commonplace throughout the Middle Ages. Keeps, gatehouses, hunting lodges and tower houses all played with this idea, and from the fourteenth century onwards there are several buildings that compare closely to Lulworth. Perhaps the most important is the great tower at Warkworth Castle in Northumberland of about 1400 (*Country Life*, 4 May 1995). It makes allusion to John of Gaunt's magnificent buildings at Kenilworth Castle and may have been conceived as a version of that residence cast in tower form. The result is one of the masterpieces of medieval design. As at Lulworth the building is conceived as a central block with four projecting towers; has a show façade; incorporates a complex system of public, private and service stairs; has a hierarchy of floors; and different types of window to denote externally the different uses of chambers.

But more modest examples of tower houses from the late fourteenth century also show an interest in similar ideas. Nunney Castle in Somerset, built in the 1370s, bears a superficial resemblance to Lulworth, designed as a central block with drum towers at each corner. And Old Wardour Castle in Wiltshire – an extraordinary house arranged round a tiny polygonal light-well courtyard – shows a concern with formal symmetry of design (Figure 6).

The style of mock fortification at Lulworth was widely anticipated in medieval architecture, where it was often used to confer the status of a castle – customarily the residence of those above the rank of baron – on buildings with no defensive capability. That Lulworth is indefensible, therefore, in no way distinguishes it from the medieval architectural tradition. Rather, it suggests the continued importance attached to the trappings of defence as the mark of a nobleman's house. Certainly until the Civil War, most great families possessed castles, and in some cases the mock fortification of seventeenth-century houses took contemporary form, as if the castle was a living, rather than an historicist, ideal.

The builder of Lulworth, Thomas Bindon, died in 1611, and it was not until 1615 that his heir, the 1st Earl of Suffolk, entertained James I there. In 1641, the property was sold to a London Catholic, Humphrey Weld. He married the daughter of the 3rd Lord Arundell – the owner of Old Wardour Castle – but the Civil War immediately put his possessions in jeopardy, and it was not until the Restoration that the family began to recover its fortunes. By the mid-eighteenth century, the family was prosperous enough to transform the interior of the castle, and George III gave permission for the then owner, Thomas Weld, to construct adjacent to it the first free-standing Catholic church in England since the Reformation. When the fire came in 1929 it exposed the complexity and riches of Lulworth's architectural past, but at the price of ruining a remarkable, living family house.

8

A Scottish Problem with Castles[*]

Charles McKean

This article examines the cultural misinterpretations that followed from the Scottish nobles' fondness for adopting the title and martial appearance of castles for their Renaissance country seats. It examines the distortions and misunderstandings that led to the continuing presumption that Scotland did not participate in the European architectural Renaissance. Using contemporary sources, the buildings themselves and recent research, it offers a cultural explanation for the seemingly martial nature of Scottish architecture in terms of expressing rank and lineage, and proclaiming political allegiance. It suggests that a reinterpretation of such buildings as self-sustaining country seats can offer much to other social and cultural aspects of British history of that period. It concludes by suggesting that the architecture of the late seventeenth century, far from indicating a classicisation or assimilation with England, represented the apogee of a confident national architecture.

The architecture of the Scottish Renaissance is curiously absent from European historiography. It figures in English historiography only since the strangely picturesque qualities of the north-east country seats like Fyvie (1598) or Craigievar (1610–25), both in Aberdeenshire, permitted their entry as a minor aberration in the steadfast evolution of a British architecture (Figure 1).[1] The reason for its absence is that no (or very little) Renaissance architecture appeared to be identifiable in Scotland according to the judgments of the time, and the Scottish nobility appeared to reside in medieval castles long after everybody else had ceased doing so. Since the architecture of such buildings followed neither contemporary trends in England, nor an identifiably classical approach, it was soon concluded that the Renaissance had largely passed Scotland by. Scots institutions shared that misconception even up to the late twentieth century. The Renaissance appeared to

[*] This article is a revised version of a paper delivered at 'The great house from the Roman villa to the stately home: perspectives and prospects' conference in the Beveridge Hall, University of London on 26–28 January 2004. The author is grateful to R. J. Morris, Michael Bath, Alan Macdonald, Charles Wemyss, Matt Davis, Kate Newland and Michael Pearce, who have shared their work with him.
[1] Sir Banister Fletcher's *A History of Architecture*, ed. D. Cruickshank (Oxford, 1996) devotes 35 pages to England 1500–1700, and 32 lines to Scotland. Scotland does not figure at all in D. Watkin, *A History of Western Architecture* (London, 1986). Sir John Summerson, in *Architecture in Britain, 1530–1830* (Harmondsworth, 1977) was more canny; stating that architecture in Scotland up to the date of the Union was as distinct from England 'as the latter is from Danish or Spanish', he relegated it to an appendix.

Figure 1. Craigievar,
Aberdeenshire,
refashioned possibly
by John Bell, 1610–26.
(AB/4962, Crown
Copyright, courtesy of the
Royal Commission on the
Ancient and Historical
Monuments of Scotland)

have fallen between the remit of the National Museum of Antiquities of Scotland
and that of the Industrial Museum of Scotland (later the Royal Museum); and
until the emergence of a brief for a new Museum of Scotland in 1986, the Scottish
medieval period was assumed to extend to 1700, when its modern period began.
The museums acknowledged little between.[2]

The ubiquitous 'heritage' presentation of Scottish Renaissance country seats
as military objects, supported by countless publications on 'Scottish castles' that
mingle genuine fortresses promiscuously with sometimes very minor country
seats, diminishes rather than enhances their interest. For the focus upon defence
distorts an understanding of how they worked as self-sustaining country houses
functioning at the centre of their estates,[3] as the centres of the regional economy,
or as the centres of regional power, culture and hospitality. Their classification as
castles isolates them from the contemporary poetic, musical, artistic and literary

---

[2] Personal communication from J. Calder to the author. See also C. McKean, *The Making of the
Museum of Scotland* (National Museums of Scotland, Edinburgh, 2000), 2–9.
[3] See particularly C. McKean, 'The Scottish Renaissance Country Seat in its Setting', *Garden History* 31 (2005), 141–62.

cultures of the country which, in many cases, were stimulated by them.[4] Indeed, when one evaluates their siting, and the manner in which their allegedly defensive panoply of turrets, gunloops, machicolations and crenellations were deployed, against contemporary European militarism, it becomes speedily evident that these castle-like houses were militarily useless. This article suggests that their martial mien was entirely metaphorical in intent, signifying lineage and rank. Furthermore, from the way in which Scottish architecture changed dramatically with each reign, it seems logical to suggest that it was also being used to express political allegiance. Thus, the architecture of the Scottish nobility was deployed, in effect, to construct rank and to proclaim politics. The resulting national architecture reached its apogee c.1680 when the controlling elite proclaimed a political self-confidence through a vigorous Scottish baroque triumphalism, exemplified in an unusual group of great and lesser houses, rather than succumbing to classical architecture as the prelude to the Union, as is the customary perspective.[5]

The principal reaction to the presumed absence of Scotland from European Renaissance culture has been to regard the country as the Albania of Renaissance Europe – isolated, violent, poverty-stricken and primitive. That assumption appears to have appealed greatly to the perverse contrariness of the Scots themselves, since it dovetailed nicely with the rewriting of Scottish history by the *illuminati* of the Enlightenment (particularly by members of the Revolution Club). Their opinion of sixteenth- and seventeenth-century Scotland may be inferred from the synoptic *Proposals for Carrying on Certain Public Works in the City of Edinburgh*, published in 1752.[6] There is good reason to believe that this was a committee document, prepared by a group fronted by Gilbert Elliot, jun., of Minto and – to judge by the language and clues left by Sir David Dalrymple – probably including Adam Smith (then in Edinburgh delivering his first lectures), Adam Fergusson, David Hume and Club members John and Robert Adam, and their cousin, Dr William Robertson.[7] 'The business was all done in the tavern, where there was a daily dinner,'[8] chaired by Revolution Club member and modernising cleric, Dr Alexander Webster.[9]

---

[4] The beautiful Wemyss manuscript of music for a 10-course lute was created by Lady Margaret Wemyss in 1643 at Wemyss castle, Fife (R. MacKillop, *Flowers of the Forest* (1998), Greentrax Recordings, CDTRAXi55, CD booklet).

[5] M. Glendinning and A. MacKechnie, *Scottish Architecture* (London, 2004), 67.

[6] *Proposals for Carrying on Certain Public Works in the City of Edinburgh* (Edinburgh, 1752) (hereafter *Proposals*).

[7] These notions are developed in greater detail in C. McKean, 'Twinning Cities: Improvement Versus Modernisation in the Two Towns of Edinburgh', in *Edinburgh – the Making of a Capital City*, ed. B. Edwards and P. Jenkins (Edinburgh, 2005), 42–64. The *Proposals*' attack on seventeenth-century Scotland uses very similar language to Robertson's own history of that period. For a wider discussion, see also C. Kidd, *Subverting Scotland's Past: Scottish Whig Historians and the Creation of an Anglo-British Identity, 1689–c.1830* (Cambridge, 1993).

[8] *Autobiography of Dr. Alexander Carlyle*, ed. J. Hill Burton (Edinburgh, 1910), 252.

[9] Alexander Carlyle liked to mock Webster as 'Dr Bonum Magnum' for his gastronomic habits, but Webster was to produce Scotland's first parish census in 1755.

As part of a much wider revisionism of Scottish history and Scottish institutions, the *Proposals* justified the case for radical change by glorifying the 1688 Revolution and the Union of the parliaments, and the blessings derived therefrom.[10] To do so, they had to vilify and falsify the aristocratic and cultural life of Scotland in the centuries immediately preceding Union in 1707. Take, for example, the statement:

Few persons of any rank, in those days, frequented our towns. The manners of our peers, of our barons, and chiefs of families, were not formed to brook that equality which prevails in cities. The solitary grandeur of a country life, at their own seats, and amidst their own vassals, suited better the stateliness and pride of these petty sovereigns.[11]

Typical of the contemporary recasting of Scottish history, it was, of course, arrant nonsense –as a glance at the countless aristocratic and gentry town houses in all towns of substance throughout Scotland might demonstrate. Indeed, one of the ways of evaluating the quality of a Scottish town or city is to identify the number and type of noble or landowner town houses that it contained. Having dismissed the aristocrats, the modernisers then dispatched Scotland's trade and culture:

No wonder then if, amidst the distractions which constantly prevailed in this country, we had neither leisure nor inclination to improve those arts which are generally the offspring of quiet times and a well-ordered state.

The nadir was reached in the seventeenth century:

We had indeed the honour to send a King to England, but this honour cost us dear. We remained in a strange equivocal situation, little better than that of a conquered province. The nation was dispirited; the little trade we had languished and decayed; every project we formed ENGLAND discouraged; our great men, who had now no wars to wage, and no court to resort to, either retired sullen to the country, or inlisting with foreign princes, vainly lavished their blood in the quarrels of strangers.[12]

That does not accord with what the buildings tell you. The boom in the construction or reformatting of country houses that had begun in the mid-1550s was reaching its peak in the first four decades of the seventeenth century in Scotland, and improvements to the yards and estates were commensurate.[13] The marquess of Huntly, as Gilbert Blakhall recorded, spent his time in furious building: 'For he was so much taken up with his newe buildings, from four hours in the morning

[10] T. Somerville, *My Own Life and Times, 1741–1830* (Edinburgh, 1861), 104.
[11] *Proposals*, 12. Kidd points out that, in writing something very similar in his essay 'On the refinement of the arts', David Hume was 'delivering a negative verdict on the former Scottish Constitution' (Kidd, *Subverting Scotland*, 176–80).
[12] *Proposals*, 14.
[13] Based upon an analysis of building dates in M. Salter, *Castles of Scotland* (5 vols, Malvern, 1993–6). See graph in C. McKean, *The Scottish Château* (Stroud, 2001), 17.

until eight at night, standing by his masons, urging their diligences, and directing and judging their worke, that he had scarce tyme to eate or sleep, much less
to wreat.'[14] At a lower rank, there is no reason to believe that Sir Christopher
Lowther's description of a typically improving landowner, Sir James Pringle at
Gala House in 1629, was in any way unusual: 'He is one of the best husbands in the
country, as appeareth by his planting … He hath a very pretty park, with many
natural walks in it, artificial ponds and arbours now a-making, and all his tenants
through his care, he hath abundance of cherry trees.'[15]

Such a reality did not suit the purposes of the Revolution Club members. The
'45 had rendered Scotland's immediate historical past – the reigns of the Stewarts
– unacceptable if not embarrassing. As Kidd puts it, 'Scotland's literati rendered
their native country a "historyless" nation.'[16] But countries need a past, an ances-
try, an inheritance, so when they required a historical memory, the Scots adopted
the mythical, politically neutral Dark Age bard Ossian as a safe substitute. Ossian
may have conferred upon Scotland the required sense of antiquity, but his bag-
gage also included heroics and martial acts. Antiquarians, some of whom were
enmeshed within the Enlightenment, now went to seek out evidence for prior
valour rather than prior cultures. Initially, they concentrated upon genuine
fortresses, but since there were not very many of those in Scotland, they were
tempted to extend the search to country seats with the characteristic militaristic
display of crenellations, gunloops and machicolations. When they found them,
they invested the houses with moats, ditches, barmkins and battlements, without
which such castle-like claims might have been questionable. Adam de Cardonnel
claimed to have found that 'every mode of fortification then in use was seldom
adequate to the defence of the Castle against the storm or blockade of the enraged
Chieftain', and this as close to the centre of Scotland as Perthshire.[17] Yet the
records do not provide evidence of such storms and blockades. A number of fatal
quarrels, feuds and street brawls, certainly, were played out by trains of noblemen
encountering each other in the market places of Stirling, Aberdeen or Edinburgh
– but of a wholly different order of magnitude to the endemic urban violence of,
say, Italy.[18] Attacks upon a country house were rare during Renaissance Scotland
– so long as one excludes periods of civil war, and the Gaidhealtachd.

The military capability of these houses was negligible, no more than a martial decoration superimposed upon a modernised living pattern. Machicolations
were solid and decorative rather than hollow and useable; the turrets (originally studies) did not provide windows to allow gunners to command the front

[14] G. Blakhall, *A Brief Narration* (Aberdeen, 1844), 170.
[15] *Our Journall into Scotland anno domini 1629* (Edinburgh, 1894), 17–18.
[16] Kidd, *Subverting Scotland*, 209.
[17] A. de Cardonnel, *Picturesque Antiquities of Scotland* (1788), pt ii, p. II.
[18] The scale of Italian urban violence is represented by a design prepared by the architect Sebastiano Serlio for a house for a 'faction leader'; taking as read that the doors of this great palazzo
would be smashed down by a rival faction, its inner hall was protected by 16 concealed gunloops.
Moreover, a nobleman's palace in Rome required both an armoury and a guardroom.

entrance; the stone cannons on the parapet were, of course, waterspouts; and the gunloops, around the decoding of which an entire subset of decorative archaeology has grown up, were mostly unusable and dangerous to the user.[19] A large number would have fired directly onto cobbles or into the walls of inner court buildings. They become slightly more operational the closer the house to the border with England, or where the owner – like Sir James Hamilton of Finnart, who had been to Europe and was something of a gunnery man – knew how to construct a *chambre à tirer*. Moreover, Scots nobles feared being walled up within their houses, and their habit during the civil war was to meet a predatory troop at the gate to the outer court. These 'castles', therefore, like so many on the Loire and elsewhere, were metaphorical structures entirely – as the French term them, *châteaux des rêves*.

Nonetheless, the recasting of Scottish history had worked. By the 1840s, Scotland's historic psyche was fixed and its primitivism taken for granted. The proof soon followed. For his *Domestic Annals of Scotland*, Robert Chambers selected from contemporary documents according to his preconception that Renaissance Scotland was a barbaric period: 'It is forced upon us that the Scots were, at this very time, a fearfully rude and ignorant people … ruder than the England of that day.'[20] (Rude', of course, had been a principal buzz word by which the Enlightenment *illuminati* characterised pre-Union Scottish society, institutions and even the parliament.[21]) Far from faithfully recording 'symptoms of advancing civilisation' and anything that illustrated the progress of the arts 'as worthy of notice',[22] as he claimed, Chambers ignored poetry, painting, music, architecture and literature in favour of war, religious turmoil, fanaticism and freaks. The former might have offered a corrective, for recent research has shown how the rituals, Renaissance thought, organisation, music and poetry of Scottish court culture, so carefully avoided by Chambers, were embedded in contemporary European culture,[23] and were not being practised in some form of distant, provincial echo. The country had followed, as the French put it, a *chantier particulier* (Figure 2).

Thus, by the mid-nineteenth century, Scottish Renaissance architecture was invariably interpreted in military terms; and in circumstances where the authentic architectural heritage appeared insufficiently ferocious, the tendency grew to

[19] For more on this, see McKean, *Scottish Château*, ch. 3.
[20] R. Chambers, *The Domestic Annals of Scotland* (3 vols, Edinburgh, [*c*.1842]), i. 5.
[21] Kidd, *Subverting Scotland*, chs. 7–9.
[22] Chambers, *Domestic Annals*, i. 521, 550.
[23] See, e.g., C. Edington, *Court and Culture in Renaissance Scotland* (East Linton, 1995); S. Mapstone and J. Wood (ed.), *The Rose and the Thistle* (East Linton, 1998); I. B. Cowan and D. Shaw (ed.), *The Renaissance and Reformation in Scotland* (Edinburgh, 1983); R. A. Mason, *Kingship and Commonweal* (East Linton, 1998); J. H. Williams (ed.), *Stewart Style 1513–42: Essays on the Court of James V* (East Linton, 1996); D. J. Ross, *Musick Fyne: Robert Carver and the Art of Music in 16th Century Scotland* (Edinburgh, 1993); R. A. Mason, 'Humanism and Political Culture', in *People and Power in Scotland*, ed. R. A. Mason and N. Macdougall (Edinburgh, 1992), 104–38; M. Bath, *Renaissance Decorative Painting in Scotland* (Edinburgh, 2003); and dissertations such as A. Thomas, 'Renaissance Culture at the Court of James V' (Unpublished Ph.D. thesis, University of Edinburgh, 1997).

Figure 2. North façade of the palace of Stirling, designed by Sir James Hamilton of Finnart, 1538–40. (B41926, courtesy of Historic Scotland)

'medievalise' it appropriately. It was not a new concept. In 1786, Sir John Dalrymple had joked about how, when he had appointed Robert Adam to refashion his ancient 'tall house' of Oxenfoord, the architect had 'really made it much older than it was'[24] --in other words, Adam had ratcheted up the romanticism. But the new medieval was distinctly more primitive than Adam's. The interior plasterwork was stripped out from St Giles's church in Edinburgh, leaving just bare stonework where that had never been intended.[25] The earliest records of St Giles's interior imply that it had been highly decorated; it was adorned with tapestries,[26] and when the Catholic Mary of Guise retook Edinburgh in 1558 after its brief occupation by the reforming lords of the congregation, she found that they had painted out its original mural decoration and replaced it with 'the Lord's Prayer, the Belief and the Commandments … patent on the kirk-walls'.[27] From its current, largely de-plastered gloom, it is difficult to imagine how vividly painted St Giles's might once have been – initially presumably with saints, then with improving religious texts, and then again (once Mary of Guise had such visual propaganda swiftly

[24] Quoted in M. Sanderson, *Robert Adam and Scotland: Portrait of an Architect* (repr. Edinburgh, 1993), 88.
[25] Below William Burn's replacement East Window, an iconic location, the stone is poor, random and keyed for plaster.
[26] Fr. A. Baillie, *True Information of the Unhallowed Offspring, Progress and Impoisoned Fruits of our Scottish Calvinist Gospel and Gospellers* (Wirtsburg, 1628), 24–8. The author is very grateful to Michael Pearce for this.
[27] It is not known what murals may have adorned St Giles's. A similar church interior – the Friary church in Konstanz – is adorned with beautiful paintings on the octagonal columns, with saints rising above them. There is only scant record of the vividness of the interior of Scottish medieval churches, such as the painting of the window embrasure of Turriff church (C. McKean, *Banff and Buchan* (Edinburgh, 1990)).

blotted out)[28] perhaps with saints once more. After the Victorians had St Giles's
stripped of its decoration and plaster, the church was ornamented instead with
crumbling regimental standards, as befitted a country of valorous soldiers.

A comparable impulse led William Nelson to pay for the reworking of the flat-
roofed belvedere above the 1575 Regent Morton's gateway to Edinburgh Castle
into a bristling, crenellated tower at least a storey higher than it had been in the
1880s. As R. J. Morris has put it, 'It was part of the recreation of Scottish identity
through a sense of violent past, a fractured history of kingship, and of a noble,
different and often persecuted religious character.'[29] For a country identifying
itself with the military values of the empire, the architecture that Scotland had
inherited from the past often proved far too peaceable for the new purpose.

The architect Robert Lorimer considered harling, the customary external
coating of rubble, to be less noble than bare stonework and, when restoring the
Renaissance houses of Dunderave, Argyll and Earlshall, Fife, he stripped it off. He
likewise removed the plaster from the vaulted hall at Lennoxlove, presumably in
conformity to the philosophy that rugged stonework added honour to a 'baronial
hall'.[30] A contemporary wrote of work carried out at Blair, Ayrshire, 'it is a pity that
the vaulted ceiling has been plastered; the original bare stonework would be so
attractive.'[31] So an assumption about a primitive past came to dominate the artistic
agenda, reinforcing the belief, widely held among historians and antiquarians,
that 'civilised' qualities had only entered the Scottish country seat after James
VI had moved down to London.[32] The past that they were thereby discounting
included the vivid interior painted decoration of the Renaissance country houses
that Duncan Macmillan has argued reflected 'the establishment of a new standard
of civil life'.[33] The 'primitive campaigns' of the later nineteenth century destroyed
much of the decorative element of that civil life.[34]

All of this formed the intellectual context within which the architects David
MacGibbon and Thomas Ross codified Scotland's castellated and domestic architecture in their five sumptuously illustrated volumes.[35] Although it was the first
time that Scottish architecture had been subjected to an examination within its
own terms, MacGibbon and Ross accepted without question the antiquarian

[28] Robert Lindsay of Pitscottie, *The History of Scotland from 1436 to 1565* (3rd edn, Edinburgh, 1778), 325.
[29] The author is greatly indebted to R. J. Morris for an advance view of R. J. Morris, 'The Capitalist, the Soldier and the Professor: the Remaking of Edinburgh Castle, 1850–1900', *Planning Perspectives* 22 (2007), 55–78.
[30] *Lennoxlove Guidebook* (Haddington, 1981).
[31] T. Hannan, *Famous Scottish Houses* (London, 1928), 119, 27.
[32] J. Warrack, *Domestic Life in Scotland, 1488–1688* (London, 1920), 99: 'But almost with the stroke of the new century there came a change.'
[33] D. Macmillan, *Scottish Art 1460–1990* (Edinburgh, 1990), 56.
[34] Photographs in the Royal Commission on the Ancient and Historical Monuments of Scotland (RCAHM (Scotland)) reveal that a number of the seats studied for *The Scottish Château* were still harled in the later nineteenth century, whereas they are not now.
[35] D. MacGibbon and T. Ross, *The Castellated and Domestic Architecture of Scotland* (5 vols, Edinburgh, 1895).

perception that the buildings they were studying were mostly castles in which defensiveness had been the primary consideration.[36] They found castles because they looked for castles, and interpreted the building plans and details accordingly. The language of medieval militaria – keep, barmkin, crenellation, machicolation, bretasche – now became the language with which country houses were analysed, and a new one – tower-house – was added.[37] Where the house was ruinous, their focus was generally the ancestral tower, and they often ignored evidence of the inner or outer courts, the galleries, guest towers, stables and service buildings – particularly where they did not fit a military analysis. MacGibbon's and Ross's approach remained largely unchallenged for over a century, and the Scottish misprision was now firmly set.

The *English* misprision of Scottish Renaissance culture pre-dated the Enlightenment by about a century. The English travellers who had come north during the seventeenth century apparently expected to find that the two ends of the island were approximately similar. Instead, they found that they had entered a foreign country with strange food, strange dress, displeasingly informal customs, and country houses bearing no resemblance to their own peaceable manor houses. Early reactions tended to be curious but neutral, like that of Sir William Brereton in 1636: 'By the way I observed gentlemen's (here called lairds) houses built all castle-wise.'[38] By the later seventeenth century, however, the tone became more venomous where it suited a broader political agenda to take the martial metaphor at face value. Thomas Kirke, who visited Scotland in 1679 to pour scorn upon the pretensions of the duke of York's court of Holyrood, had not enjoyed his stay. He had found the Scots to be 'perfect English haters' and returned the compliment by excoriating everything. He observed of the country seats that, 'indeed, all the gentlemen [sic] houses are strong castles', and then concluded, 'they being so treacherous to one another, that they are forc'd to defend themselves in strong holds'.[39] A good example of *post hoc ergo propter hoc*. Ten years later, the more balanced Thomas Morer came to a similar conclusion: 'The houses of their quality are high and strong and appear more like castles than houses made of thick stone walls, with iron bars before their windows, *suited to the necessity of those times they were built in, living then in a state of war and constant animosities between their families*.'[40]

Given the predilection of British architectural history to be predominantly English, and largely concentrated upon buildings in the southern part of the country, the dissimilarity between English Renaissance houses and their Scots counterparts was so great that it proved impossible to incorporate them within

---

[36] D. Walker, 'The architecture of MacGibbon and Ross – the background to the books', in *Studies in Scottish Antiquity Presented to Stewart Cruden*, ed. D. Breeze (Glasgow, 1984).
[37] It is not found in contemporary documents. The term 'tower' is used in the hearth tax records usually to refer to a very small and unmodernised medieval house.
[38] Sir W. Brereton, in P. Hume Brown, *Early Travellers in Scotland* (repr. Edinburgh, 1973), 149.
[39] T. Kirke, in Hume Brown, *Early Travellers*, 259.
[40] T. Morer, in Hume Brown, *Early Travellers*, 275 (author's emphasis).

the same thesis. Moreover, the attractions of classicism as the yardstick of improving culture and civilisation remain tempting for historians. For all his defence of European dispersed cultures during the Renaissance, Peter Burke nonetheless accords primacy to classicism when discussing English town halls: 'It was only after 1660 that they discovered the dignity of classical architecture.'[41] It was not therefore surprising that the warlike appearance of Scottish Renaissance country seats suited their relegation to a subsection on castles at the end of the medieval section, entirely appropriate to the English perception of the Scots character and history. It was explained as a 'time-lag': Scots were genetically slower to evolve into the paths of peacefulness.

Although research over the last fifty years slowly began to challenge this inherited intellectual mindset, beginning when John Dunbar pointed out that what looked like turrets in country houses were called 'studies' by contemporaries,[42] the persistence of martial decoration was still attributed to that notion of time-lag or cultural conservatism.[43] Three decades later, Deborah Howard finally provided a cultural context whereby the Scottish Renaissance country seat could be interpreted within the European pattern.[44] Nonetheless, the notion that Renaissance country seats were 'fortified tower houses', and that they had been designed primarily for defence, has remained obdurately prominent in subsequent scholarship.[45] It is doubtful if Scottish country seats had ever been built 'primarily for defence', judging by the indefensible sites of most of them; and it is wholly improbable that the vast rebuilding and modernisation programmes of the sixteenth and seventeenth centuries were predicated even marginally upon defence. The metaphor remains mistaken for reality.

The 'Albanian' argument holds that Scotland was remote from architectural movements on the continent as a consequence of being warring, remote and poverty-stricken. Ross Samson, for example, has suggested that Scotland did not follow the classical route because it remained in a state of ignorance for reasons of cultural isolation.[46] That is palpably not the case. In 1628, William Lithgow observed that 'the nobility and gentry of the kingdom … are courteous, discreet, learned scholars well read in the best histories, delicate linguists, the most part of them being brought up in France or Italy'.[47] As Keith Brown has shown, a European education was expected among the upper classes, despite the requirement, by a

[41] P. Burke, *The European Renaissance: Centres and Peripheries* (Oxford, 1998), 118.
[42] J. G. Dunbar, *The Historic Architecture of Scotland* (London, 1966), 76.
[43] Dunbar, *Historical Architecture*, 66–81, esp. 72.
[44] D. Howard, *Scottish Architecture from the Reformation to the Restoration 1560–1660* (The Architectural History of Scotland, Edinburgh, 1995), ch. 1.
[45] Bath, *Renaissance*, 15. T. M. Devine, *The Scottish Nation* (1999), p. xxi: 'the tower house, designed mainly for defence'.
[46] R. Samson, 'The Rise and Fall of Tower-Houses in post-Reformation Scotland', in *The Social Archaeology of Houses*, ed. R. Samson (Edinburgh, 1990), 197–243, at 224.
[47] *Scotland before 1700 from Contemporary Documents*, ed. P. Hume Brown (Edinburgh, 1893), 299.

1579 act of parliament, to seek the king's permission to receive one.[48] So far as we know, Scotland was never visited by Serlio or da Vinci (although one of Palladio's principal clients, Daniele Barbaro, was ambassador to Scotland for a few years, and Sir James Hamilton of Finnart almost certainly met da Vinci in Amboise), and no architectural treatises were translated into Scots.[49] But both English translations and Latin originals were circulating – a Serlio volume belonging to Philips Vingboons, city architect in Amsterdam in the early seventeenth century, is in the library of the Royal Incorporation of Architects in Scotland.

Moreover, Scotland had been used by France and England as both a pawn and a potential colony in the wars between them during the sixteenth century. While this brought invasion, it also brought money (in terms of bribes), cultural influence and craftsmen. Large numbers of French were domiciled in Scotland in 1538–67.[50] Far from Scotland being remote from the Renaissance cultures of Europe, it was part of them, and remained so even after French influence waned with Mary's exile in England. When King James VI made his wedding trip to Denmark in 1589/90 and visited Tycho Brahe on the Island of Ven (the only European monarch to do so), it must have come as an unpleasant shock, upon entering Brahe's palace of Uranienborg, to be faced with a portrait of his formidable tutor, George Buchanan, who had exchanged portraits with Brahe. So highly, indeed, was European travel regarded as a sign of accomplishment and breeding, that the seventeenth-century biographer Home of Godscroft felt obliged to emphasise the intellectual qualities – the knowledge of Latin and French, the understanding of triangulation – of a kinsman to excuse the inconvenient fact that he had never been to Europe.[51] The absence of European experience, it seems, was something of which to be ashamed in Renaissance Scotland, and the notion that the country was remote or isolated does not hold up.

If isolation could not explain the architecture of the Scots country seat, were nobles indeed perpetually feuding to the degree that they had to remain in defensible castles, as Kirke and Morer assumed? There had certainly been sufficient aristocratic feuding to justify James VI's 1606 'Decreet Anent Feuding', by which the king sought to end it all, but it very rarely took the form of attacking non-Highland houses during peacetime. Kill the man perhaps, but do not hurt his income, and his income derived from the estates surrounding his self-sustaining country seat.

[48] K. M. Brown, *Noble Society in Scotland: Wealth, Family and Culture from Reformation to the Revolution* (Edinburgh, 2000), 190–201; R. Johnston, *History of Scotland during the Minority of King James, Scotia Rediviva: a Collection of Tracts Illustrative of the History and Antiquities of Scotland*, ed. R. Buchanan (Edinburgh, 1836), 441.

[49] For more on Finnart, see C. McKean, 'Sir James Hamilton of Finnart – a Renaissance Courtier-Architect', *Architectural History* 42 (1999), 141–72.

[50] Both P. E. Ritchie, *Mary of Guise in Scotland 1548–60* (East Linton, 2002) and M. H. Merriman, *The Rough Wooings: Mary Queen of Scots 1542–51* (East Linton, 2000) deal with this period, although principally from a political perspective. A cultural history of the reigns of Mary Queen of Scots and Mary of Guise has yet to be written.

[51] Chambers, *Domestic Annals*, i. 120.

Figure 3. Unknown building, sometimes titled Glamis, and generally but erroneously attributed as Dalkeith. Probably a proposal for Blair, drawn by Capt. John Slezer *c.*1678. The only known representation of the multi-courtyard plan, the inner court is reached through two outer courts, and the landscape around is similarly walled. Such outer enclosures were swept into a back court in the later seventeenth century. (image taken from J. Slezer, *Theatrum Scotiae* (1693))

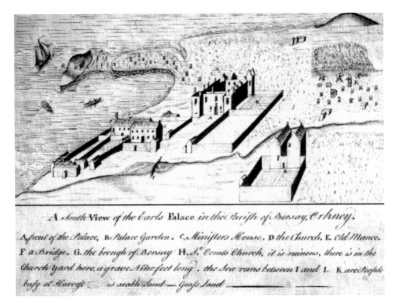

Figure 4. 'A south view of the earls [*sic*] palace in the parish of Bersay, Orkney', drawn in the late seventeenth century, showing a landscape of high walls creating microclimates for cultivation. The palace is roofless, and some of the earlier gardens, yards, butts and bowling greens that surrounded it have gone. (ORD/6/1, courtesy of the Royal Commission on the Ancient and Historical Monuments of Scotland)

The proof that these buildings were entirely metaphorical castles is demonstrated by the way in which estate activities were organised around them. Long before it was reached, the Scottish country house presented the visitor with an extensive landscape of walled enclosures between three and six metres high, for thus did the landowner control the wind and create miniature microclimates for cultivation[52] (Figures 3–4). Although they varied significantly in rank and wealth, even a fourth-rank house[53] – scarcely more than a large farm – would have had an inner court mixing higher-status chambers with service buildings like the brew house, bake house, larder, dairy, stables, barns (in which to receive the rents), a doocot (dovecote) and byres (for beasts).[54] Very rarely were these functions located within what they called 'the main house' (equivalent to the French term *corps de logis*) itself; rather, they were located in the court or – in larger establishments – the several courts that comprised the house's immediate environment. (For reasons yet to be determined, chapels were to be found far more rarely in the inner court of Scottish country seats than in their counterparts in England or Europe.)

The inner court, sometimes signified by a fountain or well of welcome, was the most important ceremonial space in a great mansion. It contained the ancestral tower (retained for reasons of filial piety, albeit often abandoned to guests or storage), the principal living quarters (the 'main house'), one or more galleries, guest accommodation, offices and household service buildings. If the gallery had the largest internal volume, it became the principal reception chamber.[55] Guest chambers were sometimes located below the gallery, as in the palace of Birsay, Orkney,[56] but more usually in a dedicated guest tower. Sometimes a library ran off the gallery overlooking the privy garden.[57] The inner court might otherwise contain the customary offices – bake house, brew house, gill house, bottle house, coal house, woman house, wine and other cellars – and a porter's lodge.[58]

The principal outer court of a larger establishment would contain the working buildings – several blocks of stables, barns and byres.[59] The privy garden would

---

[52] However, John Reid, *The Scots Gard'ner, published for the Climate of Scotland* [1683], ed. A. Hope (Edinburgh, 1988), 24, states that '4 Ells is low enough, 5 or 6 if you please' (an 'ell' being 37 inches).

[53] The suggestion of ranking in houses was first made apparent in a study of the drawings on the maps by Timothy Pont (1585–c.1608), where an obvious hierarchy is displayed (see C. McKean, 'Timothy Pont's Architectural Drawings', in *The Nation Survey'd: Timothy Pont's Maps of Scotland*, ed. I. Cunningham (East Linton, 2001)).

[54] The 1786 painting by Francis Grose of Friars' Carse, Dumfriesshire in the Riddell Collection (National Museums of Scotland) illustrates this particularly well.

[55] As in Dunnottar, by Stonehaven, Kincardineshire. W. Macfarlane, *Geographical Collections relating to Scotland*, ed. Sir A. Mitchell and J. T. Clark (3 vols, Edinburgh, 1906–8) (hereafter Macfarlane), ii. 341, iii. 233

[56] Judged by their large windows and fireplaces.

[57] As in Edzell, Saltoun and possibly Pitsligo.

[58] For more on this, see C. McKean, 'The Laird and his Guests', *Architectural Heritage* 13 (2002), 1–19.

[59] Customarily, there were three sets of stables in a larger house – court or riding stables, hunting stables and estate stables. E.g., Castle Lyon, Perthshire, had a riding stable, a hunting stable and a

customarily be set against the southern façade of the house, with the other 'yards'
upon which the household depended for food beyond.[60] The Scottish climate was
sufficiently equable to grow a surprising variety of fruit trees – even peaches,
nectarines and apricots – provided that the wind was tamed in walled orchards.[61]
Further walled enclosures included the kitchen garden (farther away), and gardens or walled enclosures for herbs, fish, vegetables, and fruit bushes like currants
and gooseberries. Tobacco was grown in the gardens at Dunrobin. In the walls
of the privy garden of his suburban villa of Pinkie, near Edinburgh, the Catholic
Stoic Lord Alexander Seton, Lord Fyvie, chancellor of the realm 1605–22, had the
following carved inscription inserted c.1600:

> D.O.M. For his own pleasure, and that of his noble descendants and all men of
> cultivation and urbanity, Alexander Seton, who above all loves every kind of cul-
> ture and urbanity, has planted, raised and decorated a country house, gardens and
> suburban buildings. There is nothing here to do with warfare; not even a ditch or
> rampart to repel enemies, but in order to welcome guests with kindness and treat
> them with benevolence, a fountain of pure water, a grove, pools and other things
> that may add to the pleasures of the place. He has brought everything together
> that might afford decent pleasures of heart and mind. But he declares that whoever
> shall destroy this by theft, sword or fire, or behaves in a hostile manner, is a man
> devoid of generosity and urbanity, indeed of all culture, and is an enemy to the
> human race.[62]

Not much about defensibility there.

Scattered throughout these walled enclosures were the gardener's house,
summer houses properly fitted up with marble tables and cane chairs,[63] hen
houses, doocots, and apple houses or garden pavilions. To judge from a court
case relating a rare attack upon a house – the invasion of the house of Hamilton
Sanquhar in 1558 – a middle-rank seat might extend to several walled orchards,
walled fishponds and four service courtyards next to the house itself, besides its
walled privy garden. After clambering laboriously over a series of walls more than
three metres high, invading soldiery armed with jack and spear would quite likely
have become mired in gooseberry bushes. The 'castle' perception of the Scottish
country seat only remains credible so long as no thought is given to it as the
centre of a working estate, and contemporary accounts are discounted.

coach stable; Panmure, Angus, had an old stable, a west stable, a coach stable, a cart horse stable
and a hunting mares stable; Kinnaird, Angus, had a hunting horse stable, a pad horse stable, a
west stable and a staigs stable; and both Glamis castle, Angus, and Floors, Roxburgh, had coach,
riding and hunting stables. (The author is indebted to Charles Wemyss for sharing his inventory
hunt.)

[60] See C. McKean, 'Galleries, Girnals and the Woman House', *Review of Scottish Culture* 11 (Edinburgh, 2003–4), 19–34.
[61] Four ells high (Reid, p. 24). For more on this, see McKean, 'Renaissance Country Seat in its Setting'.
[62] Two carved panels on the privy garden wall. This translation follows that of Bath, 99–100.
[63] Inventory of Castle Lyon c.1684 (Glamis, Glamis Papers, NRAS (S) 885 255/7/2, 16).

Furthermore, the 'castle' argument implies that a medieval living pattern persisted unchanged until 1700, as though no evolution had taken place. One can still read in contemporary scholarship that all country houses built during the Renaissance were uniformly tower-houses.[64] The evidence, however, implies that Scottish houses moved rapidly away from the medieval mode of living, in which chambers were stacked vertically above each other in the tower, to adopting the horizontal sequence of chambers known as the state apartment, following the lead of the royal palaces at Stirling, Falkland and Linlithgow early in the sixteenth century. The country house plan thereafter was organised according to the sequence of hall (or antechamber), chamber of dais (chamber) and bedchamber, on the same level.

This change from vertical to horizontal living, with its relatively novel hierarchy, privilege and privacy, meant that the original tower was either extended horizontally, or relegated to guest or service use, while a more fashionable *corps de logis* was built alongside. Unless it was later superseded by the gallery, the hall remained the most public room, and the bedchamber the most private. In the chamber between the two, the lord would sit, a canopy above the dais sometimes signifying his place of authority – hence its Scottish name, chamber of dais. In search of greater privacy, the principal floor evolved yet further in the later sixteenth century: public apartments at the centre, the bedchamber becoming a family tower to the rear, and the entrance stair tower expanding into a guest tower in the corner diagonally opposite. It mutated again in the 1590s when the family tower at the rear was relocated to the entrance façade, thus creating the typical U-plan house so much favoured by the nobles of Queen Anna's court.

One of the arguments supporting the 'defensive castle' argument was the tendency of Scottish landowners to build much higher than their English counterparts. To some extent, Scottish seats appear taller than they were partly as a consequence of the clearing away of the surrounding courts and walled gardens by eighteenth-century landscapers, and partly because the ground floor of Scottish houses contained cellars and kitchens, with the first floor being the principal. Nonetheless, given that the typical Scottish country seat might normally be up to four storeys in height, latterly capped by a viewing platform or belvedere, the culture was for higher buildings than in England, and part of the rationale may be inferred from Sir John Clerk's 1727 poem 'The country seat':

Above the Attick Floor, a Platform Roof
May be extended like a spacious Field
From whence the many pleasant Landskips round
May be with ease and with Delight survey'd …[65]

---

[64] D. Walker, 'An Historical Review', in *Restoring Scotland's Castles*, ed. R. Clow (Glasgow, 2000), 1.
[65] Sir J. Clerk, *The Country Seat* (National Archives of Scotland (hereafter NAS), GD18/ 4404/I, unpublished). The author is grateful to Sir Robert Clerk and James Simpson for this reference.

That was probably a *post hoc* rationalisation – the real agenda was one of display.[66] But this was more than display for its own sake; it was a display of rank, and appears, from the minute elevations on the maps prepared by Timothy Pont between 1585 and 1608, to have been carefully calculated.[67] In 1656, the English army captain Richard Franck reacted to the marquess of Huntly's principal seat of Bog o' Gight (later Gordon castle) exactly as expected:

> Bogagieth, the Marquess of Huntly's palace, all built with stone facing the ocean; whose fair front (set prejudice aside) worthily deserves an English man's applause for her lofty and majestick towers and turrets, that storm the air; … It struck me with admiration, to gaze on so gawdy and regular a frontispiece, more especially when to consider it is in the nook of a nation.[68]

The belief that height conveyed rank persisted into the nineteenth century. When redesigning Taymouth castle for the marquess of Breadalbane, to compete with the principal Campbell seat of Inveraray in 1806, the architect James Elliot argued for a soaring central tower on the grounds that height remained a principal signifier of nobility.[69]

A group of early seventeenth-century houses in Aberdeenshire, known as the Bell group after the family that most likely designed them, took the idea to almost an absurd degree.[70] Three further storeys were added to the top of a three- or four-storeyed tower (see Figure 1). Current research is showing that these houses, contained mostly within a twenty-eight-mile circle in north-western Aberdeenshire, are exceptional even within their own region, never mind the rest of the country. Other houses in the region are of normal height for Scotland, showing that there was no regional defensive necessity to retreat on high. The architectural impulse of the Bell group appears to have been entirely cultural. Landowner and architect decided to relocate some of the principal functions of the inner court – such as the gallery and guest lodgings – to the very heights, from which there was ready access to a belvedere on the seventh floor. The intention, as John Macky observed in 1727, was for 'the many turrets and gilded balustrades' to strike the visitor with awe and admiration – as indeed Glamis did for him (see Figure 10).[71] As Burke suggests, 'a central role in the process of innovation is often played not so much by individuals as by groups or "circles", especially if they compete

[66] M. Davis, 'Was there an Architectural School in North-East Scotland in the early 17th century?' (in progress).
[67] Manuscript maps held in the National Library of Scotland (hereafter NLS) (see Cunningham, *Nation Survey'd*).
[68] R. Franck, *Northern Memoirs*, ed. Sir W. Scott (Edinburgh, 1821), 221–2.
[69] James Elliot (NAS, Breadalbane MSS, GDII2/20, box 4).
[70] Named after a group of 14–22 country houses putatively attributed to mason/architects John, George and David Bel (M. Davis, 'The Bel Family and their Renaissance Tall Houses', *Architectural Heritage* 16 (2005), 1–13).
[71] Quoted in F. Grose, *The Antiquities of Scotland* (2 vols, 1797), ii. 87.

with others', and that appears to have been the case in early seventeenth-century north-east Scotland.[72]

If Scotland had been stuffed with recognisably Renaissance classical architecture, the 'Albanian' perception would never have arisen: but it is not. Moreover, any attempt to reassess the period, and to understand the rationale behind its unusual architecture, is hindered by the lack of known manuscripts or architectural drawings. They may yet exist, for, as a consequence of centuries of Renaissance denial, research into Scottish Renaissance cultural history remains in its infancy. Architectural drawings – even for interiors – are referred to frequently in documents,[73] but most have vanished or remain to be rediscovered.[74] Many records were destroyed or dispersed as a result of the 1715 and 1745 rebellions, and many more once Scottish families married south. More weight has to be placed, therefore, upon a reinterpretation of the buildings themselves, supported by evidence from inventories, and by the drawings on Timothy Pont's maps.[75]

It is difficult to establish a relative cultural level for Scottish architecture during the Renaissance in the face of its refusal to adopt classicism, and the lack of any contemporary manuscripts to explain why. One assumption used to be that Scotland was in a time-warp waiting, as Sir Howard Colvin put it, for an architect with knowledge of the classical language to emerge in the later seventeenth century to 'design unfortified houses for the first generation of Scottish lairds to realise that the tower house was an anachronism, and to persuade them to abandon corbel and crow-step in favour of cornice and pediment'.[76] Subsequent research has shown that Scotland's *chantier particulier* cannot be explained by cultural anachronism. Yet, if Scotland shared so much else with France during the sixteenth century, why did it diverge in its attitude to classical architecture? Classics – that is, volumes of Latin, Greek and translated poetry, philosophy and history, as well as volumes on religion from throughout Europe – dominated Scottish libraries, and their influence was pervasive.[77] The celebrations for the baptism of Prince Henry were entirely informed by classical allusion.[78] Moreover, Stoicism was adopted by two such different cultural leaders as the sternly Presbyterian George Buchanan and the staunchly Catholic Chancellor Seton. So the Scots were very far from rejecting classical ideals – only its architecture.

Deborah Howard has argued that this cultural choice derived from the Scots' perception of themselves.[79] As a consequence of at least a century of the periodic

---

[72] Burke, *European Renaissance*, 10.
[73] K. Newland, 'The Constructions of Panmure House 1666–85' (M.Phil. research, University of Dundee). See, in particular, NAS, GD 45/18.566, fo. 1.
[74] For a closer discussion of this, see McKean, *Scottish Château*, appendix.
[75] Manuscript maps held in the NLS (see Cunningham, *Nation Survey'd*).
[76] H. Colvin, 'The Beginnings of the Architectural Profession in Scotland', *Architectural History* 29 (1986), 168–82, at 173–4.
[77] See, e.g., D. Shaw, 'Adam Bothwell, a Conservator of the Renaissance in Scotland', in *Renaissance and Reformation*, 141–70.
[78] Johnston, *History of Scotland*, 480–91.
[79] See Howard, *Scottish Architecture*, esp. the final chapter.

humiliation of being a plaything between England and France, they were driven to express their sense of national individuality in architecture; and that impulse suited the way in which the Scots elite liked to express its veneration for ancestors. Thus, when reformatting his house of Glamis into the most Scottish 'great house' of them all in the 1670s, the earl of Strathmore admitted to being 'inflam'd stronglie with a great desyre to continue the memorie of my familie'.[80] As much apparent in the architecture of royal palaces and churches as in the country seat, the consequence was the predilection to adapt ancient forms and motifs to present use.[81] This intriguing argument, however, cannot be the entire explanation, since Scottish architecture also appears to have changed sharply along with the monarch, suggesting that political allegiance was just as significant.

One intriguing reason for Scotland's attitude to classical architecture is that it might have been identified too closely with Catholicism and, in particular, with the resurgent Catholicism after the Council of Trent. George Buchanan's exile in Portugal had coincided with the construction of some of its most beautiful early classical churches and abbeys, such as João de Castilho's Christ's Convent at Tomar (1530–54), and, since Buchanan taught in Coimbra, he would surely have known the delightful 1553 Fonte da Manga by João de Ruão in the garden of Coimbra's Convent of Santa Cruz. Mary Queen of Scots had worshipped in Philibert de l'Orme's chapel at Anet, which was 'modernism' at its most refined. Burke observed that Erasmus suspected classicism as being an expression of paganism,[82] and it seems quite possible that George Buchanan and John Knox regarded classical architecture as symbolic of an infection that had to be kept from their shores.

Newly constructed buildings, particularly churches, offered the greatest opportunity for classical expression, and the reformers believed that decorative and representational motifs should be abolished to permit the clear light of God to enter the building unimpeded. Yet, although the plan of Scottish reformed kirks achieved that objective,[83] the expression remained either Scottish or astylar until the use of classical architecture for reformed churches had been validated by fellow reformers in Holland. There was a distinct reluctance to use classical architecture. That was also the case for the substantial number of Scots aristocrats who remained Catholic long after the Reformation. The greatest of them – the earl (later marquess) of Huntly and the chancellor, Alexander Seton – showed no inclination overtly to structure the rebuilding of their houses according to a classical discipline, even though they made prolific use of both Catholic and

---

[80] Patrick, 1st earl of Strathmore, *The Book of Record: a Diary Written by Patrick, 1st earl of Strathmore, and Other Documents Relating to Glamis Castle, 1684–89* (hereafter Glamis Book of Record), ed. A. H. Millar (Edinburgh, 1890), 19.

[81] I. Campbell, 'A Romanesque Revival and the Early Renaissance in Scotland c.1380–1513', *Journal of the Society of Architectural Historians*, 54 (1994), 302–25; and I. Campbell, 'Tinlithgow's Princely Palace and its influence in Europe', *Architectural Heritage*, 5 (1994), 1–20.

[82] Burke, *European Renaissance*, 83–4.

[83] E.g., Burntisland, and the Tron and the Canongate kirks in Edinburgh.

Renaissance ideas in their interiors. They were compelled, of course, to make public proclamation of their adherence to the reformed church: 'many who were solely addicted to the Romish religion, yet being seazed on by fear of losing their estates, did not only swear to the Protestant religion, but also confirmed the same by subscription'.[84] So whatever they did would have to be, as it were, internalised. But rather than using classical architecture, they appeared to go into reverse. The flamboyantly medieval vaulted interiors inserted into a group of houses in north-east Scotland, which are closely associated with the Counter Reformation,[85] imply that the Scottish Catholic response to the post-Trent confidence might have been a striking reassertion of a genuine medievalism, harking back to the time when Catholicism had been the nation's accepted religion. Because this was imperceptible from the outside, the state itself could rest undisturbed. Although it remains open, therefore, whether classical architectural expression was rejected for unwelcome religious associations, the evidence before c.1640 tends in that direction.

It would be tempting to believe that Scottish architecture of the Renaissance period was the organic expression of function with the sporadic adornment of eclectic ornament. Yet, given the care and discipline with which the interiors were planned, that seems unlikely. The question arises, therefore, whether there might have been a different – non-classical – discipline underlying the design of these buildings. There is evidence of houses and churches constructed with strong inherent geometrical proportions dissimulated behind an expressively picturesque façade. Rather than function being constrained by *a priori* concepts of symmetry, these houses contain sequences of very controlled spaces organised in a loose manner appropriate to their function. The symmetrical geometrical precision of the gallery floor at Crathes, with its projecting rectangular studies, for example, is utterly concealed by a wayward façade. The proportions of 1:3.5 of the interior of King's College chapel, Aberdeen, are (like the chapel at Stirling) those of the Temple of Solomon, and its interior is divided into four equal cubes. None of that is discernible from the exterior.[86]

There are chambers in variations of squares and cubes, and façades designed to Fibunacci proportions or even, like that of Innes, to a mathematical progression,[87] with proportions often very complex and carefully contrived,[88] as though the designers were working with 'remembered spaces' from their knowledge base.

---

[84] Johnston, 372.
[85] E.g., Craig, Towie Barclay, Delgatie, Gight, the 'Wine Tower' at Fraserburgh, and perhaps even the 'summer house' in the privy garden at Edzell (see I. B. D. Bryce and A. Roberts, 'Post-Reformation Catholic Houses of north-east Scotland', *Proceedings of the Society of Antiquaries of Scotland* 123 (1993), 363–72).
[86] *King's College Chapel, Aberdeen*, ed. J. Geddes (Aberdeen, 2003). For a discussion on proportions, see A. MacKechnie, 'Geometria', *Arca*, 5 (2002), 10–13.
[87] See C. McKean, 'The Architectural Evolution of the Innes House', *Proceedings of the Society of Antiquaries of Scotland* 133 (2004), 315–42.
[88] During his restoration of Melgund, Angus, the architect Ben Tindall discovered a most impressive geometric formula governing the proportions of the rooms added by Cardinal Beaton for

That implies that there might have been an underlying geometrical discipline, possibly based upon the Art of Memory, that provided the underlying rigour to the design of these buildings;[89] an idea supported by the portrait of the architect John Mylne (d. 1657). Whereas one might have expected to see the works of Serlio or Palladio on the library shelves behind him, the titles on display are works of Archimedes, Polonius and Euclid. As Howard has pointed out, there were other expressions of classical culture than the use of the classical Orders;[90] and the curious tension between reason (geometry) and romance (the deliberately asymmetrical façade) in Scottish Renaissance architecture has yet to be adequately explained.

The architectural expression was, therefore, distinctively and deliberately Scottish, but what governed its use? Almost certainly it was rank. Scottish landowners, particularly those of the first rank, would have been perversely delighted that their ancient seats were being taken for castles, for it enhanced their sense of lineage. From the letter that Sir Robert Kerr wrote in 1632 to his son, the earl of Ancram, cautioning against removing the battlements, 'for that is the grace of the house, and makes it look like a castle, and hence so noblest',[91] it is obvious that the title 'castle' signalled rank and precedence. The custom had developed of nobles replacing the original Scottish territorial title of their ancient paternal seat with a more imposing family patronym. The house of Strathbogie, seat of the earl, later marquess of Huntly, for example, became Huntly castle (Figure 5); the house of Gloom became Castle Campbell for the earl of Argyle; Drumminor became Castle Forbes; Bog o' Gight became Castle Gordon; Muchall became Castle Fraser; Freuchie became Castle Grant; and Pettie became Castle Stewart. Even when Clanranald refashioned his country seat in South Uist in 1701–3, for his new wife, daughter of the governor of Tangiers (who had said of the original house that her father's hens were better housed),[92] he called his mansion Ormiclate castle – although, to be in keeping with his peers, it should really have been Clanranald castle. The habit persisted even into the early nineteenth century, when Sir Evan Murray Macgregor retitled his house of Lanrick, near Doune, as Gregor or Clan Gregor castle, and had it refashioned to match in the baronial manner by James Gillespie Graham.

Scottish Renaissance country seats were far from homogeneous.[93] Pont's minute elevations imply that hierarchy was expressed through differences in

Margaret Ogilvie c.1542 (B. Tindall, 'Proportions Matter', *Architectural Heritage Society of Scotland* (AHSS) *Magazine* 15 (1997), 7).
[89] D. Stevenson, *The Origins of Freemasonry: Scotland's Century, 1590–1710* (Cambridge, 1990), 87–96.
[90] Howard, 2.
[91] *Correspondence of Sir Robert Kerr, 1st earl of Ancram and his son William, 3rd earl of Lothian*, ed. D. Laing (2 vols, Edinburgh, 1875), i. 64.
[92] The author is indebted to Mary Miers for this information.
[93] There were something like 5,000–7,000 country seats of all ranks during the Renaissance, calculated by selecting random parishes from MacFarlane, comparing the seats listed therein to those that survive now, and extrapolating.

Figure 5. The palace of Huntly,
Aberdeenshire (author). The *tour
maîtresse*, or bedroom tower,
dominates on the left.

scale, function and elaboration. There was an enormous difference between the
'ancient paternal seat' of an aristocrat and the dwelling of a fourth-rank, minor
landowner, but, rather like the eighteenth-century London Building Acts, an
architectural language of finials, chimney stacks, turrets, dormer windows,
corbelling and belvederes cascaded down from rank to rank, understood like
semaphore by all those who surveyed it. All ranks might share a basic language
of turrets and crow-steps, but the lower the rank, the fewer the storeys and the
plainer the skyline. A seat of the first rank is indicated by full heraldic panoply
and a height sometimes rising to seven storeys, as in the earl of Crawford's house
of Finaven, Angus, whereas a fourth-rank house is delineated by barely more
than a modest two-storeyed dwelling with 'outshots'.

Just as the seats differed in rank, they differed in purpose. A landowner of
high rank would hold several properties, each with a different function in his life.
The most symbolic was the 'ancient paternal seat' (the ancient seat of my fathers,
as Lord Strathmore put it),[94] which performed a comparable role to the great

[94] Strathmore, *Book of Record*, 37.

circular *donjon* in French châteaux: it was the guardian and representation of lineage. This motivation appears extraordinarily powerful, for it also explains why the ancestral tower was retained at the heart of many courts of lesser rank, long after it had fallen out of use. The ancient paternal seat might have had the most elaborate embellishment, but it might no longer have remained the preferred residence. The ancient paternal seat of the Maxwells was their great triangular castle of Caerlaverock, to which they added a fine Renaissance wing in the early seventeenth century. But they rarely seem to have lived there, preferring the now vanished courtyard palace of Terregles.[95] In like manner, the Ogilvies of Airlie retained Airlie castle, but lived in the fashionable mid-sixteenth-century house of Cortachy, which they bought from a neighbour. Most striking of all, the earls of Huntly might have embellished Huntly castle and broadcast it as their seat of power, but from the 1580s, they much preferred to reside further north, in their house of Bog o' Gight, whose height and skyline so overawed its visitors. The reasons for moving appear to be the same. The original site, which might have been genuinely defensive, was no longer desirable – perhaps constrained by rivers, cliffs, moats and remoteness – and could not offer the spacious Renaissance layout, gardens and parks for which the nobles wished; or perhaps the immediate site offered inadequate space in which to construct a 'main house' in the new fashion.

Rank was also expressed through the number of properties that one owned. The earl of Huntly, for example, had principal seats at Bog (near Fochabers), Strathbogie, Ruthven in Badenoch, a splendid towered house on the castle site in Inverness, and a great mansion in Fortrose. He had town houses in Aberdeen and in Edinburgh, at least one hunting lodge at Blairfindy, and maintained the house of Melgund, in Angus, as a 'travelling house' or stopping point between Aberdeenshire and Edinburgh. The earl of Strathmore maintained Castle Huntly as a summer house, near to the River Tay, whereas his principal residence was in Glamis. Other noblemen had seaside villas, fishing pavilions, even a house for the heir (*tanist* in Gaelic) before he came into his inheritance.[96] Hunting or fishing lodges can be identified from their plan; like Huntly's Blairfindy, they were characteristically tall and narrow, with an enormous kitchen but few cellars, a large hall but few bedchambers. The implication is that cellars were not needed since the food was being caught; the large hall implies wide hospitality, but chambers were not needed since most of the throng would be living under canvas.

Even a lesser noble – a third son like Chancellor Seton – had several houses. His first act was to buy Fyvie, Aberdeenshire, and transform it into an ancient

[95] There is a painting of old Terregles in the Robert Riddell Collection in the National Museums of Scotland.
[96] Castle Stewart was the seaside pavilion of the earl of Moray at Darnaway, and Muchalls that of the Burnetts of Leys at Crathes. Gylen, on the island of Kerrera, was the fishing pavilion of the MacDougalls of Lorne. Greenknowe, in the Borders, was probably a hunting seat of the Setons of Touch. Pittulie was the house of the heir of Sir Alexander Fraser of Philorth, Sydserf of Sydserf of that ilk (who now lived at Ruchlaw), and Gagie that of the Guthries of that ilk.

paternal seat for himself and his heirs. He had it decorated in an appropriately bombastic manner (although, to judge from an eighteenth-century sketch by Robert Adam, it was not quite as flamboyant as it is now). He had a town house in nearby Elgin, whereas his seat of power was the suburban villa of Pinkie, near Edinburgh. His private family home, however, was at Dalgety, across the Forth. A fourth-rank landowner, however, would probably have had no more than his original house and its estate until he married into others.

If that provides an adequate interpretation of Scottish architectural culture during the Renaissance, it is nonetheless observable that the architectural expression of the Scottish country seat changed abruptly several times – and that those alterations coincided with regime change. Nowhere was this more striking than around the thirty-year period – 1538–68 – when Scotland teetered on the brink of becoming a colony of France. Although the Reformation in 1560 has customarily been used as a convenient point of architectural change, it is not discernible in the architecture of the country seat.[97] So far as country houses are concerned, 1560 represents an artificial break during the reign of Mary I.

The 1517 Treaty of Rouen had provided that King James V should marry a French princess, but under the direction of the king's cousin, Sir James Hamilton of Finnart, Scottish architecture appeared, rather, to be influenced by Italian examples, both at the palace of Stirling and in his own villa of Craignethan, Lanarkshire. The exceptions were the new royal lodging at Holyrood in 1529, perhaps inspired by Vincennes; and the reformatting of Falkland for the king's two French queens – the short-lived Madeleine de Valois, followed by Marie de Guise in 1538. Marie brought some of her father's craftsmen to recast the courtyard façade of the south wing, possibly in emulation of the Château du Grand Jardin, the garden pavilion of her family home of Joinville.[98] From the death of her husband in 1542 until 1568, the queen dowager, and then her daughter Mary I Queen of Scots – two French-educated women with large, mostly French, households – presided over the culture of the country. Mary I was affianced to the French dauphin, then married to a French king, and Scotland seemed destined to be a French colony. This development led to equally extreme Francophilia and Francophobia in the mid-1550s. The blind poet Sir Richard Maitland observed wryly that:

> Thair gluvis perfumit in thair hand
> Helpis meikil thair contenance,
> *Et tout est a la mode de France.*[99]

Parliament may have had to pass penal acts to stem the attacks by Scots on French soldiers in the streets, but in architecture there was no contest.

---

[97] It is the divide between the two volumes in the *Architectural History of Scotland* series, and is used as a principal division in M. Glendinning, R. MacInnes and A. MacKechnie, *A History of Scottish Architecture from the Renaissance to the Present Day* (Edinburgh, 1996).

[98] The author is grateful to Michael Pearce for this observation.

[99] *Maitland Quarto Manuscripts*, ed. W. A. C. Craigie (Edinburgh, 1920), 229. Author's emphasis.

Marie de Guise had made an extended trip to France in 1550, accompanied by her most significant nobility, and they visited Joinville, Chateaudun and Nancy as well as Paris. On their return, Bishop Lesley recorded how Scotland set about modernising itself: 'The haill realme of Scotland being this maner in quyetnes, everye man addrest him selfe to policie, and to big, plant and pleneise those rowmes quhilkis throch the trublis of the warns, be Inglismen or utheris had been wasted brint, spulyeit or distroyit.'[100] The Scots appear to have been much taken by the symbolism of the circular French *donjon*, that powerful expression of French lineal antiquity, and it is probably during this period that Scottish country houses began to sport the characteristic pepperpot studies or turrets, and to adopt the plan, of the Loire châteaux. Probably beginning with Huntly in 1553, the motif of the circular tower – as *tour maîtresse* – was added to existing houses as the expression of the final chamber in the state apartment sequence, that is, the bedchamber (see Figure 5). A tower of this kind was added by Robert Reid to his palace at Kirkwall, and by the earl of Atholl to his fortress at Balvenie. Once her French royal husband was dead, and Mary Queen of Scots returned to Scotland, a minor variant of this plan became *de rigueur* for many smaller houses. What is distinctive, however, is that the Scots were adapting French architectural ideas of the previous generation, that of Francis I, rather than the classical ways of Sebastiano Serlio, who had arrived in France eight years before the Scots embassy.

Given the embryonic Italianate nature of much of James V's architecture, it is likely that Scottish architecture was diverted from its natural evolution by its French period 1538–68, and by the subsequent backlash against it.[101] During the military posturing between Mary of Guise, the queen regent, and the lords of the congregation in 1559, it appears that the latter went out of their way to despoil Falkland palace, upon which the Guise craftsmen had worked so carefully.[102] It seems fair to deduce that they vented their wrath on the most obviously French building within reach. Once Mary Queen of Scots had been exiled to England in 1568, evidently Francophile buildings that appeared to proclaim loyalty to the disgraced regime could be politically dangerous. Even after 1572, when the civil war between what was called the French (queen's) faction and the Scottish (young king's) faction was over, the country remained uneasily divided between the two. Yet, this was a period of extensive construction:

While domestick dissentions took a little rest, the vice-roy Morton began to caste an eye upon the publicke, fortifying castles … the beautifying of the

---

[100] J. Lesley, *The History of Scotland* (Edinburgh, 1830), 243.
[101] The term 'Marian', used to categorise country seats of the period 1538–68, has been borrowed from political history where it was used only to refer to Mary Queen of Scots and her adherents, to cover the period when the culture of Scotland was led by two French-educated queens, specifically between 1550 and 1568. Mary of Guise came to Scotland in 1538, and her daughter finally lost control of her kingdom in 1568. In the 1550s, Mary of Guise's predilection for French advisers was one of the reasons adduced by the lords of the congregation for their rebellion.
[102] Current research being undertaken by Michael Pearce.

Figure 6. Claypotts, Dundee (author). The clumsiness with which the original caps of the towers have been replaced by the rectangular studies *c.*1588 implies that a very public point was being made.

kingdome with inward and outward ornaments of market places, regall structures, palaces, courts, finishing with majesticall magnificence his building at Dalkeith.[103]

Existing houses of politically astute Scots were adapted at this time in a very distinctive manner. The tops of their romantic round towers were decapitated, and a rectangular or square room or study superimposed instead. The regent himself, Morton, may have led the way at his house of Drochil, Peeblesshire, and others followed. Sometimes, the junction between the circular tower and the new square study on top was executed with a crudity that implies that a public recantation was being offered[104] (Figure 6).

This seems the most appropriate explanation of how the Loirean vertical exuberance and romanticism of the Marian period came to be replaced, during this time of enormous construction, with the much more sedate horizontally proportioned architecture of James VI's minority. Significantly, the symbolic circular bedroom tower of the Marian era, erected in emulation of the French symbol of medieval lineage, was replaced by a rectangular tower, erected in emulation of the Scottish symbol of medieval lineage. These chunky houses are frequently used to

[103] Johnston, *History of Scotland*, 396.
[104] See, e.g., Claypotts, Dundee, and Newton, Blairgowrie.

Figure 7. The House of Weem, Menzies, Perthshire, recast as Castle Menzies for the
Menzies family in 1584. The entrance/guest tower lies to the left, and the family tower to
the right, with the *corps de logis* between. (PT/1035, Crown Copyright, courtesy of the
Royal Commission on the Ancient and Historical Monuments of Scotland)

characterize Scottish Renaissance architecture, but they represented only its most
internalised phase (Figure 7).

James VI assumed power in 1585, and then married Anna of Denmark, sister of
the architectural patron Christian IV, in 1589–90. Scottish architecture shifted in
response to the queen, who was a friend and patron of architects, and cultivated a
new court architecture. The villas of her courtiers were characteristically U-plan
and horizontal in proportion, even though they remained quite deliberately
asymmetrical and, by English standards, flamboyant. There are distinct similarities between miniature Scottish villas of this period and the great Danish castles
such as Frederiksborg or Rosenberg. No ancient paternal seat was created entirely
in the form of the later Jacobean villa, although a new wing might sometimes
take that style.[105] Architecture, however, was still used to express politics – once
James VI quit Edinburgh for London, a motto carved in stone or plaster began to
appear everywhere: '106 kings have left us this unconquered.' The implication was

[105] E.g., at Cowdenknowes and at Crathes.

Figure 8. Wrichtishousis, Edinburgh, villa of the Napier family, demolished 1800 (conjectural reconstruction by the author based upon drawings by Alexander Nasmyth and others). A gallery separates the family wing (left) from the public/guest wing on the right.

that the Scots were as unwilling to permit themselves to be conquered through a reverse political takeover as they had been by force of arms.

The largely Catholic north-east Scotland, dominated by the marquess of Huntly, felt alienated from Edinburgh, never mind London; and the 'tall houses' of that region may be interpreted as expressing a more extreme form of national self-consciousness. Architectural motifs retrieved from, predominantly, the Marian period were transformed into something even more flamboyant for new purposes – hence the Bell group of houses (see Figure 1). That such construction was a matter of choice is emphasised by those who took a different architectural route. The Protestant humanist Alexander Irvine of Drum, patron of newly founded Marischal College (university) in Aberdeen, had a different perspective, although we can surmise from details that he probably deployed the same architect – John Bell – as his neighbours and peers.[106] Instead of increasing the height of his ancient tower, he opted to add a new, low-slung, U-plan wing to Drum, approximately in the form of a Lowland villa (see Figure 8). It was as strong a means of proclaiming a different sort of politics as building seven storeys into the clouds.

[106] To judge by the characteristic square or 'label' corbel used in his staircases.

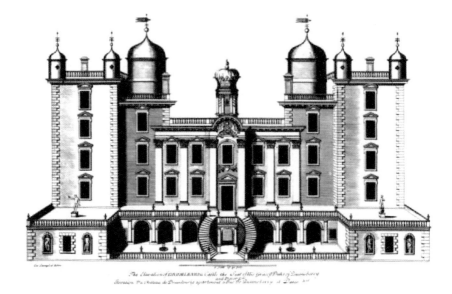

Figure 9. Drumlanrig, Dumfriesshire, possibly the most glorious exemplar of late
seventeenth-century Scottish architecture, designed by James Smith. (DFD/58/6,
courtesy of the Royal Commission on the Ancient and Historical Monuments
of Scotland)

Far less changed in Scottish architecture during the civil wars and Interregnum
period than had previously been surmised, and contrary to the suggestions of
Glendinning and MacKechnie, Scottish architectural history exhibits thereafter
much more continuity than disruption.[107] The accepted view, that 'the most obvious break with the past was the full establishment in Scotland [after 1660] of a
"mainstream" European classicism, stemming ultimately from the Italian Renaissance', is not borne out by the evidence.[108] Very few classical houses indeed were
built between 1660 and 1690, when so much construction was taking place,[109] and
the handful of such houses that can be identified – pre-eminently Kinross house,
built by James Smith and Sir Will Bruce for Bruce himself – were for new money
(that is, for those without an ancestral seat, as was also the case in France), and
– unsurprisingly, given Bruce's career in Holland – based upon Dutch models.[110]

---

[107] Glendinning and Mackechnie, *Scottish Architecture*, 217.
[108] Glendinning, MacInnes and MacKechnie, 72.
[109] C. Wemyss, 'Some aspects of Scottish Country House Construction in the Post-Restoration Period: Patrick Smyth and the Building of Methven Castle 1678–81' (Unpublished M.Phil. Thesis,
University of Dundee, 2002).
[110] See C. Wemyss, 'Merchant and Citizen of Rotterdam, Tax Collector: the Early Career of Sir
William Bruce', *Architectural Heritage* 16 (2005), 14–30. Kinross house, right down to its use of
Scamozzi orders and echoes of Amsterdam town hall, is entirely Dutch in inspiration (K. A.
Ottenheym, 'Dutch Contributions to the Classicist Tradition in Northern Europe in the 17th
century: Patrons, Architects and Books', *Scandinavian Journal of History* 28 (2003), 227–42).

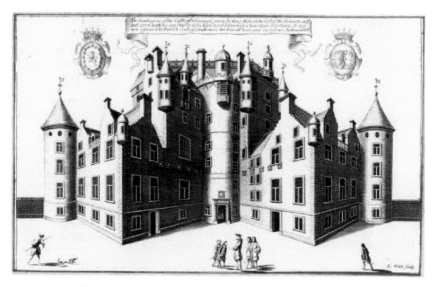

Figure 10. South elevation of Glamis, drawn c.1678 by Capt. John Slezer, and engraved in 1684. The house was not built entirely to this design. The wing on the left (west) was capped not by gables but by a flat, balustraded viewing platform of leads. (AND 20/58, courtesy of the countess of Strathmore)

Any analysis founded upon the assumption of the inevitable triumph of classicism in architecture fails to understand the burst of triumphal Scottish baroque that was taking place, led by the members of the treasury committee.

The treasury committee, consisting of key members of James, duke of York's 'court' at Holyrood, were a reincarnation of the modernisers – the Octavian – of James VI's reign, and their flamboyant seats were composed from the Scottish details and motifs of the previous two centuries used in an entirely new manner. The principal country seats erected between 1660 and 1690 (always maintaining relative rank) represent the apogee of an indigenous Scottish architecture. The main functional changes lay in the creation of parallel state and private apartments, usually on separate floors, and the relegation of the service buildings from the front courts out of sight in a new back court.[111] The axis of entry consequently moved from the rear of the building to what had earlier been the garden front, which was now aggrandised into an entrance façade, customarily framed by circular corner towers (possibly in emulation of Holyrood palace), either inherited, or made to seem so, and significantly called 'bastions'.[112] Rectangular towers, possibly the result of a need to adapt existing ones, framed some of the greatest houses, notably Hamilton palace, Panmure, Kinneil and Drumlanrig (Figure 9).

---

[111] McKean, 'Renaissance Country Seat'.
[112] Newland, 'The Construction of Panmure House 1666–86' (Postgraduate Research in Progress, University of Dundee). Circular corner towers frame or framed Brechin, Methven, Kinnaird, Dudhope, Tarbat, Tyrie, Boyndlie and many others.

Figure 11. Eastern view of the House of Hatton, Midlothian (demolished) in the later
nineteenth century. In the 1670s, it was refashioned by Charles Maitland, Lord Hatton,
into the new Scottish baroque: the addition of circular flanking 'bastions', and the cutting
down of the ancestral tower to provide a belvedere (author).

They all presented a perfectly balanced entrance façade capped by the characteristically flamboyant skyline of reinterpreted turrets, finials, heraldic motifs, turrets and belvederes. The desire to celebrate, rather than to diminish, 'Scottishness'
remained even in buildings that were modernised in the continental manner. A
house might be given a new orientation, regular fenestration and strong cornice
on one façade, as in Gardyne, Angus, while retaining its original entrance façade,
complete with towers, crow-steps and studies. The most striking example of this
Janus-like attitude to change was Hamilton palace, where James Smith added
a stupendous classical portico to the west façade of the gallery wing as a new
entry, leaving unscathed the twin-towered, dormer-windowed, high-chimneyed
Renaissance façade on the other side. It might have been cheaper to rebuild the
entire thing.

Only at Glamis, Angus, does there appear to have been intent to recreate the
architecture of a particular period of Scottish history. When Patrick, earl of King-
horne was reformatting his seat, he did not regularise it like the others, but built
most extraordinarily upon the work of his grandfather to create a design that
appeared to epitomise the French period. (Even then, practicality required that
he depart from balance to create a flat viewing platform on one side that offered
'great service to those of us who live on this side of the house'.[113]) Whatever its

---

[113] Strathmore, *Book of Record*, 38.

martial panoply, Strathmore intended that nobody should mistake his heraldic house for a castle: "There is no man more against these old fashion of tours and castles then I am."[114] To interpret this vivid and dynamic period of Scottish architectural history as a withering of the native tradition, or, as Charles Rennie Mackintosh put it, 'a mix up between Scottish Baronial & debased Elezibethan [*sic*] Italian Renaissence',[115] is fundamentally to misunderstand it (Figure 11).

The Scottish problem with castles, therefore, lies in the dichotomy between Scottish landowners seeking the nobility that the title and martial appearance of a castle might provide, and the cultural interpretations that have stemmed from it. This article has sought to demonstrate that Scottish Renaissance architecture was not the consequence of ignorance, poverty or warfare, but a deliberate cultural choice made in the full knowledge of what was being built elsewhere. That being so, it has attempted to explain how the culture of Scottish architecture during the Renaissance became misunderstood, and why, to some degree, that remains the case; and that much of the misunderstanding has arisen from the difficulty of interpreting Scotland's Renaissance culture within a British rather than a European context. Viewed within a European framework, and against the particular evolution of Scottish history between 1500 and 1700, it becomes much more comprehensible. Expressions of individuality, lineage, rank and political affiliation – tempered by both romance and nostalgia – provided an architecture much more attractive to Scottish aristocrats than the calm homogenisations of classicism.

---

[114] The *Glamis Book of Record*, quoted in A. H. Millar, *The Historical Castles and Mansions of Scotland* (Paisley, 1890), 227.
[115] C. R. Mackintosh, *The Architectural Papers*, ed. P. Robertson (Wendlebury, 1990), 63.

9

Structural Symbolism in Medieval Castle Architecture

Charles Coulson

This article is offered in the hope of assisting a juster understanding of so-called licences to crenellate as a source for the archaeologist and the architectural historian. It seeks to indicate their proper context and to relate them to their counterparts in medieval France. The social significance of seignorial authorisation to fortify has not hitherto received the attention it merits. The wider implications for architectural symbolism in general will, it is hoped, be of interest to scholars working in other fields.[1]

The medieval fortress of the castle age proper, namely the period from the twelfth to the later fifteenth century, when masonry structures were the dominant element in the fortification of Western Europe, was, in its way, as intentionally evocative and symbolic as any late eighteenth- and nineteenth-century castellated mansion of the Romantic Revival.[2] Accommodation that was sometimes truly palatial but always in some degree noble was the everyday purpose.[3] Although

---

[1] J. H. Parker, 'Houses of the Middle Ages', *Gentleman's Magazine*, new series (1856), 207–15, 323–30, 467–75, published a very faulty and incomplete list of licences to crenellate, which was later reprinted with some corrections in T. H. Turner and J. H. Parker, *Some Account of Domestic Architecture in England* (Oxford, 1851–9), III, 401–22. Parker was aware of their potential value for dating existing buildings but the issues he proposed for discussion have largely been ignored. H. Godwin, *The English Archaeologist's Handbook* (Oxford, 1867), 233–51, rearranged this list alphabetically. His text is replete with additional errors, but he was aware that in England the Crown had no monopoly of licensing. W. Mackay Mackenzie, *The Medieval Castle in Scotland* (London, 1927), 215–29, discusses 'licences to build a tower or fortalice' with a saneness of approach that resists the frequent tendency to regard authorisation as a special and reluctant royal concession, jealously restricted for fear of anarchy (see e.g. A. Hamilton Thompson, *Military Architecture in England during the Middle Ages* (Oxford, 1912), 89–90; and for an extreme example in popular vein, E. B. D'Auvergne, *The English Castles* (London, 1907), 17–19). The texts of English royal licences as a whole show how incongruous these ideas are, at least for the period after *c*.1200. A manuscript is in progress of a list 'Royal English Licences to Crenellate, 1200 to 1547', and a parallel list of French licences issued by the Crown and by subordinate magnates, necessarily incomplete, see C. L. H. Coulson, 'Seignorial Fortresses in France in Relation to Public Policy *c*.864 to *c*.1483' (unpublished doctoral thesis, University of London, 1972), Appendix B. An outline of supporting references and a minimum of secondary quotation only are included in this article.
[2] At Warwick Castle Guy's and Caesar's Towers are splendid examples of studied indifference to the danger of 'villainous salt-petre' (Henry IV, Pt I, I, iii, line 60, a true reflection by Shakespeare of chivalric nostalgia in his own day).
[3] Domestic determinants in castle ground-plans have generally been underestimated. The ideal outline purely militarily was probably the polygon of up to eight sides, which, if fairly regular and

needing also to be in very varying measure defensible, according to local and personal circumstances, the social purposes of fortresses almost always comprehended and transcended their military functions. Castles were seldom, if ever, in their own day purely functional fortifications; certainly, they were often homes as well (which fact imported an extra set of governing criteria), but, above all else, their builder sought to evoke in some manner the *moeurs* of chivalry, the lifestyle of the great, and the legends of the past.[4]

A few castles only were siege-worthy but most were capable of deterring, though not for a prolonged period of actually resisting, something less than well-equipped and organised attack; whereas common to all of them, of whatever nature their structure, was this sentiment of nostalgia. It may well be that, in this respect, the castellated architecture of the Middle Ages has closer affinities than might be supposed with so much building of the Tudor and early Stuart period in England and also, but more remotely, with that of the modern Romantic Revival in Western Europe. The symbolism of castle architecture might, in rare cases, be not much more than an accident of true functional efficiency, domestic and military, but even so it was never a purely utilitarian architecture.[5] Nor was it

---

in a layout of medium size, minimised the projection and vulnerability of the angle towers while reducing the arc of coverage required for active defence by archery and other artillery. Efficient flanking towers with well-distributed loops and reasonably thick walls can seldom be less than thirty-five feet in diameter, so a maximum of eight (exclusive of the gate-defences) was reasonable, depending on the nature of the site. Polygonal layouts of this kind are a widespread phenomenon of the earlier thirteenth century, among them Bolingbroke (Lincs.), Boulogne-sur-Mer (Pas-de-Calais), Fère-en-Tardenois (Aisne), Castel del Monte (Italy), and, in Frankish Greece, Chlemoutsi or 'Clermont' (see e.g. P. Héliot, 'Le Château de Boulogne-sur-Mer et les châteaux gothiques de plan polygonal', *Révue Archéologique*, 6th series 27 (1947), 41–59; K. Andrews, *The Castles of the Morea* (Princeton, 1953), 346–58). But quadrangular plans were much more convenient domestically, in particular, for fitting in the largest possible great hall. At Conway, in North Wales, the site precluded a long rectangle with straight sides and the resulting crooked plan was famous in illuminations (e.g. J. Evans (ed.), *The Flowering of the Middle Ages* (London, 1966), 338). Wherever the ground allowed, rectilinear layout was the norm (Carcassonne, Louvre, Dourdan etc.). In the northern type, as it were expanded tower-house castles, exemplified by Bolton (Yorks.), domestic planning is integrated closely with military. Maxstoke (Warwicks.) represents a more common European type (compare P. A. Faulkner, 'Domestic Planning from the Twelfth to the Fourteenth Centuries', *Archaeological Journal* 115 (1958), 150–83, with his 'Castle-Planning in the Fourteenth Century', *ibid.*, 120 (1963), 215–35). The evidence of castle plans falls outside the scope of this paper but tends to corroborate the conclusions presented here; components and details quite apart, in layouts pure military design is very much the exception. But it must be stressed that grandeur not cosiness was the domestic ideal for the magnate, and buildings which seem stark to us today were not *ipso facto* military.

[4] The definition of a castle propounded by the Royal Archaeological Institute, as the basis of its research project into 'The Origins of the Castle in England', does not entirely succeed in doing justice to this (e.g. *Archaeological Journal* 134 (1977), 2). C. L. H. Coulson, *Castles in Medieval Society: Fortresses in England, France and Ireland in the Central Middle Ages* (Oxford, 2003).

[5] The grim masses of talus, wall and towers at Krak des Chevaliers (Syria) are exaggerated by the loss since the 1870s of parapets and wall-tops, but this castle is as close to pure military functionalism as was possible, owing to special local factors. But there was artistry in plenty there as well: see the photographic coverage in P. Deschamps, *Les Châteaux des Croisés en Terre Sainte* (Paris, 1934), pt I, album. For examples of ecclesiastical design deliberately pruned of decorative enhancement of structure, see M. Aubert, *L'Architecture Cistercienne en France* (Paris, 1947), *passim*.

stylistically uniform; the concept was made up of deliberately chosen motifs as rich in meaning and as conscious as any coeval iconography, or as any sculptural and pictorial imagery. In what architectural elements, then, did this symbolism chiefly subsist? And how can the functionalism inherent in fortified structural features be disentangled from their evocative purpose?[6] In addition, since the two planes of operation though distinct are perforce closely related, what may be the nature of their connection and mutual accommodation? On these questions this paper attempts to supply some suggestions, based primarily on documentary sources. Obviously, in the compass of a short article only a small contribution can be made to a large and intractable subject, but it is offered in the belief that the original terminology of castellation has some quite precise information to provide in this inevitably obscure and complex field of human motivation, simultaneously artistic in nature and severely practical as it was.

Castles and Aesthetics

The castle of Dover today remains one of the most impressive of medieval fortresses in the British Isles. It crowns the lofty chalk headland facing France and, then as now, is the most memorable and conspicuous feature of the port to the visitor from across the Channel. By the time that King Henry III had made good the damage done during the siege of 1216, and had completed and extended the double concentric line of towered walls, which his grandfather Henry II had laid out and largely accomplished together with the great keep, Dover Castle was a truly magnificent spectacle. The king was justly proud of it. Normandy might have been lost in 1204 but Dover Castle frowned its defiance across the water. Never again was it to demonstrate its value to the defence of the realm of England so conspicuously as at the end of his father's reign, but the treasure he had since lavished on it was to Henry III as well spent as had been the vast expenditure incurred there between 1179 and 1214. The grandiose and ambitious scheme to rebuild the Confessor's abbey church at Westminster, to serve as a shrine for the royal saint and as a burial place and coronation church for the dynasty, now that the patrimonies of Normandy and Anjou were gone, had but lately been begun. But by 1247, King Henry had made out of the great castle of Dover, truly 'the key and redoubt of England', the most up-to-date fortress in the kingdom; fit to vie with any on the continent.[7]

---

[6] The use of drip moulds on crenels (parapet embrasures) is one such problem. On the cresting of merlons and the sills of embrasures their function as drips is obvious, but they served also to deflect arrows and by the early fourteenth century were applied also to the upright jambs. Loops in merlons were also decoratively exploited, ultimately becoming the elaborate pierced-work parapets of later medieval church towers. Machicolation was miniaturised into a mere corbel table. Such examples are too well known to require further illustration.

[7] The best compendium of information is R. A. Brown, H. M. Colvin, and A. J. Taylor, *The History of the King's Works, The Middle Ages*, 2 vols (London, 1963). For the possible link between the features of Caernarvon Castle and the romance of Emperor Maximus, a fascinating thesis of A. J. Taylor, see *ibid.*, 370–1.

In that year, Gaucher de Châtillon, a noble of north-western France, came on a visit to England. Henry III ordered his reception so as to show off possessions of recognised lordly significance in the Middle Ages, namely fine castles and well-stocked deerparks:

> Bertram de Criol, constable of Dover, is directed that when Gaucher de Châtillon shall come to Dover he shall take him into that castle and show the castle off to him in eloquent style (*faceto modo*), so that the magnificence (*nobilitas*) of the castle shall be fully apparent to him, and that he shall see no defects in it. And Gaucher is to be allowed to enter the King's park of Elham, and to hunt there two or three does as a gift from the King ... Witnessed by the King at Merton, the twenty-third day of November [1247].[8]

Castles as well as cathedrals were objects of pride to the medieval patron of architecture. Although this is hardly surprising in itself, the consequences and implications of the fact can easily be underestimated. Aesthetic pleasure in purely ornamental objects is a pronounced feature of medieval art, but that same enjoyment revelled also in architecture, which necessarily marries artistry with function and is half an art (in the recent sense of the word) and half a craft. Indeed, at no period has the integration of the two elements been so essential as in the constructions of the Middle Ages. There was aesthetic pleasure whether the purpose of the building was worship and liturgy, or defence and war, or domestic comfort and dignity.[9] But, to us, the art in the great church seems more straightforward and evident, more overtly symbolical once the basic requirements of accommodating the ceremonial processions, the shrine, altar, pilgrims, regular community and worshippers, had been satisfied. After all, the soaring aspiration of lofty vaults and blaze of pictorial colour within, stupendous towers and dizzy pinnacles outside, were meant on earth to offer a reflection of the grandeur of God in Heaven, as manifested in the Christian Church. The idiom was certainly not metaphysical but nonetheless scarcely mundane. The architecture, while highly skilful in its construction and often no less than a triumph of engineering, was at the same time unquestionably spiritual. The building, in its entirety and in its detail, was an exercise in visual education for a people whose ordinary lives were spent among wattle and thatch. Subsequent advances in building technology notwithstanding, the results, in scale and in magnitude as well as in microcosm, still evoke a response in the dulled senses of modern man. We can still understand something

---

[8] *CCR (1247–51)*, 8 is the enrolled version, in abbreviated Latin (my translation). Licences to crenellate were often associated with licences to impark. In some cases castellated pavilions in deerparks, hunting-lodges no more, were clearly intended (e.g. Bronsill Castle, Herefordshire, in 1460; *CChR (1427–1516)*, 137). The comparison with the fake ruins and classical temples typical of gardens modelled on Claude's landscapes is less remote than might appear. The longevity of the appurtenances of country seats is very notable.
[9] The various motives of the founder of a religious house are well illustrated by a charter of the Count of Nevers of 1097 in favour of St-Etienne (*Recueil des Chartes de l'Abbaye de Cluny*, ed. A. Bernard and A. Bruel (Paris, 1876–1903), v, 67–74).

of the language, be it as believers ourselves or merely in the mood of carping nostalgia of Horace's *laudator temporis acti*.

But tenuous as may be the ecclesiastical and ideological affinities between then and now there is no equivalent continuity at all between medieval and modern warfare to assist our intuitions.[10] In house building at least there is a reliable bridge. Medieval domestic building, whether strongly fortified, merely castellated or quite unadorned, can be analysed and dissected with great accuracy, for it was a very anthropocentric architecture, but it is much more difficult to assess the military specification that the castle designer had to satisfy, and to divine with reasonable certainty what degree of defensibility was demanded, and precisely what danger had to be defeated or deflected.[11] There is great vagueness today on this point, and yet exactitude is essential if we are to know what is functional and what symbolical; and what degree of each is present in any given structure at one and the same time. Lordly affectation, style and panache are too little appreciated because of the difficulty of making rigorous military analyses of this kind. The problems are severe by comparison with ecclesiastical architecture. For example, the power of siegecraft is today very much underrated, for in reality, there was no ascendancy of defence over attack but rather the reverse. By its very nature the evidence is scanty and rather intangible. Close collation of documentary with archaeological material is necessary, for a start. There must be exact and relevant historical knowledge of strictly local conditions and the state of the peace; information regarding the military skill and determination of potential attackers; and also essential is evidence regarding the cash available to the castle builder, together with some insight into his calculations of how best to allocate his revenues between his various lands.[12] Only then can the military credibility of the building itself be assessed in the light of the available means of attack, and the factor of prestige and ostentation may be isolated with some claim to accuracy and be accorded proper recognition. Seignorial ethos of recognisably medieval type no longer exists, but in the society of the European Middle Ages it defined and separated nobles, prelates, bourgeois and peasants. In architecture it was no less evident.

The condition of public order in England, apart from the marches of Scotland and Wales, and brief interludes of more widespread lawlessness elsewhere,

---

[10] Static warfare ended in 1914–18, but see K. Mallory and A. Ottar, *Architecture of Aggression* (n.p. 1973) on the period 1900–45.

[11] The classic case of confusion is Bodiam Castle, Sussex, licensed to be crenellated in 1385; compare G. T. Clark, *Medieval Military Architecture in England* (London 1884), 239–47, with H. Sands, 'Bodiam Castle', *Sussex Archaeological Collections* 46 (1903), 114–33. Clark, the former railway engineer, was undoubtedly right in stressing its defensive weaknesses. C. Hohler, in Evans, *The Flowering of the Middle Ages*, 140, pl. 16, justly calls it 'an old soldier's dream house', irrelevant to fourteenth-century warfare.

[12] See booklet (HMSO, 1978) on Caerphilly Castle, Glamorgan, by C. N. Johns for an exemplary study, on these lines. A. Emery, 'The Development of Raglan Castle and Keeps in Late Medieval England', *Archaeological Journal* 132 (1975), 151–86, on Raglan Castle great tower and its contemporaries, is very largely convincing.

tends strongly to the conclusion that military purpose should not uncritically be ascribed on the ground alone of some architectural semblance of fortification. In large measure, this caveat applies also to France, though conditions there varied greatly from province to province, and the incidence of localised warfare has to be taken into account. But in both countries it is true to say that, whereas violence was recurrent, social emulation was constant. Mind-reading across the centuries is a hazardous business, much too casually indulged in. Far too often the pre-conceptions of today are unthinkingly attributed to the past. Very occasionally, however, we can be overwhelmingly sure that the highest urgency of need, the plenitude of skill and ability, the self-evidently compelling choice of site, and the fullest resources of treasure and manpower were all at work simultaneously. Only by such a conjunction of circumstances (whether repeatedly at one location or unique in time) could a fortress of the first rank come into existence, capable of holding out without relief for a prolonged period against the full apparatus of the *siège en règle*. Such a strong place could influence campaigns by armies in the field, standing alone and unsupported.[13] If it was not so capable, then the real issue depended on the field forces and the castles were purely subsidiary. Only if the 'castle's strength could laugh a siege to scorn' would its lord regard money spent on it as equivalent to money spent on equipment, arms and mercenaries to procure him political power. Inevitably, this was seldom the case. But what of the many if this is true of the few great fortresses? Numerous fortifications, of course, merely protected lives and movables on the spot, or close vicinity, against border forays or internecine strife, against arson and momentary mob violence, and thereby still played, in every sense, a vital if unambitious role.[14] In many other instances, by contrast, a large element of ostentatious embellishment must be admitted, springing from motives more subtle than fear and more human than cool strategic calculation.[15]

Military imperatives and the assumptions of the soldierly engineer become progressively less important, and more domestic and social considerations tend to grow in prominence, as the scale of the fortification diminishes. The cause of this is not far to seek: the great lord could afford both 'guns and butter', as it were; the lesser magnate was perfectly satisfied with the simulacrum of strength appropriate to his rank, coupled with a modicum of personal safety. Castle building is a study belonging to the province of the military analyst as well as to that of the art historian, but any individual castle partakes of ideas proper to each form of scholarship in widely varying proportion. Faced with the complex imponderables of motivation it is often tempting to take refuge in the arcane subjectivism of pure *Kunstgeschichte*, or, as is commonly done with so-called military architecture, in

[13] See R. C. Smail, *Crusading Warfare (1097–1193)* (Cambridge, 1956), especially 204–15; R. Fedden and J. Thomson, *Crusader Castles* (London, 1957), ch. II.
[14] Coulson, *Castles in Medieval Society*.
[15] It is regrettable that the meticulous restoration of Castell Coch, Glamorgan, by William Burges for the third Marquis of Bute should be criticised for excess of imaginative Romanticism.

downright structural fundamentalism.[16] But medieval fortresses were not, on the one hand, pure emanations of artistic conceptualism; nor, at the other pole, were they regimental forts, like some desert outpost of the Foreign Legion. All sorts of intermediate combinations of ingredients social, military, lordly and domestic, mingle in their composition. Through the terminology of administrative records, what might be called the metaphysics of castellation may be approached with no larger danger of anachronism than is unavoidable.

The Privilege of Castellation

In the long series of licences to crenellate enrolled from c.1199 until after the reign of Henry VIII, and scattered among other abstracts of the documents issued by the English royal office of the Chancery, directly relevant material is quite plentiful. French royal and seignorial archives, published and in print, provide still more abundant and explicit evidence in the form of licences to fortify as well as other kinds of charters. Authorisation by the king, or the feudal overlord, was in most cases just honorific to the recipient. It was a courtesy of feudal convention on the part of the vassal to seek permission, which the ruler almost automatically accorded with no attempt to exploit his right financially. Authorisation was not in any political fashion obligatory.[17] On this point there has been much misunderstanding. The image of the bold, bad baron must be firmly banished as Romanticism of the wrong sort, and unhistorical. Licence was sought most usually by lesser men in order to enhance their own social status. Not infrequently this took place after the event or was sometimes altogether omitted. The text of the grant generally reflected the wording of the petition, in which frequently the works proposed, begun or completed were described. This, and the fact that the initiative was private not governmental in any way, greatly increases the value of licences for our present purposes.[18] Evidently, had they been governmental prescriptions of some sort their social interest would be far smaller. Phraseology, in fact, concentrates almost solely, but perfunctorily nevertheless, upon what we may term, the recognition features of fortification; to wit, exactly those architectural motifs in which symbolism is most expressive. They are precisely

[16] The historian must prefer the methodology exemplified by Lon R. Shelby, e.g. in 'The Education of English Master Masons', *Mediaeval Studies* 32 (1970), 1–26, esp. 14–15; and 'The Geometrical Knowledge of Mediaeval Master Masons', *Speculum* 47 (1972), 395–421. By 'structural fundamentalism' is meant the tenet that: 'castles are military architecture. All their features not obviously domestic are therefore military. Castellated residences are shams and follies not worth consideration.' Probably a majority of lay people would endorse this simplistic approach.

[17] See n. 1, above; also C. L. H. Coulson, 'Rendability and Castellation in Medieval France', *Château Gaillard Etudes de Castellologie Médiévale* 6 (1972), 59–67. In Gascony (and elsewhere in France), barons in their baronies needed no licence. In England, licences were issued by the palatinates of Durham, Chester and (after 1351) Lancaster. The Crown maintained very laxly and indifferently the right to license fortifying elsewhere. Its importance was feudal rather than political.

[18] The episcopal palace at Wells, Somerset, in 1340 was licensed for a stone wall, towers, doors and posterns, obviously repeating the petition. As built, the close was also surrounded by a moat (*CPR (1338–40)*, 466; compare *CPR (1281–92)*, 229, and *CChR (1341–1417)*, 52).

defined but with a notable peculiarity. Specific as the terms normally are, such indices of defensibility and structural solidity as the height of walls, the depth and width of ditches, the number, height, size and positioning of towers, the providing of archery loops, and the natural defensive qualities of the site itself, to name a few, are rare. In English licences from the later thirteenth century onwards, it is highly unusual to find any of them, and in French documents, which often show a greater individuality and empiricism, they still occur very infrequently, even singly. Indeed, one feature continually emphasised by modern guides and guidebooks, the thickness of walls, has been found stipulated in only one licence, in respect of a site in France or in Britain, crucial though it undoubtedly was.[19] Wall-walks or *allures*, screened by parapets, are sometimes mentioned but thinness of the wall did not preclude them, since they could be carried on internal projections, whereas mural galleries contained within the width of the wall, being usually vaulted passages with arrow loops to the field, although hardly less essential to efficient defence, are seldom if ever specified.

It emerges very clearly that those who sought licences had other preoccupations. The components of full defensibility were too well-known and too obvious to permit any other explanation of this virtual silence. Those features, on the other hand, which constantly recur have the characteristic that, while certainly military in origin and potentially defensive, they were the most striking and conspicuous, the most apt for ornamentation or, indeed, for entire conversion into decorative motifs pure and simple. Of these, obviously battlementing or crenellation was the commonest and much the most prominent. The most explicit and detailed of the English licences to crenellate are of the fifteenth century, owing to the combined effects of architectural elaboration and administrative verbosity at that period. Licences of the fourteenth century seem terse in comparison. The one issued in 1482 for Oxburgh Hall in Norfolk forms part of a comprehensive charter of seignorial privileges, including the lucrative right to hold a weekly market and giving to Sir Edmund Bedingfield the summary jurisdiction of Pye Powder (*pied poudré*). He was licensed, and also perfunctorily, though in form solemnly, pardoned for any anticipation of permission, or other transgression. The terms were:

> that he at his will and pleasure build, make and construct, with stone [*sic*], lime and sand, towers and walls in and about his manor [-house] of Oxburgh, in the

---

[19] Count Thibaut IV (1201–53) of Champagne in 1223 carefully restricted fortifications at Givry (Seine-et-Marne) to a wall fifteen and a half feet high and two and a half feet thick, around the house, and without allures, towers, or loops for archery or arbalist. His motive was to avert jealous friction with a neighbour. Height restrictions alone, leaving discretion over the thickness, occur occasionally with lay and religious precinct walls, but where full defensibility is in question the value of thick walls was clearly recognised, see *Thesaurus Novus Anecdotorum*, ed. E. Martene and U. Durand (Paris, 1717), I, cols 903–4; *Layettes du Tresor des Chartes*, ed. A. Teulet et al. (Paris, 1866), II, 252; *ibid.*, ed. J. de Laborde (Paris, 1875), III, 314; *Royal and Other Historical Letters Illustrative of the Reign of Henry III*, ed. W. W. Shirley (London, 1862), 1, 383–4, mentioning 'the thickest walls, towers and the deepest ditches' added to Rochechouart Castle (Haute-Vienne) in fear of the French, in c.1230.

county of Norfolk, and that manor with such towers and walls to enclose, and those towers and walls to embattle, crenellate and machicolate ... to hold for himself and his heirs for ever, without ... hindrance.[20]

Now Oxburgh Hall does not, of course, bear the name castle, loosely as the term was used, although in France it would certainly have been styled *château*, and we must be very wary of assuming that military purpose, in that country or in England, was the sole or even the chief contemporary qualification for the title. The limiter was far less simple than that.[21] Structurally today, Oxburgh is a moated rectangle, containing a modest brick courtyard house whose only pretensions to grandeur lie in perfunctorily crenellated stretches of parapet, which screen the roof gutters and by miniaturised proportions give an air of size; but principally it relies for its effect upon the lofty gatehouse block. In its original form, this was the only tower in the house and the only part to have crenellated parapets.[22] It was all that Bedingfield could afford. Sir Roger Fiennes, at Herstmonceux in Sussex (licensed in 1441), was able to do rather better, but his castle is simply a castellated courtyard house as well.[23] Oxburgh is one of the least demonstrative residences of its class and yet the fiction of special royal authorisation, the atavistic phraseology and pomp of the document, and the castle-like panache of the structure display all the traditional trappings and accoutrements of nostalgia. It is too brusque to dismiss these elements as pathetic pretence. Truly, they had long been typical of licences to crenellate. King Edward IV, albeit an up-to-date Renaissance despot and exponent of cynical *Realpolitik*, had no hesitation in gratifying the status-seeking ambition of his gentry, prelates of the Church included, in this time-honoured fashion. His contemporary in France, Louis XI, a man still more of the dawning age of Machiavellism, responded with similar courtesy in 1473 to the aspirations of the nuns of Cusset-en-Bourbonnais (Allier). Seignorial symbolism in France was more pronounced even than it was in England. The architectural elements specified in the king's licence for the *maison forte* of Chastellart, which the abbess and convent of Cusset desired to construct (or rebuild) were: 'walls, towers, gatehouses (*porteaulx*) and machicolation, drawbridges, bulwarks (*boulevars*), ditches, and other fortifications and defences proper and necessary to a place of strength (*place forte*)'; these were a comprehensive vocabulary of late medieval fortification.[24] In France, where the long war with the Plantagenets lasted until 1453, and its sequel with Charles of Burgundy until 1477, such recognition features of castellation were not unnaturally somewhat more warlike and

[20] *CPR (1476–85)*, 308; and Turner and Parker, *Domestic Architecture in England*, III, 291–2.
[21] Coulson, *Castles in Medieval Society*.
[22] Recent restoration work has shown that the building originally had overhanging eaves. Parapets were among the nineteenth-century additions (information supplied by Dr Richard Gem).
[23] *CChR (1427–1516)*, 33–24, licence to 'enclose, crenellate and furnish with towers and battlements', and to empark 600 acres to enlarge his park there. Hurstmonceux has gun-loops but, interestingly, they do not figure in this (or in any other English) licence, ostentatious though they were.
[24] *Recueil Général des Anciennes lois Françaises*, ed. F.-A. Isambert *et al.* (Paris, 1822–33), x, 658–9. In this case, the polite pretence of public usefulness is notably insincere.

up-to-date, but the fortress of the nuns of Cusset was evidently and undoubtedly quite as much an essay in prestige as Oxburgh Hall, or Hurstmonceux, or Kirby Muxloe, or Caister, or Tattershall. Even Raglan Castle, in the marches of Wales, cannot convincingly be differentiated from them in the nature of the motives that caused it to be built and determined its design.[25]

It may be objected that these are late examples and little more than retrospective allusions to the glories of a baronial milieu, by that period supposedly already gone, and thus rather anticipating the more blatantly nostalgic mansion architecture of the sixteenth century than genuinely characteristic of the Middle Ages. And yet, in the main, lordly society was not so very different. Precisely the same recognition features are employed in licences in France for major and serious fortifications as for castellated houses. But, more importantly, prestigious castellation was not a phenomenon of decline, nor to contemporaries was there any break in 1483 or 1485, or even as late as 1509 or 1515. The importance of the Renaissance simply as an artistic revolution, let alone as a social, political, economic or even as a cultural turning-point, has surely been greatly exaggerated. Historiographically it was the discovery of a period that had no sympathy with the era dismissively called the Middle Ages. The military affectation that continues to be seen in the dwellings of the Tudor nobility and gentry is not significantly less emphatic than it had been before. A thoroughly civilian style was a remarkably late development. Not until the advent of the classical revivalism of Inigo Jones, or even that of early eighteenth-century Palladianism, was noble architecture in England entirely dissociated from military ethos. In France, defensive reminiscence in aristocratic building never really disappeared. Survival and revival merge imperceptibly into one another. The causes of this are social not artistic. Wherever danger to life and property remained (and lawlessness was still endemic in Scotland, Ireland and the north well into the eighteenth century) defensible houses of medieval type continued to be built. Until the end of the Wars of Religion in France (1598), security in many provinces required them and thereafter, down to 1789, seignorial pretension continued to recommend an architectural *rodomontade*.

Even where the peace was fairly secure (and the Tudors, unlike the kings of France, had no standing army wherewith to enforce it), the penchant of lately ennobled families at all periods to lay claim to chivalric origins, and thus to assert their kinship with the great, served to perpetuate the old motives but little altered. After the Dissolution, the number of English nobles owning ancient castellated seats was supplemented by those who acquired former monastic residences. It was still the noble image. John Leland in his travels late in the reign of Henry VIII frequently attests it and recorded both the parvenu pretensions of the gentry and their architectural manifestations.[26] It was a tendency reinforced by the prevail-

---

[25] See n. 12 above; nor is the Hastings Tower at Ashby de la Zouche, licensed with Kirby Muxloe in 1474 (CChR (1427–1516), 242) an exception; the alleged influence of 'Bastard Feudalism' is now discredited (see n. 27 below).

[26] On *de facto* enoblement by use of weapons, see M. H. Keen, *The Laws of War in the Late Middle Ages* (London, 1965), appendix II, and *passim*; *The Itinerary of John Leland in or about the years*

ing vogue for the externals of the cult of chivalry. Henry VIII and Francis I were enthusiastic jousters, and the Emperor Maximilian I (d. 1519) liked to be known as 'the last of the knights'. Nobles and kings took it very seriously, and so perforce did craftsmen armourers. Henri II of France was killed in a jousting accident in 1559, and Henry VIII had some narrow escapes. Heraldry underwent great development. In origin a means of identifying a man wearing full armour and of denoting his followers on the battlefield, it flourished as an aristocratic symbol as never before. Tudor portraits and monuments alike display their subject's blazon. Coats of arms proclaimed antiquity and noble descent; only the architectural privilege of castellation was more conspicuous, or held greater prestige. The whole affair of Edward Stafford's Thornbury Castle, his rivalry with Wolsey, and his fall, is not intelligible in any other terms.[27] The romantic revivalism of this era, of Sir Thomas Malory and Edmund Spenser, and of so much of the ideology that imbued the lifestyle of the great, was certainly retrospective, but the previous century had been scarcely less nostalgic. Castle symbolism, in fact, goes much further back than the fifteenth century. It blossomed in the fourteenth and it would be very unwise to suppose that it cannot be found before, say, the twelfth century or indeed earlier still.

Structures and Status

The fact is that the conventional rationale is inadequate, which would explain the developments in castle architecture from the early fifteenth century in terms of a widening estrangement between house and fortress, leading ultimately to their divorce and taking separate ways, as gun-forts and ornamentally castellated mansions respectively. This schema is over-simple and subtly misleading. Long before effective battering cannon were evolved in the early fifteenth century, the great superiority of siegecraft had made the majority of castles of only marginal importance strategically, or, indeed, militarily quite irrelevant.[28] At least by the later twelfth century in north-western Europe, mechanical artillery such as mangonel and trebuchet, mining, siege-towers, and all the other 'engines' of siege, had reduced the role of the castle in most cases to personal protection and to prestige. What may be called the top league of fortresses, which, it must be stressed, were

---

1535–1543, ed. L. Toulmin Smith, 5 vols (London, 1907); see also K. B. MacFarlane, 'The Investment of Sir John Fastolf's Profits of War', *Transactions of the Royal Historical Society*, 5th series, 7 (1957), 91–116. In 1469, Caister was seized from the Pastons by the Duke of Norfolk, undoubtedly as unfitted to their lowly social position (*Paston Letters*, ed. J. Gairdner (London, 1904), v, 36–7, 40–57). Longford (Wilts.) and Lulworth. Castle (Dorset) are late Tudor examples of castellated revivalism. Burghley House (Cambs.) and, still more conspicuous, Wollaton Hall (Notts.), display similar influences.

[27] Compare W. Douglas Simpson, 'Bastard Feudalism and the Later Castles', *Antiquaries Journal*, 26 (1946), 165–70. Simpson's thesis is now untenable as a whole, but it was never credibly applicable to Thornbury.

[28] Despite its title, the posthumous book by B. H. St J. O'Neil, *Castles and Cannon* (Oxford, 1960), is no more than a study of gun-loops from *c*.1365 and a survey of the development of guns.

still palaces and symbols of lordship as well as forts, was a very select company. Symbolism in castle architecture, therefore, was a vigorous inherent element, not an uncharacteristic aberration of senescence and decline.[29]

In the year 1091, William Rufus and his elder brother Duke Robert of Normandy propounded criteria to differentiate irregular and wartime earthwork fortifications from properly established castles. They declared that their father, William the Conqueror, had in his day enforced them as a peace-keeping measure. A formula was enunciated that limited the height of the crest of the rampart above the bottom of the ditch to about nine or ten feet (a similar rule of thumb is to be found in twelfth-century Champagne and elsewhere); palisading atop the bank was to have no flanking salients or elevated sentry-walk (*alatorium*, or *allure*); and outworks (*propugnacula*) were altogether excluded.[30] It was a thoroughly practical standard, based purely on defensibility, and significantly was completed by proscribing the defensive use of any naturally isolated site, 'rock or island'. Forcible intrusion into existing and lawfully recognised castellaries and lordships by works of a sort that in the nineteenth century were termed field fortifications was the problem. Prestige did not at first accrue to their owner any more than it did to the occupant of some brigand lair or raiding base. Rather, it was associated with the stone *turris* or keep, the great earthworks of major fortresses and with the walls, towers and gates such as towns, religious precincts and noble seats displayed. But the humbler earthwork *mota* and *dongio* soon acquired seignorial connotations by prescription. The noble tenant by knight-service was frequently by his rank entitled to have earthwork moat, palisade and dwellings within. Modest even militarily negligible though they were, such establishments, for which the Victoria County Histories employ the useful term homestead moat, nevertheless on a small scale possessed all the lordly rights and attributes of the fortress.[31] As late as 1268, a verdict of the court of King Louis IX upheld that in the region of Nevers, 'a palisaded earthwork is a fortress according to the usages

[29] The best study of medieval siegecraft, much plagiarised but still unsurpassed, is to be found in the works of E. E. Viollet le Duc, e.g. *Dictionnaire Raisonné de L'architecture Française* (many editions, as Paris 1861–70), articles 'Siège', 'Engin', 'Château'; *idem*, *Essai sur L'architecture Militaire au Moyen Age* (Paris, 1854) *passim*; and *idem*, *Histoire d'une Forteresse* (Paris, n.d.) compare E. W. Marsden, *Greek and Roman Artillery* (Oxford, 1969). Accounts of major sieges (e.g. D. J. C. King, 'The Taking of le Krak des Chevaliers in 1271', *Antiquity* 90 (1949), 83–92) and the political history of castles, collectively and individually, lead to the same conclusion. The capacity to hold out against blockade (siege par excellence) depended on factors most of which were quite unrelated to the architecture of the fortress in any case.
[30] For the text of the *Consuetudines et Justicie*, see C. H. Haskins, *Norman Institutions* (New York, 1918; reprinted 1960), appendix D (esp. clause 4, on p. 282); see Coulson 'Rendability and Castellation'. For Champagne, see Coulson, 'Seignorial Fortresses', Appendix B (4).
[31] Seignorial rights and symbolism still preoccupied the French aristocracy in the seventeenth century; see e.g. Denis de Salvaing et de Boissieu, *De L'usage des Fiefs et Autres Droits Seigneuriaux* (Grenoble, 1665–8; new edn, 1731), *passim*.

and customs of the locality (*patria*). To be of gentle status, not ignoble *villanus* or *roturier*, was the essential.[32]

As is to be expected, however, from the early thirteenth century masonry elements predominate among the criteria of fortification. Expense permitting, earthwork was gradually superseded by stone as the principal material, and the modes of symbolism consequently multiplied. Prosperity allowed lesser magnates to build largely in stone, and on this the English royal licences to crenellate laid great stress. Mortared masonry possessed unique distinction. Where good ashlar is available there is great incentive to decorate and to beautify. Symbolism became somewhat freed from limitations of labour and cost as emphasis shifted from whole structures to detailed features, and a trend towards pure ornamentation began. But documents are slow to acknowledge it in respect of castellation. When Henry I agreed in 1127 that Archbishop William de Corbeil might build the great tower of Rochester, within the recently adapted area of the bailey, custody of the castle having lately been vested in the see of Canterbury, that lofty and glorious fortress-palace-to-be was referred to simply as 'a fort or tower' (*municio vel turris*). Its battlements, bratticing, angle turrets, portcullis, drawbridge and other features, at the same time functional and seigniorially eloquent, are none of them mentioned in the king's charter.[33] But a great prince of the Church naturally built according to his rank. At the end of King Stephen's reign, in 1153, his successor Henry Plantagenet, a little prematurely, rewarded Robert FitzHarding with land at Berkeley (Gloucestershire), again assuming that the castle to be built there needed no exact specification. Henry II was more precise only in regard to the jurisdictional rights of lordship that went with the land, lordship and enfeoffment.[34] Circumstances were markedly different when Pierre de Richeville promised his lord, the Count de Montfort, that he would conform the appointments of his dwelling to his status in the feudal hierarchy. In 1239 Pierre declared:

> We have given him guarantee effective against all men, saving the fealty due to the lord King of France, touching our house of Chigny, namely that we may not furnish it with any archery-loop or crossbow-loop, nor crenellation, nor shield (of

---

[32] *Les Olim*, ed. le comte Beugnot (Paris, 1839), I, 719–20; the quarrel between Hugh de Thouars and the burgesses of La Rochelle in *c*.1222 starkly reveals social attitudes; *Royal Letters*, 2, 185–6.

[33] *Regesta Regum Anglo-Normannorum*, ed. H. W. C. Davis *et al.* (Oxford, 1956), II, 356. Seals were an important medium of ideas. That of the city of Rochester (reproduced in A. Harvey, *The Castles and Walled Towns of England* (London, 1911), 64) shows the castle with the royal banner and the keep with hourding joists in position at the summit. The original parapets still survive here.

[34] *Regesta Regum*, III, 117–18, but the symbolism of crenellation was already familiar; see *ibid.*, 59; permission of *c*.1135–40 to crenellate the precinct wall of St Augustine's, Canterbury, by King Stephen (noted as spurious but now accepted as possibly genuine by the editor R. H. C. Davis in a letter to the author dated 23 April 1973, though possibly *c*.1154–1216 in date). On religious precincts as fortresses, see Coulson, *Castles in Society*, ch. III (1), and C. L. H. Coulson, 'Fortresses and Social Responsibility in Late Carolingian France', *Zeitschrift für Archäologie des Mittelalters* 4 (1976), 29–36.

arms). Around our property there we may make one ditch, twelve feet in breadth, but we may do nothing more without the Count's consent.[35]

In the enrolled licences of King John the evolution from matter-of-fact brevity (nothing more specific than 'enclosing' and 'fortifying') towards, later in the reign of Henry III, the eventual adoption of crenellation as the test par excellence, may be retraced. Though these early licences are curt and enigmatic their symbolic and lordly significance is clear, pragmatism notwithstanding. Until Henry III came of age this remained typical of the very few authorisations issued; they are, one might say, still licences to fortify rather than to crenellate. Great lords generally needed no licence. Their status admitted of no doubt, unlike their inferiors who had acquired position and power during the civil war.[36] Preserving the peace achieved by force of arms in 1217 dictated a severe practicality in the policy of the government. Security and prevention of local discord was its keynote, and the social emulation of the gentry in castellated architecture was necessarily repressed or ignored. In 1231, however, Robert de Tattershall obtained a grant of permission to fortify at his principal seat and name-place in Lincolnshire, in a form that anticipates what later became standard. He was licensed, 'freely and without hindrance to have fortified at his manor of Tattershall a house of stone and lime'. This *domus*, as it was until the extensive remodelling in brick by Ralph Lord Cromwell in the fifteenth century, was a moated fortress of some strength with a towered curtain wall.[37] The status it conferred is still not explicitly reflected in the terms of the licence, although the fact of royal endorsement was important in itself.[38] Similar to it is the licence issued by the king in 1253, to his brother Richard, Earl of Cornwall, 'to build and fortify a castle of stone and lime … on the hill above his manor of Mere' (Wiltshire).[39] The emphasis on masonry, fireproof, solid and dignified but not otherwise intrinsically castellar, is typical of English licences throughout. In France it was taken for granted.

That prestige was the prime mover is at once evident by comparing with England the situation obtaining in Ireland, where castle building was a necessity of simple survival. It was the basis of the Anglo-Norman colonisation. Lords were exhorted, encouraged, assisted and even compelled to fortify their lands, especially those 'in the march'. At home, this realistic emphasis is echoed in that, down

---

[35] Printed by the lawyer-historian or *feudiste* N. Brussel in *Nouvel Examen de l'usage des Fiefs en France* (Paris, 1727; new edn, 1750), 855.

[36] See n. 17 above. The second reissue of *Magna Carta* in 1217 (clause 47, *Stubbs Charters*, 9th edn (Oxford, 1960), 344) legislated specially against the wartime fortifications or *castra adulterina*, which, where injurious to the pacification, were demolished. In Wales and in Ireland the Crown encouraged and helped castle building, again for purely practical motives.

[37] *CPR (1225–32)*, 435; printing the licence and a mandate to the sheriff to permit the fortification.

[38] Under King Stephen and the Empress Mathilda (1135–54), Geoffrey de Mandeville had the power to create castles but was nonetheless very careful to obtain from both claimants to the throne, when in the ascendancy, due legal recognition. Even during the Anarchy de facto right was not enough (*Regesta Regum*, III, 99–103).

[39] *CPR (1247–58)*, 208. To take timber (not firewood) from scheduled forest required licence, which Earl Richard also received, namely from his wood of the manor of Mere.

to *c.*1260 the fortification of towns figures prominently among the licences issued, particularly in that part of Wales under English control. The number is still small (little more than twenty for 1216–60), and many of those obtained during the next few years betray the anxieties of the onset, hostilities and aftermath of the Barons' War of 1264–5.[40] The king's servants might cautiously be encouraged to strengthen their dwellings, but it must be done in such a way as not to provoke jealous repercussions.

In these years of stress, conditions were not propitious for the building activity and evidence we seek in licences, although one very fine illustration of the architectural ambitions of the knight bachelor class, stimulated by Simon de Montfort, can be seen at Barnwell, in Northamptonshire. It is a small but finely built castle, constructed without royal licence in *c.*1264, whose details, particularly the unique and very clumsy arrow-loops, are ostentatious and militarily unskilful.[41] This period, for a variety of reasons most of them peculiar and local, saw a marked rise in the number of licences (fourteen from 1261 to August 1264) and the phraseology exemplified by the licence of 1264, for Hood Castle (Yorkshire), became the established pattern. With progressive elaboration, this formula remained standard in Britain until the end of the Middle Ages, or as long as licences were issued. As calendared in English, it is as follows:

> Licence for John de Eyvill and his heirs to enclose a place of his called la Hode, co. York, with a dyke [i.e. earthworks] and a wall of stone and lime and to crenellate it, and to hold it so fortified and crenellated for ever.[42]

The true licence to crenellate has now arrived. Sixteen more were issued in the rest of the reign (1266–72); fifty-four by Edward I (1272–1307); sixty-seven by his son in a reign of barely twenty years (1307–27) ; and, down to the Black Death (1348–9), which called a brief halt, no fewer than 169 licences (including three for the duchy of Gascony wrongly placed on the English rolls), were obtained from the government of Edward III.[43] Wealth, peace at home, warlike leadership and success abroad, social mobility and the cult of aristocracy and chivalry make the fourteenth century the heyday of licences in England. Frequently, as before and since, they were complemented by permission to create deerparks, game-preserves, and to exercise hunting rights (free warren) within the area of the grantee's lands. Roads were often allowed to be diverted for the purpose and, clearly, the estate of the lord was expressed as much by its setting as by his seat,

---

[40] Sedgewick (Sussex) was licensed in 1258 and again in 1262; the work caused trouble locally. Perching (Sussex) was licensed twice in 1264, and again in 1268. Godstone (Surrey) was licensed in 1262 for ditches and palisading only, with the express condition, quite exceptional for England, of loyalty by the grantee (*CPR (1258–66)*, 3, 199, 206, 307, 381; *CPR (1266–72)*, 189).

[41] For permission to examine the castle my thanks are due to HRH the late Duke of Gloucester. Early in Edward I's reign the foundation of Barnwell was calmly noted by the Hundred Roll jury (*Rotuli Hundredorum*, Record Commission (London, 1818), II, 7b).

[42] *CPR (1258–66)*, 342.

[43] These provisional figures count each site in those cases where several manors or places were licensed en bloc. That this quite often occurred confirms the perfunctoriness of the procedure.

symbols alike of his status.[44] The degree of defensibility his house incorporated varied widely with local factors of security and even of prestige, for there was still distinction in a truly strong fortress suitably scaled down to the builder's purse, but licence, crenellation, moat and drawbridge met most requirements.[45] They denoted, as much as defended, a noble residence.

Architectural affirmation of nobility, by crenellation and by licensing, was naturally common also in the case of ecclesiastical buildings. The lords spiritual too, not only 'proud prelates' but humbler deans, masters of hospitals and propertied clergy, received licences. Monastic churches, precincts and gatehouses, episcopal palaces and manor-houses, churches, belfries and clerical dwellings, were all crenellated under licence, and, certainly still more, without licence. Few great magnates needed any such recognition but very many gentry, lesser prelates and even wealthy townsmen desired and obtained it not only for country mansions but also for their urban dwellings in disregard of their technical absence of nobility.[46] And burgesses corporately often received licence to crenellate walls they were building, which was one of the marks in Britain of a free borough. Grants of tolls (murage) may have been more numerous but citizens also aspired to the privilege associated with crenellation. Specific authorisation by licence was undoubtedly less purposeful than a murage grant, which afforded funds as well as implied permission, but they still coveted the licence to crenellate.

From the mid-fourteenth century, licences decline slightly in number; there are forty-four for the rest of Edward III's reign (1350–77), and sixty for Richard II including his minority (1377–99). In the fifteenth century, the rolls of Henry IV record just fifteen, his son's only two, and the long reign of Henry VI (1422–61) thirty-nine. Under Edward IV (1461–83) twenty-four were enrolled, after which, only a few. The loss of the Privy Seal records and administrative vicissitudes account partly for the much-reduced number, but evidently they had become a rather self-conscious archaism increasingly disregarded. Battlementing, and occasionally also turrets in the fifteenth century, with stone walls of enclosure, remain the standard structural features specified, irrespective of the actual details of the building proposed or already executed.[47] Sometimes the licence repeats a justificatory phrase evidently from the petition, referring to the exposed loca-

---

[44] Dovecots and fishponds were lordly symbols too and were also important in France.

[45] For William Heron, lord of the strong fortress of Ford, Northumberland, crenellation alone (in 1338) was not enough. In 1340 he received express licence to call it a castle and gained extensive hunting rights nearby. Defence here was very necessary but status was no less important (*CPR (1338–40)*, 114; see *CPR (1343–5)*, 409, and *CChR (1327–41)*, 468–9 for this and the exposure of Ford to Scottish raids).

[46] Town houses, in London particularly, were also licensed. The grantees were mostly members of the merchant patriciate, but in 1293, Edmund Earl of Lancaster obtained a licence for the Savoy Palace, west of the City (*CPR (1292–1301)*, 30).

[47] A few licences were technically pardons for anticipating the permission to crenellate. Occasionally work was officiously interrupted for lack of a licence, but obtaining it was a mere formality not even fiscally exploited by the Crown. Only a small Chancery (hanaper) fee was payable, as for any other document of title.

tion of the site, as 'in the north marches' or 'on the coast', or allusion is made to the public-spirited motives professed by the grantee. It was fashionable also in contemporary France to allege public utility in this way. Sometimes such phrases occur as 'to enclose ... and crenellate ... and make a castle and fortress', but comparison with architectural remains and consideration of the grantee's rank and wealth seldom, if ever, substantiate any special seriousness.[48] Correlation with known facts of military need rarely suggests these formulae were anything more than lip-service and special pleading. Taken as a whole, the English licences are a part of socio-architectural history, and the same, with remarkably little mutation, is true of France. They dignified the recipient who sought them and paid the small Chancery fee. Just as he might covet rank, title, noble connections, jurisdiction and military renown for himself and his family, so for his residence the ostentatious parade of battlementing, and the king's patent authorising it, was desired when not actually needed, and the noble symbolism was cherished whatever the structural ranking of the place between the extremes of functional efficiency and spurious military braggadocio. Personal security depended, the marches apart, on the king's peace rather than on walls and a moat. Massive fortifications were highly costly to build and could only become effective when guarded by armed men, which was only done in rare emergencies. At other times, the civilian households within their walls were almost as vulnerable to aggravated burglary as the occupants of a castellated manor house. Such attacks, even in peaceful England, were far from rare, but fear of them did not convert the pleasant and spacious courtyard castle-house and palace into the grim tower-house of the Borders. Style of life mattered too much for that to happen; dignified comfort ignored danger whenever it could.

Some French Comparisons

Crenellation, then, occupies a special position in the English licences and their symbolism, almost one of monopoly to judge from the documents alone. In common with their emphasis on building in stone, this characteristic is unique and curious, and so is the habitual security of tenure formula. The clerks of the royal Chancery worked in a quite distinct idiom, employing a wholly different official phraseology, when they were dealing with the duchy of Gascony.[49] As in France generally, seignorial awareness and lordly pride in the duchy were well-developed, perhaps rather more so than in Britain, although facile comparisons are hazardous. At any rate, its architectural expression was undoubtedly much

---

[48] This form was in fashion under Richard II, for example. But *fortalicia* was a word (like *castrum*) meaning the semblance as well as the reality of strength. Modern preoccupations frequently cause too unsubtle and literal an interpretation of medieval terminology.

[49] See Coulson, 'Rendability and Castellation', and *idem*, 'Seignorial Fortresses', Appendix B (3), for these and the points following. The duchy licences mentioned are printed at length in *Rôles Gascons*, ed. Ch. Bémont (Paris, 1896), Supplement to vol. I, 42, 47–8, 50; *ibid.* (Paris, 1900), II, 43, 45, 115–16, 125; *ibid.* (Paris, 1906), III, 428.

more diversified. A whole range of castellar recognition features was in vogue. In Gascony as in England, however, these do not become evident in licences issued by the king as duke, or by his deputy, until late in the thirteenth century. In 1255 three licences were issued for *maisons fortes* in the texts of which prosaic defensibility is all that is emphasised, leaving both functional and ornamental details to the builder's fancy, and to be determined by his financial resources. Edward I recorded two similar grants in 1278, the first in favour of one 'Garsias de Salmund, knight', for 'an adequate fortification' near Amou in the Landes; and the second, in a hybrid form combining English and Gascon phraseology, for a 'secure house', which was to be crenellated and thus held by the grantee and his heirs. These, though distinctive, are comparable to contemporary English licences. But the characteristic Gascon formula was to develop soon afterwards. Apart from occasional errors by the royal scribes the two forms were henceforth kept rigidly apart. Feudal convention in this particular had come to differ despite the closeness of the links between the duchy and the kingdom.

Helpfully, the Gascon licences are much more explicit. In 1280 the Bishop of Agen and his brother obtained one, for 'a strong house girt about with walls, towers and ditches'. Others were yet more precise; in the year following Edward I was petitioned by a minor lord, Amanieu de Loubens, *domicellus*, to the effect that his wish 'to construct a house or manor for his residence and without any great or undue fortification' (*sic*) had been jealously, or perhaps officiously, obstructed by the king's seneschal. Edward's decision, based no doubt on his deep personal knowledge of the duchy, was to order an enquiry 'as to what kind [i.e. degree] of fortification' was proposed by Amanieu. In the interim, he was authorised to complete the timber portion of his house, the curtilage about it of earthwork or palisading and also the tiling of the roof, but was temporarily forbidden to erect 'any other enclosure, any palisading or device (*ingenium*) such as a drawbridge, or rather greater ditches and other features of major fortification'. Significantly, the normal bank, hedge or moat surrounding the manor place to demarcate as much as to protect it, was still regarded as a fortification. Quality and degree were aspects that the medieval mind differentiated clearly.[50]

In the Gascon licences of Edward I and Edward II, the fashion in various parts of the duchy for minor nobles' houses to have ditches, wooden stockades, stone walls, drawbridges and gate-towers is frequently alluded to. Of these elements the drawbridge (often *pons levaticius*) occurs the most often and seemingly possessed particular significance, but details are much less standardised than in English licences. In 1304, one occurs for 'a strong house with crenels and archery loops', without further particular; and in the border province of the Agenais (Lot-et-Garonne), tower-houses with stone gate defences and other crenellated

---

[50] Regulation of dress (especially the gradation of fur trimmings to robes), of attendants or retainers, and of the mode of hospitality, considered proper to each degree of nobility was also part of the same medieval concept of rank and station; see F. E. Baldwin, *Sumptuary Legislation and Personal Regulation in England* (Baltimore, 1926), *passim*.

fortifications were acknowledged proper to the nobility.[51] Similar problems of lawlessness, abduction and ransoming, raids and sudden attacks obtained here as in the northern counties of England, with similar architectural consequences.

Of seignorial manifestations in castellation in the other regions and provinces of what is now France only brief discussion is possible. Gascon practice is undoubtedly typical and is, for example, closely comparable to the ways which prevailed in another great honour, the palatine county of Champagne and Brie.[52] It was very similar, too, in the county of Ponthieu, in the north-west. This was an area of weak comital authority, very much dominated by the burgesses of the powerful commercial towns. In 1214–15 Count William II, to satisfy the townsmen of Rue (Somme), agreed to content himself with only minor buildings and defensive constructions at the nearby earthwork site of Gard. Despite his feudal status, he promised them by charter that he would erect there:

> no greater fortification … than … atop the bank a fence, and a bridge which can be lifted [or retracted], and a gateway of timbers without any outworks; and over the entry a chapel or bedchamber, or a room for storing corn and oats.

Because such a dwelling, although demonstratively noble, was still of degree appropriate to only a minor lordling, the men of the commune of Rue would not have any encroachment on their own court's jurisdiction to fear, nor incidentally, any risk that Gard-lés-Rue might be used as a siege-castle, or base for the harassment of the town in any war.[53]

The size and materials, then, of residential buildings and more especially their degree of conformity or approximation to the substance or outward appearance of the first-rank fortress, were the gauge and measure of the social and feudal standing of the noble owner. The structural features of castellation, however massive or however perfunctory, always possessed a symbolical importance irrespective of what the modern student regards as military criteria. A few further points only need be noted in conclusion. First, that lords corporate (urban communes and, of course, religious communities) as well as individuals were involved. The point is perhaps less obvious in the case of towns, and deserves illustration. In 1284, King Philip III heavily mulcted the townsmen of Lille (Nord) for disregarding his authority as overlord of the county of Flanders, in various ways. He pardoned them for having without permission fortified the city and accorded them

[51] See n. 49 above. The drawbridge, whether pivoted or merely removable presupposed a ditch or moat, but, less prosaically, it had strong symbolic significance. In 1302, a messenger sent by King Philip IV to serve a summons was adjudged to have been treated with contempt because the drawbridge of a *maison forte* was raised to keep him from entering. Gate defences in general, in France, were often conspicuously damaged by judicial verdict to punish *lèse majesté* and to advertise for a stated period the culprit's humiliation (*Les Olim*, III, 86–7; compare *ibid.*, II, 208, 346–7; and *ibid.*, III, 822–3).
[52] The word *camera* was used in the licence of 1267 by Henry III to describe the tower-house to be walled, fortified and crenellated by John Comyn at Tarsett, Northumberland. It was to be modelled on Heaton tower (*CPR (1266–72)*, 178).
[53] *Recueil des actes des Comtes de Ponthieu (1026–1279)*, ed. C. Brunel (Paris, 1930), 353–4.

the right to hold and maintain their defences and, in future, to construct new
fortifications, namely 'ditches and walls, with crenels and towers, after the fashion
of fortresses'. Towns were indeed 'the castles of communities', and very frequently
in France were termed castles, which fact deserves more notice. Very naturally
the seignorial privileges with which they were often corporately endowed were
evidenced architecturally as was appropriate.[54] Whatever its size or form, the fortification connoted lordship, be it a great *ville fermeé* or a mere embattled manorial curtilage or religious precinct wall. *Droit de châtellenie* comprised rights of
wide scope and type. To protect the crowded and vulnerable world within walls
of the medieval town certainly required that its defences be effective, but in
the invariable mode of the Middle Ages they were symbolic also. We find the
burgesses of Isle-en-Périgord (Dordogne) authorised in 1309 to put crenels on
their houses but debarred from creating fortifications strong enough to injure the
town defences or to be liable to jeopardise the peace. The inhabitants of two new
towns (*bastides*) licensed in 1329 and 1332 in a frontier region where self-defence
was crucial, received the right not just to fortify but explicitly to construct 'walls,
merlons [i.e. crenellation], ditches and towers'; and like any individual aspirant
to lordly rank they were granted the right to have fish-ponds and dovecots, usually perquisites of gentlefolk. Unquestionably it was their wish to proclaim their
newly won status in stone and they used the conventional aristocratic method of
doing so.[55]

Crenellation, as we have seen, was not so prominent in non-functional importance in France as it was in Britain. In French building it was one symbol among
several. Archery loops, in verdicts of the king's court of 1266–8, were declared 'to
have been hitherto emblems of fortification', and in 1309–10 the deciding factor
was the presence of 'two strong towers'. Both were cases of disregard of the right
possessed over his tenants by the lord of the fief to consent to their fortifying. The
lord cited his contumacious vassal to the royal court, and the king's judges duly
upheld him after verifying the facts of feudal law and tenure at issue. Such structural elements proclaimed that the dwellings concerned were not just technically
but, as it were, spiritually and demonstratively fortified. They were the *signa fortericie*. It was because of seignorial pretension, rather than of any conceivable
warlike hazard, which only a major fortification could present, that they were
subject to the lord's ban. It was the feudal obligation of the king to be solicitous
of a vassal's honour as a good overlord should be.[56] Such criteria in France were
admittedly more empirical and varied, even perhaps more serious and realistic,

---

[54] Viz., '*juxta modum fortaliciarum*', *Ordonnances des Roys de France de la Troisième Race*, ed. E.
J. de Lauriere, *et al.* (Paris 1723–1840), 11, 358–9. The phrase is that of A. Hamilton Thompson
(*Military Architecture in England*, viii). The connection between castle ownership and capital
jurisdiction ('high justice') is repeatedly affirmed in the records.

[55] *Ordonnances*, XI, 417–20; *ibid.*, XII, 500–2, 522–5. Within towns, houses built like towers, or
with lofty turrets, were a common form of architectural emulation. San Gimignano in Italy still
preserves this feature.

[56] *Les Olim*, I, 226, 719–20, 730; *ibid.*, III, 296, 460–1.

but the symbolism was always the heart of the matter. It is probably true that in later fifteenth-century French licences the recognition features, since they were common to military and to prestigious works, tended to be more in tune with the contemporary arts of war and siege. In English licences they are distinctly conservative, in fact deliberately atavistic and nostalgic. But the contrast merely reflected the more warlike context of life across the Channel. Pretentious affectation had to conform to a more overtly militant mode in order to be in the aristocratic fashion. There was no difference in social significance. Thus, a licence granted in 1469 to Louis XI's trusted secretary Baudes Meurin, explicitly for the enhancement of his recently gained nobility speaks nonetheless of the full panoply of militant architecture. It authorised 'walls, towers, machicolation, crenels, barbicans, drawbridges, bulwarks, and ditches … such as shall be necessary and proper'. In contrast, the licence issued in 1459 by Henry VI to Thomas FitzWilliam, 'king's squire', in respect of Mablethorpe, Lincolnshire, though ostensibly for reasons of defence (a not uncommon fiction as we have seen), the place being 'on the sea coast', nevertheless more modestly empowered him 'to put a ditch to his manor [-house] and enclose the same with walls of *breke*, stone and mortar and crenellate and embattle it, and make towers and fortresses [fortifications] there, and so hold it to him and his heirs'. The spirit of both royal charters is identical.[57]

Nostalgia is an ineradicable human habit and the myth of a golden age is extremely old. Belief in Progress, stemming from the eighteenth-century Enlightenment, has made remarkably small inroads on them. As an influence on building styles, nostalgia tends constantly to historicism and is the commonest form of symbolism; in addition to being Romantic, it implies that the patron's family made its debut socially a long time since. Whereas the aristocrat in the later seventeenth and eighteenth century commissioned a mansion of classical style, and often himself dabbled in its design, so as to demonstrate that he had gone on the Grand Tour and thereby belonged to the select circle of men of taste, discernment and sound principles in art, in religion perhaps, and in politics, the great men of the Middle Ages (but still more the knightly class) built castles and castellated dwellings to assert their kinship with aristocratic modes. Whenever personal safety gave them the latitude to do so, their residences were clothed in the symbolic appurtenances of castle architecture commensurate with their wealth and status.

Acknowledgements

For reading this article in draft and generously giving their comments and advice upon it I am indebted in considerable though varying measure to Sir John Summerson, H. M. Colvin, H. R. Loyn, R. D. H. Gem and F. R. H. Du Boulay, and for

---

[57] *Ordonnances*, XVII, 219; *CChR (1427–1516)*, 131–2.

his support and encouragement to A. J. Taylor. While I take entire responsibility for what I have written their help has been of the greatest value.

The British Archaeological Association gratefully acknowledges a grant from the Twenty-Seven Foundation towards the cost of publication.

10

Specimens of Freedom to Crenellate by Licence

Charles Coulson

Self-advertising noblemen, ecclesiastics, gentry and merchants, between 1200 and 1578, obtained licence to fortify 409 castles and manors, 43 religious establishments, and about 55 towns and town houses. Taking fifteen case-studies, put in context, Dr Charles Coulson illustrates the results of aristocratic aspiration on the ground and in the records.

The truth about licences to crenellate is as remote from tradition as it is with Bodiam Castle (*Fortress* 10 (1991), 3–15). Since the error is widespread we need only refer to the late David Cathcart King's great *Castellarium Anglicanum* to give the essence of it. He wrote of early baronial fortresses: 'the king's concern with these private castles was inevitable. Over their foundation he had the negative control of requiring licences to crenellate.'[1] This he modified for the reigns of the first three Norman kings, believing that 'in general, barons built castles where they pleased on their fiefs', caution more than confirmed by Richard Eales (1990) and the present writer.[2] Traditional ideas derive from the notion that feudalism was essentially anarchic, and 'private castles' as hostile to the peace and to royal power as the 'turbulent barons' who built them; combined with faith in the virility of monarchy in England, unlike Europe. So David King then qualified his previous realism: 'the requirement of a licence to crenellate enabled the kings to control the building of new castles so well that, from the reign of Stephen onwards, it is impossible to think of more than one permanent castle built for a purpose hostile to the Crown'. He had in mind 'the remote and sinister Dunstanburgh'.

But relatively few castles were founded after the great post-Conquest explosion. Regulation of additional fortification (e.g. Thomas of Lancaster's Pontefract) not of new castles was needed if kings really had wished to check them, strong ones particularly. In fact, the famous 'adulterine castles' of the 1135–54 Anarchy were simply objectionable to the few contemporary clerics who used the term, not unlicensed. Until the reign of King John there are no true licences; and when

---

[1] D. J. C. King, *Castellarium Anglicanum*, 2 vols (New York, 1983), i, ch 2.
[2] R. Eales, 'Royal Power and Castles in Norman England', in *Medieval Knighthood* 3, ed. C. Harper-Bill and R. Harvey (Woodbridge, 1990), 48–78, reprinted *ANC*, 41–67; C. Coulson, 'The Castles of the Anarchy', in *The Anarchy of Stephen's Reign*, ed. E. King (Oxford, 1994), 67–92, reprinted *ANC*, 179–202; C. Coulson, 'Hierarchism in Conventual Crenellation', *Medieval Archaeology* 26 (1982), 69–100.

they begin to be known their character is honorific not restrictive. They signified royal favour, like other privileges, but most castle-builders did not trouble to ask for it.

The whole view that 'private' military capacity was wrong in the Middle Ages (be it armed tenantry, personal arsenals, castles or 'private war') betrays strange misconceptions. In Victorian Britain it would have been odd, and the historians of Bishop Stubbs' generation assumed that strong kings had to stop it, castles included. In truth, castles were defensible landed seats of the gentry and nobility, which they were fully entitled to build. War, in any case, was an occasion, whereas the *panache* of militant architecture was the aristocratic norm. It is remarkably strange that the castellated residences of the pre-Tudor nobility have been treated, particularly in England, as the ancestors of the national state's artillery forts and strategic defensive planning, when they were really the progenitors of the country house and stately home. Functional (and diminishing stylistic) links connect them with the Continental *château* and *Schloss* of the later seventeenth, eighteenth and nineteenth centuries. The socio-architectural approach that Mark Girouard has made particularly his own[3] needs only to be extended to the Middle Ages. The whole culture is expressed by its buildings, and nothing is more eloquently medieval than its castles and cathedrals. If Talleyrand was right to say 'war is much too serious a thing to be left to military men', then castles cannot possibly be abandoned to the military historian.[4]

Licences to crenellate have much to do with the aristocratic culture of knighthood. A military aura was part of the social fabric of the landed arms-bearing class. Their values infiltrated the Church from top to bottom, the gentry ubiquitously and the merchant princes of proud town corporations, putting battlements everywhere. Aggressive ostentation was the universal aesthetic but it was far more than ornament. Fortification meaning 'serious defence' mattered just as much. Buildings today often called 'fortified manor houses' to contemporaries were 'castles and manors'. The owner's rank counted most. By modern fashion, places like Allington (licensed in 1281), Amberley (1377), Belvoir (1203), Beverstone (1229), Bishop's Stortford (1346), Bodiam (1385), Bolton-in-Wensleydale (1379), Bronsill (1460), Brougham (1309), and Bungay (1294), to go no further, are set apart from the majority as fortresses first and dwellings second, as though the two functions were opposed. The structural remnants on the ground are not so simple; and the contemporary social realities were infinitely more complex. The same phraseology, for instance, covered a Dunstanburgh (1315) and an Acton Burnell (1284).

The English 'military' obsession is an insular oddity, due in part to the ruin of most castles during or before the Civil War. Britain is out of step in ignoring most of the cultural aspects meant by *castellologie* and by *Burgenkunde*. Licences require them. Crenellation meant fortification architecturally and metaphysically:

---

[3] For example, M. Girouard, *Life in the English Country House* (New Haven, 1978), esp. chs 2, 3.

[4] For example, C. Coulson, 'Some Analysis of the Castle of Bodiam, East Sussex', in *Medieval Knighthood* 4, ed. C. Harper-Bill and R. Harvey (Woodbridge, 1992), 51–107.

equipment with the panoply of ditches, walls, towers and crenels.[5] It is a travesty to say: 'licences are by no means only in respect of castles or fortifications of any kind; they were licences to *crenellate*, and all manner of medieval buildings were topped with a crenellated parapet – often merely ornamental'. Why they were apparently so indiscriminate requires explanation. Modern logic would expect a two-tier system, with careful rationing of 'serious' defences to loyal major lords. The initiative, in reality, lay entirely with the builder not the Crown. The large unlicensed majority, having the symbols or some substance of architectural defence, could not otherwise have escaped official disapproval, whether for being 'strong' and 'dangerous', or merely 'ornamental' and 'arrogant'. Actually, less than half a dozen of any kind achieved any such notice.[6] The puzzle can only be resolved by considering the way licences were granted, as well as the reasons some propertied people had for choosing to get one. Individuals' motives varied as widely as the structures they sometimes proceeded to build.

The Sociological Context

The more than 220 volumes of published Patent, Close, Fine and Charter Rolls translate and condense, or give in *extenso* transcript, the Chancery clerks' summaries of nearly every privilege, grant, appointment and mandate sent out under the Great Seal.[7] These enrolments, enormous in bulk and detail, began abruptly to be kept in 1199 and disclose the everyday workings of a centralised bureaucracy of great sophistication, but spurious modernity.[8] In the vast majority of entries the impression of authoritarianism is an illusion. Most are due to petitions sent in directly, or (from the early fourteenth century) via the Privy Seal Office, often forwarded by an influential friend at Court. Very few arose from royal or Council action. The administration for most issues was set on autopilot, responding automatically to routine demands. Checking and verification procedures do not support any idea that fortification was planned or supervised as something special and peculiarly affecting the public; indeed, the contrary. Appointing local juries to find out who might be affected usually preceded grants of new markets and fairs, or permitting roads to be diverted further from noble mansions, or for monks and friars to have posterns in town walls. Rights of way were highly regarded. Imparking and crenellation received no such precautions. Nor were honorific privileges in general fiscally exploited, whereas bequests to the Church

---

[5] C. Coulson, 'Structural Symbolism in Medieval Castle Architecture', *Journal of the British Archaeological Association* 132 (1979), 73–90.

[6] D. J. C. King, *The Castle in England and Wales* (Beckenham, 1988), 22. Hartlebury (1268) is conjectural; Marham (1271), Barnwell (1274), Swine (1352) and Wigton church (1374) were perfunctorily noticed.

[7] HMSO *c.*1890–: Record Commission 1830s. The English is archaic and indexes unreliable but the series is very under-used.

[8] T. F. Tout, *Chapters in the Administrative History of Medieval England*, 6 vols (Manchester, 1920–33).

(mortmain) paid an approximate *ad valorem* duty and 'fines' were levied for most lucrative rights and getting special judicial enquiries. Instead, like the improving of a manor-seat with exclusive deer park, hunting preserve or warren, permission to crenellate passed the Privy Seal and then through Chancery virtually automatically. Grants habitually recite uncritically the terms of the petition.

Requests by towns for *murage* were rarely refused, sometimes checked, verified only when royal revenue was affected. Occasional details, beyond the standard phraseology of different periods, repeat, as in the case of Bodiam, what the applicant said. Seemingly restrictive licences normally just declare what the petitioner wished to build. Neighbouring lords, and towns especially, might be touchy. Patents, especially if read out by the Sheriff in full County Court, were prestigious and inexpensive; the modest 'fee of the seal', payable on all grants sued out, merely covered clerks' costs in parchment, wax and labour, with a profitable surplus. Licensing was not at all like planning permission.[9]

Had royal patronage (like royal justice) been sold, licences would have been controlled by the rigorous procedures of the Exchequer, backed by the itinerant judges and system of informers. As it is, in 1371 the Commons in Parliament blandly asked to be dispensed altogether from the nominal obligations to sue out a licence to crenellate. Even during the torrent of licences under Edward III (213 sites 1327–77) it was a technical formality. Fortunately for socio-architectural history it was not accepted, although licences decline sharply in numbers after about 1399.[10] A series of Acts of Resumption beginning in 1404, expressly declared that the 'making of castles' and enclosing of parks were 'in no way prejudicial to the Crown' (or its revenues) and should continue to be licensed on request.[11] As noted by N Denholm-Young, 'like any other medieval licence (e.g. mortmain) a licence to crenellate would be granted to any applicant … if he could afford it'.[12] To this he added tendentiously, 'if he was not openly hostile to the crown'. Anyone out of favour might find access to the machinery of Chancery less easy than it was for a courtier. Political opponents were not barred as such.

The range of public figures, notable in their counties, in the Commons, or even nationally, who obtained licences, is very wide. Those who pulled the levers of the fruit-machine of patronage include princes of the blood such as Richard of Almain (Mere, 1253), Edmund of Lancaster (Savoy Palace, 1293, case 3 below), and Humphrey of Gloucester (Greenwich, 1433 and 1437). Among the earls are Hubert de Burgh of Kent (Hadleigh, 1230); Richard de Clare of Gloucester (Manhall 'Manor', Southwold and Tonbridge 'Manors' and towns also, and the Isle of Portland, 1259); Humphrey de Bohun of Hereford (batch of nine sites including the old castle of Saffron Walden, 1347); Henry de Percy of Northumberland (Alnwick Town, 1434); and Edward Stafford, duke of Buckingham (Thornbury,

---

[9] All these matters are to be examined in my book *Castles, Kings and Courtiers: Fortifying, Privilege and Defence in England, Ireland and Wales* (in preparation).

[10] Statistics are: 59 sites 1200–72; 57, 1272–1307; 67, 1307–27; 58, 1377–99; 41, 1400–61; 59, 1462–1578.

[11] *Rotuli Parliamentorum* 2, no. 34, 307; 3, no. 14, 548 (19), etc.

[12] N. Denholm-Young, *The Country Gentry in the Fourteenth Century* (Oxford, 1969), 36.

1510). As courtiers and civil servants, it is unsurprising to find twenty-eight bishops, including Bath and Wells, Chichester, Coventry, Durham, Exeter, Lincoln, Norwich, Salisbury and Winchester (the richest of all) among them. Building and living in castles denoted baronial and noble rank. The majority was not licensed. Civil War or earlier ruin has damaged the palace aspect, but Alnwick, Arundel, Belvoir, Raby, Warwick and Windsor show what castles once were. Many great men's castles had no licence: de Blundeville's Beeston, Bolingbroke and Chartley; de Valence's Goodrich; de Montfort's and Lancaster's Kenilworth; York's Fotheringhay; Stanley's Lathom and Percy's Warkworth. Episcopal Eccleshall (Coventry) and la Rose (Carlisle) had licences (1200; 1336 and 1355) but, in general, caprice and personal circumstances were decisive. 'Strong' or 'weak', new creations or routine refortifications, interior or borderlands, mattered not at all.

The prelates of the religious orders had somewhat less direct access to the bureaucrats, normally under an episcopal Chancellor, but there are 58 conventual licences, including repeats (precincts, gatehouses, dwellings etc.). That towns and inns account for nearly as many (29 for town walls, about 25 for other buildings and town houses, suburban or intramural) shows that non-noble birth was in England no obstacle to this privilege, although six of the town licences went to their lords and ten of the town houses were the inns and *hôtels* of bishops and nobles.

Between the social extremes of the great lords and the town patricians lies the great bulk of the 470 sites licensed (67 twice, 6 thrice and one four times). Lay manors and castles total 349, compared with 60 ecclesiastical, structurally similar but tending to be closer to magnate type. It would be wrong to treat this majority as no more than a very long tail to the castle species. Seignorially eloquent crenellated and moated residences, a tiny fraction of them licensed and those mostly the property of wealthier gentry, are vividly known sometimes from excavations and contemporary descriptions (dower partitions; inquisitions *post mortem* etc.). Like the whole class of *Herrensitze* they combined the noble accommodation with barns and farmyards, suitably demarcated. Classifying some as 'castles', others as 'strong houses', and more as 'rejects', often on the basis of whether the situation is 'strong', or ignoring them entirely unless of early earthwork type, cannot be justified, even by convenience. This class was not pseudo-castles but simply little ones. Hugh Braun (1936), Colin Platt (1982), Michael Thompson (1987) and Norman Pounds (1990)[13] have begun the move away from the notion that the 'real' castle was a Krak des Chevaliers or a Salses de Roussillon.[14] Licences to crenellate, the particulars of their recipients and subjects, individually and in the aggregate, provide an architectural sociology of castles. Moor End (Northamptonshire) is

---

[13] H. Braun, *The English Castle* (London, 1936), ch. 5; C. Platt, *The Castle in Medieval England and Wales* (London, 1982), chs 7, 8; M. W. Thompson, *The Decline of the Castle* (Cambridge, 1987), ch. 5; N. J. G. Pounds, *The Medieval Castle in England and Wales* (Cambridge, 1990), ch. 10.

[14] For example, I. Hogg, *The History of Forts and Castles* (London, 1981), 104–5; cf. my 'Castellation in the County of Champagne in the Thirteenth Century', *Château Gaillard* 9–10 (Caen 1982), 347–64.

not now impressive but it was licensed (1347) to be crenellated, made a fortress (*fortalicium*) and embellished with a deerpark (*CPR (1345–1348)*, 270). To its royal and princely owners it was truly a castle (1363, 1451, 1478) but to David King 'more a habitation than a fortress'. Where the great led, lesser men followed, so far as their resources allowed.

Specimens of Licensed Crenellation

Representing so many sites, a great many 'vanished', extending over nearly four centuries, by a mere fifteen specimens is not easy. The variety is enormous and it coexisted at all periods. There was no 'decline' from earlier 'real castles' to later fake ones. Castle-symbolism indeed differed but slightly in earthwork and timber form. We have shunned the most familiar examples in order to reduce automatic associations.

Figure 1.
Whittington: remains
of thirteenth-century
curtain. (Arnold Taylor).

1. *Whittington Castle, Shropshire* (Figure 1)

One phase of the continual updating of early castles, for administrative, defensive and residential use, was officially noticed at Whittington, on the Welsh March. The civil war was barely over and the king still a child. Personal letters went from the Regent, Hubert de Burgh, to the earl of Chester and to the sheriff notifying them that 'the king' had 'granted licence to Fulk fitz Warin to fortify his castle adequately' (*competenter*), since Fulk had promised no consequent breach of the peace (*Rotuli Litterarum Clausarum*, ed. T. D. Hardy, Record Commission, I, 1204–24, (1833–4), 460 (1221)). Local friction the sheriff was to pacify. Ranulf of Chester's local interests, like Hubert's own, were not to lead to interference with the work. Such precautions characterise this period of pacification. The king's theoretical right to license fortification could occasionally (as at Dudley, Staffordshire, in 1262; Leybourne, Kent, 1260) be used to inhibit local provocation. The troubled era of the Barons' War (1264–5) has a few other examples like those of 1216–27. To 'fortify' (*firmare*) often meant only munitioning, and may well do so here; but such warlike preparation might threaten neighbours more than any slow and merely demonstrative repair of an old castle.

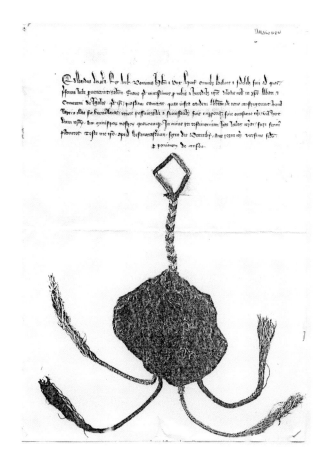

Figure 2.
Halesowen Abbey: original issue-copy patent with great seal (private collector), 1293. (*Birmingham City Archives*)

2. Halesowen Abbey, Worcestershire (Figure 2)

The full surviving issue-version of a patent, sealed on a multicolour tag and open
to inspection by all, looks imposing but was one of many thousands by Edward I's
government. His titles are in full, the 'address' and dating clauses are unabbrevi-
ated and only a few words are in shorthand. The seal, showing him sitting in state
in a throne more elaborate than the one in Westminster Abbey made to contain
below the seat the Stone of Scone, authenticates the grant. On a letter close it had
to be broken. The text reads:

> Edward by the grace of God King of England and Lord of Ireland and Duke of
> Aquitaine, to all his bailiffs and faithful to whom these letters shall come, greeting.
> Know that we have granted for ourselves and our heirs to our beloved in Christ the
> abbot and convent of Hales that they may crenellate certain buildings [cameras]
> which they have constructed anew within the Abbey and may hold them thus
> crenellated to themselves and their successors in perpetuity without interference
> [occasione] by ourselves or by our heirs or by any of our ministers. In witness of
> which we have caused these are letters to be made patent. Witness myself at West-
> minster on the sixth day of December, in the twenty- second year of our reign. By
> petition made to the Council. (CPR 1292–1301), 55 [1293]

3. The Savoy Palace, London (Figure 3)

In the Strand, just outside Temple Bar, was the London mansion of Peter of Savoy,
brother-in-law of Henry III and builder of much of the inner ward of Pevensey
Castle. His nephew, Edmund of Lancaster, obtained licence in 1293 (CPR (1292–
1301), 3) 'to crenellate his house called Sauvey in the parish of St Clement Danes'.
In Rymer's full transcript (Foedera, 1, 2, 789) it is 'to fortify and crenellate [firmare
et kernellare] … with a wall of stone and lime and, to hold it to himself and his
heirs in perpetuity thus crenellated and fortified'. The permanency is that of realty
grants, and the crenellation is the form used from c.1265 until 1377 and beyond,
with variations. Greatly enlarged by John of Gaunt (duke 1362–99), the Palace
(destroyed in 1830) was an immense complex of apartments, halls, chapels, shops
and offices, which, for a time, housed the captive King John of France (1356–64).
The City liberties were suspended 1285–99 and Edmund may have got his brother
the King's licence in order to disarm, or perhaps to defy, the citizens' resentment.
It narrowly escaped sacking in 1376 but not in 1381, when described as 'a lodging
to be compared with no other in the kingdom for beauty and nobility'. It may have
begun a fashion: ten London houses were licensed 1305–85.

4. Brougham Castle, Westmorland (Figure 4)

This, like most grants increasingly from Edward I's reign, began with a Privy
Seal warrant to the Chancery, but no Great Seal licence exists. All we have of the
surviving order is: 'Mandate to make letters patent granting to Robert … that he
may crenellate his castles of Brouham and Pendragon' (July?) 1309 (Calendar of
Chancery Warrants, 1, 291). The Privy Seal office did not enrol its writs, but more

Figure 3. The Savoy Palace: elevation from the Thames by G. Vertue, 1736.
© London Metropolitan Archives, City of London

Figure 4. Brougham Castle: early but massive diagonal buttresses, later heightened.
(Arnold Taylor). Reproduced by permission of Historic England Archive

than a few such abortive orders are unlikely. It must be Robe rt de Clifford, who got his mother's Vipont lands in 1295, but not the Appelby barony until late 1308. He may have celebrated coming into his own with the large rebuilding attributed stylistically to the early fourteenth century, including the outer gatehouse with its fine accommodation and most of the south curtain with the chapel, hall, chamber and kitchen. Since he was killed in the disaster of Bannockburn (1314) he must have built fast. His son was in wardship until 1318 and was executed in 1322. Robert's pride in his new work may be presumed, although the inscription above the archway 'thys made Roger' is believed to be due to the fifth Lord Clifford and to have been moved to the gatehouse from the southern lodgings range. Keep and gatehouses, inner and outer, made a fine and strong lordly residence, with most elegant fenestration.

5. Bampton Castle, Oxfordshire (Figure 5)

Aymer de Valence, earl of Pembroke, prominent rival at Edward II's court of Thomas of Lancaster, chose to build for himself a castle, which John Blair has described as 'a huge square enclosure, symmetrically planned with corner towers and intermediate corbelled out turrets' (Ham Court). Goodrich Castle and

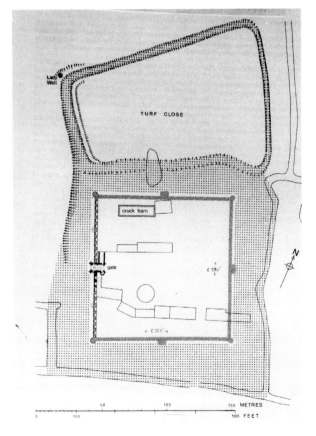

Figure 5. Bampton Castle, Oxfordshire. (*By courtesy of Dr D. W. Blair*)

Wallingford also belonged to Aymer. Bampton's early date is notable. Despite its truly magnatial scale 'its closest analogies are with late fourteenth century castles and fortified houses' (*Medieval Archaeology* 32 (1988), 268). Dr Blair has recovered the original layout from the small remnant (gateway, chamber block and short stretch of curtain), from the ground, and using a drawing of 1668 and the 1827 enclosure map. Of the princely apartments almost nothing is left. It was while spending the night here in 1312 with his countess that earl Guy, whom Piers Gaveston had called the Black Dog of Warwick, abducted the king's captive favourite from Deddington rectory nearby, when under Aymer's sworn safe-custody. Gaveston was beheaded soon after, to Edward's bitter anger. Bampton had been in the Valence family since at least 1256 but the place must have had deep resonances in 1315 (May) when Aymer obtained his licence. King Edward authorised it directly (*CPR (1313–1317)*, 278).

6. Dunstanburgh Castle, Northumberland (Figure 6)

The King's first cousin, Thomas of Lancaster, is an enigma and his licence especially so. One skirmish ended his revolt in 1322. He was arraigned in his own great hall at Pontefract Castle and executed. From 1314 until Boroughbridge he was the most powerful English magnate. When in virtual control of the government, having displaced Pembroke, he had himself licensed for Dunstanburgh. Work had been started on the great coastal promontory over two years before his licence (1315, August). Quarries were opened in May 1313 when Bannockburn and the subsequent Scottish inroads were equally unimaginable. A few licences are expressed technically as pardons, but not this. Thomas by May 1315 had taken over (from Pembroke) the defence of the North, but discharged it laxly. In the new conditions, some trumpeting of his patriotism (however mendacious) might have been expected in the licence but there is none. His castle is well-placed and large enough to receive refugees, as it happens.[15] The ostentatious great gatehouse

Figure 6. Dunstanburgh: land-face of the peninsula from the south. (Arnold Taylor). Reproduced by permission of Historic England Archive

[15] C. H. Hunter Blair and H. L. Honeyman, HMSO Guide (1955).

is one of the largest and latest, but the cliff-top enclosure though vast is weakly defended, requiring modification by John of Gaunt to form an economically defensible inner ward. It is all highly demonstrative, like the superfluous licence itself (*CPR (1313–1317)*, 344).

7. Westenhanger Castle, Kent (Figure 7)

For the sub-baronial order of the knighthood and country gentry a licence was straightforwardly fashionable, especially during the long and militarily most glorious reign of Edward III. Westenhanger was the seat of the Criolls or Kiriels, an established family with widely scattered lands in east Kent. Men of this class did a wide variety of governmental jobs. John de Kiriel in 1339 was put in charge of the defence of the Isle of Thanet. His licence to crenellate was obtained in August 1343 (*CPR (1343–1345)*, 106). In April 1346 he had licence in mortmain to found and endow a chantry dedicated to St Thomas (Becket) adjoining the parish church, and died not long after. Piety and fashion for a dynastic burial-place and prayer-centre commonly caused those who had the means to copy in miniature such great religious castle-colleges as. Kenilworth, Maxstoke, Warwick and Tattershall. The noble and chivalric Kiriel castle, with its eight round and rectangular towers, set in an extensive deerpark (now the Folkestone racecourse), was broken into by night in 1382 by Sir John de Cornwall and his accomplices, using ladders to scale the wall. Forcing the widow Lady de Kiriel into marriage was frustrated because she 'hid in some water'. There were gracious lodgings all round the spacious courtyard, according to a plan of 1648.

Figure 7. Westenhanger: north-east angle. The evolution of castle into *château*, rare in England, is charted by the styles of window. (Arnold Taylor).
Reproduced by permission of Historic England Archive

Figure 8. Oxford Town: thirteenth-century angle-tower with typical arrow loops. (Arnold Taylor). Reproduced by permission of Historic England Archive

8. *Oxford Town* (Figure 8)

Since townsmen were authorised automatically to levy tolls (*murage*) to pay for building and repairing walls, gates and towers (also for bridges and paving), they evidently needed no permission to fortify. Walls, or ditches at least, were an attribute of the chartered free borough.[16] Large sums were confidently entrusted to them, sometimes of potential royal revenue, checked by occasional audits. With towns, most clearly, licence to crenellate (29 cases) was a symbolic optional extra. Wells' (1341, with five years' murage) and Oxford's (*CPR (1381–1385)*, 16), uniquely, were revoked; Wells' licence because the bishop probably found out and resented his burgesses' presumption; and Oxford's 'because granted at the time of the insurrection of the commons'. Certainly 'a ditch 200 feet wide' was exorbitant. The city walls reflect Oxford's murage grants (1226–40, 1251–5, 1257–68, 1285–9, 1301–6, 1321–6, 1347–51). Pride in their walls and jealous monopoly of their control

---

[16] H. L. Turner, *Town Defences in England and Wales* (London, 1971), ch. 6; C. Coulson, 'Battlements and the Bourgeoisie: Municipal Status and the Apparatus of Urban Defence in Later-Medieval England', in *Medieval Knighthood* 5, ed. S. Church and R. Harvey (Woodbridge, 1995), 119–95.

were municipal characteristics. Royal backing for levies to repair and man them (on the slightest pretext) was often sought and granted. Oxford did so in 1378. In 1380 a renewed order was directed at obstruction by the scholars of Merton. Getting clergy to contribute and stopping posterns and denial of access to the walls were always problems.

9. *Wells Cathedral Close and Palace, Somerset* (Figure 9)

Prominence in public service provided wealth, incentive and opportunity to make of the whole Close and adjacent Palace a towered and castellated enclave of ecclesiastical lordship. First, Bishop Robert Burnel, two years after his personal glorification with licensed Acton Burnell (1284), had his own Chancery make him out a licence for the precinct and canons' houses, providing 'sufficient gates and posterns to be opened at dawn' (*CPR (1281–1292)*, 229). Bishop Ralph got this repeated 'for the glory of God, the honour of the Cathedral … and the saints whose bodies repose therein and the security and quiet of the canons …' (*CPR (1340–1343)*, 466). Towers and the bishops' dwelling were included, but the citizens' daytime rights of way were again safeguarded. Perhaps provoked to rivalry, they got their own short-lived licence (*CChR (1341–1417)*, 6–7). Bishop Ralph in 1346, as elsewhere (Lichfield, Lincoln), went one further, having the precinct exempted from lodging, and entry, of royal officials. In 1451, Bishop Thomas had discretion to close the various gates at night confirmed, together with leave to complete the towered and moated Palace, as granted in 1340. Worldly and Divine glory did not seem so distinct as they do today, although the Middle Ages too had its puritans.

Figure 9. Wells: symbolic crosslet-oillet loops typically combine with windows and drawbridge. (Arnold Taylor). Reproduced by permission of Historic England Archive

Figure 10. Thornton abbey: only the oriel above the central archway has been added, and the tiny porter's sentry-box. (Arnold Taylor). Reproduced by permission of Historic England Archive

10. Thornton Abbey, Lincolnshire (Figure 10)

The opulent great gatehouse here, one of the finest, conveys a similar message; exactly as it was meant to do. Built largely of brick, it is carefully faced in stone. Thornton was among the wealthiest of Augustinian canons' abbeys. In August 1382, licence was issued 'to build and crenellate a new house over and next to their abbey gate' (*CPR (1381–1385)*, 166), and in May 1389 to crenellate the abbey in general (*CPR (1388–1392)*, 28). These highly expressive gateways, copied in lay mansions down to the Stuart period, figure quite humbly in licences as 'a chamber over the gate', etc. (Peterborough; St Augustine's, Canterbury, 1308; Evesham, 1332) although at Temple Bruer it was 'a great gate' (1306). Thornton's has side archways (one only at Battle, 1338). Slender octagonal turrets and, inside, miniaturised cruciform loops and saints' statues in canopied niches, make a composite picture (compare the King's Gate, Caernarfon). The canons were proprietors of an annual fair, but in 1345 had to ask for its cancellation because of 'insults, assemblies and disputes which they are unable to pacify or restrain'. They may have reasserted their lordly authority somewhat with the 1380s programme. Such reactive castellation was not unusual.

Figure 11. Sheriff Hutton: the northern style generally favoured square towers like 'peels'.
(By courtesy of Anthony Emery)

11. *Sheriff Hutton Castle, Yorkshire* (Figure 11)

The 'plot in his own ground' which John de Nevill of Raby, knight, was licensed (*CPR (1381–1385)*, 108) 'to enclose with a wall of stone and lime and to crenellate' became a rather irregular northern-type castle, not unlike Bolton (1379). The misleading phrase used in several of Richard II's licences then follows: 'and to make a castle out of it'. In 1378, John had obtained the bishop of Durham's licence (akin to Chester and Lancaster palatinates but longer-lasting) to fortify the ancestral castle of Raby, whose name he assumed. His new lordly seat at Sheriff Hutton resembles Wressle and many others. Lacking a moat and defensive loops, the bold square towers and quite large exterior windows present an aesthetic contrast but share the purpose of such southern courtyard castles as Bodiam. John was a rising man, having married the Latimer heiress, become a retainer of John of Gaunt and Steward of the King's Household until removed in 1376. He died in 1388 holding manors in more than nine counties, castles at Bamburgh, Snape, Middleham, Danby and Sheriff Hutton, and, in London, 'a great tenement with a garden by the city wall'. Ralph, his son, was created earl of Westmorland.

12. *Wingfield Castle, Suffolk* (Figure 12)

Michael de la Pole rose and fell further and faster, following the fortunes of Richard II, which gained him the Chancellorship and earldom of Suffolk (September 1385) but made him one of the victims of the Lords Appellant in February 1387. Arising from a merchant-banking dynasty of Hull, he made his chief country seat at the moated and lofty walled castle, with its East Anglian flint flushwork, square and multangular towers and stately apartments, called as late as 1553 'the

Figure 12. Wingfield Castle: the classic assemblage of moat, towers, double-towered gatehouse and lodgings, revealed by windows in the walls and chimneys above. (Arnold Taylor). Reproduced by permission of Historic England Archive

manor, mansion and castle of Wingfield'. His licence (April 1385; *CPR (1381–1385)*, 555) covered Sternfield and Huntingfield as well, where no work is known, and his heirs in addition to himself. Also unusual is 'with a wall of stone and lime or paling of timber' and (for a patent) including imparking. He called himself 'lord of Wingfield' already in 1379. The links of family, affinity and patronage are shown by the foundation terms of the Carthusian chantry he set up outside Hull (1379). The monks were to pray for the de la Pole family, for John de Nevill of Raby, Richard le Scrope (of Bolton) and for Michael's late wife, Richard's sister. In 1383, Michael obtained the earl of Stafford's daughter in marriage for his son, restored in 1397.

13. *Wardour Castle, Wiltshire* (Figure 13)

This ingenious, 'logical' and sumptuous courtyard castle was so badly damaged in 1643 and modified in Elizabeth's reign by enlarging the windows, that it is most easily appreciated in the reconstruction by Beric Morley. Set within a large outer

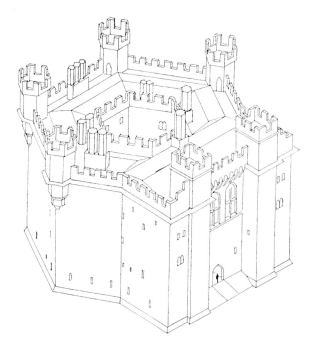

Figure 13. Wardour Castle: from *Essays in Memory of Stuart Rigold* (Maidstone 1981), 112. The western quarter was mined in 1643 and the grounds vindictively destroyed by the Parliamentarians. (By courtesy of Beric Morley)

ditched enclosure, the plan is a hexagon, the angles capped by romantic 'bartizan' turrets with effective chunky corbelling, and the entry set between square towers with recessed wings and beneath machicolation. It is a bijou hunting-box of a castle, licensed in February 1393 (*CPR (1391–1396)*, 261) for John, Lord Lovel, 'to crenellate and make into a castle'. Apart from his castle's affinities with Bodiam, Lovel was a Council colleague of Dallingridge after 1390. Other members were John Devereux, licensed for Penshurst in 1392, and John de Cobham (Cooling, 1381). The Lovel lands were in Northamptonshire (Titchmarsh), and Wardour was a recent acquisition. The designer employed was a master architect. Wardour was a house satisfactory (like Percy Warkworth) to Tudor tastes, which combines the compactness of a tower house with the allure of a southern castle. The windows may have been rather larger than shown, lighting about eight separate suites of rooms, with the Great Hall set over the entrance, magnificently illuminated.

14. *Tonford Manor, Canterbury* (Figure 14)

This little-known near-contemporary of Herstmonceux (licensed 1441), Hellifield (Yorkshire, 1440), Greenwich (Kent, 1433, 1437, vanished) and Cartington (Northumberland, 1442) was one of a batch of six sites licensed in 1448 to Thomas Browne, a prominent Lancastrian Exchequer official, sheriff and MP, in a grand package of lordly rights (*CChR (1427–1516)*, 102). Of the 43 licences by charter, all but six are of this type (imparking, free warren, frankpledge, etc) and there are 47 more on the Patent Roll, 18 per cent of all licences. In many other cases lordly perquisites came in separate grants. Thomas is the classical *arriviste* who rose to

Figure 14. Tonford Manor: north surviving side of the diminutive enceinte with classic house. (cf. Westenhanger, Figure 7)

be a member of Henry VI's household. Knight of the shire (1445–6), he escaped more than verbal violence from the Cade rebellion (1450) and was sheltering in the Tower when the Yorkists captured the king in 1460 near Northampton. His landed interests were in east Kent (Betchworth, Surrey, also licensed, is an outlier). Tonford, conveniently near Canterbury, has the miniature square gatehouse and turreted curtain wall needed to establish him among the landed aristocracy. His gatehouse lacks not only hinges and bar-sockets but also even gates; the nostalgic allusion was quite sufficient.[17]

15. *Baconsthorpe Castle, Norfolk* (Figure 15)

The quality and longevity of the castellated emblems of nobility are perhaps the chief socio-architectural lesson of the licences to crenellate. The castle-home proclaimed status and lordly lifestyle. Licence alone seems to have done so too. The Heydons of Baconsthorpe rose (like the Scropes) by practising the law, began their turreted quadrangle before 1480, continued it under Henry Heydon (1480–1504) with the substantial rectangular inner gatehouse of flint with stone dressings, but obtained no licence until 1561, when the family was securely established among the north Norfolk gentry, under Christopher Heydon (1551–79) 'the Queen's servant'.[18] He added the outer gatehouse, with its cupola-topped stair-turret, square label-framed archway in distant courtesy to the traditional drawbridge,

---

[17] Career details in R. A. Griffiths, *The Reign of King Henry VI* (Berkeley and Los Angeles, 1981).
[18] S. E. Rigold, *Baconsthorpe Castle* (HMSO, 1966). The Bacon family name, despite prolonged Heydon tenure, was not erased.

Figure 15. Baconsthorpe
Castle: Christopher
Heydon's outer Gatehouse
of *c.*1561. (Arnold
Taylor). Reproduced by
permission of Historic
England Archive

and battlemented architrave to the door-case, to fulfil his patent 'to fortify, embattle and build towers' there (*CPR (1560–1563)*, 219). Nothing much had changed.
The Spenserian cult of chivalry even reinvigorated tradition, one of innumerable
signs being Leicester's Gatehouse at Kenilworth. The impact of the Renaissance
upon a medievalism that had no need of revival was little more than ornamental
until the slow advent during the Stuart era of Palladianism. Only then was the
militant cloak of the noble mansion discarded in favour of the strait-jacket of an
alien classicism.

Acknowledgements

For the illustrations for Figures 1, 4, 6, 7, 8, 9, 10, 12 and 15 I am indebted to Arnold
Taylor and to the skills of the University of Kent photographic department. Mr J.
D. Warner-Davies of Birmingham City Archives provided Figure 2, the Guildhall
Library Figure 3, and the kind courtesy of Dr W. J. Blair permitted me to use
Figure 5, from *Medieval Archaeology* 32 (1988), 269. I am grateful to Anthony
Emery for Figure 11 and to Beric Morley for Figure 13. The kind hospitality of
Mr and Mrs Charles Barker of Tonford Manor (Figure 14) is also most gratefully
acknowledged.

11

Some Analysis of the
Castle of Bodiam, East Sussex*

Charles Coulson

I. The Significance of Bodiam

The castle of Bodiam, blandly ensconced in its lily-pond of a moat, is well-known, but can scarcely be said to be well-understood.[1] It represents the popular ideal of a medieval castle, and its inheritors from the Marquis Curzon of Kedleston, the National Trust, style it simply '*the* favourite castle' in their tourist leaflet, and 'everyone's fairy-tale castle' in their 1985 Guide.[2] That it has had so compelling and so enduring an impact, not least today six centuries since it was completed, triumphantly proves its success. In the modern literature of castle studies it has held a special position, which would have pleased Sir Edward Dallingridge, who sought and duly obtained licence, in October 1385, to build what has also been

---

* A brief summary of this paper appears in *Fortress*, 10 August 1991, entitled 'Bodiam Castle: Truth and Tradition'.

[1] Dr W. Douglas Simpson commented that 'few English castles have been more thoroughly studied or more extensively written about', since 1831: 'The Moated Homestead, Church and Castle of Bodiam', *Sussex Archaeological Collections* (hereafter SAC) 72, (1934), 69–99 (hereafter Simpson 1931). The present paper enlarges upon my note 11 (p. 76) in 'Structural Symbolism in Medieval Castle Architecture', *Journal of the British Archaeological Association* 132 (1979), 73–90 [p.00 in this volume]. Acknowledgement is gratefully made for the benefits of discussion of a résumé of this paper to Michael Clanchy, Richard Eales, Anthony Emery, Richard Gem, Robert Higham, Lawrence Keen, John Kenyon, Beric Morley, Michael Prestwich, Derek Renn, Andrew Saunders, Nigel Saul, Arnold Taylor and Michael Thompson. For communicating in November 1990 full details of the landscape survey done in 1988 by the Royal Commission on the Historical Monuments of England, my special thanks are due to Paul Everson of RCHME Keele, National Archaeological Record, Southampton, NAR no. TQ 72 NE1; also *Medieval Archaeology* 34 (1990), 155–7 (hereafter RCHME i and ii)) and their very generous help in providing the specially drawn site plan (Figure 2) and 'viewing platform' detail (Figure 3), together with photographs (Figures 10, 17, 18) where indicated, is most gratefully acknowledged. Mr Everson also discusses the landscaping aspects in CBA *Research Report* no. 78 (1991), *Garden Archaeology*, ed. A. E. Brown, esp. 9–10. For less tangible but great benefits I am indebted, as always, to the late Otto (R. C.) Smail.

[2] A. Yarrow, *Bodiam Castle* (Norwich, 1985) (1985 Guide) contains an excellent brief treatment of the domestic and seignorial aspects. Curzon's book (*Bodiam Castle*, 1926) was good for its date and circumstances (cf. Curzon and H. A. Tipping, *Tattershall Castle* (Lincolnshire, 1929), *passim*). He bought Bodiam in 1916, conserved it and left it to the Trust in 1925. A new Guide by D. Thackray is understood to be in preparation. The form Dallingridge is adopted in preference to the variant medieval phonetic spellings (viz. Dalling Ridge near East Grinstead) approximating to Dalyngrigge.

called 'the most spectacular private castle of the decade'.[3] The fairy-tale cannot be sustained and questioning analysis rather than enthusiastic advocacy is our present purpose. The equivocation of Bodiam comment, finely balanced between lurking ugly disbelief and uninhibited romantic enjoyment, to be found almost universally in all kinds and levels of work, must be resolved.[4]

The building remains profoundly significant in a perhaps surprising variety of ways. It has been assumed to be the most notable (indeed, virtually the sole) exception to the scenario of post-Edwardian (military) 'decline', and it is certainly something of a test-case for the understanding of licences to crenellate. These royal patents (or charters), ostensibly authorising the construction of stone walls and battlements (and occasionally of other fortifications), usually phrased as additions to an existing dwelling, come formally into being with the commencement of enrolment under King John and last until the early Stuart period. From c.1200 until 1578 over 500 sites were licensed (some several times), nearly half of them (217) during the reign of Edward III.[5] They have traditionally been regarded as prohibitive in purpose, reluctantly conceded, and thought to bear the imprint of a supposed royal disfavour towards noble castellation.[6] It has also been implied that they are prescriptive, implementing some national defence plan. This latter is the particular claim made for Bodiam; namely that the licence, in saying that the new castle was for 'the defence of the adjacent countryside' and for the 'resisting of the king's enemies', in effect, 'designated what was otherwise a privately-owned residence and stronghold as forming part of a coastal or second-line (sic) national defence scheme' (see Figure 1). Its construction is further attributed to the danger of French raids and to the loss of 'control of the Channel' between 1372 and 1387.[7] If the licence were indeed, as W. D. Simpson has claimed, the result of central and

---

[3] D.J. Turner 'Bodiam, Sussex: True Castle or Old Soldier's Dream House?' (274), in *England in the Fourteenth Century: Proceedings of the 1985 Harlaxton Symposium*, ed. W. M. Ormrod (Woodbridge, 1986), 267–77 (hereafter Turner).

[4] Recent comment remains 'military' in emphasis or equivocates, e.g. R. Allen Brown, *English Medieval Castles* (London, 1954), 95–6; slightly modified in *English Castles* (London, 1976), 144–6; C. Platt, *The Castle in Medieval England and Wales* (London, 1982), 114–18; D. J. C. King, *Castellarium Anglicanum* (New York, 1983), 469 (hereafter King); M. W. Thompson, *The Decline of the Castle* (Cambridge, 1987) (hereafter Thompson), 17, 36–7, 111, penetrates more deeply but substantially adheres to the traditional view (*pers. comm.*, 6 October 1990).

[5] Coulson 1979 (n. 1 above); more generally, 'Hierarchism in Conventual Crenellation: an Essay in the Sociology and Metaphysics of Medieval Fortification', *Medieval Archaeology* 26 (1982), 69–100.

[6] The view is ubiquitous, but see the summary by Daniel Williams 'Fortified Manor Houses', *Transactions of the Leicestershire Archaeological and Historical Society* 1 (1974–5), 1–16. For an early denial, see W. Mackay Mackenzie, *The Medieval Castle in Scotland* (London, 1927), appendix A; and recently, R. Eales, 'Castles and Politics in England, 1215–1224', *Thirteenth-Century England* 2 (1988), esp. 39–40, reprinted *ANC*, 367–88; and 'Royal Power and Castles in Norman England', in *Medieval Knighthood* 3, ed. C. Harper-Bill and R. Harvey (Woodbridge, 1990), *passim*, reprinted *ANC*, 41–67.

[7] Simpson 1931 (845 *et passim*), citing the sack of Rye by Jean de Vienne in 1377, attacks on Rye and Winchelsea, 1380, etc. The fashion for 'military' explanations has received apparent support from the terms of the 1385 licence, which have been taken uncritically with rare exceptions, e.g. T. F. Tout's weighty dubiety (see n. 74 below), *Chapters in the Administrative History of Medieval*

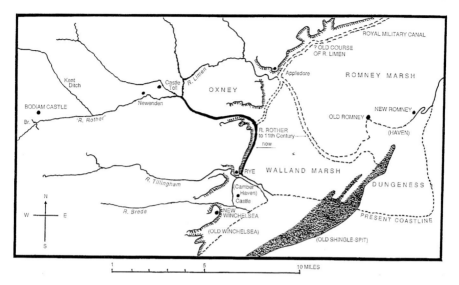

Figure 1. Sketch plan showing position of Bodiam Castle in relation to changes in the coastline in the neighbourhood of Romney Marsh since Saxon times. (Adapted with kind permission from B. K. Davison, *Medieval Archaeology* 16 (1972), 124)

royal *dirigisme* and granted only for these reasons of public benefit, then it would truly be unique.

Very fortunately, the building itself offers the most eloquent testimony since it is entirely of one period and almost entirely of one build. Far from standing alone against the weight of the general evidence (of licences to crenellate most notably), both the structure and the historical circumstances of Bodiam Castle when re-examined are found to concur. The nearly complete remains and the very suggestive documentary evidence corroborate each other. The militant array of walls and towers, which primarily concerns us here, is almost intact. The interior, although stripped out, still retains substantial traces of the lodgings and apartments, but the outer shell being virtually undamaged it is possible to address directly the key issue that has focused controversy, namely the degree of its 'seriousness as a fortification'. The debate goes back to the early commentators and still continues as a live issue. Some reconsideration may achieve a certain general clearing of the ground and restore to the fellowship of chivalry a long-lost brother, redeemed from the ranks of the military.

England, 6 vols (Manchester, 1920–33), iii, 411 n. 1; also J. R. Maddicott, *Past and Present*, Suppl. i (1975), 64–5.

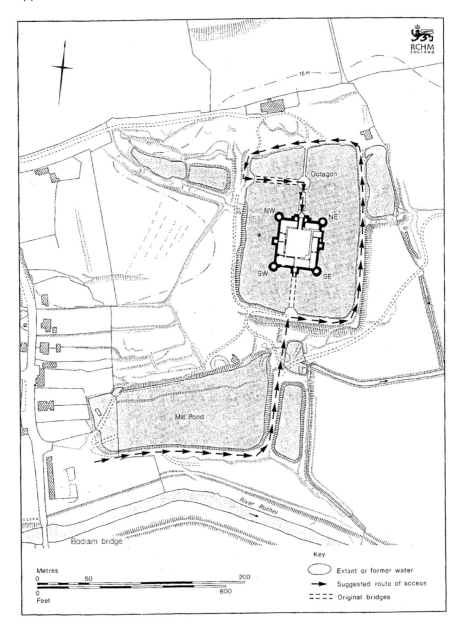

RCHM
ENGLAND

15 m

Octagon

NW   NE

SW   SE

Mill Pond

River Rother

Bodiam bridge

Key

Metres
0   50   200

0   600
Feet

⬭ Extant or former water

→ Suggested route of access

▪▪▪▪ Original bridges

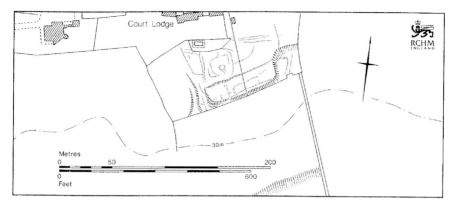

Figure 3 Bodiam castle, 'viewing platform' or belvedere.
© Crown copyright. Historic England Archive
'On the crest of the high ridge (about 750 feet) to the N of the castle, and some 30m
(nearly 100 feet) vertically above it, is an earthwork known as the Gun Garden …
interpreted following limited excavations in 1961 as a medieval building platform … The
earthworks consist … of broad terraces backed by what may be the sites of buildings
… obviously ornamented and grand in scale. It is most likely to have been a garden
or pleasance … but it must surely also have functioned as a viewing platform for the
landscaped setting of the castle below. Whether it … was physically linked to the castle
is now unclear …' (C. Taylor, P. Everson and R. Wilson-North, *Medieval Archaeology* 34
(1990), 155–7, 156 is the complete original plan of the entire site, including the viewing
platform here treated separately by kind agreement of RCHME)

Figure 2 (opposite) Bodiam castle, site and landscape plan. (RCHME, Feb. 1991)
© Crown copyright. Historic England Archive
'The earthworks surrounding Bodiam castle form an elaborate and contrived setting for
the building, of a coherence not previously perceived. Most striking is the use of sheets
of water to create a staged landscape, not only to be passed through but to be viewed
from above …'
(C. Taylor, P. Everson and R. Wilson-North, *Medieval Archaeology* 34 (1990), 155–7,
including the plan on which the above is based, specially adapted by great courtesy of
the Royal Commission on the Historical Monuments of England, by P.M.Sinton)

Notes
1 Since 1988 the NE moat sluice has been restored by the National Trust, together with
the NE overflow pond.
2 The principal route of access proposed above supplemented the direct NW approach
along the side of the two NW ponds, not marked here.
3 The 'viewing platform' (Figure 3) lies about 750 feet NNW from the N margin of the
main moat.

II. The Problem of Bodiam

It will be sufficient to mention the principal existing views to show the extent and nature of the central problem of interpretation and to illustrate the equivocation referred to.

The authority of G. T. Clark still stands high. He began his monographs in the 1830s and was incautious only when unduly influenced by E. A. Freeman, to whom he dedicated his collected papers, published in 1884 as *Medieval Military Architecture in England*. He was able to employ the services of record-searchers but his work does somewhat lack historical context.

When dating masonry from stylistic or structural signs alone Clark was most careful not to make attributions earlier than the mid-twelfth century and resisted the strong expectations for Anglo-Saxon castles of masonry. On stone-work he was impervious to the pressures of contemporary fashion, but he did succumb notoriously in thinking some earthwork moues to be pre-Conquest.[8] His description (1874) of the *assiette* of Bodiam shows him at his best:

> A sort of platform was selected upon the sloping ground, about thirty feet above the river (Rother)'s level and in it was excavated a rectangular basin, 180 yards north and south, by 117 yards east and west, and about seven feet deep [see Figure 2]. To the east the containing bank was wholly artificial, formed of the excavated material, as was also the case with the contiguous parts to the north and south … In the centre, or nearly so, of the excavation was left a rectangular island of rather above half an acre in area, raised artificially about four feet … (giving) a wet moat from thirty-five to sixty-five yards broad.[9]

Clark was struck by the defensive incongruity of the post-medieval sluice then used 'for the occasional emptying of the moat' (originally quite frequently needed for cleaning out the silt and issues of the garderobes) and thought that 'probably something of the sort was originally constructed, though it would, of course, be concealed (*sic*)'. Realism nevertheless required him to remark that, 'the fact is, however, that a few vigorous workmen could at any time have cut through the bank in a few hours, and thus have deprived the castle of one of its defences' (see

---

[8] George Thomas Clark was a civil engineer and scholar who had worked with Brunel (see King xii). His prefatory chapters to his collected papers (1884, next note) incurred the ire of J. H. Round (anonymously but typically in *The Quarterly Review* 179 (1894), 27–57; and, more aggressively, *Archaeologia* 58 (1902), 313–40, targeting also Freeman) and of E. S. Armitage (*Early Norman Castles of the British Isles*, 1912, *passim*). See also J. M. B. Counihan, 'Castle Studies in England and on the Continent since 1850', *Anglo-Norman Studies* 12 (1988), *passim*. But Clark's reputation rests solidly on his pioneering castle monographs.

[9] *Medieval Military Architecture* (1884), i, 239–47, reprinting *Archaeologia Cantiana* 9 (1874), cv–cxvi. The 'basin' was actually partly excavated and partly levelled up with the spoil (see Figure 10). The Royal Commission 1988 landscape survey (RCHME i, 4) gives the moat as on average 115 m x 155 m and the water depth as about 2 m. The central 'platform' is slightly to the S of centre of the tapering rectangle of water (see Figure 2).

Figure 4. Bodiam castle (June 1970), S front looking W, showing: silt deposited since 1920, bulldozed; the impermeable bed of the moat; the S bank (left-hand side) with postern bridge-pier facing diminutive cheek wall barbican-platform; machicolation to part of flank only; the SE tower (right-hand side); SW tower beyond.

Figure 5. Bodiam castle (June 1970), postern tower from S bridge-pier, showing: trestle-bridge footings; the moat water-level mark on the plinth (partly rendered by Curzon); hall lower window (right-hand side) in the SE curtain; the postern barbican, an afterthought (not bonded).

Figure 6. Bodiam castle (March 1991), detail of the postern archway, showing: no chain holes, pit or pivots; closure by thin portcullis and doors (early modern) lacking bar-hole(s) and socket(s); specious 'drawbridge' rebate; screens passage beyond.

Figure 7. Bodiam castle (June 1970), E side looking N, showing: vulnerable E bank (right-hand side); large single-light windows; small ground-floor lights to SE tower (non-defensible); hall window (left-hand side); moat overflow to NE, lately restored with NE pond (see Figure 2).

Figures 4, 5, 7, 11, 12, 19). Enchantment resumed its sway next sentence with – 'the mud, however, until dry would be an even better protector than the water'.[10]

With much careful factual detail and some very illuminating asides, Clark then turns to the building on the 'platform'. The rectangle, exclusive of tower-projections, measures 152 feet north and south, by 138 feet east and west (184 by 171 feet overall).[11] The curtain walls are forty feet and a half high from moat to parapet copings and six and a half feet thick at the bottom, the round or 'drum' angle towers being twenty-nine feet in external diameter. Aesthetically the ensemble of 'eight mural towers, four cylindrical and four rectangular' (but the Main Gate is rectilinear *rectius*) provides, in Clark's words, 'an agreeable variety to the outline'. It would be naive to suppose this effect was accidental (see Figure 13). Proportions are assisted also by the stair turrets to the towers (dummies covering the stairwells), which are 'crested with miniature battlements in the late-Perpendicular manner'. Clark faithfully describes the gunloops found only in the Main Gate, but has difficulty in believing the reputed defensive purpose of the round holes in the vaults of the gate passage. These so-called 'murder-holes' occur in both chambers of the Main Gate passage, where the vaults are fallen, and in the intact vault of the Postern gate passage. 'The openings', he says, 'are, of the central boss, six inches, and of the others, four inches diameter. These apertures can scarcely have been meant for defence; they are too small, and do not command the four corners of the passage ...' Fantasies involving boiling oil and molten lead (hazardous even with a stone ceiling) are summarily dismissed but without any alternative explanation being offered.[12]

[10] There are now concrete capped overflows in the centre of the S bank and near the NE corner (lately replaced by a restored spillway). Cleaning was evidently done by cutting the bank. There was no morass but only eighteen inches of silt on the firm bottom in 1970, accumulated since the 1920 emptying. Sewage in a latrine shoot did not deter the French in 1204 at Château Gaillard. Laying brushwood and planking was standard procedure, normally countered by deep ditches. Simpson 1931, 88, dismissed Clark's objection (although Curzon had accepted it) and argued that 'to cut through the bank' (about six feet thick at the top) 'would scarcely be an easy job, or one of a few hours, under the full command (*sic*) of parapets and towers lined by the finest archery in Europe'. Such archers (had Dallingridge been able to pay them) would not have been allowed to skulk at an inland site remote from the threatened coast (see Figure 1). Any attackers would also possess archery and might be numerous.

[11] RCHME i, 4. Clark did err in saying there are chain-holes in the upper corners of the Main Gate 'drawbridge' rebate. As with the Postern, this is precluded by the location and dimensions of the portcullis slot, in any case (see Figures 6, 14). The building may still have been ivy-clad in 1874. Its small scale is shown by Colchester 'keep' (about 154 by 113 feet excluding projections); Caerphilly inner ward (about 200 feet internally) and Beaumaris (about 175 by 190 feet internally). Expanding Bodiam's dimensions by a third, or slightly more, would give it the 'Edwardian' size its designer conveys by careful proportioning. Clark surely knew of the licence to crenellate (terms summarised by J. H. Parker, n. 14 below) but curiously was not misled or influenced (i, 240).

[12] The brick flooring (probably nineteenth century) to the chamber over the passage complicates measurement, but the central hole is seven inches diameter and the others about six inches. All are now blocked (one with ?early-modern brick), perhaps a late medieval modification for domestic convenience. Very effective defensive holes, of different design, can be seen without the doors of Henry VII's Deal Castle.

The rest of his description is devoted to the halls, chambers and 'domestic' offices of the manor-house enveloped by the walls and filling every interior space, including the towers. He concludes with the shrewd comment that 'the drum towers look older than their real date, their gorge walls, general proportions and arrangements, well-staircases and lancet and often trefoiled windows, savouring of the Edwardian period' and contrasting, he feels, with the Perpendicular mood of the interior details. Despite some doubts caused by the unpracticality of the putative though vanished right-angled trestle bridge approach to the Main Gate via the Octagon (in fact, an authentic feature), 'Castle Clark's' main conclusion firmly annexes Bodiam to his province. 'It was', he declares, 'a castle, not a manor-house, nor palace.'[13] Whether this view reflects a sensitive or contemporary understanding of what such a castle truly was (let alone a fair assessment of the actual structure) must be questioned, but it was the verdict also of John Henry Parker in 1859 in still less acceptable form. For Parker, Bodiam 'is altogether more of a castle than a house; it was habitable but built chiefly for defence'. Somewhat more perceptive, of atmosphere at least, is his comment that 'the windows in the towers are small, narrow and round-headed, just like Norman or Early English'.[14]

Not remotely subtle or sympathetic is the paper published in 1903 by the local antiquarian Harold Sands, in the *Sussex Archaeological Collections*. We find here a military rationale of the most undiluted variety, but strenuous advocacy makes light of the difficulties. Mr Sands's work is a bizarre tribute to the militant aura, which the unknown designer so cleverly created. The position, fourteen miles up the now shrunken but just tidal river Rother from Rye, lying ten and a half miles inland from the nearest coast by Hastings, possesses, we are told, 'considerable strategical advantages'.[15] The 'higher ground', which, in fact entirely overlooks the

---

[13] Clark's 101 other monographs nearly all deal with much earlier and major castles, to which he tried to assimilate Bodiam. His reservations are the more telling, as a result, and his omissions more understandable. Subsequent general surveys of castles have regrettably discarded his careful case-study method, and popular synthesis has (D. F. Renn, *Norman Castles in Britain* (1968), and King, excepted) been repetitively superficial.

[14] J. H. Parker (and T. Hudson Turner), *Some Account of Domestic Architecture in England ...*, 3 vols in 4 (Oxford, 1851–9), iii, 312–14 (still basic; cf. M. E. Wood, *The English Medieval House*, 1965). Parker published the first 'List of Licences to Crenellate from the Patent Rolls' (iii, 401–22). Seriously incomplete though it is, his preliminary comments are percipient. Unfortunately, William Stubbs and many since took him as proof of the existence of some restrictive policy and system of royal licensing; and not of crenellating but of fortifying (n. 6 above).

[15] H. Sands, 'Bodiam Castle', SAC 46 (1903), 114–33 (115); the 1985 Guide (caption to first photograph) claims a harbour and an estuary in 1385. The actual estuary S of Rye was in constant danger from the coastwise drift of shingle (later to form Dungeness; see Figure 1). The fourteen miles of now partly canalised meandering stream, now crossed by six bridges, some doubtless once fords, flowing from Bodiam to Camber (on the Haven, now inland, in the late fifteenth century; see *Medieval Archaeology* 8 (1964), 259) was not a waterway to compare, e.g. with the Arun or the Medway. Bodiam administratively represented the upper extremity of the port of Winchelsea, e.g. in the 1400 enquiry into the improper shooting of ballast, blamed for blocking the (seaward) channel (*CPR (1399–1401)*, 346). In 1349 a dam at *Knellesflote* allegedly blocked the upper river (N. Saul, *Scenes from Provincial Life: Knightly Families in Sussex 1280–1400* (Oxford, 1986), hereafter Saul, 164). It was clearly quite narrow. The small rivulet at Bodiam combines with four others (now the Kent Ditch, two miles downstream; the Newmill Channel; the Royal Military

site especially on the western side, 'was not', we are assured, 'within the range of the offensive weapons in use at the time of its foundation' (see Figure 13). This reads oddly since Sands's own drawing shows the ground level at bowshot, or 220 yards radius from the castle to the west, to be about ten feet above the tower tops and nearly thirty feet above the curtain parapets (see Figure 10). Crossbows, longbows, mechanical artillery in the form of mangonels and trebuchets, as well as rapidly developing cannon, were all in use in the 1380s. Those 'murder-holes' in the gate passages (despite Clark, from whom much detail is taken unacknowledged) were for 'thrusting down posts to stop a rush … or for casting down that

Canal, of *c*.1800; and the Union Channel) before flowing around the dominant bluff of Rye, with its coeval Ypres Tower, and (in 1385) into the enclosed basin of Camber Haven. The upper part at least could easily be barred (e.g. by piling, as was quite customary on the coast) at many points (notably at Newenden, four and a half miles below Bodiam), but the river gave access to no attractive inland target, nor would French raiders have preferred slow and small barges to swift horses or direct marching had deep invasion ever been attempted. The late fourteenth-century water-table may have been slightly higher, but John Leland was told 'the water is a little brakkische' at Bodiam bridge, just above the castle, which suggests not, if sea-level has not changed. He reported also very credulously that 'the fresch water or ryver' flowed eastwards to Appledore, which it had ceased to do by the end of the twelfth century at the latest (see below). Traditions of the old river 'Rother' alias Limen long outlived the reality, and still survive. It had flowed to the sea at Old Romney or perhaps to Lympne and Hythe at the eastern end of the Marsh (*The Itinerary … in or about 1535–1543*, ed. L. Toulmin Smith (1964), v, 62–3, 68). He seems to have picked up a folk tradition of the era of the Danish raids when Newenden and Appledore stood on true estuaries and were easily accessible to seaborne raiders, as Rye (and, to a lesser extent, (New) Winchelsea) continued to be (see *Medieval Archaeology* 16 (1972), 124 map). The text typically adopts the Bodiam tradition of 'blocking French raids up the Rother'; also *ibid*. viii (1964), 81–6). Dallingridge's fiction may itself have been prompted by local folklore. The 'ancient ship' found in 1823 (sixty-four feet long by fifteen feet beam) six miles below Bodiam (Sands, 117–18), being undated and relating probably to the old river course E to the Romneys, is no proof of late fourteenth-century 'navigability', particularly of the sinuous and shallow upper reaches; nor, in any case, could Bodiam interdict passage unless a large field-force was based there. Only in full-scale invasion could Bodiam be reached. In Leland's time this was a real fear, but he treats Bodiam as of no relevance, for this it could neither resist nor stop. Turner (271–2, Figure 1) relies on a more than necessarily conjectural sketch map of the coastal region not, as he believes, as it was in the late fourteenth century but in fact as it was in the ninth or tenth century. The once great port town of Old Romney, chiefest of the Cinque Ports but by then decayed, Turner's map would place not high and dry far inland but some miles out to sea (and its contemporary successor New Romney, like some Lyonesse, still more deeply submarine). Even for the Danish era, it exaggerates the probable breadth of the ancient estuary S of Oxney. Turner, while attempting to allow for more recent work, has only carried to extremes the fantasy Sands and Simpson have propagated, amalgamating local folklore with a credulous acceptance of Dallingridge's meretricious licence. Ancient swamps and marshes, like secret subterranean passages, are powerful myths. The present course of the Rother was created, about ten miles downstream of Bodiam, by choking and silting of the old course, diverting the river S to Rye and (Old) Winchelsea. Recent work strongly indicates this in fact occurred, not in the great storms of 1287 as is customarily held, but 'by at least the late twelfth century': T. Tatton-Brown, 'The Topography of the Walland Marsh Area …', in *Romney Marsh: Evolution, Occupation, Reclamation*, ed. J. Eddison and C. Green (Oxford 1988), 105–11 (ref. due to R. Eales); cf. M. Beresford, *New Towns of the Middle Ages* (London, 1967), 15, on Old Winchelsea. Maritime access, but for barges only, from Yarmouth, is rather more plausibly advanced for John Fastolf's Caister by Simpson and H. D. Barnes (*Antiquaries Journal* 32 (1952), 33–52), but a touch of the same curious aquatic obsession may be present here too.

favourite medieval defensive agent, powdered quicklime'. Froissart does mention this, but for external use only.[16]

We are told that between the two cheek-walls outside the Postern entry there was once the pit of a lifting bridge, the outer end supposedly spanning a gap between the masonry abutment and the trestle-bridge crossing the moat. Remains of this bridge and of a similar long fixed timber catwalk to the Octagon in front of the main entrance were investigated in 1919–20 and in 1970 when the moat was again emptied for cleaning. Although none of the characteristic traces of a *pont à bascule* occur in the masonry of either entry or of the Barbican (the recess framing the Postern doorway in particular contradicting the notion) each bridge had a lifting span at its outer end instead (see Figures 5, 6, 12, 14). This, in the case of the Main Entry at least, was not quite original but a contemporary afterthought. The gaps afforded some defence but scarcely beyond a symbolic and ceremonial interruption of the access. Simple removable spans of timber are all that the little platforms, or revetted aprons, in front of the Main and Postern entries (and of the Barbican), can have allowed. These are far removed from the massive combined bridge and doorway-closures of Caerphilly and elsewhere, where a pit received the inner counterbalanced end. Harold Sands, however, confidently believed in his 'drawbridges' and even advanced the view 'that originally there was a line of exterior defences, possibly and not improbably in stone, and certainly in wood, running partially or entirely round that part of the outer edge of the bank which retains the waters of the moat' (i.e. on the south and east sides). Sands unfortunately had in mind not so much the dauntless and gallant *escarmouches* and *appertises d'armes* at the 'barriers' so beloved of Jean Froissart, as his own personal vision of a warlike fortress armed at all points. In the sketch plan he attached he omits this imaginary outer defence but transforms the two half-piers to the trestle-bridges on the north-west (main entrance) and south (postern) banks into full-blown and large octagonal tower foundations. Still more visionary, among his other suggestions, is that the Rother level and its 'navigability' were such as to permit a large dock for sea-going ships below the site immediately to the south (assimilating Bodiam to Beaumaris).[17] Equally aberrant is his idea that the angle

---

[16] See the valuable summary by J. R. Kenyon, 'Early Artillery Fortifications in England and Wales: a Preliminary Survey and Reappraisal', *Archaeological Journal* 138 (1981), 205–40; Sands, fig. 26 *et passim*; *Chroniques ... de Jean Froissart*, ed. J. A. C. Buchan, 2nd edn enlarged (Paris, 1835), 4 vols, e.g. i 91 (siege of Aubenton, 1340). Simpson's citations (1931, 90) do not relate to gate passages. Definite examples of water shoots are exterior, placed to soak the doors (e.g. Caerphilly, inner face of main east gatehouse; Leybourne, Kent; see S. Toy, *The Castles of Great Britain* (London, 1953), 239–40)). Richard II's Bloody Tower, London, has similar vault-holes as also has contemporary Donnington. Voice-communication for the porters, or surveillance and intimidation, are possible, but not shooting. 'Eyes' in vault-bosses are found in other contexts.

[17] See n. 15. Romantic imagination has also made a 'tilt-yard' of the large embanked area to the SSW (see Figure 2). This was another enclosed pond well above river level, probably a mill-pond to supply which the local springs were supplemented by a new leat from Salehurst (n. 84; RCHME i, 9–11). These outer ponds, to the S above the Rother and to the NW, and E of the moat were 'water features all intended to enhance the visual appearance' (RCHME, 11). Sands elsewhere (e.g. 'Some Kentish Castles', in *Memorials of Old Kent*, ed. P. Ditchfield and G. Clinch (1907), 150–237)

towers 'were probably covered by high conical roofs, not being large enough to carry engines'. Their structure indicates otherwise, to go no further. Elsewhere Sands shows he is aware of the cultural and domestic elements in the castles of this era, but no attempt is made to reconcile them in a fashion true to the period and its works. The image of an anarchic Middle Ages, 'red in tooth and claw', is not easily relinquished.

It is worth persisting a little longer with this most unsatisfactory paper, which compounds its errors by both plagiarising and denigrating G. T. Clark (by picking a quarrel, chiefly on the garderobe chamber doors), because it demonstrates (albeit in ludicrous extremity) the kind of literal-minded, materialistic anachronism that has prevented Bodiam Castle from being properly appreciated, or its ethos comprehended. Sands regarded it essentially as a military fort, citing the thirty-three remaining fireplaces, several ovens and twenty-eight garderobes as proof 'that the castle was intended to be manned by a large garrison, certainly not less than a hundred men'. While emphasising the powers of the contemporary longbow (but entirely ignoring these at the disposal of an attacking party), Sands could still pass over without remark the entire absence of arrow-loops throughout the place, whether in the merlons of the parapets or elsewhere (see e.g. Figure 7). He saw the chief defence of the castle as lying in 'the passive strength afforded by the moat, the external barbicans, and the machicolations above the gates'. In reality, the structural solidity of Bodiam is spurious within and without.

Anachronistic popularisation is the last accusation seemingly to be made against Alexander Hamilton Thompson, but his very solid work focused expressly on 'military architecture'. He also took literally that tendentious phrase in the licence and believed that 'the defensive nature of the works at Bodiam is very clearly apparent, not only in the strength (sic) of the walls, the height of which is equal to the height of the walls at Harlech, but in the provision made for the defence of the approaches'. The facts of contemporary siegecraft he omits. He likens the moat to that of late-thirteenth-century Leeds (Kent), praising the careful revetting of 'the islands in the lake' but does not grasp the major differences, notably the crucial weakness of the purely earthen banks which at Bodiam pound it up (see Figures 7, 10). Whereas the revetments protected the foundations and earth infill from the erosion of the water, almost stagnant though it is, the retaining banks on the south and east have neither lining nor core of masonry.[18] This is

shows great realism. On Bodiam he equivocates between fantasy (e.g. that the interior had timber platforms for projectile engines, 122) and the sober locating of the castle at some (ill-defined) stage between the Tudor manor house and 'the sterner forms of military architecture of Norman times'. Many good comparisons are drawn, and siegecraft is carefully discussed (129–30), but this pragmatism succumbs to the seduction of Bodiam. Even Sidney Toy, 213, describes the moat as 'fed from the river'. Of the fallacy of regarding castles 'strategically', even in Palestine, the classic refutation is R. C. Smail, *Crusading Warfare* (Cambridge, 1956), ch. I. For the bridges, see n. 32 below.

[18] A. H. Thompson, *Military Architecture in England during the Middle Ages* (Oxford, 1912), 322–7, 338; cf. the criticism of 'the military point of view', as a whole, and Thompson in particular, for defining (232) a castle as 'a military post which may include one or more dwelling houses within

not the sort of misjudgement that an engineer, like G.T. Clark, or an architect with strong historical insights, is likely to commit. Hugh Braun in his 'little book' *The English Castle* (1936) characterises Bodiam as 'a fortified manor-house' (surely the essential nature of castles, at whatever level), and rightly praises it as 'one of the most perfect ... as well as possibly the most beautiful' example of the genre. As usual, he then tags on a discussion of the alleged danger of French raids, which supposedly made Bodiam different, relying again on the licence, chiefly supported by a superficial impression of the apparently elaborate defences. Braun, like Clark and also Parker, remarks on its 'looking much more like a castle of a century earlier', but he goes much further than they in treating these fourteenth-century castles in general as 'toy fortresses', attributable to the 'fashionable craze' for chivalry. The last of the 'real castles', in his eyes, was Beaumaris in Anglesey, begun in 1295 and still unfinished twenty years later. Despite their affinities of plan, the later 'so-called castles', he declares, or 'more properly fortified manor-houses ... would not have stood up to a trebuchet and the artillery of the Civil War crumpled them up like a pack of cards'. His view is uncompromising:

> Nothing would suit such marvellous persons as these ... lords and ladies but that they must live in castles. The fact that there was very little need for such was a small consideration; those who had not already a (more or less obsolete) castle had to see about building one as soon as they could afford it and acquire the necessary (*sic*) licence.[19]

Christopher Hohler has since then (1966) condensed Braun's view, shorn of qualification, into the trenchant judgement that Bodiam, 'though planned in accordance with sound military principles (*sic*) is ... really an old soldier's dream-house and could never have played a significant part in a late-fourteenth century war'.[20] With the latter point it is impossible to disagree, but Bodiam should not be dismissed as mere *braggadocio* on that account. The middle ground must be explored. Hohler's view is still very much the minority opinion. But there is a

---

its walls', by Mackay Mackenzie, appendix B, on the modern concept of 'the keep'. For Thompson the Bodiam licence had for its 'main object ... to provide against a French attack upon the ports of Rye and Winchelsea (*sic*) at the mouth of the Rother ...' (cf. Figure 1, and n. 15 above). Comparison with the great dams at Leeds, Caerphilly, Kenilworth, and also at London would have been corrective. Commonsense would too. The Bodiam embankment is structurally barely adequate even without hostile interference (*pers. comm.*, 24 June 1970, Mr L. E. Hole). The revetments of the outer bridge piers are not quite original, it seems (n. 32 below).

[19] H. Braun, *The English Castle* (London, 1936), 102 *et seq.* Licences were acts of royal patronage, patents of architectural nobility. Braun's comment on Beaumaris may in purely 'military' terms have some justification, but culturally and historically it has none. It is a strange and widespread modern arrogance to reject so many places contemporaries called 'castles' as though we better understood their true nature.

[20] The quadrangular towered plan is not exclusively 'military'. Hohler's phrase has provoked, but if indeed 'a man is not on oath in lapidary inscriptions', captions should also be excused. (C. Hohler, 'Kings and Castles: Court Life in Peace and War', in *The Flowering of the Middle Ages*, ed. J. Evans (London, 1966), 140.

compromise hypothesis, that advanced by Dr W. Douglas Simpson of Aberdeen in the 1940s.

Simpson argued in a closely related group of papers in 1939–46 that 'bastard feudalism' decisively affected the later castles.[21] It is an attempt to construct a socio-economic explanation (in this case strongly tinged by the Tudor 'feudal anarchy' myth and by revivalist militarism), which constitutes the most sustained effort so far to bring to bear upon a series of buildings, in a systematic manner, many of the wide range of relevant issues. Simpson devoted a long paper (1931) to Bodiam and contributed in 1961 a Guidebook on the castle for the National Trust. His doctrine has persisted in steadily more diluted guise.[22] For the enemy without, by and large, Simpson substituted the enemy within – potentially restive and mutinous household troops, on whose disaffection the pay packet allegedly exercised less restraint than had formerly the personal loyalty to their lord of men who were his feudal dependants, doing him unpaid service during brief periods of warfare. Architecturally the case depends on proving that the quarters assigned by the scheme (often on flimsy evidence) to these retainers were defensibly separated from those of the lord's family (in the restricted and modern sense), which goes far beyond the expression of degrees of rank and differences of use effectuated by ordinary doors, stairways, ante-chambers and passages.[23] Also, the pronounced trend at this time towards greater privacy for the lord and his closest companions affected even monasteries and has to be allowed for. In fact, at all periods, separate defensibility of component units (essentially the 'keep' concept) is, to the 'military' interpreter, frustratingly unusual. The whole thesis in short presents innumerable difficulties. Standing or long-term garrisons, for one thing,

[21] Most notably 'Bastard Feudalism and the Later Castles', *Antiquaries Journal* 26 (1946), 145–71; also 'Castles of Livery and Maintenance', *Journal of the British Archaeological Association*, 3rd ser. 4 (1939), 39–54 with some extra material. Simpson did not apply the interpretation to Bodiam in 1931. In 1935 it was still evolving ('The Affinities of Lord Cromwell's Tower House at Tattershall', *Journal of the British Archaeological Association* 40 (1935), 177–92), but was nearly developed by 1938–9 ('Warkworth: a Castle of Livery and Maintenance', *Archaeologia Aeliana* 15 (1938), 115–36; 'Dunstanburgh Castle', *ibid.* 16 (1939), 31–42; 'Belsay Castle and the Scottish Tower Houses', *ibid.* 17 (1940), 75–84; 'The Castles of Dudley and Ashby de la Zouche', *Archaeological Journal* 96 (1939), 142–58). The architectural relevance at least of the phenomenon (e.g. C. Carpenter, 'The Beauchamp Affinity: a Study of Bastard Feudalism at work', *English Historical Review* 95 (1980), 514–32; cf. G. A. Holmes, *The Later Middle Ages* (London, 1962), 27–30, 165–7) is by no means generally accepted (e.g. Stewart Cruden, *The Scottish Castle* (Edinburgh, 1960), 87–91). Patrick Faulkner (n. 25 below) had no need of the hypothesis.

[22] Changes of tone and detail are found between the 1961, 1975 (Catherine Morton) and 1985 *Guides*. The large room in the NW range has been 'Stables?', 'Garrison', and again 'Stables'. The 1975 text keeps 'retainers' (e.g. 16) but the Plan has 'Servants' Hall'. In 1961 and 1975 (16, 17) 'that necessity of all good (*sic*) castles the dungeon' is put in the NW Tower basement, but 1985 admits 'the lake water' would flood it, suggesting instead the two cavities (inaccessible; lit by loop-lights) under the porters' chambers in the Main Gate, which are equally implausible.

[23] Most clearly formulated by Simpson in 1946 (n. above) 151–2. Internecine Scottish ambiance may have contributed. The theory was even stretched to Edward Stafford's Thornbury, Gloucs. (licensed 1510). At Doune Castle, Perths. (*ibid* 148) his whole case depends on a single door closure, between the Servants' Hall and lord's suite (cf. his excellent 'The Tower Houses of Scotland', in *Studies in Building History*, ed. E. M. Jope (1961), 229–42).

were prohibitively expensive in whatever manner they were remunerated, nor are mercenary soldiers confined to the era of the 'Hundred Years War'.[24]

Simpson's attempt at Bodiam to link contemporary society to the architecture must still be commended. His insistence that Bodiam Castle 'is a strong fortress erected, as the terms of its licence show, to subserve national military needs', cannot, however, be accepted. His presumption of dominant military purpose must be compared with the very careful analysis done on the interior by P. A. Faulkner, who has convincingly shown that providing suites of lodgings for persons of varying rank is the clue to much castle-planning in the later thirteenth century and in the fourteenth. At Bolton in Wensleydale this technique is particularly illuminating.[25] At Bodiam, Simpson asks us to 'note that the retainers' quarters (the western range) are completely isolated (*sic*). They communicate neither with the gatehouse (Main Gate) at their own end nor with the lord's suite at the other' (unless the bold retainer were to stroll across the courtyard). The well, which Clark was unable to find in 1874 (nor any piping, as at Leeds, from an exterior spring), and which Sands expected in the central courtyard, has been located, by Simpson, in the basement of the SW Tower where it serves 'both the Lord's Kitchen and the Retainers' Hall'. This, he feels, is important as 'the water supply … is under the lord's control' – which conjures up some intriguing visions of rival scullions warring over the water-pots. Faulkner's analysis of the entire surviving accommodation, focusing especially on access-linkages, is wholly to be preferred to Simpson's internecine variety of militarism, and it alone makes sense of the ways in which the tower chambers communicate with the interior and with the wall-walks (allures) of the curtains.[26]

The architectural grandeur, and powerful effect of Bodiam are, however, beyond dispute and are justly extolled by W. Douglas Simpson (1961) and epitomised by the heraldic displays on the two gate towers (see Figures 5, 14). The difficulty lies in discerning how far the visual impact and the symbolic significance inherent

---

[24] Space precludes discussion here. Separately defensible sections (e.g. Château Gaillard) or units were valuable anyway for prolonged defence against external enemies, as Caerphilly abundantly but most exceptionally shows (e.g. C. N. Johns, *Caerphilly Castle*, HMSO (Cardiff, 1978), 51, 68 *et passim*). The 'keep-gatehouse' here, at least, is a reality. On privacy, see Wood (n. 14 above), 129–36; also M. Girouard, *Life in the English Country House* (Harmondsworth, 1978), 30, quoting Langland c.1362, and ch. 3 *passim*.

[25] Simpson appreciates the aesthetics of the seignorial role, but Faulkner consistently follows the practicalities through to the details of the building: P. A. Faulkner, 'Domestic Planning from the Twelfth to the Fourteenth Centuries', and 'Castle Planning in the Fourteenth Century', *Archaeological Journal* 115 (1958); 150–83; *ibid.* 120 (1963), 215–35 (Bodiam, 230–4). His comments command acceptance in almost all respects, notably that the customary duplication (e.g. of Halls) was to provide separately for the occasionally resident lord and the permanent manorial staff.

[26] Simpson (1931, 91–2) admitted he was puzzled by the seemingly haphazard presence or absence of wall-walk doorways. The present 'well' seems to be only a cistern, despite the 1985 *Guide* (7). Pollution from the 'lake', to which its level corresponds, would be a danger. The soldiery Simpson believed Dallingridge kept here figure alternatively as 'his well-tried free companions' and as the unruly mercenaries upon whose existence his 1946 thesis depends (e.g. 161). The notion that some French commando raid might hunt down their old adversary here is most imaginative (1985 *Guide*, 1).

in battlemented panoply have affected particular features and exaggerated them in the familiar contemporary fashion whereby art enhanced structural function. Working the same transformation upon the defensive elements of fortification, such as the crenellation, flanking towers, archery loops (absent here), portcullis and drawbridge, can so perfectly integrate the military and the psychological that separately analysing the contribution of each becomes very difficult. The wisest course is to resist the temptation to write off any feature as 'sham', or to take any element as purely 'functional' (by which 'defensive' is intended normally). It is an artful combination that expresses, and most deliberately evoked for contemporaries, all the complex seignorial associations of the medieval castle-image, which included the deterring (and, if necessary, the defeating) of attack at whatever level was appropriate in the personal, local and wider circumstances. Given that the age of Richard II was one of the most sophisticated and cultured of the whole era of medieval European civilisation, it would be as well to jettison the crude dichotomy implicit in the assertion that Bodiam is 'a late but genuinely military castle, no mere residence'.[27] It is a gross anachronism in any medieval period but especially in this (see Figure 18).

III. The Structural Evidence of the Castle Proper[28]

Because the wider questions of location and historical context are best dealt with in concluding, and flow from considering the exterior and its *assiette*, we will examine first the significant details as seen from within, in order to address the central issue of this paper, namely the precise sense in which it may be affirmed that Bodiam is truly a castle.

Interior Impressions

The preservation of the building is remarkably complete, having suffered no apparent damage when surrendered in 1483 nor during the Civil War, when so many castles were vindictively dismantled and disfigured. Opportunistic pre-Victorian quarrying for the worked ashlar, and the effects of time, are alone visible. Fortunately, building stone is quite readily available in quarries scattered across the area (Wadhurst stone). Much of the interior, where some of the internal

---

[27] 1975 *Guide* 9. It is simplistic to regard the 'noble display' of the south front, and to write (truly) of the north side 'as one of the noblest facades (*sic*) of medieval military architecture' ('... the Great Gatehouse, broad lofty and browbeating') as meaning that they necessarily therefore constitute 'a formidable fortification' (Simpson 1961, 6, 9), although they might be acceptably described as 'a grand parade of feudal pride' (see Figures 11, 13). Wholly to be preferred is the sensitive analysis by Beric Morley of fourteenth-century castle design, in *Essays in Memory of Stuart Rigold*, ed. Alec Detsicas, Kent Archaeological Society (Maidstone, 1981), 104–13.

[28] Warm acknowledgement is due for invaluable help to Mr J. H. Past, custodian, and to Mr L. E. Hole, the contractor, in June 1970, and to the late Derek Cassleton-Elliott of Vinehall Farm, Robertsbridge, for his intermediary good offices. Any unattributed information in this and the following section IV is due to them. Other details derive from examination mostly in August and October 1989. All are easily verifiable with no more equipment than unprejudiced observation.

Figure 8. Bodiam castle (March 1991), detail of the SE tower-base and curtain junction: note plinth; masonry detail; bevelled lights (right-hand side damaged, not modified for cannon); accessibility from boat in moat.

Figure 9. Bodiam castle (March 1991), NE tower and main gate E summits, showing: stair-well narrow lights; allure door; cap of stair projection below (dummy) turret; curtain parapet destroyed; machicolation not over allure junction with main-gate flank.

walls and partitions may have been of timber and plaster, and an uncertain but considerable amount of masonry, have disappeared, although a great deal still remains.[29] The embankments pounding up the lake for some space of time may have been breached and left with the water drained off, but this was clearly not part of any 'slighting'. Only the most conveniently accessible stonework has been taken, namely most of the northern Barbican, much of the domestic ranges and all the parapets of the curtains except for the north and south-east (see Figures 9, 18). The destruction has been mild and freestone detail has not generally been wrenched out.[30] The towers have largely been spared: the summits of the Main Gate, of the NE, NW and SE angle towers almost entirely so; and of the rectangular mid-wall towers the East Tower is largely unscathed and the others (apart from the Mid-West Tower) have lost little more than some of the merlons of their parapets. The machicolated portions of parapet would have been especially easy to destroy. Even the dainty and attractive stair turrets are intact, and most of the elegant chimneys. The 'defences' are barely touched, the Main Gate gunloops being unmodified and in pristine condition. The only conspicuous medieval

[29] Edward's son, John Dallingridge, died in 1407 and another John in March 1443 (*CCR (1441–7)*, 94–5). Bodiam, not held in-chief, passed to the Lewknors. In the Buckingham revolt, November 1483, a commission significantly including Richard Lewknor, obtained its surrender (*CPR (1476–85)*, 370). The large calibre integral cast-iron bombard found in 1919 in the moat was not a garrison weapon, being much too large to fit the Main Gate gunloops. If a relic of the supposed attack, it cannot have been used since there is no visible damage, unless to the (largely vanished) Barbican. The interior may have been partially gutted, as happened then to Buckingham's own Maxstoke (J. D. Mackenzie, *The Castles of England …*, 2 vols (1897), i, 360), but Bodiam stayed in some sort of occupation until the early seventeenth century. It fitted Simpson's thesis to believe the tradition of a Civil War siege (1931, 97–8) nominally on the strength of an alleged cannon battery, near the top of the slope overlooking the north front, 'known of old as the Gun Garden or Gun Battery Field'. Found to be medieval in 1960, the Royal Commission interpret this as 'a viewing platform for the landscaped setting of the castle below' (RCHME i, 13–15; ii, *passim* (see Figure 3); and *Medieval Archaeology* 6–7 (1962–3), 334–5). Bodiam does not figure in the list of 150 known Parliamentary 'slightings' (including Bolton, Donnington, Maxstoke, Sterborough and Wressel, all comparable) compiled by M. W. Thompson (138–57, appendix 3). There are no apparent defensive modifications, despite allegations (e.g. 1975 *Guide* 13: the SE Tower ground-floor lights needed no enlargement; traces are equivocal and in the wrong place for flanking (see Figure 8); no other lights have been tampered with) and wild assertions, e.g. that the 'towers were later provided with gun-ports for covering-fire all round the castle by adapting arrow-loops' (*sic*), among other embroidery in P. S. Fry, *The David and Charles Book of Castles* (Newton Abbot, 1980), 91, 190–1. Cannon on the wall-tops are most improbable (Kenyon 1981, 209). Stone chips (from the original construction) were found in the moat in 1970, but no traces of any attack.

[30] Signs were found in 1970 that grass or rushes had grown on part of the area, at a level about eight inches below the modern slime of lily detritus (Curzon?) and about ten inches above the original bed. The masonry taken was all accessible from the interior. In 1778 the pond was full (print, 1975 *Guide*). Clark noted (1874) that 'enough, and not too much, has been done to arrest the effects of time and weather. The repairs have been well executed, and in Wadhurst stone, the proper material …' (Clark i, 240). Certainly, they are not now evident. Simpson (1931, 96–9) argues over-ingeniously that 'slighting', not quarrying, was responsible. Even 'penal slighting', to punish Lord Thanet, would not have spared the 'defences'. But he may be right to ascribe the direct northern earthen causeway (rather questionably replaced by a timber cat-walk recently) to the late medieval period (see Figure 12). Of his alleged widening of the main entrance for carts by cutting away the basal jamb mouldings, however, there is no conclusive sign (see Figure 17). The hub not the cart tyre required the greatest width in any case, and leaves distinctive marks.

alteration is the supplementary portcullis chamber built onto the inner ground floor of the Main Gate, extending the passage inwards to meet the interior building alignment. The details show this was a contemporary afterthought, which with the cheek walls and platform added outside the Postern Tower form the chief exceptions to the masterly foresight with which the whole closely combined scheme has been carried out. The consistency of detail and in the dimensions of standard features (e.g. doorways, stairs and windows) is most notable. Preparatory earthworks (principally to the moat) could have begun at the time of the licence in October 1385, and the masonry revetments and foundations at the start of the next building season. The variety of coloration of the ashlar suggests batches of material of diverse provenance. It is economically employed (see e.g. Figure 8). In all, with the limited means at Dallingridge's disposal and allowing for competition for the services of peripatetic masons, a quite prolonged construction period is indicated, perhaps as much as eight 'seasons'. Such mild gaucheness and crudity of execution as is visible in the lintels to some allure doorways, and in the construction of the lesser arches in general, strikes the eye only because of the contrast with the careful plugging of the putlog (scaffolding) holes, the elegant parapet crestings, nicely moulded corbels to the machicolation (particularly of the Main Gate) and the charmingly proportioned and sturdy mouldings of the single-light exterior windows to be seen everywhere.[31] For reasons of safety and convenience some parts of the castle are not ordinarily accessible. The upper chambers of the Main Gate can be inspected but not its summit, nor the eastern ground floor. The only usable portion of wall-walk is that linking the Main Gate to the NW Tower, all levels of which are open, as also is the case with all but the upper floor of the Postern. Otherwise, only the 'basements' (ground floors) can be seen closely, but these limitations do not materially affect the present investigation.

The Postern Tower, Doorways and 'Programme'

The Postern is a scaled-down version of the main entrance, lacking any gunloops and with one portcullis chase instead of three. The doors at the inner side of the

[31] The thesis of defence crisis has tended to predicate speedy construction, just as belief in a 'slighting' fitted the military interpretation, although Curzon (to whom Simpson normally defers) thought the construction 'took several years' (Simpson 1931, 89). Notably, all parts went up at once, not defences first and apartments later. Dallingridge's means were piecemeal and diverse, and his local and national preoccupations considerable, especially as a royal councillor from 1389 until shortly before his death, c.1394 (nn. 83, 84). 'Wadhurst stone', from a number of local quarries, is a coarse but enduring material varying from pale buff to greenish light grey. Many standard items, such as newel-stair treads (about ten and a half inches high except in the upper Main Gate where of twelve inches riser), windowheads and jambs, were supplied ready-made from the quarry. The sporadic use of lintels reinforces the 'job-lot' impression. Lesser arches made of large soffit-hollowed bed-tilted blocks, not radial voussoirs, are normal at this period. Masons' marks have been found on some underwater ashlars. On building seasons and duration, see J. G. Edwards, 'Edward I's Castle-Building in Wales', *Proceedings of the British Academy* 32 (1944), esp. appendix I; D. Knoop and G. P. Jones, *The Medieval Mason* (Manchester 1949), 131–4; L. F. Salzman, *Building in England down to 1540* (Oxford, 1952), *passim*.

entry chamber open directly into the Screens Passage (see Figure 6). The chamber vault and its 'murder holes', in the bosses at the intersections of the ribs, are all intact. It is, in all, a lightly protected private access, or more probably, a 'trades-man's entrance', conveniently placed to supply the adjacent kitchens. Indeed 'Postern' is a misnomer, but traditional. Exteriorly, the straight wooden trestle-bridge once debouched upon the narrow space between the low cheek walls. Around the archway into the tower is the emphatic square recess, which might ordinarily be taken for a drawbridge rebate. It closely resembles that on the Main Gate, but neither there nor here is there any sign of a pit, nor any trace of chain holes in the spandrels.[32] The portcullis groove is of reasonable size for a thin oak grating, similar to the fragment remaining in the Main Gate. No traces of any winch can be found.[33] The only other closure to this gate passage are the doors at either end, the inner archway opening onto the Screens Passage (with the fine triple service doorways still intact on the left-hand side), the outer closed by an old, but not original frame and (vaguely linenfold) panel, two-leaf door, set in a rebate four and a half inches deep with the hinge-hooks still in place. No trace of the normal defensive closure, by means of one or two substantial timber bars set in a deep hole and drawn across to engage in a socket in the opposite jamb, can be found. Indeed, none of the Bodiam doorways, not even the defensively vital ones (such as the access to the staircase from the entry chamber), are so provided. Closure was effected by small (metal) bolts mounted on the door, engaging in small shallow sockets. It is of purely domestic character nor can arrangements now gone explain it: even a pivoting bar on one of the leaves of the original Postern door, engaging not in the jambs but in a bracket on the other, would be very weak in such an exposed position.

[32] 'Meutriere' is the French Romantic modernism but for an archery loop ('archère' *rectius* for *arbalisteria* or *archeria*); see E. E. Viollet le Duc, *Dictionnaire Raisonné de l'Architecture Française ... art.* 'Meutrière' for details of loops. Base timbers (e.g. sleeper beams) of the main trestle bridge were found in 1920, and in 1970 on the Postern approach (see Figure 5) by David Martin (*Hastings Area Archaeological Papers* i, 1973; summarised *Medieval Archaeology* 15 (1971), 148; and more fully, with context, by S. E. Rigold, 'Structural Aspects of Medieval Timber Bridges' (p. 77), *Medieval Archaeology* 19 (1975), 48–91). Both at first were uninterrupted but (probably soon) altered to provide lifting spans to new stone-encased semi-octagonal abutments, i.e. such defences as these approaches possessed are not attributable to the 1385–6 coastal-defence crisis. Both were carefully dismantled, the N bridge (?) when the causeway was built (the N side of the gap is reverted, see Figure 12). The cheek walls to the Postern were also after-thoughts (not bonded), the result being a diminutive version of Warwick's barbican, or those of York and Alnwick town walls (see Figure 4). Even when there was no actual drawbridge, such square recesses around portal archways become standard symbolism, e.g. the brick gatehouse at Rye House, Herts. (licensed 1443; *CChR (1427–1516)*, 38); Maxstoke (1345) has 'murder holes' but again no drawbridge to its recess. The obligatory portcullis slit occurs and also provision for parapet crenel-shutters (Binney, n. 41 below, pls 9, 10).

[33] The Postern portcullis chase (see Figure 6) measures five by four and a half inches, slightly slimmer than the remains (seen by Clark in 1874 and probably medieval) at the Main Gate (chases four by three inches and six by four and a half inches deep), which consist of halving-jointed (oak) bars, iron plated and secured with rivetted-over wrought-iron nails. All the other chases are empty. They show no wear and may never have been fitted with gratings (built *in situ* or inserted from above, where space allows).

Hinge-hooks and depths of rebates give the rough thickness of doors, and also of window shutters. Here the hinges seem mostly to have been set in wooden plugs fixed in cut-out sockets, and many have disappeared. But the resultant recesses cannot be mistaken for drawbar holes. Doors and shutters universally were evidently of planks on fragile battens, seldom exceeding two inches in thickness and mostly under one inch in all.[34]

The Postern passage chamber is generously lit by two windows of the type standard throughout. These look along the adjacent curtains but can in no sense be termed 'loops', still less 'slits', the unaltered example being thirteen inches wide by twenty-six inches high, with traces of iron bars, shutter rebate and hinges (see Figure 4). In the castle as a whole four basic types of outward window can be distinguished. They illustrate the 'programme' to which the designer was working. Any fortification was advertised as such. The *signa fortericie* such as crenellation, towers, moats, drawbridge and portcullis, of course, but also the arrow-slits, or later the gunloops, were made evident. Whereas the message of power and deterrence compelling respect was a by-product in works of conspicuous solidity and defensive efficiency (e.g. major castles), magnates of lesser motivation or more modest means, needs and social pretensions chose to convey it by the studied exaggeration of features of defensive origin, which have been called 'the vocabulary of fortification'. This lesser class of building is best termed 'militant architecture'. When this embroidery of the substance develops (with no obvious point of transition as Bodiam shows) into outright mannerism and hyperbole (as at Herstmonceux), other means than physical force have clearly taken over that message of power and status. Contemporaries knew the language and would have read aright those Bodiam windows. It is the modern observer who may be deceived.[35]

The Windows and Loop-Lights

The window openings are, then, as eloquent as the doorways. Originally they were equipped with shutters and bars, except only for the narrow loop-lights to the garderobe chambers. Little original ironwork remains, but the indications at

[34] Clearances between hinge-hooks and rebate face seldom indicate doors more than three-quarters of an inch (2 cm) thick even allowing for strap-hinges fixed directly to planking itself nailed to battens or to a complete frame. Traces of brick blocking in the jambs of the inward Postern passage doorway cannot have been bar-hole and socket. Minor adaptations, some in brick, show the continued convenience of the house into the Jacobean period, although Leland disliked its archaism. His dismissive reference suggests he did not inspect it ('an old castle', *Itinerary* iv, 68), cf. the appreciative 1538 survey of Warkworth, Northumberland (Turner and Parker iii, 204).

[35] Cf. Turner, 277 and consider Louis d'Orléans' castles of Vez, La Ferté Milon and Pierrefonds whose documentation and *construction de prestige* are analysed by Jean Mesqui and Claude Ribéra-Pervillé in *Bulletin Monumental* t. 138, 3 (1980), 293–345, esp. 320–3. At a humbler level, and for *signa fortericie* see C. L. H. Coulson, 'Castellation in the County of Champagne ...', *Château Gaillard Etudes ... 9–10* (Caen, 1982), 347–64. For the Breton gentry, see M. Jones *et al.*, 'The Seigneurial Domestic Buildings of Brittany ...', *Antiquaries Journal* 69 (1989), 73–110; also the important discussion by Thompson ch. 5. ('A Martial Face'), which concentrates attention on the fifteenth century but discusses illuminatingly the 1360–90 additions at Warwick.

the accessible windows show they were protected by a vertical bar and up to five horizontal (saddle) bars in the largest, to prevent illicit entry. Many are within quite easy reach from a boat or raft (see e.g. Figure 8). Some have traces of incised glazing grooves (on one side only) but they are shallow, with no sign of lead cames, and probably one of the sixteenth- or seventeenth-century refinements. Originally there may well have been small glass panes set in the shutters but not in the few surviving, probably early-modem replacements. Outward and inward windows are treated indifferently. Shutters cannot much have exceeded three quarters of an inch in thickness, most being half an inch thick, that is slightly thinner than the doors. They too were secured by sliding metal bolts of small dimension. Some of the open effect of these plentiful apertures was modified by the shutters, by which light and draughts were regulated, but the powerful contemporary crossbow particularly, or the English longbow, would find in them little obstruction.[36] Disregarding the various forms of window-head and mould-ings, the four types referred to are: the standard, medium size in the towers and curtains, exemplified by the Postern gate chamber; secondly, rather smaller 'base-ment' lights, most readily seen in the SE Tower (five and a half inches wide by twenty-eight and a half inches high, minimum opening) and in the SW ('Well Tower' two and a half inches wide by twenty-five inches high, exceptionally, and having no splay at all to the outer thirteen inches of their jambs, making them quite useless for shooting); and thirdly, the large and multi-light special purpose windows of the Lord's Hall and Chamber, in the SE curtain and of the Chapel (see Figure 18). Finally, and of the most interest for defensive potential, because most flank the curtains in good enfilading positions and open through relatively thin walls, are the loop-lights to the latrines and some of the stair-wells.[37]

The positioning of the windows in the tower rooms should first be noted. It is quite unrelated to flanking (the defensive *raison d'*être of projecting towers), being upon the outward half of the perimeter so as to get the best light, leaving the thickened junctions with the curtains to accommodate the vice stairs. Essen-tially, above the ground floor each of the drum towers contains three storeys, each chamber provided with three of these windows, a fireplace and a compact garde-robe closet opening off a short passage, the stair being on the opposite side. Very

---

[36] The late fourteenth-century windlass-crossbow was formidable and widely used and could out-range the longbow (R. Payne-Gallwey, *The Crossbow* (London, 1958), 20–30, 90–1 *et passim*). The combination of crossbowmen (behind their pavises), archers, trebuchets, mangonels and cannon in contemporary sieges is clear in MSS, e.g. H. W. Koch, *Medieval Warfare* (1978), 80, 149; nn. 39, 41 below; also E. E. Viollet le Duc, *Dictionnaire du Mobilier Français* vi, 215–21, art. 'Pavois'.

[37] Despite wish-fulfilment assertions, the windows along the most vulnerable west side are not smaller but conform to the general pattern of their type. The medium size in the Postern Tower is thirteen by twenty-six inches (ground floor), ten by forty-nine (first floor); in the Sacristy (next the Chapel) ten by thirty-five; N Tower ten and a half by forty-eight generally. The Well (SW) Tower basement lights (not 'loops') are the only examples here to suggest even remotely the *soupirail* type, raked steeply to light and ventilate foundation-pit chambers. The dovecot in the SW Tower summit is convenient for both kitchens (oddly, Sands did not claim this was for carrier-pigeons to send messages in time of siege).

skilful planning was required to fit all this, and suitably proportioned openings for each, into the limited space, even with walls only six feet thick. Descending privy shoots (discharging below the moat surface) and ascending fireplace flues are the verticals determining the placing of the windows which, where possible (for structural and visual advantage) are staggered, although many do vertically coincide (see Figure 7). The effect is admirable. Wall-masses everywhere predominate and yet excellent illumination, well distributed and balanced, is achieved. The window seats are on the sill aprons to make the most of the limited space, and the arched heads to the splayed recesses are most elegant and attractive. The voids are as large as harmonious proportion allowed. The skin of this house may be a castellated one, but John Harvey's comment is very just that 'the building is certainly not the work of an unaided country contractor'. Domestic convenience and a certain modest elegance prevail throughout.[38] Lacking niches (the jambs are simply splayed) and without rake to the sills, these windows would scarcely be usable even by a crossbow-man and in no way resemble defensive slits. Experiments at Whitecastle (Gwent) have shown that archers (and a crossbowman with slightly better success) were able at twenty-five yards distance from the walls to put nearly a third of their arrows (or bolts) through slits a mere one and a half to two inches wide. Even with the slight protection of shutters, the entire interior of Bodiam Castle would be exposed and men crouching behind the merlons of the parapets above would be scarcely less vulnerable. Had they been there at all, Edward Dallingridge's 'trusty companions in arms' would have been hard-pressed even by a band of peasant archers with their war-bows in which so many were well-practised.[39]

[38] Bodiam, though castellated with such *panache*, has an almost bourgeois cosiness quite absent from such grand magnatial lodgings as John of Gaunt's hall-suite at Kenilworth. J. Harvey (*Henry Yevele* (London, 1940), 41, 80) believed that 'the position of Dalyngrigge (i.e. at Court) and the simple powerful (*sic*) design of the castle, strongly suggest Yevele as the architect'. He was involved at Cooling and at Canterbury (cathedral nave and city walls) and the 'gatehouse' at Saltwood has 'the appearance of being Yevele's'. In Harvey's *The Perpendicular Style* (London, 1978), 107, these buildings are definitely ascribed 'to Yeveley or to his associates' on 'various combinations of structural evidence and records'. Yevele, it must be stressed, was a large-scale omnicompetent contractor and not especially a 'military' architect. A very capable site-supervisor or master mason must have been in day-to-day charge at Bodiam if Harvey is right, for Yevele, like Dallingridge, can have spent very little time here.
[39] Dr Derek Renn and Peter Jones ('The Military Effectiveness of Arrow-Loops', *Château Gaillard* 9–10 (1982), 445–56) confirmed also how such niched loops were used in defence (cf. Viollet le Duc, n. 32 above). Whitecastle's mid-thirteenth-century loops have long slits with the rare refinement of staggered cross-slots (here it is argued for wider view rather than field of fire, cf. Viollet le Duc). These may have raised the success-rate, but the rubber tips fitted to the arrows, to avoid damage to English Heritage property, would have reduced it. A standard thirteenth-century arrow loop measuring one and a half inches by (say) seven feet long presents about 130 square inches. The smaller medium Bodiam windows are a compact area of about 340 square inches, implying a 75 per cent success-rate at the very least shooting from the bank. The modern crossbow tested by Renn and Jones did slightly better. French galleys were manned by crossbowmen (nn. 36, 41). By the mid-fourteenth-century, *via* transitional forms (e.g. Swansea; Llanblethian; Lewes barbican; Bishop's Palace, Wells), the crosslet-oillet (or cruciform) loop, with circular expansions to the end of each arm (horizontal as well as vertical) had been evolved. Amberly (n.

The last resort of the military analyst looking for archery loops would be those apparently very well-placed garderobe closet and stair loop-lights, set in the flanks and squinch walls of all eight towers (see Figures 9, 18). Perhaps here a covert 'active defence' might lie concealed, much as the *bourgeoisie* (and clergy sometimes) wore steel caps under their bonnets and jacks under their peaceful cloaks. If so Bodiam could perhaps plausibly be labelled, as some have suggested, 'fortified manor-house', a category imagined to be a sort of lesser castle. The arbalist, after all, was used from many a cramped space, given sufficient lateral clearance for its short (by the 1380s, steel) bow. It was aimed and discharged like a modern hand-gun, the stock to the shoulder, and the crossbowman could dwell on his aim and snap-shoot. Longbows were much more demanding.[40] Many of these inconspicuous stair and latrine-ventilating loops, by minor design changes, could so easily have been of defensive value. Their standard exterior dimensions are two and three quarter inches wide by fifteen inches high, but even when the lintel to the opening is at or above eye-level shooting out of them is virtually impossible because the sill is much too high and is horizontal. No longbowman could use them and an acrobatic crossbowman would have the greatest difficulty. The NW Tower shows the rejected opportunity to perfection and also, on its first and second main floors, has windows, which perfectly command the Barbican and causeway to the Main Gate. The lower position especially would have been perfect for an enfilading gunloop, but the architect has chosen to put these in conspicuous but very poor positions frontally in the Main Gate (see Figure 16).

The real preoccupations are shown by the very large Chapel, Chamber and Lord's Hall windows to the east and south-east, which demonstratively flaunt their vulnerability. The effect from outside, nicely set off by the elegant chimneys peeping over the battlements (not yet quite in the ostentatious Tudor manner), is of palatial comforts peering through the castle walls – an enticingly veiled hint of the seignorial conveniences within. Putting them here (they could well, in fact, have opened on the Courtyard) where they overlook the Rother meadows, gave more light and a better view. It enhanced also the scenic effect of the open aspects of the site (see Figures 10, 18). On the other side, facing the dull, steeply rising

76; licensed 1377) has an inept and showy compromise form. On defensive loops, see also H. G. Leask, *Irish Castles and Castellated Houses* (Dundalk, 1951), 20, for a careful description of the features distinguishing them from ventilation slits.

[40] Viollet le Duc, *Mobilier* v, *arts.* 'Arbalete', 'Gambison'; vi, *art.* 'Jacque'. Clergy and bourgeoisie were not of the legitimate arms-bearing class, unlike the gentry or (on special summons) the peasantry and urban levies (e.g. permission, 1347, for Philippe V to a Toulouse merchant for him and two attendants to be covertly armed: *Actes du Parlement de Paris* ii, ed. H. Furgeot *et al.* (Paris, 1960), 201 no. 7560). It is very remarkable that, despite the importance in English warfare of the longbow, its special requirements behind walls (very long, shallowly raked sills; overhead space etc., e.g. Caernarvon, mural gallery to Menai Strait) are very rarely met, loops continuing to be of crossbow type. The late fourteenth-century rebuild of Bothwell, Lanarks., with its 'French' crossbow loops (short, double-ended slit; deep internal niche), continuous curtain and tower machicolation, and drawbridge 'à flèches' (as at Herstmonceux) is a most instructive comparison showing deep differences of circumstances and response (e.g. Cruden, ch. 8; cf. B. J. St. J. O'Neil, *Castles and Cannon* (Oxford, 1960), esp. pls 3–10 of gunloops).

Figure 10. Bodiam castle (February 1989) from SSE near the stream (Rother), showing: raised central moat area; vulnerable SE angle of the embankment; hill slopes to W (left-hand side) and N (see Figure 2). © Crown copyright. Historic England Archive

Figure 11. Bodiam castle (June 1970), N front looking across original line of entry to octagon (left-hand side), showing: bridge gap; barbican remnants; second gap; main entry; NW tower (right-hand side) and W tower; special treatment of N curtain parapets.

ground to the west and north, they would have spoiled the cultivated effect of the elongated entry and frowningly sombre Main Gate, preceded by its Octagon and Barbican (see figure 13). Their placing may be discreet, but it is not defensive; it is on the south and east that any attacker would cut the moat bank, and the steepness of the further slope spoils visibility of the crucial ground from the wall and tower tops.[41]

Parapets, Machicolation and Planning

Of the eight towers the parapets are conveniently accessible only with the Postern and NW towers, and of the curtain allures solely the NW. Such, however, is the consistency of details and dimensions, and so closely does the summit machico-lation of the Postern Tower replicate that of the Main Gate, that the evidence is tolerably complete. Crenellation, whether to plain or overhanging parapets, has always been the essential mark of castellated architecture and was retained when other 'emblems of fortification' (such as the emphatic archery loops of the later thirteenth century) went out of vogue. Similarly, chemical artillery created at once a new military practice and a new aesthetic mode, which is reflected by the gunloops flaunted by the Main Gate. Machicolation, which is of more recent ped-igree, was here a mannerism, put where it is to differentiate the two gate towers, giving them an up-to-date appearance, and to heighten the contrast with those archaic-looking drum and mural towers, and also with the 'Edwardian' aspect of the windows, which so struck J. H. Parker and G. T. Clark (see Figures 12, 19). At Scotney, coeval and nearby, Roger de Ashbumham opted for machicolated drum towers and the effect is strikingly different.[42] Whereas the mason-technique at

[41] The placing of the chapel window (of severe but up-to-date Perpendicular design) is strongly reminiscent of the Clintons' Maxstoke, a castle that almost disdains pretence (plates in M. Bin-ney, *Country Life* 18 (11 April 1974), 842–5, 930–3). The chimneys in elaborate brickwork (some dummy) added by the Howards to Framlingham have their antecedents here, although Clark (i, 246, cf. 242, 245) resisted the implications. The concave southern counterscarp, down to the Rother (see Figure 10), is not well 'commanded' (*pace* Simpson 1931, n. 10 above, cf. Kenyon, 1981, 209). Pavises were regularly used to screen crossbowmen particularly. Defenders would be exposed at windows or crenels. The defenders of Poole c.1405 against Don Pero Niño's Castilian raiders are said to have used house-doors, 'propping them up on stakes and sheltering behind them in the battle … for fear of the arbalests which used to kill many of them' (*The Unconquered Knight – a Chronicle of the Deeds of Don Pero Niño, Count of Buelna*, trans. and ed. Joan Evans (London, 1928), 124–5). (My thanks are due to Richard Eales for drawing my attention to this text.) Behind such a barricade, direct and plunging 'fire' would eliminate any active resistance while the bridges were stormed and doors stove in or the bank was cut, even in full daylight. Escalade would quickly overwhelm the place. The fall at this time of so many English-held for-tresses in France to brutally effective siege methods, seconded now by cannon, is the reality of contemporary warfare (n. 61 below).

[42] Simpson's very penetrating comments on the aesthetic aspects consort with vagueness on the military. He justly remarks (1931, 92) that 'French fashion' at this date would have prescribed machicolation all round (e.g. Charles V's Bastille, Paris). Confining it 'to the gatehouses is a characteristically English mannerism' (but cf. Nunney). Also 'Bodiam's plan is entirely within English evolution' (*ibid.* 85–6), although the internationalism of European culture must still not be underrated, especially in this phase of the Wars. Such token castellation as Maxstoke did not satisfy Dallingridge's generation. Simpson was able to measure the downward-looking apertures

Figure 12. Bodiam castle (June 1970), site of main approach looking NE, showing: solid earth N causeway with hedges, perhaps late medieval (left-hand side: see n. 60), lately replaced by timber catwalk; octagon; barbican; NW tower base; wall foundations, found to be shallow on silt pan.

Bodiam is true to its date, the ashlar blocks being nearly square, little longer in the bed than in the perpend (which is economical usage but less well bonded), the machicolation does make its desired point. Recessing the wings of the Main Gate precluded flanking loops but emphasised the agglomerated corbel clusters to the doubled corners. The canting off of the corners nicely reduced an otherwise awkward and disproportionate diagonal projection (see Figure 11). Using flattish three-centred (almost segmental) arches to carry the parapets, in place of semi-circular, was very modish and enhances the counterpoint of rectilinear mid-wall

(*machicoulis*) of the Main Gate parapets (see Figure 9). They compare closely with those of the Postern (about twelve inches broad; from two feet six inches up to three feet six inches long between corbels). Bold chamfering of these corbels (and of arrises throughout) gives a solid effect heightened by delicate drip moulds at the base of the parapets of the other six towers by way of contrast. Crenellation is the oldest of symbols; it denoted the *corona* of the Roman *praefectus castrorum*. It occurs much earlier in Egyptian and Assyrian bas reliefs and is ubiquitous in medieval borough seals. The *formulae* equating crenels with fortification in English licences to crenellate became standard from c.1264, with Hood Castle, Yorks. (*CPR (1258–66)*, 342; P. Connolly, *Greece and Rome at War* (London, 1981, 244); Y. Yadin, *The Art of Warfare in Biblical Lands* (London, 1963), 228, 390–1). No real improvement or radical departure in gunloop design from arbalist patterns occurs until the 'gunport' type of splayed rectangular embrasures was evolved, mainly for harbour defences (e.g. Kingswear, Devon, O'Neil 1960, Plate 10a). Cf. the heraldic *cross pommée*, closely resembling the crosslet-oillet loop form (C. Boutell, *English Heraldry* (London, 1907, 56–7).

towers to cylindrical angle towers. It is a studied and ingenious compound, cleverly blended, made to seem all rather larger and somewhat more ancient than it really is. Nostalgia and topicality are neatly juxtaposed. Machicolation, if needed at all, would be more useful on the projected angles, and on the gate towers it is an outward display, frontally threatening but neglectful or indifferent to covering the curtain allure doorways below (see Figures 9, 19). Round fronts to the west and east mural towers would have been more solid, with less 'dead ground'; and why was the broad but shallow Main Gate crammed into the short side of the rectangle when it could have strengthened the long side confronting the western slope? No satisfactory answers can be in structural or military terms. Although now obscured by trees, the aesthetic effect of the castle, set in its lake and once surrounded by lesser pools, is fully apparent in the semi-aerial view from the hill to the north (see Figures 2, 3, 13). That this was fully intended cannot for an instant be doubted.[43]

Details and dimensions of the parapets tell us less than do the windows. Proportions overall are very satisfying and, again, largely consistent, although the north curtain parapets receive specially dignified treatment. Modern concrete platforms rather disfigure the Postern and NW Tower-summits but the parapets of the latter are intact, with some reinstatement of original stones. Corbels and beam-sockets below indicate low-pitched, leaded timber roofs whose narrow wall-walk-cum-gutter discharged rainwater via the plain-cut spouts just below the string-course. Allowing for the thickness of the concreting, merlons were about six and a half feet high over the roll-moulded coping and are six feet eight inches wide, crenels being two feet one inch, their plain flat sills being (originally) about two feet seven inches high. The crenel-to-merlon ratio (1:3.1) gives an admirably solid, indeed atavistic, effect, confirmed by omitting vertical mouldings to the sides of the embrasures. Nor do they occur on the up-to-date machicolated parapets of the two gates, which also conform to the severe mien displayed everywhere by plain chamfers and mouldings, in the windows most conspicuously.[44]

---

[43] Bodiam's is much more elegant than (Yevele's) outer gatehouse at Cooling whose small drum towers look top-heavy with their full-sized machicolation. At Saltwood and Canterbury West Gate solecism is avoided by machicolating only the parapet between the frontal turrets. Donnington omits the feature entirely. The lesser Cobham seat at Hever by Tonbridge (licensed 1383, CPR (1381–5), 326) also has a very crowded main front, but the rectangular plan of the (altered) gatehouse (partly machicolated) simplified the difficulty. Archaisms in medieval architecture do occasionally break the normal tendency to ruthless modernisation (e.g. naves of Canterbury and Winchester cathedrals). Yevele's nave at Westminster respected not the details but the effect of Henry III's work. Atavistic allusion, it seems, can be imitative or conceptual; specific (great towers at Tattershall and Ashby de la Zouche) or more general, as at Raglan.

[44] St Giles church tower has equally spaced crenels and merlons, both being coped (as are the north curtains of the castle), which is an ecclesiastical variant, also probably due to Dallingridge (Simpson 1931, 82). Outward roll-mouldings gave horizontal emphasis and could stop or deflect arrows, as could vertical rolls framing embrasures (e.g. Eagle Tower, Caernarvon, c.1320). Both were soon ubiquitously adopted in miniaturised ornament style; cf. the compromise adopted by the stair-turret crowns, Figures 13, 18). The full French flowering of castellated symbolism with exuberant tall chimneys, pinnacles, roof crestings, bartizans, échauguettes and tall conical roofs (which make Bodiam seem most reticent) is shown in the Très Riches Heures pictures of Jean

Dimensions of the Postern parapets are similar, in both cases giving just adequate cover. Here the machicolation can be inspected; the slot between the corbels is thirteen inches deep, lacking any water-drip or arrow-deflecting moulding (see Figure 5). As noted, it does not completely wrap around the flanks of the tower, only the external and most visible portion, not the crucial curtain-junctions below (nor the rear), being covered.[45] It all 'doth protest too much' with splendid mendacity.

No incongruity obtrudes because proportion is so well kept, but these parapets are no more than thin and weak screen-walls, just over one foot thick and constructed of large blocks stood on edge. The long coping stones afford some stiffening and bond to the merlons, but what strength there is depends on the cohesion of the mortared beds and perpends. Any greater thickness would have thrown out the delicate illusion of 'Edwardian' scale. Ashlar-faced rubble-concrete, though much stronger would have looked impossibly gauche. The stair-turrets, however, give the game away (human occupants could not be dwarfed). There is one to each of the eight towers. Their ostensible character as watch-towers masks their real function of covering the six feet six inch diameter stair wells. Below parapet level, hexagonal expansions, where the gorge wall merges with the curtain, contain the stair (except with the NW and E mid-towers, and the Main Gate). Above, the octagonal dummy caps are skilfully set upon the broader mass below (see Figures 9, 18). Internally they are covered over by saucer domes in small rubble but exteriorly they are turrets, battlemented in miniature as though they were accessible and usable échauguettes.[46]

The height of the walls, however, is no illusion; the accommodation within and outward show both dictated it. Although little thicker than structural stability

de Berri's castles (e.g. Saumur, Flowering of the Middle Ages, 134; cf. R. Morris, Cathedrals and Abbeys of England and Wales (London, 1979), 29 for alternative trans. of the Sir Gawain and the Green Knight extract. This is an important contemporary aesthetic statement.).

[45] On the sectioning function of towers and defence of their lateral doorways, see Viollet le Duc, Architecture ... art. 'Tour'. The concrete roofing (marked '1962') to the Postern does not encroach upon the wall-walk (cf. NW Tower) permitting accurate measurement. The surviving merlons are five feet three inches high, plus fourteen inches of coping. Crenels are again twenty-five inches wide, the flat sills three feet four inches from the floor. These dimensions are kept to the bare minimum for proportion's sake. Modern stature cannot exceed medieval averages by more than three to four inches, and headgear must be allowed for. For machicolation in France, of all types, see Viollet le Duc, art. 'Mâchicoulis' esp. figs 9 'D' and 12 'P'. Bodiam has no hourding holes although bretasches were still very much in use (Viollet le Duc, art. 'Hourd').

[46] Some sort of stair-top hutch just would not do! Access could only be by ladder (as Sands realised) from the main summit, but four of the surviving six turret-tops are domed and could not be walked on, nor is there any gap in the sketchy (maximum waist-height) parapet. The clear aerial photograph in P. Johnson, The National Trust Book of British Castles (London, 1978), 133, shows flat platforms to the E and W mural towers' turrets only. Lofty watch-turrets were a favourite conceit (royal apartments, Conway). They magnify Bodiam most powerfully (see Figure 13). Stairs are not unduly steep despite contraction of the castle's lateral scale even in the upper storeys of the Main Gate (twelve-inch risers, cf. many church-tower stairs). Rubble infill and large rough blocks compose the stair-wells. Only in the NW Tower, where the stair-well intercepts the east-side allure doorway, has an awkward mis-alignment had to be overcome (n. 48 below). Such infelicities are rare here.

required, grappling hooks and ladders from boats or rafts below would doubtless target the windows. The distance to the parapet tops would be about forty-eight feet if the moat were drained. But the omission of bow-slits from the merlons of the parapets is conspicuous, and evidently as deliberate as the design of the garderobe loop-lights (even Maxstoke had shutters to its crenels). The much grander construction of the North Front curtain parapets clinches the matter. They are one and a half times the normal thickness (i.e. eighteen inches), but the merlons are narrower (four feet nine inches), probably to fit three crenels into the short length. Dallingridge intended, perhaps, ceremoniously to man the walls, for important visitors, along the NW curtain, which overlooks the angled main approach (see Figure 11). The height of these merlons is also less than usual (five feet ten inches overall), doubtless to counter the disproportion (even to make his 'honour guard' more visible), and the standard-width crenels uniquely have coped sills. Where artifice is so subtly contrived, even minor variations from standard treatment must be given considerable weight. The North Front is very much the showpiece of the whole place. The door from this allure into the Main Gate, it may be remarked at this point, opens outwards and has no defensive development, although the quarters supposedly occupied by 'the garrison' were in the adjoining range. From the wall-walk here the platform over the vault of the inward extension of the entry passage, with its 'murder holes' strikes an incongruous note. The upper chamber itself, under a lean-to roof, was reached by an afterthought stairway, also not internally defensible.[47]

The Main Gate and Gunloops

Here it is the gunloops that chiefly require attention and are not the least ambiguous feature of the castle. Entering from the NW curtain allure (no defences and no machicolation overhead), the first feature is a garderobe chamber of high rank (ribbed vault) lit by the familiar pattern of loop-light. On the opposite (east) side of the Gate is a matching example. Even a contortionist crossbowman could not use these slits. The Gate block is a screen-like structure, frontally imposing but without depth.[48] From the chamber above the entrance, on the second floor, opens

[47] Insofar as the remains indicate, this and the wing-walls outside the Postern are of somewhat cruder masonry (n. 32 above). The segmental inner archway and rough adaptation of the two moulded capitals to take formeret and diagonal ribs of the additional vault suggest on-site extemporisation. The gate-passage otherwise would have debouched unceremoniously on whatever chamber was to have completed the range on this side (much as the Postern entry does into the Screens Passage). Chancellor Richard Scrope's Bolton was not so fastidious, but an enemy who won through to the small inner courtyard would be trapped, facing defended doorways all around. Exteriorly his towers and walls are much higher, and more solid, well beyond reach of ladders. Bolton, however, afforded quite as good accommodation and was as well adapted to its northern environment as was Bodiam to the softer conditions of the south, for all that Bolton has no moat.
[48] Both allure doorways, to the NW Tower and to the W side of the Main Gate, had to be awkwardly screened to adjust the levels via short flights of stairs, an expedient rare at Bodiam and avoided on the other side, so probably inadvertent (see Figures 11, 16). Prominent gatehouses, some predating the 'Edwardian' fashion, in many fourteenth-century cases produced what David King

Figure 13. Bodiam castle (February 1989) from NW, dominated by rising ground. Note: rivulet beneath the banks in distance; semi-aerial overview from the 'viewing platform' higher up (Figure 3); massing on N (show) front; the impact of alternating round and rectilinear towers. © Crown copyright. Historic England Archive

the upper of two small 'gunloops', which are contrived diagonally in the re-entrant angle of the outer recess of the entrance archway (see Figure 14). Seen from out-side, they would appear to be most cunningly placed to look north-westwards, over the trestle-bridge to the Octagon, and to cover the low Barbican roof and part of the causeway linking it to the gate below. They are part of a telling façade: the eye travels upwards, past the iron-plated and powerfully symbolic portcullis, to the thin screen-wall arch above, framed within the emphatic (but meretri-cious) drawbridge rebate; then pauses to absorb the trio of armorial shields (Dal-lingridge flanked by de Wardedieu and Radynden) in a row beneath the large and solemn central window, surmounted in turn by Sir Edward's helm with unicorn crest and mantle displayed (perhaps once all coloured). To this theme of chivalric panache the 'gunloops' in question provide a corroborative hint of ruthless force; the one adjacent to the row of heraldic shields, the other above it, not far beneath the framing arch with its sectioned slot (machicoulis or *assommoir*), which dou-bles the threat from the machicolation high overhead. Here are all the elements of the medieval castle image, repeated with variations down to the Tudor age of Spenserian revivalism.[49] The gatehouses of stately red-brick Buckden Palace,

---

(1983) has aptly called 'gatehouse castles' (e.g. Boarstall, 1312; Bywell, and Donnington). Bodiam's debt to this tradition is less apparent because the Main Gate does not monopolise attention to the same extent.

[49] Leland has much of Tudor attitudes as well as of the then condition of castles' repair (Thomp-son, 171–8), e.g. Harringworth is 'a right goodly manor-place ... buildid castelle-like'; Bagworth had 'ruines of a manor-place, like castelle building'; Shirburn was 'a strong pile or castelet';

Figure 14. Bodiam castle (March 1991), main-gate central panel, showing: the large window over the portcullis slot and above consorts with oblique gunloop-form squints and heraldry' an *assommoir* (and also machicolation) overhead but no 'drawbridge' below, despite spurious recess.

among many such, and of Henry VIII's pretty little granite gun-fort of Pendennis at Falmouth (*c*.1540) display it quite as fully. But it is far harder to go behind the mask and assess the exact amount of incorporated force deemed necessary to give to the symbols of noble status in contemporaries' eyes the physical substance appropriate to the personal and local situation: to establish how forcible was the force; who was meant to be impressed, deterred, and, if necessary, defeated by

contemporary Pendennis and St Mawes are still 'castle or fortress' simply; Warwick is 'magnificent and strong', always admired; whereas the structurally insignificant upstart Fulbrook is 'a praty castle made of stone and brike', which 'was an eyesore to the Erlis that lay in Warwike Castle, and was cause of displeasure betweene each Lord'. Even the crenellated close of Lichfield was (most percipiently) 'somewhat castle-like'; Bolton was 'a very fair castelle', and Chideock 'a castle or a fair house'. Such views are very close to the later medieval aesthetic, concentrating on scenic quality and seignorial allusion. Leland also had an interested eye for portcullis grooves, e.g. Sleaford, Denbigh and Tenby town (*Itinerary* i, 13, 20, 114–15, 196, 200; ii, 40–1, 46–8, 99, 102; iv, 27, 108; and ii, 26–7; iii, 97–8, 116–17).

it – and precisely how. *Kunstgeschichte* alone cannot do it, and nor can any purely 'military' rationale (see Figures 2, 3).

Examination of the two 'gunloops' does, in this case, provide limited, prosaic but quite clear answers. The upper specimen measures on the outer face twenty-six inches by three and a half inches broad in the slot, apart from the small circular oillet expansion at the foot. Through this loop the further part only of the approach, beyond the Octagon, and part of the path around the NW corner of the moat can be seen, but the sill is horizontal, putting the near approaches out of the line of sight.[50] The splay is very narrow and the traverse for any weapon extremely restricted, observations equally true of the loop on the floor below, opening off the portcullis chamber, which differs but slightly in dimensions. The embrasure is again of the habitual contemporary gunloop pattern, 'pierced' through a thick (seven inch) frontal plate, which interiorly projects from the plane of the splay of the jambs, virtually precluding alternative defensive use. The general inefficiency of this pattern is at its worst at Bodiam. The faults are found also in the ground-floor gunloops as well as in the double-oillet 'dumb-bell' shaped loops on either side of the entry (see Figures 15, 16, 17). The design gravely restricts the angle of vision. Both of the diagonal upper-floor loops must, in fact, be regarded as no more than spy-holes enabling the porter, and perhaps occupants of rank, to make ready for new arrivals, spotted approaching the entry to the north-west – surely with due ceremony, herald and trumpet; scarcely 'in manner of war'. They are, in short, porter's lodge squints in the guise of miniature gunloops, a topical allusion like the machicolation.[51]

[50] Poor translation, loose expression and low standards of proof vitiate the art-historical treatment by A. Tuulse, *Castles of the Western World* (London, 1958). The diagonal embrasure is very narrow, the horizontal bed about thirty-three inches from the floor and three inches below the bottom of the oillet (about five inches diameter); i.e. a very small gun on a shallow trunk might conceivably have used it, but only firing dead ahead and horizontally, since the sighting-slot is parallel-sided and the oillet is a cylindrical hole about seven inches deep and but slightly bevelled on the outer and inner arrises (in Canterbury city wall the contemporary gunloops, many in good enfilading positions, have larger oillets 'piercing' much thinner blocks, which, despite generally poor condition where unrestored, were evidently splayed or heavily bevelled). By propping up the trunk and packing the charge with wadding a slight downward deflection would be possible, which the high position of many such loops (e.g. Carisbrooke barbican) necessitated; but the target here at least would be wholly out of sight without extraordinary contortions (cf. Kenyon, 1981, 209). A stock-mounted shoulder-held gun, like a crossbow, would have had some potential but not the contemporary 'firework on a pole' type of gun (Koch, 132, 159, 200–1; all fifteenth century; Viollet le Duc, *Mobilier* vi, 325–33). See discussion of the problem by D. F. Renn in *Medieval Archaeology* 8 (1964), 226–8 on the Southampton Arcade.

[51] Apart from very rare 'espringald' embrasures (e.g. Tortosa, Palestine) only bow-loops were previously known. Their deep splays would resist the blows of mechanical artillery. Comparison disposes of any possibility that early gunloops (see for examples O'Neil, 12–13, showing the exaggerated plate-front at Bodiam) were built to resist heavy impact breaking away the facing stones. Fronts are thicker, with the usual slight chamfering of the exterior arrises (of slit and oillet) but nothing suggests fear of bombardment was a factor, despite their especially massive character here (see Figures 16, 17). The studiedly ambivalent message is still more pronounced in the most conspicuous pair looking onto the platform outside the main doors. The parallel-sided slot and oillet run through no less than ten inches (three and a quarter inches wide, six and a quarter inches diameter respectively). The interior is gravely exposed by such wide openings

Figure 15. Bodiam castle (March 1991), main entry W side, showing: the octagon edge, left-hand side foreground; above, remnants of the barbican, partly masking frontal main gunloop(s); small gunloop-form garderobe-chamber light (right-hand side) set in recessed wing (design precludes flank defence).

Figure 16. Bodiam castle (March 1991), main entry W side: gunloop does not bear; none is in an ideal position in the NW tower (right-hand side); lesser 'gunloop' entirely masked by salient; 'dumb bell' loop to apron-platform (far left-hand side, just apparent); awkward junction of curtain parapet to NW tower, showing afterthought alteration.

Figure 17. Bodiam castle
(March 1991), main gate,
showing: detail of W jamb
of archway, with bevelled
edge and (below) broach
stop; 'dumb bell' double-
oillet loop, showing
exaggeratedly thick
'plate front' design, from
porters' lodge.

From the accessible western ground-floor chamber opens the largest pattern of the gunloops, regarded by the 1975 Guide (after Simpson, 1961) as 'grim
reminders of the new weapon cannon, that would sound the death knell of the
feudal castle'. That it manifestly did nothing of the kind is less to the present point
than that, Bodiam being supremely well-planned, any lack of skill, if these loops

approachable closely from without. A cannon here with its muzzle laid into the foot-oillet would
strike its partner directly opposite if fired. The 'dumb-bell' pattern vaguely apes the crossbow
slit (e.g. Bothwell, n. 40 above) but owes more to symbolism than to utility. The gunloop type
of plate-fronted embrasure (notably since the slot facings project obstructively from the splay-
plane) was, in addition, highly inconvenient for crossbows and still more for the longbow, and
yet this is the normal and ubiquitous pattern until the later fifteenth century. J. R. Kenyon argues
that the elaborate cruciform-oillet loops to the Great Tower at Raglan were for ventilation only
and light, and that some of the other oillets of gunloop type were purely psychological (*Essays in
Honour of D. J. Cathcart King* (Cardiff, 1987), 164–5, *et passim* 161–72). Outward guise and covert
personality in medieval art were often tenuously connected. The same mentality was equally at
work in its castellated architecture.

ought to represent 1380s state-of-the-art technology, deserves to be pondered. The architect was certainly no country practitioner; nor was his patron some rustic *hobereau*. There are four of the larger loops of the 'inverted keyhole' type, all placed frontally, not in flanking positions but, at any rate, where horizontal fire was theoretically possible. The two largest examples are located in the advanced portions of the towers, and a smaller version in each of the recessed wings (see Figures 11, 15). Of these four, that in the (inaccessible) east wing of the Gate could not bear on the approaches at all, and its larger fellow only with great difficulty, being originally largely masked by the Barbican. None flank the curtain walls in any way. Had they done so the problems of lack of lateral traverse would be less crucial. The pair on the western side, between them would seemingly cover the eastern (inner) part of the trestle-bridge and a little of the Octagon platform, most of which is concealed by the Barbican. Internal inspection, however, heavily damages the apparent efficacy even of the western pair. The smaller loop opens off a typical small cramped garderobe chamber, which its function was clearly to light and ventilate. Dimensions, design and purpose are all closely comparable to the diagonal squints on the upper floors, although the splay is less narrow. Admitting any secondary function is difficult, but it could conceivably be used by an archer. Lateral space, on one side, is insufficient for an arbalist. Essentially, it is a loop-light with an oillet foot, simulating the external appearance of a gunloop of the type familiar since *c*.1370.[52] Its larger fellow, in the 'Guard Chamber' (*recte* Porters' Lodge), because of its greater internal space and size, was undoubtedly usable by a small cannon fixed to a 'trunk' bed. Its excellent condition is not likely to be due to Curzon, more probably to its never having experienced the shock or smoke of gunpowder. Vertically, including the ten-inch diameter oillet, it measures twenty-seven inches, the sighting slot being three and a quarter inches wide, both again bevelled on the exterior edges but lacking splay to the outer seven inches. Scarcely any deflection of the gun would be possible; fortunately so since, to the right, any shot fired would strike the frontal turret on the flank of the Barbican. Sir Edward must have intended having a saluting base whence to greet honoured guests with his own personal *Crakkys of Warre* firing 'blank', for which this one gunloop would be quite adequate (see Figure 3).

The details of the 'dumb-bell' loops on either side of the entry show that a display of aggression, not any real vindictiveness, was in the designer's mind Indeed, their width seriously exposed the interior to a bowman outside (see

---

[52] The earliest loops were apparently plain circular handgun (?) apertures set in splayed recesses, datable to 1365 (D. F. Renn, *Archaeological Journal* 125 (1968), 301–3). If Simpson is right that the earthen causeway (until recently) linking the Octagon to the north bank was a medieval modification, which the dismantling and salvaging of the bridge timbers tends to support (nn. 32, 60), then the western gunloops soon became equally inapt to close defence of the entry. The two 'gunloops', to the privies opening off the Porters' Lodges, are placed lower down than the other garderobe lights and convey an outward illusion of defence that the latter eschew (see Figure 15). Any more might have been unduly pretentious for a *nouveau riche* cadet, albeit of an old knightly family (Turner, fig. 2, showing an 'inverted keyhole' gunloop has been printed upside down).

Figures 16, 17). Clearly also, the architect and his patron did not expect the vital doorways, opening from the gate passage on either side (itself lacking two-leaved doors to the putative portcullises) to be in any danger of being hostilely kicked in, to judge from the feeble bolt sockets in the jambs and the thinness of the doors, disclosed by the hinge-hooks. From the opposite door is reached the stair, giving direct access to the rest of the Gate, but even here there are no drawbars, nor were there any, still more surprisingly, to the main outer two-leaved doors, presently represented by a pair of respectable, but not remarkable, solidity. Behind it, the bravado of double portal chambers, 'murder holes' and three portcullises, is mere *rodomontade* when the lateral doors are so weak. There is no 'military' logic in trebling the main closures while leaving a short and direct approach to a weak back door (Postern), which entirely lacks elaboration. But there is powerful psychological sense nonetheless: it is closer to Jean Froissart (and perhaps also to Franz Kafka) than it is to Vegetius or to the Sieur de Vauban.[53] The fairy-tale element is here, allusive and romantic.

IV. The Moat, Siting and Circumstances

At the outset of this discussion we referred to the common opinion that Bodiam Castle is significant chiefly as an exception to a discerned general trend of 'decline' since the great days of Edward I. It is seen as a sort of Paul of Tarsus castle: one born out of due time, and thus not quite worthy to be called a castle; and yet fully one really, and a belated vindication of a certain materialistic view of medieval civilisation. Indeed the 1985 Guide tells us that 'it was one of the last English medieval castles to be built, the final flowering of 300 years of castle design'. This is profoundly wrong: not so much for ignoring such a place as Raglan; nor even the awesome power of siegecraft, which had long since defied the utmost art of the military engineer; but because it disregards the whole medieval and sub-medieval procession of castellated architecture across five centuries and more of European cultural and social history. Bodiam's true importance and its authentic castle-character consist in its exalting of the castle-image *Anglice modo*, exploiting all the demonstrative opportunities available, while (most interestingly of all) spurning even a covert or secondary defensive capability. 'Fortification' was most surely metaphysical as well as material; a matter of imagery and symbolism, not

---

[53] The 'psychological warfare' element cannot be supposed to involve actual deception: contemporaries were not (for long) fooled by spurious gunloops, but they did assert the power of the owner, expressed according to the new aesthetic, which thus deterred (Coulson, 1982 (1), 84–91; cf., on the 'psychology of gun warfare', Renn, *Medieval Archaeology* 8 (1964), 226–8; Kenyon 1981, 217; Turner, 277). The pristine condition of all the gunloops notwithstanding, G. T. Clark's assurance (n. 30 above) covers the risky era of 'restoration' (c.1820–60). Fixed lines of fire, slowness of loading and haphazard performance must have made early guns in such loops far inferior to contemporary 'espringalds' even against fixed siege engines. Lack of lateral range could only be mitigated by gunloops in enfilade positions.

just of technology. It comprehended the soldierly imperatives of Woolwich Arsenal and of the Ecole Militaire, but also transcended them.

Second only in the esteem of the gentry to crenellated walls, fine towers and lodgings of ashlar masonry, in central and southern England, came water-filled moats. No modern rationalisation of this phenomenon in terms of defence against mining, or from violent (but hydrophobic) bands of brigands can satisfactorily account for it. It was a fashion that began early. Thus the Staffordshire knight William of Caverswall (licensed to crenellate here in 1275) caused an epitaph to be inscribed on his tomb-slab proclaiming to posterity that it was he who 'erected the castle, with dwellings, moats and works of masonry'. His boast provoked the spleen (though the castle of Caverswall was quite modest) of some unknown, who retorted with this scrawled translation and jibe, apparently in the Tudor period:

'William of Caverswell here lye I,
That built this Castle and the pooles herebye':
William of Caverswell here then mayest lye
But thy Castle is down and thy pooles are dry.[54]

Bodiam and Dallingridge have been more fortunate. His out-lying pools are likewise dry but not the principal pond (see Figure 2). His own, and his castle's credit (however misconceived) have stood high. It would have afforded him no little grim amusement to find his extravagant conceits so credulously received.

Moat and Siting

The 'lake' was drained twice in the twentieth century, by Curzon and in the summer of 1970. It is a revealing experience to see the castle without its mirror of water. The seven or eight feet of extra height add something but also transform

[54] Tudor architectural emulation pursued similar ideals. No fortress that could be assaulted outright was likely to be mined, making the moat defensively superfluous. My thanks are due to Dr John Blair for sending me a copy of his 'Cavers99wall (Staffs.): an exceptionally early indent', *Bulletin of the Monumental Brass Society* 35 (Feb. 1984); reconstructed *sic – Hic facet Willehnus de Kavereswelle Miles + castri structor eram domibus fossisque cum cemento perficiens op eram – nunc claudor in hoc monumento*. Last recorded in 1291, he 'appears as an unexceptional member of the knightly community, executing the usual round of duties as commissioner and justice' (Blair). The moated 'quadrangular castle, with four small towers and a gatehouse' (King, 1983) was initially rebuilt as a castellated late-Elizabethan mansion, rather resembling Lacock Abbey (M. Girouard, *Robert Smithson…*, 1966, reproducing 1686 engraving; also Mackenzie (1897), i, 390–1). On the supposed causal linkage between moats and lawlessness, see n. 80 and e.g. C. Platt, *Medieval England* (London, 1978), 111–15, 266–7; D. Wilson, *Moated Sites Research Group, Report* 9 (1982) (and *Reports* 1973–86 *passim*), but the 'prestige' explanation receives emphasis, e.g. in *Medieval Moated Sites*, ed. F. A. Aberg, CBA Research Report no. 17 (1978), 9–13; a large proportion of licences to crenellate concern such *gentilhommières* and motives of social *arrivisme* predominate. Places regarded as 'major' castles (though equally powerless to resist mechanical artillery) might be so engendered, whether built by the aspirant knighthood (Barnwell, Northants. c.1264) or by careerists at their name-place or patrimony (Anthony Bek's, Somerton, Lincs., 1281; Acton Burnell, Salop., licensed 1284). Moats in literature also figure strongly (e.g. *Langland*, trans. Coghill (1959), 47; *Sir Gawaine and the Green Knight*, n. 44; and even *King Richard II*, Act ii, scene i). As a curtilage 'fence' to demarcate a gentry seat they were unrivalled and probably more cost-effective than a wall in most situations.

Figure 18. Bodiam castle (February 1989) from SE, showing: the view displayed to arrivals from the SW (Bodiam bridge) who would pass along the SE and E bank, around the N side to the NW entry point (see Figure 2). Note *inter alia* the stair-capping turrets to the SW (left-hand side) and NE (right-hand side) towers. © Crown copyright. Historic England Archive

Figure 19. Bodiam castle (June 1970) from SE; without the magnifying and romanticising effect of water, still impressive but prosaic and reduced in scale; once the centrepiece of an entire system of water features (Figure 2)

the proportions, showing how small the place really is (see e.g. Figures 18, 19). The fine continuous plinth is completely uncovered but illusion and magic are gone. The sense of remoteness and intangibility of walls and towers reflected by still water also glorifies Queen Isabella's favourite residence of Leeds (Kent) and Warin de Lisle's Shirbum (Oxon., licensed 1377) and many a Continental *Wasserburg*. Moats conventionally segregated the lord's own courtyard from the manorial offices and *basse cour*, dignifying the castle proper, but they had their drawbacks.[55] In this case, lack of through-flow of water to scour out the sewage would have necessitated quite frequent cleansing while the house was in occupation. In 1970, having emptied the water via the two modern sluices on the south and north-east, about 15,000 cubic yards of silt, partly decayed lily humus, covering the bed about eighteen inches deep, were scraped off with mechanical diggers and dumped in the meadow to the SE. The castle was left, in the words of *The Times* headline to its photograph (6 May 1970) 'high, dry and defence-less' – and here is the crucial issue: in the contractor's estimation, about a dozen labourers (using only picks, spades and shovels), starting work at dusk, would be able to cut completely through the retaining embankment at almost any point along the S and E sides before daybreak. His opinion, indeed, was that the water must regularly have been emptied in this way for cleaning while the house was inhabited. Probably this was done near the newly restored overflow slightly north of the mid-point of the east bank, where it is flanked outside by an embanked area, now again a pond, from which the water would have been conducted by a ditched channel into the southern ponds, or directly into the river (see Figure 2). At this point of the moat a channel was left where the bank merges into the slope. Scour could be minimised by gradually deepening the cut in the bank, which here would be least likely to do damage. Since the bank is not 'clayed' (water-proofed with a lining of puddled clay) but composed of the impermeable heavy loam, which overlies the sub-stratum of compacted fine grey cohesive sand, no re-proofing would be needed when the breach was partially re-closed with packed earth. It would be such a simple operation that no proper sluices or reinforcements of the bank to accommodate them were thought desirable by the builder or designer. The features of this pool link it with the ubiquitous manorial mill-ponds, fish-stews and growing fashion for ornamental lakes rather than with proper 'water defences' with their stone-cored or revetted substantial earthwork

---

[55] In Germany the fashion lasted well into the eighteenth century (K. E. Mummenhoff, *Wasserburgen in Westfalen* (Berlin-Munich, 1958), *passim*; E. Thomson and G. baron von Manteuffel-Szoege, *Schlösser and Herrensitze im Baltikurn* (Frankfurt, 1963), with many early engravings). Descriptions of manor-house complexes, particularly dower and co-heiress partitions, often show that a moat divided the 'chief messuage' from its appendages. The jurors give no hint of defensive factors being involved, even when 'drawbridges' and 'gatehouses' are among the features. Examples 1352–70 are Woking, Surrey; Conington, Hunts.; Barton, Cumbria; Mulbarton and Brundall, Norfolk; Shenley, Bucks.; Slaugham, Sussex (CIPM x, nos 46, 484; xi, no. 317; xii, nos 79, 348, 404). Valuable barns, stables and byres usually lay outside such protection as the moat afforded. At Bodiam all the 'offices' (e.g. stables and dovecot) were apparently fitted into the one enclosure, which, to modern eyes, (falsely) enhances its 'castle' character.

dams. The springs, moreover, which feed it and break out all along the northern and western margin of the basin, are not streams, and a simple small pipe once sufficed for the overflow. In 1970 it took six months to restore the water to its normal level. This was quite a dry summer, but in the fourteenth century it would have been much the same at this elevation.[56]

The site, nonetheless, does offer some exceptional advantages. Defensively most awkward, being a terraced shelf partly cut into the hillside and partly built up, the creation here of a relatively wide moat and subsidiary ponds was so greatly facilitated and rendered so inexpensive by natural features that its disadvantages were quite unimportant (see Figures 5, 10, 13). Strategic reasons for the location are inherently most implausible. They alone would not have caused the old manor-site, probably the 'moat' close to the parish church to the NE, to be superseded. Rather, the exceptional qualities of the new position must have been decisive. Having married the de Wardedieu heiress and established his tenure of Bodiam manor by begetting a son by her, Dallingridge would have desired a dwelling of dignity and visual impact commensurate with his fortuitously prominent status in the county and reflecting his role in the national politics of Richard II's regency. It would fittingly crown his long career in royal service and perpetuate his family renown. Numerous castles were built for such reasons. Overlooking the Rother valley, conspicuous to the south and east, it would have prominence and 'prospect' lacking at the old 'homestead moat', which lies near the tributary valley bottom, slightly higher up but tucked away behind the ridge north of the new castle. The village has no nucleus, apart from St Giles church.[57] Although the

[56] The RCHME (n. 1 above) view the majority of the water-holding and other earthworks around the moat as medieval and probably part of the original conception, including the 'viewing platform', *alias* 'Gun Garden' (Figures 2, 3). The spring flow, allowing for seepage, need not have exceeded the present, to maintain this extensive system. The abutments of Bodiam bridge (documented 1313), two and a quarter miles above the junction with the stream of the Kent Ditch, do not suggest the water-table has been more than slightly higher (see n. 15 above). Stone brought here by water (as it probably was) came evidently by barge, not by ship, and perhaps to the wharves once just downstream from the Bridge. The supposed spring-catchment basin in the NW slope is regarded by RCHME as the lower of two partly artificial ponds, possibly forming a cascade, flanking the NW entrance roadway (not marked in Figures 2). They describe the earthworks as 'massive' as well as extensive, but it is to be noted that the SE moat bank had to be reinforced for safety in 1970 (horizontal thrust of the water, cf. the north dam at Caerphilly). It is not much less vulnerable than that of Michelham Priory, Sussex, especially on the east side, opposite to the monks' imposing fourteenth-century gatehouse, which has also traditionally been ascribed to fear of French raids (e.g. Saul, 89).

[57] From Simpson's still valuable local survey (1931, 69–71, 73–83), a further motive for his castle's assertiveness and for the new site is inferable in that Edward shared the parish church with surviving de Wardedieus and de Bodehams. He seems only to have completed the tower. It may be that his own tomb was not there but in Robertsbridge Abbey, where his son John's (d. *c*.1407) probably was (1975 *Guide* 23; effigy fragment in the Castle Museum). Conspicuously independent of St Giles church, the new position would be a natural response. Excavation on the 'old manor site', 350 yards NNE of the church, at TQ 784264 and rather closer to the Kent Ditch than the castle is to the Rother, has revealed a late thirteenth-century hall with service bay and solar wing of timber on dry-stone sleeper walls, within the moat (*Medieval Archaeology* 6–7 (1962–3), 335; and 15 (1971), 165–6). The excavators 'confirmed that the use of the moat was domestic and not defensive' (*sic*). Edward followed his elder brother Roger (d. *c*.1380 in his 70s) into the Arundel

Rother marshes would afford excellent water defences, a site upon the flood-plain would be both unhealthy and subject to flooding. Closeness to Bodiam bridge was evidently unimportant, nor was a change of site in conflict with the terms of the licence to crenellate. The great majority relate in terms to existing sites but a fair proportion are associated with a change of manorial *caput*. All in all, to a builder whose ambition was a place as magnificent as he could afford and capable of being conspicuously moated with the maximum economy of labour and materials, the attractions of this position despite its defensive weakness must have been both obvious and decisive.[58] Examination on site suggests that there may originally have been a natural pooling of water, breaking the surface. Traces of what may once have been reeds and rushes, showing up in 1970 as dark bands of humus and rust-coloured streaks in the firm scraped pan of silt, might be so interpreted. And the constructional sequence may reasonably be deduced. Loamy topsoil was excavated, chiefly along the western and part of the northern sides and carted across to form the southern and eastern embankments, with a little levelling up of the area to the east as well. The water-absorbent silt-pan was stripped to the nearly horizontal natural bed, no attempt being made to achieve greater depth in mid-moat, nor shallower margins to reduce the water-thrust exerted on the embankments, thin and decidedly weak though they are (see Figures 4, 7, 19). The lime mortar had to be laid in dry conditions, but the slight summer spring-flow could easily have been channelled away (or penned up with a coffer dam). In 1970 exploratory spadework indicated that the depth of the wall footings varied but did not exceed two to three feet below the bed. In the places tested in this fashion no drystone rubble packing was found beneath the bottom course of ashlar, showing that it was laid completely dry.[59] The central rectangle of shallow foundation trenches could thus be laid out (almost exactly north–south) and dug with such accuracy. Stone revetments, battered inwards by about three

affinity and was his heir. Their father had died in 1335 (Saul 38, 67–8). J. G. Hurst does not rule out a previous manor on the castle site (*Medieval Archaeology* 6–7 (1962–3), 140) but his context was one of extreme caution.

[58] Licence expressed as for the *mansum manerii* even technically did not preclude such a shift, and there is considerable evidence that new administrative centres were thereby seen as ratified; cf. Simpson (1931, 72) '... the building of a strong military castle on a site selected ... so as to command the waterway of the Rother, up which, during the weak reign of Richard II, French naval raids were feared ...'. It is at the castle by the bridge that any such raiders (presumably in punts or wherries) would surely disembark (and be resisted) should they come so far (and so slowly) by water. The nearest part of the castle (SW Tower) is about 340 yards distant, recessed into the shoulder of the hill and barely visible from the bridge, well beyond effective range with scant (even visual) 'command'. The river is now about 260 yards from the S front of the castle, extreme range at best (n. 15; Figures 1, 2).

[59] Special thanks are due to Mr L. E. Hole for conducting these trials for me. For the investigations by David Martin in 1970, see n. 32. Footings on the E side seem no deeper so the whole central platform probably rests on the natural subsoil (corroborated by the absence of differential movement). The refinement that the latrine shafts discharge below water-level doubtless reduced the (often very chilly) updraught and some of the smell, but far superior arrangements were being provided at Langley (Northumberland) or Southwell (Notts.); see Wood, 377–8 – garderobes grouped in turrets over cess-pits.

feet in a rise of nine, encased the made-earth of the central platform and revetted the Barbican and Octagon (either from the first or subsequently, on construction of the half-piers of the modified trestle-bridge responds). Elsewhere revetment was dispensed with, thanks to the steep angle of rest of the heavy loam, and if any piling was needed to consolidate the earth no trace of it has been discovered.

It was all superbly economical. Sections vertically through the central raised area show how little earth had to be moved (1961 Guide centre-fold). Only the courtyard is significantly built up. The sloping plinth at the foot of the walls, rendered by Curzon in cement to reduce erosion and water seepage, is of rather cruder workmanship than elsewhere. Only the top two feet or so are normally visible (see Figures 5, 12). The design effectively resisted the pressure of the water-logged semi-plastic mass within. No subsidence has occurred anywhere and the success of the engineering, with its rigorous economy of means, speaks as highly as does the more visible architecture above water-level of the skill of the builder. Much of the visual satisfaction is attributable to the walls' rising almost sheer from the water (with no 'berm' around as at Maxstoke), but this is yet another by-product of the natural aptitudes of a site carefully chosen and skilfully exploited.

Before turning from the structure to its historical context, the purpose of the originally angled main approach should be considered (see Figures 5, 13). Any semblance of exposing to archery the shieldless (and supposedly defenceless) right-hand-side of foot soldiers (a horseman's mount was always vulnerable), as they advanced across the trestle-bridge towards the Octagon, springs not from medieval cunning but from modern imagination. Indeed, these long outer bridges, highly vulnerable to destruction, which would isolate the castle and preclude the sorties that were an essential part of an active defence, are themselves more demonstrative than defensive in nature. Everyday convenience dictated the direct and shorter approach to the Postern, and also the subsequent shortening of the main approach itself (see Figure 12), whereby the perishable timber span was replaced by an earthen causeway, lattetly (1990) altered to a bridge on piles.[60] Courtly ceremony is the most likely reason. Affinities must lie with the already long tradition of lordly residences comprising a *basse cour*, approached obliquely to the main axis, from which in turn the *cour d'honneur* was entered.

[60] Simpson (nn. 32, 52 above) cited principally as evidence of medieval alteration the stone-reverted gap left before the Octagon (see Figure 12), although Clark believed this masonry to be modern (in spite of thinking the direct causeway original). Devious approaches are a normal device both ancient (British hill forts; Greek acropolis) and medieval. The RCHME case that they were carried here to very great lengths (Figure 2), diverting the approach from the bridge along and between the southern ponds, up to the moat bank, on the central axis, facing the Postern Tower, and then anti-clockwise along the E side to the NW entrance, not only agrees with all the evidence examined in this paper, but is in general analogous with e.g. the circuitous lices-entrance at Pierrefonds and with Tattershall with its double moats. Such impressive approaches, affording closer and closer glimpses of the house, fully evolved later in the parks of sub-medieval mansions culminating in the landscape gardening of the seventeenth and eighteenth centuries. A late-medieval (c.1460) and much enlarged version of oblique approaches with moats and detached barbicans is ducal Castello Sforzesco at Milan (sixteenth-century drawing in *The Horizon Book of the Renaissance*, ed. J. H. Plumb (1961), 178), but its elements are moated-sites' vernacular.

The Chantilly picture of Jean de Berri's nearly coeval castle of Poitiers shows the arrangement to perfection, including the lifting bridge section. Bishop Anthony Bek's Somerton Castle (Lincs., licensed 1281), which housed the captive John the Good; Ashburnham's nearby Scotney Castle, Broughton Castle (Oxon.), licensed in 1406 to William of Wykeham's heir, and Sir John Fastolf's Caistor by Yarmouth are the best known of very many examples in England. At Bodiam the feature may well have compensated for the lack of an outer courtyard of stables and offices. Rather inconveniently (though the castle-impression gains thereby), these had to be fitted into the main building, along with the dovecot housed inconspicuously in the summit of the SW Tower, seignorial symbol though it was.

At the outer 'barriers', having negotiated the circuitous water-girt roadways, a guest of the greatest honour would be courteously received by the Lord; conducted past the specious challenge of Dallingridge tenantry and deferential domestics, via the Octagon and Barbican, each point doubtless the occasion of ceremony (see Figure 2). Lesser folk perhaps would dismount at the Octagon, the great within the inner courtyard suitably impressed by portcullis, 'murder holes' and mummery. In all things, the stately *pavanne* of chivalric encounter, along with the humdrum business of manorial administration, and the whole routine life of a knightly household, were most effectively expressed and provided for, in necessities and military ethos alike.

Some Contemporary Considerations and Context

Campaigning in Brittany and Picardy in the 1360s, as a mature soldier of fortune, Dallingridge would have been well aware of the draconian steps taken by Charles *le Sage* as Regent of France after Poitiers (1356), and subsequently as king (1364–80), both north of the Loire and later in almost all provinces, to counter the forays of English, Navarrese and 'Free Companies'.[61] Seignorial fortresses *en pays de guerre* were subjected to a degree of royal (central or regional) direction highly rare or quite unknown in England, although Ireland and the Scottish March offer some intimations. Exhortation was backed up by supervision of munitioning and repair, with demolition the ultimate sanction. Increasingly, direct Crown takeover of castles, towns, fortified monasteries and precincts (forts of every variety)

---

[61] The spirit of Bodiam is one of remoteness from the grim harshness of war (e g. *Froissart* i, ch. c, shows a knightly distaste for 'scorched earth' in Hainault in 1340). Dallingridge wished, while eschewing the daintiness of Saumur, to proclaim not brutal *arrivisme* but legitimate and established social position and public service. Much material for French royal defence policy is among the *Mandements et Actes Divers de Charles V (1364–80)*, ed. L. Delisle (Paris, 1874). *La Guerre de Cent Ans vue à Travers les Registres du Parlement (1337–1369)*, ed. P-C Timbal *et al.*, CNRS (Paris, 1961), 105–300 cites and summarises entries about the repair, administration and resort to castles and towns (indifferently fortresses). C. T. Almand, *The Hundred Years War* (Cambridge, 1988), 76–82 shows great walled towns were the chief refuges and army bases. Philippe Contamine, *War in the Middle Ages*, trans. Michael Jones (Oxford, 1984), collates details on cannon (193–207), and his *Guerre, Etat et Société à la fin du moyen Age* (Paris, 1972), deals with the military reforms of Charles V and their sequel *inter alia multa* (135–233). The success of Bodiam as a 'fortification' was not in the utilitarian sphere of the art for, indeed, 'it could never have played a significant part in late fourteenth-century war' (n. 20 above).

by the local Captain or royal Lieutenant, was resorted to. Proclamations ordered the people of the *plat pays* to withdraw, 'themselves and their goods' *ès forteresses*, namely the nearest viable refuge whatever it was, free of entry or exit dues. Quite rapidly new *de facto* castellanies evolved and *guet et garde* liabilities were redefined to accord with the military realities, the judges of the *Parlement* freely overriding traditional liens and subordinations. Places too small to accommodate refugees and chattels, moved to deny targets and subsistence to the enemy, or too weak to deter sufficiently the privateering bands attracted by such concentrations of booty; or castles and forts whose lords (increasingly subsidised, from local war-taxation) could not or would not man and strengthen them, were all ordered to be entirely razed to prevent their being used as 'lodgements' and raiding bases. A considerable proportion of the castellated gentry-residences and *neufs châteaux*, which had arisen within the old *châtellenies* since the later twelfth century, must have been affected in the devastated provinces. Raid counter-measures reduced not multiplied, fortifications. Even 'incastellated' churches, namely those occupied and munitioned as bases, might suffer. Summing up his survey of this policy Pierre-Clément Timbal (1961) comments: 'Mieux vaut, en somme, un nombre limité de châteaux solides et bien pourvus qu'une multitude de fortins inefficaces; c'est ce dont se persuade facilement le régent Charles au lendemain de Poitiers.'[62]

After 1380, under the lax confusion of Charles VI's regencies and subsequently, these powers were still exercised but tended to devolve upon the great magnates in their apanages. When in his turn Henry V set about combating irregulars after Agincourt, the lieutenants in his conquests regularly had powers to take over or to demolish all fortresses that 'cannot be conveniently kept to our advantage.' Public necessity, combined with the feudal takeover powers of *rendability*, justified a royal *dirigisme*, which, in England, was rarely applied even to a few especially important and vulnerable towns.[63]

---

[62] Timbal 1961, 106–7. In England in this period we have found no such precautionary demolitions ordered, but only the clearance of houses and obstructions to town defences (e.g. Chichester, 1377; but also inland at Winchester, 1378; *CPR (1377–81)*, 72, 111). Local levies to help man royal castles were ordered sporadically, e.g. Hadleigh, Queenborough, Rising, Trematon, Tintagel, Restormel, Launceston (*CPR (1377–81)*, 2, 271, 455; *CPR (1381–5)*, 566, 600); cf. the French *guet et garde* system; but Portchester in February 1381 had only its tiny peacetime complement (*CCR (1377–81)*, 441–2). All Scottish March castles were loosely supervised by the Wardens but direct aid or takeover was minor and notably rare (*CPR (1377–81)*, 80, 455; *CPR (1381–5)*, 182, 344). Precautions concentrated on the coast, and the coastwise 'maritime lands' but extended from Newcastle-upon-Tyne in the NE round to SW Wales. In contrast Irish absentee lords had long been obliged to man and maintain castles, against internal enemies, although exemptions were not infrequent by this period (*CPR (1377–81)*, 528, 608).

[63] 'Rôles Normands et Français … par Bréquigny …' in *Mémoires de la Société des Antiquaires de Normandie* 3 ser. iii (Paris, 1858), no. 197 (1418, bailiwick of Evreux etc.). The noted soldier Nicholas Dagworth (October 1377) was empowered to compel the repair and defence of Irish fortresses, royal and seignorial (*Rymer's Foedera*, Record Commission (1830) iv (HMSO, 1869), 21–2). In 1380, John of Gaunt had a similar commission for *omnia et singula castra, villas et fortalitia* 'in the March of Scotland' (*ibid.* 97). Even for coastal England measures were traditional, e.g. 'compelling … knights and esquires … with suitable habitations … (in Cornwall) to remain upon their lands during the present summer'; to arraying all able-bodied men and stopping them fleeing

The public-defence role ascribed to Bodiam and the pure patriotism credited to Sir Edward Dallingridge are, in this general context, equally implausible. Close cross-Channel links serve to highlight the contrasts. Individual magnates had long been required (in England during invasion scares; in Ireland, continually) to reside upon their manors within the marches, or within 'the maritime lands', but this had no apparent impact upon the pattern of crenellating, with licence or without.[64] Problems in France and crisis at home made it politic for members of the governing council to profess public spirit, and the inscription put up by Dallingridge's colleague John de Cobham upon his outer gate at Cooling (Kent, licensed 1381), boldly proclaimed his unselfishness. And his protestations do have some credibility. The site lies on the Thames estuary. The spacious inner and outer enclosures would be well able to accommodate refugees and movables, and Cooling is placed just where a show of defiance might deter enemy galleys from landing.[65] Being cut off inland was no part of the tip-and-run strategy of harassment by coastwise raiders and even that chivalrous paragon of the species, Don Pero Niño with his Castilian galley squadron (1404–6), did not care to risk it (see Figure 1). Works at Rochester and at Queenborough, in Sheppey, and at Hadleigh on the Essex side, from the late 1360s, and the re-walling at great cost of Southampton and of the city of Canterbury (which it would have been a great

(Isle of Thanet) and overhauling the beacon warning system (Isle of Purbeck); *CPR (1377–81)*, 166, 455, 474. In May 1380 the monks of Netley were told (or obtained authority) to arm themselves and put the abbey in a state of defence being 'situate in a perilous place upon the sea shore between … Southampton and the high sea suitable for the enemies' landing', details undoubtedly taken from their petition (*CCR (1377–81)*, 311). The danger here was real (see next note) but such alarms were initiated more, often locally than centrally and had many non-altruistic motives.

[64] H. J. Hewitt, *The Organization of War under Edward III 1338–62* (Manchester, 1966), ch. I 'defence'. Resistance depended largely on local leadership; e.g. in July 1377, John de Clinton was directed to reside at his castle of Folkestone 'near the sea'; and Archbishop Sudbury in September 1380 had his men stay at Saltwood 'upon the coast' (one mile inland) thereby exempting them from array (*CCR (1377–81)*, 6, 404). The earliest approach to what Simpson in particular (1961, 3) propounds for Bodiam is apparently Richard Guldeford's licence for a coastal defence fort below Rye at Camber in 1487 (see n. 15). In 1547 Sir William Paulet had a fully explicit licence and commission, including powers of distraint, to enlarge and garrison the new fort on the exposed Netley abbey site (*CPR (1485–94)*, 151; *CPR (1547–8)*, 66–8).

[65] In October 1380, and again in February 1381 when Cooling was licensed, John de Cobham headed commissions to survey likely enemy landing-places around the Hoo coast 'and cause them to be fortified by the erection of pales and the repair of dykes' ('piles and trenches', 1381: *CPR (1377–81)*, 577, 596, 629). In 1386 the warlike Bishop Despenser of Norwich built three 'bastides' to protect Great Yarmouth but lesser measures were preferred (*CPR (1385–9)*, 177, 258–9; *CCR (1385–9)*, 169). His licences to crenellate next year (Gaywood, North Elmham; *CPR (1385–9)*, 381) were of purely manorial type. Thanet had old entrenchments and 'turreted walls both upon and below the cliff of that island', for resisting enemy landings. In England only the Scottish March approached the French system of organised refuge. The castles of Dunstanburgh (see W. D. Simpson, *Archaeologia Aeliana*, 4th ser. 16 (1939), 31–42), Bamburgh and Tynemouth Priory were much used. Wholesale evacuation and retreat south was occasionally resorted to after Bannockburn (1314) to escape major Scottish inroads. For this and many searching points, see M. C. Prestwich, 'English Castles in the Reign of Edward II', *Journal of Medieval History* 8 (1982), 159–78.

coup, but also a major task to take and sack), were all costly and protracted.[66] Extempore timber *bretasches*, stockades and entrenchments at landing-places, manned by local levies, and barricading of town circuits and weak spots, could respond to emergencies but have left little trace, even in the printed records. When long-term dangers did beyond doubt generate defensive building by the gentry and baronial class it is of a rather distinct type, for the most part variations on the tower-house formula. Endemic raiding, cattle rustling and abducting for ransom produced, on the Scottish March and in the Lowlands, a host of tall compact,dwelling-towers, single or aggregated, sometimes with a small barmkin, their roofs sheltered by the parapets. They effectively protected the lord and his household from marauders, too hasty and ill-equipped for sieges.[67] But the architectural result lacked the castle-image, however cost-effective, and wherever security permitted the more spacious courtyard layout (castellated or otherwise) was nearly always preferred. Bodiam has the unusually demonstrative militancy common to others of its decade in slightly higher degree, but is true to its general type in all other respects.[68]

[66] The building contracts for Cooling (incomplete; W. A. Scott Robertson, *Archaeologia Cantiana* 11 (1877), 128–44; facsimile of inscription, p. 134) total only £974; manor receipts in 1300 were £26 *p.a.* Minor works at Rochester (1367–70) cost £2,262; the new castle at Queenborough (1361–75, for protecting the populace; *CChR (1341–1417)*, 211–12 (1368) cost about £20,000, and the refortification of Hadleigh (1361–70) over £2,288, which last is attributable to other causes largely (*HKW*, 812–13, 792–804, 665–6). Bodiam might have cost as much as Cooling, although it covers only just over half an acre compared with over eight acres of usable space. C. Kightly (*Strongholds of the Realm* (London, 1979, 134)) summarises Pero Niño's evidence (see n. 41 above) emphasising the customary case for French raids and seeing Bodiam as 'well-equipped' to resist them, but he implies dubiety as to its exposure and rejection of access by the Rother. Sandwich, near the Stour mouth, suffered, but Canterbury would have taken major overland invasion, as would Winchester and other inland towns where reactions seem to be a compound of panic and opportunistic manipulation (see discussion of the same problem by Hewitt, esp. 2–5).

[67] Just how satisfactory the tower-house formula was can be seen all over the Lowlands, Cumberland, Westmorland, Northumberland, Durham and parts of Yorkshire and Lancashire, as also in Ireland, whether in castle-style like Bolton or humble dwelling-tower like the Vicar's Peel, Corbridge. Rarely can major non-royal castle-building be ascribed to ephemeral crises (cf. Henry VIII's 1538 gun-castle scheme; Edward I's N Welsh castles, particularly the response to the 1294 uprising with Beaumaris). Commons' petitions in Parliament (often manipulated) show anxiety that the savagery of French war could come to England (e.g. 1378, commonalty of Kent) and concern that lords should stay on local defence; Scarborough asked for a naval guard (1379); Sussex wanted Bramber Castle to be kept against possible French seizure and use as araiding-base (1388), and coastal towns (also some far inland, as Salisbury, Northampton, Bath, Norwich and Winchester) were affected by, the widespread and indiscriminate furore (*Rotuli Parliamentorum* iii, 20, 30, 42, 46, 53, 63, 70, 80–1, 146, 161, 200–1, 213, 251, 255; cf. K. Fowler, *The Age of Plantaganet and Valois* (London, 1967), 165–72). The 'navy' was not then capable of 'controlling the Channel' (cf. Simpson 1931, 84; 1961, 3, citing the period 1372–87 between the defeat off La Rochelle and Cadzand). Major invasion ostensibly was feared but coastal harassment and opportunistic exploitation by parties at home are most to be inferred from the records. The archaeological evidence overall also supports caution if not scepticism.

[68] Licensed examples, 1380–90, are Hemyock (Devon), Cooling, Sheriff Hutton (Yorks.), Farleigh Hungerford (Som.), Thornton Abbey (Lincs.). Towers are still 'castles' in Scotland. William Heron, licensed in 1338 to crenellate Ford (Northumberland) obtained supplementary lordly rights in 1340 including that he should hold it *per nomen castri* (a unique instance). Ford was a quadrangular castle, suffering with Chillingham a Scots raid in 1344; sacked in 1385 (*CPR (1338–40)*,

Reasoning from illusive defensive effects mechanistically back to imagined military causes has, in the case of Bodiam, led to the famous licence of October 1385 being taken at its face value, so that its subtleties have not been grasped. Because no study has been done of licences to crenellate as a whole (and only a very incomplete bare list has so far been published), many misjudgements have arisen purely from lack of contextual awareness. The construction invariably put upon this particular licence illustrates how essential is the administrative as well as the archaeological context. In four crucial respects it errs: first, in thinking of licences as prescriptive royal directions; secondly, in believing the special pleading incorporated in its terms, undoubtedly by the petitioner's own intervention; thirdly, in supposing that licences were reluctantly and selectively granted; and finally, in assuming that such allusions to local dangers are peculiar or, indeed, at all specially significant. As a *corpus* and also individually licences to crenellate are most valuable evidence, illuminating a wide range of local, genealogical and chivalric questions; but so also are the licences to create parks and warrens, to exercise hunting rights, and to divert roads for the privacy of residences, privileges often associated with castellation, licensed or unlicensed. Licences to crenellate will not, in short, bear the political weight put upon them; nor can Bodiam's carry the elaborate structure of tendentious supposition that has been chiefly founded upon it.[69]

Dallingridge's patent has more individuality than many but adhered to the standard form, progressively modified from late in the reign of Henry III. Granted by the usual 'special grace' common to most types of gracious privilege, it authorised him 'to fortify with a wall of stone and lime the dwelling-place of his manor of Bodiam next to the sea (*sic*) in the county of Sussex, and to construct and make thereof a castle (*castrum*) for the defence of the adjacent country and for the resisting of our (unspecified) enemies'. The habitual security of tenure formula of realty grants then concludes the document.[70] Occasionally petitioners had their

---

114; *CPR (1343–5)*, 409); *CChR (1327–1341)*, 468–9; *Rotuli Parliamentorum* 255–6). The 1415 survey listing some seventy-eight Northumberland fortresses in some cases equivocates between *turris* and *fortalicium*, but the *castra* (including *ffurde*) are mainly the more established (printed C. J. Bates, *The Border Holds of Northumberland*, 'vol. i', Newcastle-upon-Tyne, 1891), 13–19; cf. 78–9, facsimile of 1584 Plat). For the 'rival' courtyard house alternative (castellated still, but distinctively), see Thompson, ch. 4; e.g, Eltham Palace, Haddon Hall (56, 61).

[69] Lt Col A. H. Burne's 'inherent military probability' (*The Crécy War* (London, 1955, 12)) approach will not do for castles. Simpson (1961, 3) believed that 'the terms of the licence appear to be unique (though there may be similar earlier instances on the Welsh and Scottish borders)'. Turner and Parker iii, 419, gave it undeserved prominence by quotation at length. W. D. Peckham, on 'The Architectural History of Amberley Castle' (SAC, 62 (1922), 21–63) even supposed (30–1) that it would be 'very unlikely that a Bishop in the Home Counties would dare fortify first and ask leave afterwards under … the third Edward'. In fact Edward III's Chancery issued licences for no fewer than 217 sites, a few certainly retrospective. Amberley's was from the regency (10 Dec. 1377), as was Bishop Erghum's (1377) for ten sites in a batch, including six manors, his London inn, his palace at Salisbury and the city itself, in rivalry with the *citizens* (CPR (1377–81), 9, 76).

[70] The 'king' granted *pro nobis et heredibus nostris*, as usual, but also *quantum in nobis est*, i.e. without prejudice to existing susceptibilities or rights, caution common in duchy of Gascony licences but rare in English ones. Here it may possibly reflect Chancery fears of a resumption of

licences phrased to refer to the work being on a new site, but the normal wording employed here was not literally construed. Licences often marked the setting up of a new manor-site, or signalised its definitive acquisition (often without building done), or some notable step into the local or national social hierarchy by the grantee. The presumed move from the old 'moat' below Bodiam church is thus unremarkable. *Juxta mare* is less acceptable when the nearest coast by Hastings is ten miles and more to the south. Unlike the Bodiam apologists the licence significantly does not make any case based on proximity to the river, that erstwhile 'water of Limen', which had once flowed into the sea south-eastwards at Romney (see Figure 1). Dallingridge preferred to exploit the prevailing fear of coastal attack, not the remoter danger of invasion.[71] Justificatory references to local dangers, as 'in', 'near' of 'upon' 'the March of Scotland', do sometimes occur in licences and were, as a rule, copied in turn by the Privy Seal then by the Great Seal office clerks, with other details from the recipient's draft or petition; but where more precise locations are given, such as 'situated on the sea coast', they are for whatever reason accurate. Only Bodiam is not virtually on the beach. Dallingridge here too was 'drawing the long bow' and the absence of verification of claims by the Chancery, coupled with his strategic personal advantages, ensured that he got away with it. So far as the texts of the licences (duly abbreviated, enrolled and mostly as calendared) permit us to judge, very few petitioners pleaded public utility, and none with his effrontery, so far as castles are concerned.[72]

the friction with John of Gaunt, which had caused an affray in June 1384 and Dallingridge's brief imprisonment (Saul, 28–9, 75, 92–3, 191). The vagueness of *inimici nostri* may not be without significance. The patent was doubtless shown off to his coterie and dependants to proclaim that Edward *Dalyngrigge chivaler ... rnansum manerii sui de Bodyham juxta mare in Comitatu Sussex muro de petra et cake firmare et kernellare et castrum inde in defensionem patrie adjacentis et pro resistencia inimicorum nostrorum consrruere et facere [Possit] et mansum predictum sic firrnatum et kernellaturn et castrum inde sic factum tenere possit sibi et heredibus suis in perpetuum sine impedimento nostro et heredum nostrorum aut ministrorum nostrorum quorumcunque* (*Rot. Pat.* 9 Ric II p. 1 memb. 21; 21 October 1385, Westminster; *CPR (1385–9)*, 42).

[71] See nn. 15, 56 above (cf. the bizarre notion that via the Rother the French might sail around 'behind the Cinque Ports', Turner, 271–2). Bodiam certainly established Dallingridge's (largely absentee) 'presence', which might calm nerves, but it could scarcely accommodate local refugees with their chattels (see unique Kent–Sussex coastal refuge order April 1385, n. 74 below) nor resist direct assault, in case of actual invasion. Its existence in no way defended Rye or Winchelsea or Hastings (Figure 1, *pace* A. H. Thompson, n. 18 above). Small surprise that 'no French force ever broke its teeth upon the guarded (sic) walls of Bodiam' (Simpson, 1961, 3–4); but Dallingridge did thereby show his local commitment, his leading position among the east Sussex county gentry and perhaps some 'championship of local autonomy' (Saul, 68).

[72] The genuine cases put Bodiam in its true light. Nearness to the Scots is cited in the licences for Scaleby, Drumburgh (1307), Triermain (1340) and Penrith (1397, 1399), in Cumberland; also for Blenkinsop (1340, Northumberland) and for Hartley (1353, Westmorland), places all known to have suffered Scots forays. Licensed sites 'on the sea coast', or similar, are Flamburgh (1351, Yorks.); Fish-house and Quarr Abbey, Isle of Wight (1365, see n. 52); Chideock (Dorset 1370, 1380); and Mablethorpe (Lincs. 1459). Juries at *inquisitions ad quod damnum* (at least nominally) checked before Chancery licensed diverting water conduits or roads or creating parks and warrens. *Post hoc* complaints about crenellating nevertheless are remarkably rare (Marham 1271, Wells City 1341, Swine 1352, Oxford town 1381). Unlicensed Barnwell *c.*1264 was reported calmly in 1275–6 (*Rot. Hund.* 7b).

Such pleas are, by contrast, habitual in the case of town authorities requesting power to tax merchandise, to pay not only for fortification (murage) but equally for bridge repairs (pontage), paving and other projects of 'common utility'. Communal and civic prestige was also involved, but benefit to the local populace and to the realm was regularly asserted and almost always accepted. Tax remissions confirm that the favourable administrative instinct would concede quite large cash sums, with only the nominal Hanaper fee taken for all grants offsetting the loss of revenue.[73] The public advantage was frequently and most explicitly cited in a number of petitions for licence to crenellate towns, notably by Hull (1327), Rye (1369), Leominster (Herefordshire, 1402), Kingswear (Devon, 1402), Plymouth (1404), Harwich (1405), Winchelsea (1415) and Alnwick (1434), all of which at the time were in clear potential danger. Thus Rye in 1369 was licensed to be walled 'in view of the perils which may ensue', and the 1415 licence for Winchelsea (to select the two examples nearest to Bodiam) referred to the king's liking such places to be strengthened '... (being) on the sea coast and frontier of the king's enemies and as it were a key of those parts'. Such language is, with very few exceptions indeed, significantly absent in this period respecting castles. When it does occur the location, circumstances and surviving structures fully justify it.[74]

Of the Bodiam licence to crenellate one element remains that has been especially fruitful of misunderstanding. It is the clause *et inde castrum facere*; that is, having fortified the *mansum manerii* with a crenellated stone wall, licence 'to make thereof a castle'. It means at once much less than appears, for 'castle' was a term of elusive subtlety, and the phrase occurs in five other licences of Richard II alone; but also much more, because it raises the whole question of what, in

---

[73] Occasional and emergency direct royal takeover of port-town defence (most notably Southampton e.g. *CPR (1377–81)*, 7, 76, 80, 448; and construction of a royal tower, 174 etc.) contrasts with the normal governmental non-interference. Certainly urban enlightened self-interest (less so with castles) had some 'public benefit', but again motives, e.g. of prestige, distort the picture (H. L. Turner, *Town Defences in England and Wales* (London, 1971), 87–94; also appendix B and C, somewhat incomplete). Implied licence was thought insufficiently honorific in some twenty-nine cases and formal licence to crenellate was obtained (by the burgesses twenty-three; by lords six). Border towns (e.g. Shrewsbury; Carlisle) do figure continually but the underlying reality is as much one of royal response as initiative. The Council was hardly a Ministry of War or a defence-forces General Staff.

[74] He appropriated the 'defence of the adjacent country' phrase used elsewhere with discrimination (e.g. at Ford, 1340, n. 68 above; Penrith, 1399, *CPR (1396–9)*, 524). Tout (n. 7 above) commented on the peculiar wording: 'this was an excuse, or the result of panic, as Bodiam is far from the sea' (Figure 1). Tynemouth Priory (Northumb.) 'was reputed a castle' (1388), receiving defence-aid, having been 'in time of war the castle and refuge of the whole country' (1390; *CPR (1385–9)*, 494; *CPR (1388–92)*, 194), which combines the symbolic and military senses in almost modern fashion. In the invasion scare of April 1385 (*CPR (1381–5)*, 553, n. 71 above), believed to threaten 'the people and fortalices on the English Coast', in almost French style 'all the inhabitants ... with their families and goods', within six miles of Dolier, Rye and Sandwich and from Thanet and Oxney were ordered 'to withdraw before 3 May under pain of imprisonment to the said castle and towns'. For Rye and Winchelsea, see particularly *CPR (1367–70)*, 224; *CPR (1381–5)*, 518–19, 525, 532, 588; *CPR (1413–16)*, 224, 273, 368–9; *Rotuli Parliamentorum* iii, 70, 201. The official strategy in 1385 was to concentrate manpower and valuables at the coastal targets, which were large enough and capable of defence. It was not to flee inland.

contemporary terms, constituted a 'castle'. That their usage was not ours is a fact that cannot be over-emphasised. Whereas the first point is quickly dealt with, the administrative and literary meanings of *castrum*, *castellum* and *château* are quite beyond the present scope, so a few suggestions must suffice.[75]

The immediate context of the Bodiam licence offers numerous insights. In the reign of Richard II a total of fifty-six sites was licensed, of which forty-three may be termed 'manorial' (whether in lay or clerical possession); five are conventual or ecclesiastical establishments; another seven are for entire towns or individual town houses, and the other is for the bridge-houses of Kilkenny town in Ireland. This diversity is typical and significant. Most of the manor site licences conform to Edward III's standard formula but Sheriff Hutton (Yorks., 1382), Bodiam (1385), Donnington (Berks., 1386), Harringworth (Northants., 1387), Lumley (Co. Durham, 1392), and Wardour (Wilts., 1393) all contain minor variants of the *et inde castrum facere* phrase. No particular weight can be given to it. Not only are Amberley (Sussex, 1377), Bolton-in-Wensleydale (Yorks., 1379) and Cooling omitted, but of those so dignified Donnington was very weak. Harringworth has vanished but was seemingly not structurally notable, and Old Wardour is essentially a tower-house, although of unique design with a courtyard or central light-well.[76] Here, however, lurks a deep pitfall – beyond all doubt we are quite on the wrong track when we casually apply originally medieval terms of status and structural style as though they were an architectural terminology equivalent to their modern derivatives. Degrees of social rank within the *bourgeoisie*, gentry and nobility and their appropriate manifestation, preoccupied contemporaries, whereas gradations of structural strength seldom did so, even in an explicitly military context. The linkage between structure and rank is esoteric and highly elusive. Bodiam may help to clarify the problem but not if, with the Royal Archaeological Institute, we define the castle as 'a fortified residence which might combine administrative and judicial functions but in which military considerations were paramount'. The strenuous efforts to prove that Bodiam is, in Curzon's words, 'a genuine military castle' represent one of the innumerable aberrations

---

[75] For the castle in literature, see K. Reyerson and F. Powe (ed.), *The Medieval Castle, Romance and Reality* (Dubuque, Iowa 1984), *passim* (reference due to R. Eales), in particular see 147–74; M. A. Dean, 'Early Fortified Houses: Defenses and Castle Imagery 1275–1350 with evidence from the S.E. Midlands', a valiant attempt to establish architectural criteria. The range of the contributions far exceeds that indicated by the title. The various styles of champagne gentry-seats in succeeding thirteenth-century fief rolls offer some illumination also (Coulson, 1982 (2), 353–6). On the metaphysics of 'fortification', see Coulson 1982 (1).

[76] Reconstruction with its bartizan turrets in B. Morley, 112. Two of the fifty-six (Penrith, Thornton Abbey) are repeated; Chudleigh and Sherburn (Rest Park) have *fortalicium* instead. Bishop Rede's Amberley (nn. 39, 69 above) sited on the edge of the wide flood plain, cut through the Downs by the splendidly navigable Arun, and near the bridge (or ford), might much more plausibly have been ascribed to fear of coastal raiders (Arundel Castle could not have 'blocked' them even if heavily manned), but no such tradition has arisen here. Its licence is standard and it entirely lacks Bodiam's panache. The 'make a castle' licences are *CPR (1381–5)*, 108, cf. 333; *CPR (1385–9)*, 42, 156; *CPR (1391–6)*, 188, 261; cp. *CPR (1377–81)*, 377; *CChR (1341–1417)*, 307.

this approach has caused.[77] Ironically, by these very criteria we could not regard Bodiam as qualifying at all, whereas by the proper standards of its own *milieu*, Bodiam by its social function and its architecture fully deserves the coveted style of 'castle' (see Figures 13, 18).

The rank and landed estate of the lord who held it and the deference he evoked quite as much as any dignity of structure, in fact, in later medieval England, conferred the title as also did popular nomenclature. Dallingridge needed to compensate for his lack of pedigree. Lords of consequence lived in 'castles', just as bishops do in 'palaces', even if on archaeological grounds the comfortable VCH term 'homestead moat' would be applied to their mansions. Nicholas de la Beche had such a place at Beams (Berks., licensed 1338), which is styled 'castle' in the enquiries into the forcible abduction from it in 1347 of his widow Margery, the king's young son Lionel of Antwerp being in residence at the time. The *mansum* of Melbourne (Derbys., licensed 1311) had as defences only a gate-house and turreted curtain but achieved castle status in Henry of Lancaster's inquisition *post mortem* in 1361. As for the equally modest works of Moor End and Maxey (Northants., licensed 1347, 1374) royal and ducal tenure lent that dignity. Contrariwise, major and ancient feudal *capita* tended to be 'castles' regardless of their occupancy or architecture. Quite frequently also the title was popularly conferred, as at Bagworth (Leics., licensed 1318) reported by inquisition jurors in 1371 as 'a capital messuage called the castle'. Mettingham in Suffolk (licensed 1343), also structurally not very distinguished, was *castellum* in 1366 and (to our eyes more justly) so was Cooling, but only on the forfeiture of John de Cobham in 1398.[78] Occasionally there are hints that quadrangular towered and moated places as such qualified. Titchmarsh (Northants., licensed 1304) was styled *fortalicium* in 1314 and described as 'a capital messuage enclosed like a castle with water and a stone wall', in 1347 (i.e. 'in castle-fashion', not 'in imitation of a castle'). But no sort

---

[77] E.g. C. and B. Gascoigne, *Castles of Britain* (London, 1975), 54, for some notably imaginative Bodiam comment. The definition was for the RAI research project into the origins of the castle in England (*Archaeological Journal* 134 (1971), 2) but is almost as inadequate for the Conquest period. See e.g. Giraldus Cambrensis's description of the amenities of Manorbier (Pembs.; R. A. Brown, 1954, 177); also the emphasis on the fertile environs of rebuilt Templar Saphet, in Palestine (c.1240–60), as well as on its formidable defences (V. Monet and P. Deschamps, *Recueil de Textes relatifs a l'histoire de l'architecture* ,,,, ii (Paris 1929, 261–4)). Literary allusions are equally clear (nn. 44, 75). Resentment of social pretension seems to have been felt most keenly by the Shire gentry. The 1363 Sumptuary Laws and the 1379 graduated categories of Poll Tax payers illustrate clearly the contemporary sense of hierarchy (*Rotuli Parliamentorum* ii, 278–9; iii, 57–8).

[78] Earlier usage of *castrum* for major 'public' works and ancient walled towns (e.g. as a place-name element in Anglo-Saxon England designating all kinds of former Roman sites) has constantly been neglected. 'Castle' took on subsequently strong seignorial connotations, giving birth to the later medieval concept, but the laboured contrast with 'communal' and 'pre-feudal' fortification is highly suspect, e.g. in 1227 and 1317 the Salisbury cathedral clergy petitioned to 'have the stones built in their minster and houses within (*sic*) the castle of Salisbury (i.e. Old Sarum hillfort) for their work of (new) Salisbury' (cf. R. A. Brown, M. C. Prestwich, C. Coulson, *Castles: A History and Guide* (Poole, 1980), 10–11); *Rotuli Parliamentorum* i, 174–5; *Calendar of the Chancery Warrants* i, 470–1). The CIPM references are ix, 236–8; xi, 92–116; xii, 51–3; xiii, 237–40; see also *CPR (1408–13)*,195; *CFR (1391–9)*, 257–8; *CFR (1445–52)*, 239.

of consistency was observed. It was mostly tradition in the eye of the beholder. Sir Reginald de Cobham's Sterborough (Surrey, licensed 1341) with its erstwhile seven towers, curtain, gatehouse and moat was described (1369) as a *forcelet-tum ad modum castri*, but while noting its 'strong walls' the jurors were just as impressed by 'the park containing deer measuring a league in circuit'. Numerous posthumous surveys show that the appurtenances contributed quite as much as the mansion-place to the renown of a noble residence. Established castles, even decaying earthworks, still possessed a prestige that put them above later arrivals, whose aim was therefore to imply respectable antiquity, though seldom as brashly as Dallingridge did.[79]

The Enigma of Bodiam

It may now be possible to venture some explanations for the enigmatic conjunction at Bodiam of an exaggeratedly militant outward ostentation, which is so deliberately contradicted by the domesticity of all the features of detail. That its defensive panoply accords with the typological evolution of the southern quadrangular castle, which flourished ever more luxuriantly during the era of its military decline, must be emphasised. What is misleading at Bodiam is the apparently purposeful assertiveness of the militant overlay, but comparison with its own generation of licensed castles, to go no further (Chideock 1370, 1380; Nunney, 1373; Claxton, 1376; Shirbum, 1377; Bolton 1379; Cooling, 1381; Sheriff Hutton, 1382; Farleigh Hungerford, 1383; Lumley, 1392; Wardour, 1393; Penrith, 1397) is corrective. Bodiam is only locally exceptional. Dallingridge's circumstances do indeed offer more clues, but hyperbole is often a symptom of irrelevance. As castles' defensive value diminished, be it against foreign invasion, riot or civil conflict as well as in *guerre à outrance*, so the integral and incorporated symbolic element was emancipated to become explicit and in time fully autonomous with a life of its own. It could then develop without imposed constraints through stages, which may be represented by Penshurst (re-licensed 1392), Faulkebourne (Essex, licensed 1439), Herstmonceux, Tonford (Kent, 1448), Sudeley (Gloucs., 1458), Gidea Hall (Essex, 1466), Oxburgh (Norfolk, 1482), Athelhampton (Dorset, 1495), Thornbury (Gloucs., 1510) and ultimately by such revivalist manifestations as Cowdray (Sussex, 1533) and Baconsthorpe (Norfolk, 1561). Its energy even then was far from spent as can be seen at Hardwick, Burghley House and Wollaton Hall, Nottinghamshire. Licences to crenellate continuously chart this aesthetic progression, until they and it peter out with the advent of Palladianism late in the reign of Elizabeth. At no point were 'defence' and domesticity divorced. Seignorial symbolism kept the outward and inward aspects of the castle-image in harmony throughout, and it may well be possible to show that this conjunction,

---

[79] Even abandoned sites were 'the old castle' or *situm castri*. Judicial and administrative functions often continued. For Titchmarsh, see CIPM v, 289–90; ix, 24–5; for Sterborough xii, 326–9. On the Anglo-Saxon lordly display of burh-geat, see A. Williams, 'A Bell-House and a Burh-geat: Lordly Residences in England before the Norman Conquest', *Medieval Knighthood* 4 (1992), 221–40, reprinted *ANC*, 23–40.

embodied in the gentry residence, began very much earlier. That it was already in existence in the later thirteenth century can scarcely be denied; but more to the present purpose are the problematic effects of security-consciousness in the violent late Middle Ages.

Rather unconvincing attempts have been made to attribute the very numerous moated *gentilhommières* to the defensive rather than to the socially symbolic function of noble architecture, and thereby to fit them into the ready-made military scenario as a response to the endemic problems of law and order. Burglaries of manor-houses, even in daylight and by determined bands of malefactors, were certainly not uncommon but they were obviously not deterred by the level of 'defences' typified by the castle of Beams. The sophisticated amalgam of deterrence, status-affirmation and some limited degree of physical protection, characteristic of this class of 'fortified manor-house', should not be too roughly dissected. Any single, or simple, system of explanation will certainly be inadequate.[80] The full range of analysis certainly must be brought to the understanding of Bodiam. French practices of the *chevauchée* would have placed it very low in the category of place not requiring engines to capture. It could scarcely have resisted the bands of peasant *réfractaires*, forced into copying the tactics of the Free Companies, let alone a mass uprising or *jacquerie*; nor, to judge from English *oyer et terminer* commissions, would it have been at all secure from aggravated house-breaking. Descriptions copied from the petitions of aggrieved householders may well exaggerate. But attacks holding a place 'besieged in manner of war', described in vivid detail including the culprits suspected and stating the value of the goods stolen and the damage done, are still important evidence. Their flagrancy and mass violence are very striking. One of them details an assault in October 1381 upon the Kiriel (Crioll) family castle of Westenhanger (Kent, licensed in 1343), situated four miles inland from the coast at Hythe. The destruction of many such castles has made Bodiam seem far more special than it really was. Westenhanger was once an impressive and substantially constructed, moated, roughly quadrangular castle with a gate and seven other towers, somewhat larger than Bodiam but of comparable design and siting. The attackers, led by Sir John Cornwall, according to Lettice widow of Sir John de Kiriel, 'with ladders scaled by night and entered

---

[80] The almost ritualised response to violence by ineffective legal processes is analogous to that by crenellating, illustrated most clearly with conventual precincts (Coulson 1982 (1), esp. 84–92; cf. H. R. T. Summerson, 'The Structure of Law Enforcement in Thirteenth-Century England', *American Journal of Legal History* 23 (1979), 313–27. (I owe this reference and helpful discussion to Dr Michael Clanchy.) A psychological rather than a materialistic reaction is inferable. The phenomenon of 'rogue gentry' has generated a large literature, e.g. R. W Kaeuper, 'Law and Order in Fourteenth-Century England …', *Speculum* 54 (1979), 734–84 (e.g. 741, *oyer et terminer* commissions 1272–1377); also, more broadly, in *War, Justice and Public Order* (Oxford, 1988) (esp. ch. 2). Moat-digging (and other works) are ascribed to lawlessness by C. Platt, 1978 (n. 54 above), 111–15; and 1982, ch. 5; but in Sussex the problem was absent or inconspicuous (Saul, 75). Licences to crenellate suggest a broader gamut of social motives (cf. 1371 Commons' petition to dispense with the formality of licensing *Rotuli Parliamentorum* ii, 307). Beams Castle consists today of 'the remains of a moat and some earthworks'; otherwise 'a square moat', and 'traces of an earthwork' (VCH Berks. i, 271; iii, 268; King, *Castellarium Anglicanum*, Berks.).

her castle ..., broke her houses and chambers, searched for her so closely that she was compelled to hide in some water, narrowly escaping death thereby'. The attempted ravishment failed but the raiders stole twelve horses valued at forty li., saddlery, jewellery and other goods. One of the culprits, not accused by Lady Lettice, received pardon nearly two years later 'for having with others broken the gates, doors and windows (*recce fenestre*, i.e. 'shutters') of the Lady of Kiriel's Castle of Estrynghangre and besieged her there ...', so it was no mere sneak attack.[81] Jealous or opportunistic near-dwellers and the perversion of the chivalric code among the war-calloused aristocracy were a serious social problem, most certainly, but the *insouciance* of the architectural response may not be too hard to comprehend.

Even when the lord was himself in residence, gentry households would seldom have been numerous enough or equipped to fight off such attacks. Tower houses needed few defenders and suited conditions of continued lawlessness much better, but the castellar fashion of central and southern England prescribed quadrangular and gracious courtyard castles. To describe the male members of the normal knightly *familia* as a 'garrison' is to distort the realities. The personnel aspect quite as much as the architectural *matériel* determined what resistance could be offered. A resident force comprising a handful of porters, kitchen-hands and manorial record-keepers was totally inadequate. Nor would this skeleton staff be much enlarged on occasion by the 'riding household' of their peripatetic lord. Dallingridge's old patron, Richard earl of Arundel, in his own honourable and ancient castle of Lewes, with its modernised shell-keep and outer gatehouse, was himself not untouched by the more coordinated commotions of 1381. He obtained (February 1383) a commission of enquiry into an attack by Lewes 'insurgents', who 'came armed to Lewes, broke his closes and the gates, doors and windows (i.e. shutters) of his castle there, threw down his buildings, consumed and destroyed ten casks of wine, value 100 li. (*sic*) and burned his rolls, rentals and other muniments'. Manorial records were a natural and frequent target of the Commons in 1381. Protecting them was particularly important, but in the castellated building of the decade following the Peasants' Revolt, seignorial reassertion (as on previous occasions) is the chief discernible response, not defence

---

[81] Bodiam's doors would not have withstood any kind of battery. If there was warning enough to raise the lifting bridges, they could be forced or by-passed; if time to remove the bridge-spans (Figures 5, 11, 15), the narrow gaps could quickly be crossed by ladder or beams to the platforms without the entries; failing which the 'lake' would be crossed or the water drained (under cover of dark if necessary) and ladders put up. Accounts of such attacks show how determined they often were. Wrenching out the bars, with rope and grapple (Figure 8) would give easy entry particularly via the Chapel or Hall windows. 'Siege', as such, would not be required. Plans of Westenhanger (as it was in 1648 and 1887) in J. F. Wadmore, *Archaeologia Cantiana* 17 (1887), 200; *CPR (1381–5)*, 133, 319, 548. Lettice outlived her son Nicholas, who died in 1380 leaving a widow and baby. Any husband could expect a lucrative administration of Lettice's dower (the castle and advowson). The Criolls held of the archbishop and had also Eynsford 'castle and manor', with lands at Mongeham and Walmer in E Kent. The deer park at Westenhanger (now the racecourse) was still famous in Tudor times (CIPM xv, 100–1).

precautions.[82] Restive peasants, like cannon and French raids, all seem to have been blandly disregarded. An alternative explanation, both peculiar and general, is obviously needed. Only the former can be attempted here.

Because time has damaged or eliminated so many of Bodiam's architectural compeers, its special quality has certainly been exaggerated. In the local context it does stand out – indeed, exactly as it was meant to do; it is a most studied *coup de théâtre* (see Figure 2). To understand its intended dramatic impact the necessary background lies in Edward Dallingridge's standing in the county. His was an acutely rank-conscious society, which prescribed to each grade by blood, acquired rank or by possessions the 'conspicuous consumption' deemed proper. So, having bruised the conventions, why does he soften the impact of his castle by giving us drawbridge recesses with no drawbridges, 'gunloops' which do not work, doors without drawbars, projecting towers which do not flank, and a fragile pond for water-defences, among less conspicuous oddities, all set in an elaborately contrived *scène* of aquatic *divertissements* (see Figures 2, 3)? Castellated fashion explains the features but does not fully account for their *bravura* nor adequately for their self-deprecation. It is a curious impressario who sabotages his own show, and yet Bodiam is militarily speaking a piece of splendid tongue-in-cheek bluff. Its covert contradictions are so many coded disclaimers of undue social pretension, whose message, we may be sure, was perfectly clear to the audience Dallingridge and his architect were addressing. There may well have been a touch of cynical humour in all that bluster and undoubtedly much romantic self-indulgence.

The case is necessarily speculative and depends largely on the peculiar position of Sir Edward during the 1380s and early 1390s in local affairs and national politics. Dr Nigel Saul has recently illuminated the local situation, and further light has been shed upon the brush with John of Gaunt in June 1383. Dallingridge was an elderly man at the time of his licence to crenellate, but aggressive and only belatedly in a position to gratify ambitions quite possibly stimulated originally by his service in the French wars (*c.*1340–75), as were those of other aspiring gentry, many of whom figure among the recipients of licences. His military activities there and later at home are not exceptional for men of his class and type, nor is his traditional enrichment in France more than supposition. His opportunities, however, both locally and at Court in the 1380s, were distinctly

---

[82] *CPR (1381–5)*, 259; Saul, 35. The Kentish 'insurgents' also 'broke' Rochester Castle 'and all the king's gaols in Kent' (*CPR (1381–5)*, 409; *CCR (1396–9)*, 171–2). They attacked properties of Sir William de Etchingham, some of the culprits being Bodiam men (Saul, 82). On the defensive capabilities, in such circumstances, of northern tower-houses see Kightly, 120–7. He well shows the value of first-floor entrances, vaulted ground-floors and summits, and of skilful flanking-loops (e.g. 158, 168–9) but (the last feature excepted) the formula is essentially that of the supremely cost-effective twelfth-century dwelling-tower (styled 'keep' by the Victorians' prejudice for 'real' castles: see Pugin's skit on 'the modern castellated mansion', in M. Girouard (1978), 244, also ch. 2, 'The medieval household' for a general discussion of domestic logistics).

beyond the norm.[83] As also for his colleague Sir Richard Abberbury, licensed to build a castle soon after (1386, June) at Donnington, ready access to the machinery of the Chancery facilitated getting a variety of grants and favours. Ten times knight of the shire for Sussex (1379–88) and especially having been one of three shire representatives on the 1380 commission investigating abuses during King Richard's minority, Dallingridge evidently could put drafts of what he wanted to the appropriate chancery clerk, in the usual way of inner-circle courtiers. Bribes and the low Hanaper fee, paid on collection after the grant was duly engrossed and enrolled, financed the office and yielded a profit. He and his like could purchase very much what they wanted. In February 1386 he got another licence, this time to divert a watercourse (often a very sensitive issue) 'from Dalyngreggesbay in Salehirst' to Bodiam Mill (pond below the Castle). His commissions, in July 1380 to advise how and at whose expense Winchelsea might be 'fortified', and in March 1386 to see to the defence and fortifications of Rye (he was, in fact, 'in the king's company in Scotland', in June 1385) imply no particular expertise, being part of the habitual general-purpose employment by the Crown of the active gentry. Nor should the extent of his local commitment in Sussex be exaggerated. Neither he nor Abberbury, king's knights though they were, supported Suffolk at his impeachment (1386), and he defected soon after to the Appellants; but not for very long. His conduct suggests the adroit trimmer, quick to collect the benefits of privilege, by violence or sharp practice if necessary, while avoiding, so far as

[83] On 'the peerage of soldiers', see M. H. Keen, *The Laws of War in the Late Middle Ages* (London, 1965), 254–7. Dallingridge probably built in this spirit. The *ex spoliis Gallorum* tradition is investigated by K. B. McFarlane on Fastolf in *Transactions of the Royal Historical Society*, 5th ser. 8 (1957), 91–116 on Caistor. See S. Walker, 'Lancaster v. Dallingridge; a Franchisal Dispute in Fourteenth-Century Sussex', *SAC* 121 (1983), 87–94; Saul 28–9, 43, 67–8, 75, 98n, 191 on Gaunt's attempt as lord of Pevensey to assert his rights and hold his hundred court at Hungry Hatch (near Sheffield Park, seat of Sir Roger Dallingridge, d. *c.*1380). Gaunt 'met with considerable provocation from a group of local landowners led by Sir Edward'. Bodiam Manor was held of the queen's Rape of Hastings. Arundel's temporary eclipse at Court enabled Gaunt to have Edward tried and briefly imprisoned. In July 1386, Gaunt left England for his Iberian ventures. Sussex is notable for apparent immunity from 'magnate feuding' and from 'the disruptive activities of the outlaw gangs' (n. 80 above). The position of men like Sir Edward was enhanced 'by the relative absence of magnate lordship' (72). He acted as Gaunt's master forester in Ashdown Forest and abused his position with impunity. He had served under Sir Robert Knollys, and in 1367 under Lionel of Clarence (*CPR (1367–70)*, 41). Knight of the royal household (1377), he married Elizabeth de Wardedieu and inherited his elder brother's lands *c.*1380. His acquisition (after July 1376) of Bodiam Manor is noted in 1381 in a transaction for the sale of timber from 'a wood in Bodyham park between Bodyham pond [was this on the present castle site? see above] and the lands of Thomas Colepepere, knight', to be taken to the sea and shipped to Calais (*CPR (1377–81)*, 611). In 1380 he was one of the shire knights on the parliamentary commission for the reform of the king's household; Shire member in 1379–88; assiduous member of the royal council 1389–93; commissioner for peace with France 1390, keeper and escheator of London, 20 June to 22 July 1392, during Richard's dispute with the citizens (among them Henry Yevele), which office was doubtless lucrative (see Tout iii, 352, 411, 413n, 469n, 470n, 480–1; J. F. Baldwin, *The King's Council in England during the Middle Ages* (London, 1913 (1969), 132–3, 300n, 489 *et seq.*, showing he can seldom have been in Sussex; *CFR (1391–1399)*, 49, 51. He died *c.*1394 (Tout, Saul '1393').

possible, the odium of office at a moment of especial unpopularity for the royal councillor and acquisitive courtier.[84]

His career does much to explain the éclat of Bodiam. His chivalry moreover, was evidently of the war-hardened and brutal Robert Knollys variety, and his 'toy fortress' swaggers with assumed self-confidence, as Nunney (1373), Cooling and Wardour do also in their own way, shrugging off the facts of defeat abroad. But there is very little of France about the styling of Bodiam. Not for him the majestic Pierrefonds-type double-crowned tower summits of Guy's and Caesar's towers, added to the great baronial castle of Warwick, although modernity received the gesture of his machicolation and inverted keyhole gunloops. Bodiam fits not uncomfortably its stylistic and social niche, but a more specific context might tentatively be proposed, namely that of 'reassertive castellation', a phenomenon demonstrated by several of the licences to crenellate. Having gathered to himself family lands, heiress-wife and son, profits of office and opportunity, and having confronted the great Duke of Lancaster and King of Castile, a grandiloquent statement of his triumph very naturally followed (see Figure 13).

The instance most local and most characteristic is the case of 'Shoford', near Maidstone. It is typical in that the circumstances suggest that the chief motive for obtaining the licence was to answer back to some slight or insult. Dallingridge may have suffered himself in the disturbances of 1381. Arundel, his patron, certainly did. But the offence could be any event derogatory to personal standing. Near Maidstone, in early June 1381, the house of an unpopular local official, William

[84] Abberbury at Donnington founded also a chapel and hospital (VCH *Berks* iv, 96, 137, 456, 508). Edward's elder (and perhaps less assertive) brother Roger had an active career latterly in Shire politics 1360–77, dying c.1380 in his 70s. He gained the de la Lynde lands, joined the Arundel retinue and fought in France with the de Poynings in 1338–46 (Saul 36, 67–8). In many ways Edward succeeding as head of the family built upon his achievement. The writs of 'expenses' for his Parliamentary attendances 1379–84, at four shillings per day total nearly £60 (*CCR (1377–81)*, 356, 497; *CCR (1381–5)*, 133, 453; *CCR (1385–9)*, 119, 495). He had also ten shillings a day as a royal Councillor 1389–93, and 100 marks *p.a.* for life and perquisites (e.g. two tuns of Gascon red wine annually). Of the thirty-plus councillors he was the most 'industrious', attending e.g. for 207 days between 8 January 1392 and 21 February 1393. He is styled in the council journal *Monsire* and served with John sire de Cobham, Lord Lovell and John Devereux (Baldwin, n. 83 above). These three all had licence to crenellate (Cooling, Wardour, Penshurst). 'Like any other medieval licence (e.g. Mortmain), a licence to crenellate would be granted to any applicant, if he was not openly hostile (*sic*) to the Crown, and could afford it' (N. Denholm-Young, *The Country Gentry in the Fourteenth Century* (Oxford, 1969), 36). Edward's licence for the mill-leat (smoothed by the subtlety that the water was to be channelled 'by an ancient dyke on his own ground to his said mill at Bodiam'), dated 3 February 1386, presumably indicates that the water-holding earthworks were then quite far advanced and the inadequacy of water for the mill was apparent. The licence cost him half a mark, good value for a lucrative sign of lordship. In the summer 1385 invasion crisis quite significantly he was exempted (June) from arraying men in Sussex in order to be with the king. He backed Arundel and the Appellants in 1387–9, and in March 1388 was one of the trusties empowered to receive oaths of loyalty from Sussex notables. In January 1389 he secured the keeping of the local alien priory of Wilmington for 100 marks *p.a.*, doubtless profitably (*CPR (1385–9)*, 6, 98, 123, 405–6; *CPR (1377–81)*, 566; *CFR (1383–1391)*, 278). Invested in Bodiam Castle these combined resources yielded lasting gains, cannily safeguarded by John Dallingridge's cultivation of Henry of Derby, which was duly rewarded after the revolution of 1399 (Saul, 70). In 1412 the Sussex lands yielded £100 *p.a.* (G. Mathew, *The Court of Richard II* (London, 1968), 206).

de Topcliffe, was 'thrown down by the common people' who had been incited by a gang responsible for sacking several manor-houses in the area and destroying manorial documents. No licence was actually needed to rebuild but, perhaps, adding some crenellation and support from the new archbishop (successor of the murdered Sudbury) William de Courtenay, in getting it out of Chancery, all served to reassert Topcliffe's status and his association with the great and to scorn those who had humiliated him.[85]

Popular resentments, smouldering among the broken promises of 1381, may be an additional reason for disclaiming motives of aggrandisement, as does Dallingridge by the wording of his licence and John de Cobham even more publicly. Impressing the knightly class risked irritating the common people, especially by treating them like French peasantry. Cooling Castle was being completed about the time the earthworks at Bodiam were begun. Both belong to that recovery of confidence by divinely ordained authority, once the levelling doctrines of John Ball had been repressed. But there is a note of self-exculpation and unease nonetheless –

> Knowyth that be-th and schal be
> That I am mad in help of the cuntre –
> In knowyng of whyche thyng
> Thys is chartre and wytnessyng.[86]

Being worsted in his quarrel over franchisal rights of jurisdiction by John of Gaunt's local agents in 1384 must have sharpened all these motives and may well have pushed Dallingridge to the bravado of Bodiam. Its studied archaisms asserted his lineage while its touches of modernity advertised his present power. The 'frontier-castle' allusion could disregard the realities of the March; nothing more poetic than that castle in a valley can be imagined. In a region, since the decline early in the century of the Warenne power, and lacking intermediate magnates, the upper gentry in East Sussex seem to have got rather above themselves. At Bodiam, Dallingridge shared the parish church, had a park only in name and suffered from all the stigma of being a newcomer. The lordly emblems and appurtenances of deer park, minor jurisdiction and rights of free warren were esteemed as much as the castle-seat itself. Dallingridge, whether bruised by his set-down

[85] Probably in Mote Park, SSE of the town centre, see Coulson 1982 (1), 85–6. The cases of 'Hales' recte Halesowen (see Zvi Razi, on abbot–tenantry friction, in Essays in Honour of R. H. Hilton, ed. T. H. Ashton et al. (Cambridge, 1983), 151–67; ref. due to M. C. Prestwich), Waltham and Abingdon are also revealing monastic instances. On Lewes in 1381, see n. 82 above. That the chivalrous ambiance exists mostly in modern preconception is argued by John Gillingham on William the Marshal's History (Thirteenth Century England 2, 1988).

[86] See n. 66 above. The plaque has beth (i.e. 'be-eth') and mad in help (not 'made'). John Harvey (1944, 39) commented that 'Lord Cobham was taking no chances of arousing hostility among the peasants by the building of the castle' (but the licence is dated 10 Feb. 1381). '...The inscription is in blue enamel on a copper plate, made in the form of a charter with strings and seal.' Except that a lead flashing has been inserted at the top as a rain-drip, this well-known (but still remarkable) manifesto (?c.1385) is in pristine condition.

or emboldened by coming off well, evidently set out to make his castle at Bodiam in compensation as assertive as a careful choice of site, an excellent architect and economical expenditure of his local and central sources of income allowed.[87] It is all 'up front'. The 'castle-in-a-lake' look is still supremely effective; in its original setting the effect must have been stunning (see Figure 2). Perhaps he was thereby somewhat stepping beyond his proper station in life, but *de facto* ennoblement by arms and subsequent royal service produced similar symptoms of architectural *hubris* in numerous members of his class. King Richard's minority, unsettled local conditions both foreign and domestic, and the experience of 'heavy lordship' at Lancaster's hands, undoubtedly explain the building that we can examine today in its singular completeness and splendour. Its ambiguity may perhaps be resolved by borrowing from the repertoire of animal behaviourism: a gregarious intruder, conscious of his strength but reluctant to provoke resentment, sends out conflicting and simultaneous signals of aggression and of submission, at once eager to compel respect while anxious not to offend unduly the hierarchical proprieties of his own time and species.[88]

Addendum, September 1992

The 1917–25 correspondence (copy generously supplied 2. ix. 92 by Dr D. W. R. Thackray) chiefly of William Weir (architect), E. E. Bowden (site-supervisor) and Curzon, reveals *inter alia multa* that: the MOAT, contrary to the opinion quoted

---

[87] See nn. 52, 71, 82–4 above; also n. 83 for Bodiam park. That crenellation was merely one of many prestigious elements is most obvious in the licences under charter (forty-five covering sixty-six sites including six town and three castle-building jurisdictional franchises) where the 'fortification' is part of an entire complex of seignoralia (e.g. Boughton Malherbe, Kent 1363; Harringworth, Northants., 1387; Ketdewell in Craven, Yorks., 1405: *CChR (1341–1417)*, 174, 307, 427). A few by letter patent are also packages combining in one document that whole array of cherished and lucrative rights appurtenant to lordly rank in terms of which Sir Edward Dallingridge's Bodiam Castle should be analysed and understood.

[88] It has been unavoidably necessary in this paper to take issue with a good many statements which have previously gone unchallenged, have been continually reiterated, but which are clearly erroneous; and also to confront some interpretations which would appear to be poorly substantiated. The result may seem rather more combative than courteous. It is indeed the third demand of that threefold test of justified utterance that is the hardest to satisfy. 'Is it true? Is it necessary? Is it kind?' The more the others are served the more elusive becomes the last.

Further Note The latest National Trust guidebook has been published since writing (David Thackray, *Bodiam Castle*, The National Trust (June 1991), 60pp, numerous illustrations). Use of custodianship records has supplied valuable details of early conservation work (26–30) notably by the Fuller family (1829–64), by George Cubitt (1864–1916) and by Lord Curzon (1916–25). Interestingly, it was he who had the Main Gate 'prison pits' dug out (37). There is also a variety of useful but flawed historical material. Some telling architectural indicators such as the absence of hinges for doors to the barbican, are noted (although doors are still alleged behind the mid- and inner portcullises to the main entry) and a chapter is included on 'The Setting' (55–8) not quite fairly presenting the views of RCHME, but the work as a whole is substantially traditional, attempting to assimilate contradictory evidence mentioned selectively. A few errors seem to be entirely new (since Curzon), notably Dallingridge's age and the omission of his elder brother (genealogy, 22). To catalogue them all would risk emulating J. H. Round's pungent index entry on 'Freeman, Professor' in his *Feudal England*, 1895.

of L. E. Hole (1970) did need clay puddling on the S and E banks; refilling 1920–1 took over twelve months owing to poor spring-flow aggravated by leakage; the old sluice was of 'portcullis' penstock type, replaced by manhole and plugged pipe; Curzon had the lilies removed (and, less successfully, rushes from his 'Tiltyard'). BRIDGES: attempts were made to find 'pits' outside both gates; the stone-cased causeway S from the Barbican was eventually accepted as a contemporary after-thought and largely refaced (in new stone). PARAPETS were extensively re-set or reinstated with original ashlar from the moat and interior; entire 'restoration' was rejected on cost (£950 estimated). The INTERIOR was largely dug out ('exca-vated') then partially re-filled; efforts to find true basements (Main Gate, SW and SE Towers) as 'dungeons' were frustrated by water-seepage; the 'well' found in the SW Tower (probably *recte* a cistern for rainwater and once lead-lined) filled up as the Moat level rose (1920–1). The WORK AS A WHOLE (cost £5,780, 1919–21, by Curzon's summary) was creditably conservative once the 1917 total 'restoration' scheme, costed at £20,000, was providentially declined by Lord Curzon.

12

English Castles in the Reign Of Edward II

Michael Prestwich

Why did castles not play a more dominant role in the troubles of Edward II's reign? There were no major sieges like those of Bedford or Kenilworth in the thirteenth century, and castles failed to protect the north against Scottish raids. It was not so much that their walls and battlements were inadequate, but rather that garrisons and supplies were often insufficient. Frequent changes of command partly reflected the political difficulties of the period, but were also a result of administrative confusion. In several English towns there was considerable trouble between the constable of the local castle and the urban populace. Royal attempts to overawe opposition by placing large numbers of castles in a state of defence seem to have had little effect, while baronial castles rarely held out for long under attack. Architectural developments reflected the changing role of castles. The traditions of Edward I's castle-building declined, and there was a greater emphasis on the domestic aspects of castles, rather than on the fortifications. Much building was on a relatively small scale, in response to local disorder rather than national emergency.

It was not very often that the castles of medieval England were put to the test.[1] The reign of Edward II, however, witnessed both civil war and invasion by the Scots, and it is striking that castles did not play the dominant role that they had a century previously. The warfare at the end of John's reign and in Henry III's minority had largely centred on castles. Sieges such as those of Rochester, Dover and Bedford were important turning points. Later, in the mid-thirteenth century, the protracted defence of Kenilworth in the final stages of the Barons' Wars amply demonstrated the efficacy of strong defences against a massive mobilisation of resources. Yet under Edward II, sieges were usually very brief, as when the king's favourite, Piers Gaveston, surrendered at Scarborough in 1312, or when the king took Leeds in Kent in 1321. Thomas of Lancaster's supporters in 1322 did not attempt to hold out behind strong walls as Simon de Montfort's had done in 1266. Nor, apparently, did castles do much to deter the Scots on their frequent and highly profitable raids into the north of England. Yet although the military importance of castles appears to have declined by the early fourteenth century, questions regarding their custody were politically significant. Architecturally, too,

---

[1] My thanks are due to the Travel and Research Fund of the University of Durham for financial assistance with the preparation of this article. Unless otherwise stated, all MS sources are in the PRO, London [now TNA].

the period was important, for it witnessed the last attempts to build in the grand manner that Edward I's great master mason, James of St George, had employed in north Wales, while at the same time some building works presaged the future direction that military architecture was to take.

The question of the appointment of castle constables was obviously one of great importance. A castle was of little military value if its commander was unreliable, while at the same time the power to appoint constables was a valuable form of royal patronage. In March 1308, when baronial rebellion first threatened after Edward II's coronation, thirteen castles changed hands. Among those removed from office were Payn Tibetot, John Botetourt and Robert Clifford, who had all placed their seals on the Boulogne Declaration of January 1308, indicating their dissatisfaction with the state of the realm. Members of the royal household were prominent among the new appointees (Maddicott 1970, 77–8; CFR (1307–19), 17–19). Some appointments were highly contentious. Edward I had granted Isabella de Vescy custody of Bamburgh Castle, and in 1310 the terms of the appointment were made more generous, Edward II conceding that she need make no payments to the exchequer. Although there is no evidence to suggest that the castle was particularly badly maintained or equipped while in her hands, the Ordainers demanded her removal from office in 1311 in adamant terms (Prestwich 1971, 148–52). Another unpopular appointment was that of the household sergeant Robert Lewer to Odiham. The castle was entrusted to him in 1311, and although the Ordainers demanded his expulsion from the household in that year his post was confirmed in 1312. In 1317, however, he was replaced by the younger Despenser, who was rising rapidly in royal favour, and until 1322 the two seem to have been keen rivals for the castle. Lewer rebelled twice against the king, and in 1322 even laid siege to the castle he had once commanded. It is very likely that it was his replacement in office by Despenser that caused him to turn against the king (CFR (1307–19), 103; CPR (1307–13), 481; CPR (1317–21), 46; Fryde 1979, 153–4).

Another example of the way in which argument over the custody of a castle had implications for national politics is that of Leeds in Kent. Although Queen Isabella had been promised the reversion of the castle on the death of Edward I's queen Margaret, the castle was in fact granted to Bartholomew Badlesmere, steward of the royal household, in 1318, in exchange for the much more financially valuable manor of Adderley in Shropshire. When Badlesmere deserted the royal cause in 1321, Edward II deprived him successively of the custody of Dover and Tonbridge castles, but not initially of Leeds. Then in a clever move the king sent Isabella to demand lodging at the castle. Badlesmere was not present, but his wife refused the queen admittance: to have allowed her in might have been seen as a tacit recognition of her claim to the castle. This act of refusal gave Edward the opportunity he needed to move against Badlesmere, and the castle was duly besieged and taken by royal troops (HKW, 69; Martin 1869, 111–16).

It was not only the problems of conflicting claims and political argument that made the crown's task of appointing castle constables a difficult one: the government did not always possess the right information, and at times one department appears to have been ignorant of the actions of another. In 1308, the chancery drew up a list of castles and their constables in an attempt to simplify the task, but in five cases the clerk left a complete blank, while five others were simply noted as being in the king's hands, with no constable named.[2] In 1312, William de Montacute and John de Percy were appointed to inspect ten castles, and to appoint reliable local men to those that they found to lack constables. Their task was not an easy one, for the ten included Bedford and Buckingham, the first of which had been demolished in 1224, while the second had never existed at all (*CPR (1307–13)*, 469; *HKW*, 559). In the autumn of 1311 and early in 1312, there was remarkable confusion over the custody of Carlisle. The council nominated Andrew Harclay for the post, but the king, apparently ignorant of this, gave his backing to a household knight, John de Castre. On 1 April 1312, a writ was issued expressing surprise at de Castre's reluctance to obey orders, and instructing him to hand the castle over to Harclay, yet on 11 March, John de Weston had been appointed to replace de Castre, and on 31 March it had been granted to Piers Gaveston (*CFR (1307–19)*, 118, 120, 123, 128–9; *CPR (1307–13)*, 450). Although a royal writ, in a slightly different context, spoke of 'the circumspect providence of the royal majesty, which according to the qualities of things and the events of the times, must often change ministers and officials and transfer them from place to place and from office to office', the rapid changeover of castle constables which is characteristic of the reign of Edward II was more an indication of the crown's weakness than of its strength in operating the system of patronage (*CFR (1319–27)*, 78).

In times of crisis, special measures were sometimes taken to try to ensure that the king's nominees as castle constables would not be replaced by men appointed by his opponents. At the end of the reign there were even special countersigns agreed with the constable of Caerfili Castle in Glamorgan, so that he could be sure of the authenticity of royal commands (*CFR (1319–27)*, 430). Extraordinary difficulties could arise; in 1312, Bartholomew Badlesmere and Henry Percy swore not to hand over their respective castles of Bristol and Scarborough to any one save the king, and in both cases there was trouble when authentic royal orders were disregarded. At Scarborough the garrison even refused to accept the instructions of the king when he appeared in person and ordered them to hand the castle over. Percy was not himself present, and later excused the men's action on the grounds that he had foolishly made them swear not to deliver the castle to anyone save himself, never thinking that the king would come to the castle in person (*CPR (1307–13)*, 429, 431–2; Palgrave 1830, 47–8).

There were no echoes in this period of the type of argument that had been so important a century earlier, in Henry III's minority, as to whether particular castles were royal or private (Turner 1904, 277–9). There was, rather, a view that

---

[2] C 47/2/23/13. This MS is undated, but from the names of the castle constables it provides, it can safely be attributed to 1308.

at least in time of war the king should himself take on some of the responsibilities of castle-holders. Yet although various private castles in the north were given royal garrisons, there are no indications that Edward II made direct appeal to the feudal doctrine of 'rendability', which would have entitled him to take charge of castles held from him in feudal tenure in time of need.[3] Rather, the custodians of castles were themselves anxious to see the crown shoulder responsibilities that were highly onerous, while accidents of descent placed various castles in the king's hands. As early as 1310, it was agreed with Isabella de Vescy that in time of war the king should supply Bamburgh with victuals, and repair the structure of the castle (*CPR (1307–13)*, 405). In the next year, the earl of Pembroke's constable at Bothwell in Scotland surrendered his charge to the king 'on account of the defects of its munition and to prevent it falling into the hands of the king's enemies', but after revictualling it, Edward regranted the castle to be held as in the past (*CPR (1307–13)*, 408). The bishop of Durham similarly handed Norham Castle over to the crown in 1314, but it was soon restored to him. A later royal offer to garrison and victual Norham, in 1322, was rejected (*CPR (1313–18)*, 163; Bain 1887, no. 770). In the years after the disastrous defeat at Bannockburn in 1314, several previously private castles in the north appear in royal wardrobe accounts with royal constables and garrisons, notably Alnwick, Appleby, Barnard Castle, Egremont, and Skipton-in-Craven.[4] This was through accident rather than policy. It was the deaths of Robert Clifford in 1314, the earl of Warwick and Henry Percy in 1315, and of Thomas de Multon in 1318 that brought the castles into royal hands because of the minority of the heirs. Such major wardships could hardly have been granted out by the king in the political atmosphere after the Ordinances of 1311, with their attempt to control royal patronage, but the responsibility for the castles does not appear to have been welcomed by the crown. When the royal household knight, John de Felton, to whom Alnwick had been entrusted, was captured by the Scots in 1318, the castle was handed over to the young Henry Percy, even though he was not yet of age. In the same year the young Roger Clifford was likewise granted custody of the castles that were his by inheritance, although he too was a minor (*CFR (1307–19)*, 208, 212, 219, 267–8, 370–1, 378–9). The one example of the crown taking over a private castle in the north completely is that of Wark, whose owner, William de Ros, gave up his rights in 1317 in exchange for lands further south. His decision to do so may well have been influenced by the fact that his claim to Wark was a distinctly fragile one (Bain 1887, no. 577).[5]

---

[3] In a brief discussion C. L. H. Coulson (1976) has suggested that this doctrine whereby an overlord could demand that an enfeoffed fortress should be rendered back to him in time of necessity was of Carolingian origin, in which case it would almost certainly have been applicable in England. Richard (1968), however, argues that this practice only developed in twelfth-century France, so it is possible that it was not a valid principle in England.

[4] See the sections on the garrisoning of castles in Society of Antiquaries MSS 120, 121, and also E 101/378/4, which together cover the period 1316–20.

[5] William de Ros' father had received Wark in 1296 when his brother joined the Scots. His brother's co-heirs, Margaret and Isabel, however, had a strong claim to Wark, which the crown recognised in 1313 (Sanders 1960, 149n).

With a few possible exceptions, it would be hard to argue that the crown made bad appointments to the custody of its castles, unpopular as some of its nominees were. William de Anne, who held Tickhill for Edward II at the time of Lancaster's rebellion in 1322, was not an entirely reputable figure. Yet as constable he performed highly creditably, holding Tickhill against the king's enemies and providing him with valuable information (Maddicott 1970, 306- 7). Predictably, royal household knights, and of course the king's personal favourites, dominate the lists of those appointed to the custody of castles. As with any form of royal patronage, there were inevitable jealousies and conflicts. Analysis of the appointments made in the reign does not, however, suggest any strong reasons as to why castles did not play a more dominant role in the warfare of the period. In 1322, Edward II berated the constables of Bamburgh, Warkworth, Dunstanburgh and Alnwick, as the Scots, after 'infesting the neighbourhood of the castles … taking ransoms and hostages from his subjects, have got away without challenge or damage from the garrison, to the constable's dishonour and shame' (Bain 1887, no. 783). The reasons for the relative ineffectiveness of the castles, however, were more complex than the simple question of the personal capabilities of the constables, and Edward's accusation was hardly fair. It was no use providing castles with constables if garrisons were not adequate, and victuals and arms not sufficient. By Edward II's reign there could no longer be any question of relying upon the old traditional feudal service of castle-guard. In those cases where this had not been wholly forgotten, it had been commuted into a cash payment and integrated with the other revenues from rents and dues that were owed to a castle. In times of emergency it might be possible to persuade the local inhabitants to keep watch in a castle, as happened at Scarborough in 1321 (CPR (1317–21), 596), but in general garrisons at this period were all composed of paid men. The normal revenues available to a castle constable were rarely sufficient to maintain a full garrison for any length of time. In peaceful times, garrisons were kept at very low levels: at Warwick in 1323 there were only a constable, a janitor, a watchman and a keeper of the warren.[6] When there was a threat of invasion or of civil war, however, numbers were sharply increased.

There was a contrast between the comparatively large garrisons employed in the north of England near the Scottish border, and those placed in castles further south in efforts to prevent or contain civil war. The largest forces were concentrated at Berwick and Carlisle: in 1314, there were 84 men-at-arms, 30 hobelars, or lightly armed cavalry, and 326 archers in the castle and town of Carlisle (Bain 1887, no. 403). Eight years later, the castle was defended by five knights, 34 men-at-arms, 40 hobelars and 40 archers. At the same date, Warkworth held 31 men-at-arms and 70 hobelars, and Barnard Castle, not a major fortress, was held by William Ridel under the terms of an indenture obliging him to garrison it with 10 men-at-arms and 20 footsoldiers. Dunstanburgh, taken over by the crown after

[6] SC 6/1040/24.

Lancaster's rebellion, was held by 30 men-at-arms and 100 hobelars.[7] The cost of such forces was very considerable: in 1316–17 the royal wardrobe paid out £17,065 on castle garrisons, and £10,465 in the following year.[8]

When orders were issued for various castles to be placed in a state of defence in 1317 because of the danger of civil war, the writs specified the numbers of men in the garrisons. Wallingford and York were to have forty men each, and other castles twenty or thirty. Accounts show that at Wallingford and York at least, the royal orders were strictly adhered to, but the great bulk of these forces were simply archers, without the substantial proportion of skilled men-at-arms that featured in the border garrisons.[9] Scarborough in 1322 was only garrisoned by twenty archers.[10] Such forces were not kept in being for a moment longer than necessary, because of their cost: in 1322, the keeper of Warwick castle dismissed the soldiers he had recruited when he first heard rumours that the baronial forces had dispersed, rather than wait for royal orders.[11]

There is less evidence to show how private castles were garrisoned, but the evidence does not suggest that they were better provided for than those of the crown. Although the earl of Lancaster kept a huge retinue, and spent lavishly on castle-building, he had no more than a constable and six archers in Kenilworth Castle in 1313–14.[12] He did not keep a permanent garrison at Bolingbroke in Lincolnshire: in 1318 he wrote to his constable there, ordering him to keep the castle securely, and suggesting that he take a dozen or more men from the local lordship to garrison it (Thompson 1965, 168). When Leeds was taken in 1321, Edward II had thirteen of the garrison hanged, which does not suggest that the castle was defended by a large force (Martin 1869, 114).

Victualling was a considerable problem. Food supplies had to be adequate to last out a siege, yet it was obviously not practicable to keep large stocks for long periods in castles that had little more than a skeleton staff. When danger threatened, special arrangements had to be made. In 1312, orders were issued for the victualling of various castles. Oxford with a garrison of eighteen was to receive 30 quarters of wheat, 60 of malt, four tuns of wine, 10 quarters of salt, 10 beef carcases, 40 sides of bacon and 500 stockfish (*CCR (1307–13)*, 402, 420). Such quantities would have been sufficient for up to six months, but the evidence of inventories suggests that it was rare in practice for a castle to have a full and sufficient range of supplies in store. At Bamburgh in 1312, the stores consisted of 34 quarters of wheat, 141 quarters of malt, 41 quarters of barley, 14 quarters of oats and one beef carcase.[13] At Scarborough in late 1321, there were sufficient

[7] British Library, MS Stowe 553, fo. 62v.

[8] Society of Antiquaries MSS 120, fo. 46; 121, fo. 22.

[9] Society of Antiquaries MS 121, fo. 19v.

[10] E 101/16/2.

[11] SC 6/1040/24.

[12] DL/29/1/3, m. 12d.

[13] SC 6/950/2.

wheat, beans, salt and wine, but no meat, fish, malt or oats.[14] The only enquiry to reveal a more or less satisfactory state of affairs was one into the state of the castles in north Wales in the 1320s: Caernarfon had 100 quarters of wheat in store, and a sufficiency of other supplies with the exception of wine and fish.[15] Although castle constables could use the right of prise, or compulsory purchase, in order to stock their castles (*CCR (1318–23)*, 418), it could be a costly business to ensure that a garrison was well-fed. In 1316, the sub-eschaetor of Cumberland took steps to prepare Cockermouth Castle because of the Scottish danger. He provided it with food worth £111, and garrisoned it with a substantial force of 159 men, who received their wages in kind. The cost for three weeks came to almost £100 (*CCR (1313–18)*, 496). The situation was particularly difficult, of course, at that time because of the severe famine that had begun in 1315. At Berwick in the winter of 1315–16, the garrison suffered severe privations, being reduced to eating their horses as they died. The garrisons of Appleby and Brougham were forced to resort to seizing by force food supplies that were being taken to the priory at Carlisle (Bain 1887, nos. 470, 542).

The evidence of the stores of arms and equipment maintained in castles in this period is one of decay and neglect. Indentures drawn up when one constable handed over to another are a dreary catalogue of rusty armour and broken siege engines. The inventory for Bamburgh in 1312 began with two old breastplates, three rotten haubergeons, eight rotten iron helmets, two further helmets and parts of a third, and six broken crossbows. There were 8,000 usable crossbow bolts, but the total value of the stock belonging to the castle was only £3 16s. 3d. There were, however, in addition some supplies that belonged to Isabella de Vescy, including 22 crossbows in good condition.[16] At Scarborough in 1321, virtually all the armour listed was too rusty to be of any use, while the great beam of one of the two siege engines was broken.[17] At Wallingford in the 1320s, royal officials found along with some useless armour a sad relic of the early years of the reign, in the form of sixty shields painted with the arms of the king and Piers Gaveston.[18] Baronial castles were no better stocked with weapons and armour than royal ones. The dilapidated remains of siege engines last used at Kenilworth in 1266 that were found at Wigmore can have been of little value.[19] When Warwick Castle came into the king's hands, all the royal officials found there were two horses, two crossbows and some armour, worth in all only £5.[20]

In comparison with an earlier period, it is plain that castles were not as well manned or supplied. There is nothing equivalent to the carefully worked out system for garrisoning and victualling the Clare castles in south Wales that is

[14] E 101/16/2.
[15] E 101/17/11.
[16] SC 6/950/2.
[17] E 101/16/2.
[18] E 101/17/11.
[19] E 163/4/48.
[20] SC 6/1049/24.

revealed by the account for their custody by Humphrey de Bohun in 1262–3, which shows carefully calculated weekly rations for the men and their horses.[21] Rochester in 1264 was stocked with 211 quarters of wheat, 255 quarters of barley, 163 quarters of oats, and large quantities of meat, fish and miscellaneous food-stuffs.[22] It is not, therefore, surprising to find that castles did not play a more important part in the conflicts of Edward II's reign, although of course the problems of garrisoning and victualling do not provide a full explanation of this.

In the north of England the problem was not so much that castles could be easily taken by the Scots, in the way that the English-held castles in Scotland were (Barrow 1976, 274–9). The Scots did not completely disregard English defences, but as their intention was simply to raid and plunder, rather than acquire territory, they could afford to bypass castles rather than besiege them. They did have some success against castles, notably in 1318, when they took Wark, Harbottle and Mitford, and after winning the town of Berwick through treachery, starved the garrison of the castle into surrender. Yet in 1315, the failure of their attempt to take Carlisle showed that although they were adept at the surprise attack, they lacked experience in siege warfare proper. On that occasion the great movable siege tower, or belfry, that they had built became literally bogged down as it was being moved up to the walls (Barrow 1976, 338). Two major sieges of Norham failed, although an attack by local marauders in time of truce in 1323 was successful (Bain 188, no. 814; Stevenson 1836, 147; Blair and Honeyman 1966, 6–7). The Scots were not wholly unconcerned about English castles: they made the destruction of Harbottle a condition for a truce, and in 1321 Edward II ordered it to be razed 'as secretly as possible' (Barrow 1976, 341; Bain 1837, nos. 738–9). In 1323, one condition of truce was that Edward should build no new castles in the north (Rymer 1816, 521). For the most part, however, the Scots were able to ignore the castles of the north: garrison forces were neither large enough nor mobile enough to halt their raids.

There is some evidence of forays made by castle garrisons. On three occasions in 1315, Roger Damory led a troop from Knaresborough to assist magnates operating further north[23] (Figure 1). In 1317, a combined force drawn from the garrisons of Warkworth, Bamburgh and Alnwick took Bolton and Whittingham from the rebels at the close of Gilbert de Middleton's rebellion (Bain 1887, no. 623). But raids could prove dangerous: Andrew Harclay lost twenty-two horses in one attack on the Scots in 1314, and a sortie made by the exhausted and desperate men of the Berwick garrison in 1316 ended in almost total disaster. In one petition, the men of the northern marches complained that the defences of the Border were quite inadequate, and requested the king's personal presence with a large force. All that the council could suggest was that Andrew Harclay should do all he could to harass the enemy from Carlisle: it is quite evident that it was the

---

[21] SC 6/1020/1.
[22] E 101/3/3.
[23] E 101/376/7, fo. 61v.

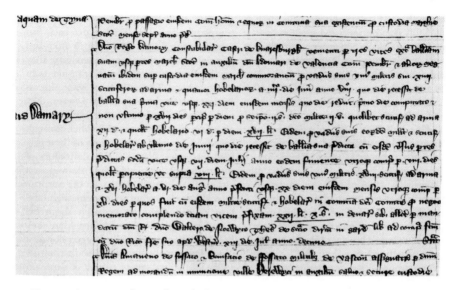

Figure 1. A section of a royal wardrobe account book detailing payments to Roger Damory, constable of Knaresborough Castle, for going north with members of the garrison on three occasions in 1315. Public Record Office [now TNA], E 101/376/7, fo. 61v. Crown Copyright material reproduced by kind permission of the Controller of H.M. Stationery Office.

inefficiency of such operations that had prompted the petition in the first place (Bain 1887, nos. 77, 470, 799).

Many undoubtedly responded to the Scottish danger by fleeing south: in 1322, the king even ordered the sheriff of Yorkshire to aid those who were driving their cattle away from danger (Bain 1887, no. 784), and the canons of Bridlington in the same year removed all their valuables to safety in Lincolnshire (Stubbs 1883, 80). But castle walls did provide a refuge for some at least at times of Scottish invasion, though a high price was exacted. A petition from the men of Cumberland and Westmorland complained that the charges exacted by lords and constables of castles were so extortionate that they preferred to evacuate their lands rather than pay up to 6s. 8d. for two or three nights in safety.[24] At Bamburgh the local people complained bitterly of the fees demanded for entering and leaving the castle, and for storage of goods in it (Bain 1887, no. 463). There, the presence of the castle did not even protect the immediate vicinity from the ravages of the enemy, and tenants could not be found for vacant holdings because of the fear of attack. In 1322, no grain for stocking the castle could be found locally, and supplies had to be brought north from Pontefract. In 1318–19, the castle revenues, which normally stood at over £100 a year, sank to £53 as a result of enemy attacks. The accounts even reveal that there were no rabbits to be sold, as the warrens had

[24] SC 8/4147.

been destroyed by the Scots.[25] There is much evidence from the north as a whole
of severely depleted manorial revenues as a result of the Scottish raids, which
testifies to the inadequacy of the castles as a defensive network (Scammell 1958,
385–90; Miller 1976, 15).

The crown certainly hoped that by placing its network of castles in a state
of readiness, civil war might be prevented. The first occasion when orders were
issued to prepare them was in December 1307, prior to the king's departure overseas for his marriage, and the second was soon after his coronation in 1308, when
opposition was beginning to mount. In the following month Edward expressed
his desire 'that his castles should be defended for the greater security and tran-
quillity of his people'. The king's attempt to regain the political initiative after
the production of the Ordinances by his opponents in 1311 was accompanied by
much activity concerning the castles of the realm: in January and July, orders
went out for the safe-keeping of the major royal fortresses (CCR (1307–13), 29,
35, 50, 402, 540). Again in November 1317, when the violence of Thomas of Lancaster's retainers threatened to develop into civil war, twenty-three castles were
ordered to be garrisoned (CCR (1313–18), 504–5). In 1321, Robert Wodehouse,
an important royal clerk, was sent to report on the condition of the castles in
Wales when the rising of the Marchers against the Despensers threatened, and
measures were taken to put them in a defensible state (HKW, 234). Lancaster's
rebellion prompted royal requests that sixty-three castles be placed in a condition
of military readiness (CCR (1318–23), 511–13). Such instructions may have had
some effect, but a number of incidents suggest that castles were hardly adequate
protection for either side in the civil conflicts of Edward II's reign.

The most celebrated example of misplaced trust in the security of a castle was
Gaveston's ill-fated stay in Scarborough in 1312, when he was forced to surrender
after no more than ten days, as his garrison was inadequate and supplies non-
existent (Denholm-Young 1957, 24). In the autumn of 1317, the earl of Lancaster's
associates had little difficulty in taking Knaresborough, even though much money
had been spent on the defences there earlier in the reign. At the same period,
earl Warenne lost his castles of Sandal and Conisborough to Lancaster (HKW,
689–90; Maddicott 1970, 207–8). In the rising of the Marcher lords against the
Despensers in 1321, the powerful castles held by the latter were of little avail. The
constables offered little resistance, although Ralph de Gorges was injured at Cardiff, and Newport held out for four days (Denholm-Young 1957, 110; Fryde 1979,
44). The story of the fall of Lancaster in 1322 again suggests that castles could
not be relied upon. Kenilworth, which had held out so magnificently in the final
stages of the civil wars of Henry III's reign, surrendered without a struggle, and
there was no resistance from the garrisons at Tutbury and Pontefract. The earl
himself had intended to hold out at the latter castle, but was dissuaded by his supporters, notably Roger Clifford, who preferred to retreat towards the earl's newest
castle at Dunstanburgh. Defeat at Boroughbridge came before they could reach

[25] E 372/174, mm. 50–1.

the questionable security of Dunstanburgh's unfinished defences (Maddicott 1970, 310–11; Brie 1906, 217). The only castle to resist attack successfully was the royal one at Tickhill, where William de Aune held out against Lancastrian forces.

The king's castles did not even prove entirely satisfactory as prisons for those captured in the campaigns of 1321–2. Roger Mortimer succeeded in escaping from the Tower of London, and at Wallingford the prisoners under Maurice de Berkeley seized the castle itself with some outside aid. Only when a large force was gathered did they agree to surrender. Edward II himself, of course, was to succeed at least once in escaping from Berkeley Castle after his deposition in 1327 (Denholm-Young 1957, 129–31; Fryde 1979, 156, 161, 201–6).

It is perhaps not surprising, in view of events in the course of the reign, that castles were not given a very prominent position in the arrangements for defence against invasion in 1326. Although Walter Stapledon was instructed early in the year to survey and strengthen the castles of the south-west, his orders were later cancelled (*CPR (1324–7)*, 244–5). No general instructions to place large numbers of royal castles in a state of readiness were issued, in contrast to the earlier crises of the reign. Conwy in north Wales was something of an exception, however, for orders were issued to make the castle ready to hold a garrison of a hundred men for six months (*CFR (1319–27)*, 418). This was presumably in response to the extraordinary fear expressed by the royal council that Queen Isabella and her allies might choose to make a landing in those parts.[26] In the event, when Isabella did land near Orwell in Suffolk, she faced little resistance from royal forces, whether in castle garrisons or otherwise deployed. It was only the garrison of Caerfili that held out, astonishingly, until March 1327 (Fryde 1979, 22).

Although castles may not have played a very central role in the major civil conflicts of the reign, at least in comparison with the experience of the twelfth or thirteenth centuries, they did feature significantly in disputes at a local level. The presence of a castle in a town often, far from overawing the local populace, provided a cause of friction and unrest. The best known example is that of Bristol. Bartholomew Badlesmere was appointed constable of the castle there at the beginning of the reign, and his conduct did much to exacerbate the complex disputes between the townspeople and the crown, which lasted from 1312 to 1316. On two occasions the men of Bristol actually laid siege to the castle, building a crenellated wall opposite it on the first occasion, and draining the moat and deploying siege engines on the second. In the end it was forces from outside, not those of the castle garrison, which restored order (*CPR (1313–17)*, 69; *CCR (1313–18)*, 424; Fuller 1894–5).

The events at Bristol were to some extent mirrored at Nottingham. There the constable, John Segrave, initially appointed in 1308, incurred deep hostility. There were many complaints against him: his forced seizures of foodstuffs were particularly resented, and there was trouble over ditches dug by members of the garrison through private property. The central issue in the dispute was the right of the

[26] C 47/5/16.

town to have its own gaol, and a *cause-célèbre* was provided by the murder of the mayor in 1313. The culprit was taken and imprisoned in the castle: an attempt was made by some of the townspeople to rescue him. They forced an entry and gave the man a tonsure in an apparent attempt to provide him with clerical immunity. Two years later the castle was actually besieged by the townspeople for a week. Although an enquiry into Seagraves' conduct was held in 1317, he was not dismissed from his post. Rather, it was in that year that he became banneret of the royal household[27] (Cameron 1971, 68–75; *Rotuli Parliamentorum* 1, 328, 417).

Another example of rivalry between castle and town is provided by Builth in mid-Wales. The castle there was granted to the unpopular royal chamberlain, John Charlton, early in 1314. In May of the following year, the tenants complained bitterly that they had paid Charlton £120 so that they could enjoy their traditional customs, but nevertheless he had extorted services from them. Three weeks later they accused the garrison of coming out of the castle secretly, feigning a siege of it, and then using this as an excuse to attack and imprison many of the townspeople. The story is a remarkable one, and it is perhaps more likely that the men of Builth had simply attacked the castle themselves (*CPR (1313–18)*, 322, 325).

It may be significant that in the cases of Bristol, Nottingham and Builth, the constables were men of national importance, associated with the royal household, with the result that some of the bitterness of national politics spilled over into local affairs. There were, however, many other examples of discontent at the activities of castle constables and their subordinates. Problems often arose over the right of prise: at Scarborough in 1314, those appointed to provide timber for the repair of the castle were assaulted, and in 1315, a Londoner who had been purveying goods for the Tower was pursued into the precincts of the fortress itself and attacked (*CPR (1313–17)*, 141–2, 314). At Berwick, a commission was set up in 1317 to inquire into disputes between the burgesses and the garrison, as these were thought to be endangering the security of the town. It may well be that this situation contributed to the loss of Berwick in the following year, for the Scots were admitted to the town by a disaffected burgess Peter of Spalding (Bain 1887, no. 589: Barrow 1976, 341). When the constable of Conisborough went to the local church to audit the accounts of royal bailiffs, and to see to the collection of royal revenue, he was attacked and besieged in the building (*CPR (1324–7)*, 232). It was, of course, nothing new for the local inhabitants to resent a castle and its custodians, but the frequency of conflict under Edward II is striking, as is the boldness of those who challenged the power of such castle constables as Badlesmere and Segrave.

It would be wrong to exaggerate the extent to which attitudes towards castles differed in Edward II's reign from those of earlier periods. Motives were complex, and the fact that, for example, Lancaster's men did not attempt to hold out within castle walls reflects, perhaps, a genuine reluctance to oppose the king by force of arms as much as fear that they would suffer the fate of the Leeds garrison,

---

[27] Society of Antiquaries MS 121, fo. 37.

hanged by Edward II as an example 'so that no one in future would dare to hold fortresses against him' (Denholm-Young 1957, 116). Turning finally, however, to the developments in military architecture in this period, it is again possible to detect a changing approach to the problems of fortification.

The tradition established by Master James of St George under Edward I, of massive twin-towered gatehouses, round flanking towers and concentric lines of defence, did not die at once. Thomas of Lancaster's magnificent gatehouse at Dunstanburgh in Northumberland is very recognisably 'Edwardian' in style (Figure 2). For all his great financial resources, the earl never completed the castle, which in his day probably consisted of little more than the gatehouse overshadowing a simple, and probably inadequate, curtain wall. Just as Lancaster's death meant that Dunstanburgh was never completed on the scale and in the style originally intended, so equally the death of Gilbert de Clare, earl of Gloucester, at Bannockburn in 1314 brought the works at the south Welsh castle of Langibby, or Tregrug, to an end. Like Dunstanburgh, this castle enclosed a vast area. Its gatehouse was perhaps in conception the grandest of all the twin-towered 'Edwardian' entrances, featuring four stair-turrets rather than the normal two. A unique feature of the castle was the Lord's Tower, a great D-shaped building with two turrets on the courtyard side, resembling half a gatehouse and forming in effect a powerful keep. The architectural vocabulary used by Edward I's masons in north Wales was

Figure 2. The gatehouse of Dunstanburgh Castle, Northumberland, built by Thomas, earl of Lancaster. (*M. Prestwich*)

Figure 3. The keep of Knaresborough Castle, Yorkshire, built early in the reign of Edward
    II. The king took a great personal interest in the building works. (*M. Prestwich*)

being used in a rather different way at Tregrug. The absence of concentric lines of
defence and the presence of a type of keep suggest a reversion to earlier traditions
of castle-design (Cathcart King and Perks 1956, 96–132).

The greatest of the Clare fortresses was, of course, Caerfili. The building history of the castle is unfortunately ill-documented, but it is evident that there the
death of the unfortunate Earl Gilbert did not mean an end to the work of fortification. During his tenure of the castle, the younger Despenser was probably
responsible for the hall in its present form, and for much of the outer defences.
The concentric tradition was very strong here, but the angular outer gatehouse
contrasts strikingly with the round towers of the thirteenth-century work, and
shows one way in which style was changing (Pugh 1971, 423–6). Other examples
of building under Edward II, however, show a much clearer break with the concepts so brilliantly executed by Master James of St George.

Edward II himself, as befitted the son of a great castle-builder, took a keen
personal interest in the design of fortifications. In the early stages of the reign he
spent heavily on Knaresborough, and was probably responsible for the design of
the great keep or tower-house there, which significantly departed from the almost
universal fashion for round towers (Figure 3). On the courtyard side the plan
was rectangular, while to the exterior the tower presented a three-sided front,
with a round projection on the central face (*HKW*, 689–90). The reversion to the

concept of one single main tower was also to be seen at Dudley in Worcestershire, where John de Somery crowned the old Norman motte with a keep of four-lead clover plan. There was possibly also a keep built at the Despenser castle of Hanley, another Worcestershire castle, where Edward II spent lavishly on his favourite's property (Brown 1976, 137; *HKW*, 66–9).

In addition to the works at Knaresborough, Edward II authorised some fairly extensive building at Carlisle early in his reign. In view, however, of the danger front the Scots, it is surprising that he did not do more work on the castles of the north. A peel, or enclosure, was built at Haywra in 1316, and others were built at Northallerton and Staward, but these were very minor fortifications (*HKW*, 235). The king's unfortunate experience in 1322, when he narrowly escaped capture by the Scots, probably prompted him to order new works at nearby Pickering Castle. In the last years of the reign, a new outer bailey was built at a cost of about £950. The two towers and the gatehouse were square, rather than circular, and far inferior to anything that Edward I had built in Wales (*HKW*, 780: Thompson 1965). A similar reversion to rectangular towers is to be seen at Dunstanburgh, where the Lilburn Tower, probably dating from the 1320s, stands in striking contrast to Thomas of Lancaster's works (Blair and Honeyman 1955, 17 18) (Figure 4).

Figure 4. The Lilburn Tower at Dunstanburgh Castle, Northumberland, probably built in the reign of Edward II, and showing the trend to build square rather than round towers. (*M. Prestwich*)

It does not appear that the threat of Scottish invasion and of civil war was such as to prompt much castle-building on the grand scale. Thomas of Lancaster certainly spent a great deal on building, but with the notable exception of Dunstanburgh and Pontefract, where he built a new tower, most of the works were intended to improve the accommodation within his castles, rather than their defences (Maddicott 1970, 26). But although few major castles were built in Edward II's reign, the period did see much fortification on a lesser scale. Plenty of licences to crenellate were issued: seven in 1311, and the same number in 1318, but the bulk of them were for what can have been little more than lightly fortified manor houses, while one was issued to the London oligarch, John de Wengrave, for his chamber in Breadstreet in the City (*CPR (1313–17)*, 118). A more typical example of the type of site that was licensed in this period is Markingfield Hall in Yorkshire, a moated manorial complex for which a licence was granted in 1310. Building of this type was not wholly new, but followed a pattern established in the late thirteenth century (Le Patourel 1973, 17, 22). A royal example of the relatively simple fortification of a manorial site is that of Eltham in Kent, where a contract for building a new surrounding wall was made in 1315 (*HKW*, 930–1), while the earth and timber peel built at Thundersley in Essex fits into a similar pattern (*HKW*, 660n).[28] Such buildings were probably a response to the tide of lawlessness, of localised gang warfare, rather than to the uncertainties of national politics.

It is likely that in the north of England the threat of Scottish raids prompted men to build simple fortfications. Aydon castel, near Corbridge, in Northumberland, was licensed in 1305, and its lord, Robert de Raymes, later described it as having been fortified with a crenellated wall of stone and mortar against the king's Scottish enemies (Figure 5). It was in fact a fairly simple rectangular stone hall-house, to which a courtyard was added (Craster 1914, 344–5, 350–66). The majority of the minor fortifications of the north are impossible to date with any accuracy, but at Cartington in Northumberland, another hall-house, some architectural details resemble Lancaster's building at Dunstanburgh (Dodds 1940, 375). Some tower-houses may date from the early fourteenth century: it has been suggested that the Vicar's Peel at Corbridge was built at this time, although the first documentary evidence for it dates from 1415 (Figure 6). These lesser defences were hardly invulnerable against attack: Aydon was captured twice in Edward II's reign (Craster 1914, 209, 345). Yet they represented a more realistic response to the problems of the day than a major fortification such as Dunstanburgh, for a large number of minor castles could defend the country from ravaging and looting better than a single major fortress, whose garrison was incapable of patrolling a wide tract of territory. It should be stressed, however, that the great majority of tower houses and similar structures in the north were almost certainly built much later than Edward II's reign, in periods when the Scottish menace was not so immediately pressing.

---

[28] Society of Antiquaries MS 120, 1.18.

Figure 5. Aydon Castle, Northumberland, built by Robert de Raymes as a defence against the Scots, and fairly typical of the minor fortifications of the north. (*M. Prestwich*)

Much of the evidence regarding castles in Edward II's reign is of a depressing nature. For the most part they were badly garrisoned and poorly equipped, while in many cases their physical structure was in poor condition. At Lincoln, for example, one tower collapsed during the lifetime of Henry de Lacy, who died in 1311, while another fell while Thomas of Lancaster held the castle (*HKW*, 705). It was perhaps too long since the king's castles had been needed to defend the crown against insurrection to expect too much of them. Steps such as those taken to place the king's Welsh castles in readiness when the Marcher rebellion threatened in 1321 had little effect, while equally the king's opponents placed little trust in their own defences. At a local level, castle garrisons did as much to cause trouble as to prevent it. In the north of England, the network of castles did not provide an adequate defence against the Scots. Yet castles were far from irrelevant to the history of the reign. Grants of their custody were an important element of royal patronage, and the rapid changeover of con- stables, on occasion marked by considerable administrative muddle, helps to illuminate one aspect of Edward II's misgovernment. The desire of many to defend their manor houses with moat and crenellated walls shows that the concept of the castle was far from dead, even if such buildings should be seen in a context of local gang violence rather than of national politics and strategy. Early in the reign, John de Somery clearly saw castle-building as a means of establishing his mastery in Staffordshire: it was

Figure 6. The Vicar's Pele, Corbridge, Northumberland, an early example of a northern
tower-house, probably dating from the early fourteenth century. (*M. Prestwich*)

said that he forced men to buy his protection either with money, or by helping
him to build his castles (*CPR (1307–13)*, 369). There was, however, no question of
the crown undertaking a castle-building programme on the scale of Edward I's
undertaking in Wales, which had cost at least £80,000 (*HKW*, 1029), despite the

king's personal interest in building, which was demonstrated at Knaresborough. What building there was largely abandoned the traditions of the great castles in Wales; there was, instead, something of a revival of the concept of the keep, and in places a reversion to square rather than round towers. The military history of the reign suggests that questions of garrisoning and victualling were of greater importance in military terms than architectural developments; the period did not see new developments in siege techniques spurring fresh defensive methods. The development of the castle in the fourteenth and fifteenth centuries was to stem more from the increasing complexity and sophistication of the domestic aspects than from elaboration of the fortifications. Edward II's reign did much to show that the castle could no longer play the role in warfare that it had done in the twelfth and thirteenth centuries, although its functions as a residence, as a centre of administration, and as a physical demonstration of aristocratic wealth and power still remained.

Bibliography

Bain, J. ed. (1887) *Calendar of documents relating to Scotland*, 3. *1307–1357*. Edinburgh.

Barrow, G. W. S. (1976) *Robert Bruce and the community of the realm of Scotland*. Second edition. Edinburgh.

Blair, C. H. Hunter, and H. L. Honeyman (1966) *Dunstanburgh Castle*. Official Guidebook. London.

Brie, F. W. D. ed. (1906) *The Brut*, I. Early English Text Society, London.

Brown, R. A. (1976) *English castles*. Third edition. London.

Cameron, A. (1971) 'William de Amyas and the community of Nottingham, 1308–50', *Transactions of the Thoroton Society* 75, 68–78.

Cathcart King, D. J., and J. C. Perks (1956) 'Llangibby Castle', *Archaeologia Cambrensis* 105, 96–102.

Coulson, C. L. H. (1976) 'Fortresses and social responsibility in late Carolingian France', *Zeitschrift fur Archaeologic des Mittelalters* 4, 29–36.

Craster, H. E. (1914) *A history of Northumberland*, 10. Newcastle upon Tyne.

Denholm-Young, N. (1957) *Vita Edwardi Secundi*. London.

Dodds, M. H. (1940) *A history of Northumberland*, 15. Newcastle upon Tyne.

Fryde, N. M. (1979) *The tyranny and fall of Edward II, 1321–1326*. Cambridge.

Fuller, E. A. (1894–5) 'The tallage of 1312 and the Bristol riots', *Transactions of the Bristol and Gloucestershire Archaeological Society* 19, 172–278.

Le Patourel, H. E. J. (1973) *The moated sites of Yorkshire*. London.

Maddicott, J. R. (1970) *Thomas of Lancaster 1307–1322*. Oxford.

Martin, C. Wykeham (1869). *The history and description of Leeds Castle, Kent*. London.

Miller, E. (1976) 'Farming in northern England during the twelfth and thirteenth centuries', *Northern History* 11, 3–16.

Palgrave, F. (1830) *Parliamentary writs*, 2. *1307–1327*. Record Commission. London.

Prestwich, M. C. (1971) 'Isabella de Vescy and the custody of Bamburgh Castle', *Bulletin of the Institute of Historical Research* 44, 148–52.

Pugh, T. B. (1971) *Glamorgan County History*, 3. The Middle Ages. Cardiff.

Richard, J. (1968) 'Le château dans la structure féodale de la France de l'est au XII siècle', *Probleme des 12. Jahrhunderts. Reichenau Vortrage* 1965–7, 169–76.

Rotuli parliamentorutn, I. 1272–1326.1767. London.

Rymer, T. (1816) *Foedera*, 2(i). Record Commission, London.

Sanders, I. J. (1960) *English baronies*. Oxford.

Scammell, J. (1958) 'Robert I and the north of England', *English Historical Review* 73, 385–403.

Stevenson, J. ed. (1836) *Scalacronica* by Sir Thomas Grey of Heton, Knight. Maitland Club, Edinburgh.

Stubbs, W. ed. (1883). *Chronicles of the Reigns of Edward I and Edward II*, 2. RS. London.

Thompson, M. W. (1965) 'An alert in 1318 to the constable of Bolingbroke Castle, Lincolnshire', *Medieval Archaeology* 9, 167–8.

Turner, G. J. (1904). 'The minority of Henry III', *Transactions of the Royal Historical Society*, new series 18, 245–95.

13

Castles of Ward and the Changing Pattern of Border Conflict in Ireland

T. E. McNeill

Throughout the Middle Ages, on any definition of that term, Ireland was a land of borders. Competing early medieval kingdoms were followed by the incursion of lords owing allegiance to the English king who never succeeded in controlling the whole land. We find the term, the March, being used from the time of King John, and so too was the term 'the land of war', to be contrasted with the land of peace.[1] The terms came from Wales, but the two countries were different; there was no such thing in Ireland as March law, nor was there a group of baron distinguishable from their fellows by holding land in the March.

We must stress that in Ireland we are not looking at a single border, but at many individual borders, between different lordships, English and Irish. Inevitably the response to the question of control of these borders will have varied through both space and time. In terms of the archaeology, we may distinguish between three sorts of buildings: earthworks, predominantly mottes; castles of ward, and tower houses. It should be stressed that we are talking here about responses to situations, not necessarily about systems; these may simply be tendencies to be picked out, not clear-cut types.

The early phase of this evolution has already been discussed:[2] a considerable increase of motte building (with more baileys) along the frontier as it developed. Only some of the English lordships erected a border screen of mottes. This is partly a measure of the threat they perceived, greater for Meath, Oriel and Ulster than for Munster or Leinster. Not all borders were considered the same, and militarisation, constructing many mottes, was not always worth the effort involved. I wish, however, in this paper to concentrate on the next period, covering the bulk of the thirteenth and fourteenth centuries. Here we may see two sorts of castles on the borders. One is a major stronghold, a first-rate castle in Irish terms at least, in the area concerned: the other is the building of castles of ward, lesser enclosures to be manned by small, temporary garrisons. The former are not true border castles, but mark attempts to expand lordships to new areas.

---

[1] B. Smith, 'The Concept of the March in Medieval Ireland', *Proceedings of the Royal Irish Academy* 88 (1988), 257–69.
[2] T. E. McNeill, 'Hibernia pacata et castellata', *Château Gaillard* 14 (1988), 261–76, reprinted *ANC*, 259–71; K. O'Conor, 'The Earthwork Castles of Medieval Leinster' (Ph.D. thesis, University of Wales, 1993), chapter 5.

We can see the beginnings of the idea of warding in the garrisons placed in areas of tension at the time of the Justiciar's war leading to the attempted establishment of a motte and bailey at Clones, Co. Monaghan in 1211–12, at a time when mottes also marked borders. It is in Ulster, however, that we can see the emergence of a type of castle that seems to have been built for the defence of the border, a castle of ward. The remains of the small castle of Seafin can be identified with the castle that the Justiciar in 1252 caused to be fortified 'in a fit place in Ulster'. This place was on a small but steep hill overlooking the river Bann, in the client Irish kingdom of Ui Echach Cobha, but an outpost to the Earldom of Ulster faced with a period of aggression from Brian O'Neill of Cenel Eoghain. Excavation at the castle showed that it had been built in two phases.[3] The final form was of a small enclosure surrounded by a wall, polygonal in plan with a base batter: the entrance was simply a gap in the wall, but there was a tower attached to the western side.

Further north in Ulster lies Doonbought in Co. Antrim, sited on the border between the Earldom and the small Irish kingdom of Ui Tuirtre. It is undocumented but excavation showed it to have been constructed in the thirteenth century.[4] All that it consisted of was a polygonal wall with a crude base batter around a courtyard some 30 metres across. Along the coast at the foot of one of the two glens reached from Glenravel and Doonbought lies Court McMartin. Again this consists of a polygonal wall with a base batter enclosing the top of a small, steep hill: the line of the wall is completed by a section of unquarried rock. Beside one of the few crossing points over the lower Bann river, the western border of the Earldom of Ulster, lay Cross castle, planned and described in the 1830s before its destruction. It consisted of a mound revetted and topped by a battered polygonal wall, with the traces apparently of one or two buildings inside (Figure 1).

These four sites are in similar positions, on the tops of steep hills with good views, except for Cross, set in the river valley but covering an important crossing point. They consist either mainly or entirely of a polygonal enclosure about 25–30 metres across surrounded by a wall. This wall is less than 1.80 metres wide above its crude base batter. The sites of Seafin, Doonbought and Cross all relate to vulnerable points in the borders of the Earldom of Ulster, while Court McMartin could well be connected to communications with Scotland. They were not important places, unlike the larger castles of the Earl, at Carrickfergus, Dundrum or the two Green Castles.

South of Ulster lay the lordship of Oriel, where there is evidence of a small number of stone structures replacing a line of mottes along the border. Some may have been recorded in the eighteenth century by Wright, who produced plans of six mottes with hexagonal or octagonal structures on top of them. Only one of

[3] D. M. Waterman, 'Excavations at Seafin Castle and Ballyroney Motte and Bailey', *Ulster Journal of Archaeology* 18 (1955), 83–104.
[4] T. E. McNeill, 'Excavations at Doonbought fort, Co. Antrim', *Ulster Journal of Archaeology* 40 (1977), 63–84.

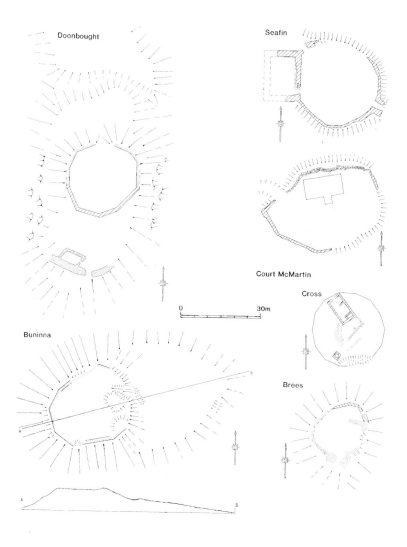

Figure 1. Small polygonal enclosures in Ulster and Connacht.

these, Faughart, now has remains of some sort of walling visible, which excavation might clarify.[5] Castle Ring motte also has traces of a surrounding wall; in 1301 an Irishman was paid £ 2-0-0 to defend it, under the name of Castle Frank.[6]

The conquest of Connacht under William de Burgh, completed in 1235, was one of the last major expansions of English lordship in medieval Ireland, resulting

[5] V. Buckley and D. Sweetman, *Archaeological Survey of Co. Louth* (Dublin, 1991), 282–91.
[6] Reports of the Deputy Keeper of Public Records, no. 38, 53.

in De Burgh lands of Galway and south Mayo, and the Fitz Gerald lands in Sligo and north-east Mayo. Two sites concern us here (Figure 1). One is Brees, sited on a steep hill on the northern edge of the De Burgh lands. It is a small polygonal enclosure with possible traces of a tower. The other is Buninna, a lesser castle of the De Berminghams on the coast road west of Sligo. It appears to have been built on a motte, although the mound may be largely natural. On the top are the remains of a polygonal enclosure, again with traces of what might have been a small tower. Unfortunately, owing to a mis-identification of the site, this site has appeared in print described as a ringwork.[7]

The lordship of Leinster had two borders: the one with the Wicklow hills within the area of the lordship and one to the north-west facing Laois and Offaly, linking up with the Butler lands of Ormonde. Leinster's history was complex because, after the death of the last Marshal lord, the Liberty was partitioned into five holdings, some of which were themselves further sub-divided. Because none of the inheritors was normally resident in Ireland, and because the Wicklow hills were near to Dublin, the King's Justiciar found himself having to hold together and direct the affairs of the counties of the Liberty, rather than leaving it in the hands of its lord. As a result, the borders of Leinster loom very large in the royal records from the later thirteenth to the later fourteenth centuries.[8]

The castles associated with the borders vary. We have two examples of the polygonal stone enclosures. Borrisnafarney in north Tipperary overlooks a pass through the Silvermines mountains south from Nenagh.[9] It is set on the top of a steep ridge, cut off at the base by two ditches. On the top are the remains of a polygonal wall around about half the area concerned; presumably erosion has accounted for the other half. Ballyvollen lies in the narrow corridor between the Wicklow hills and the sea. Landscaped and altered by the construction of a bungalow and its garden are the remains of a polygonal walled enclosure, with the wall about 1.5 metres wide and, for one length, some four metres high, and a ditch outside it (Figure 2). Unusually the castle is sited on level land, but there are few hills in the immediate vicinity.

Two sites are rectangular raised earthworks, which might be described as square mottes, reinforced by stone perimeter walls. At Aghaboe in south Laois, this walling is visible along the top of the earthwork, apparently without reverting down the slope, or the addition of towers.[10] The Archbishop of Dublin's castle at Castle Kevin in Wicklow is located near the old monastic site of Glendalough. It

[7] B. Graham, 'Medieval Timber and Earthwork Fortifications in Western Ireland', *Medieval Archaeology* 32 (1988), 123.

[8] R. Frame, 'English Officials and Irish Chiefs in the 14th Century', *English Historical Review* 90 (1975), 748–77.

[9] G. Stout, *Archaeological Survey of the Barony of Ikerrin* (Roscrea, 1984), 114.

[10] G. Cunningham, *The Anglo-Norman advance into the south-west Midlands of Ireland* (Roscrea, 1987), 159–61; K. O'Conor, *Earthwork Castles*, chapter 10.

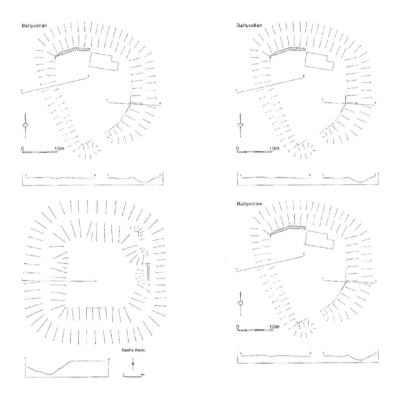

Figure 2. Border castles in Leinster.

too is a rectangular mound fortified with a stone wall (Figure 2).[11] The wall, however, clearly rose from the base of the deep surrounding ditch to revet the mound. There was a tower projecting forward at the entrance and providing the abutment of a bridge; at the north-east angle are the remains apparently of a tower, and the line of the ditch may betray the same on the two western angles.

Newcastle McKynegan is a little north and east of Castle Kevin, and was the main royal manor between the sea and the mountains. Basically the castle consists of a low, broad, circular platform, set at the end of a ridge (Figure 2).[12] This probably dates from around 1200 when the manor first comes to our attention, but between 1276 and 1282, and then in 1294–5, we find money being spent on its fortification. This is stated to include the building of a wall around it, and a tower. The base of the latter is probably still to be seen in the present masonry

---

[11] G. H. Orpen, 'Castrum Keyvini, Castlekevin', *Journal of the Royal Society of Antiquaries of Ireland* 38 (1908), 17–27.

[12] G. H. Orpen, 'Novum Castrum McKynegan, Newcastle, Co. Wicklow', *Journal of the Royal Society of Antiquaries of Ireland* 38 (1908), 126–40.

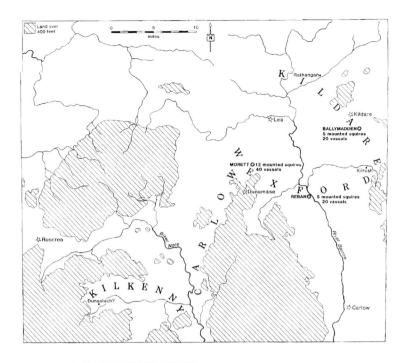

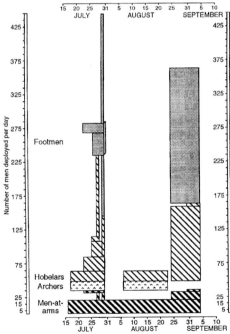

Figure 3. John de Sandford's disposition of troops along the northern border of Leinster in 1288–9; the wages paid by John Morice during his action in Wicklow in 1342.

structure: a small twin-towered gate house walled up in the sixteenth century and used a tower house. A similar broad, flat mound probably constituted the castle of Reban, now much quarried away.

The documentary references to the use of border castles in Leinster includes a number of places: Dunlavin, Ballymore Eustace, Saggart and Ballyteny (Powerscourt, Co. Wicklow), which now have no remains of castles. Baltinglass, the site of prominent abbey with a later tower, is also mentioned in the documents: so are the large castles of Clonmore and Ferns. The last are interesting for two reasons: neither are particularly defensible, nor are they more prominent in the records than the lesser castles. Wicklow castle, a rock stack surrounded by a wall built of straight sections, might be included here. Undocumented and undated, but possibly relevant might be the late, dry-stone polygonal wall found on the prehistoric hillfort of Rathgall on the southern slopes of the Wicklow mountains. Rathangan appears, possibly referring to the use of the powerful ring fort in the town. The overwhelming impression is that of a mixed bag of places; that any mildly defensible enclosure will do.

Two documents show these castles in action (Figure 3). The first is the account of the measures taken by the Justiciar John de Sandford on the Laois border of Leinster in 1288–9.[13] He was faced with a situation described as 'the war of Offaly and Leys (Laois) … and that those parts were then very hostile'. To cope with this he mobilised the seneschals of the four parts of the Liberty of Leinster to guard stated lengths of border, and posted men hired for the year at Ballymadden, Reban and Morett. Two things are striking. The number of men is very small: 22 mounted men and 80 footmen in total, presumably to act as the basic core to be reinforced by levies from each Liberty as needed. They are not stationed in the major castles, as we might expect, but at lesser places. In the case of Lea, this might be because it lay outside the Liberty, and Carlow was perhaps too far south to be effective, but both Kildare and Dunamase are conspicuous by their absence.

The wages bill for John Morice's expedition against Wicklow Irish in 1342[14] shows that there were two bodies of men concerned. The first was a small force under the command of Morice consisting of 20 men at arms for the whole period, with 15 hobelars (light horse) and 14 foot archers for most of the time: John de Bermingham commanded 3 men at arms and 5 hobelars for the whole time too. Added to this were two forces present for very short periods, during 25–29 July and between 24 August and 4 September; on 29 July 514 men were paid, 347 of them foot men. There was a small long-term, defensive force, with more men mustered for two raids, one lasting five days, and the other twelve. In one sense this is a fifty-day war but most of it was probably phoney. Yet the problem engaged the attention of major figures in the administration, as did the problem of 1288–9; it is worth recalling the description then of the Irish as 'very hostile'.

---

[13] H. S. Sweetman (ed.), *Calendar of Documents Relating to Ireland*, vol. 3 (London, 1875), 265–77.
[14] Reports of the Deputy Keeper of Public Records of Ireland, no. 53, 44–5.

If we look at royal expenditure on castle at the end of the thirteenth century, when more was spent than at any other time, we can get an idea of the priorities of the Crown. The border castles did not fare well.

Castle	Years	Expenditure
Roscommon	1275–85	£3,500
Roscrea	1278–85	£ 875
Castle Kevin	1276–9	£ 471
Newcastle McKynegan	1276–82	£ 197
" "	1294–5	£ 156

If we can talk of a system here, it is of building structures to accommodate small groups of men hired to guard districts. There is a typical castle, the small polygonal enclosure, but in Leinster especially, other castles are pressed into service. Their function is to house a garrison to stiffen the local levies in the case of trouble, who will track and intercept raiders coming into the lordship concerned. The only actual dates that we have for such sites are the two thirteenth-century ones for Seafin and Doonbought. The siting of the others, and the dates from Castle Kevin and Newcastle McKynegan, can all be linked to the borders of lordships in the thirteenth and fourteenth centuries. As such these would be described as the 'fortalicia' that we find occasionally mentioned in documents, rather like the 'peel' or 'municipio' of Edward I's Scottish wars.[15] They are only just castles, lacking the administrative functions of lordship that a true castle should have. The term has caused confusion in Ireland, with it being claimed that it should be translated as our modern 'tower house'.[16]

The idea of defending a border in this manner became obsolete some time after the middle of the fourteenth century, because the nature of the lordships themselves changed. None of the great lordships founded before 1250 survived to 1350. The lordships that dominated the next two centuries – Ormonde, Desmond and Kildare – were not based on the same idea of territorial integrity. There was decentralisation of all levels of lordship. It started with the power of the English king, which shrank drastically through the fourteenth century and did not recover until the sixteenth. It applied within the lordships as well, as they tended to become looser federations of allegiances of men, the latter often cadets of the lord's family, and control of quite small parcels of land; a world articulated by the mini-castles called by us tower houses. It took time for Dublin civil servants to come to terms with this, especially if they tried to revive the earlier facts of royal power. The last kick of their line of thought was the Pale, a linear earthwork, which would define and protect the civilised from the rest, with all the efficiency of an unmanned Maginot Line.

[15] G. Nielson, 'Peel, its Meaning and Derivation', *Transactions of the Glasgow Archaeological Society*, new series 2 (1893), 121–53.
[16] C. Cairns, *Irish Tower Houses* (Athlone, 1987), 9.

Significantly the late Middle Ages are notable for the Irish lords joining the castle-building world, for this structure of local, fragmented power was one that they could align with easily. It was a society in some ways reminiscent of the earlier stages of the European feudal revolution, with a network of small castles articulating a distribution of control that often paid little attention to the patterns of the past. It is nowhere better illustrated than in Harry Avery's castle in west Tyrone, built by a younger son of the ruling O'Neill. It was established in an area that had been for long the subject of fighting between the O'Neills and the O'Donnells. Establishing a younger son in a disputed area, which he controlled through the construction of a castle, and then which provided his sons with a power base, is pure early feudalism.

This is where discussion of castles, lordship, borders and war all come together. Castles of ward were used in wars involving small numbers of men fighting for short periods. Between 1250 and 1400, during the time of the wars of the three Edwards in England, Wales, Scotland and France, it is difficult to think of more than one time when Ireland saw armies of more than a thousand men operating for more than a month or two at a time. That occasion was when the Scots under Edward Bruce invaded Ireland, so it is hardly surprising that the Irish lords took three years to defeat Bruce's veterans.

To contemporaries, these were true wars, as they were wars to kings of the early Middle Ages, and were celebrated as such in the same way, in annals and praise poems. The nearest sort of activity and society was that of the Anglo-Scottish Border in the late Middle Ages. The scale is similar, and there was the same sort of contrast between their normal raiding and full war, when the armies of either government descended on them. So too the best parallel with the Irish castles of ward is the small castle of Bewcastle in Cumbria.

These raids took up much of the time of the Dublin government officials who had to lead the troops out on these expeditions, and to organise and muster the wards, so they loom large in modern accounts too. In *The New History of Ireland*[17] Lydon has a chapter entitled 'The land of war' to describe the end of the thirteenth century, leading up to his account of the Bruce invasion. When we look the size of the wards and at the structures associated with them we can see how this is hyperbole. It was serious to those lives and stock were destroyed, but it cannot have caused the changes we see in fourteenth-century Ireland. They lie in the economic problems of the period, in the recession at the margins of Europe, and the structure of lordship of the late Middle Ages, which may have led to the fragmentation of control and to raiding, but the raids were neither full war nor the prime cause of cultural change.

---

[17] A. Cosgrove (ed.), *A New History of Ireland* (Oxford, 1987).

14

The Donjon Of Knaresborough: The Castle As Theatre

Philip Dixon

The important royal castle of Knaresborough has received surprisingly little attention despite the originality of the arrangements of its donjon. Here it will be argued that the form of the donjon was due to very specific political conditions in the North at the end of the first decade of the fourteenth century, and that the tower's builder conferred on it a deliberate element of theatrical propaganda, which explains otherwise perplexing details in its design.

Knaresborough Castle stands on the edge of a steep cliff above the River Nidd, about three miles from Harrogate and seventeen miles from the city of York (Figure 1). The remains consist of a large courtyard, measuring about 120 metres by 90 metres, once sub-divided by a cross wall, the fragmentary remains of a gateway and small 13-shaped towers, a late medieval domestic building, now heavily rebuilt, and the larger part of a massive five-sided tower of the very early fourteenth century, which was partially demolished as a result of slighting during the Civil War (Figure 2). During most of the Middle Ages the castle was in royal hands, or in the tenure of royal kinsmen, and the majority of the surviving masonry can be ascribed to royal initiatives.

Of the early castle, first recorded in 1129–30,[1] little can now be seen apart from the rock-cut ditches, which were probably the object of King John's expenditure of £1,300 between 1203 and 1214.[2] The small towers, which still survive, and the much-damaged gatehouse on the town side of the castle, are built with solid interiors and gently splayed bases, and thus seem to be of an early design, similar to those at Conisborough Castle, Yorkshire. Unfortunately, too little remains for certainty about their date, but the details of their plinths suggest a date much later in the thirteenth century. They were clearly additions to a comparatively low curtain wall, for their rear faces are grouted against a former smooth surface; nothing else can now be seen above ground that can have belonged to the pre-Edwardian castle.[3] The king's writs and accounts which give details of the early fourteenth-century works at the castle show that the present donjon occupies the

---

[1] Pipe Roll, 31 Henry 1, 31.
[2] *HKW*, 688.
[3] W.A. Atkinson, 'Some Remarks on Knaresborough Castle', *Yorkshire Archaeological Journal* 31 (1934), 114–32, discusses the pre-Edwardian castle in the light of the then recent excavations. His view of the late date of the outer courtyard is poorly supported, and his location of the early great

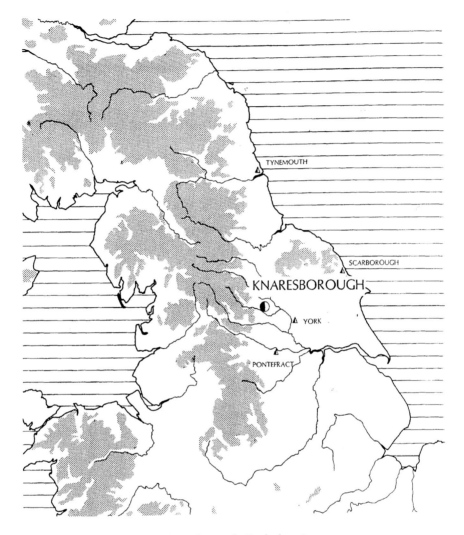

Figure 1. Knaresborough Castle, location map.

site of an older tower, demolished at the end of 1307 or early in 1308.[4] The demolition appears to have been a significant operation, and in view of the small size of
the surviving towers of the castle, it is reasonable to consider this old tower an
earlier great tower, presumably part of the twelfth-century castle; the documents,
unfortunately, are too vague for certainty on this point.

tower is likely to be incorrect, but it is hard to disagree with his conclusion that none of John's
masonry now stands above ground.
[4] *HKW*, 688–91, gives the fullest details of the cost of these building works, and unless otherwise
stated the figures in the present paper are derived from this source.

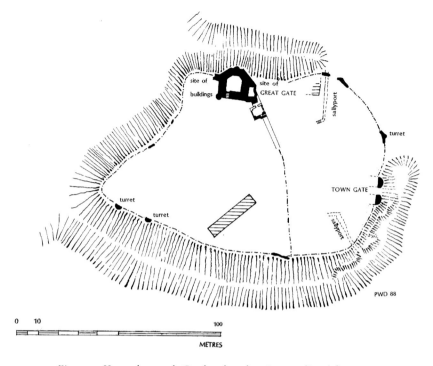

Figure 2. Knaresborough Castle, plan showing medieval features.

The castle reverted to the crown at the death without issue of the King's cousin, Edmund earl of Cornwall, in 1300, and for the next few years modest sums were spent on its repair, and on the rebuilding of the great gate (1304), which may be the 'new gate' whose gutters were being leaded in 1305.[5] Shortly after his accession in July 1307, Edward II ordered the demolition of the old tower, and the construction of a new one. Between September 1307 and March 1312, when the roof received its lead and the windows their glass, he spent no less than £2,174 on the building, a very large sum for a single tower. Apart from a short period during the uprising of 1317, when one of Lancaster's retainers seized it, the castle remained in royal hands until the end of Edward's reign, but it passed into the hands of Queen Isabella in 1327, during the disturbances that followed Edward's deposition and murder, and finally was granted to John of Gaunt: it continued in the control of the Duchy of Lancaster throughout the Middle Ages, becoming part of the crown estates again with the accession of Henry of Lancaster to the throne in 1399. After Edward II's reign, however, Knaresborough attracted little interest, and the details of works imply no more than belated repairs to keep the building in order.

Despite the interest of its history and its buildings, Knaresborough has remained comparatively unstudied and seldom visited, a site of only local importance. Clark discussed it, and was responsible for promulgating the view that the

[5] CCR (1302–1307), 292.

donjon formed a thoroughfare from one ward to the other.[6] This very odd notion, based largely on the misidentification of a window as a door, survived at least as late as 1912, when we can read 'The rectangular keep of Knaresborough is entirely of the fourteenth century: it stood between an outer and inner ward, and its great peculiarity is that the only passage from one to the other was through the first floor of the keep'.[7] In more recent studies of castles Knaresborough has played little part,[8] though Toy gave a concise and accurate description of what he called 'an exceptionally interesting structure', adding, however, that 'the reason for some of the features of this building is now obscure'.[9] Archaeological work on the site earlier in the twentieth century showed up several features of importance, but the quality of the operation was no better than one might expect of the 1920s, and the report is quite inadequately illustrated and very hard to use.[10] More recent excavations took place only in the outer courtyard, and so have little of relevance to the present theme, the nature and role of the donjon.[11]

Description
(Figures 3–7)

The Knaresborough donjon still stands to a maximum height of about 17 metres, a little below the original wallheads. It contains four storeys: a vaulted basement, a vaulted chamber at ground-floor level, a tall first-floor hall, and a chamber on the second floor, which must have been covered by a roof of very slight pitch. The basement is reached by a straight flight of stone steps from an entrance door whose sill is some three metres below the present ground level. The present steps from the outside of the building down to this door are modern. The original arrangement involved a passage covered with a plain pointed tunnel vault, which ran parallel to the face of the tower, and was presumably entered by a stair from the buildings that once stood to the west of the donjon. At ground-floor level the principal room is entered from the courtyard by a broad pointed door. The main chamber, about eight metres square, is covered by an elegant ribbed vault resting

[6] G. T. Clark, 'Knaresborough Castle', *Archaeological Journal* 6 (1880–1), esp. 105–6; reprinted in *Medieval Military Architecture in England* ii (1884), 168–76.
[7] A. Hamilton Thompson, *Military Architecture in England during the Middle Ages* (Oxford, 1912), 311–12. The 'donjon as through-passage' was decisively disproved by W. A. Atkinson in 'A Note on Knaresborough Castle', *Yorkshire Archaeological Journal* 36 (1944–7), 198–208.
[8] R. A. Brown, *English Medieval Castles* (London, 1954), for example, only lists the donjon, and in the 1976 edition draws attention chiefly to the unmilitary appearance of the courtyard façade (140). C. Platt, *The Castle in Medieval England and Wales* (London, 1982) does not notice it at all.
[9] S. Toy, *The Castles of Great Britain* (London, 1953), 207. Early accounts are collected by Atkinson, 'A Note on Knaresborough'.
[10] S. C. Barber, 'Excavations at Knaresborough Castle, 1925–1928', *Yorkshire Archaeological Journal* 30 (1930–1), 200–24.
[11] J. Le Patourel, 'Knaresborough Castle', *Yorkshire Archaeological Journal* 41 (1963–5), 591–607. For our purposes this report does, however, show the position of Barber's cutting on the cross wall of the castle, and publishes the sixteenth-century drawing of the castle from the north (plate I, facing p. 594).

Figure 3. Donjon from the east, showing (extreme left) staircase, (centre left) ante-room, (centre) audience chamber with arch. The site of the great gatehouse is in the foreground.

on two pillars, and was heated by a fireplace in the west wall. Two small chambers, one provided with a garderobe, are contrived in the thickness of the walls, and before the demolition there is likely to have been another in the north-eastern side of the donjon. A small vaulted chamber in the south-western corner of the tower at this level is separately entered by a small two-centred door; traditionally called the record room, it is probably the 'treasure house' of Cumberland's survey of 1538.[12] At the south-eastern corner, a pair of small chambers, similarly isolated from the main part of the donjon, provided accommodation for a porter immediately within the passage between the baileys (Figures 8–9).

At the south-eastern corner of the large vaulted room a short passage leads to a narrow newel staircase, which today provides the sole access to the upper storeys of the tower. It leads to a small mural lobby, and so to the first-floor hall, and formerly continued to the second-floor chamber. These two upper floors have suffered badly in the seventeenth-century demolition, and little more than half of their walls survive. On the western side we can see what Toy called a 'wide recess'

[12] A transcript of the survey is in Barber, 'Excavations', 224.

Figure 4. Donjon from south-west, showing great window of the audience chamber.

and Atkinson a 'trough recess',[13] with a large fireplace to its north, and a very large window, once traceried, to its south.[14] A second fireplace, smaller than the first, stands in the southern wall near the staircase door. The ingo of a window of reasonable size is still preserved in the northern wall opposite this latter fireplace. Its outer face is now destroyed, but the sixteenth-century drawing of the castle indicates that at that date, at least, it had four narrow lights, arranged like an oriel in the central turret of the northern face of the castle. The topmost floor is still more ruinous, but was clearly somewhat lower than the hall. At present it is inaccessible, but some details are clear: it was heated by a fireplace whose

[13] S. Toy, *Castles*, 207; Atkinson, 'A Note', his fig. b, 205.
[14] For this window, see Atkinson, 'A Note', esp. 198–204. E. King [in a paper in *Archaeologia* 6 (1782), 321–6] gives a drawing of the window (which he identified as a doorway) at a time when some tracery still remained. It appears to be a form of Y-tracery, eminently suitable for the early fourteenth-century date of the building.

Figure 5. Donjon from south-east, showing porch and remains of staircase. The site of
the gatehouse is on the right, foreground.

jamb survives in the western wall, and a length of dressed stone to the north of
this fireplace may have been the side wall of a garderobe passage, since shoots
are traceable in the walls below this point. The surviving window at this level
is of only modest size:[15] since the missing walls were exposed to the exterior of
the castle, it is very unlikely that any windows in them were larger. This makes
still more remarkable the huge opening on the first floor. Only a fragment now
remains of the arrangements of the space to the east of the main chamber. There
must have been some room from which the topmost portcullis was operated, and
a newel staircase, which begins at second-floor level in the south-eastern corner
of the donjon, may have given access to this, and the roof of the building. It is now
impossible to be certain whether these defensive works were approached from

---

[15] The head of the window on the southern side is four-centred with a rectangular label, and can
hardly be earlier than the fifteenth century; its rear arch, however, seems to be original.

Figure 6. Jamb of staircase window and the window of the ante-room, from the south.

within the donjon (which would require the provision of doors from the chamber through the now-destroyed eastern wall of the tower), or from the upper storeys of the great gate beside the donjon.

The internal newel staircase from the ground to first floors is only 80 cm wide, and is a quite unsuitable access to a grand first-floor hall, but fortunately just enough survives at the eastern side of the tower to reconstruct the original approach, and this is shown in a cut-away axonometric projection as Figure 10. About seven metres to the south east of the donjon two walls still stand of a small square gatetower. This evidently consisted of a large outer and inner portal, each capable of being secured against the exterior; the outer side of the gatehouse lay towards the east, where a pedestrian gate allowed a bypass to the main door, an arrangement that resembles the conventional layout of a monastic gatehouse. In view of the alignment of the cross wall located by Barber, precisely on the outer face of the gatehouse, there is every reason to accept the conventional opinion

Figure 7. The staircase head (extreme left), ante-room (left), and defended door to the audience chamber, before the recent clearance of the floor debris.

that this fragmentary structure was the passage between the outer, eastern, and inner, western baileys. Its oddity is that it must have been weak for this purpose, with little provision for defence beyond two simple wooden doors, and that the gatepassage was elaborately vaulted with extensive use of finely cut mouldings.

Within this gate passage, immediately to the north of the thoroughfare, lay a staircase of comparatively gentle ascent. Its lower portions have been lost, and their relationship with the gatepassage must remain a matter of conjecture until proved by excavation, but its western side is visible in the stub of wall that protrudes from the south-eastern corner of the donjon, and it was clearly constructed with an elaborate ribbed vault and a shapely cut handrail. It appears, furthermore, to have been designed with a gentle curve amounting to about 30 degrees deflection, and must have been a noble approach to the first floor of the tower. Access to the foot of the stair from within the gatehouse may have been checked by a portcullis.[16] At the head of the stair the groove for a second portcullis can be traced, immediately outside the jamb of a door. Beyond lay a small chamber, lit by a reasonably large traceried window, and containing a stone bench. Between this chamber and the main hall of the donjon once stood a fine large doorway, whose shape has been revealed by the recent removal of debris and tarmac, which had long covered the ground-floor vault. This doorway was very securely closed

---

[16] The survey of 1538 states that there were three portcullisses on this stair [see n. 17, below]. One survives at the head of the stair, another may be that between the ante-room and the chamber, and so at least one other must have lain in the now-destroyed portion of the staircase.

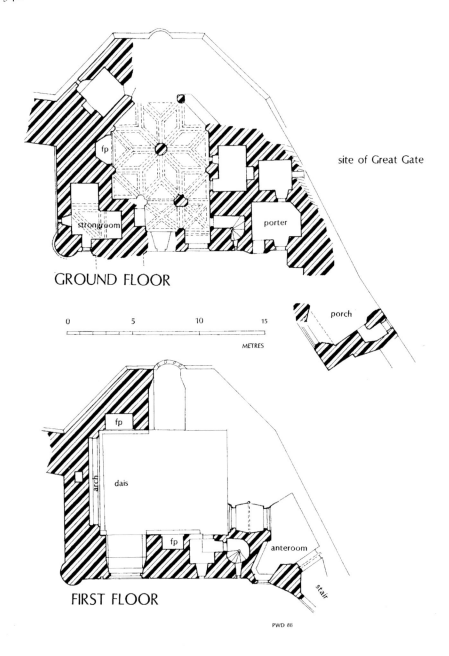

Figure 8. Donjon, ground- and first-floor plans.

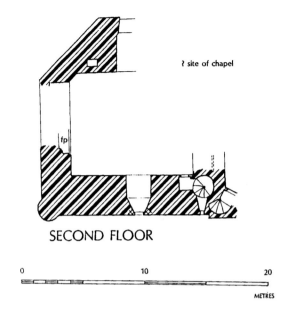

? site of chapel

SECOND FLOOR

0   10   20
METRES

EAST-WEST SECTION

PWD 88

Figure 9. Donjon, plan of second floor and east–west section

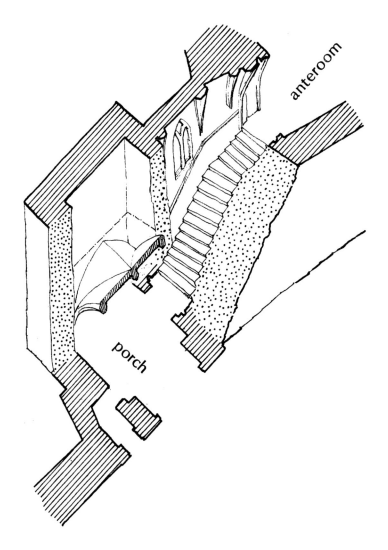

Figure 10. Knaresborough Castle, axonometric reconstruction.

with two two-leaved doors separated by a portcullis. The contrast is quite striking between the elegant staircase and the security of the approach: the 1538 survey makes the point clearly when it describes the donjon as 'strongly fortified with work and man's ingyne to abide all assaults and hath but one stare upwards and that defended with three gates and three portcullesses albeit they be but of timber and aloft above the stair a strong vawt with open vents to make war downwards'.[17]

---

[17] Taken from Cumberland's survey, as printed in Barber, 'Excavations', 223–4.

The Role of the Knaresborough Donjon

The oddities of this building, referred to by most of those who have alluded to it, may be made less strange by a consideration of the political situation in the early years of Edward II's reign. The intimate relationship between Edward and his Gascon favourite, Piers Gaveston, was well known, and had led to scandal in the closing years of Edward I's reign. Gaveston was, indeed, sent into exile in 1307,[18] and the old king is said on his deathbed to have instructed the earls of Lincoln and Warwick not to allow him to return.[19] The immediate cause of the exile was Prince Edward's request for a grant for his favourite of the county of Ponthieu or the earldom of Cornwall. Knaresborough, until the death of Edmund, earl of Cornwall, in 1300, had been part of the Cornwall estates, and Edward lost no time on his accession in recalling Gaveston and creating him earl of Cornwall. Gaveston thus became lord of Knaresborough. In the first year of his reign Edward held the South securely, and had the support of the greater barons; in the North, however, the abandonment of the campaign against Scotland of 1307, during which Edward I had died, led to mounting disaffection among those northern lords whose estates were vulnerable to Scottish attacks, and within two years of his accession Edward's rule in the north had a rival in the authority of his cousin, Thomas earl of Lancaster, whose own great landholding and retinue was augmented by the support of a large body of lesser barons, and from time to time that of almost all the earls, and even the Queen herself, united in their hatred of Gaveston. In such circumstances some display of royal authority was needed, and Edward attempted to provide this by supporting Gaveston as a northern lord.[20] The donjon at Knaresborough was the largest of the king's works in the region at this time, and it is significant both of Edward's policy and his relationship with Gaveston that though the favourite held the lordship and the castle, it was the king who paid for the new building.

This background provides us with the necessary evidence to understand the design of the Knaresborough donjon. In the basement and the ground floor, both entered independently from the inner bailey, was provision for stores and, probably, a privy kitchen with mural chambers for staff. The narrow newel staircase provided the necessary access of attendants to the principal room on the first floor. The normal approach to this room, however, was contrived in such a way as to make a much greater impression on the visitor. It began outside the donjon in a gracefully vaulted gatepassage, rose by a (probably) broad set of gentle steps,

---

[18] H. Johnson, *Edward of Caernarvon 1284–1307* (Manchester, 1946), 122–4.
[19] F. W. D. Blue (ed.), *The Brut* [Early English Text Soc., 1st series, 131 (1906)], i, 202–3.
[20] The best account of the rivalry and factions is given by J. R. Maddicott, *Thomas of Lancaster* (Oxford, 1970), esp. 67–130; I. R. S. Phillips, *Aymer de Valence, earl of Pembroke, 1307–1324* (Oxford, 1972), gives a similar account of these events, but underemphasises the role of Lancaster. It should be noted that Lancaster's favourite castle was only some 15 miles away from Knaresborough at Pontefract, and that Lancaster spent much time there and loved it 'plus qe nul autre qil aveit en la terre' [the French Brut, quoted Maddicott, *Thomas*, 26: cf. *ibid.*, 331, and Lancaster's itineraries, 339–47].

covered in elaborate vaulting, and paused in an ante- or waiting room, lit by a fine window, provided with seats around its walls, and perhaps heated by a fireplace in the missing eastern wall.[21] While waiting here, the visitor could admire the vaulting, the tracery, and an imposing doorway with twin leaved doors, which led to the audience chamber. Once permitted within this doorway the visitor would be confronted by a large chamber, surrounded by benches, and directly facing him a dais set against the opposite wall. A fireplace warmed the dais, but this would be largely out of sight of the door. Small windows opened towards the field on the northern side, but the majority of the light in the room would be at the far end, where the great traceried window, facing southwards, would have let in a flood of sunlight directly on the dais, and on the lord's chair, which was framed by the huge ashlar-built pointed recess in the western wall, whose purpose, like that of a proscenium arch, was to focus attention on the principals. This *coup de théâtre* may be an explanation too for another incongruity: until the arrival in the audience chamber the approach road was elaborately vaulted. The chamber itself, however, was very simple, apart from the treatment of the dais, and was celled merely in timber. It may have been the intention that the visitor should be impressed by the grandeur of the building while approaching the chamber, and while waiting for admission in the ante-room, but once admitted should not be allowed to be distracted by quality of the chamber from the necessary awe at the presence of the castle's lord, the brightest object in the room, with his courtiers sitting in a discrete twilight on benches around the walls.

The theatricality of the scene is clear, but it would make a significant political point, the nobility of the new lord of the castle, and neither Edward nor his father scorned the use of propaganda, as can be seen in the design of the new Rome at Caernarvon, the charade (if not true, then at least believed in as early as the second quarter of the fourteenth century) of the princedom of Wales, or indeed the royal performance of the translation of the bones of Arthur at Glastonbury.[22] A writ of 14 September 1307 demonstrates that the king himself had taken an interest in the design.[23] The show, in the event, proved insufficient. In 1312 Gaveston and the king were pursued from Newcastle to Tynemouth, and fled to Scarborough Castle, newly fortified and provisioned against mounting baronial revolt; Edward himself pressed on to York, leaving Gaveston in Scarborough. After a short siege the favourite surrendered to the earls, and was taken southwards under safeconduct, but was intercepted near Oxford, was led to Lancaster's estate near Kenilworth, and was executed after a somewhat irregular trial by

---

[21] The donjon contained a chapel, perhaps an oratory off the second-floor chamber in the eastern part now destroyed, above which was a chimney, which needed repair in 1538 [Barber, 'Excavations', 224]. This would provide a flue in the vicinity of the ante-room, even if the chapel itself were large enough to need a fireplace.

[22] See *HKW*, 371 and note 1, and p. 373.

[23] The writ ordering the constable and the clerk of works to begin operations at Knaresborough, 'as we have more fully indicated to them' [*si come nous lour auoms plus pleinement deviser*]: *HKW*, 689.

Lancaster and his adherents, while Edward himself took refuge in the new tower at Knaresborough.[24] The *King's Works* quite rightly points out that documentary evidence is inadequate to enable us to say whether Gaveston or Edward himself was to be the intended occupant of the tower,[25] and later tradition named the audience chamber very clearly the 'King's Hall'.[26] The point is perhaps not very significant, since Gaveston was evidently envisaged as Edward's representative in the region, but on balance the favourite is the more likely incumbent, since he remained the lord of the castle, and required the trappings of *dominium* much more than did the king himself. Furthermore, it is hard to believe that at the beginning of his reign Edward thought the great strength of the donjon necessary for his own security: he already had clear evidence, however, of the unpopularity of his favourite, and the building of a strong towerhouse for his protection in the North would be no more than simple prudence.

In this context the design and role of the Knaresborough donjon may well seem by now clear. Consideration of some recent royal building works makes the intention of the architectural design still more plain. Among the castles built for Edward's father in Wales the plan of Flint is unusual, since it was dominated by a cylindrical donjon in an arrangement apparently a little out of fashion by the standards of late thirteenth-century England, and the tower itself has an internal layout that lacks any grand room: from the outside it would have appeared to be a solid traditional donjon; inside a ring of small chambers surrounded a tiny courtyard. Taylor has very plausibly suggested that this was intended to provide a lodging for the justiciar of Chester when hearing pleas at Flint.[27] Caernarvon Castle was designed with a massive courtyard house, suitable for royal occupation, in its upper ward. In the lower ward the Eagle Tower, with the trappings of power and propaganda in the sculptures on its battlements, was built as a self-contained residence, presumably for the justiciar, Otto de Grandison.[28] Both were for royal officers, whose authority was being emphasised by their accommodation in a donjon. So, too, at Knaresborough, where the newly fashionable polygonal form of tower was adopted for the northern face of the donjon:[29] The connection with the Welsh castles may be still closer, for the Knaresborough tower was built immediately next to the main gate of the castle. Its eastern wall, beside the gate, is very ruined, but clearly was set at an angle to the main tower. It seems possible that this was the western side of a polygonal chamber behind the main gate: the arrangement envisaged here would closely resemble that of the King's gate at Caernarvon, or, indeed, the gatehouse at Denbigh Castle, built by Henry de Lacy,

---

[24] Maddicott, *Thomas*, 124–30; Phillips, *Aymer*, 32–7.
[25] *HKW*, 690.
[26] Barber, 'Excavations', 224.
[27] *HKW*, 317, n. 4.
[28] *HKW*, 373.
[29] For the prestige of polygonal towers, see A. J. Taylor, 'The Castle of St. Georges-d'Espéranche', *Antiquaries Journal* 33 (1953), esp. 46.

earl of Lincoln, but with royal assistance, and the presence of the king's mason, James of St George.[30]

Acknowledgements

I am grateful to Susan Content of New Hall, Cambridge [now Murray Edwards], for assistance in the survey, and to Mary Kershaw of the Harrogate Borough Museum for showing us her excavations on the site of the great gate, which are currently in progress, and for discussion of the problems of the donjon.

[30] *HKW*, 333–4.

15

The Architecture of Arthurian Enthusiasm: Castle Symbolism in the Reigns of Edward I and his Successors[1]

Richard K. Morris

The castles of King Edward I in North Wales have long been acknowledged as one of the crowning achievements of European military architecture.[2] They mark the culmination of almost two centuries of development, from the first crusading experience in the Near East, through the castles of the Plantagenets and Philip Augustus in France; resulting in virtually impregnable fortresses relying on such features as concentric walls and heavily fortified gatehouses. The Edwardian castles are a virtuoso demonstration of such ideas, characterised especially by their enormity of scale and their variety of type. Flint has a detached keep, Conwy is planned for consecutive defence, Harlech and Beaumaris rely on concentric defences of near perfect symmetry; Caernarfon experiments with polygonal towers, Conwy with a very early example of stone machicolation, and so on. The impression is firmly given of an elite group of men-of-war, long-standing comrades in arms of the king, indulging in an orgy of military architectural expression on an almost unlimited budget:[3] a medieval forerunner of the American 'star-wars' programme.

No-one doubts that the English castles in North Wales represent an overkill. One has only to compare a castle of the Welsh princes, such as Dolbadarn in

[1] Versions of this paper were given to various audiences, starting as a series of undergraduate course lectures in 1974; its major previous public airings were to the British Archaeological Association in 1979 and Le Comité International d'Histoire de l'Art in 1985. Its content has benefited from the comments of many people too numerous to acknowledge individually. I thank them all, and I am particularly grateful to Professor Alan Gowans, whose teaching at the University of Victoria (Canada) introduced me to socio-architectural history: and to Professor Julian Gardner and other staff and students in the History of Art and English Departments at the University of Warwick for their continuing interest in this subject and to the Harlaxton Symposium committee for the opportunity finally to publish it.
[2] The standard modern account is by Arnold Taylor, *HKW*, 293–408; reissued with minor revisions as A. J. Taylor, *The Welsh Castles of Edward I* (London, 1986). See also the Cadw Guidebook series – *Beaumaris Castle* (1988), *Caernarfon Castle* (1993), *Conwy Castle* (1990), *Flint Castle-Ewloe Castle* (1995), *Harlech Castle* (1988), *Rhuddlan Castle* (1987). I am much indebted to Dr David Robinson (Cadw) for considerable assistance with the Welsh material in this paper.
[3] For example, Sir Otto de Grandison (Edward's closest friend), Sir William de Cicon and the engineer Master James of St George; see further *HKW*, 293–408. For a study of the potentially withering firepower from some of these castles, see Q. Hughes, 'Medieval Firepower', *Fortress* 8 (1991), 31–43.

Figure 1. Caernarfon
Castle, the Eagle Tower.
© History of Art Photo
Library, University of
Warwick (*R. K. Morris*)

Figure 2. Caernarfon Castle, river façade.
© Crown Copyright (2016) Cadw

Figure 3. Caernarfon Castle, the King's Gate.
© Crown Copyright (2016) Cadw

Figure 4. Harlech Castle, general view from the south-west.
© Crown Copyright (2016) Cadw

Figure 5. Conwy Castle, view across the estuary to the inner ward.
© Crown Copyright (2016) Cadw

Figure 6. Dolbadarn
Castle, the tower. (*R. K.
Morris*) © History of Art
Photograph Collection,
University of Warwick

Snowdonia,[4] with Harlech or Conwy to gain a visual appreciation of this phenomenon (Figures 4, 5, 6). Clearly the explanation for these excesses goes beyond basic military function, and two further motives will be examined here – artistic effect and symbolism – as exemplified particularly at Caernarfon, the viceregal centre of the English administration after 1284.

The idea that real castles might also incorporate decoration found no place in Sidney Toy's style of military history,[5] but Caernarfon displays a series of features that can be construed as consciously artistic. Decoration can be observed earlier in the fabric of some Anglo-Norman keeps, like that at Castle Rising, Norfolk (c.1140), and modern research has heightened our awareness of such factors at work in the twelfth century.[6] Nevertheless, the extent of the decorative vocabulary at Caernarfon marks it out as a turning point: the progenitor of the late medieval castle as a work of art. The relevant effects include geometrical variety in plan, banded masonry in the walls, a surfeit of turrets, and battlements carved with figures; to all of which we shall return shortly. Probably the feature most symptomatic of the new spirit, however, and one that has received least attention from scholars, is the façade of the King's Gate (Figure 3). Here the presence of an elaborate sculpted niche enclosing the seated figure of a king appears to have been inspired by the imperial precedent of Frederick II's triumphal gate at Capua,[7] which Edward or a member of his court was likely to have seen during his return from crusading. In 1272 he wintered in southern Italy, and in February 1273 he travelled north to the papal court at Orvieto. The design of the King's Gate is repeated in the gatehouse of the lordship castle at Denbigh, with the additional chequer-board pattern of coloured stones above emphasising the artistic effect.[8] Caernarfon and Denbigh appear to incorporate the first surviving examples in England – perhaps even in northern Europe – of castle gatehouses adorned with carved imagery, an idea more familiar in ecclesiastical entrances of the period.[9] It thus stands at the head of a trend that became the fashion for pretentious castles in the later Middle Ages, such as the gatehouses at Bodiam and Herstmonceux, or Pierrefonds and La Ferté-Milon in France (Figures 7, 19).

[4] See further R. Avent, *Castles of the Princes of Gwynedd* (Cardiff, 1983); and Cadw Guidebook *Dolwyddelan Castle–Dolbadarn Castle* (Cardiff, 1994).

[5] S. Toy, *A History of Fortification from 3000 B.C. to A.D. 1700* (London, 1955).

[6] T. A. Heslop, 'Orford Castle, Nostalgia and Sophisticated Living', *Architectural History* 34 (1991), 36–58.

[7] For a reconstruction of this gate, see C. A. Willemsen, *Kaiser Friedrichs II Triumfihtor zu Capua* (Wiesbaden, 1953), pl. 106.

[8] See D. W. Dykes (ed.), *Alan Sorrell. Early Wales Re-Created* (Cardiff, 1980), 61, for an artist's impression. It is possible that the Denbigh gatehouse façade was actually completed before that at Caernarfon. Both presumably stem from a general design probably established in the 1280s, though not completed for several decades at Caernarfon; see further *HKW*, 333–4 and 388 (reference of 1320 to *ymaginem Regis* over the King's Gate); and J. M. Maddison, 'Building at Lichfield Cathedral during the Episcopate of Walter Langton (1296–1321)', in *Medieval Archaeology and Architecture at Lichfield*, British Archaeological Association Conference Transactions 13, ed. J. M. Maddison (Leeds, 1993), 77–8.

[9] For example, the Judgement porch of Lincoln Cathedral Angel Choir (1255–80).

Figure 7. Herstmonceux
Castle, the gatehouse. (*A.
Watson*) © History of Art
Photograph Collection,
University of Warwick

Symbolism of a political kind has been discerned in the fabric of Caernarfon,
linking it with the antiquity of the location – the Roman Segontium – and with
a wider imperial imagery. The most salient points are the carved eagles of the
eponymous west tower, and especially the imitation of the late fourth-century
Theodosian walls of Constantinople through the combination of polygonal
towers with bands of two different colours in the wall fabric (Figure 2).[10] Affirmation of the link with Constantinople is provided by the contemporary record in
the *Flores Historiarum* that the body of Magnus Maximus, the legendary father
of the Emperor Constantine, was discovered when preliminary work was under
way on the castle in 1283. All this information and its interpretation has been

---

[10] The Theodosian walls are stone and tile, whereas the Caernarfon walls are two types of stone
(carboniferous limestone with darker bands of carboniferous sandstone); see Royal Commission
for Ancient and Historic Monuments (RCAHM) (Wales), *Caernarvonshire*, II, *Central* (1960),
130.

precisely recorded and analysed by Arnold Taylor.[11] However, one may venture to suggest that the intended symbolism goes beyond the merely political to a specific association with the fashionable contemporary world of Arthurian romance: and herein lies the main objective of this paper.

At this juncture, it is necessary to turn away temporarily from the Welsh castles to consider the historiography of Arthurian art. In 1938, when Roger Sherman Loomis and Laura Hibbard Loomis published their survey, *Arthurian Legends in Medieval Art*, they found only modest evidence in England in the decorative arts and in a few undistinguished manuscripts.[12] This was all the more surprising for, as they remarked, medieval England was 'the homeland ... of some of the finest versions of Arthurian story';[13] and subsequently R. S. Loomis was to go on to detail one aspect of the story in his article 'Edward I, Arthurian Enthusiast'.[14] Alison Stones has usefully updated our knowledge of 'Arthurian Art since Loomis', though keeping to literal representations of Arthurian episodes and characters mainly in manuscript illumination, as the Loomises had done.[15] There is thus still a place for an examination of the potential architectural examples of 'Arthurian enthusiasm'; even though it must be admitted at the outset that identifications will be less definitive because of the abstract language of building fabric and the need to argue through association.

Since the early versions of this paper over twenty years ago, the academic climate has become more receptive to my main hypothesis, particularly regarding changing attitudes to secular architecture. Charles Coulson has diagnosed the 'structural symbolism' of castellation, whilste Colin Platt and Michael Thompson have introduced respectively the terms 'castles of chivalry' and 'show castles' for later fourteenth- and fifteenth-century castles.[16] Thompson has also brought out the contemporary realism of the *Gawain*-poet's description of the Green Knight's

[11] *HKW*, 369–71. For the identity of 'Constantine', see J. J. Parry, 'Geoffrey of Monmouth and the Paternity of Arthur', *Speculum* 13/3 (1938), 271--7; and R. S. Loomis, 'From Segontium to Sinadon; the Legends of a "Cité Gaste"', *Speculum* 22 (1947), 520–33. For an archaeological account of Segontium, see P. J. Casey (*et al.*), *Excavations at Segontium (Caernarfon) Roman Fort*, Council for British Archaeology Research Report, 90 (London, 1993).
[12] R. S. Loomis with L. H. Loomis, *Arthurian Legends in Medieval Art* (New York, 1938), 40–1 (stained glass and the Winchester round table), 44–8 (the Chertsey tiles), 68 and 79 (misericords), 138–9 (manuscripts).
[13] *Ibid*, 138.
[14] R. S. Loomis, 'Edward I, Arthurian Enthusiast', *Speculum* 28 (1953), 114–27.
[15] M. A. Stones, 'Arthurian Art since Loomis', in *Arturus Rex*, ed. W. van Hoecke (*et al.*), II (Leuven, 1991), 21–55, especially 27–30 for Britain; 'Arthur's Hall' at Dover Castle is noted, but without any discussion of the architecture.
[16] C. L. H. Coulson, 'Structural Symbolism in Medieval Castle Architecture', *Journal of the British Archaeological Association* 132 (1979), 73–90; C. Platt, *The Medieval Castle in England and Wales* (London, 1982); M. W. Thompson, *The Decline of the Castle* (Cambridge, 1987). Critical reviews of changing attitudes to castle studies are D. Stocker, 'The Shadow of the General's Armchair', *Archaeological Journal* 149 (1992), 415–20; and C. L. H. Coulson, 'Freedom to Crenellate by Licence – an Historical Revision', *Nottingham Medieval Studies* 38 (1994), 87 137.

Castle,[17] and the relationship of military architecture to romance literature now warrants a section in a general textbook like Tom McNeill's English Heritage book of *Castles*.[18] Away from castles, a milestone has been Paul Binski's re-assessment of the decorative scheme in the former Painted Chamber of Westminster Palace, demonstrating *inter alia* the association of its Maccabees cycle with Edward I's heroic notion of kingship and with the Arthurian climate of the late thirteenth century.[19]

In addition it is pertinent to note here three other discoveries that are strongly suggestive of the Arthurian climate in Edward's time, and which could not have been known to R. S. Loomis or were not identified by him. The first is the recent revelation through scientific dating methods that the famous Round Table hanging in the former great hall of Winchester Castle was formed from trees that are now known to have been felled c.1250–80.[20] Thus although the extant Arthurian painting of the surface belongs to the early Tudor period, the table was almost certainly created initially for one of the royal round table festivities of Edward's reign.[21]

As in life, so in death: for, secondly, a case can be made that Edward's tomb chest, surprisingly austere among the regal splendours of Westminster Abbey, is based on or related to the former tomb of Arthur at Glastonbury.[22] The latter had been inspected personally by Edward and Queen Eleanor in 1278, and as a result of this visit the remains of Arthur and Guinevere were reburied with ceremony before the high altar, where their tombs were displayed for the rest of the Middle

[17] M. W. Thompson, 'The Green Knight's Castle', in *Studies in Medieval History Presented to R. A. Brown*, ed. C. Harper-Bill *et al.* (Woodbridge, 1989), 317–25. I am grateful to Dr Christopher Norton for first drawing my attention to this reference. See also A. Putter, '*Sir Gawain and the Green Knight' and French Arthurian Romance* (Oxford, 1995), 38, for Gornemant's castle in the *Conte du Graal* 'fully abreast of the latest developments in castle construction'.

[18] T. E. McNeill, *Castles* (London, 1992), 109–11.

[19] P. Binski, *The Painted Chamber at Westminster*, Society of Antiquaries Occasional Paper, New Series 9 (London, 1986), especially ch. 3 and Conclusion; also see P. Binski, *Westminster Abbey and the Plantagenets: Kingship and the Representation of Power* (New Haven and London, 1995), especially 104–6, 139, 197–8, for images of Edward's kingship.

[20] M. Biddle and B. Clayre, *Winchester Castle and the Great Hall* (Winchester, 1983), 37 and 40; see further M. Biddle (ed.), *King Arthur's Round Table: An Archaeological Investigation* (Woodbridge, 2000).

[21] Biddle and Clayre, *Winchester Castle*, 40, 'the [scientific tests] place the making of the table … in the later part of the reign of King Henry III … or the earlier part of the reign of King Edward I … with the latter being for various reasons – scientific, political, personal – the more likely'. Loomis, *Arthurian Legends*, 40–1, noted that the table was potentially earlier than Tudor, but could not tell what date.

[22] This association, which I first expounded publicly in a lecture to the British Archaeological Association in 1979, has also been suggested by Paul Binski and Nicola Coldstream. See respectively M. A. Stones, 'Aspects of Arthur's Death in Medieval Illumination', in *The Passing of Arthur: New Essays in Arthurian Tradition*, ed. C. Baswell and W. Sharpe (New York, 1988), 52–86 (n. 38 citing personal communication with Binski); and N. Coldstream, *The Decorated Style: Architecture and Ornament 1250–1350* (London, 1994), 127, where she also suggests a link with the tomb of Louis IX of France.

Ages:[23] which suggests how highly Edward regarded his association with them. The salient points of comparison between the Westminster and Glastonbury tomb chests are that both were fashioned from 'marble' and were devoid of an effigy on the lid,[24] the latter a remarkable omission in the case of Edward's tomb and distinguishing it from all the other comparable monuments at Westminster. The suggestion that the use of marble may also have been intended to evoke associations with antiquity through the porphyry sarcophagi of royal burials in southern Europe[25] need not preclude the Arthurian connection, for the visual imagery of Edward's monarchy was multiple and eclectic.[26] Indeed, the only English tomb surviving to a member of the royal family actually called Arthur – the Tudor Prince Arthur (d. 1502) buried in Worcester Cathedral – quotes the same formula of a marble topped tomb chest without an effigy.[27] This observation has not been made before to my knowledge, and it tends to corroborate the Arthurian association for Edward's earlier memorial.

The employment of romance imagery owed as much to his courtiers as to the king himself, and their tombs provide an insight into the chivalric lifestyle of English noble society. Here we are concerned with the meaning of the cross-legged pose for military effigies, which constitutes the third piece of contextual evidence not considered by Loomis. Significantly the posture is almost entirely restricted to English monuments,[28] appearing during the first half of the thirteenth century in a few effigies mainly connected with the Knights Templar and becoming fashionable in a wider context at about the beginning of Edward's reign, from the 1270s to the 1340s; including notably the tomb of Edward's brother, Edmund, earl of Lancaster, in Westminster Abbey, with chivalric details in the gable tympanum and elsewhere.[29] The suggestion that the pose denoted a Crusader has long

---

[23] A. Gransden, 'The Growth of the Glastonbury Traditions and Legends in the Twelfth Century', *Journal of Ecclesiastical History*, 27 (1976), 355, citing Adam of Domerham. See also E. K. Chambers, *Arthur of Britain* (London, 1927), 125; Loomis, 'Edward I, Arthurian Enthusiast', 114–16; and J. Vale, *Edward III and Chivalry: Chivalric Society and its Context, 1270–1350* (Woodbridge, 1982), 19.

[24] For Arthur's tomb, see Chambers, *Arthur of Britain*, n. 23, 125–6; and Gransden 'Glastonbury Traditions', 349–57. For depictions in manuscript illumination, see Stones, 'Aspects of Arthur's Death', n. 22, 61–4. For Edward I's tomb, see Royal Commission for Historical Monuments in England, *London*, I, Westminster Abbey (London, 1924), 29 and Pl. 48; his tomb is made of English Purbeck marble, as presumably was Arthur's at Glastonbury.

[25] See J. Deer, *The Dynastic Porphyry Tombs of the Norman Period in Sicily* (Cambridge, MA, 1959); and B. Rosenman, 'Tomb Canopies and Cloister at Santes Creus', in *Studies in Cistercian Art and Architecture*, II, ed. M. P. Lillich (Kalamazoo, 1984), 229–31, for the tomb of Peter III of Aragon (d. 1285).

[26] See Binski, *The Painted Chamber at Westminster*, Conclusion; and Binski, *Westminster Abbey*, 104–6.

[27] Illustrated in N. Pevsner, *Worcestershire* (Harmondsworth, 1968), Pl. 44.

[28] For a survey of English cross-legged effigies and reference to continental examples, see H. A. Tummers, *Early Secular Effigies in England: The Thirteenth Century* (Leiden, 1980), 107–26. The continental specimens are restricted to Spain, to a small group of the later thirteenth century in northern Castile; and a link with England through Edward's Spanish marriage would be worth investigating further.

[29] *Ibid.*, 112.

since been replaced by the more general idea of the knight as 'soldier of Christ',[30] but it may have been associated more specifically in contemporary minds with romance allusions to the knights on quest. In the case of the Grail Quest, with its potential for personal salvation, this might be highly appropriate as an image for a knight's tomb.[31] The most obvious visual parallel is the depiction on a series of early fourteenth-century ivories of Gawain on the Perilous Bed, in an agitated pose in full armour, and usually with his legs crossed, an episode probably derived from the *Conte du Graal* of Chrétien of Troyes.[32] The bed translates well into a tomb chest; or vice versa, for it cannot be certain that the version in the portable arts preceded the monumental tombs. In manuscript illumination, sleeping cross-legged figures in full armour that also relate to this theme include 'Lancelot asleep as the Grail appears' and 'the soul of Roland carried to heaven'.[33]

Perhaps the most extreme version of this pose in sepulchral monuments comes towards the end of the trend, in three well-known East Anglian tombs depicting cross-legged knights lying on beds of stones; of which that to Oliver de Ingham (d. 1344) at Ingham in Norfolk (Figure 8) is considered here. Various explanations have been proposed for this peculiar imagery, including Andrew Martindale's suggestion of a possible link with the Roman statue of a recumbent river-god, misinterpreted in the Middle Ages as depicting Mars.[34] However, in the early nineteenth century Stothard recorded painted hunting and forest scenes as the backdrop to the Ingham effigy. Taken together with Sir Oliver's restless slumber, his right hand resting (formerly) on the pommel of his sword, this suggests an allusion to the knight on quest, sleeping rough in the forest; vowing never to sleep twice in the same place until he achieved his goal.[35] This was the vow of Perceval

[30] See Coldstream, *The Decorated Style*, 111–12.
[31] See further M. Whitaker, *Arthur's Kingdom of Adventure: The World of Malory's Morte D'Arthur* (Cambridge, 1984), ch. 4.
[32] Cited in Loomis, *Arthurian Legends*, 71–2 and Figs 136–42; but without drawing any parallel with monumental tombs.
[33] The former illustrated in M. A. Stones, 'Sacred and Profane Art: Secular and Liturgical Book Illumination in the Thirteenth Century', in *The Epic in Medieval Society*, ed. H. Scholler (Tubingen, 1977), Figs 5 and 6 (two depictions, dated to c.1285 and c.1315–25); the latter in M. Keen, *Chivalry* (New Haven and London, 1984), Fig. 8 (*Les Grandes Chroniques de France*). Obviously one must beware of the pose being employed as a convention for sleep, as for example in some of the sleeping knights in the carved Easter sepulchres at Heckington and Hawton; which is why the extra visual and contextual evidence is vital at Ingham.
[34] A. Martindale, 'The Knights and the Bed of Stones: a Learned Confusion of the Thirteenth Century', *Journal of the British Archaeological Association* 142 (1989), 66–74, where all three tombs at Ingham, Reepham and Burrough Green are described and illustrated; including Stothard's record of the painting on the back wall of the Ingham recess (Pl. XVIIB). Related to this group is the monument at Saleby (Lincolnshire) showing a cross-legged knight lying on a bed of flowers; I am grateful to Loveday Gee for this observation. For a suggestion that the Ingham knight's pose signifies a 'penitent spirit', see J. and M. Vale, 'Knightly Codes and Piety', in *Age of Chivalry: Art and Society in Late Medieval England*, ed. N. Saul (London, 1992), 26–7.
[35] For example, *Sir Gawain and the Green Knight*, ed. W. R. J. Barron (Manchester, 1974), lines 691–739, e.g. 'Almost slain by the sleet, he [Gawain] slept in his irons night after night amongst the naked rocks' (729–30). For a convenient selection of forest episodes from old French romance, see Putter, 'Sir Gawain and the Green Knight', 16–20.

Figure 8. Ingham parish church, Norfolk, tomb of Sir Oliver de Ingham (*R. K. Morris*)

in the *Conte du Graal*, and its continuing significance for the Edwardian period is emphasised by its use as a model for the chivalric oaths taken at the Feast of the Swans in Westminster Palace in 1306, as noted by Loomis.[36]

What the Ingham example demonstrates, together with the other tombs cited, is how the general interest in Arthurian romance in continental Europe, evidenced in relatively 'mass produced' personal artefacts like ivory caskets and mirror-backs, manifests itself in England rather in monumental works of art that are more specifically personal in patronage. The conclusion to be drawn is that certain elements in the circle of Edward I had adopted Arthurian ideals as a life-style, more so than even Loomis had envisaged when he wrote of Edward's 'Arthurian enthusiasm'.[37] This corresponds with how his military activities in Wales and Scotland may be viewed almost as re-enactments at sites associated with Arthur by poets and chroniclers;[38] and, in artistic terms, with how the English Decorated

---

[36] Loomis, 'Edward I, Arthurian Enthusiast', 122–3; see also A. Gransden, *Historical Writing in England c.550 to c.1307* (London, 1974), 453–4.

[37] Loomis, 'Edward I, Arthurian Enthusiast', 114, '... in his cult of Arthur Edward was influenced by a vogue not exclusively English but shared by most of the aristocracies of Christendom in his day'. See also Vale, *Edward III and Chivalry*, 16–24, for the international Arthurian prestige of Edward I and English knights.

[38] See Loomis, 'From Segontium to Sinadon', 521–9.

style magnified small-scale ornament (often of foreign derivation) into monumental architectural creations.[39]

Armed with such ideas, we may return to Caernarfon to consider the full
meaning of the castle's architectural sources. In 1283, the year work began, Edward
received the crown of Arthur from the Welsh, and in the following year he held
a round table festivity at Nefyn, south-west of Caernarfon and the Snowdonia
range.[40] Moreover, 'Sinadon' (Snowdon) or Segontium had long been known to
conteurs and writers of Arthurian romance as the birthplace of Perceval and a
site 'where Arthur sits at the Round Table'.[41] In such circumstances it would be
astonishing if contemporaries did not recognise automatically that the incontro-
vertible architectural links with Constantinople (as described above) also implied
an association with Arthur, as grandson of Constantine, following the pedigree
stemming from Geoffrey of Monmouth's *Historia Regum Britanniae*.[42] The continuing relevance of the latter is shown by Edward's use of Arthurian material
from the *Historia* in a letter to the pope in 1301 to support his claim to Scotland.[43]
Overall it is hard to accept Loomis's assertion that, with Edward's re-use of stones
from Segontium for his new castle, 'the magic departed'.[44] Rather the evidence
suggests that Caernarfon is an Arthurian castle in all but name.

The potential implications of this conclusion for the design of castellated
architecture will now be examined. It would be naive to imagine that every feature discussed below bears a connotation that must be specifically or exclusively
Arthurian. Nor can it be certain that images are always being transferred from
literature to architecture, rather than vice versa.[45] Vinaver has demonstrated that
the interaction between visual art forms and the constructions of romance story-
telling could be very close.[46] The later thirteenth century in England was a period
of great artistic invention, known best through the development of the Decorated
style. So it is to be expected that architects, like poets, would wish to entertain
and dazzle their patrons, designing works of novelty and complexity as far as
the constraints of the architectural process would permit. In certain instances,
their creations would be derived from the content, or inspired by the climate, of
Arthurian romance, as the largest body of literary chivalric material available.
But it is important to stress that the general application of artistic imagination to

---

[39] Especially in tracery patterns: see J. Bony, *The English Decorated Style: Gothic Architecture Transformed 1250–1350* (Oxford, 1979), ch. 3; Coldstream, *The Decorated Style*, 35–52.

[40] Loomis, 'Edward I, Arthurian Enthusiast', 117.

[41] Loomis, 'From Segontium to Sinadon', 527–8.

[42] See Parry, 'Geoffrey of Monmouth and the Paternity of Arthur', 271–7 for how Geoffrey conflated
three historical Constantines, including Constantine the Great. See also Loomis, 'From Segontium to Sinadon', 521–4.

[43] Gransden, *English Historical Writing*, 443, 477–8.

[44] Loomis, 'From Segontium to Sinadon', 531.

[45] For example, the (admittedly later) *Gawain*-poet's famous description of Sir Bertilac's castle may
be based on an existing castle; see Thompson, 'The Green Knight's Castle', 318–19.

[46] E. Vinaver, *The Rise of Romance* (Oxford, 1971), ch. 5.

castle architecture is potentially as relevant to the theme of this paper, even where no specific literary source can be discovered.

At Caernarfon, the turrets of the Eagle Tower and the variety of geometrical planning may be interpreted as such attributes of Arthurian enthusiasm. Both constitute decorative features well beyond the requirements of military and domestic function, evoking the wonder and excitement of the wish-fulfilling castles of romance.[47] A single turret projecting above the battlements of a tower can be justified as a look-out post and as housing a staircase; even two turrets can evolve from the latter purpose, as in the later Guy's Tower at Warwick Castle. However, the employment of three turrets in the Eagle Tower was unprecedented and, though logical explanations have been posited,[48] the telling impression which it still produces today suggests that it was designed rather (or also) for con-scious effect (Figure 1). Here, then, is an important progenitor of the spectacular fighting decks of some later medieval towers, such as Caesar's Tower at Warwick (after 1356) and the gatehouse at Herstmonceux (c.1440, Figure 7).[49] A similarly visual approach to the deployment of turrets is found at Conwy Castle, where single turrets crown each of the four corner towers of the inner ward and thus signify the position of the royal apartments (Figure 5). This idea is more familiar in later palaces, notably the turreted ranges of the royal lodgings at Richmond (c.1498–1501) and the show façade to the royal lodgings at Nonsuch (1537–47),[50] both taking inspiration from the chivalric castle image. By this date continental intermediaries also deserve consideration, such as the existing rooftop architec-ture of the châteaux of the Loire, but behind all these streams may lie the Edward-ian castles as a fundamental source.

Analysis of the plan of Caernarfon Castle reveals a designer playing with geometrical shapes for effect. The plan for the King's Gate seems to be based on three octagons linked in a triangular formation, the rear octagon intended as a vaulted reception hall presumably with side doors leading out to both wards. Strategists would argue that the 'bent entrance' is good defence, as appreciated at the better-preserved example of this gatehouse design at Denbigh: but it is also dramatically chivalric, in the same spirit of display as the five sets of doors and six portcullises for which the King's Gate was provided. For the plan of the Eagle Tower, a decagon was chosen, with both hexagons and octagons employed for the smaller mural chambers.[51] The intended effect may be to impress and entertain

---

[47] Whitaker, *Arthur's Kingdom of Adventure*, ch. 2.

[48] For example, imperial and heraldic meanings in *HKW*, 370–1; also Professor John White, in a personal communication, has suggested to the author that such a large tower could require three observation positions in a military contingency.

[49] There is no need to look invariably, or ultimately, to French precedent for these; see further R. K. Morris, 'The Architecture of the Earls of Warwick in the Fourteenth Century', in *England in the Fourteenth Century*, ed. W. M. Ormrod (Woodbridge, 1986), 172–4.

[50] See S. Thurley, *The Royal Palaces of Tudor England: Architecture and Court Life 1460–1547* (New Haven and London, 1993), 27–32 (Richmond), 60–5 (Nonsuch).

[51] The only published plans that show the geometrical intricacies of the Eagle Tower satisfactorily are in RCAHM (Wales) *Caernarvonshire*, II, between 150–1. The best study of the geometry of

the visitor, rather like the social circuit of variously shaped and decorated rooms in the 'social house' of the eighteenth century.[52] A similar repertoire of octagons, hexagons and triangles appears in miniature in the Eleanor Crosses of the 1290s, a suggestively chivalric series of monuments in the homage they pay to a lady (herself a known collector of romances)[53] and in their heraldic display. Elsewhere in castles of Edward's period, unusual geometry is used in the triangular plan of Caerlaverock (c.1300–10), which suggests that the castle's association with the chivalric poem the *Siege of Caerlaverock* may be more than coincidental.[54] The visual qualities of triangular and polygonal geometry continued to hold an attraction for some later medieval castle-builders in England and on the continent, in spite of the dominant uniformity of quadrangular planning. The Château du Clain of John, Duke of Berry, shown as triangular in the month of July page of the *Très Riches Heures*, may be related to Caerlaverock; and hexagonal planning is to be seen, for example, at Old Wardour and Raglan Castles. The compact courtyard house at Wardour (1393) is an amazingly creative piece of planning, an architectural evocation of the world of romance: with a first-floor hall contrived above a fan-vaulted entrance passage, and formerly with a labyrinth of chambers more in keeping with the ingenious Elizabethan designs of Robert Smythson.[55]

Water defences and castellation are two other military features that lend themselves as well to an Arthurian interpretation in certain examples from Edward I's reign. It goes without saying that the origin of wet moats generally relates to issues of security, and that numerous castles were built adjacent to a river for strategic reasons. Nevertheless, new meanings could be added in the course of time, and it is proposed here that the romance image of the 'castle across water' is such a development, blurring the distinction between the real castle (originally the model for the literary image) and the castle in literature. In the thirteenth century *La Mort le Roi Artu*, the Castle of Douloureuse Garde is approached across a river, and King Arthur could see the arrival of the boat carrying the body of the maid of Escalot from the hall windows of Camelot,[56] and there are many more examples

the Welsh castles and its influence is J. M. Maddison, 'Decorated Architecture in the North-West Midlands: An Investigation of the Work of Provincial Masons and their Sources' (unpublished Ph.D. thesis, University of Manchester, 1978), especially ch. 1. It is worth noting that the decoration of the Eagle Tower, like that of the King's Gate, was not finally completed until the second decade of the fourteenth century.

[52] M. Girouard, *Life in the English Country House* (New Haven and London, 1978), ch. 7, esp. 194–8.

[53] See Loomis, 'Edward I, Arthurian Enthusiast', 116; Binski, *The Painted Chamber at Westminster*, 97.

[54] Caerlaverock was probably built by the English in the 1290s, and is described in the poem as shaped like a shield; B. H. St J. O'Neil, *Caerlaverock Castle* (Edinburgh, 1952), 3. For the poem and roll of arms, see Vale, *Edward III and Chivalry*, 23; she observes that Edward I is implicitly identified with King Arthur in the poem.

[55] For the design of Wardour (Wiltshire), see B. Morley, 'Aspects of Fourteenth-Century Castle Design', in *Collectanea Historica: Essays in Memory of Stuart Rigold*, ed. A. Detsicas (Gloucester, 1981), 111–12. Robert Smythson was familiar with Wardour from the conversion works he carried out there in c.1576–8; M. Girouard, *Robert Smithson and the Elizabethan Country House* (New Haven and London, 1983), 78–81.

[56] J. Cable (ed.), *The Death of King Arthur* (Harmondsworth, 1971), 71, 92.

Figure 9. Wells, Bishop's Palace, detail of chapel roofline (*R. K. Morris*)

Figure 10. Leeds Castle, general view of the moat (*R. K. Morris*)

throughout romance literature. A castle from Edward I's reign that would fit this identification is Leeds in Kent, well away from the active 'war zones' of the later thirteenth century.[57] It was acquired by King Edward and Queen Eleanor in 1278, and became one of their favourite residences, more of a country house in usage

---

[57] In that there was no French threat to the south coast during the castle's main period of rebuilding, in contrast, say, to the situation a century later when Bodiam Castle was constructed. Charles

Figure 11. Leeds Castle, the *gloriette* (*R. K. Morris*)

than a castle. For today's visitor the most striking feature is the moat that surrounds the two islands of the castle like a lake, and contributes to the picturesqueness of the whole (Figure 10). That contemporaries thought similarly about the castle is implied by its thirteenth-century nickname, 'La Mote', and the fact that the smaller island housing the king's chamber was known as 'La Gloriette' (Figure 11).[58] Significantly 'glorieta' is a Spanish word almost certainly introduced into England by Queen Eleanor of Castile, deriving from the Arabic term meaning a 'garden pavilion'.[59] In this respect, the Gloriette at Leeds compares to a toy castle, and the delicacy of its pedestrian bridge (originally wooden) conjures up in the romantic imagination the episode of Lancelot balancing on the sword-bridge as he crosses the water to rescue Guinevere from Meleagant's castle.[60] The visual and symbolic qualities that can thus be inferred for the moated setting at Leeds suggest that the perceived images of some other water-borne castle sites should be reconsidered. One thinks of Warwick, for example, with its association with Guy of Warwick; and Kenilworth, formerly flanked by its great mere, the setting

---

Coulson's recent re-assessment has overstated the case against Bodiam's military capacity; C. H. L. Coulson, 'Bodiam Castle: Truth and Tradition', *Fortress* 10 (1991), 3–15.

[58] *HKW*, 695–6. The term 'gloriette' is also used at Corfe Castle from this period; *idem*, 622.

[59] J. H. Harvey, *Medieval Gardens* (London, 1981), 106. See also T. Tolley, 'Eleanor of Castile and the "Spanish" Style in England', in *England in the Thirteenth Century*, ed. W. M. Ormrod (Woodbridge, 1991), 167–92.

[60] For the popularity of toy castles at Edward I's court, see Binski, *The Painted Chamber at Westminster*, 74–5. For depictions of the Lancelot episode, see Loomis, *Arthurian Legends*, 70–1 and Figs 136–8.

for Roger Mortimer's round table event in 1279 and where Queen Elizabeth I was welcomed by the Lady of the Lake in 1575.[61] Indeed, at Bodiam Castle, the moats have recently been reinterpreted as 'landscape features'.[62]

Evaluating the extent to which battlements might be perceived to be primarily for display is complicated by the relative lack of surviving or unrestored examples, especially from earlier periods like Edward I's reign. Indeed a full survey still needs to be published of merlons, loops and other such military fixtures. The documentary research of Charles Coulson into the socio-architectural implications of royal licences to crenellate validates the perception of such features as evoking a chivalric culture, while warning against classifying some smaller castles as 'merely ornamental' or 'sham', such as Acton Burnell.[63] It might be supposed that militarily functional battlements may be identified by the occasional survival of slots or sockets on the merlons to house shutters in the embrasures as, for example, on the south tower of Stokesay Castle (c.1291) and at Maxstoke Castle (c.1345). There is evidence, though, that such fixtures could be added later, thus potentially confusing the historical record.[64] Anyway, it appears that the more complete the array of military apparatus, the better it came to suit the literary romance image, as the description of Sir Bertilac's castle in *Sir Gawain and the Green Knight* suggests.[65]

On the other hand, display is clearly intended (in addition to any other function) where merlons are surmounted with carved figures, as on the Eagle Tower at Caernarfon (Figure 1) and the contemporary residential tower of Roger Bigod at Chepstow Castle.[66] Additionally, battlements that survive without any signs of protecting the embrasures and without loops in the merlons are potentially nonmilitary in function, especially where other circumstances are favourable. Such a case is the great hall and chapel added to the bishop's palace at Wells by Edward's chancellor and most trusted official, Bishop Robert Burnell, in c.1285–90 (Figure 14). The enormous windows beneath the crenellated parapets visually contradict any idea of defence, even though iron bars and shutters actually provided

[61] For the Kenilworth round table, see Loomis, 'Edward I, Arthurian Enthusiast', 116–17. For Elizabeth's visit, see F. J. Furnivall (ed.), *Robert Laneham's Letter: Describing a Part of the Entertainment unto Queen Elizabeth at the Castle of Kenilworth in 1575* (London, 1907), 6–7.

[62] Coulson, 'Bodiam Castle', 11–15, citing the RCHME survey of 1988.

[63] See C. H. L. Coulson, 'Specimens of Freedom to Crenellate by Licence', *Fortress* 18 (1993), 3–6. I am grateful to Charles Coulson for several discussions on matters concerning crenellation, and for setting me right about the 'sham' nature of Acton Burnell.

[64] See L. F. Salzman, *Building in England Down to 1540: A Documentary History* (Oxford, 1952), 90: in 1313 at the Tower of London, John de Lynne was paid for 'piercing into the battlements for the insertion of hekkes [hatches]'.

[65] Thompson, 'The Green Knight's Castle', 318–22. Pierced merlons are common in micro-architecture in painting, e.g. in the Painted Chamber at Westminster, and the Peterborough Psalter (Brussels); see respectively Binski, *The Painted Chamber at Westminster*, colour Pl. III, and R. S. Loomis, 'The Allegorical Siege in the Art of the Middle Ages', *American Journal of Archaeology* 13 (1919), 255–69, Fig. 4.

[66] For the wider context, see Coldstream, *The Decorated Style*, 45–6. The Caernarfon eagles are virtually unrecognisable today, and evidence presented by Arnold Taylor implies that they have been restored and augmented at least once; 'The King's Works in Wales', 371, note 1.

security, as also probably the enclosure of the site.[67] Moreover, the archaeology of the chapel's roof-line shows that the creasing was once higher, suggesting that the parapet may not have afforded adequate protection for men-at-arms (Figure 9).[68]

The fabric of Burnell's other famous surviving work, Acton Burnell Castle in Shropshire (c.1284), provides evidence just as compelling for viewing its castellation as primarily for effect. It is a compact rectangular house with crenellated walls and four crenellated angle towers (Figure 12), and has been compared to Anglo-Norman keeps.[69] Though much disfigured through ruin and later use as farm buildings, the original interior organisation can still be clearly read in its fabric. At the upper end of a first-floor hall was a two-storey chamber block, through which was the only purpose-built access to the wall-walk by way of a first-floor staircase in the south-west tower (Figure 13).[70] As these were the best chambers, the design is distinctly inconvenient had its intentions been primarily military. The building's impracticality for this purpose is further revealed by the fact that it must originally have had a service range attached to the east wall, apparently timber-framed. The obvious prominence given to symbolism at Acton Burnell has been interpreted as establishing personal political authority,[71] but chivalric fashion may also be relevant to the crenellated appearance. Edward and his retinue stayed at Acton Burnell in 1283,[72] and more visits may have been anticipated, which would have encouraged Bishop Burnell to build in a style suitable for court entertainment: rather like the later builders of Elizabethan prodigy houses. In which case, the battlemented settings that appear in contemporary ivories and manuscript illumination, forming a backdrop to enactments of the 'Castle of Love' and other such festivities, are as pertinent an image for a courtier's residence.[73]

Architectural settings influenced by romance literature may also be detected in some churches of the period, especially those with a strong reliance on baronial patronage and in regions with a tradition for inventive stone-carving.[74] One related example is the unusual flower-patterned vault over the mausoleum of the

---

[67] For the palace, see R. W. Dunning, 'The Bishop's Palace', in *Wells Cathedral: A History*, ed. L. S. Colchester (West Compton, 1982), ch. 10. Dunning (235) asserts that the moat and outer walls are works of c.1340, but it seems highly probable that some form of enclosure existed before this date.

[68] This point needs checking further with measurements and a thorough investigation of the roof.

[69] J. West, 'Acton Burnell Castle, Shropshire', in *Collectanea Historiana: Essays in Memory of Stuart Rigold*, 91, n. 55.

[70] *Ibid.*, Fig. 14, for plans.

[71] *Ibid.*, 92.

[72] *Ibid.*, 90. Exactly when Burnell built this part of his castle – for there obviously was more – is an interesting issue, as implied in West's ultimately inconclusive text. The conventional view is that the work follows on from Edward's 1283 visit and the 1284 licence to crenellate, but it could predate them.

[73] For the Castle of Love and related images, see Loomis, 'The Allegorical Siege', 255–69; and Binski, *The Painted Chamber at Westminster*, 74–5.

[74] Here I refer particularly to early Gothic architecture in the west of England, which includes features antipathetic to the orthodoxy of French Gothic; see H. Brakspear, 'A West Country School of Masons', *Archaeologia* 81 (1931), and more recently M. Thurlby, 'The Lady Chapel of Glastonbury Abbey', *Antiquaries Journal* 75 (1995), 115–27.

Figure 12. Acton Burnell Castle, exterior from the south. (*R. K. Morris*)
© History of Art Photograph Collection, University of Warwick

Figure 13. Acton Burnell Castle, interior looking west. (*R. K. Morris*)
© History of Art Photograph Collection, University of Warwick

Figure 14. Wells, Bishop's Palace, general view from the north. (*R. K. Morris*)
© History of Art Photograph Collection, University of Warwick

Despenser family in the sanctuary of Tewkesbury Abbey (*c.*1320–40), perhaps evoking the Paradise Garden and the spiritual salvation of a knightly class.[75] Another is the east arm of St Augustine's Abbey at Bristol (now the cathedral), which was the burial place of the lords of Berkeley Castle throughout this period, a family risen to prominence in the military service of Edward I. The work, dating mainly to *c.*1310–40, is relatively small but enjoys an unique reputation among English churches for combining a hall church elevation with internal bridges across the aisles.[76] It also represents the earliest example in England of horizontal transoms consistently applied to a series of ecclesiastical windows (Figue 16).[77] Both the bridges and the transoms are redundant in a general structural sense, in that much larger aisles and windows had been constructed successfully in preceding Gothic buildings; for example, Lincoln Cathedral, or Tintern Abbey, to name a more local and monastic comparison.

The designer's purpose may have been no more than to show off his artistic virtuosity, which in itself is relevant to our theme: but a deeper symbolism may

[75] R. K. Morris, 'Tewkesbury Abbey: the Despenser Mausoleum', *Bristol and Gloucestershire Archaeological Society Transactions* 93 (1974), 142–55.

[76] The bridges and Bristol's numerous other idiosyncrasies have generated a considerable literature; see Bony, *The English Decorated Style*, 35–6, n. 9.

[77] Earlier occurrences of the 'transom' derive from French Rayonnant ecclesiastical tracery effects, such as the group of Yorkshire churches of the late thirteenth century/early fourteenth century (e.g. York Minster nave, Bridlington Priory); from which derive 'feature' windows like Howden west window, which come closest to the Bristol form but only in single windows.

Figure 15. Wells, Bishop's Palace, great hall interior. (*R. K. Morris*)
© History of Art Photograph Collection, University of Warwick

also have been intended. A clue lies in the mimetic form of the bridges, which loosely recalls such features of contemporary timber construction as arch braces and tie-beams, and perhaps crown-posts too (Figure 16).[78] The quotation, though not literal, is from the open roof of a secular great hall, and this is as likely a source for the transoms at Bristol as French rayonnant curtain tracery. Transoms had been used in an English secular context since at least the great hall of Winchester Castle (1222–36), and by the late thirteenth century they were fashionable in aristocratic great halls. Excellent examples survive in the west in the castles of Goodrich, Chepstow and Acton Burnell; and, finest of all, in Burnell's great hall at Wells (Figure 15), which might even have influenced the Bristol design.[79] In these hall windows the transom was employed to divide a lower area with shutters and grilles from a glazed upper area, which might also have shutters, as may be seen in the background of many fifteenth-century Flemish paintings such as Jan van Eyck's *Arnolfini Wedding Portrait* (London, National Gallery). At Bristol, the transom loses any such function and has been subsumed under the fully glazed format of ecclesiastical traceried windows. It has been copied for effect, which the context here suggests is to make an association with a secular hall. It is a singular fact that the tombs of the Berkeleys line the aisles, which

---

[78] See Bony, *The English Decorated Style*, 36. The analogy with a crown-post roof (Bony's 'king-post') is based on the way the ribs spring from a point in the centre of the bridge (equivalent of a collar beam), recalling the curved braces diverging from a crown-post.

[79] The great hall at Berkeley Castle also has transomed windows, though with simpler tracery and of slightly later date (c.1320–40).

Figure 16. Bristol Cathedral, south choir aisle and Berkeley tombs.
© Conway Library, Courtauld Institute of Art

incorporate the transomed windows and mimetic bridges (Figure 16); whereas
the abbots are buried in the centre vessel (choir and Lady Chapel) under a more
conventional Decorated lierne vault and devoid of secular architectural associations. The image from romance literature that would best explain the various references of the Bristol aisles is the Grail Hall, where the successful knight errant
meets his Maker. The imaginative filigree stellar recesses that house the effigies

intensify the other-worldly effect (Figure 16, right).[80] Overall this is as appropriate an architectural setting for knightly burial as is the quest iconography of Ingham for an individual knight's monument.

A possible corollary of this interpretation is that some secular great halls were themselves viewed by contemporaries as evoking the Grail Hall or the feasting hall of one of the other romance castles.[81] The case would be stronger if the great hall is particularly magnificent, or if the site has relevant historical associations: criteria that are both satisfied at Burnell's great hall at Wells. The splendour of its windows and its display of crenellations has already been noted, and it was also one of the largest aristocratic halls to have been built in England in its time, at 115 feet by 59½ feet. Historically the most significant factor is the palace's situation only five miles from Arthur's resting place at Glastonbury. Burnell was building on a regal scale probably in anticipation of further royal visits, following that to Glastonbury in 1278. However, it could also be that the conception of the hall was influenced by a local Arthurian micro-climate recreated by Edward's opening of Arthur's tomb.

The image may have continued to capture men's minds in later periods, such as the rebuilding of the great halls at Westminster Palace and Kenilworth Castle in Richard II's reign. In favour of this interpretation at Kenilworth is the former approach to the castle across water and the documented Arthurian festivities there in the thirteenth and sixteenth centuries, described above. The great hall itself is one of the most sumptuously appointed large halls surviving from the later Middle Ages (Figure 18). Everything about it excites wonder in the beholder[82] – the symmetry of the hall and towers seen from across the mere; its elevation to the first floor as an extension of the state apartments: the elaborately carved porch entrance and the enormous double-transomed windows: the fireplaces decorated with the latest Perpendicular tracery patterns, and with provision for tapestries to hang above. The builder of the hall and new apartments was John of Gaunt, duke of Lancaster, in whose circle of patronage it has been suggested that the *Gawain*-poet may have worked.[83] Moreover, Lancaster was commemorated in a chivalric style tomb in Old St Paul's, dressed in full armour beneath a shrine-like canopy

---

[80] Bristol also has crenellated parapets like the Wells hall, and is thus one of a select group of churches at the head of a fashion that became popular in late Gothic architecture.

[81] See Thompson, 'The Green Knight's Castle', 324, for the importance of the great hall in *Sir Gawain and the Green Knight*.

[82] Contemporary literary interest in fantastic halls, though architecturally more surreal than related to built examples, is represented in Chaucer's Hall of Fame, *c*.1379–80; see J. A. W. Bennett, *Chaucer's Book of Fame: an Exposition of 'The House of Fame'* (Oxford, 1968), ch. III.

[83] R. S. Loomis, *Arthurian Literature in the Middle Ages* (Oxford, 1959), 529, n. 6. More recently Bennett has suggested that the poem was written to entertain the itinerant royal household; M. J. Bennett, 'The Court of Richard II and the Promotion of Literature', in *Chaucer's England: Literature in Historical Context*, ed. B. Hanawalt (Minneapolis, 1992), 3–20, esp. 12–15. Goodman found no actual proof that Gaunt commissioned a literary work or rewarded an author, though he was a patron of Chaucer and one of his retainers was 'a voluminous writer of courtly verse'; A. Goodman, *John of Gaunt: the Exercise of Princely Power in Fourteenth-Century Europe* (Harlow, 1992), 37–8.

Figure 17. London, Old St
Paul's Cathedral, tomb of
John of Gaunt (Dugdale,
*History of St Paul's
Cathedral*, 2nd edn, 1716).
(*R. K. Morris*) © History
of Art Photograph
Collection, University of
Warwick

hung with the knightly accoutrements of lance, helm and shield (Figure 17):[84] a
more orthodox rendition of themes from knightly tombs of the earlier fourteenth
century and ultimately of Edward I's reign.

---

[84] See Goodman, *John of Gaunt*, for Gaunt's 'lifelong delight in the finer points of jousting' (37) and
as 'a devotee of the combat' (360). It was fairly common practice in the period for a knight's military accoutrements to be given to the church in which he was buried; see J. and M. Vale, 'Knightly
Codes and Piety', 27. Gaunt's tomb follows the general pattern of that of the Black Prince (d. 1376)
in Canterbury Cathedral. For the latter, see C. Wilson, 'The Medieval Monuments', in P. Collin-
son *et al.* (eds), *A History of Canterbury Cathedral* (Oxford, 1995), 494–8, where the practice of
hanging arms on knightly graves is discussed; and Binski, *Westminster Abbey and the Plantagenets*, 197–8, placing the tomb firmly in a chivalric context.

Figure 18. Kenilworth Castle, great hall, view from the keep. (*R. K. Morris*)
© History of Art Photograph Collection, University of Warwick

Figure 19. La Ferté-Milon, entrance façade. (*R. K. Morris*)
© History of Art Photograph Collection, University of Warwick

The architecture of his reign has been the main subject of this paper, which has endeavoured to show that at a particular moment in time, in particular buildings, Arthurian symbolism informed their design through the aspirations of their patrons and the imagination of their craftsmen. The Edwardian court had captured the spirit of Arthurian romance literature and, more significantly, had created a style that had given its ideals permanent monumental expression in stone. This new perception of castle architecture is as much a part of the Decorated style as the curvilinear tracery of churches, and its influence at least as great in late medieval Europe. The vocabulary of the Arthurian castle worked out in Edward's reign is the language of Warwick, Herstmonceux, Mehun-sur-Yèvre and la Ferté-Milon (Figures 7, 19); even if the phraseology becomes more clichéd and mannered as it enters the vernacular of late Gothic architecture.

16

Medieval Ornamental Landscapes

Christopher Taylor

In recent years archaeologists in Britain have found many examples of what have been called 'ornamental landscapes' of medieval date. These landscapes comprise the archaeological remains of former lakes, ponds, moats, causeways, gardens, deer parks and other features, and are associated with castles and other high-status buildings. They seem to have been intended to enhance the setting of these buildings as well as to provide places of entertainment and recreation. This paper recounts the discovery of these landscapes and describes their archaeological components and some of their related buildings. It analyses the evidence from documents and illustrations for their existence and appearance. It discusses their creators, the motives behind their creation and their influence on the development of later ornamental landscapes. The paper concludes with an examination of the problems of defining such landscapes.

Analytical field archaeology, that is the discovery, recording and interpretation of upstanding archaeological remains, has made many contributions to landscape history. It is thus appropriate that in the first issue of a new journal concerned with this subject there should be a paper devoted to some of the results of this method of research. Until relatively recently, analytical field archaeology was almost entirely concerned with utilitarian sites and landscapes of all periods. But in the 1970s and 1980s field archaeologists began to find and record the remains of former pleasure gardens, mainly of sixteenth-century and later date. One result of this was the realisation that abandoned gardens are one of the commonest type of archaeological sites in Britain (Taylor 1983, 1997, 1998a). Later fieldwork led to the discovery of medieval gardens, which turned out to be much more varied in form than garden historians had hitherto believed (Brown and Taylor 1991; Everson *et al.* 1991, 54; Blood and Taylor 1992; Rose 1994). The wider understanding of these former gardens was only achieved by co-operation with workers in other disciplines. Similarly, this paper, although based on the results of analytical field archaeology, could not have been written without the work of other scholars.

During the 1980s the writer and two of his colleagues recorded the medieval and later archaeological sites in part of Lincolnshire for the Royal Commission on the Historical Monuments of England. Among a number of the achievements of that work, arguably the most important for landscape studies was the discovery of what turned out to be a medieval ornamental landscape at Stow (Everson *et al.* 1991, 184–5). The site was not impressive. At the northern end of a medieval deer park, the interior of which was an arable prairie and the surrounding bank and ditch of which had been all but ploughed to extinction, was a small moated site. This had been the site of a palace of the bishops of Lincoln from at least the mid twelfth century until the mid-fifteenth century. Examination of the surrounding land revealed a number of related features that had been almost destroyed by ploughing, including the traces of the dams of three lakes to the north of the moat. The middle dam had also once carried the main approach road to the palace. These, and the boundary of an outer walled enclosure, visible as a soil mark, indicated that originally the north side of the palace had had a strikingly ornamental appearance with the approach drive seemingly passing over large sheets of water.

The documented history of Stow confirmed that the palace and its park was a place of retreat, entertainment and administration. The licence to crenellate, granted in 1336 (Thompson 1998, 167), suggested a date for the creation of this landscape. However the significance of these hitherto unrecognised arrangements, as well as their perhaps earlier date, was established by the fact that in about 1186 Stow formed the setting for Giraldus Cambrensis's tale of St Hugh's pet swan. Giraldus, who knew Stow, then described it as 'delightfully surrounded with woods and ponds' (Dimcock 1887; Douie and Farmer 1962, 104–9). All this implied that the medieval palace there had had a landscape deliberately contrived to produce an ornamental approach and a pleasing view from the palace. But was Stow unique or merely the only site of its type to be recognised?

Over the succeeding years first the writer and Paul Everson and then a number of other workers began to recognise similar sites, which came to be called 'medieval ornamental landscapes'. As archaeological sites, which is what they were, almost all of them had characteristics similar to Stow. They all had the remains of dams, leats and other water-management and control features. These were of such a scale or complexity that the provision of sheets of water and other ponds and their arrangement to provide an ornamental outlook or approach seemed to have been a prime consideration. Most of them had associated deer parks, many also contained the remains of enclosed gardens, and all seemed to be adjacent to high-status buildings. The majority seem to have been so arranged that they could be viewed from above, from local eminences, from the upper floors or roofs of the buildings or from special 'standings' or pavilions, often known as 'gloriettes' (Harvey 1981, 44).

An early discovery was that at the site of a palace of the bishops of Ely at Somersham, Cambridgeshire (Figure 1; Taylor 1989; 1998b, 30–1). The palace and its formal gardens lay inside a moated site. One side of this was not a typical, broad, water-filled ditch but a narrow stream set in a wide valley-like feature. The approach to the palace was past the parish church, between paddocks produced by the clearance of the existing village of Somersham and its relocation over its own fields some distance away. As this drive neared the palace it ran across a causeway set between two large artificial lakes before entering the moated site on a stone bridge. On the opposite side of the palace another causeway on the same axis as the first led into the adjacent deer park. On either side of the latter

Figure 1. Somersham Palace, Cambridgeshire, from the south. The palace, surrounded by a moat, lay immediately beyond the modern farmstead. The rectangular field above it is the site of a lake. Another lay to the east, right. In the foreground are the cropmarks of a moated gazebo, ponds and raised terraced walks. A deer park occupied the foreground.

causeway were extensive gardens, the archaeological remains of which included a moated gazebo and associated ponds, raised terraces, the planting ridges of an orchard and several other ponds. These last included a line of three increasing in width from east to west, probably in an attempt to correct the effect of perspective. The whole site could be viewed from the rising ground just inside the deer park.

Other sites that were discovered included the landscape at Old Bolingbroke Castle, Lincolnshire, where the remains of a large lake as well as other ponds are arranged around three sides of the moated castle (Beresford and St Josep. 1979, 150–2, where the lake was not recognised; Taylor 1998b, 38–9). Another was Framlingham Castle, Suffolk, where there are again the remains of a large mere below the castle, the site of a formal garden and a deer park (Raby and Baillie Reynolds 1987; Brown and Pattison 1997; Taylor 1998b, 40–1).

Elsewhere the moated Ravensworth Castle, North Yorkshire (Figure 2), has been shown to have lain within a great lake, with an attached walled deer park and with formal gardens on the approach drive (Ryder 1979; Lofthouse 1997). Leeds Castle, Kent, is still surrounded by its lake, and there is evidence of a second lake,

Figure 2. Ravensworth Castle, Yorkshire, from the east. The remains of the castle, rebuilt
in the later fourteenth century, lie surrounded by a moat and on the marshy ground
that marks the encircling lake. In the foreground, below the approach drive, are traces
of former ponds and gardens. A deer park lay in the background. © Copyright reserved
Cambridge University Collection of Aerial Photography

at least two sets of ponds that were visible from the upper floors of the detached
gloriette, a deer park and a possible valley-side platform for viewing the whole
site (Colvin 1963, 695–7; Taylor 1996; 1998b, 36–7).

There are also other sites, which were discovered many years ago and which
were then interpreted in functional terms. Their arrays of ponds and watercourses
were described as fishponds, breeding-tanks, leats and channels, mill sites and
defensive moats. While these functional interpretations still stand it is now possible to see such sites as having aesthetic elements and thus to reclassify them
as medieval ornamental landscapes. They include the complex arrangements of
ponds and watercourses at the site of the palace of the bishops of Worcester at
Alvechurch, Worcestershire, and the double-moated arrangement, ponds and
surrounding park at Beckley Park, Oxfordshire (Aston 1970–2; Bond 1988 and
1989).

A simpler but related form of ornamental landscape has also been recognised.
One is at the site of the house and deer park of the priory of Wenlock at Great
Oxenhold, Shropshire, where the setting of the house was enhanced by an adja-
cent large lake, the outlines and dam of which survive (Everson 1998).

Another is at the deer park at Harringworth, Northamptonshire. If the documented late thirteenth-century lodge was in the same position as and was similar to the surviving fifteenth-century building there, a stone structure with a first-floor viewing platform, it overlooked both the open centre of the park and an extensive lake (RCHME 1975, Harringworth (9); RCHME 1984, Harringworth (32)). An almost identical instance of a late medieval lodge overlooking a lake within a deer park has been noted at Kelsale, Suffolk (Hoppitt 1992). A very small example, created by the earls of Lincoln in the later thirteenth century, is that at Wadenhoe, Northamptonshire. There, the hill-top, semi-fortified manor house or hunting lodge, lay within and overlooked a tiny 32-acre (13 ha) stone-walled park and associated garden (Brown 1998).

The use of buildings both to support the interpretation of medieval ornamental landscapes and to assist the recognition of similar examples further augments the archaeological evidence. The remarkable landscape at Bodiam Castle, Sussex, had a contrived approach route around lakes, ponds and moats, over bridges as well as terraces, cascades and waterfalls, and a building for viewing the whole from an adjacent hillside. Understanding of the site has been given additional depth by work on the castle itself by Dr Coulson. He has drawn attention to the symbolic and non-military nature of Bodiam, to which the fantastic surroundings were admirably suited (Everson 1996; Coulson 1992). Likewise, the lake, ponds and park at Leeds Castle have much greater meaning and coherence when the significance of the detached thirteenth-century gloriette from which the landscape was viewed is appreciated (Harvey 1981, 103–6; Taylor 1996). On a larger scale, the broad traceried windows of the late fourteenth-century first-floor hall at Kenilworth, Warwickshire, which overtop the curtain walls and give views over the adjoining Chase and across the extensive Mere, indicate that this lake was much more than simply a fishpond (Harvey 1981, 106–7; Taylor 1997, 20; 1998b, 34–5).

Analysis of a building can also lead to the recognition of ornamental landscapes. Old Wardour Castle, Wiltshire, built in 1393, is a non-defensive courtyard house masquerading as a castle (Saunders and Pugh 1991). All of the private apartments were on the south side at first-floor level, overlooking what superficially resembles an eighteenth-century lake. However, the lake is depicted on a seventeenth-century map together with an adjacent deer park containing lines of ponds (WRO). Although almost all trace of this park has been removed by eighteenth-century landscaping and the ponds altered or destroyed, the evidence for an earlier, presumably late fourteenth-century, ornamental landscape is clear.

A similar case is Harewood Castle, Yorkshire. The castle lies in the north-eastern corner of the eighteenth-century park of Harewood House on the south side of the Wharfe valley. It was built, or rebuilt, in about 1367 and has all of its principal rooms on the upper floor as well as a walkway on the roof. Both afforded spectacular views along the lower Wharfe valley and also over most of the adjacent deer park. Archaeological field survey and excavation there have shown that there were also medieval gardens around the castle, which included an array of ponds (Moorhouse 1989; Emery 1996, 339–44; Gaimster *et al.* 1990, 222–3).

Another example of the contribution of buildings to the understanding of these landscapes is Middleham Castle, Yorkshire (Figure 3). In the early fifteenth century its twelfth-century keep and fourteenth-century walls were transformed into an elaborate domestic dwelling. Then, in the late fifteenth century, an addition, the precise form and function of which is not clear, was made to the upper part of the first-floor great hall. It was either a clerestorey to provide extra light to the hall below, or a separate great chamber above the hall (Weaver 1993, 18). If it was the latter, it would have provided spectacular views along Wensleydale through its great windows. But, even if only a clerestorey, the fact that its relatively thin walls are set on corbels on the inside edge of the massive keep walls means that there was a paved walkway protected by a parapet, which allowed the same views. This walkway, and that at Harewood Castle, would have been similar to and in the same tradition as the roof walks on sixteenth- and seventeenth-century country houses (Heward and Taylor 1996, 31 and *passim*). With such a viewing place the various deer parks that lay around Middleham Castle, as well as the traces of gardens and of a former lake or lakes to its south, have added significance. These late

Figure 3. Middleham Castle, Yorkshire, from the east. The twelfth-century keep surmounted by the fourteenth-century addition with its great windows stands within the curtain walls. To the south, left, are the remains of one of the lakes. © Copyright reserved Cambridge University Collection of Aerial Photography

medieval buildings and their associated ornamental landscapes suggest that there may have been similar landscapes in other locations where, because of alterations and destruction or the lack of documentation, there is now no evidence for them. Buildings such as Nunney Castle, Somerset of 1373, based on a French design (Rigold 1956), Maxstoke Castle, Warwickshire of 1346 (Binney 1974; VCH 1947, 133–6), or Kirby Muxloe, Leicestershire of 1480–4 (Pevsner 1992, 192–4), are possible examples.

Another way of identifying medieval ornamental landscapes is through the documentary record. This is particularly valuable when later activities again have obscured the physical remains. The best is the landscape of the royal palace of Woodstock, Oxfordshire, now submerged beneath the eighteenth-century park of Blenheim Palace. Thirteenth-century descriptions and accounts show that the landscape of Woodstock comprised a park, the palace itself, which was approached by a road passing on a causeway between lakes, and the detached lodging and walled garden of Everswell with its own gloriette. As early as the twelfth century the park contained exotic wild animals (Bond and Tiller 1987, 23–7; Harvey 1981, 10, 50, 64, 80). Less certain perhaps is Manorbier Castle in Pembrokeshire, the birthplace of Giraldus Cambrensis (1147–1220). In 1188 he described it as having 'a noble pool of deep water and a very beautiful orchard by it, shut in by a wood of hazels on a rocky eminence' (Harvey 1981, 10). The existence of an adjoining deer park increases the interest here too. Further instances, judging from the documentary details, may have been Clarendon Palace, Wiltshire, and King's Langley manor, Hertfordshire (McLean 1981, 98–9, 102).

One final source of information is illustrative material. There is no recognised contemporary depiction of such landscapes in Britain but two types of illustration exist which show ornamental landscapes and, by providing evidence of botanical arrangements, fill the inevitable lacuna that dependence on archaeological and architectural remains produces. The first is cartographic. There are a number of sixteenth- or early seventeenth-century maps that show landscapes similar to those described. None can be proved to be medieval and some are certainly later. But these maps probably portray traditions as well as layouts that originate in medieval times. The evidence from the seventeenth-century map of Old Wardour Castle has already been noted.

Another example is John Norden's map of Windsor of 1607, which shows the castle and its park (Harvey 1981, plate 40). As is the case with other ornamental landscapes, the castle has an enclosed garden and orchard below and an adjacent deer park with a 'standing' or viewing tower. But the map also shows the drive to the park lodge lined with trees, in effect an avenue, and a U-shaped arrangement of trees. Another example, although certainly of late sixteenth-century date, is Holdenby, Northamptonshire. Two maps of 1580 and 1587 respectively show the parish before and after Sir Christopher Hatton enclosed its common fields and created a deer park as a backdrop to his new house and elaborate gardens. The maps show that a string of small ponds was transformed into a lake and existing woodland had intersecting rides inserted (RCHME, 1981, Holdenby (3, 4, 7), plates 16, 17). The park, woodland and lake could all be seen from the house and gardens on the adjacent hilltop, from a nearby viewing tower or from a prospect mound. Here again are the elements of medieval ornamental landscapes being carried into a new one of the sixteenth century.

The other type of illustration is the illuminated manuscript or painting. This source is largely continental in origin and mainly fourteenth and fifteenth century in date. The backgrounds of many paintings depict what were, presumably, ideal or idealised landscapes. Although this paper is concerned only with medieval ornamental landscapes in Britain, there is no doubt that they were common all over western Europe and that they are well documented. The best-known and the one which, because of its political connections, must have been influential in Britain, was the great castle, gardens, gloriette, lakes and parkland at Hesdin, in Burgundy, of late thirteenth-century date. But John Harvey has collected a number of documentary references, which demonstrate the existence of ornamental landscapes in Europe from at least the twelfth century (Van Buren 1986; Harvey 1981, 10 and *passim*).

Paintings are an additional source for the existence of ornamental landscapes, and they are especially useful for the botanical aspects of these landscapes. For example, in a painting of *The Virgin with Angels* of about 1490 and now in the Capilla Real, Granada, Spain, the foreground figures look out of an upper window, perhaps of a detached gloriette, down into a formal garden backed by a mansion. But beyond is a landscaped park with swans on a meandering river. More interesting is the painting for April in the *Très Riches Heures* created for Jean Duc de Berry in 1409–16 now in the Musée Condé, Chantilly. The background shows the Château de Dourdan and its landscape. The latter has all of the features of a medieval ornamental landscape including parkland with trees arranged in lines or within straight-edged plantations and a lake with boats. In the foreground is a detached gloriette with its own garden (Harvey 1981, plates IVB, VIIA, Musée Conde 1969, plate 5).

Particularly important is the painting of *The Miraculous Draught of Fishes* by Konrad Witz of 1446 now in the Musée d'Art et d'Histoire, Geneva. This is one of the few late medieval paintings said to be of a real landscape, the shores of Lake Geneva. The background includes a hunt within a landscaped park (Hofstötler 1968, 181). Another illustration is a fresco in the chapel of the Palazzo Medici-Ricardi, Florence, *The Journey of the Magi* by Benozzo Gozzoli, of *c.*1459–63 (Gombrich 1997, plate 168). The background shows a landscaped park with the approach to its associated castle lined by trees or shrubs. Further examples can be seen in many late medieval paintings and illuminated manuscripts (e.g. Paul Getty Museum 1997; National Gallery, London).

A particularly important painting because of its British associations is the Donne triptych of 1479–80 by Hans Memlinc, now in the National Gallery, London. The background to the scene of the Virgin and Child with angels, donors and saints includes a towered castle overlooking a pastoral landscape. This contains a meandering river with swans, a watermill, copses and even a horseman riding across open parkland. The interest of the painting for this paper lies in the fact that its 'donor' was Sir John Donne of Kidwelly (d. 1503), soldier, administrator, diplomat and loyal supporter of the House of York. The painting was executed when, after a lifetime of royal service in Europe, Donne settled in England and acquired a landed estate in Buckinghamshire (McFarlane 1971; Campbell 1998, 374–91). Among the offices that he held was keeper of the royal park at Princes Risborough (VCH 1908, 264).

This then is the evidence from a variety of sources for the existence in medieval times of ornamental landscapes with contrived access, displays of water, arranged tree-planting, formal gardens and space for indulging in, and provision for observing, recreational activities such as hunting, fishing and boating. But the identification of such landscapes raises a number of questions. The most important of these are: when were these landscapes created? Who created them? Where did the ideas for them come from? And what was their purpose?

The chronology of ornamental landscapes is not in doubt, even if individual sites cannot be dated closely. If the evidence of Giraldus Cambrensis is accepted then either Manorbier, perhaps mid-twelfth-century, or Stow, which seems to have been in existence by the 1180s, is the earliest known. Woodstock could be even earlier, perhap. 1129–30 when Henry I converted the existing hunting lodge, or even about 1110 when he fenced the park for his menagerie (Stubbs 1887–9, 485). Certainly Woodstock had an ornamental landscape by the 1170s when Henry II installed his mistress, Rosamund de Clifford, in the detached palace and garden at Everswell (Bond and Tiller 1987, 25–6). Although the illustrative evidence for an ornamental landscape at Windsor is post-medieval, the garden there was begun in 1110 and the park existed by 1156 (Harvey 1981, 10, 11; McLean 1981, 92, 99–100). A few other landscapes, including Framlingham, may date from about 1200 or a little later. Another small group of landscapes are of the late thirteenth century and include Leeds Castle, Clun Castle, Shropshire (Morris 1990; Nerk et al. 1993, 279–80; Stamper 1996, 8, plate 4), Odiham, Hampshire (Roberts 1995), and Stokesay, Shropshire (Munby 1993, 10, 34; Taylor 1998a, 5). A larger group are dated only generally to the fourteenth century. Among them are Alvechurch, Bolingbroke Castle, Lincolnshire (Thompson 1966), Braybrooke, Northamptonshire (RCHME 1979, Braybrooke (1)), Shotwick Castle, Cheshire (Figure 4; Everson 1998, 35–6) and Somersham.

However, the majority of ornamental landscapes fall into the second half of the fourteenth century, and among them are those with the most elaborate layouts. This group includes those surrounding the castles at Bodiam, Harewood, Ravensworth, Scotney, Sussex (National Trust 1987), Sheriff Hutton, Yorkshire (Dennison 1997), Wardour, Whorlton, Yorkshire (Everson 1998, 33–5), and perhaps Beckley Park and Bishops' Waltham, Hampshire (Hare 1987; Roberts 1998, 81). The additions to Kenilworth are early fifteenth-century (Taylor 1998a, 4–5), while Middleham Castle and Collyweston, Northamptonshire (RCHME 1975, Collyweston (8)), are of the later fifteenth century. Similar landscapes continued to appear in the sixteenth century, as at Kettleby, Lincolnshire (Everson et al.

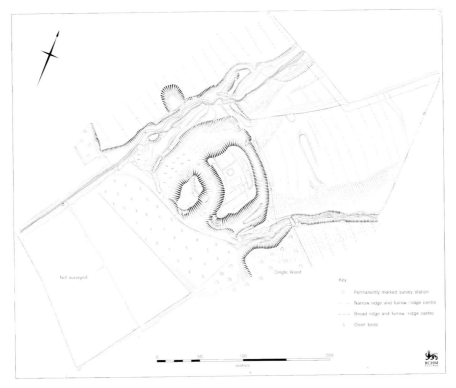

Figure 4. Shotwick Castle, Cheshire, survey plan. The original motte and bailey are clear.
To their north-west are the remains of lakes with a raised approach causeway, from the
north-east, passing between them. For the interpretation, see Everson, 1998, 37.
© Crown copyright. Historic England Archive

1991, Bigby (1)), Baconsthorpe Castle, Norfolk (RCHME, n.d.) and Holdenby. The
dating of European landscapes seems to be as wide as in Britain. The evidence
from paintings is, of course, relatively late as is the documentary evidence for
complex landscapes such as Hesdin. John Harvey's collection of documentary
references to undoubted ornamental landscapes in France begins as early as the
late eleventh century (Harvey 1981, 10; 1991, 438–9).

If ornamental landscapes were being created throughout the medieval period,
who was responsible for them? The crown took a leading role, with Woodstock in
the early to mid twelfth century, Leeds in 1270–90, Odiham in the 1290s, Bolingbroke in the fourteenth century and the Pleasance in the Marsh at Kenilworth
in 1415. The leading aristocratic families were also involved. The Nevilles created
the landscape at Sheriff Hutton in 1382–1400 and probably that at Middleham in
1460–80. The Bigods were responsible for Framlingham and Kelsale in the early
thirteenth century and the FitzAlans at Clun a little later. Major clerics also laid out
landscapes around their palaces and lodges. The bishops of Ely made Somersham
in the fourteenth century. Alvechurch was created by the bishops of Worcester,

Bishops' Waltham by the bishops of Winchester and Great Oxenbold by the prior of Wenlock. Lesser nobles too were involved. The Zouches at Harringworth were only minor aristocracy in the late thirteenth century while Whorlton, despite its sophisticated layout, seems to have been made by a family of modest status. Most remarkable is the landscape around Stokesay Castle, which seems to have been laid out by Laurence de Ludlow in the 1290s to go with his new domestic 'castle'. De Ludlow was no feudal magnate or Marcher lord, but a sheep farmer and a wool merchant, albeit probably the wealthiest in England.

It is possible that institutions too created ornamental landscapes. Byland Abbey, Yorkshire, is surrounded by the remains of water-management structures including the dams of two large ponds, various leats and two water mills. But on the north side of the low ridge on which the abbey stands is the site of a huge lake, the waters of which almost lapped against the walls of the abbey church. This lake was too large for fish-farming, and in any case the abbey had perfectly good fishponds elsewhere. For visitors arriving at Byland from the north, east or west, many on a road crossing a dam, the lake would have reflected the abbey and the buildings themselves would have appeared to be rising out of it (Harrison 1990; Aston 1993, 96–7). The date of this lake is not known but it must be after 1177 when the much-travelled Byland monks finally settled here. There are other monastic houses that have remains similar to those at Byland and which, if re-examined, might also prove to be ornamental landscapes.

Although in general terms the creators of these landscapes extend across a wide range of the upper ranks of medieval society, if the crown and ecclesiastics are excepted, a large proportion of those involved had recently risen or were about to rise in status when their landscapes were laid out. That at Clun Castle was probably created around the time that the FitzAlans became earls of Arundel and thus made the jump from Marcher lords to landed aristocracy. Harewood Castle, and presumably its landscape, were the work of Sir William Aldeburgh who had just become, or soon became, Lord Aldeburgh. Old Wardour Castle was built, and perhaps its landscape laid out, when John, fifth Lord Lovel, unexpectedly inherited. The castle and landscape at Ravensworth were the work of Henry, third Lord FitzHugh, who began as a professional soldier but became Chamberlain to Henry IV and ultimately Treasurer of England. Sheriff Hutton was the work of John, third Lord Neville, and his son Ralph. Although the Nevilles were to rise higher in the fifteenth century it was John who took the family from northern lords to national magnates. He had distinguished military and administrative careers and amassed fortunes from both. His wealth was augmented by two judicious marriages, and with it he enlarged and consolidated his northern estates and rebuilt the family homes at Raby, Northumberland, Middleham and Sheriff Hutton. Ralph, fourth Lord Neville, who completed Sheriff Hutton, was also a soldier, and one of the most powerful men in northern England. In 1396 he married Joan Beaufort, daughter of John of Gaunt, and this brought him yet more wealth and influence. In 1397 he was made Earl of Westmorland by Richard II. Two years later Neville abandoned his king and supported Henry of Lancaster in his bid for the throne. His reward was to be made Marshall of England and to be granted the Honour of Richmond. This was the man for whom the ornamental landscape at Sheriff Hutton was created. In sharp contrast, Laurence de Ludlow, of Stokesay, was a very rich wool merchant yet he too was the most successful of all his family. Bishops may have created landscapes as part of the apparent desire to live away from their see palaces, the locations of which brought them into conflict with the deans and chapters or priors and convents (Thompson 1998, 91).

Where did ornamental landscapes come from? They seem to have been widespread on the continent and in Britain by the twelfth century, perhaps even by the eleventh. As with so many aspects of early medieval life, culture and landscapes, the lack of unequivocal documentation for the centuries before 1100 means that it is difficult to identify either the origins or development of ornamental landscapes (see Lewis et al. 1996, 229–33 for the same problem over villages). Received wisdom is to look to the Islamic world, either directly or via Spain, for many of the elements of European gardens (Harvey 1981, chapters 1–4). But, while the influences are clear, the mechanism for the transfer of ideas into western Europe is not. Early Christendom was always an integrated whole where trade, religion, warfare, literature, art, architecture and family connections all interlocked. To attempt to trace lines of development and places of origin for the ornamental landscapes here described in a poorly documented and little researched period is perhaps beyond the scope of this paper.

There are, however, two hypotheses. Ornamental landscapes could have been an entirely new concept resulting from changing perceptions of art, architecture and literature. Or, and perhaps more likely, they developed gradually from earlier landscapes, which were designed primarily for functional purposes, either economic or defensive. The evolution of ornamental landscapes thus would have mirrored that of their associated buildings as their owners moved from purely defensive concerns to those of status and ostentation. If this was so then their origin lies with the development of the castle, on the Continent (e.g. Teyssot 1998; Zimmer 1998). Even so this hypothetical process may be evident in Britain. An example is Shotwick Castle, Cheshire, situated on the estuary of the River Dee (Figure 4). There the twelfth-century motte-and-bailey was transformed in the fourteenth century. The motte was reduced and given a polygonal crenellated enclosure with towers and a gatehouse. The bailey became an enclosed garden, three lakes were created to the north-east and an elaborate embanked approach drive, around and between the lakes, was devised. In addition, a huge 1,000-acre (405 ha) hunting park was laid out in the surrounding land (Everson 1998, 35–7).

A more pertinent question concerns the function of these ornamental landscapes. There can be no doubt that ornamental landscapes had a utilitarian role. The archaeologists who first recorded some of them were correct in identifying the fishponds and mill sites within them. And even the fishponds did not produce only fish (Roberts 1986). They were also used for keeping wild fowl, driving mills, providing rushes for thatching and were often cultivated in a complex fish/arable rotation (RCHME 1979, lix, Braybrooke (1)). Park woodland also was managed to

afford a variety of resources including grazing on wood pasture, pannage, coppic-
ing and pollarding for hurdles and fuel, timber trees for building materials, and
food, especially game (Rackham, 1986, chapters 5 and 6). Deer parks too were not
just for hunting. They provided food from deer, grazing for cattle and horses and
often had rabbit warrens in or adjacent to them.

But there were other motives for ornamental landscapes. Obvious ones are
those followed by gardeners and landscape designers through the centuries.
That is to adapt or mould the landscape in order to produce pleasurable views,
to enhance and beautify the settings of dwellings and to gain delight from the
deliberate arrangement of plants. Certainly these reasons seemed obvious to
this writer when ornamental landscapes were initially recognised (Taylor 1989).
And there is little doubt that ornamental landscapes were indeed, in part at least,
intended to give enjoyment to the viewer. Further, there are numerous references
in medieval literature to the pleasure that medieval people gained from plants,
gardens and landscapes (Harvey 1981, *passim*). From these it is clear that landscapes, both natural and ornamental, were appreciated in medieval times, as they
are today.

Another use of ornamental landscapes was for recreation. A major activity in
many such landscapes was hunting, although only a few of the many medieval
deer parks were ornamental landscapes. Indeed the parks of the bishops of Winchester have been described as both 'playgrounds and larders' (Roberts 1998). But
medieval hunting was far from being merely the pursuit of deer and other animals. As much contemporary literature makes clear, it was just one of the aspects
that made up medieval culture. Hunting was a way in which physical skills were
displayed and helped to prepare a weapon-bearing class for warfare. As such it
ennobled the participants by the display of the skills involved. Hunting was also
a social occasion. Hunting parties sometimes included ladies, servants with food
and furniture, and even chaplains with tented chapels and portable altars. It had
its own ceremonies, etiquette and rituals (Thiebaux 1967). Seen in this light, the
association of deer parks with ornamental landscapes and their standings, gloriettes, lodges with gardens and other forms of observation platforms, even of a
temporary nature, is hardly surprising (Myers 1969, 1158).

Other pastimes that took place in ornamental landscapes included boating
and fishing. Boats are depicted on the many late medieval illustrations, and there
are also archaeological remains. The detached Pleasance of 1415 at Kenilworth
could only be approached by boat, and indeed had its own wharf or dock at the
end of a short canal linking it to the great Mere. At Framlingham a possible landing stage or 'harbour' on the edge of the mere below the castle has been identified.

An equally significant aspect of ornamental landscapes is that of symbolism
and imagery. These were deeply embedded in medieval culture and have been
re-examined recently in the context of gardens and ornamental landscapes and
of their associated buildings (Everson 1998, 32–3, 37; Stocker 1993; Stocker and
Stocker 1996). Many of the 'castles' associated with ornamental landscapes, especially those from the late thirteenth century onwards, are hardly castles at all. Or

at least their military aspect is only a minor part of their function. Many seem to have a meaning that has more to do with imagery or symbolism. Both Whorlton and Bodiam Castles, and thus perhaps their landscapes, are emblems of chivalry. More complex, as Paul Everson has shown, are the networks of interlocked symbolism that occur. The swans at Stow perhaps indicate sincerity and thus purity and grace that might invoke the Virgin. But they could also be 'part of the teeming variety and wonder of all creation: they were routinely part of the intertwined imagery of hunting rituals and courtly love as well as evoking the early legend of the Swan Knight with its dynastic significance'. The adoption of the swan as the emblem of Bishop (St) Hugh is also noteworthy (Everson 1998, 32–3). Much the same is true of the depiction of other animals, and in particular deer and rabbits, in many illustrations of ornamental landscapes as well as in numerous legends (Harvey 1981, plate MB; Savage 1928; Stocker and Stocker 1996).

The symbolism of water in ornamental landscapes is also important, whether it be part of the complexities associated with mirrors or reflections, or in the relation of water to Paradise. The contrast between 'rocky' landscapes and watery landscapes, emphasised by Giraldus Cambrensis at Manorbier, may be a precursor of the *paysage moralisé* – the path of virtue is rocky but that of vice runs through pleasant, well-watered orchards.

Related to symbolism was status and fashion. All upper levels of medieval society displayed their position, actual, perceived or intended, through their way of life, servants, marriages, heraldry, buildings, and perhaps their landscapes too. As was pointed out many years ago, even the ubiquitous medieval moated sites were as much a fashionable status symbol for the middle orders of medieval society as castles were for its aristocracy (Taylor 1972). A landscaped park would enhance the setting of an actual or pseudo-castle, impress visitors and illustrate taste and wealth just as an eighteenth-century park did for a Georgian country house. A contrived approach around and across lakes with towers reflected in sheets of water would do the same.

Fashion must also have played its part. The numbers of late fourteenth-century ornamental landscapes can hardly be fortuitous. Travel, commerce, war, art and literature must all have contributed to the Europe-wide fashion for ornamental landscapes. Certainly some of the late medieval semi-fortified domestic structures have close European parallels that were probably derived from their owners' direct experience. The windows of the lower hall at Harewood Castle are comparable with ones of an identical date in northern France (Emery 1996, 340), while the whole design of Wardour Castle seems to be based on the Château de Concressault in France of the same date. It has been suggested that it was Lord Lovat's presence there during the Hundred Years War that lay behind the use of the design at Wardour (Saunders and Pugh 1991, 3). If such architectural connections existed, then so could designs and layouts for landscapes even if, as yet, these latter connections have not been identified.

Two further points about ornamental landscapes are worth making. The first is the influence of these landscapes on later ones, particularly in Britain. These landscapes continued to be created until at least the late sixteenth century, and from the seventeenth century there is a well-documented tradition of landscape design, which extends through to the nineteenth century. The effect both of the tradition and of the survival of medieval landscapes on later ornamental ones has not yet been studied but it may have been considerable.

The final point about ornamental landscapes is one of definition. This paper has been concerned with those sites that, in the judgement of the writer, are unequivocal examples of ornamental landscapes. But where does the definition of ornamental landscapes begin and end? On it April 1268 Gilbert de Clare (1243–95), Earl of Gloucester and Hertford, Lord of Glamorgan, later son-in-law of Edward I and then only twenty-five years old, began building Caerphilly Castle in Glamorgan. When it was finished it was probably 'the finest castle in the English realm, at least rivalling, perhaps exceeding, the greatest of Edward I's castles in North Wales …' (Allen Brown 1989, 67). Its concentric-towered inner ward and outer bailey lie first within its own moat and then centrally within a great lake. The latter was created by the construction of a moated dam with its own curtain walls and towers and connected to a similarly fortified and moated barbican. Between them they controlled the water supply and protected the north and south approaches to the castle. To the west, also within the lake, a walled island outwork protected that side. When completed the castle was, militarily, the most sophisticated defence work in Britain, possibly in western Europe, and could easily have withstood any besieging army (Renn 1997).

But Caerphilly was much more than a castle. In the 1280s a great vaulted D-shaped tower was added on the sunny south side of the middle ward, forming part of a group of sumptuous rooms for a great lord. Elsewhere were all the necessary domestic offices and lodgings for the household of a feudal magnate. Later, after Gilbert de Clare's death, a magnificent great hall was added, probably by Hugh Despenser the Younger, who married Gilbert's elder daughter and thus acquired the best of the Clare lands. Caerphilly was thus a statement of its owner's position in contemporary society. Gilbert de Clare was the greatest of the distinguished family of that name. The Clares had begun in England, in the late eleventh century, with lands in Kent and East Anglia granted to them by William the Conqueror. Thereafter the family marched, metaphorically and literally, westwards, founding towns, establishing castles, endowing religious houses, becoming Marcher lords and Irish conquerors, and all the time rising in wealth, status and influence. Hugh Despenser too was a member of a family that aspired to greatness. Edward II made him earl of Winchester in 1322, although he was hanged for treason in 1326.

Caerphilly, with its water features, wooded islands, contrived approaches, views from its towers, luxurious apartments and even the so-called sally ports into the lake from whence boating parties could have been launched, is the closest there is to a medieval ornamental landscape without actually being one. Or is it indeed an ornamental landscape?

Bibliography

Allen Brown, R. (1989) *Castles from the Air*, Cambridge.

Aston, M. A. (1970–2) 'Earthworks at the bishop's palace, Alvechurch, Worcestershire', *Transactions of the Worcestershire Archaeological Society*, 3rd series 3, 55–9.

—— (1993) *Monasteries*, London.

Beresford, M. W. and St Joseph, J. K. S. (1979) *Medieval England: An Aerial Survey*, 2nd edition, Cambridge.

Binney, M. (1974) 'Maxstoke Castle, Warwickshire', *Country Life* 155, 842–5, 930–3.

Blood, N. K. and Taylor, C. C. (1992) 'Cawood: an archiepiscopal landscape', *Yorkshire Archaeological Journal* 64, 83–102.

Bond, J. (1988 and 1989) 'The medieval park at Beckley, Oxfordshire', *Oxfordshire Local History*, 3.1, 1–13; 3.2, 47–61.

Bond, J. and Tiller, K. eds. (1987) *Blenheim: Landscape for a Palace*, Stroud.

Brown, A. E. (1998) 'The medieval landscape', in *The Story of Wadenhoe*, ed. R. Duffey, Wadenhoe History Group. 42–50.

Brown, A. E. and Taylor, C. C. (1991) 'A relict garden at Linton, Cambridgeshire', *Proceedings of the Cambridge Antiquarian Society* 80, 62–7.

Brown, M. and Pattison, P. (1997) *Framlingham Mere, Suffolk*, RCHME Field Survey Report: NMR no. TM26 SE1.

Campbell, L. (1998) *The Fifteenth Century Netherlandish Schools*, London.

Colvin, H. M. ed. (1963) *History of the King's Works*, Vol. II, HMSO, London.

Coulson, C. (1992) 'Some analysis of the castle at Bodiam, East Sussex', in *Medieval Knighthood* 4, ed. C. Harper-Bill and R. Harvey (Woodbridge, 1992), 51–107.

Dennison, E. (1997) 'Sheriff Hutton Castle', *Archaeological Journal* 154, 291–6.

Dimcock, J. F. ed. (1887) *Giraldus Cambrensis*, Vol. 7, Longman, London, 73.

Douie, D. L. and Farmer, H. ed. (1962) *The Life of St Hugh of Lincoln*, Vol. 1, Thomas Nelson, London.

Emery, A. (1996) *Greater Medieval Houses of England and Wales 1300–1500*, Vol. 1, Cambridge.

Everson, P. L. (1996) 'Bodiam Castle, East Sussex: castle and designed landscape', *Château Gaillard: etudes de castellologie medievale* 16, 79–84.

—— (1998) 'Delightfully surrounded with woods and ponds', field evidence for medieval gardens in England', in *There by Design*, ed. P. Pattison, RCHME, London.

Everson, P. L., Taylor, C. C. and Dunn, C. J. (1991) *Change and Continuity*, HMSO, London.

Gaimster, D. R. M., Margeson, S. and Hurley, M. (1990) 'Medieval Britain and Ireland in 1989', *Medieval Archaeology* 34, 222–3.

Gombrich, E. H. (1997) *The Story of Art*, London.

Hare, J. N. (1987) *Bishops Waltham Palace*, English Heritage, London.

Harrison, S. A. (1990) *Byland Abbey*, English Heritage, London.

Harvey, J. (1974) *Early Nurserymen*, Chichester.

—— (1981) *Medieval Gardens*, London.

—— (1990) 'Pleasance', in *The Oxford Companion to Gardens*, ed. G. and S. Jellicoe, Oxford, 438–9.

Heward, J. and Taylor, R. F. (1996) *The Country Houses of Northamptonshire*, RCHME, Swindon.

Hofstätler, H. H. (1968) *The Art of the Late Middle Ages*, London.

Hoppitt, R. (1992) 'A study of the development of parks in Suffolk from the eleventh century', unpublished Ph.D. thesis, University of East Anglia.

Lewis, C., Mitchell-Fox, P. and Dyer, C. (1997) *Village, Hamlet and Field*, Manchester.

Lofthouse, C. (1997) *Ravensworth Castle and environs*, RCHME Field Survey Report: NMR no. NZ10 NW1.

McFarlane, K. B. (1971) *Hans Memling*, Oxford.

McLean, T. (1981) *Medieval English Gardens*, London.

Moorhouse, S. (1989) 'Earthworks around Harewood Castle, West Yorkshire', *Council for British Archaeology Forum* (Newsletter of CBA Group 4), 4–7.

Morris, R. K. (1990) *Clun Castle, Shropshire: an Outline History*, Herefordshire Archaeology Series 69.

Munby, J. (1993) *Stokesay Castle*, English Heritage, London.

Musée Condé, Chantilly (1969) *Les Tres Riches Heures du Duc de Berry*, London.

Myers, A. R. ed. (1969) *English Historical Documents IV 1327–1485*, London.

National Gallery, London *The Virgin and Child* by Lorenzo di Credi (1480–1500), acc. no. 593.

National Trust (1987) *Scotney Castle*, National Trust, London.

Nerk, B. S., Margeson, S. and Hurley, M. (1993) 'Medieval Britain and Ireland in 1992', *Medieval Archaeology* 37, 279–80.

Paul Getty Museum (1997) *Illuminated Manuscripts*, London.

Pevsner, N., Williamson, E. and Brandwood, G. (1992) *Leicestershire and Rutland*, London.

Raby, F. J. E. and Reynolds, P. K. Baillie (1987) *Framlingham Castle*, English Heritage, London.

Rackham, O. (1986) *The History of the Countryside*, London.

Renn, D. (1997) *Caerphilly Castle*, Cadw, Cardiff.

Royal Commission on the Historical Monuments of England (RCHME) (1975) *Northamptonshire* Vol. I, HMSO, London.

— (1979) *Northamptonshire* Vol. II, HMSO, London.

— (1981) *Northamptonshire* Vol. III, HMSO, London.

— (1984) *Northamptonshire* Vol. VI, HMSO, London.

— (no date) *Baconsthorpe Castle, Norfolk*, Field Survey Reports: NMR no. TG13 NW1, 15 and 16.

Rigold, S. E. (1956) *Nunney Castle*, HMSO, London.

Roberts, E. (1986) 'The Bishop of Winchester's fishponds in Hampshire 1150–1400', *Proceedings of the Hampshire Field Club* 42, 123–38.

— (1995) 'Edward III's lodge at Odiham, Hampshire', *Medieval Archaeology* 39, 91–106.

— (1998) 'The Bishop of Winchester's deer parks in Hampshire 1200–1400', *Proceedings of the Hampshire Field Club* 44, 67–86.

Rose, P. (1994) 'The medieval garden at Tintagel', *Cornish Archaeology* 33, 170–82.

Ryder, P. F. (1979) 'Ravensworth Castle, North Yorkshire', *Yorkshire Archaeological Journal* 51, 81–100.

Saunders, A. D. and Pugh, R. B. (1991) *Old Wardour Castle*, English Heritage, London.

Savage, H. L. (1928) 'The significance of the hunting scenes in *Sir Gawain and the Green Knight*', *Journal of English and German Philology* 22, 38–46.

Stamper, P. (1996) *Historic Parks and Gardens of Shropshire*, Shrewsbury.

Stocker, D. (1993) 'The shadow of the general's armchair', *Archaeological Journal* 149, 415–20.

Stocker, D. and Stocker, M. (1996) 'Sacred profanity. The theology of rabbit-breeding and the symbolic landscape of the warren', *World Archaeology* 28.2, 264–72.

Stubbs, W. ed. (1887–9) *Gesta Regum* Vol. 11, Public Record Office, London.

Taylor, C. C. (1972) 'Medieval moats in Cambridgeshire', in *Archaeology in the Landscape*, ed. P. J. Fowler, John Baker, London, 237–48.

— (1983) *The Archaeology of Gardens*, Aylesbury.

— (1989) 'Somersham Palace, Cambs: a medieval landscape for pleasure?', in *From Cornwall to Caithness*, ed. M. Bowden, D. Mackay and P. Topping, British Archaeological Reports, British Series 209, 211–24.

— (1996) 'Leeds Castle Park', unpublished field report for Leeds Castle Limited (copy in National Monuments Record).

— (1997) 'The place of analytical fieldwork in garden archaeology', *Journal of Garden History* 17.1, 18–25.

— (1998a) 'From recording to recognition', in *There by Design*, ed. P. Pattison, RCHME, Swindon, 1–6.

— (1998b) *Parks and Gardens of Britain*, Edinburgh.

Teyssot, J. (1998) 'Les fortresses urbaines', *Château Gaillard* 18, 231–8.

Thiebaux, M. (1967) 'The medieval chase', *Speculum* 42, 260–73.

Thompson, M. (1966) 'The origins of Bolingbroke Castle', *Medieval Archaeology* 10, 152–8.

— (1998) *Medieval Bishops' Houses in England and Wales*, Aldershot.

Van Buren, A. H. (1986) 'Reality and literary romance in the park of Hesdin', in *Dumbarton Oaks Colloquium in the History of the Landscap*. 9, ed. E. B. MacDougall, 117–34.

Victoria History of the Counties of England (VCH) (1908) *Buckinghamshire*, Vol. II, London.

— (1947) *Warwickshire*, Vol. IV, Oxford.

Weaver, J. (1993) *Middleham Castle*, English Heritage, London.

W R O (Wiltshire Record Office), undated seventeenth-century map of Wardour, Wiltshire.

Zimmer, J. (1998) 'Zur wahl des burgbauplatzes', *Château Gaillard* 18, 257–67.

17
Otherworld Castles in Middle English Arthurian Romance

Muriel A. Whitaker

Castles in Middle English Arthurian romance may vary from Malory's generally undifferentiated 'fair' castles to the *Gawain*-poet's splendid Hautdesert, which is as real as the castles at Windsor and Carlisle and as ideal as those in Gothic illuminations, with their pink stone walls, azure pinnacles, and gilded gables. Whenever it appears in romance, the castle is a hierarchic image implying the existence of a mythic aristocratic society unhampered by the constraints of everyday life. The realistic aspects are drawn from contemporary models. The supernatural aspects are likely to reflect motifs in Celtic tales of heroes' journeys to the Otherworld.

When the hero of *Sir Orfeo*,[1] a Middle English metrical romance (*c*.1300), follows a cavalcade of splendid ladies through a rocky barrier, he emerges into a brilliantly lit green plain dominated by a crystal castle. Its hundred towers are wonderfully high, its buttresses pure gold, its vaulting elaborately enameled, its spacious apartments radiant with precious stones, its poorest pillar of burnished gold. No man might describe or imagine 'the riche werk that ther was wrought'. The formulaic combination of crystal, gold, and jewels in a castle of consummate beauty and brilliance indicates that Sir Orfeo has entered a fairyland of marvelous beauty.

The Otherworld journey is an archetype of early Irish literature.[2] Teigue Mac Cian, traveling across the seas, finds a silver fortress with posts of burnished gold, corridors of varicolored marble, a silver-floored hall with golden doors and diamond-studded walls.[3] Finn and his companions, accepting the invitation of a supernatural host to enter his *sidh* (a *faerie* mound), are greeted by a hospitable company seated on crystal benches. They are entertained with harp music played by the host's beautiful daughter, served the newest meat and the oldest liquor, and given a marvelous cup that produces whatever drink is desired. An essential

---

[1] *Sir Orfeo*, ed. A. J. Bliss (Oxford, 1966).
[2] Particularly useful in analyzing motifs are T. Peete Cross, *Motif-Index of Early Irish Literature* (Bloomington, 1939), and D. Bruce Spaan's illuminating doctoral dissertation, 'The Otherworld in Early Irish Literature' (Unpublished Ph.D, Thesis, University of Michigan, 1980). See also H. R. Patch, *The Other World According to Descriptions in Medieval Literature* (1950; rpt New York, 1970). Translations of early Irish literature that I have consulted include M. Dillon, *Early Irish Literature* (Chicago, 1948); J. Gantz, *Early Irish Myths and Sagas* (Harmondsworth, 1981); R. Meger, *The Voyage of Bran*, 2 vols (Dublin, 1895–7); S. H. O'Grady, *Silva Gadelica*, 2 vols (London, 1892); T. P. Cross and C. H. Slover, *Ancient Irish Tales* (1936; rpt New York, 1969).
[3] On marvelous castles made of crystal and precious metal, see Cross, *Motif Index*, F 163.3; and Patch, 'The Otherworld', 56, n. 67.

part of the happy Otherworld is the beautiful, generous *fée* who is all too willing
to become a mortal's mistress. Ruad Mac Rigdon not only enjoys making love to
nine gorgeous girls on nine successive nights but also receives from each one a
golden cup as his reward. The sacrifice involved in returning to the natural world
is expressed by Dunlang O'Hartugan just before the Battle of Clontarf:

> 'Alas, O king,' said Dunlang, 'the delight that I have abandoned for thee is greater
> … namely, life without death, without cold, without thirst, without hunger, with-
> out decay; beyond any delight of the delights of the earth to me.'[4]

However, the Celtic Otherworld is not only a Land of Promise; it is also a Land
of the Dead. Its ambivalence is apparent to Sir Orfeo when he enters the castle
gate; for inside the crystal walls is a horrifying company of mutilated mortals,
some without heads, some without arms, some wounded, some mad, some stran-
gled, some drowned, some burned, some suffering the pains of childbirth. These
people who have been snatched from the natural world at noon provide a striking
contrast to the powerful King Pluto and his 'fair and swete' Queen whose crown
and clothes dazzle Orfeo's eyes. According to A. C. L. Brown, the Happy Otherworld (called Tír Taingiri, 'The Land of Promise'; Tír na noc, 'The Land of the
Young'; Mag Mell, 'The Delightful Plain') is never far from Tír na Fer, the Dolorous Tower.[5] Derived, as Brown suggests, from Pluto's flame-protected iron tower,
which Virgil describes in the *Aeneid* (Bk. VI, ll. 548–55), the Dolorous Tower is
an abode of the dead, controlled by the Fomorians. An ugly, evil race who drove
the supernatural Tuatha Dé Danann into the mounds and islands, these giants
represent darkness and winter. When they themselves were displaced by the Sons
of Mil, they also retreated to the realms of the occult.[6] Their dark towers, containing dungeons, ferocious animals, piles of bones, and impaled heads, signify the
oppression and death that the hero must confront. Brown associates the color
red with the Fomorians and their towers, an attribute that is of some importance
when these giant warriors reappear as the hero's opponent in Arthurian romance.[7]

If fairyland is aesthetically and morally ambiguous, its location is equally
confusing. It may be identified specifically with Ireland (as it is in the Welsh
Spoils of Annwfn), with the Isle of Man,[8] or even with Spain. It may be located
inside a hollow hill or on an island or may suddenly materialize as a castle in a
thick forest. It is cut off from this world by a Perilous Passage. Transition usually

[4] J. H. Todd, *The War of the Gaedhil with the Gaill* (London, 1867), 173, quoted by Spaan, 'The Otherworld', 187.
[5] A. C. L. Brown, *The Origin of the Grail Legend* (New York, 1943), p. 16. For a complete list of Otherworld names, see Spaan, 'The Otherworld', Appendix IV, 428–9.
[6] On the complex interrelationships of Irish gods of the Underworld, Celtic gods of Gaul who survived in Irish mythology, and the gods of the supernatural faerie world, see M. Dillon and N. Chadwick, *The Celtic Realms* (1967; rpt London, 1973), 173ff. The authors conclude that the writers of later legends called them all Tuatha Dé Danann. On the Fomorians (Fomoiri) as a type of evil oppressor, see 187–8.
[7] Dillon and Chadwick, *The Celtic Realms*, 18, n. 7; 89–90; 98–9; 109–10; 356–8; and Cross, *Motif-Index*, F 178.1.
[8] See Cross, *Motif-Index*, F 130–7; and Spaan, 'The Otherworld', 4, n. 2.

involves some form of water: a druidical mist; a shower of hail, rain, or snow; a lake; a tumultuous river; the sea. In addition, a thick forest, an icy mountain, a fiery rampart, or a metal palisade may bar the way.

Even in the late Middle Ages, the idea of a third Otherworld was not inadmissable. Having met the fairy queen by the Eildon Tree and mounted her supernatural steed, Thomas the Rhymer is shown three roads. The narrow road beset with thorns and briars is the path of righteousness, the wide road across the plain is the path of wickedness, and the bonny road among the hills is the road to fair Elfland.[9] The ways to Heaven and Hell may be discovered by choice, that to Elfland by arbitrary direction only. The chosen hero is summoned by a dwarf,[10] a giant, a *fée*, or a guide animal such as a deer or hound, for such purposes as education, testing, lifting a curse, defending an Otherworld character, or gaining a mistress or wife. Transition is most easily effected at Samhain (1 November), the end and beginning of the Celtic year, for then the barriers disappear and the established order is dissolved 'as a prelude to its recreation in a new period of time'.[11] The idea of regeneration is implicit in the literary Otherworld journey.

The definition of Otherworld castles cannot be separated from the appearance and functions of their inhabitants since the hero's journey is motivated by a predetermined relationship that an Otherworld man or woman has planned. Cuchulainn is the Irish hero whose adventures most closely resemble Gawain's, motivated as they are by a desire for personal and tribal honor and prestige. The ritualistic pattern of his life includes an unusual conception in an Otherworld fortress, youthful successes against supernatural opponents, and instruction in battle skills from the warrior woman Scáthach (Shadow), who is a prophetess. Two adventures in particular, *The Wasting Sickness of Cuchulainn* (Serglige Con Culainn) and *Bricriu's Feast* (Fled Bricrend), are sources of romance materials.[12] Having offended the *fées* LiBan and Fand (appearing as birds) by trying to shoot them, Cuchulainn is overcome by a wasting sickness. The spell can only be broken, LiBan tells him, if he will help King Labraid to free his *sidh* from three tyrants. As a reward, he will receive gold, silver, plenty of wine, and the love of LiBan's sister, Fand. Unwilling to accept a woman's invitation, Cuchulainn twice sends his charioteer with LiBan to spy out the situation. Loeg reports that in the king's house there are 'Fifty beds on the right side / and fifty on the floor; / fifty beds on the left side / and fifty on the dais / Bedposts of bronze, / white gilded pillars; / the candle before them / a bright precious stone.' There is also a vat of mead that is always full. As for Fand,

[9] H. C. Sargent and G. L. Kittredge (ed.), *English and Scottish Popular Ballads* (Boston, MA, 1904), no. 37, 63–6.
[10] See V. J. Harwood, *The Dwarfs of Arthurian Romance and Celtic Tradition* (Leiden, 1958).
[11] P. MacCana, *Celtic Mythology* (London, 1970), 127. On the significance of Samhain, see also Spaan, 'The Otherworld', 409; Dillon and Chadwick, *The Celtic Realms*, 185–6; A. Rees and B. Rees, *Celtic Heritage: Ancient Tradition in Ireland and Wales* (London, 1961), 89–92.
[12] For a detailed study of English and French analogues related to Bricriu's Feast, see G. L. Kittredge, A *Study of Gawain and the Green Knight* (1916; rpt Gloucester, MA, 1960).

> she appears with yellow hair
> and great beauty and charm.
> Fair and wondrous
> her conversation with everyone,
> And the hearts of all men break
> with love and affection for her.[13]

Persuaded, Cuchulainn makes the Otherworld journey at Samhain, defeats the tyrants, spends a month as Fand's lover (in the absence of her husband, the shape-shifting god, Manandan), and returns to his wife.

Bricriu's Feast contains the Irish version of the Beheading Game (Champion's Bargain), also found in *Sir Gawain and the Green Knight* and *The Turk and Gawain*. Having prepared a sumptuous feast for the Ulstermen, Bricriu purposely stirs up trouble by urging each of three heroes, Loegaire Buadach, Conall Cer nach, and Cuchulainn, to claim the champion's portion. After a series of tests, which Cuchulainn inevitably wins but which the others refuse to accept as conclusive, they are sent for judgment to CuRoi, the enigmatic king of a mysterious citadel, which revolves nightly under his spell.[14] As a *gruagach*,[15] a form assumed by the supernatural king when he is testing and judging a hero, CuRoi later appears at the High King's court:

> It seemed to them that there was not in all Ulaid a warrior half as tall. His appearance was frightful and terrifying: a hide against his skin, and a dun cloak round him, and a great bushy tree overhead where a winter shed for thirty calves could fit. Each of his two yellow eyes was the size of an ox-cauldron; each finger was as thick as a normal man's wrist. The tree trunk in his left hand would have been a burden for twenty yoked oxen; the axe in his right hand, whence had gone three fifties of glowing metal pieces, had a handle that would have been a burden for a team of oxen, yet it was sharp enough to cut hairs against the wind.

He announces that he has never found a man to keep his bargain, but since the Ulstermen 'surpass the hosts of every land in anger and prowess and weaponry, in rank and pride and dignity, in honor and generosity and excellence', let one of them keep faith. The three rival champions agree to cut off the churl's head, and on each occasion the decapitated churl rises and walks away, leaving the house full of blood. Only Cuchulainn, who has smashed the head into fragments, waits to receive the return blow:

> He stretched his neck until it reached the other side of the block. ... The churl brought the axe down, then, upon Cu Chulaind's neck – with the blade turned up.[16]

---

[13] Gantz, *Early Irish Myths and Sagas*, 167–8.
[14] On revolving castles, see Patch, *The Other World*, 56, n. 68; and Cross, *Motif-Index*, F 163.1.1.
[15] A *gruagach* is a huge, surly peasant; also called a *bachlach*. Cf. Spaan, 'The Otherworld', 411.
[16] Gantz, *Early Irish Myths and Sagas*, 251–5.

CuRoi declares the hero supreme in courage, skill, and honor; he is the rightful possessor of the champion's portion.

In summary, these Irish tales provide a number of motifs associated with the visit to an Otherworld castle: a messenger who summons the hero by challenging him or asking his help; a perilous passage marked at the point of transition by some form of water; a threatening giant with magical powers who lives in a demonic castle; a hospitable host who is a shape-shifter; a sumptuous feast where the hero is provided with whatever food and drink he most desires; a magical cup; a powerful woman (sometimes old and ugly) who teaches and tests the hero; and a beautiful, amorous young woman who gives rewards in the form of sexual gratification and magical gifts. If a substantial number of these motifs occur in certain Middle English romances, we may speculate that a journey to fairyland underlies the adventure, rationalized though it may be. An understanding of the motifs' significance in Irish literature provides clues to interpreting the later works.

The Turk and Gawain (*c*.1500), *The Carl of Carlisle* (fourteenth or early fifteenth century), *Sir Gawain and the Green Knight* (*c*.1400), Malory's 'Tale of Sir Gareth', and various adventures associated with Lancelot in Malory's *Morte Darthur* (1470) all exemplify the use of a strange castle as a means of revealing the hero's character. With the exception of the Lancelot material, none of these romances has a known source, though numerous analogues have been found in Old French romances. Kittredge suggests that at least one, *The Turk and Gawain*, is an Irish folk tale that came to England by way of Scotland.[17] It is unnecessary here to account for the process by which the matter of Celtic myth and saga reached the authors of Middle English romance except to say that R. S. Loomis's theory of minstrel transmission from Wales and Cornwall to Brittany seems plausible,[18] as does the link between Breton minstrels and French court poets.[19] The close cultural relationships between France and England in the twelfth and thirteenth centuries would have furthered the process of transmission. If, as Michael J. Bennett proposes, a middle-class poet from the remote Northwest of England was one of the court retainers who accompanied Richard II to Ireland, then the author of *Sir Gawain and the Green Knight* might have encountered the Cuchulainn saga at first hand.[20]

Of the romances under discussion, *The Turk and Gawain*, though the latest in date, is the most primitive in form.[21] It survives uniquely and partially in that

---

[17] Kittredge, *A Study of Gawain*, 280.

[18] See 'The Oral Diffusion of the Arthurian Legend', in *Arthurian Literature in the Middle Ages*, ed. R. S. Loomis (Oxford, 1959), 52–63; 'By What Route did the Romantic Tradition of Arthur Reach the French?', in *Studies in Medieval Literature: A Memorial Collection of Essays by Roger Sherman Loomis* (New York, 1970), originally published in *Modern Philology*, 33 (1936), 225–38.

[19] Cf. R. S. Loomis, *Arthurian Tradition and Chrétien de Troyes* (New York, 1949). For a contrary view regarding Celtic influences in Chrétien's work, see C. Luttrell, *The Creation of the First Arthurian Romance* (London, 1974).

[20] M. J. Bennett, 'Courtly Literature and Northwest. England in the Later Middle Ages', in *Court and Poet*, ed. Glyn S. Burgess (Liverpool, 1981), 75–6.

[21] The text is printed in Sir Frederic Madden's *Syr Gawayne: A Collection of Ancient Romance-Poems by Scottish and English Authors Relating to that Celebrated Knight of the Round Table* (London,

section of the Percy Folio which Sir Humphrey Pitt's housemaid was using to light her infamous fire. About 288 lines constituting half the poem are lost, but the work's archetypal nature makes it possible to reconstruct the contents. A dwarf (Turk) enters Arthur's hall while the king and court are eating and issues a challenge to anyone who is so hardy as 'to give a buffet and take another'. Gawain rides off with the Turk so that he may receive the return blow at a later date in a different place. The challenge turns out to be a device for acquiring the assistance of a champion as well as ending a spell. According to Kittredge, this romance has developed from the folk tale type of hero who is assisted by an animal in the completion of seemingly impossible tasks.[22] Ackerman suggests as sources a version of the Beheading Game and a story about a king's visit to his rival's palace.[23] Neither mentions that the work describes an Otherworld journey in which the hero encounters more than one form of the mysterious country.

Gawain proceeds northward for two days with the dwarf, who taunts him about his loss of dainty food and, like the guide in *Sir Gawain and the Green Knight*, emphasizes the terrors that lie ahead. They approach a hill that opens to admit them, then closes again – obviously the entrance to a *sidh*. At the same time, a sudden shower of snow and rain descends, marking the transition from one world to another. Gawain's remark that 'Such wether saw I never afore / In noe stead where I have beene' suggests the uniqueness of the experience. Having completed the perilous passage, they come upon a richly decorated castle in which a feast has been prepared – 'All manner of meates & drinks there was / For groomes that might it againe.' As Gawain is by now extremely hungry, he wants to fall to, but is prevented from doing so by the Turk. *Geasa* related to eating *faerie* food are common.[24] What surprises the hero even more than the prohibition is the fact that 'I see neither man nor maid / Woman nor child soe free.'

This splendid castle with its sumptuous feast and strange emptiness recalls an episode in *The Voyage of Maeldune*[25] when the starving voyagers reach an unknown island, on which is a marvelous dun

> and a high wall around the dun, as white as if it was built of burned lime ... When Maeldune and his men went into the best of the houses they saw no one in it but a little cat.[26]

The palace is decorated with jeweled brooches, collars of gold and silver, and great swords. In one room is a whole roasted ox and large vessels of wine that the

    1839; rpt New York, 1971), 243–55.
[22] Kittredge, *A Study of Gawain*, 274.
[23] R. W. Ackerman, 'English Rimed and Prose Romances', in *Arthurian Literature in the Middle Ages*, 496–7.
[24] Cf. J. R. Reinhard, *The Survival of Geis in Medieval Romance* (Halle, 1933), 92–5; and Cross, *Motif-Index*, C 211.1.
[25] According to Patch, *The Other World*, 31, some scholars date the work as early as the first half of the ninth century, others as late as the beginning of the eleventh century.
[26] Lady Gregory, *The Voyages of Saint Brendan the Navigator and Stories of the Saints of Ireland* (Gerrards Cross, 1973), 59–60.

travelers consume. But when one of the brothers takes a necklace, the cat leaps through him and burns him to ashes. Such a fate awaits those who flout the *geis* laid on a place.

The next stage of Gawain's adventure involves traveling across water to 'a castle faire / Such a one he never saw yare / Noe where in noe country'; it is located on the Isle of Man, which, as we have seen, is identified with the Otherworld. This is a Dolorous-Tower type, inhabited by a heathen sultan and his gang of giants, strong, stout, pugnacious, and ugly[27] – cognates of the Fomorians who, as the Irish imagined, also lived in the Isle of Man. The hero is subjected to a variety of tests at which he succeeds with the help of the Turk, whose assistance is so important that Gawain is reluctant to obey the decapitation order. Compliance, however, effects the breaking of the spell. The Turk turns into a Te Deum-singing, Christian knight, Sir Gromer, who accepts the kingship of Man, which Arthur bestows. Gawain, for his part, having survived the terrors of the castle, releases the prisoners and receives the giants' treasures, a basin of gold and a sword. Thus, the journey to a strange castle tests the hero's courage and obedience, establishes him as paramount knight, and provides him with material rewards.

The second of the Middle English trilogy utilizing the Beheading Game in conjunction with an Otherworld journey is *The Carl of Carlisle*. Two versions survive, the late fifteenth-century MS Porkington 10 and the Percy Folio version (*c.*1650), which, though shorter and even less sophisticated, includes the essential act of decapitation as a means of returning the bespelled Carl to his original form.[28] Kittredge notes Scandinavian analogues (the winning of the troll's daughter) but sees the Temptation motif as Celtic.[29]

To bring Gawain and his companions, Kay and Bishop Baldwin, into contact with the supernatural, the device of a hunt is used. According to M. B. Ogle, the essential features of the stag-messenger episode are an apparently voluntary hunt of a stag that escapes unhurt, a meeting with a lady (usually at a fountain, a place associated with *fées*), and the union of the hunter and the lady.[30] As Lucy A. Paton points out, a splendid castle is also part of the conventional pattern.[31] An Irish analogue occurs in the twelfth-century *Acallamh na Senorach*, a collection of stories about Finn and the *fiana*, who are a band of roving men principally occupied with hunting and fighting.[32]

---

[27] According to Dillon and Chadwick, *The Celtic Realms*, 187, the Fomoiri (Fomorians) lived in the Hebrides and Isle of Man.

[28] Madden publishes the Porkington version as *Syre Gawene and the Carle of Carelyle*, 187–206, and the Percy version, 256–74. See also R. W. Ackerman's edition of *Syre Gawene and the Carle of Carelyle* (Ann Arbor, 1947); and D. B. Sands (ed.), *Middle English Verse Romances* (New York, 1966), 348–71, II. 262–4 and 485–9, from which my quotations are taken.

[29] Kittredge, *A Study of Gawain*, 257–73.

[30] M. B. Ogle, 'The Stag-Messenger Episode', *American Journal of Philology* 37 (1916), 387–416.

[31] L. A. Paton, *Studies in the Fairy Mythology of Arthurian Romance*, 2nd edn (1903, New York, 1970), 229–32.

[32] Rees, *Celtic Heritage*, 62. The camaraderie of the group, in contrast to the Ulstermen's rivalry, suggests the fellowship of the Round Table Knights.

As seven of us chased a beautiful fawn, it suddenly vanished underground and we were immediately engulfed in a heavy snowstorm. Seeking shelter, I went over the south side of the mountain, where I found a rich, well-lighted *sidh*. Entering, I sat in a crystal chair. On one side were twenty-eight warriors, each with a beautiful woman; on the other were six yellow-haired maidens while a seventh maiden sat in the center playing a harp and drinking from a horn.[33]

The lord of the *sidh* admits that the deer was one of the maidens, sent to lure the warriors into the *sidh* so that they might defend it against a supernatural army.

Riding out from Cardiff (a mistake for Carlisle) at 'grease time', the Arthurian hunters follow a hart from sunrise to noon (a time when 'the veil between this world and the unseen world was very thin').[34] The animal suddenly disappears as a mist rises over the moor. Now, as the informed reader is aware, the barriers are dissolving so that the protagonists can enter a world of supernatural characters and uniquely significant adventures. Baldwin suggests that they take shelter in the castle of the Carl of Carlisle, despite the host's reputation for mistreating his guests. In appearance the Carl is a *gruagach*. The 'dredfull man' has an arrogant face, large aquiline nose, and a grey beard lying across his chest like a fan. He is a span between the eyebrows, two yardsticks between the shoulders, and nine yards high.

> Ther was no post in that hall,
> Grettyst growand of hem all,
> But his theys wer thycker.

The first trial, at which only Gawain succeeds, is a courtesy test based on the treatment of the host's little horse. Subsequently, the hero's obedience, prowess, and self-control are tested when he is required to hurl a spear at the host's face; lie in bed with the beautiful, amiable wife without engaging in intercourse; and strike off the Carl's head with a sword.

The castle combines antithetical elements suggesting the ambiguous fortress of Cu Roi and other Celtic *bruiden*. In its paradisal aspect it provides feasting, music, and love, not to mention a plentiful supply of wine contained in one of those enormous vessels that can never be emptied. The beautiful daughter who plays on the harp is a *fée*-like heroine. Her hair shines like gold wire, her jewel-studded garments are worth a thousand pounds, and she lights up the hall as a sunbeam does. Gawain feels no guilt at spending the night with her, especially as he has the host's encouragement:

> 'My blessynge I geyfe yow bouthe to,
> And play togeydor all this nyght.'
> A glad man was Syr Gawen

---

[33] Spaan, 'The Otherworld', 360–1.
[34] Rees, *Celtic Heritage*, 92.

Sertenly, as I yowe sayne,
Of this lady bryght.

The dark side of this setting is represented by the malignant porter, the Carl's ferocious whelps (a wild bull, a boar, a lion, and a bear), and the chamber full of bloody mail and human bones, the remains of the fifteen hundred men who have failed the obedience test.

The termination of the spell enables the Carl to fulfill unrestrainedly the role of Hospitable Host, as he does when he welcomes King Arthur into his regenerated hall, where the walls, gleaming like glass and diapered in gold, azure, and grey, signify the transformation of a Dolorous Tower into a magnificent 'happy Otherworld'. He has already, as CuRoi did for Cuchulainn, judged Gawain to be a non-pareil. The two ladies, each of whom Gawain finds sexually attractive, correspond to the two types of Otherworld woman in Irish literature, the Queen whose function is to test the hero and the maiden who provides the reward. The former, being married, is unavailable as a mortal's wife; the latter, being unmarried, can become the hero's wife, as she does in *The Carl of Carlisle*. The interest afforded by this romance extends beyond its usefulness as an example of the Beheading and Temptation, motifs more complexly exemplified in *Sir Gawain and the Green Knight*.

Of the Arthurian romances under discussion, *Sir Gawain and the Green Knight*[35] may seem least to need critical comment, yet the fact that it still inspires a diversity of interpretations attests to its problematic nature. Earlier in the twentieth century, the Celtic analogues were discussed in important studies by G. L. Kittredge, Alice Buchanan, and J. R. Hulbert.[36] Recent criticism has shown more interest in syntax, style, symbolism, and Gawain's moral and spiritual dilemma. I make no apology, therefore, for returning to the Celtic archetypes associated with the Otherworld journey to a strange castle, in an effort to understand the roles of Gawain, Bercilak, Bercilak's wife, and Morgan le Fay.

As the New Year's feast is being celebrated at Camelot, Arthur's *geis* is satisfied by the sudden appearance of a green giant, whose intrusion is not unlike that made by CuRoi into the Ulstermen's meadhall, axe in hand. Though the challenger's color has been taken as evidence that he is a folkloric Green Man, a Vegetation God, Death, or the Devil,[37] the simplest explanation is to see his

---

[35] J. R. R. Tolkien and E. V. Gordon (ed.), *Sir Gawain and the Green Knight*, ed. Norman Davis, 2nd edn (1925; Oxford: Clarendon, 1967).

[36] Kittredge, *A Study of Gawain*; Alice Buchanan, 'The Irish Framework of Gawain and the Green Knight', *PMLA* [*Journal of the Modern Languages Association of America*] 47 (1932), 315–38; J. R. Hulbert, 'Syr Gawayn and the Grene Knyght', *PMLA* 13 (1915), 433–62, 689–730.

[37] See, for example, A. C. Spearing, *The Gawain-Poet: A Critical Study* (Cambridge, 1970), 179–80; J. Speirs, *Medieval English Poetry: The Non-Chaucerian Tradition* (London, 1957), 219–26; D. B. J. Randall, 'Was the Green Knight a Fiend?', *Studies in Philology* 57 (1960), 479–91; A. H. Krappe, 'Who was the Green Knight?', *Speculum* 13 (1938), 206–15; H. Zimmer, *The King and the Corpse* (New York, 1956), 76–7.

greenness as a link to the Celtic Otherworld.[38] The relationship of Gawain to the
Green Knight clearly resembles the role of Cuchulainn in the Ulster cycle. Each
is the paramount hero of his tribe who protects the social center, whether Tara or
Camelot, from Otherworld incursions even though the duty necessitates a con-
flict with an Otherworld lord. That we are not to identify the Green Knight as a
Fomorian-type giant is evident from his shapeliness:

> For of bak and of brest al were his bodi sturne,
> Both his wombe and his wast were worthily smale,
> And alle his fetures folȝande, in forme þat he hade,
> ful clene.
>
> (II. 143–5)

His churlish manner, however, and his taunts and insults both at Arthur's court
and at the Green Chapel link him to the *gruagach* form in which the Otherwold
King tests the hero. His name Bercilak, in fact, has been derived from *bachlach*
(peasant or churl).[39]

It is significant that Gawain, like Cuchulainn and other Celtic heroes, begins
his journey at Samhain, the time of year when the barriers are down and the *sidh*
mounds open. The sense of immanent death felt by the Arthurian court and by
the hero himself is intensified when we remember that at Samhain 'man seems
powerless in the hand of fate'.[40] Rain, sleet, mountain streams, and icicles are the
watery forms marking the perilous passage. Equally significant is the fact that
the forest near Bercilak's Castle Hautdesert consists of oaks, hazels, and haw-
thorn, all of them fairy trees.[41] The castle itself suddenly appears as if by magic.
It stands on a hill, which the poet actually calls a *syde*, surrounded by a park-like
meadow, which is enclosed within a palisade. It shimmers and shines through
the bright oaks (the arboreal attribute suggests that winter has been banished
within this magic circle). At closer quarters, it is seen to be a work of consummate
craftsmanship:

> A better barbican bat burne blusched vpon neuer.
> And innermore he behelde bat halle ful hyȝe,
> Towres telded bytwene, trochet ful þik,
> Fayre fylyoleȝ at fyȝed, and ferlyly long,
> With coruon coprounes craftyly sleȝe.
> Chalkwhyt chymnees tier ches he innoȝe
> Vpon bastel rouez, bat blenked ful quyte;

[38] Hulbert, 'Syr Gawayn', 455, provides examples. On green as a fairy color, see also A. D. Hope, *A Midsummer Eve's Dream* (Canberra, 1970), 13.
[39] In an unpublished doctoral dissertation (University of Alberta 1981), A. Flemming-Blake sug-
gests that the name derives from *bercelet*, the name of a hound used to drive game to waiting
hunters.
[40] Rees, *Celtic Heritage*, 91.
[41] See A. Porteous, *Forest Folklore, Mythology, and Romance* (London, 1928), *passim*; and D. Mac-
Manus, *The Middle Kingdom: The Faerie World of Ireland* (Gerrards Cross, 1973), 51–63.

So mony pynakle payntet watz poudred ayquere,
Among þe caste] carnelez clambred so pik,
Þat pared out of papure purely hit semed.

(II. 793–802)

A better barbican that knight had never beheld. And further in he saw the lofty hall, towers regularly spaced and thickly battlemented, fair pinnacles that fitted, marvellously tall, with carved tops, craftily worked. Many chalk-white chimneys he noticed on the tower roofs that whitely gleamed. So many painted pinnacles were powdered everywhere among the castle embrasures, clustered so thickly, that faultlessly pared out of paper it seemed.

The combination of a supernatural challenger who provides a motive for a journey, a November departure, a perilous passage marked by showers of rain and snow, the specific mention of trees with *faerie* associations, and the brilliant castle surrounded by a palisaded park makes it impossible to avoid the conclusion that this is an Otherworld setting.

Inside, the superlative hospitality verifies this identification. The welcome is enthusiastic, the food so copious and delicious that even a fast seems a feast. The music sounds as gaily and the wine flows as freely for Gawain as it did for the Irish heroes. The Hospitable Host is genial almost to excess, so anxious is he to provide pleasant entertainment. Bercilak's lady is far too aggressive to be regarded as a courtly love heroine, a type who must be 'daungerous', standoffish, until persuaded by a knight's humility, obedience, and service to show him pity. However, if we identify the wife as a would-be fairy mistress, then her brash ardor is perfectly explicable:

'3e ar welcum to my tors,
Yowre awen won to wale,
Me behoue3 of fyne force
Your seruaunt be, and schale.'

(II. 1237–40)

You are welcome to my body to take your pleasure. I must be your servant and shall be.

Even before reaching Mag Mell, Cuchulainn was told that Fann wanted to get him into bed. A show of reluctance does not characterize the *fée*. Accepting a protective amulet is also part of the love and reward pattern applicable to the hero–fairy mistress relationship, as is the willingness to lie in bed rather than participate in the hunts.[42]

The second lady of the castle is so extraordinarily ugly that a medieval audience would have identified her as one who had been magically transformed or

---

[42] Cf. 'The Voyage of Maeldune' in Gregory, *The Voyages of Saint Brendan*, 67–9, where Maeldune's supernatural mistress, the Queen of the island, urges him to stay in the house and do no work.

as a witch. She is Gawain's aunt Morgan le Fay, whose derivation from the Irish Morrigan[43] reminds us that the latter was a white-haired hag and a shape-shifter. Further, she may be related to one aspect of the Otherworld Queen in Spaan's classification, the *Cailleach* (hag or witch), who embodies 'the antithesis of the Queen's ideal beauty and decorum'.[44] Her expressed hatred of Guinevere reflects both the jealousy and malice of the Irish goddess.

Whether Bercilak is her pawn and a victim of her shape-shifting powers or, as I think, an active participant who has changed his own shape in order to test and judge the hero, it is evident that he enjoys his role. Having given the three strokes, he leans on his axe, observing how the brave Gawain stands fearlessly before him and 'in hert hym lykes.' This line does not suggest to me a gloating over the knight's discomfiture. On the contrary, like CuRoi he pronounces the champion a non-pareil:

> As perle bi þe quite pese is of prys more,
> So is Gawayn, in god fayth, bi oþer gay kny3tez.
>
> (ll. 2364–5)

As a pearl is more precious than a white pea, So is Gawain, in good faith, compared with other fair knights.

He goes on to minimize Gawain's fault in refusing to hand over the love-lace; he acted not from covetousness but from love of life, an understandable motive.

In mythological stories, supernatural characters seem incapable of leaving the world of men alone. Gawain is summoned to the Otherworld so that his courage and truth may be tested. He expects that the New Year's meeting with the Green Knight at the demonic Green Chapel[45] will be the climax of his quest, but he learns that the more important test has occurred in the castle, as the riddling fairies decreed. Alwyn Rees and Brinley Rees suggest that the Celts used riddles to bring opposites together. Questions and answers in *The Wooing of Ailbe* that require 'finding a degree beyond the superlative'[46] seem particularly applicable to this English romance:

> What is sweeter than mead? – Intimate conversation
> What is blacker than a raven? – Death
> What is whiter than snow? – Truth
> What is sharper than the sword? –Understanding
> What is lighter than a spark? – The mind of a woman between two men.

---

[43] Patron, *Studies in the Fairy Mythology*, 148–53. Note that the Morrigan lived in a *sidh* and that she 'stands in specially intimate relationship to Cuchulinn'. See also Dillon and Chadwick, *The Celtic Realms*, 183–4.

[44] Spaan, 'The Otherworld', 410–11.

[45] See Hulbert, 'Syr Gawayn', 457, with regard to the idea that the Green Chapel is a *sidh* (fairy mound).

[46] Rees, *Celtic Heritage*, 350.

Critics associate Malory's 'Tale of Gareth'[47] with the preceding romances because it contains a supernatural knight whose severed head can be rejoined to his body. However, Gareth's encounter with the phantom is not an isolated event but the penultimate stage of a fairy mistress story that begins at Arthur's court during the Pentecostal Feast.

After the unrecognized Gareth has spent a year as a kitchen boy in King Arthur's castle, a damsel arrives seeking a champion to free her sister from a 'tyr-raunte that besegyth her and destroyeth hir londys'. The knights decline to accept the quest because the messenger will not reveal what the lady is called or where she dwells. Having been granted the quest by Arthur and secretly knighted by Lancelot, Gareth sets out. The journey in the forest is trying, not only because Gareth must overcome at 'perilous passages' a succession of strangely colored knights – Black, Green, Red, and Blue – but also because his scornful guide deni-grates his gentility and prowess.

That the Lady Lyonesse's oppressor, the Red Knight of the Red Lands, has supernatural origins is suggested by the blood-red color of his arms, armor, and horse, his great size, and his sevenfold strength, which increases as the sun rises to its zenith. Like the defender of the Sidh Bri Ele in the Finn Cycle, this knight kills everyone who approaches the maiden to woo her because he himself loves her. The nearby trees are macabrely decorated with forty good knights hanging by the neck.

The fact that Lady Lyonesse's castle and that of her brother Sir Gringamour are located on the island of Avalon encourages us to assign Otherworldly ori-gins. Lynet, Lyonesse, and Gringamour, like LiBan, Fand, and Labraid, require a champion to free their land from a supernatural tyrant. Lynet acts as messen-ger and guide and as an enchantress who twice calls up a gigantic, light-giving, axe-wielding phantom to forestall premarital consummation. She is also a super-natural healer who not only heals Gareth's wounds but reassembles the head that Gareth has chopped into a hundred pieces and tossed out the window. Lyonesse is the fairy mistress whose magic ring makes her so beautiful that Gareth, meeting her in Gringamour's castle, fails to recognize her. Later she gives this ring with its protective and shape-shifting powers to Gareth. The jovial brother, Gringa-mour, as hospitable host, provides 'all maner of gamys and playes, of daunsyng and syngyne', not to mention great couches and feather-beds where Lyonesse, encouraged by her brother, lies down beside the hero. In this tale, rationalization has obscured but not obliterated the Celtic patterning.

---

[47] This tale has no immediate extant source. On the question of Malory's responsibility for its con-tents, see E. Vinaver (ed.), The *Works of Sir Thomas Malory*, 2nd edn (Oxford, 1967), III, 1427–34; W. L Guerin, '"The Tale of Gareth": the Chivalric Flowering', in *Malory's Originality*, ed. R. M. Lumiansky (Baltimore, 1963), 99–117; L. D. Benson, *Malory's Morte Darthur* (Cambridge, MA, 1976), 92–108; V. D. Scudder, *Le Morte Darthur of Sir Thomas Malory* (London, 1921), 217–18; R. H. Wilson, 'The Fair Unknown in Malory', *PMLA* 58 (1943), 2–21; R. S. Loomis, 'Malory's Beau-mains', *PMLA* 54 (1939), 656–68. Loomis proposes that Gareth is a form of Gawain.

The one Arthurian castle generally acknowledged to have Celtic origins is the Grail castle, Carbonek.[48] Among Malory's castles, it is the most difficult to define. For the Grail knights, it is, as Jean Marx suggests, 'inaccessible, invisible, sauf pour l'invité, l'appelé ou l'elé'.[49] Its ruler, King Pelles, introduces himself as 'kynge of the forayne contré'. Lancelot, Bors, Perceval, and Galahad traverse endless forests, wastelands, and seas before arriving at their destination. Yet in the secular milieu, Balin, Lancelot, Gawain, and Bors seem to have no difficulty finding it. When Elaine completes her visit to Camelot, King Arthur and a hundred knights bring her on her way through the forest as if her home were nearby. This sense of multiple locations is characteristically Celtic as are such specific features as Lancelot's midnight arrival at a seaside castle described as 'rych and fayre', the open doors, the apparent emptiness, Bars' Perilous Bed adventure, the hospitable entertainment of an elite at a feast where 'the Sangreall had fulfylled the table with all metis that ony harte myght thynke', the sense of unseen powers when 'all the doorys of the palyse and wyndowes shutte withoute mannys honde'.

From its first appearance in 'The Tale of Balin', the castle is enigmatic. The custom that allows only a knight accompanied by a lady to be admitted to the feast may reflect the hedonistic pairings of Mag Mell. But inside is Garlon of the Black Face, the invisible slayer of good knights, who provokes his own death by slapping Balin's face. Hotly pursued by the Grail Keeper Pellam, Balin rushes into the Grail Chapel, an apparently ideal and permanent setting. Yet when he has struck the Dolorous Blow with the magical lance, the castle shatters, the walls crumble, many of the inhabitants are killed, and the surrounding lands laid waste.

Carbonek next appears as part of an adventure designed to release an oppressed maiden. Elaine, the daughter of King Pelles (who seems to be Pellam's son), has been boiling in scalding water for five years because two jealous *fées*, Morgan and the Queen of North Galys, have bespelled her. She can only be released by the best knight in the world. Gawain has failed the test.[50] Lancelot succeeds. At the celebratory feast, the Grail provides the usual desirable plenty. (One does not ask why its powers could not break the *fées'* spell.) Now that Lancelot has been lured into the castle, Pelles must find a way of getting him into bed with his daughter, for

> the kynge knew well that sir Launcelot shulde gete a pusyll upon his doughtir, whyche shulde be called sir Galahad, the good knyght by whom all the forayne cuntrey shulde be brought oute of daunger. (Vinaver ed., II, 794, ll. 4–8)

Fortunately, he has in his castle, passing as Elaine's nurse, one of those powerful supernatural women who effects the consummation through a magical drink and

---

[48] See, for example, A. C. L. Brown, *The Origin of the Grail Legend*; R. S. Loomis, *The Grail from Celtic Myth to Christian Symbol* (Cardiff and New York, 1963); Jean Marx, *La Légende Arthurienne et Le Graal* (Paris, 1952).

[49] Marx, *Légende Arthurienne*, 140.

[50] The greatest hero of the Middle English metrical romances has been replaced by the French hero Lancelot.

a golden ring. It is not the first time that a mortal has been summoned to the Otherworld to engender a son who represents 'a rebirth of himself'.[51]

Of course, Carbonek is predominantly Otherworldly in a Christian sense, for it exists to enshrine the Holy Grail and to permit the enactment of the appropriate rituals.[52] In the Grail chapel, filled with angels, disembodied voices, unearthly music, and supernatural light, the consecration of bread and wine makes transubstantiation visible. Like a sacred mountain, this castle links earth with heaven and time with eternity, replacing a horizontal temporal myth with a vertical timeless paradigm. Paradoxically, in the moment of its completeness, it is disestablished. The holy objects, which it had contained for more than four centuries, are transferred to Sarras (Jerusalem) and then to heaven.

The Middle English Arthurian romances that we have been discussing depict a world in which Christianity and chivalry refine, change, and obscure the Celtic mythology, though the magic, the love of fine possessions, and the paramountcy of women are retained. Indeed, the ancient stories of Ireland in their extant forms have themselves been rationalized by Christian scribes. Modernization is architectural and social. As has been pointed out, Bercilak's castle with its machicolations and its pinnacles resembles the Duc de Berry's castle, which the Limbourg Brothers depicted in their September calendar scene [see McKenzie fig. 18, p. 212].[53] The Carl's refurbished hall contains canopied chairs and diapered walls. The King of Man has an enormous brass tennis ball and 'an iron forke made of steele', which the Turk uses to cause the drowning of one of the giants by holding him down in a cauldron of boiling lead. Castle occupants lounge comfortably in front of fireplaces, sleep in curtained beds, and participate in such aristocratic pastimes as hunting and jousting. When he is entertaining King Arthur, the Carl of Carlisle demonstrates his new-found gentility by serving swans, pheasants, cranes, partridges, plovers, and curlews, dishes that were de rigueur at a royal feast in the fourteenth century.[54]

The overriding concept that makes the Arthurian romances quite different in tone from the Irish tales is the formers' concern with courtesy. This word, expressing the virtue of courts, subsumes, says Henre Dupin, an antithesis between 'courtois' and 'vilain'; the performance of ritual gesture associated with hospitality; the moral qualities of loyalty, faith, generosity, and compassion; an atmosphere of joy; an observance of 'mesure'; and the experience of that particular

---

[51] Spaan, 'The Otherworld', 408–9.

[52] Malory's source, the Old French 'La Queste del Saint Graal' (1215–30), was written to exalt the ascetic ideal and to explain particular doctrines, such as those relating to grace. See Albert Pauphilet, *Etudes sur la Queste del Saint Graal* (Paris, 1921); F. Locke, *The Quest for the Holy Grail: A Literary Study of a Thirteenth Century French Romance* (Stanford, 1960); E. Gilson, 'La mystique de la grace dans la Queste del Saint Graal', *Romania* 51 (1925), 321–37.

[53] For example, in Joan Evans (ed.), *The Flowering of the Middle Ages* (London, 1966), 134–5; *Les très riches heures du Duc de Berry*, ed. J. Longnon and R. Cazelles (London, 1969), fo. 9, 9.

[54] See H. L. Harder, 'Feasting in the Alliterative Morte Arthure', in *Chivalric Literature: Essays on Relations between Literature and Life in the Later Middle Ages*, ed. L. D. Benson and J. Leyerle (Kalamazoo, 1980), 53–4.

kind of love known as 'amour courtois'.[55] The Carl of Carlisle eschews courtesy: 'My lorde can no corttessye,' says the porter. Yet the first test that the three visitors undergo involves this virtue. Bishop Baldwin and Kay are knocked down for failing, Gawain praised for succeeding.

Gawain's reputation for courtesy, acknowledged on all sides when he visits Bercilak's castle, may have suggested to the conspirators the form their test would take. Unfortunately for Gawain, in the context of this poem, he cannot accept the *fée*'s proposition because his courtesy is composed of the moral and spiritual values that the pentangle symbolizes, rather than depending on his skill as a lover.[56] What makes this complex poem so intriguing and entertaining is the poet's subtle examination of courtesy in all the aspects defined by Dupin.

Malory's 'Tale of Gareth' contains the author's most thorough examination of courtly love in the context of romantic adventure. The hero's gentility, prowess, humility, loyalty, obedience, and devotion to his lady mark him as an ideal courtly lover. When it seems that the courtly virtue of 'mesure' will be abandoned and the lover's honor lost through overhastiness, the power of magic is invoked. The conclusion of the tale epitomizes the concept of courtesy as aristocratic virtue and order. Not only does Gareth marry Lady Lyonesse, but his brother Gaheris marries her sister Lynet and his brother Agravain marries Laurel, Lyonesse's beautiful and wealthy niece. The knights whom the hero has defeated in his progress to the besieged castle are made officers of the feast, the only occasion when Malory distinguishes a courtly celebration by designating individually the honorary members of the king's household.

Because fidelity to his lady Guinevere is the paramount aspect of Lancelot's courtesy, he cannot marry either Elaine of Carbonek or Elaine of Astolat. Nor can he separate the secular virtue from its religious form. Ignoring the prohibition, he rushes into the Grail chapel to assist the priest who seems in danger of collapsing under the weight of the chalice. Struck down by a fiery breath, he lies unconscious for twenty-four days, signifying the years of his adultery. For this knight who is the 'flower of chivalry', his courtesy is his doom.

Rose Macauley has called the castle 'a formidable image, a powerful, intimidating fantasy of the human imagination'.[57] When combined with man's irrepressible dream of a remote yet accessible country of delight, it produces one of the most powerful images in Western literary tradition.

[55] H. Dupin, *La Courtoisie au Moyen Âge* (d'après les Texes du XIe et du XIIIe siècle) (Paris, 1906).
[56] See D. S. Brewer, 'Courtesy and the Gawain-Poet', in *Patterns of Love and Courtesy: Essays in Memory of C. S. Lewis*, ed. J. Lawlor (London, 1966), 68–78.
[57] *The Pleasure of Ruins*, ed. C. B. Smith (London, 1964), 266.

Guide to Further Reading

This guide is not in any way intended to be exhaustive; rather, it should be seen as an introduction into the specialised literature. Castle studies are fortunate that annual bibliographies of published work have been collated for many years by John Kenyon and now by Gillian Scott (née Eadie) for the Castle Studies Group (for details, see www.castlestudiesgroup.org.uk). These bibliographies, together with Kenyon's earlier lists published by the CBA, have now been comprehensively updated in J. R. Kenyon, *Castles, Town Defences and Artillery Fortifications in the United Kingdom and Ireland: A Bibliography 1945–2006* (Shaun Tyas, Donington, 2008), and this volume represents the starting point for those seeking references or to research a particular castle. For individual sites D. J. Cathcart King, *Castellarium Anglicanuum* (Kraus International, New York, 1983) remains an invaluable work of scholarship, containing as it does references to primary sources and antiquarian literature. Much new work is published each year by the Castle Studies Group, while the bi-annual Château Gaillard conference proceedings remain the principal publication for work on castles from across Europe. The guide below should be read in conjunction with the footnotes in the introduction to this volume, together with the bibliography in R. Liddiard (ed.), *Anglo-Norman Castles* (Woodbridge, 2003), with due allowance for some inevitable overlap.

The political context of the majority of articles included in the present study is best approached by the two relevant volumes in the New Oxford History of England series, namely M. Prestwich, *Plantagenet England, 1225–1360* (Oxford, 2005) and G. Harriss, *Shaping the Nation: England 1360–1461* (Oxford, 2005).

On the historiography of castles, D. Stocker, 'The Shadow of the General's Armchair', *Archaeological Journal*, 149 (1992), 415–20 is an important review article, complemented by M. W. Thompson, 'The Military Interpretation of Castles', *Archaeological Journal* 151 (1994), 439–45 and by S. Speight, 'British Castle Studies in the Late Twentieth and Twenty-First Centuries', *History Compass* 2 (2004), 1–30. Charles Coulson's 'Cultural Realities and Reappraisals in English Castle-Study', *Journal of Medieval History* 22 (1996), 171–207 is a detailed survey of historiographical trends up to that date. It is instructive to compare the approach taken in two books published in the Shire series, but separated by nearly twenty years: R. Allen Brown, *Castles* (London, 1985), and O. Creighton and R. Higham, *Medieval Castles* (Princes Risborough, 2003). More recent reflections on the subject are R. Higham, 'Castle Studies in Transition: A Forty Year Reflection', *Archaeological Journal* 167

(2010), 1–13; C. Platt, 'Revisionism in Castle Studies: A Caution', *Medieval Archaeology* 51 (2007), 83–102; O. Creighton and R. Liddiard, 'Fighting Yesterday's Battle: Beyond War or Status in Castle Studies', *Medieval Archaeology* 52 (2008), 161–9; O. H. Creighton, 'Castle Studies and Archaeology in England: Towards a Research Framework for the Future', *Château Gaillard* 23 (2008), 79–90.

There are many discussions of castle-building during the late medieval period, either on its own as or as part of the broader 'castle story'. R. Allen Brown, *English Castles*, 3rd edn (London, 1976) is the classic study, but see also C. Platt, *The Castle in Medieval England and Wales* (London, 1982); M. W. Thompson, *The Decline of the Castle* (Cambridge, 1987); D. J. C. King, *The Castle in England and Wales – an Interpretative History* (London, 1988); N. J. G. Pounds, *The Medieval Castle in England and Wales* (Cambridge, 1990); M. W. Thompson, *The Rise of the Castle* (Cambridge, 1991); T. McNeill, *Castles* (London, 1992). The first decade of the twenty-first century saw the publication of other general works that took a different focus. Chief among these is C. Coulson, *Castles in Medieval Society* (Oxford, 2003), which is a major study written from a historical background; more archaeological approaches can be found in M. Johnson, *Behind the Castle Gate: From Medieval to Renaissance* (London, 2002) and R. Liddiard, *Castles in Context* (Macclesfield, 2005). On castle architecture, see now J. Goodall, *The English Castle* (New Haven, 2011).

The key treatment of royal castles remains R. Allen Brown, H. M. Colvin and A. J. Taylor, *The History of the Kings Works*, vols 1 and 2, *The Middle Ages* (London, 1963). Aspects of thirteenth-century development are discussed in J. R. Kenyon and R. Avent (eds.), *Castles in Wales and the Marches* (Cardiff, 1987) and A. J. Taylor, *The Welsh Castles of Edward 1* (London, 1986), with the Edwardian castles receiving important revision in D. M. Williams and J. F. Kenyon (eds.), *The Impact of the Edwardian Castles in Wales* (Cardiff, 2010).

On the buildings themselves, some sites have dedicated volumes, notably E. Impey (ed.), *The White Tower* (New Haven and London, 2008), but the most comprehensive survey of aristocratic building in general is Anthony Emery's magisterial three-volume *The Greater Houses of England and Wales, 1300–1500* (Cambridge 1996–2006), which contains much useful information on many castle sites and a series of important essays on general themes. The most detailed single-volume treatment of castle architecture must now be John Goodall, *The English Castle, 1066–1650* (New Haven and London, 2011), which extends the chronology of castle-building up to the Civil War. Residential development and sophistication are discussed in B. Morley, 'Aspects of Fourteenth-Century Castle Design', in *Collectanea Historica: Essays in Memory of Stuart Rigold*, ed. A. Detsicas (Maidstone, 1981), 104–13; J. A. Ashbee, '"The Chamber called Gloriette": Living at Leisure in Thirteenth- and Fourteenth-Century Castles', *Journal of the British Archaeological Association* 157 (2004), 17–39; C. Curry et al., 'Dartington Hall and the Development of Double-Courtyard Design in English Late Medieval High-Status Houses', *Archaeological Journal* 161 (2005), 189–210, with social background discussed in C. M. Woolgar, *The Greater Household in Medieval England*

(New Haven and London, 1999). The theatricality in structuring the approach to lordly chambers is discussed in P. Dixon, 'Design in Castle Building: the Controlling of Access to the Lord', *Château Gaillard* 18 (1998), 47–57.

The subject of royal licencing is dominated by the work of Charles Coulson. The most detailed treatment is C. Coulson, 'Freedom to Crenellate by Licence: An Historiographical Revision', *Nottingham Medieval Studies* 38 (1994), 86–137, but other important articles include Coulson's, 'Hierarchism in Conventual Crenellation: An Essay in the Sociology and Metaphysics of Medieval Fortification', *Medieval Archaeology* 26 (1982), 69–100; 'Castellation in the County of Champagne in the Thirteenth Century', *Château Gaillard* 9–10 (1982), 347–64; 'The Sanctioning of Fortresses in France: "Feudal Anarchy" or Seigneurial Amity?', *Nottingham Medieval Studies* 42 (1998), 38–104; and 'Battlements and the Bourgeoisie: Municipal Status and the Apparatus of Urban Defence in Later-Medieval England', *Medieval Knighthood* 5 (Woodbridge, 1995), 119–95. The subject is also discussed in R. W. Kaeuper, *War, Justice and Public Order: England and France in the Later Middle Ages* (Oxford, 1988).

For Scottish castles, see S. Cruden, *The Scottish Castle* (London, 1960); C. Tabraham, *Scottish Castles and Fortifications* (Edinburgh, 2000), with a useful overview of historiographical trends in R. D. Oram, 'Castles, Concepts and Contexts: Castle Studies in Scotland in Retrospect and Prospect', *Château Gaillard* 23 (2008), 349–60. A series of useful essays is to be found in R. D. Oram and G. P. Stell (eds.), *Lordship and Architecture in Medieval and Renaissance Scotland* (East Linton, 2005); and see also F. Watson, 'The Expression of Power in a Medieval Kingdom: Thirteenth-Century Scottish Castles', in *Scottish Power Centres from the Early Middle Ages to the Twentieth Century*, ed. S. Foster, A. MacInnes and R. MacInnes (Glasgow, 1998), 59–78.

The study of Irish castles was set on its modern footing by H. G. Leask, *Irish Castles and Castellated Houses* (Dundalk, 1941, see also 3rd edn 1977); for more recent overviews, (and with contrasting approaches), see T. McNeill, *Castles in Ireland: Feudal Power in a Gaelic World* (London, 1997), and D. Sweetman, *The Medieval Castles of Ireland* (Woodbridge, 1999); much new work is to be found in T. O'Keeffe, *Medieval Irish Buildings, 1100–1600* (Dublin, 2015). A useful collection of essays is brought together in John R. Kenyon and K. O'Conor (eds.), *The Medieval Castle in Ireland and Wales* (Dublin, 2003).

Tower houses remain a subject for much debate: see P. Dixon, 'Towerhouses, Pelehouses and Border Society', *Archaeological Journal* 136 (1979), 240–52; C. Tabraham, 'Smailholm Tower: A Scottish Laird's Fortified Residence on the English border', *Château Gaillard* 13 (1987), 227–38; C. Tabraham, 'The Scottish Medieval Tower-House as Lordly Residence in the Light of Recent Excavation', *Proceedings of the Society of Antiquities of Scotland* 118 (1988), 267–76; T. Barry, 'Harold Leask's "Single Towers": Irish Tower Houses as Part of Larger Settlement Complexes', *Château Gaillard* 22 (2006), 27–33.

Discussions of the military role of the castle are often found within broader accounts of medieval warfare more generally, for which see P. Contamine, *War in the Middle Ages*, trans. M. Jones (London, 1985); Maurice Keen (ed.), *Medieval Warfare: A History* (Oxford, 1999); D. Nicolle, *Medieval Warfare Sourcebook*, 2 vols (London, 1996); M. Prestwich, *Armies and Warfare in the Middle Ages: the English Experience* (London, 1996). An overview of historians' attitudes to siege warfare is to be found in Bernard S. Bachrach, 'Medieval Siege Warfare: A Reconnaissance', *The Journal of Military History* 58 (1994), 119–33, while J. Bradbury, *The Medieval Siege* (Woodbridge, 1992) provides a chronological narrative. Much good material on siege warfare is to be found in Matthew Strickland and Robert Hardy, *The Great Warbow* (Stroud, 2005), and also in I. Corfis and M. Wolfe (eds.), *The Medieval City Under Siege* (Woodbridge, 1995). For early discussion of the use of gunpower weapons in castle buildings, see B. O'Neil, *Castles and Cannon: A Study of Early Artillery Fortifications in England* (Westport, 1975); also J. R. Kenyon, 'Early Artillery Fortifications in England and Wales', *Archaeological Journal* 138 (1981), 205–40, and A. Saunders, *Fortress Britain* (Liphook, 1989). An important study of the sociology of medieval conflict is R. Jones, *Bloodied Banners: Martial Display on the Medieval Battlefield* (Woodbridge, 2010).

The subject of 'castles and landscapes' has almost become a sub-discipline in its own right. An early work, but one that pointed up later approaches, is D. Austin, 'The Castle and the Landscape', *Landscape History* 6 (1984), 69–81, while the potential of landscape evidence is discussed in P. Everson, '"Delightfully Surrounded with Woods and Ponds": Field Evidence for Medieval Gardens in Britain', in *There by Design: Field Archaeology in Parks and Gardens*, ed. P. Patterson (BAR British Series 267, 1998), 32–8. The key text is O. Creighton, *Castles and Landscapes* (London, 2002), but see also his *Designs Upon the Land* (Woodbridge, 2009). Useful articles include O. Creighton and R. Higham, 'Castle Studies and the Landscape Agenda', *Landscape History* 26 (2004), 1–18, and O. Creighton, 'Castle Studies and the European Medieval Landscape: Traditions, Trends and Future Research Directions', *Landscape History* 30 (2009), 5–20. A useful case study of what the landscape approach can contribute to the wider study of an individual castle is to be found in P. Everson, G. Brown and D. Stocker, 'The Earthworks and Landscape Context', in *Ludgershall Castle, Excavations by Peter Addyman, 1964–1972*, ed. P. Ellis, Wiltshire Archaeology and Natural History Society Monograph No. 2 (Devizes, 2000), 97–115. The work on Bodiam castle looms large in this topic, but the original publication remains one of the best pieces of writing on the landscape context: C. Taylor, P. Everson and R. Wilson-North, 'Bodiam Castle, Sussex', *Medieval Archaeology*, 34 (1990), 155–7; for a recent review of the subject and the suggestion that modern notions of 'design' might not be wholly applicable to the Middle Ages, see R. Liddiard and T. Williamson, 'There by Design? Some Reflections on Medieval Elite Landscapes', *Archaeological Journal* 165 (2008), 520–35.

Much new information continues to come to light through archaeological excavation. Three reports in particular show how important excavations are to understanding castle sites: D. Austin, *Acts of Perception: A Study of Barnard Castle in Teesdale*, 2 vols (English Heritage and the Architectural and Archaeological

Society of Durham and Northumberland, 2007); A. Saunders, *Excavations at Launceston Castle, Cornwall* (Society for Medieval Archaeology Monograp. 24, 2006); and C. Caple, *Excavations at Dryslwyn Castle, 1980–95* (Society for Medieval Archaeology Monograp. 26, 2007).

The place of the castle as a cultural icon in medieval society is a subject that has not attracted widespread attention, or at least not directly. One of the best works is a collection by K. Reyerson and F. Powe (eds.), *The Medieval Castle: Romance and Reality* (Minnesota, 1984), which contains a series of essays on the depiction of castles in literature and in the context of noble architecture more generally. A more recent treatment is A. Wheatley, *The Idea of the Castle in Medieval England* (York, 2004).

The focus of this volume is the British Isles, but for those seeking the European context the starting point for French castles is probably C. Laurent, *L'Atlas des Châteaux-forts en France* (Strasbourg, 1977) ; but see also G. Fournier, *Le Château dans la France Médiévale* (Paris, 1978); J. Gardelles, *Les Châteaux de Moyen-Âge dans la France du Sud-Ouest: La Gascogne Anglaise de 1216 â 1327* (Geneva, 1972); J. Mesqui, *Châteaux et Enceintes de la France Médiévale: De la Défence à la Résidence*, 2 vols (Paris, 1991); J. Mesqui, *Les Châteaux-Forts en France* (Paris, 2000) ; and two important publications by Marie-Pierre Baudry, *Les Fortifications des Plantagenêts en Poitou 1154–1242* (Paris, 2001); Marie-Pierre Baudry (ed.), *Les Fortifications dans le Domains Plantagenêt, XIIe–XIVe siècle* (Poitiers, 2000); see also M. Casset, *Les Évêques Aux Champs: Châteaux et Manoirs des Évêques Normands au Moyen Âge (XIe–XVe Siècles)* Caen, 2007), which discusses the landscape of bishops' residences and is highly relevant to castle studies.

For an overview of German castles, see H. W. Böhme *et al.* (ed.), *Burgen in Mitteleuropa. Ein Handbuch*, 2 vols (Stuttgart, 1999) and a collection of essays (which include abstracts in English) in G. Ullrich Grossmann and H. Ottomeyer (ed.), *Die Burg. Wissenschaftlicher Begleitband zu den Ausstellungen 'Burg und Herrschaft' und 'Mythos Burg'* (Dresden, 2010). The evolution of lordly castles is examined in T. Biller, *Die Adelsburg in Deutschland: Entstehung – Gestalt – Bedeutung* (München, 1998), while J. Zeune, *Burgen. Symbole der Macht. Ein neues Bild der mittelalterlichen Burg* (Regensburg, 1996) discusses 'symbolism' in a German context.

Spanish castles are discussed in E. Cooper, *Castillos Señoriales de Castilla* (Salamanca, 1991); A. Ocaña, *El Castillo de Santiago en Sanlúcar de Barrameda* (Cádiz, 2007); F. Cobos and J. Castro, *Castilla y León: Castillos y Fortalezas* (Valladolid, 1998). Danish castles have formed the basis for a recent publication in English: V. Etting, *The Royal Castles of Denmark during the Fourteenth Century* (Copenhagen, 2010).

For crusader castles, see D. Pringle, 'Castellology in the Latin East: An Overview', *Château Gaillard* 23 (2006), 361–77. A good discussion of castle-warfare in the Levant is to be found in C. Marshall, *Warfare in the Latin East, 1192–1291* (Cambridge, 1992); N. Housley, *Crusading and Warfare in Medieval and Renaissance Europe* (Aldershot, 2001) extends the discussion beyond the end of the

Middle Ages. On the buildings and their historical context, see T. E. Lawrence (with introduction by D. Pringle), *Crusader Castles* (Oxford, 1988); H. Kennedy, *Crusader Castles* (Cambridge, 1994); D. Pringle, *Fortification and Settlement in Crusader Palestine* (Aldershot, 2000). See also the important excavation report, D. Pringle *et al.*, *Belmont Castle: The Excavation of a Crusader Stronghold in the Kingdom of Jerusalem*, British Academy Monographs in Archaeology, vol. 10 (Oxford, 2000).

Index

Page numbers in bold type indicate illustration or diagram